W9-BDC-588

Get the eBook FREE!

(PDF, ePub, Kindle, and liveBook all included)

We believe that once you buy a book from us, you should be able to read it in any format we have available. To get electronic versions of this book at no additional cost to you, purchase and then register this book at the Manning website.

Go to https://www.manning.com/freebook and follow the instructions to complete your pBook registration.

That's it!
Thanks from Manning!

Windows
PowerShell in Action
Third Edition

BRUCE PAYETTE
RICHARD SIDDAWAY

MANNING

SHELTER ISLAND

For online information and ordering of this and other Manning books, please visit
www.manning.com. The publisher offers discounts on this book when ordered in quantity.
For more information, please contact

Special Sales Department
Manning Publications Co.
20 Baldwin Road
PO Box 761
Shelter Island, NY 11964
Email: orders@manning.com

Manning Publications Co.   Development editor: Jennifer Stout
20 Baldwin Road   Technical development editor: Tobias Weltner
PO Box 761   Project editors: Kevin Sullivan, Janet Vail
Shelter Island, NY 11964   Copyeditors: Linda Recktenwald, Jodie Allen
Proofreader: Elizabeth Martin
Technical proofreader: James Berkenbile
Typesetter: Dennis Dalinnik
Cover designer: Marija Tudor

ISBN: 9781633430297
Printed in the United States of America

For my father.

—Bruce

To Ann for everything. I couldn't have done this without your help and support.

—Richard

brief contents

contents

8 *Using and authoring modules*   270

9 *Module manifests and metadata*   314

preface

The second edition of this book was based on PowerShell v2. Since then we've seen a number of PowerShell releases—the current one is v5.1 with v6 in beta as we write. PowerShell use has grown astronomically to the extent that the PowerShell community is large enough to support independent conferences in North America, Europe, and Asia. User groups are available in all parts of the world.

PowerShell v2 was a big release bringing modules, remoting, and jobs. Subsequent releases have been as big in terms of their impact—PowerShell v3 brought PowerShell workflows and the CIM cmdlets; PowerShell v4 brought Desired State Configuration; and PowerShell v5 brought the ability to write classes in PowerShell. Those are only the headline items—under the covers there are a host of other changes that extend and improve PowerShell. All of this change demands a new edition of the book.

One big difference to the previous editions is that this book requires two authors. Between us we bring you the experience and knowledge of creating and developing PowerShell coupled with extensive practical experience using PowerShell to solve real-world problems. Even with two authors creating the third edition has been a mammoth task. We had to drastically prune the material in the second edition to make room for the new material we had to cover. At one point, we even discussed the book spanning two volumes! We settled on a single volume and even though we've had to put some topics as being out of scope we've covered all of the new functionality.

So why write the book? The answer is the same now as it was then—we wanted the PowerShell community to have a way to see "inside the box" and have a more intimate insight into the goals and motivations behind PowerShell. Although PowerShell draws heavily from existing technologies, it combines them in novel ways. This leads to misunderstandings which then turn into urban myths, like PowerShell does X because its designers were kitten-eating aliens. (Trust us—they're not.) We've also added material covering the practical use of PowerShell to solve your problems.

Speaking at conferences, and answering questions on forums, shows that there were a number of questions that were being asked repeatedly. These questions would arise as a result of prior language experience that the user had or a lack of understanding of a new feature in PowerShell. Typically, a simple explanation was all it took to clear up the confusion. Unfortunately, we couldn't keep answering these questions over and over on a one-to-one basis. That couldn't scale. There needed to be a way to gather this information in one place. This third edition of *Windows Powershell in Action* is our attempt to continue to address that problem.

It's amazing how much power comes out of the synergy of all the technologies underlying PowerShell. We see this in the internal uses of PowerShell at Microsoft, the talks at conferences describing what people are doing in their organizations, and what the community has done with it. And so, a continuing goal of this edition was to try to foster that creativity by conveying just how capable PowerShell is.

A final word from Bruce: This is the book I wanted to read. I love programming languages and the best books are the ones that explain not only what but also why. Look at the books that continue to sell year after year: Kernighan and Ritchie's *The C Programming Language*, Stroustrup's book on C++, and Ousterhout's book on TCL. The TCL book in particular, which describes a very early version of the TCL language, has never been updated, and yet it continues to sell. Why? Because these books give the reader something more than technical detail. They convey a sense of the overall design and some element of the intent of the designer.

Let us know if we succeeded in meeting our goals, okay?

acknowledgments

There wouldn't be a PowerShell book without a PowerShell product in the first place and PowerShell wouldn't exist without the vision of its chief architect Jeffrey Snover. His guidance and comments over the years have been invaluable.

Thanks also to the PowerShell team for making Jeffrey's vision into a reality and helping build the thriving community that exists today.

To all the MEAP readers and reviewers, many thanks for your feedback. We've incorporated as much of it as possible. In particular, we'd like to thank the following who reviewed the manuscript at various stages: Benoît Benedetti, Braj Panda, Chris Frank, Craig Forrester, Edgar Knapp, Jan Vinterberg, Lincoln Bovee', Michel Klomp, Mike Taylor, Nick Selpa, Zalán Somogyváry, Stephen Byrne, Thomas Burl, and Wayne Boaz. Thanks to all of you for your patience. This book took way, way too long to complete.

Finally, special thanks to everyone at Manning who did their usual wonderful job to make this happen: Michael Stephens, Jenny Stout, Linda Recktenwald, Jodie Allen, Elizabeth Martin, Kevin Sullivan, Corbin Collins, Janet Vail, and all the others who worked behind the scenes. All we can say is thank you—this book wouldn't have happened without you.

And more super-special thanks to Tobias Weltner, our technical development editor, who started some very interesting conversations and our technical proofreader James Berkenbile who checked our code.

From Bruce: Thanks to Richard for putting up with me and making this book a reality. It wouldn't have been possible without him. I'd also like to thank Jason Shirk,

Sergei Vorobev, and Jim Truher for their feedback and suggestions for the material on classes (chapter 19). Finally I'd like to thank my wife Tina for putting up with this madness called writing a book.

From Richard: I'd also like to thank Bruce for the opportunity to work on this book. It's been an interesting experience (eight time zones between authors makes for some odd communications) and an honor. I've learned a lot while working with Bruce and hope we've managed to bring that out in the book.

about this book

Windows PowerShell is the next-generation scripting environment created by Microsoft. It's designed to provide a unified solution for Windows scripting and automation, able to access the wide range of technologies such as .NET, COM, and WMI through a single tool. Since its release in 2006, PowerShell has become the central component of any Windows management solution. In addition, due to PowerShell's comprehensive support for .NET, it has broad application potential outside of the system administration space. PowerShell can be used for text processing, general scripting, build management, creating test frameworks, and so on. With PowerShell v6 being available on Linux and macOS as well as Windows, the benefits of PowerShell now extend cross-platform bringing a unified approach to system management.

The authors have extensive experience with PowerShell. Bruce was one of the principal creators of PowerShell. Richard has been using PowerShell since it first became available to apply automation techniques to many organizations. Using many examples, both small and large, this book illustrates the features of the language and environment and shows how to compose those features into solutions, quickly and effectively.

Note that, because of the broad scope of the PowerShell product, this book has a commensurately broad focus. It was not designed as a cookbook of pre-constructed management examples, like how to deal with Active Directory or how to script Exchange. Instead it provides information about the core of the PowerShell runtime and how to use it to compose solutions the "PowerShell Way." After reading this book, the PowerShell user should be able to take any example written in other languages like C# or Visual Basic and leverage those examples to build solutions in PowerShell.

Who should read this book?

This book is designed for anyone who wants to learn PowerShell and use it well. Rather than simply being a book of recipes to read and apply, this book tries to give the reader a deep knowledge about how PowerShell works and how to apply it. All users of PowerShell should read this book.

So, if you're a Windows sysadmin, this book is for you. If you're a developer and you need to get things done in a hurry, if you're interested in .NET, or just if you like to experiment with computers, PowerShell is for you and this book is for you.

Roadmap

The book is divided into 20 chapters and an appendix. Our aim is to provide a comprehensive tour of the PowerShell language and runtime. The goal is to introduce new PowerShell users to the language as well as to provide experienced users with a deep insight into how and why things are the way they are.

We look at all aspects of the PowerShell language including the syntax and the type system. Along the way, we present examples showing how each feature works. Because the goal of the book is to focus on the individual features of the environment, most examples are quite small and are intended to be entered in an interactive session. We do include some larger examples that bring the individual features together to build larger applications.

Chapter 1 begins with the history and the rationale for why PowerShell was created. We then examine PowerShell's elastic type system, including aliases, and how PowerShell parses commands. The way that PowerShell uses the pipeline is unique among scripting languages. We examine the pipeline in depth and explain how to get the most from it. The chapter closes with a review of the closely linked topics of formatting and output.

Chapter 2 introduces the PowerShell type system and discusses its relationship to .NET. This chapter also presents the syntax for each of the PowerShell literal data types. PowerShell's methods for working with collections are examined and show how type conversions can be handled.

The discussion of operators and expressions (PowerShell has lots of these) begins in chapter 3 which covers the basic arithmetic, comparison, and assignment operators. It also covers the wildcard and regular expression pattern matching operators. The logical and bitwise operators close the chapter. Chapter 4 continues the discussion of operators with the advanced operations for working with types, arrays (indexing, slicing) and objects (properties and methods). It also covers output redirection and the formatting operator, and introduces PowerShell variables.

Chapter 5 covers the PowerShell language constructs like if statements and loops.

Chapter 6 introduces programming in PowerShell and covers basic functions, variable scoping, and other programming-related topics. Chapter 7 builds on the material in chapter 6, covering advanced function metadata, scripting, and how to create in-line documentation for scripts and functions.

Chapter 8 covers the basics of how to use PowerShell modules and how to create your own basic modules. The PowerShell gallery, an online repository of community written modules is examined and we show how to discover and download modules. Chapter 9 looks at more advanced module features covering module manifests and how to use them to add information like a version number, dependences, and nested modules. We also examine publishing modules to a repository such as the PowerShell gallery.

Chapter 10 builds on the material in chapters 7–9, introducing advanced programming techniques like object construction and extensions. It also covers first-class functions (scriptblocks) and shows how to extend the PowerShell language itself using these features.

Chapter 11 introduces PowerShell remoting, starting with basic configuration and setup. It then covers the forms of remoting (interactive and non-interactive) and how to apply these techniques. Creation of custom remoting endpoints, including constrained endpoints, is included as well.

Chapter 12 covers the PowerShell workflows—introduced with PowerShell v3. This coverage includes workflow overview and concepts—when to use them and when they aren't appropriate. The workflow keywords are all explained with examples and we show how to parameterize your workflows as well as explaining the common workflow parameters. There're a number of cmdlets available for working with workflows that we explain.

PowerShell jobs were introduced with PowerShell v2 and their reach has been extended with each subsequent release. In chapter 13 we explain the issues with synchronous processing and show how PowerShell jobs enable you to work asynchronously. The way jobs work, and the various job types, is explained as we review the PowerShell cmdlets for managing jobs. PowerShell workflows can make extensive use of jobs especially when suspending a workflow because the machine on which the workflow is operating has been rebooted. The chapter closes with an examination of how PowerShell jobs can work with the Windows task scheduler through scheduled jobs.

Chapter 14 introduces you to error handling concepts in PowerShell such as how to deal with terminating and non-terminating errors. We also examine how you can use event logs to record information as your script executes.

Chapter 15 covers the features in PowerShell for debugging scripts. We start with script instrumentation and capturing session output. We then examine the PowerShell debugger including debugging workflows, jobs, and remote runspaces.

In chapter 16 we shift focus slightly by looking at how PowerShell can be used to attack the kind of text processing tasks that have traditionally been the domain of languages like Perl. This chapter begins with basic string processing, then introduces file processing (including handling binary files), and finishes up with a section on working with XML documents. We look at how to work with COM objects. This includes using the application automation models to script applications like Microsoft Word with PowerShell. We close by looking at how to use CIM (WMI) from the command line and in scripts to inspect, update, and manage a Windows system.

In chapter 17, we look at how we can explore and apply the vast capabilities of the .NET framework. We cover locating, exploring, and instantiating types in the .NET framework, including generic types. Then we look at numerous applications using these types, including network programming and graphical programming with WinForms and WPF. Chapter 17 also looks at the asynchronous eventing subsystem in PowerShell. Eventing allows PowerShell scripts to respond to external events in real time—an important characteristic in systems automation.

Desired State Configuration (DSC) is a mechanism for managing the configuration of your servers in a declarative manner. Chapter 18 opens by reviewing the need for DSC and then covers the DSC theory and architecture. We introduce the DSC modes push and pull. We show how to create configurations and push them to a target server. Creating a pull server from which a machine can pull its configuration information is explained and we show how to prepare configurations to be pulled. We also examine the role of partial configurations and how to create and apply them.

Chapter 19 discusses PowerShell classes. We examine how to create classes and enums in PowerShell and explain the differences from creating a class in C#. A detailed discussion of properties and methods in PowerShell classes is followed by a review of class initialization and construction. We close by explaining how to create DSC resources using PowerShell classes.

Chapter 20, our final chapter, covers the PowerShell and runspace APIs. We discuss the PowerShell API and how to perform isolated and concurrent operations. Runspaces, runspace pools, and remote runspaces are covered, followed by runspace management techniques.

The appendix introduces PowerShell v6 starting with the PowerShell open source project. We discuss .NET core and its implications for PowerShell. Installing PowerShell v6 on Windows and Linux is covered followed by an examination of the techniques required for PowerShell remoting between Windows and Linux machines. We close by showing how to manage the configuration of your Linux machines using DSC.

Code conventions

Because PowerShell is an interactive environment, we show a lot of example commands as the user would type them, followed by the responses the system generates. Before the command text there is a prompt string that looks like this: PS>. Following the prompt, the actual command is displayed. PowerShell's responses follow on the next few lines. Because PowerShell doesn't display anything in front of the output lines, you can distinguish output from commands by looking for the prompt string. These conventions are illustrated as follows:

```
PS> Get-Date

12 July 2017 10:40:55
```

Sometimes commands will span multiple lines. When you type or paste the code into PowerShell you'll see >> on the second and subsequent lines. We've not shown the >> for ease of copying from the ebook. In the text of the book, we show:

```
PS> 1..3 |
foreach {"+" * $_}
+
++
+++
```

Whereas in the interactivePowerShell session you'll see:

```
PS> 1..3 |
>> foreach {"+" * $_}
>>
+
++
+++
```

If we think there may be confusion between the code and output we've left a blank line to separate them. Note that the actual prompt sequence you see in your PowerShell session will be somewhat different than what is shown in the book. The prompt display is user-controllable by redefining the "prompt" function—for more information about prompts see:

```
PS> Get-Help about_Prompts
```

Code annotations accompany many of the listings, highlighting important concepts. In some cases, numbered bullets link to explanations that follow the listing.

Source code downloads

Source code for all working examples in this book is available for download from the publisher's website at www.manning.com/books/windows-powershell-in-action-third-edition.

Book forum

Purchase of Windows PowerShell in Action, Third Edition includes free access to a private web forum run by Manning Publications where you can make comments about the book, ask technical questions, and receive help from the author and from other users. To access the forum, go to https://forums.manning.com/forums/windows-powershell-in-action-third-edition. You can also learn more about Manning's forums and the rules of conduct at https://forums.manning.com/forums/about.

Manning's commitment to our readers is to provide a venue where a meaningful dialogue between individual readers and between readers and the authors can take place. It is not a commitment to any specific amount of participation on the part of the authors, whose contribution to the forum remains voluntary (and unpaid). We suggest you try asking challenging questions lest the authors' interests stray! The forum and the archives of previous discussions will be accessible from the publisher's website as long as the book is in print.

About the authors

BRUCE PAYETTE is one of the founding members of the Windows PowerShell team. He is co-designer of the PowerShell language along with Jim Truher and the principal author of the language implementation. He joined Microsoft in 2001 working on Interix, the POSIX subsystem for Windows. Shortly after that, he moved to help found the PowerShell project. Prior to joining Microsoft, he worked at various companies including Softway (the creators of Interix) and MKS (producers of the MKS Toolkit) building UNIX tools for Windows. He lives in Bellevue, Washington, with his wife, many computers, and two extremely over-bonded codependent cats.

RICHARD SIDDAWAY has been using PowerShell since the early beta versions of PowerShell v1. He has introduced PowerShell to many organizations while producing automation-based solutions to their problems. He has written, and co-authored, a number of PowerShell books for Manning including *PowerShell in Practice*, *PowerShell and WMI*, and *PowerShell in Depth*. His books on Hyper-V and Active Directory contain many practical PowerShell examples. An active blogger and speaker, Richard has also received Microsoft's PowerShell MVP award for 10 years.

About the title

By combining introductions, overviews, and how-to examples, the *In Action* books are designed to help learning and remembering. According to research in cognitive science, the things people remember are things they discover during self-motivated exploration.

Although no one at Manning is a cognitive scientist, we are convinced that for learning to become permanent it must pass through stages of exploration, play, and, interestingly, retelling of what is being learned. People understand and remember new things, which is to say they master them, only after actively exploring them. Humans learn in action. An essential part of an In Action book is that it is example-driven. It encourages the reader to try things out, to play with new code, and explore new ideas.

There is another, more mundane, reason for the title of this book: Our readers are busy. They use books to do a job or solve a problem. They need books that allow them to jump in and jump out easily and learn just what they want just when they want it. They need books that aid them in action. The books in this series are designed for such readers.

about the cover illustration

The figure on the cover of *Windows PowerShell in Action, Third Edition* is a "Mufti," the chief of religion or the chief scholar who interpreted the religious law and whose pronouncements on matters both large and small were binding to the faithful. The illustration is taken from a collection of costumes of the Ottoman Empire published on Jan. 1, 1802, by William Miller of Old Bond Street, London. The title page is missing from the collection and we have been unable to track it down to date. The book's table of contents identifies the figures in both English and French, and each illustration bears the names of two artists who worked on it, both of whom would no doubt be surprised to find their art gracing the front cover of a computer programming book ... two hundred years later.

The collection was purchased by a Manning editor at an antiquarian flea market in the "Garage" on West 26th Street in Manhattan. The seller was an American based in Ankara, Turkey, and the transaction took place just as he was packing up his stand for the day. The Manning editor did not have on his person the substantial amount of cash that was required for the purchase and a credit card and check were both politely turned down. With the seller flying back to Ankara that evening the situation was getting hopeless. What was the solution? It turned out to be nothing more than an old-fashioned verbal agreement sealed with a handshake. The seller simply proposed that the money be transferred to him by wire and the editor walked out with the bank information on a piece of paper and the portfolio of images under his arm. Needless to say, we transferred the funds the next day, and we remain grateful and impressed by this unknown person's trust in one of us. It recalls something that might have happened a long time ago.

The pictures from the Ottoman collection, like the other illustrations that appear on our covers, bring to life the richness and variety of dress customs of two centuries ago. They recall the sense of isolation and distance of that period—and of every other historic period except our own hyperkinetic present.

Dress codes have changed since then and the diversity by region, so rich at the time, has faded away. It is now often hard to tell the inhabitant of one continent from another. Perhaps, trying to view it optimistically, we have traded a cultural and visual diversity for a more varied personal life. Or a more varied and interesting intellectual and technical life.

We at Manning celebrate the inventiveness, the initiative, and, yes, the fun of the computer business with book covers based on the rich diversity of regional life of two centuries ago—brought back to life by the pictures from this collection.

Welcome to PowerShell

1

This chapter covers

- Core concepts
- Aliases and elastic systems
- Parsing and PowerShell
- Pipelines
- Formatting and output

> *Vizzini: Inconceivable!*
>
> *Inigo: You keep on using that word. I do not think it means what you think it means.*
>
> —*William Goldman,* The Princess Bride

It may seem strange to start by welcoming you to PowerShell when PowerShell is ten years old (at the time of writing), is on its fifth version, and you're reading the third edition of this book.

> **NOTE** PowerShell v6 is under development as we write this. The appendix covers the changes that this new version will introduce.

In reality the adoption of PowerShell is only now achieving significant momentum, meaning that to many users PowerShell is a new technology and the three versions of PowerShell subsequent to this book's second edition contain many new features. Welcome to PowerShell.

> **NOTE** This book is written using PowerShell v5. It'll be noted in the text where earlier versions are different, or work in a different manner. We'll also document when various features were introduced to PowerShell or significantly modified between versions. We treat v5 and v5.1 together as v5 as the differences are relatively minor.

Windows PowerShell is the command and scripting language from Microsoft built into all versions of Windows since Windows Server 2008. Although PowerShell is new and different (or has new features you haven't yet explored), it's been designed to make use of what you already know, making it easy to learn. It's also designed to allow you to learn a bit at a time.

Running PowerShell commands

You have two choices for running the examples provided in this book. First is to use the PowerShell console. This provides a command-line interface. It's the tool of choice for interactive work.

The second choice is the PowerShell Integrated Scripting Environment (ISE). The ISE supplies an editing pane plus a combined output and interactive pane. The ISE is the tool of choice when developing scripts, functions, and other advanced functionality.

The examples in the book will be written in a way that allows pasting directly into either tool.

Third-party tools exist, such as those supplied by Sapien, but we'll only consider the native tools in this book.

Starting at the beginning, here's the traditional "Hello world" program in PowerShell:

```
'Hello world.'
```

But "Hello world" itself isn't interesting. Here's something a bit more complicated:

```
Get-ChildItem -Path $env:windir\*.log |
Select-String -List error |
Format-Table Path,LineNumber –AutoSize
```

Although this is more complex, you can probably still figure out what it does. It searches all the log files in the Windows directory, looking for the string "error", and then prints the full name of the matching file and the matching line number. "Useful, but not special," you might think, because you can easily do this using cmd.exe on Windows or bash on UNIX. What about the "big, really big" thing? Well, how about this example:

```
([xml] [System.Net.WebClient]::new().
    DownloadString('http://blogs.msdn.com/powershell/rss.aspx')).
        RSS.Channel.Item |
            Format-Table title,link
```

Now we're getting somewhere. This script downloads the RSS feed from the Power-Shell team blog and then displays the title and a link for each blog entry. By the way, you weren't expected to figure out this example yet. If you did, you can move to the head of the class!

One last example:

```
using assembly  System.Windows.Forms
using namespace System.Windows.Forms
$form = [Form] @{
    Text = 'My First Form'
}
$button = [Button] @{
    Text = 'Push Me!'
    Dock = 'Fill'
}
$button.add_Click{
    $form.Close()
}
$form.Controls.Add($button)
$form.ShowDialog()
```

This script uses the Windows Forms library (WinForms) to build a GUI that has a single button displaying the text "Push Me!" Figure 1.1 shows the window this script creates.

When you click the button, it closes the form and exits the script. With this you go from "Hello world" to a GUI application in less than two pages.

Let's come back down to Earth for a minute. The intent of chapter 1 is to set the stage for understanding PowerShell—what it is, what it isn't, and, almost as important, why the PowerShell team made the decisions they made in designing the PowerShell language. Chapter 1 covers the goals of the project, along with some of the major issues the team faced in trying to achieve those goals. First, a philosophical digression: while under development, from 2002 until the first public release in 2006, the codename for this project was Monad. The

Figure 1.1 When you run the code from the example, this window will be displayed.

name Monad comes from *The Monadology* by Gottfried Wilhelm Leibniz, one of the inventors of calculus. Here's how Leibniz defined the Monad:

> *The Monad, of which we shall here speak, is nothing but a simple substance, which enters into compounds. By "simple" is meant "without parts."*
>
> —*Gottfried Wilhelm Leibniz,* The Monadology (translated by Robert Latta)

In *The Monadology*, Leibniz describes a world of irreducible components from which all things could be composed. This captures the spirit of the project: to create a toolkit of simple pieces you compose to create complex solutions.

1.1 *What is PowerShell?*

What is PowerShell, and what can you do with it? Ask a group of PowerShell users and you'll get different answers:

- PowerShell is a command-line shell.
- PowerShell is a scripting environment.
- PowerShell is an automation engine.

These are all part of the answer. We prefer to say PowerShell is a tool you can use to manage your Microsoft-based machines and applications that programs consistency into your management process. The tool is attractive to administrators and developers in that it can span the range of command line, simple and advanced scripts, to real programs.

> **NOTE** If you take this to mean PowerShell is the ideal DevOps tool for the Microsoft platform, then congratulations—you've got it in one.

PowerShell draws heavily from existing command-line shell and scripting languages, but the language, runtime, and subsequent additions, such as PowerShell Workflows and Desired State Configuration, were designed from scratch to be an optimal environment for the modern Windows operating system.

Most people are introduced to PowerShell through its interactive aspects. Let's refine our definitions of shell and scripting.

1.1.1 *Shells, command lines, and scripting languages*

In the previous section we called PowerShell a command-line shell. You may be asking, what's a shell? And how's it different from a command interpreter? What about scripting languages? If you can script in a shell language, doesn't that make it a scripting language? In answering these questions, let's start with shells.

Defining a shell can be tricky because pretty much everything at Microsoft has something called a *shell*. Windows Explorer is a shell. Visual Studio has a component called a shell. Heck, even the Xbox has something called a shell.

Historically, the term *shell* describes the piece of software that sits over an operating system's core functionality. This core functionality is known as the *operating system kernel* (shell ... kernel ... get it?). A shell is the piece of software that lets you access the functionality provided by the operating system. For our purposes, we're more interested in the traditional text-based environment where the user types a command and receives a response. Put another way, a shell is a command-line interpreter. The two terms can be used for the most part interchangeably.

SCRIPTING LANGUAGES VS. SHELLS

If this is the case, what's scripting and why are scripting languages not shells? To some extent, there's no difference. Many scripting languages have a mode in which they take commands from the user and then execute those commands to return results. This mode of operation is called a *read-evaluate-print loop*, or REPL. In what way is a scripting language with a REPL not a shell? The difference is mainly in the user experience. A proper command-line shell is also a proper UI. As such, a command line has to provide a number of features to make the user's experience pleasant and customizable, including aliases (shortcuts for hard-to-type commands), wildcard matching to avoid having to type out full names, and the ability to start other programs easily. Finally, command-line shells provide mechanisms for examining, editing, and re-executing previously typed commands. These mechanisms are called *command history*.

If scripting languages can be shells, can shells be scripting languages? The answer is, emphatically, yes. With each generation, the UNIX shell languages have grown increasingly powerful. It's possible to write substantial applications in a modern shell language, such as Bash or Zsh. Scripting languages characteristically have an advantage over shell languages in that they provide mechanisms to help you develop larger scripts by letting you break a script into components, or *modules*. Scripting languages typically provide more sophisticated features for debugging your scripts. Next, scripting language runtimes are implemented in a way that makes their code execution more efficient, and scripts written in these languages execute more quickly than they would in the corresponding shell script runtime. Finally, scripting language syntax is oriented more toward writing an application than toward interactively issuing commands.

In the end, there's no hard-and-fast distinction between a shell language and a scripting language. Because PowerShell's goal is to be both a good scripting language and a good interactive shell, balancing the trade-offs between user experience and script authoring was one of the major language design challenges.

MANAGING WINDOWS THROUGH OBJECTS

Another factor that drove the need for a new shell model is, as Windows acquired more and more subsystems and features, the number of issues users had to think about when managing a system increased dramatically. To help users deal with this increase in complexity, the manageable elements were factored into structured data objects. This collection of *management objects* is known internally at Microsoft as the *Windows Management Surface*.

> **NOTE**   Microsoft wasn't the only company running into issues caused by increased complexity. Most people in the industry were having this problem. This led to the Distributed Management Task Force (dmtf.org), an industry organization, creating a standard for management objects called the *Common Information Model* (CIM). Microsoft's original implementation of this standard is called *Windows Management Instrumentation* (WMI).

Although this factoring addressed overall complexity and worked well for GUIs, it made it much harder to work with using a traditional text-based shell environment.

Windows is an API-driven operating system, compared to UNIX and its derivatives, which are document (or text) driven. You can administer UNIX by changing configuration files. In Windows, you need to use the API, which means accessing properties and using methods on the appropriate object.

Finally, as the power of the PC increased, Windows began to move off the desktop and into the corporate datacenter. In the corporate datacenter, there were a large number of servers to manage, and the graphical point-and-click management approach didn't scale. All these elements combined to make it clear Microsoft could no longer ignore the command line.

Now that you grasp the environmental forces that led to the creation of Power-Shell—the need for command-line automation in a distributed object-based operating environment—let's look at the form the solution took.

1.2 PowerShell example code

We've said PowerShell is for solving problems that involve writing code. By now you're probably asking "Dude! Where's my code?" Enough talk, let's see some example code! First, we'll revisit the `Get-ChildItem` example. This time, instead of displaying the directory listing, you'll save it into a file using output redirection like in other shell environments. In the following example, you'll use `Get-ChildItem` to get information about a file named somefile.txt in the root of the C: drive. Using redirection, you'll direct the output into a new file, c:\foo.txt, and then use the `type` command to display what was saved. Here's what this looks like:

```
PS> Get-ChildItem -Path C:\somefile.txt

    Directory: C:\

Mode                 LastWriteTime         Length Name
----                 -------------         ------ ----
-a----        29/05/2017     13:58          25424 somefile.txt
```

> **NOTE**   PowerShell has aliases for many cmdlets so `dir C:\somefile.txt` and `ls C:\somefile.txt` would both work. It is best practice to reserve aliases for interactive usage and not use them in scripts. We'll usually use the full cmdlet name but may occasionally use aliases to save space.

Next, instead of displaying the directory listing, you'll save it into a file using output redirection as in other shell environments. In the following example, you'll get information about a file named somefile.txt in the root of the C: drive. Using redirection, you direct the output into a new file, c:\foo.txt, and then use the `Get-Content` (you can use the alias of `cat` or `type` if you prefer) command to display what was saved. Here's what this looks like:

```
PS> Get-ChildItem -Path C:\somefile.txt > c:\foo.txt
PS> Get-Content -Path C:\foo.txt

    Directory: C:\

Mode               LastWriteTime        Length Name
----               -------------        ------ ----
-a----       29/05/2017      13:58       25424 somefile.txt
```

As you can see, commands work more or less as you'd expect. Let's go over other things that should be familiar to you.

NOTE On your system choose any file that exists and the example will work fine, though obviously, the output will be different.

1.2.1 Navigation and basic operations

The PowerShell commands for working with the file system should be pretty familiar to most users. You navigate around the file system with the `cd` (alias for `Set-Location`) command. Files are copied with the `copy` or `cp` (aliases for `Copy-Item`) commands, moved with the `move` and `mv` (aliases for `Move-Item`) commands, and removed with the `del` or `rm` (aliases for `Remove-Item`) commands. Why two of each command? One set of names is familiar to `cmd.exe`/DOS users and the other is familiar to UNIX users. In practice, they're aliases for the same command, designed to make it easy for people to get going with PowerShell.

NOTE In PowerShell v6 Core on Linux or macOS these common aliases have been removed to prevent conflict with native commands on Linux and macOS. The aliases are present in the Windows versions of PowerShell v6 Core.

Keep in mind that, although the commands are similar, they're not exactly the same as either of the other two systems. You can use the `Get-Help` command to get help about these commands. Here's the output of `Get-Help` for the `dir` command:

```
PS> Get-Help dir

NAME
    Get-ChildItem

SYNOPSIS
    Gets the items and child items in one or more specified locations.

SYNTAX
    Get-ChildItem [[-Filter] <String>] [-Attributes {ReadOnly |
Hidden | System | Directory | Archive | Device |  Normal |
 Temporary | SparseFile | ReparsePoint | Compressed | Offline |
  NotContentIndexed | Encrypted |IntegrityStream | NoScrubData}]
```

```
[-Depth <UInt32>] [-Directory] [-Exclude <String[]>] [-File]
[-Force] [-Hidden][-Include <String[]>] -LiteralPath <String[]>
[-Name] [-ReadOnly] [-Recurse] [-System] [-UseTransaction]
  [<CommonParameters>]

    Get-ChildItem [[-Path] <String[]>] [[-Filter] <String>]
[-Attributes {ReadOnly | Hidden | System | Directory |
Archive | Device | Normal | Temporary | SparseFile |
ReparsePoint | Compressed | Offline | NotContentIndexed |
Encrypted | IntegrityStream | NoScrubData}] [-Depth <UInt32>]
[-Directory] [-Exclude <String[]>] [-File] [-Force]
[-Hidden] [-Include <String[]>] [-Name] [-ReadOnly] [-Recurse]
[-System] [-UseTransaction] [<CommonParameters>]
```

DESCRIPTION

    The Get-ChildItem cmdlet gets the items in one or more specified
    locations. If the item is a container, it gets the items inside the
    container, known as child items. You can use the Recurse parameter to get
    items in all child containers.

    A location can be a file system location, such as a directory, or a
    location exposed by a different Windows PowerShell provider, such as a
    registry hive or a certificate store.

RELATED LINKS
    Online Version: http://go.microsoft.com/fwlink/?LinkId=821580
    Get-Item
    Get-Location
    Get-Process
    Get-PSProvider

REMARKS
    To see the examples, type: "get-help Get-ChildItem -examples".
    For more information, type: "get-help Get-ChildItem -detailed".
    For technical information, type: "get-help Get-ChildItem -full".
For online help, type "get-help Get-ChildItem -online"PowerShell help system

PowerShell help system

The PowerShell help subsystem contains information about all the commands provided with the system and is a great way to explore what's available.

In PowerShell v3 and later, help files aren't installed by default. Help has become updatable and you need to install the latest versions yourself. See `Get-Help about_Updatable_Help`.

You can even use wildcard characters to search through the help topics (v2 and later). This is the simple text output. The PowerShell ISE also includes help in the richer Windows format and will let you choose an item and then press F1 to view the help for the item. By using the `–Online` option to `Get-Help`, you can view the help text for a command or topic using a web browser.

```
PS> Get-Help Get-ChildItem
```

(Continued)

displays the information in the help file stored locally.

```
PS> Get-Help Get-ChildItem -Online
```

displays the online version of the help file.

Using the -Online option is the best way to get help because the online documentation is constantly being updated and corrected, whereas the local copies aren't.

1.2.2 Basic expressions and variables

In addition to running commands, PowerShell can evaluate expressions. In effect, it operates as a kind of calculator. Let's evaluate a simple expression:

```
PS> 2+2
4
```

Notice as soon as you typed the expression, the result was calculated and displayed. It wasn't necessary to use any kind of print statement to display the result. It's important to remember whenever an expression is evaluated, the result of the expression is output, not discarded. PowerShell supports most of the basic arithmetic operations you'd expect, including floating point.

You can save the output of an expression to a file by using the redirection operator:

```
PS> (2+2)*3/7 > c:\foo.txt
PS> Get-Content c:\foo.txt
1.71428571428571
```

Saving expressions into files is useful; saving them in variables is more useful:

```
PS> $n = (2+2)*3
PS> $n
12

PS> $n / 7
1.71428571428571
```

Variables can also be used to store the output of commands:

```
PS> $files = Get-ChildItem
PS> $files[1]

    Directory: C:\Users\Richard\Documents

Mode                LastWriteTime         Length Name
----                -------------         ------ ----
d----        16/02/2017     18:36                Custom Office Templates
```

In this example, you extracted the second element of the collection of file information objects returned by the `Get-ChildItem` command. You were able to do this because you saved the output of the `Get-ChildItem` command as an array of objects in the `$files` variable.

> **NOTE**   Collections in PowerShell start at 0, not 1. This is a characteristic we've inherited from .NET. This is why `$files[1]` extracts the second element, not the first.

Given PowerShell is all about objects, the basic operators need to work on more than numbers. Chapters 3 and 4 cover these features in detail.

1.2.3   *Processing data*

As you've seen, you can run commands to get information, perform some basic operations on this information using the PowerShell operators, and then store the results in files and variables. Let's look at additional ways you can process this data. First, you'll see how to sort objects and how to extract properties from those objects. Then we'll look at using the PowerShell flow-control statements to write scripts that use conditionals and loops to do more sophisticated processing.

SORTING OBJECTS

First, sort the list of file information objects returned by `Get-ChildItem`. Because you're sorting objects, the command you'll use is `Sort-Object`. For convenience, you'll use the shorter alias `sort` in these examples. Start by looking at the default output, which shows the files sorted by filename:

```
PS> cd c:\files
PS> Get-ChildItem

    Directory: C:\files

Mode                LastWriteTime     Length Name
----                -------------     ------ ----
-a---        21/01/2015     18:10          9 File 1.txt
-a---        11/07/2015     15:14      15986 File 2.txt
-a---        21/01/2015     18:10          9 File 3.txt
-a---        21/01/2015     18:10          9 File 4.txt
```

The output shows the basic properties on the file system objects, sorted by filename. Now sort by filename in descending order:

```
PS> Get-ChildItem | sort -Descending

        Directory: C:\files

Mode                LastWriteTime     Length Name
----                -------------     ------ ----
-a---        21/01/2015     18:10          9 File 4.txt
-a---        21/01/2015     18:10          9 File 3.txt
-a---        11/07/2015     15:14      15986 File 2.txt
-a---        21/01/2015     18:10          9 File 1.txt
```

There you have it—files sorted by filename in reverse order. Now you'll sort by something other than the filename: file length.

> **NOTE** Many examples in this book use aliases (shortcuts) rather than the full cmdlet name. This is for brevity and to ensure the code fits neatly in the page.

In PowerShell, when you use the `Sort-Object` cmdlet (alias `sort`), you don't have to tell it to sort numerically—it already knows the type of the field, and you can specify the sort key by property name instead of a numeric field offset. The result looks like this:

```
PS> Get-ChildItem | sort -Property length

        Directory: C:\files

Mode                LastWriteTime       Length Name
----                -------------       ------ ----
-a---        21/01/2015     18:10            9 File 3.txt
-a---        21/01/2015     18:10            9 File 4.txt
-a---        21/01/2015     18:10            9 File 1.txt
-a---        11/07/2015     15:14        15986 File 2.txt
```

This illustrates what working with pipelines of objects gives you:

- You have the ability to access data elements by name instead of using substring indexes or field numbers.
- By having the original type of the element preserved, operations execute correctly without you having to provide additional information.

Now let's look at other things you can do with objects.

SELECTING PROPERTIES FROM AN OBJECT

In this section we'll introduce another cmdlet for working with objects: `Select-Object`. This cmdlet allows you to select a subrange of the objects piped into it and specify a subset of the properties on those objects.

Say you want to get the largest file in a directory and put it into a variable:

```
PS> $a = Get-ChildItem | sort -Property length -Descending |
Select-Object -First 1
PS> $a
        Directory: C:\files

Mode                LastWriteTime       Length Name
----                -------------       ------ ----
-a---        11/07/2015     15:14        15986 File 2.txt
```

> **NOTE** You'll notice the secondary prompt >> when you copy the previous example into a PowerShell console. The first line of the command ended in a pipe symbol. The PowerShell interpreter noticed this, saw the command was incomplete, and prompted for additional text to complete the command. Once the command is complete, you type a second blank line to send the command to the interpreter. If you want to cancel the command, you can

press Ctrl-C at any time to return to the normal prompt. The code examples in the book won't include the >> to make copying from the electronic version simpler for the reader.

Now say you want only the name of the directory containing the file and not all the other properties of the object. You can also do this with `Select-Object` (alias `select`). As with the `Sort-Object` cmdlet, `Select-Object` takes a `-Property` parameter (you'll see this frequently in the PowerShell environment—commands are consistent in their use of parameters):

```
PS> $a = Get-ChildItem| sort -Property length -Descending |
Select-Object -First 1 -Property Directory
PS> $a

Directory
---------
C:\files
```

You now have an object with a single property.

PROCESSING WITH THE FOREACH-OBJECT CMDLET

The final simplification is to get the value itself. We'll introduce a new cmdlet that lets you do arbitrary processing on each object in a pipeline. The `ForEach-Object` cmdlet executes a block of statements for each object in the pipeline. You can get an arbitrary property out of an object and then do arbitrary processing on that information using the `ForEach-Object` command. Here's an example that adds up the lengths of all the objects in a directory:

```
PS> $total = 0
PS> Get-ChildItem | ForEach-Object {$total += $_.length }
PS> $total
16013
```

In this example you initialize the variable `$total` to `0`, then add to it the length of each file returned by the `Get-ChildItem` command, and display the total (you'll get a different total on your system).

PROCESSING OTHER KINDS OF DATA

One of the great strengths of the PowerShell approach is once you learn a pattern for solving a problem, you can use this same pattern over and over again. Say you want to find the largest three files in a directory. The command line might look like this:

```
PS> Get-ChildItem | sort -Descending length | select -First 3
```

Here, the `Get-ChildItem` command retrieved the list of file information objects, PowerShell then sorted them in descending order by length, and then selected the first three results to get the three largest files.

Now let's tackle a different problem. You want to find the three processes on the system with the largest working set size. Here's what this command line looks like:

```
PS> Get-Process | sort -Descending ws | select -First 3
Handles  NPM(K)    PM(K)      WS(K) VM(M)   CPU(s)     Id ProcessName
-------  ------    -----      ----- -----   ------     -- -----------
   1337    1916   235360     287852  1048    63.23   2440 WWAHost
    962      55    94460     176008   692   340.25   6632 WINWORD
    635      40   136040     140088   783     6.42   2564 powershell
```

This time you run `Get-Process` to get data about the processes on this computer, and sort on the working set instead of the file size. Otherwise, the pattern is identical to the previous example. This command pattern can be applied over and over.

NOTE   Because of the ability to apply a command pattern repeatedly, most of the examples in this book are deliberately generic. The intent is to highlight the pattern of the solution rather than show a specific example. Once you understand the basic patterns, you can effectively adapt them to solve a multitude of other problems.

1.2.4   Flow-control statements

Pipelines are great, but sometimes you need more control over the flow of your script. PowerShell has the usual flow-control statements found in most programming languages. These include the basic `if` statements, a powerful `switch` statement, and loops like `while`, `for` and `foreach`, and so on. Here's an example showing the `while` and `if` statements:

```
PS> $i=0
PS> while ($i++ -lt 10) { if ($i % 2) {"$i is odd"}}
1 is odd
3 is odd
5 is odd
7 is odd
9 is odd
```

This example uses the `while` loop to count through a range of numbers, printing only the odd numbers. In the body of the `while` loop is an `if` statement that tests to see whether the current number is odd, and then writes a message if it is. You can do the same thing using the `foreach` statement and the range operator (`..`), but much more succinctly:

```
PS> foreach ($i in 1..10) { if ($i % 2) {"$i is odd"}}
```

The `foreach` statement iterates over a collection of objects, and the range operator is a way to generate a sequence of numbers. The two combine to make looping over a sequence of numbers a very clean operation.

Because the range operator generates a sequence of numbers, and numbers are objects like everything else in PowerShell, you can implement this using pipelines and the ForEach-Object (alias foreach) cmdlet:

```
PS> 1..10 | foreach { if ($_ % 2) {"$_ is odd"}}
```

These examples only scratch the surface of what you can do with the PowerShell flow-control statements. (Wait until you see the switch statement!) The complete set of control structures is covered in detail in chapter 5 with lots of examples.

1.2.5   *Scripts and functions*

What good is a scripting language if you can't package commands into scripts? Power-Shell lets you do this by putting your commands into a text file with a .ps1 extension and then running that command. You can even have parameters in your scripts. Put the following text into a file called hello.ps1:

```
param($name = 'bub')
"Hello $name, how are you?"
```

Notice the param keyword is used to define a parameter called $name. The parameter is given a default value of 'bub'. Now you can run this script from the PowerShell prompt by typing the name as .\hello. You need the .\ to tell PowerShell to get the command from the current directory.

> **NOTE**   Before you can run scripts on a machine in the default configuration, you'll have to change the PowerShell execution policy to allow scripts to run. Use Get-Help about_execution_policies to view detailed instructions on execution policies. The default settings change between Windows versions, so be careful to check the execution policy setting.

The first time you run this script, you won't specify any arguments:

```
PS> .\hello
Hello bub, how are you?
```

You see the default value was used in the response. Run it again, but this time specify an argument:

```
PS> .\hello Bruce
Hello Bruce, how are you?
```

Now the argument is in the output instead of the default value. Sometimes you want to have subroutines in your code. PowerShell addresses this need through functions. Let's turn the hello script into a function. Here's what it looks like:

```
function hello {
param($name = "bub")
"Hello $name, how are you"
}
```

The body of the function is exactly the same as the script. The only thing added is the `function` keyword, the name of the function, and braces around the body of the function. Now run it, first with no arguments as you did with the script

```
PS> hello
Hello bub, how are you
```

and then with an argument:

```
PS> hello Bruce
Hello Bruce, how are you
```

Obviously, the function operates in the same way as the script, except PowerShell didn't have to load it from a disk file, making it a bit faster to call. Scripts and functions are covered in detail in chapter 6.

1.2.6   *Remote administration*

In the previous sections, you've seen the kinds of things you can do with PowerShell on a single computer, but the computing industry has long since moved beyond a one-computer world. Being able to manage groups of computers, without having to physically visit each one, is critical in the modern cloud-orientated IT world where your server may easily be on another continent. To address this, PowerShell has built-in remote execution capabilities (remoting) and an execution model that ensures if a command works locally it should also work remotely.

> **NOTE** Remoting was introduced in PowerShell v2. It isn't available in PowerShell v1.

The core of PowerShell remoting is `Invoke-Command` (aliased to `icm`). This command allows you to invoke a block of PowerShell script on the current computer, on a remote computer, or on a thousand remote computers. Let's see some of this in action. Microsoft releases patches for Windows on a regular basis. Some of those patches are critical, in that they resolve security-related issues, and as an administrator you need to be able to test if the patch has been applied to the machines for which you're responsible. Checking a single machine is relatively easy—you can use the Windows update option in the control panel and view the installed updates as shown in figure 1.2.

Alternatively, you can use the `Get-HotFix` cmdlet:

```
PS> Get-HotFix -Id KB3213986

Source  Description   HotFixID  InstalledBy         InstalledOn
------  -----------   --------  -----------         -----------

W510W16 Security Update KB3213986 NT AUTHORITY\SYSTEM 12/01/2017 00:00:00
```

This shows you the hotfix is installed on the local machine.

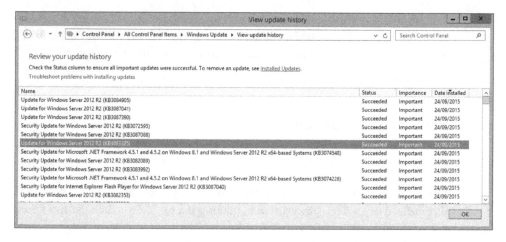

Figure 1.2   Viewing the installed updates on the local (Windows Server 2012 R2) machine

> **NOTE**   Updates for Windows 10 and Windows Server 2016 tend to be cumulative so your machine may not have KB3213986 installed.

But what about all your other machines? Connecting to each one individually and using the control panel or running the `Get-HotFix` cmdlet is tedious. You need a method of running the cmdlet on remote machines and having the results returned to your local machine.

`Invoke-Command` is used to wrap the previous command:

```
PS> Invoke-Command -ScriptBlock {Get-HotFix -Id KB3213986} `
-ComputerName W16DSC01

Description         : Security Update
HotFixID            : KB3213986
InstalledBy         : NT AUTHORITY\SYSTEM
InstalledOn         : 11/01/2017 00:00:00
PSComputerName      : W16DSC01
```

> **NOTE**   `Get-HotFix` has a `-ComputerName` parameter, and, like many cmdlets, is capable of working directly with remote machines. Cmdlet-based remoting often uses protocols other than WS-MAN. Using `Invoke-Command`, as in a PowerShell remoting session, is more efficient, as you'll see in chapter 11.

You have many machines that need testing. Typing in the computer names one at a time is still too tedious. You can create a list of computers, either from a text file or in your code, and test them all:

```
PS> $computers = 'W16DSC01', 'W16DSC02'
PS> Invoke-Command -ScriptBlock {Get-HotFix -Id KB3213986} `
-ComputerName $computers |
Format-Table HotFixId, InstalledOn, PSComputerName -AutoSize
```

```
HotFixID   InstalledOn          PSComputerName
--------   -----------          --------------
KB3213986 11/01/2017 00:00:00  W16DSC02
KB3213986 11/01/2017 00:00:00  W16DSC01
```

An error is generated on a computer that doesn't have the patch installed, and results appear on the computers that do.

> **NOTE** In a production script you'd put error handling in place to catch the error and report that the patch wasn't installed. This will be covered in chapter 14.

`Invoke-Command` is the way to programmatically execute PowerShell commands on a remote machine. When you want to connect to a machine to interact with it on a one-to-one basis, you use the `Enter-PSSession` command. This command allows you to start an interactive one-to-one session with a remote computer. Running `Enter-PSSession` looks like this:

```
PS> Enter-PSSession -ComputerName W16DSC01
[W16DSC01]: PS C:\Users\Richard\Documents> Get-HotFix -Id KB3213986 |
   Format-Table -AutoSize

Source    Description     HotFixID  InstalledBy         InstalledOn
------    -----------     --------  -----------         -----------
W16DSC01 Security Update KB3213986 NT AUTHORITY\SYSTEM 11/01/2017 00:00:00

[W16DSC01]: PS C:\Users\Richard\Documents> Get-Date

05 March 2017 15:35:07

[W16DSC01]: PS C:\Users\Richard\Documents> Exit-PSSession
PS>
```

When you connect to the remote computer, your prompt changes to indicate you're working remotely. Once connected, you can interact with the remote computer the same way you would a local machine. When you're done, exit the remote session with the `Exit-PSSession` command, which returns you to the local session. This brief introduction covers some powerful techniques, but we've only begun to cover all the things remoting lets you do.

At this point, we'll end our "cook's tour" of PowerShell. We've only breezed over the features and capabilities of the environment. In upcoming chapters, we'll explore each of the elements discussed here in detail and a whole lot more.

1.3 Core concepts

The core PowerShell language is based on the mature IEEE standard POSIX 1003.2 grammar for the Korn shell, which has a long history as a successful basis for modern shells like Bash and Zsh. The language design team (Jim Truher and Bruce Payette) deviated from this standard where necessary to address the specific needs of an object-based shell and to make it easier to write sophisticated scripts.

PowerShell syntax is aligned with C#. The major value this brings is PowerShell code can be migrated to C# when necessary for performance improvements, and, more importantly, C# examples can be easily converted to PowerShell—the more examples you have in a language, the better off you are.

1.3.1   *Command concepts and terminology*

Much of the terminology used in PowerShell will be familiar if you've used other shells in the Linux or Windows world. Because PowerShell is a new kind of shell, there are a number of terms that are different and a few new terms to learn. In this section, we'll go over the PowerShell-specific concepts and terminology for command types and command syntax.

1.3.2   *Commands and cmdlets*

Commands are the fundamental part of any shell language; they're what you type to get things done. A simple command looks like this:

```
command -parameter1 -parameter2 argument1 argument2
```

A more detailed illustration of the anatomy of this command is shown in figure 1.3. This figure calls out all the individual elements of the command.

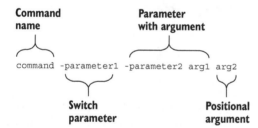

Figure 1.3   The anatomy of a basic command. It begins with the name of the command, followed by parameters. These may be switch parameters that take no arguments, regular parameters that take arguments, or positional parameters where the matching parameter is inferred by the argument's position on the command line.

All commands are broken down into the command name, the parameters specified to the command, and the arguments to those parameters. You can think of a parameter as the receiver of a piece of information and the argument as the information itself.

> **NOTE**   The distinction between *parameter* and *argument* may seem a bit strange from a programmer's perspective. If you're used to languages such as Python and Visual Basic, which allow for keyword parameters, PowerShell parameters correspond to the keywords, and arguments correspond to the values.

The first element in the command is the name of the command to be executed. The PowerShell interpreter looks at this name and determines which command to run, and which *kind* of command to run. In PowerShell there are a number of categories of commands: cmdlets, shell function commands, script commands, workflow commands, and native Windows commands. Following the command name come zero or more parameters and/or arguments. A parameter starts with a dash followed by the name of the parameter. An argument, conversely, is the value that will be associated with, or *bound to*, a specific parameter. Let's look at an example:

```
PS> Write-Output -InputObject Hello
Hello
```

Here, the command is `Write-Output`, the parameter is `-InputObject`, and the argument is `Hello`.

What about the positional parameters? When a PowerShell command is created, the author of that command specifies information that allows PowerShell to determine which parameter to bind an argument to, even if the parameter name itself is missing. For example, the `Write-Output` command has been defined such that the first parameter is `-InputObject`. This lets you write:

```
PS> Write-Output Hello
Hello
```

The piece of the PowerShell interpreter that figures all this out is called the *parameter binder*. The parameter binder is smart—it doesn't require you to specify the full name of a parameter as long as you specify enough for it to uniquely distinguish what you mean.

> **NOTE** PowerShell isn't case-sensitive but we use the correct casing on commands and parameters to aid reading. It's also a good practice when scripting, as it's easier to understand the code when you revisit it many months later.

What else does the parameter binder do? It's in charge of determining how to match the types of arguments to the types of parameters. Remember PowerShell is an object-based shell. Everything in PowerShell has a type. PowerShell uses a fairly complex type-conversion system to correctly put things together. When you type a command at the command line, you're typing strings. What happens if the command requires a different type of object? The parameter binder uses the type converter to try to convert that string into the correct type for the parameter. If you use a value that can't be converted to the correct type you get an error message explaining the type conversion failed. We discuss this in more detail in chapter 2 when we talk about types.

What happens if the argument you want to pass to the command starts with a dash? This is where the quotes come in. Let's use `Write-Output` to print out the string "-InputObject":

```
PS> Write-Output -InputObject "-InputObject"
-InputObject
```

And it works as desired. Alternatively, you could type this:

```
PS> Write-Output "-InputObject"
-InputObject
```

The quotes keep the parameter binder from treating the quoted string as a parameter.

Another, less frequently used way of doing this is by using the special "end-of-parameters" parameter, which is two hyphens back to back (`--`). Everything after this sequence will be treated as an argument, even if it looks like a parameter. For example, using `--` you can also write out the string "-InputObject" without using quotes:

```
PS> Write-Output -- -InputObject
-InputObject
```

This is a convention standardized in the POSIX Shell and Utilities specification.

The final element of the basic command pattern is the *switch parameter*. These are parameters that don't require an argument. They're usually either present or absent (obviously they can't be positional). A good example is the `-Recurse` parameter on the `Get-ChildItem` command. This switch tells the `Get-ChildItem` command to display files from a specified directory as well as all its subdirectories:

```
PS> Get-ChildItem -Recurse -Filter c*d.exe C:\Windows

    Directory: C:\Windows\System32

Mode                LastWriteTime          Length Name
----                -------------          ------ ----
-a----        11/11/2016     09:56         187520 CloudStorageWizard.exe
-a----        16/07/2016     12:42         232960 cmd.exe
```

As you can see, the `-Recurse` switch takes no arguments. We've only shown the first folder's worth of results for brevity.

> **NOTE**   Although it's almost always the case that switch parameters don't take arguments, it's possible to specify arguments to them. We'll save our discussion of when and why you might do this for chapter 7, which focuses on scripts (shell functions and scripts are the only time you need this particular feature, and we'll keep you in suspense for the time being).

Now that we've covered the basic anatomy of the command line, let's go over the types of commands that PowerShell supports.

1.3.3   *Command categories*

As we mentioned earlier, there are four categories of commands in PowerShell: cmdlets, functions, scripts, and native Win32 executables. PowerShell v4, and later, also has configurations (see chapter 18).

CMDLETS

The first category of command is a cmdlet (pronounced "command-let"). *Cmdlet* is a term that's specific to the PowerShell environment. A cmdlet is implemented by a .NET class that derives from the `Cmdlet` base class in the PowerShell Software Developers Kit (SDK).

NOTE Building cmdlets is a developer task and requires the PowerShell SDK. This SDK is freely available for download from Microsoft and includes extensive documentation along with many code samples. Our goal is to coach you to effectively use and script in the PowerShell environment, so we're not going to do much more than mention the SDK in this book.

This category of command is compiled into a dynamic link library (DLL) and then loaded into the PowerShell process, usually when the shell starts up. Because the compiled code is loaded into the process, it's the most efficient category of command to execute.

Cmdlets always have names of the form Verb-Noun, where the verb specifies the action and the noun specifies the object on which to operate. In traditional shells, cmdlets correspond most closely to what's usually called a *built-in command*. In Power-Shell, though, anybody can add a cmdlet to the runtime, and there isn't any special class of built-in commands.

FUNCTIONS

The next type of command is a *function*. This is a named piece of PowerShell script code that lives in memory as the interpreter is running, and is discarded on exit. Functions consist of user-defined code that's parsed when defined. This parsed representation is preserved so it doesn't have to be reparsed every time it's used.

Functions in PowerShell v1 could have named parameters like cmdlets but were otherwise fairly limited. In v2 and later, this was fixed, and scripts and functions now have the full parameter specification capabilities of cmdlets. The same basic structure is followed for both types of commands. Functions and cmdlets have the same streaming behavior.

PowerShell workflows were introduced in PowerShell v3. Their syntax is similar to that of a function. When the workflow is first loaded in memory a PowerShell function is created that can be viewed through the function: PowerShell drive. Workflows are covered in chapter 12.

SCRIPTS

A *script command* is a piece of PowerShell code that lives in a text file with a .ps1 extension. These script files are loaded and parsed every time they're run, making them somewhat slower than functions to start (although once started, they run at the same speed). In terms of parameter capabilities, shell function commands and script commands are identical.

NATIVE COMMANDS (APPLICATIONS)

The last type of command is called a *native command*. These are external programs (typically executables) that can be executed by the operating system. Because running a native command involves creating a whole new process for the command, native commands are the slowest of the command types. Also, native commands do their own parameter processing and don't necessarily match the syntax of the other types of commands.

Native commands cover anything that can be run on a Windows computer, so you get a wide variety of behaviors. One of the biggest issues is when PowerShell waits for a command to finish but it keeps on going. Say you're opening a text document at the command line:

```
PS> .\foo.txt
```

You get the prompt back more or less immediately, and your default text editor will pop up (probably `notepad.exe` because that's the default). The program to launch is determined by the file associations that are defined as part of the Windows environment.

> **NOTE** In PowerShell, unlike in `cmd.exe`, you have to prefix a command with `./` or `.\` if you want to run it out of the current directory. This is part of PowerShell's "Secure by Design" philosophy. This particular security feature was adopted to prevent Trojan horse attacks where the user is lured into a directory and then told to run an innocuous command such as `notepad.exe`. Instead of running the system `notepad.exe`, they end up running a hostile program that the attacker has placed in that directory and named `notepad.exe`.

What if you specify the editor explicitly?

```
PS> notepad foo.txt
```

The same thing happens—the command returns immediately. What if you run the command in the middle of a pipeline?

```
PS> notepad foo.txt | sort-object
<exit notepad>
```

This time PowerShell waits for the command to exit before giving you the prompt. This can be handy when you want to insert something such as a graphical form editor in the middle of a script to do processing. This is also the easiest way to make PowerShell wait for a process to exit (you can also use `Wait-Process`). As you can see, the behavior of native commands depends on the type of native command, as well as where it appears in the pipeline.

A useful thing to remember is the PowerShell interpreter itself is a native command: `powershell.exe`. This means you can call PowerShell from within PowerShell. When you do this, a second PowerShell process is created. In practice, there's nothing unusual about this—that's how all shells work. PowerShell doesn't have to do it often, making it much faster than conventional shell languages.

The ability to run a child PowerShell process is particularly useful if you want to have isolation in portions of your script. A separate process means the child script can't impact the caller's environment. This feature is useful enough that PowerShell has special handling for this case, allowing you to embed the script to run inline. If you want to run a fragment of script in a child process, you can by passing the block of script to the child process delimited by braces. Here's an example:

```
PS> powershell { Get-Process *ss } | Format-Table name, handles

Name   Handles
----   -------
csrss      386
csrss      385
lsass     1778
smss        51
```

Two things should be noted in this example: the script code in the braces can be any PowerShell code, and it will be passed through to the new PowerShell process. The special handling takes care of encoding the script in such a way that it's passed properly to the child process. The other thing to note is, when PowerShell is executed this way, the output of the process is *serialized objects*—the basic structure of the output is preserved—and can be passed into other commands. We'll look at this serialization in detail when we cover *remoting*—the ability to run PowerShell scripts on a remote computer—in chapter 11.

DESIRED STATE CONFIGURATION

Desired State Configuration (DSC) is a configuration management platform in Windows PowerShell. It enables the deployment and management of configuration data for software services and the environment on which these services run. A configuration is created using PowerShell-like syntax. The configuration is used to create a Managed Object Format (MOF) file that's passed to the remote machine on which the configuration will be applied. DSC is covered in chapter 18.

Now that we've covered the PowerShell command types, let's get back to looking at the PowerShell syntax. Notice that a lot of what we've examined this far is a bit verbose. This makes it easy to read, which is great for script maintenance, but it looks like it would be a pain to type on the command line. PowerShell addresses these two conflicting goals—readability and writeability—with the concept of *elastic syntax*. Elastic syntax allows you to expand and collapse how much you need to type to suit your purpose. We'll cover how this works in the next section.

1.3.4 *Aliases and elastic syntax*

We haven't talked about aliases yet or how they're used to achieve an elastic syntax in PowerShell. Because this concept is important in the PowerShell environment, we need to spend some time on it.

The cmdlet `Verb-Noun` syntax, although regular, is, as we noted, also verbose. You may have noticed that in some of the examples we're using commands like `dir` and `type`. The trick behind all this is aliases. The `dir` command is an alias for `Get-ChildItem`, and the `type` command is an alias for `Get-Content`. You can see this by using `Get-Command`:

```
PS> Get-Command dir

CommandType    Name
-----------    ----
Alias          dir -> Get-ChildItem
```

This tells you the command is an alias for `Get-ChildItem`. To get information about the `Get-ChildItem` command, you then do this:

```
PS> Get-Command Get-ChildItem

CommandType Name           Version Source
----------- ----           ------- ------
Cmdlet      Get-ChildItem 3.1.0.0 Microsoft.PowerShell.Management
```

To see all the information, pipe the output of `Get-Command` into `fl`. This shows you the full detailed information about this cmdlet. But wait—what's the `fl` command? Again, you can use `Get-Command` to find out:

```
PS> Get-Command fl

CommandType     Name
-----------     ----
Alias           fl -> Format-List
```

PowerShell comes with a large set of predefined aliases. Two basic categories of aliases exist: *transitional* and *convenience* . By *transitional aliases*, we mean a set of aliases that map PowerShell commands to commands that people are accustomed to using in other shells, specifically `cmd.exe` and the UNIX shells. For the `cmd.exe` user, PowerShell defines `dir`, `type`, `copy`, and so on. For the UNIX user, PowerShell defines `ls`, `cat`, `cp`, and so forth. These aliases allow a basic level of functionality for new users right away.

NOTE   PowerShell v6 for Linux and macOS removes these aliases to avoid confusion with native commands.

Convenience aliases are derived from the names of the cmdlets they map to. `Get-Command` becomes `gcm`, `Get-ChildItem` becomes `gci`, `Invoke-Item` becomes `ii`, and so on. For a list of the defined aliases, type `Get-Alias` at the command line. You can use the `Set-Alias` command (the alias of which is `sal`, by the way) to define your own aliases—many experienced PowerShell users create a set of one-letter aliases to cover the cmdlets they most often use at the command prompt.

NOTE   Aliases in PowerShell are limited to aliasing the command name only. Unlike in other systems such as Ksh, Bash, and Zsh, PowerShell aliases can't include parameters. If you need to do something more sophisticated than simple command-name translations, you'll have to use shell functions or scripts.

This is all well and good, but what does it have to do with elastics? Glad you asked! The idea is PowerShell can be terse when needed and descriptive when appropriate. The syntax is concise for simple cases and can be stretched like an elastic band for larger problems. This is important in a language that's both a command-line tool and a scripting language. Many scripts that you'll write in PowerShell will be no more than a few lines long. They will be a string of commands that you'll type on the command line and then never use again. To be effective in this environment, the syntax needs to be concise. This is where aliases like `fl` come in—they allow you to write concise command lines. When you're scripting, though, it's best to use the long name of the command. Sooner or later, you'll have to read the script you wrote (or worse, someone else will). Would you rather read something that looks like this?

```
gcm|?{$_.parametersets.Count -gt 3}|fl name
```

or this?

```
Get-Command |
  Where-Object {$_.parametersets.count -gt 3} |
    Format-List name
```

We'd certainly rather read the latter. (As always, we'll cover the details of these examples later in the book.)

There's a second type of alias used in PowerShell: *parameter*. Unlike command aliases, which can be created by end users, parameter aliases are created by the author of a cmdlet, script, or function. (You'll see how to do this when we look at advanced function creation in chapter 7.)

A parameter alias is a shorter name for a parameter. Wait a second, earlier we said you needed enough of the parameter name to distinguish it from other command parameters. Isn't this enough for convenience and elasticity? Why do you need parameter aliases? The reason you need these aliases has to do with *script versioning*. The easiest way to understand versioning is to look at an example.

Say you have a script that calls a cmdlet `Process-Message`. This cmdlet has a parameter `-Reply`. You write your script specifying

```
Process-Message -Re
```

Run the script, and it works fine. A few months later, you install an enhanced version of the `Process-Message` command. This new version introduces a new parameter: `-Receive`. Only specifying `-Re` is no longer sufficient. If you run the old script with the new cmdlet, it will fail with an ambiguous parameter message; the script is broken.

How do you fix this with parameter aliases? The first thing to know is PowerShell always picks the parameter that exactly matches a parameter name or alias over a partial match. By providing parameter aliases, you can achieve pithiness without also making scripts subject to versioning issues. We recommend always using the full parameter name for production scripts or scripts you want to share. Readability is always more important in that scenario.

Now that we've covered the core concepts of how commands are processed, let's step back and look at PowerShell language processing overall. PowerShell has a small number of important syntactic rules you should learn. When you understand these rules, your ability to read, write, and debug PowerShell scripts will increase tremendously.

1.4   *Parsing the PowerShell language*

In this section we'll cover the details of how PowerShell scripts are parsed. Before the PowerShell interpreter can execute the commands you type, it first has to parse the command text and turn it into something the computer can execute, as shown in figure 1.4.

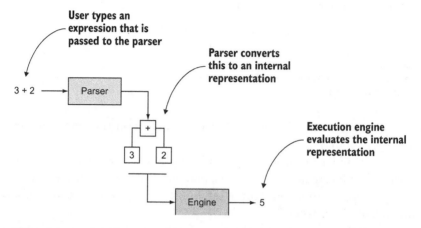

Figure 1.4   **Flow of processing in the PowerShell interpreter, where an expression is transformed and then executed to produce a result**

More formally, parsing is the process of turning human-readable source code into a form the computer understands. A piece of script text is broken up into tokens by the *tokenizer* (or *lexical analyzer*, if you want to be more technical). A token is a particular type of symbol in the programming language, such as a number, a keyword, or a variable. Once the raw text has been broken into a stream of tokens, these tokens are processed into structures in the language through syntactic analysis.

In syntactic analysis, the stream of tokens is processed according to the grammatical rules of the language. In normal programming languages, this process is straightforward—a token always has the same meaning. A sequence of digits is always a number; an expression is always an expression, and so on. For example, the sequence

```
3 + 2
```

would always be an addition expression, and "Hello world" would always be a constant string. Unfortunately, this isn't the case in shell languages. Sometimes you can't tell what a token is except through its context. In the next section, we go into more detail on why this is, and how the PowerShell interpreter parses a script.

NOTE   More information on this and the inner workings of PowerShell is available in the PowerShell language specification at www.microsoft.com/en-us/download/details.aspx?id=36389. The specification is currently only available up to PowerShell v3.

1.4.1 How PowerShell parses

For PowerShell to be successful as a shell, it can't require that everything be quoted. PowerShell would fail if it required people to continually type

```
cd ".."
```

or

```
copy "foo.txt" "bar.txt"
```

On the other hand, people have a strong idea of how expressions should work:

```
2
```

This is the number 2, not a string "2". Consequently, PowerShell has some rather complicated parsing rules, covered in the next three sections. We'll discuss how quoting is handled, the two major parsing modes, and the special rules for newlines and statement termination.

1.4.2 Quoting

Quoting is the mechanism used to turn a token that has special meaning to the PowerShell interpreter into a simple string value. For example, the `Write-Output` cmdlet has a parameter `-InputObject`. But what if you want to use the string "-InputObject" as an argument? To do this, you have to quote it by surrounding it with single or double quotes:

```
PS> Write-Output '-InputObject'
-inputobject
```

If you hadn't put the argument in quotes an error message would be produced indicating an argument to the parameter `-InputObject` is required.

PowerShell supports several forms of quoting, each with somewhat different meanings (or semantics). Putting single quotes around an entire sequence of characters causes them to be treated like a single string. This is how you deal with file paths that have spaces in them, for example. If you want to change to a directory the path of which contains spaces, you type this:

```
PS> Set-Location 'c:\program files'
PS> Get-Location
Path
----
C:\Program Files
```

When you don't use the quotes, you receive an error complaining about an unexpected parameter in the command because `c:\program` and `files` are treated as two separate tokens.

NOTE   Notice the error message reports the name of the cmdlet, not the alias used. This way you know what's being executed. The position message shows you the text that was entered so you can see an alias was used.

One problem with using matching quotes as shown in the previous examples is you have to remember to start the token with an opening quote. This raises an issue when you want to quote a single character. You can use the backquote (`` ` ``) character to do this (the backquote is usually the upper-leftmost key, below Esc):

```
PS> Set-Location c:\program` files
PS> Get-Location
Path
----
C:\Program Files
```

The backquote, or *backtick*, as it tends to be called, has other uses that we'll explore later in this section. Now let's look at the other form of matching quote: double quotes. You'd think it works pretty much like the example with single quotes; what's the difference? In double quotes, variables are expanded. If the string contains a variable reference starting with a $, it will be replaced by the string representation of the value stored in the variable. Let's look at an example. First assign the string "files" to the variable $v:

```
PS> $v = 'files'
```

Now reference that variable in a string with double quotes:

```
PS> Set-Location "c:\program $v"
PS> Get-Location

Path
----
C:\Program Files
```

The directory change succeeded and the current directory was set as you expected.

NOTE   Variable expansion only occurs with double quotes. A common beginner error is to use single quotes and expect variable expansion to work.

What if you want to show the value of $v? To do this, you need to have expansion in one place but not in the other. This is one of those other uses we had for the backtick. It can be used to quote or escape the dollar sign in a double-quoted string to suppress expansion. Let's try it:

```
PS> Write-Output "`$v is $v"
$v is files
```

Here's one final tweak to this example—if $v contained spaces, you'd want to make clear what part of the output was the value. Because single quotes can contain double quotes and double quotes can contain single quotes, this is straightforward:

```
PS> Write-Output "`$v is '$v'"
$v is 'files'
```

Now, suppose you want to display the value of $v on another line instead of in quotes. Here's another situation where you can use the backtick as an escape character. The sequence `n in a double-quoted string will be replaced by a newline character. You can write the example with the value of $v on a separate line:

```
PS> "The value of `$v is:`n$v"
The value of $v is:
files
```

The list of special characters that can be generated using backtick (also called *escape*) sequences can be found using `Get-Help about_Escape_Characters`. Note that escape sequence processing, like variable expansion, is only done in double-quoted strings. In single-quoted strings, what you see is what you get. This is particularly important when writing a string to pass to a subsystem that does additional levels of quote processing.

1.4.3 *Expression-mode and command-mode parsing*

As mentioned earlier, because PowerShell is a shell, it has to deal with some parsing issues not found in other languages. PowerShell simplifies parsing considerably, trimming the number of modes down to two: expression and command.

In expression mode, the parsing is conventional: strings must be quoted, numbers are always numbers, and so on. In command mode, numbers are treated as numbers, but all other arguments are treated as strings unless they start with $, @, ', ", or (. When an argument begins with one of these special characters, the rest of the argument is parsed as a value expression. (There's also special treatment for leading variable references in a string, which we'll discuss later.) Table 1.1 shows examples that illustrate how items are parsed in each mode.

Table 1.1   Parsing mode examples

Example command line	Parsing mode and explanation
2+2	Expression mode; results in 4.
Write-Output 2+2	Command mode; results in 2+2.
$a=2+2	Expression mode; the variable $a is assigned the value 4.
Write-Output (2+2)	Expression mode; because of the parentheses, 2+2 is evaluated as an expression producing 4. This result is then passed as an argument to the Write-Output cmdlet.

Table 1.1 Parsing mode examples *(continued)*

Example command line	Parsing mode and explanation
`Write-Output $a`	Expression mode; produces `4`. This is ambiguous—evaluating it in either mode produces the same result. The next example shows why the default is expression mode if the argument starts with a variable.
`Write-Output` `$a.Equals(4)`	Expression mode; `$a.Equals(4)` evaluates to true and `Write-Output` writes the Boolean value `True`. This is why a variable is evaluated in expression mode by default. You want simple method and property expressions to work without parentheses.
`Write-Output $a/foo.txt`	Command mode; `$a/foo.txt` expands to `4/foo.txt`. This is the opposite of the previous example. Here you want it to be evaluated as a string in command mode. The interpreter first parses in expression mode and sees it's not a valid property expression, so it backs up and rescans the argument in command mode. As a result, it's treated as an expandable string.

Notice in the `Write-Output (2+2)` case, the opening parenthesis causes the interpreter to enter a new level of interpretation where the parsing mode is once again established by the first token. This means the sequence `2+2` is parsed in expression mode, not command mode, and the result of the expression (4) is emitted. Also, the last example in the table illustrates the exception mentioned previously for a leading variable reference in a string. A variable itself is treated as an expression, but a variable followed by arbitrary text is treated as though the whole thing were in double quotes. This allows you to write

```
PS> cd $HOME/scripts
```

instead of

```
PS> cd "$HOME/scripts"
```

As mentioned earlier, quoted and unquoted strings are recognized as different tokens by the parser. This is why

```
PS> Invoke-MyCmdlet -Parm arg
```

treats `-Parm` as a parameter and

```
PS> Invoke-MyCmdlet "-Parm" arg
```

treats `"-Parm"` as an argument. There's an additional wrinkle in the parameter binding. If an unquoted parameter like `-NotAparameter` isn't a parameter on `Invoke-MyCmdlet`, it will be treated as an argument. This lets you say

```
PS> Write-Host  -this -is -a parameter
```

without requiring quoting.

This finishes our coverage of the basics of parsing modes, quoting, and commands. Commands can take arbitrary lists of arguments, so knowing when the statement ends is important. We'll cover this in the next section.

1.4.4 *Statement termination*

In PowerShell, there are two statement terminator characters: the semicolon (;) and (sometimes) the newline. Why is a newline a statement separator only *sometimes*? The rule is that if the previous text is a syntactically complete statement, a newline is considered to be a statement termination. If it isn't complete, the newline is treated like any other whitespace. This is how the interpreter can determine when a command or expression crosses multiple lines. For example, in the following

```
PS> 2 +
>> 2
>>
4
```

the sequence 2 + is incomplete, so the interpreter prompts you to enter more text. (This is indicated by the nest prompt characters, >>.) But in the next sequence

```
PS> 2
2
PS> + 2
2
```

the number 2 by itself is a complete expression, so the interpreter goes ahead and evaluates it. Likewise, + 2 is a complete expression and is also evaluated (+ in this case is treated as the unary plus operator). From this, you can see that if the newline comes after the + operator, the interpreter will treat the two lines as a single expression. If the newline comes before the + operator, it will treat the two lines as two individual expressions.

Most of the time, this mechanism works the way you expect, but sometimes you can receive some unanticipated results. Take a look at the following example:

```
PS> $b = ( 2
>> + 2 )
>>
At line:1 char:9
+ $b = ( 2
+         ~
Missing closing ')' in expression.
    + CategoryInfo          : ParserError: (:) [],
  ParentContainsErrorRecordException
    + FullyQualifiedErrorId : MissingEndParenthesisInExpression
```

NOTE The example code applies to the PowerShell console. If you use ISE you'll get the error immediately after pressing the Enter key after typing the first line.

This behavior was questioned by one of the PowerShell v1 beta testers who was surprised by this result and thought there was something wrong with the interpreter, but in fact, this isn't a bug. Here's what's happening.

Consider this text:

```
PS> $b = (2 +
>> 2)
```

It's parsed as $b = (2 + 2) because a trailing + operator is only valid as part of a binary operator expression. The sequence $b = (2 + can't be a syntactically complete statement, and the newline is treated as whitespace. On the other hand, consider this text:

```
PS> $b = (2
>> + 2)
```

In this case, 2 is a syntactically complete statement, so the newline is now treated as a line terminator. In effect, the sequence is parsed like $b = (2 ; + 2)—two complete statements. Because the syntax for a parenthetical expression is

```
( <expr> )
```

you get a syntax error—the interpreter is looking for a closing parenthesis as soon as it has a complete expression. Contrast this with using a subexpression instead of the parentheses alone:

```
PS> $b = $(
>> 2
>> +2
>> )
PS> $b
2
2
```

Here the expression is valid because the syntax for subexpressions is

```
$( <statementList> )
```

How do you extend a line that isn't extensible by itself? This is another situation where you can use the backtick escape character. If the last character in the line is a backtick, then the newline will be treated as a simple breaking space instead of a newline:

```
PS> Write-Output `
>> -InputObject `
>> "Hello world"
>>
Hello world
```

Finally, one thing that surprises some people is strings aren't terminated by a new-line character. Strings can carry over multiple lines until a matching, closing quote is encountered:

```
PS> Write-Output "Hello
>> there
>> how are
>> you?"
>>
Hello
there
how are
you?
```

In this example, you see a string that extended across multiple lines. When that string was displayed, the newlines were preserved in the string.

The handling of end-of-line characters in PowerShell is another of the trade-offs that keeps PowerShell useful as a shell. Although the handling of end-of-line characters is a bit strange compared to non-shell languages, the overall result is easy for most people to get used to.

1.4.5 *Comment syntax in PowerShell*

Every computer language has some mechanism for annotating code with expository comments. Like many other shells and scripting languages, PowerShell comments begin with a number sign (#) and continue to the end of the line. The # character must be at the beginning of a token for it to start a comment. Here's an example that illustrates what this means (echo is an alias of `Write-Output`):

```
PS> echo hi#there
hi#there
```

In this example, the number sign is in the middle of the token hi#there and isn't treated as the starting of a comment. In the next example, there's a space before the number sign:

```
PS> echo hi #there
hi
```

Now # is treated as starting a comment and the following text isn't displayed. It can be preceded by characters other than a space and still start a comment. It can be preceded by any statement-terminating or expression-terminating character like a bracket, brace, or semicolon, as shown in the next couple of examples:

```
PS> (echo hi)#there
Hi
```

```
PS> echo hi;#there
hi
```

In both examples, the # symbol indicates the start of a comment.

Finally, you need to take into account whether you're in expression mode or command mode. In command mode, as shown in the next example, the + symbol is included in the token hi+#there:

```
PS> echo hi+#there
hi+#there
```

In expression mode, it's parsed as its own token. Now # indicates the start of a comment, and the overall expression results in an error:

```
PS> "hi"+#there
>>
At line:1 char:6
+ "hi"+#there
+      ~
You must provide a value expression following the '+' operator.
    + CategoryInfo          : ParserError: (:) [],
  ParentContainsErrorRecordException
    + FullyQualifiedErrorId : ExpectedValueExpression
```

The # symbol is also allowed in function names:

```
PS> function hi#there { "Hi there" }
PS> hi#there
Hi there
```

The reason for allowing # in the middle of tokens was to make it easy to accommodate path providers that used # as part of their path names. People conventionally include a space before the beginning of a comment, and this doesn't appear to cause any difficulties.

MULTILINE COMMENTS

In PowerShell v2, *multiline* comments were introduced, primarily to allow you to embed inline help text in scripts and functions. A multiline comment begins with <# and ends with #>. Here's an example:

```
<#
 This is a comment
    that spans
 multiple lines
#>
```

This type of comment need not span multiple lines; you can use this notation to add a comment preceding some code:

```
PS> <# a comment #> "Some code"
Some code
```

In this example, the line is parsed, the comment is read and ignored, and the code after the comment is executed.

One of the things this type of comment allows you to do is easily embed chunks of preformatted text in functions and scripts. The PowerShell help system takes advantage of this feature to allow functions and scripts to contain *inline documentation* in the form of special comments. These comments are automatically extracted by the help system to generate documentation for the function or script. You'll learn how the comments are used by the help subsystem in chapter 7.

Now that you have a good understanding of the basic PowerShell syntax, let's look at how commands are executed by the PowerShell execution engine. We'll start with the pipeline.

1.5   How the pipeline works

A pipeline is a series of commands separated by the pipe operator (|), as shown in figure 1.5. In some ways, the term *production line* better describes pipelines in PowerShell. Each command in the pipeline receives an object from the previous command, performs some operation on it, and then passes it along to the next command in the pipeline.

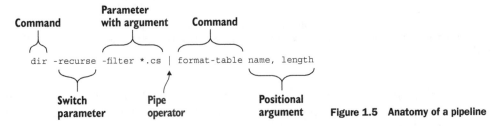

Figure 1.5   Anatomy of a pipeline

> **NOTE**   This, by the way, is the great PowerShell heresy. All previous shells passed strings only through the pipeline. Many people had difficulty with the notion of doing anything else. Like the character in *The Princess Bride*, they'd cry, "Inconceivable!" And we'd respond, "I do not think that word means what you think it means."

All the command categories take parameters and arguments. In

```
Get-ChildItem -Filter *.dll -Path c:\windows -Recurse
```

`-Filter` is a parameter that takes one argument, `*.dll`. The string "c:\windows" is the argument to the positional parameter `-Path`.

Next, we'll discuss the signature characteristic of pipelines: streaming behavior.

1.5.1   Pipelines and streaming behavior

Streaming behavior occurs when objects are processed one at a time in a pipeline. This is one of the characteristic behaviors of shell languages. In stream processing, objects are output from the pipeline as soon as they become available. In more traditional programming environments the results are returned only when the entire result set has been generated—the first and last results are returned at the same time. In a pipelined shell, the first result is returned as soon as it's available and subsequent results return as they also become available. This flow is illustrated in figure 1.6.

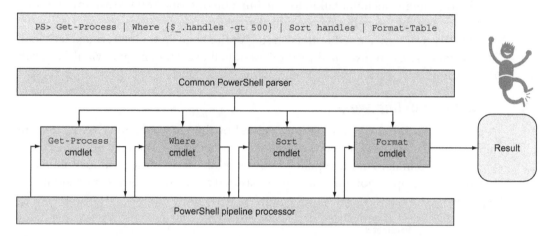

```
PS> Get-Process | Where {$_.handles -gt 500} | Sort handles | Format-Table
```

Figure 1.6   **How objects flow through a pipeline one at a time. A common parser constructs each of the command objects and then starts the pipeline processor, stepping each object through all stages of the pipeline.**

At the top of figure 1.6 you see a PowerShell command pipeline containing four commands. This command pipeline is passed to the PowerShell parser, which figures out what the commands are, what the arguments and parameters are, and how they should be bound for each command. When the parsing is complete, the pipeline processor begins to sequence the commands. First it runs the begin clause of each of the commands once, in sequence from first to last. After all the begin clauses have been run, it runs the process clause in the first command. If the command generates one or more objects, the pipeline processor passes these objects one at a time to the second command. If the second command also emits an object, this object is passed to the third command, and so on.

When processing reaches the end of the pipeline, any objects emitted are passed back to the PowerShell host. The host is then responsible for any further processing.

This aspect of streaming is important in an interactive shell environment, because you want to see objects as soon as they're available. The next example shows a simple pipeline that traverses through C:\Windows looking for all the DLLs with names that start with the word "system":

```
PS> Get-ChildItem -Path C:\Windows\ -recurse -filter *.dll |
where Name -match "system.*dll"
    Directory: C:\Windows\assembly\GAC_MSIL\System.Management.Automation\1.0.
    0.0__31bf3856ad364e35
```

```
Mode                LastWriteTime           Length Name
----                -------------           ------ ----
-a----      16/07/2016      12:43          3010560 System.Management.
   Automation.dll


    Directory: C:\Windows\assembly\GAC_MSIL\System.Management.Automation.
    Resources\1.0.0.0_en_31bf3856ad364e35

Mode                LastWriteTime           Length Name
----                -------------           ------ ----
-a----      16/07/2016      23:51           253952 System.Management.
   Automation.Resources.dll


    Directory: C:\Windows\assembly\NativeImages_v4.0.30319_32\System\08da6b66
    98b412866e6910ae9b84f363

Mode                LastWriteTime           Length Name
----                -------------           ------ ----
-a----      16/07/2016      12:44         10281640 System.ni.dll
```

With streaming behavior, as soon as the first file is found, it's displayed. Without streaming, you'd have to wait until the entire directory structure has been searched before you'd see any results.

In most shell environments streaming is accomplished by using separate processes for each element in the pipeline. In PowerShell, which only uses a single process (and a single thread as well by default), streaming is accomplished by splitting cmdlets into three clauses: BeginProcessing, ProcessRecord, and EndProcessing. In a pipeline, the BeginProcessing clause is run for all cmdlets in the pipeline. Then the ProcessRecord clause is run for the first cmdlet. If this clause produces an object, that object is passed to the ProcessRecord clause of the next cmdlet in the pipeline, and so on. Finally, the EndProcessing clauses are all run. (We cover this sequencing again in more detail in chapter 5, which is about scripts and functions, because they can also have these clauses.)

1.5.2 *Parameters and parameter binding*

Now let's talk about more of the details involved in binding parameters for commands. *Parameter binding* is the process in which values are bound to the parameters on a command. These values can come from either the command line or the pipeline. Here's an example of a parameter argument being bound from the command line:

```
PS> Write-Output 123
123
```

And here's the same example where the parameter is taken from the input object stream:

```
PS> 123 | Write-Output
123
```

The binding process is controlled by declaration information on the command itself. Parameters can have the following characteristics: they're either mandatory or optional, they have a type to which the formal argument must be convertible, and they can have attributes that allow the parameters to be bound from the pipeline. Table 1.2 describes the steps in the binding process.

Table 1.2　Steps in the parameter binding process

Binding step	Description
1. Bind all named parameters.	Find all unquoted tokens on the command line that start with a dash. If the token ends with a colon, an argument is required. If there's no colon, look at the type of the parameter and see if an argument is required. Convert the type of argument to the type required by the parameter, and bind the parameter.
2. Bind all positional parameters.	If there are any arguments on the command line that haven't been used, look for unbound parameters that take positional parameters and try to bind them.
3. Bind from the pipeline by value with exact match.	If the command isn't the first command in the pipeline and there are still unbound parameters that take pipeline input, try to bind to a parameter that matches the type exactly.
4. If not bound, then bind from the pipe by value with conversion.	If the previous step failed, try to bind using a type conversion.
5. If not bound, then bind from the pipeline by name with exact match.	If the previous step failed, look for a property on the input object that matches the name of the parameter. If the types exactly match, bind the parameter.
6. If not bound, then bind from the pipeline by name with conversion.	If the input object has a property with a name that matches the name of a parameter, and the type of the property is convertible to the type of the parameter, bind the parameter.

As you can see, this binding process is quite involved. In practice, the parameter binder almost always does what you want—that's why a sophisticated algorithm is used. Sometimes you'll need to understand the binding algorithm to get a particular behavior. PowerShell has built-in facilities for debugging the parameter-binding process that can be accessed through the `Trace-Command` cmdlet. Here's an example showing how to use this cmdlet:

```
PS> Trace-Command -Name ParameterBinding  -Option All `
-Expression { 123 | Write-Output } -PSHost
```

In this example, you're tracing the expression in the braces—that's the expression:

```
123 | Write-Output
```

This expression pipes the number 123 to the cmdlet `Write-Output`. The `Write-Output` cmdlet takes a single mandatory parameter, `-InputObject`, which allows pipeline input by value. The tracing output is long but fairly self-explanatory, so we haven't included it here. This is something you should experiment with to see how it can help you figure out what's going on in the parameter-binding process.

And now for the final topic in this chapter: formatting and output. The formatting and output subsystem provides the magic that lets PowerShell figure out how to display the output of the commands you type.

1.6   *Formatting and output*

One of the issues people new to PowerShell face is the formatting system. As a general rule, we run commands and depend on the system to figure out how to display the results. We'll use commands such as `Format-Table` and `Format-List` to give general guidance on the shape of the display, but no specific details. Let's dig in now and see how this all works.

PowerShell is a type-based system. Types are used to determine how things are displayed, but normal objects don't usually know how to display themselves. PowerShell deals with this by including formatting information for various types of objects as part of the extended type system. This extended type system allows PowerShell to add new behaviors to existing .NET objects or extend the formatting system to cope with new types you've created. The default formatting database is stored in the PowerShell install directory, which you can get to by using the `$PSHOME` shell variable. Here's a list of the files that were included as of this writing:

```
PS> Get-ChildItem $PSHOME/*format* | Format-Table name

Name
----
Certificate.format.ps1xml
Diagnostics.Format.ps1xml
DotNetTypes.format.ps1xml
Event.Format.ps1xml
FileSystem.format.ps1xml
Help.format.ps1xml
HelpV3.format.ps1xml
PowerShellCore.format.ps1xml
PowerShellTrace.format.ps1xml
Registry.format.ps1xml
WSMan.Format.ps1xml
```

The naming convention helps users figure out the purpose of files. (The others should become clear after reading the rest of this book.) These files are XML documents that contain descriptions of how each type of object should be displayed.

> **TIP** These files are digitally signed by Microsoft. Do *not* alter them under any circumstances. You'll break things if you do.

These descriptions are fairly complex and somewhat difficult to write. It's possible for end users to add their own type descriptions, but that's beyond the scope of this chapter. The important thing to understand is how the formatting and outputting commands work together.

1.6.1 Formatting cmdlets

Display of information is controlled by the type of the objects being displayed, but the user can choose the "shape" of the display by using the `Format-*` commands:

```
PS> Get-Command Format-* | Format-Table name

Name
----
Format-Hex
Format-Volume
Format-Custom
Format-List
Format-SecureBootUEFI
Format-Table
Format-Wide
```

By *shape*, we mean things such as a table or a list.

> **NOTE** `Format-Hex` is a PowerShell v5 cmdlet that is used to create displays in hexadecimal. The `Format-SecureBootUEFI` cmdlet receives certificates or hashes as input and formats the input into a content object that is returned. The `Set-SecureBootUEFI` cmdlet uses this object to update the variable. These two cmdlets are outside the scope of this section.

Here's how they work. The `Format-Table` cmdlet formats output as a series of columns displayed across your screen:

```
PS> Get-Item c:\ | Format-Table

    Directory:

Mode                LastWriteTime      Length    Name
----                -------------      ------    ----
d--hs-       06/06/2017      09:06                C:\
```

PowerShell v5 automatically derives the on–screen positioning from the first few objects through the pipeline—effectively an automatic -Autosize parameter. This change was introduced because -Autosize is a blocking parameter that caused huge amounts of data to be stored in memory until all objects were available.

> **Format-Table -Autosize parameter**
>
> In PowerShell v1 through v4 `Format-Table` tries to use the maximum width of the display and guesses at how wide a particular field should be. This allows you to start seeing data as quickly as possible (streaming behavior) but doesn't always produce optimal results. You can achieve a better display by using the -AutoSize switch, but this requires the formatter to process every element before displaying any of them,

> **(Continued)**
>
> and this prevents streaming. PowerShell has to do this to figure out the best width to use for each field. The result in this example looks like this:
>
> ```
> PS> Get-Item c:\ | Format-Table -AutoSize
>
>     Directory:
>
> Mode           LastWriteTime Length Name
> ----           ------------- ------ ----
> d--hs- 06/06/2017     09:06         C:\
> ```
>
> In practice, the default layout when streaming is good and you don't need to use -Autosize, but sometimes it can help make things more readable.

The `Format-List` command displays the elements of the objects as a list, one after the other:

```
PS> Get-Item c:\ | Format-List

    Directory:

Name          : C:\
CreationTime  : 22/08/2013 14:31:02
LastWriteTime : 06/06/2017 09:06:56
LastAccessTime : 06/06/2017 09:06:56
```

If there's more than one object to display, they'll appear as a series of lists. This is usually the best way to display a large collection of fields that won't fit well across the screen.

The `Format-Wide` cmdlet is used when you want to display a single object property in a concise way. It will treat the screen as a series of columns for displaying the same information:

```
PS> Get-Process –Name s* | Format-Wide -Column 8 id

1372    640    516    1328   400    532    560    828
876     984    1060   1124   4
```

In this example, you want to display the process IDs of all processes with names that start with "s" in eight columns. This formatter allows for a dense display of information.

The final formatter is `Format-Custom`, which displays objects while preserving the basic structure of the object. Because most objects have a structure that contains other objects, which in turn contain other objects, this can produce extremely verbose output. Here's a small part of the output from the `Get-Item` cmdlet, displayed using `Format-Custom`:

```
PS> Get-Item c:\ | Format-Custom -Depth 1

class DirectoryInfo
{
```

```
PSPath = Microsoft.PowerShell.Core\FileSystem::C:\
PSParentPath =
PSChildName = C:\
PSDrive =
  class PSDriveInfo
  {
    CurrentLocation =
    Name = C
    Provider = Microsoft.PowerShell.Core\FileSystem
    Root = C:\
    Description = C_Drive
    Credential = System.Management.Automation.PSCredential
  }
```

The full output is considerably longer, and notice we've told it to stop walking the object structure at a depth of 1. You can imagine how verbose this output can be! Why have this cmdlet? Mostly because it's a useful debugging tool, either when you're creating your own objects or for exploring the existing objects in the .NET class libraries.

1.6.2   *Outputter cmdlets*

Now that you know how to format something, how do you output it? You don't have to worry because, by default, things are automatically sent to (can you guess?) Out-Default. Note the following three examples do exactly the same thing:

```
dir | Out-Default
dir | Format-Table
dir | Format-Table | Out-Default
```

This is because the formatter knows how to get the default outputter, the default outputter knows how to find the default formatter, and the system in general knows how to find the defaults for both. The Möbius strip of subsystems!

As with the formatters, there are several outputter cmdlets available in PowerShell out of the box. You can use the Get-Command command to find them:

```
PS> Get-Command Out-* | Format-Wide -Column 3

Out-Default      Out-File      Out-GridView
Out-Host         Out-Null      Out-Printer
Out-String
```

Here there's a somewhat broader range of choices. We've already talked about Out-Default. The next one we'll talk about is Out-Null. This is a simple outputter; anything sent to Out-Null is discarded. This is useful when you don't care about the output for a command; you want the side effect of running the command.

> **NOTE**   Piping to Out-Null is the equivalent to redirecting to $null but invokes the pipeline and can be up to forty times slower than redirecting to $null.

Next, we have Out-File. Instead of sending the output to the screen, this command sends it to a file. (This command is also used by I/O redirection when doing output to a file.) In addition to writing the formatted output, `Out-File` has several flags that control how the output is written. The flags include the ability to append to a file instead of replacing it, to force writing to read-only files, and to choose the output encodings for the file. This last item is the trickiest. You can choose from a number of text encodings supported by Windows. Here's a trick—enter the command with an encoding you know doesn't exist:

```
PS> Out-File -encoding blah
Out-File : Cannot validate argument on parameter 'Encoding'. The argument
"blah" does not belong to the set "unknown,string,unicode,bigendianunicode,ut
f8,utf7,utf32,ascii,default,oem" specified by the ValidateSet attribute.
Supply an argument that is in the set and then try the command again.
At line:1 char:20
+ Out-File -encoding blah
+                    ~~~~
    + CategoryInfo          : InvalidData: (:) [Out-File],
  ParameterBindingValidationException
    + FullyQualifiedErrorId : ParameterArgumentValidationError,Microsoft.
  PowerShell.Commands.OutFileCommand
```

You can see in the error message that all the valid encoding names are displayed.

NOTE Tab completion can be used to cycle through the valid encodings. Type `Out-File -Encoding` and then keep pressing the tab key to view the options. Tab completion works with cmdlet names, parameters, and values where there's a predefined set of acceptable values.

If you don't understand what these encodings are, don't worry about it, and let the system use its default value.

NOTE Where you're likely to run into problems with output encoding (or input encoding for that matter) is when you're creating files that are going to be read by another program. These programs may have limitations on what encodings they can handle, particularly older programs. To find out more about file encodings, search for "file encodings" on http://msdn.microsoft.com. Microsoft Developer's Network (MSDN) contains a wealth of information on this topic. Chapter 5 also contains additional information about working with file encodings in PowerShell.

The `Out-Printer` cmdlet doesn't need much additional explanation; it routes its text-only output to the default printer instead of to a file or to the screen.

The `Out-Host` cmdlet is a bit more interesting—it sends its output back to the host. This has to do with the separation in PowerShell between the interpreter or engine, and the application that hosts that engine. The host application has to implement a special set of interfaces to allow `Out-Host` to render its output properly. (We see this used in PowerShell v2 to v5, which include two hosts: the console host and the Integrated Scripting Environment (ISE).)

NOTE `Out-Default` delegates the work of outputting to the screen to `Out-Host`.

The last output cmdlet to discuss is `Out-String`. This one's a bit different. All the other cmdlets terminate the pipeline. The `Out-String` cmdlet formats its input and sends it as a string to the next cmdlet in the pipeline. Note we said *string*, not *strings*. By default, it sends the entire output as a single string. This isn't always the most desirable behavior—a collection of lines is usually more useful—but at least once you have the string, you can manipulate it into the form you want. If you do want the output as a series of strings, use the `-Stream` switch parameter. When you specify this parameter, the output will be broken into lines and streamed one at a time.

Note this cmdlet runs somewhat counter to the philosophy of PowerShell; once you've rendered the object to a string, you've lost its structure. The main reason for including this cmdlet is for interoperation with existing APIs and external commands that expect to deal with strings. If you find yourself using `Out-String` a lot in your scripts, stop and think if it's the best way to attack the problem.

PowerShell v2 introduced one additional output command: `Out-GridView`. As you might guess from the name, this command displays the output in a grid, but rather than rendering the output in the current console window, a new window is opened with the output displayed using a sophisticated grid control (see figure 1.7).

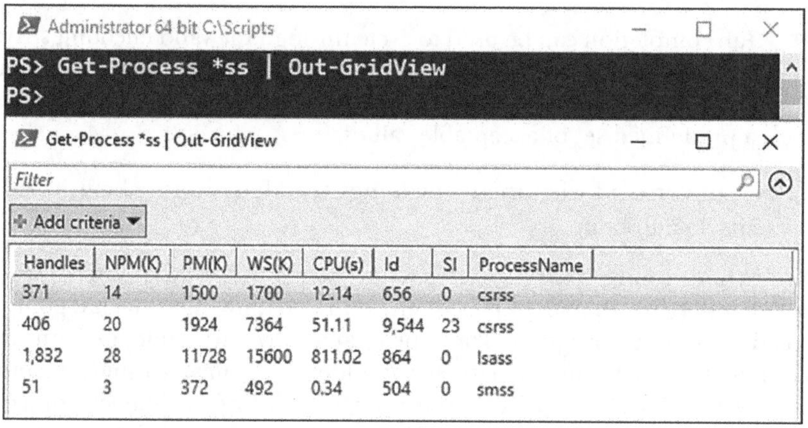

Figure 1.7 Displaying output with `Out-GridView`

The underlying grid control used by `Out-GridView` has all the features you'd expect from a modern Windows interface: columns can be reordered by dragging and dropping them, and the output can be sorted by clicking a column head. This control also introduces sophisticated filtering capabilities. This filtering allows you to drill into a dataset without having to rerun the command.

That's it for the basics: commands, parameters, pipelines, parsing, and presentation. You should now have a sufficient foundation to start moving on to more advanced topics in PowerShell.

1.7   Summary

- PowerShell is Microsoft's command-line/scripting environment that's at the center of Microsoft server and application management technologies. Microsoft's most important server products, including Exchange, Active Directory, and SQL Server, now use PowerShell as their management layer.

- PowerShell incorporates object-oriented concepts into a command-line shell using the .NET object model as the base for its type system, but can also access other object types like WMI.

- Shell operations like navigation and file manipulation in PowerShell are similar to what you're used to in other shells.

- Use the `Get-Help` command to get help when working with PowerShell.

- PowerShell has a full range of calculation, scripting, and text-processing capabilities.

- PowerShell supports a comprehensive set of remoting features to allow you to do scripted automation of large collections of computers.

- PowerShell has a number of command types, including cmdlets, functions, script commands, and native commands, each with slightly different characteristics.

- PowerShell supports an elastic syntax—concise on the command line and complete in scripts. Aliases are used to facilitate elastic syntax.

- PowerShell parses scripts in two modes—expression mode and command mode—which is a critical point to appreciate when using PowerShell.

- The PowerShell escape character is a backtick (`` ` ``), not a backslash.

- PowerShell supports both double quotes and single quotes; variable and expression expansion is done in double quotes, not in single quotes.

- Line termination is handled specially in PowerShell because it's a command language.

- PowerShell has two types of comments: line comments that begin with # and block comments that start with <# and end with #>. The block comment notation was introduced in PowerShell v2 with the intent of supporting inline documentation for scripts and functions.

- PowerShell uses a sophisticated formatting and outputting system to determine how to render objects without requiring detailed input from the user.

Now that you have the basics, we'll start digging into the details starting in the next chapter with how PowerShell works with types.

Working with types

2

This chapter covers
- Type management
- Types and literals
- Collections
- Type conversion

> *"When I use a word," Humpty Dumpty said, in rather a scornful tone, "it means just what I choose it to mean—neither more nor less."*
>
> *—Lewis Carroll,* Through the Looking Glass

Most shell environments can only deal with strings, so the ability to use objects makes PowerShell profoundly different. And where you have objects, you also have object *types*. Much of PowerShell's power comes from the innovative way it uses types. In this chapter, we'll look at the PowerShell type system, show how to take advantage of it, and examine some of the things you can accomplish with types in PowerShell. One of the biggest impacts of an object's type is how it's displayed.

46

2.1   Type management in the wild, wild West

Shell languages are frequently, though inaccurately, called *typeless* languages. In practice, you can't have a typeless language because programming in any form is all about working with types and typed objects like numbers, strings, dates, and so on. For any given programming language, one of the most important characteristics is how it deals with types and how much work the language expects from you up front versus at runtime. Languages that require you to provide a lot of up front explicit guidance are called *statically typed*, because all the types of objects they can deal with must be known up front. Languages that don't require much (if any) up front guidance are called *dynamically typed*, where the set of types can change dynamically throughout the program's run. PowerShell falls into the latter dynamic camp.

In *statically typed* languages, the initial guidance you provide allows the language processor to do a lot of work for you, but only if you stick to the types you initially planned for. At runtime, if your program encounters types you didn't plan for, the rigid nature of a static language can make it difficult to accommodate these new types. By analogy, if your program only handles square pegs, encountering a round peg is going to be a big problem.

In contrast, with *dynamically typed* languages, the user provides little type information up front. Instead, their programs deal with the types as encountered. If all the program is interested in is things that are blue, the shape of the object doesn't matter. Round, square, or triangular—the program doesn't care. Even if the object doesn't have a color property, it doesn't matter to the program—it's not blue so it's ignored.

These days, it's rare to see a purely static language (reality has a nasty habit of intruding upon academic notions of purity) and so most languages have some level of support for dynamic data types. The amount of support largely depends on the domain of application. For example, there isn't much that's dynamic in an accounting program. But in the area of IT systems management, PowerShell's domain of application, there's something of an excess of riches regarding dynamic types.

2.1.1   Types and classes

If we're going to talk about types, it's useful to have a common understanding of what a *type* is. There are many thick books in the fields of philosophy, science, and mathematics that try to address this question. We'll ignore them all. Why? Because you already know what a type is! You look at an object and say "that's a bird." Well, what *type* of bird is it? It's a robin. What properties do robins have? A red breast. What about its "parent class," birds? What properties do birds have? Wings, feathers, a beak, and so on. What do birds do? They fly, eat worms, poop on your car. Now you're an expert in object orientation along with everyone else on the planet. Computer people always like to make things more formal, so we'll use specific words when we talk about types, as noted in table 2.1.

Table 2.1 Classes, types, and members defined

Term	Example	Notes
Type	Robin, Bird	A type is a description of an object—what it looks like and what it can do. That description is associated with the type name. The relationship between an object and its type is called an is-a relationship (though the PowerShell operator for this is -is, not is-a). Some examples of this relationship are Robin is-a bird or Mickey is-a mouse. In PowerShell the code would be Robin -is bird and Mickey -is mouse respectively.
Class	Robin, Bird	Class is the keyword used in PowerShell v5 and later to define a new type. You'll see the words "type" and "class" frequently used interchangeably but when we define a type we use the class keyword. See chapter 19.
Property	BreastColor, Size, Weight	A property of an object is some piece of data describing the object. The property is defined on a class but only has value on an instance; for example, the class Bird defines a property Color but only an individual bird has a color. All Bird classes have the property Color. A crow has the property Color == black
Method	StartFlying(), EatWorm(),	Methods define behaviors on a class. In some object-oriented languages methods are called messages, because, for example, calling the StartFlying() method effectively sends a message to the bird to start flying.
Member	Size, EatWorm()	Member is a general term that includes all aspects of a type, both methods and properties.
Event	OnButtonDown, PoopOnCar	Events are a special kind of method except you don't call them directly. The object invokes them as a consequence of some other action on the object. If you tell a bird to fly by calling the StartFlying() method, this might trigger the event PoopOnCar().
Generic type	List<integer>, Dictionary<string, integer>	A generic type contains instances of other types such as a List of Integers or a dictionary mapping a name to a number. See section 2.5.2 for more information about generics.

Table 2.1 covers all the major concepts used by PowerShell when dealing with objects and object-oriented programming. In later chapters, we'll discuss additional variations on these terms, but what we've covered so far is sufficient for now. Before we move on, here's a brief note on terminology.

SCHEMA AND CLASSES AND TYPES, OH MY!

In table 2.1, you see the words "class" and "type" can be used interchangeably. In practice, there are a few more synonyms for "type" that you might run into, especially the term *schema*, which is used a lot with XML and databases. In the databases case, schema defines the set of tables a database uses and the structure of the rows in each table. The definition of schema in the Oxford dictionary is "a representation of a plan or theory in the form of an outline or model." Look—this definition defines yet another term, *model*.

Again, these terms are all equivalent though the representations may differ significantly. Some of this is due to the fact that object-oriented terminology grew out of languages designed to help programmers deal with complexity by "modeling" the real world. When modeling something, it's important to remember the model is a simplification of the thing you're trying to model. A model Tyrannosaurs Rex isn't 30 feet high and rarely eats lawyers.

The model should only include the information necessary to solve the problem at hand. This may sound easy, but designing a model, especially in a fluid medium like software and IT, requires thought. Whatever you design initially will have to grow and evolve as requirements change. Fortunately, there are guiding patterns and principles that will help you write flexible models. We'll discuss these principles in chapter 19 when we look at writing classes in PowerShell. We'll also look at modeling in more detail when we look at Desired State Configuration (DSC) management in chapter 18.

Whew—that was abstract, so let's return from our intellectual clouds and focus on how all of this stuff works in PowerShell.

2.1.2   *PowerShell: A type-promiscuous language*

Using the definitions for static and dynamic typing we looked at in the beginning of section 2.1, it's pretty clear we should characterize PowerShell as a dynamically typed language. But an even better description is PowerShell is a *type-promiscuous* language (sounds salacious, doesn't it?). By type-promiscuous, we mean PowerShell will expend a tremendous amount of effort, much more than a typical dynamic language, trying to turn what you have into what you need with as little work on your part as it can manage. When you ask for a property Y, PowerShell doesn't care if the object foo is a member of class X. It only cares whether foo has a property Y.

People who are used to strongly typed environments find this approach, well, disturbing. It sounds too much like "wild, wild, West" management. In practice, the PowerShell runtime is careful about making sure its transformations are reasonable and no information is unexpectedly lost. This is particularly important when dealing with numeric calculations. In PowerShell, you can freely mix and match different types of numbers in expressions. You can even include strings in this mix. PowerShell converts everything as needed without specific guidance from the user, as long as there's no loss in precision. Table 2.2 presents some example conversion scenarios. It includes both examples of successful conversions and of conversions the runtime fails because they could result in an unintended loss of information.

Table 2.2   Examples of PowerShell type management

Example	Result Type	Comment
`PS> 2 + 3.0 + '4'` `9`	`System.Double`	Everything widened to double-precision floating-point number.
`PS> 2 + '3.0` + 4` `9`	`System.Double`	Everything widened to double-precision floating-point number.
`PS> (3 + 4)` `7`	`System.Int32`	Integer as expected because all elements are integers.
`PS> 6/3` `2`	`System.Int32`	Integer as expected because all elements are integers and 3 is a factor of 6.
`PS> 6/4` `1.5`	`System.Double`	System switch to double to avoid loss of precision.
`PS> 1e300 + 12` `1E+300`	`System.Double`	In effect, adding an integer to a number of this magnitude means the integer is ignored. This sort of loss is considered acceptable by the system.

`PS> 1e300 + 12d`
`Value was either too large`
`or too small for a Decimal.`
`At line:1 char:1`
`+ 1e300 + 12d`
`+ ~~~~~~~~~~~`
`    + CategoryInfo`
`: OperationStopped: (:) [],`
`OverflowException`
`    + FullyQualifiedErrorId :`
`System.OverflowException`
		This results in an error because when one of the operands involved is a `decimal` value, all operands are converted to decimal first and then the operation is performed. Because `1e300` is too large to be represented as a decimal, the operation will fail with an exception rather than lose precision.

The .NET `GetType()` method, or `Get-Member`, is used to look at the base type of the results of the various expressions as shown in figure 2.1. You can also pipe the results from a cmdlet (or pipeline) to `Get-Member` to discover its output type.

From these examples, you can see that although the PowerShell type-conversion system is aggressive in the types of conversions it performs, it's also careful about how it does things.

Now that you have a sense of the importance of types in PowerShell, let's look at how it all works.

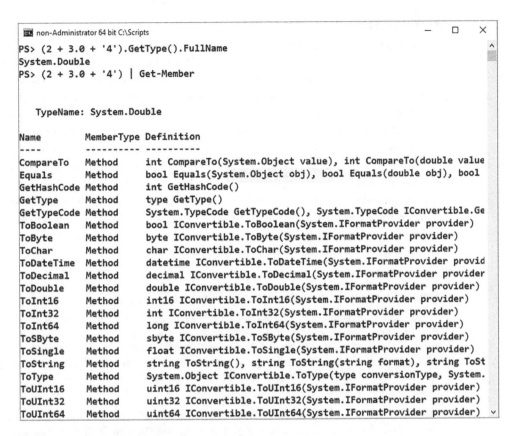

```
non-Administrator 64 bit C:\Scripts                                       —    □    ×
PS> (2 + 3.0 + '4').GetType().FullName
System.Double
PS> (2 + 3.0 + '4') | Get-Member


   TypeName: System.Double

Name         MemberType Definition
----         ---------- ----------
CompareTo    Method     int CompareTo(System.Object value), int CompareTo(double value
Equals       Method     bool Equals(System.Object obj), bool Equals(double obj), bool
GetHashCode  Method     int GetHashCode()
GetType      Method     type GetType()
GetTypeCode  Method     System.TypeCode GetTypeCode(), System.TypeCode IConvertible.Ge
ToBoolean    Method     bool IConvertible.ToBoolean(System.IFormatProvider provider)
ToByte       Method     byte IConvertible.ToByte(System.IFormatProvider provider)
ToChar       Method     char IConvertible.ToChar(System.IFormatProvider provider)
ToDateTime   Method     datetime IConvertible.ToDateTime(System.IFormatProvider provid
ToDecimal    Method     decimal IConvertible.ToDecimal(System.IFormatProvider provider
ToDouble     Method     double IConvertible.ToDouble(System.IFormatProvider provider)
ToInt16      Method     int16 IConvertible.ToInt16(System.IFormatProvider provider)
ToInt32      Method     int IConvertible.ToInt32(System.IFormatProvider provider)
ToInt64      Method     long IConvertible.ToInt64(System.IFormatProvider provider)
ToSByte      Method     sbyte IConvertible.ToSByte(System.IFormatProvider provider)
ToSingle     Method     float IConvertible.ToSingle(System.IFormatProvider provider)
ToString     Method     string ToString(), string ToString(string format), string ToSt
ToType       Method     System.Object IConvertible.ToType(type conversionType, System.
ToUInt16     Method     uint16 IConvertible.ToUInt16(System.IFormatProvider provider)
ToUInt32     Method     uint32 IConvertible.ToUInt32(System.IFormatProvider provider)
ToUInt64     Method     uint64 IConvertible.ToUInt64(System.IFormatProvider provider)
```

Figure 2.1   Discovering the type of an expression

2.1.3   *Type system and type adaptation*

In the previous section we said that when looking for a `Color` property, PowerShell doesn't care what type the underlying object is as long as it has a `Color` property on it. That's an oversimplification. The PowerShell code the user writes doesn't have to care. But the PowerShell runtime cares deeply as it does all the hard work of finding that property for you. A main goal of the type system is to allow the user to work with a wide variety of data types and sources like .NET, XML, WMI, and other ingredients in the alphabet soup that makes up computer science.

Let's talk about the member resolution algorithm. Member resolution is done through a set of layers. In PowerShell v1 and v2, there are two layers: synthetic members and native members. In PowerShell v3 a new layer was added providing for fallback members.

There are three phases of member resolution: synthetic, native, and fallback. The PowerShell member resolver code goes through each of these phases and stops as soon as it finds an appropriate match. Let's look at what happens in each layer.

SYNTHETIC MEMBERS

In section 2.1.1, we said that the members on an object are determined by that object's type or class. *BWAHAHAHA*—we lied to you. PowerShell has an extra layer it checks first, called the PSObject wrapper. This wrapper allows the end user, who didn't define the type, to change the set of members on that type (sort of). For any given instance of an object, you can add new properties or methods at runtime. You can even over-shadow existing members possibly changing their behavior to something more appropriate to the task at hand. But doing this only affects the current instance. The class itself isn't changed. For this reason, these members are sometimes called *singletons* as they're only defined for a single instance of the object. PowerShell includes ways to add these members to every object of a class but they're still singletons—each one is unique to the object it's attached to. It's even possible to build an object purely out of synthetic members with no "native" properties at all. You'll see more about this in chapter 10 when we discuss metaprogramming.

PowerShell versions and synthetic members

There was one significant change in implementation in this area between Power-Shell v2 and PowerShell v3. In PowerShell v1 and v2, every object was wrapped in a PSObject container that also held its synthetic members. This caused a number of obscure bugs, because storing an object with synthetic members in a strongly typed variable would result in the wrapper getting "lost" along with the values of the synthetic members.

In PowerShell v3 and later, to fix these bugs, the implementation was changed to use a "look-aside" mechanism. Instead of wrapping the object, the extensions are kept in a separate table and are looked up when needed. This fixed all the data-loss problems resulting from using wrappers but introduced a new even more obscure problem.

Certain types of objects like numbers are constant so there's only ever one instance for any value of that type. For example, there's only ever one instance of the number 1. If you add a synthetic member to the number 1 using look-aside, then that member will be the same everywhere that 1 is used. This caused a real bug where a v2 programmer was using the different instances of a number (different wrappers) to carry around extra information. In v3, that information was always the same because there was only ever one look-aside object for the number. By using what was considered a bug in v2, the code was broken in v3 when the bug was fixed. It was an extremely obscure situation, but it does provide an object lesson in that no matter how benign or obscure a change, it can break people's programs.

NATIVE MEMBERS

Native members are what we talked about in section 2.1—they're the members defined by the object's type. If you know the type, then you know all the native members of that object. In the PowerShell environment, there are multiple native types—.NET being the primary, but also WMI and COM, where the type defines its members. These members can be discovered by using the Get-Member cmdlet as follows:

```
PS> Get-Date | Get-Member
   TypeName: System.DateTime

Name                  MemberType     Definition
----                  ----------     ----------
Add                   Method         datetime Add(timespan value)
AddDays               Method         datetime AddDays(double value)
AddHours              Method         datetime AddHours(double value)
:
DisplayHint           NoteProperty   DisplayHintType DisplayHint=DateTime
:
Date                  Property       datetime Date {get;}
Day                   Property       int Day {get;}
DayOfWeek             Property       System.DayOfWeek DayOfWeek {get;}
DateTime              ScriptProperty System.Object DateTime {get=if ((& {...
```

The output from this example has been trimmed significantly (there are about 59 members on a DateTime object) to show examples of each type of property. The first thing you see is the type of the object followed by a list of its members. Notice this list also includes information about any synthetic members attached to the instance such as DisplayHint and DateTime along with the native properties like Day and methods like AddDays().

FALLBACK MEMBERS

Fallback members are a final phase of member resolution. Unlike synthetic members, which are added by the end user on native members defined in the class, fallback methods are defined by the PowerShell runtime itself. Presently, there's no way for the end user to add any new ones. Fallback members resolve last—if something isn't found, then the member resolver falls back (duh!) to this type of member. Fallback members were first introduced in PowerShell v3 to solve an interoperation problem with PowerShell Workflow.

Then in PowerShell v4, new ones were added as part of the DSC management feature. In both cases, the members were designed to make it simpler for the script author to work with collections. You'll see examples of this in chapter 4.

Now, at last, what you've been waiting for: what you can do with PowerShell, or at least what the basic types of objects are that you can represent and manipulate in a script.

2.1.4 Finding the available types

One thing you'll have noticed is that there appear to be a lot of types available by default. This is correct—the PowerShell runtime loads and uses many .NET (native) types. Unfortunately, there's no out-of-the-box way to find all of those types—there's no Find-Type cmdlet. Let's jump ahead a bit and write one. First you need to know how .NET arranges its types. Within the host process, the .NET runtime creates an Application Domain, or AppDomain. PowerShell is an application that, not too surprisingly, runs inside an AppDomain. That's the first step. You can find your AppDomain using the .NET `AppDomain` class:

```
[System.AppDomain]::CurrentDomain
```

> **NOTE** The `AppDomain` class isn't available in .NET core which means this technique can't be used on Linux or Mac machines running PowerShell v6.

Next you need to find the types in the AppDomain. Individual types (or classes as they're sometimes called in this context) are organized into *assemblies*—modules similar to the PowerShell modules you'll see in chapters 8 and 9. To get a list of assemblies, you use the `GetAssemblies()` method:

```
[System.AppDomain]::CurrentDomain.GetAssemblies()
```

Once you have all the assemblies, you need to get a list of all the types in each assembly. You call the—wait for it—`GetTypes()` method. You have to do this once for each assembly returned by `GetAssemblies()`. You could use a `foreach` statement (see chapter 5) but instead here you'll use one of the fallback methods. The type of fallback method you're going to use is a bit unusual because it isn't a specific method. One of the things the fallback method resolver does is, if the method isn't found on the object but the object is a collection, it tries to see if the method exists on the members of the collection. It's exactly what you need to call a method: `GetTypes()` on each member of the collection returned by `GetAssemblies()`. And so you get:

```
[System.AppDomain]::CurrentDomain.GetAssemblies().GetTypes()
```

The result is a pretty powerful one-liner. But there's one last thing you need to do. What you have now will return all the types available. In fact with

```
[System.AppDomain]::CurrentDomain.GetAssemblies().GetTypes().Count
```

the result will be in the tens of thousands depending on which modules you've loaded. You want to filter the result but now you can go back to PowerShell and use the `Select-String` cmdlet. Let's see all the types that mention `DateTime`:

```
[System.AppDomain]::CurrentDomain.GetAssemblies().GetTypes() |
Select-String datetime
```

Note this will still produce a lot of output. You can use more sophisticated regular expressions (see section 3.4 for more information on regular expressions).

The last step is to turn this into a function that looks like the following:

```
function Find-Type {
    param
    (
        [regex]$Pattern
    )
```

```
    [System.AppDomain]::CurrentDomain.
    GetAssemblies().GetTypes() |
    Select-String $Pattern
}
```

You now have a tool to find which types you've loaded. But you can also do the opposite. Suppose you want to find out which assemblies contain a type? Well, this is a property on the [type] object. You can see where the [PowerShell] type comes from using

```
[PowerShell].Assembly
```

This will give you lots of information about the assembly. If you want the location of the filename, then

```
[PowerShell].Assembly.Location
```

will do the trick. And, if you're a developer, it can be useful to know when the assembly was modified. Again, you can mix the type expression with PowerShell:

```
PS> [PowerShell].Assembly.Location |
Get-ChildItem |
foreach LastWriteTime

28 April 2017 01:32:49
```

Now you have a couple of tools that will make discovering types and assemblies much easier.

PowerShell comes pretty much "batteries included" with respect to the set of types you can use. In the next section, we'll cover the basic set of types you'll likely use most often and how to express them in PowerShell.

2.2   Basic types and literals

All programming languages have a set of basic or primitive types from which everything else is built. These primitive types usually have some form of corresponding syntactic literal. *Literal tokens* in the language are used to represent literal data objects in the program. In PowerShell, there are the usual literals—strings, numbers, and arrays—but there are other literals that aren't typically found outside of dynamic languages: dictionaries and hashtables. PowerShell also makes heavy use of *type literals* that correspond to type objects in the system. In this section, we'll go through each of the literals, illustrate how they're represented in script text, and explore the details of how they're implemented in the PowerShell runtime.

2.2.1   String literals

There are four kinds of string literals in PowerShell: single-quoted strings, double-quoted strings, single-quoted here-strings, and double-quoted here-strings, shown in this order in figure 2.2. Each string type will be discussed in detail later in this section. The underlying representation for all these strings is the same, an object of type System.String.

Figure 2.2   **String types in PowerShell**

NOTE   It's recommended to use single-quoted strings and here-strings, unless you're explicitly using variable expansion in the strings.

STRING REPRESENTATION IN POWERSHELL

In PowerShell, a string is a sequence of 16-bit Unicode characters and is directly implemented using the .NET System.String type. Because PowerShell strings use Unicode, they can effectively contain characters from every language in the world.

Encoding matters

The encoding used in strings is obviously important in international environments. If you're interested in the nitty-gritty details of the encoding used in System.String, here's what the MSDN documentation has to say:

- Each Unicode character in a string is defined by a Unicode scalar value, also called a Unicode code point or the ordinal (numeric) value of the Unicode character. Each code point is encoded using UTF-16 encoding, and the numeric value of each element of the encoding is represented by a Char. The resulting collection of Char objects constitutes the String.
- A single Char usually represents a single code point (the numeric value of the Char equals the code point). However, a code point might require more than one encoded element. For example, a Unicode supplementary code point (a surrogate pair) is encoded with two Char objects.

Refer to the MSDN documentation for additional details.

There are a couple of other characteristics that strings in PowerShell inherit from the underlying .NET strings. They can also be arbitrarily long and they're *immutable*—the contents of a string can be copied but can't be changed without creating an entirely new string.

> **NOTE** In almost all modern languages, strings are immutable. The biggest exception to this we're aware of is Apple's new language Swift. Probably due to the need for backward compatibility with Objective-C, Swift's strings are mutable. It will be interesting to see how that works out.

SINGLE- AND DOUBLE-QUOTED STRINGS

Because of the expression-mode/command-mode parsing dichotomy described in section 1.5.3, strings can be represented in several ways. In expression mode, a string is denoted by a sequence of characters surrounded by matching quotes, as shown in the following examples:

```
PS> "This is a string in double quotes"
This is a string in double quotes

PS> 'This is a string in single quotes'
This is a string in single quotes
```

Literal strings can contain any character, including newlines, with the exception of an unquoted closing quote character. Embedding closing quotes in a string is achieved in the following manner:

```
PS> "Embed double quote like this "" or this `" "
Embed double quote like this " or this "

PS> 'Embed single quote like this '' '
Embed single quote like this '
```

> **NOTE** In single-quoted strings, the backtick isn't special. This means it can't be used for embedding special characters such as newlines or escaping quotes.

Double-quoted strings (sometimes called *expandable strings*) support variable substitution.

> **NOTE** Arguments to commands without explicit quotes are treated as though they were in double quotes, so variables will be expanded in that situation as well. You'll see examples of this later on.

Let's look at an example of string expansion:

```
PS> $foo = "FOO"
PS> "This is a string in double quotes: $foo"
This is a string in double quotes: FOO

PS> 'This is a string in single quotes: $foo'
This is a string in single quotes: $foo
```

In the preceding lines, you can see $foo in the double-quoted string was replaced by the contents of the variable—namely, FOO—but not in the single-quoted case.

Expandable strings can also include arbitrary expressions by using the *subexpression* notation. A subexpression is a fragment of PowerShell script code, including statement lists, that's replaced by the value resulting from the evaluation of that code. Here's an example where the subexpression contains three simple statements:

```
PS> "Expanding three statements in a string: $(1; 2; 3)"
Expanding three statements in a string: 1 2 3
```

The result shows the output of the three statements concatenated together, space separated, and inserted into the result string. Using a subexpression in a string is one way to quickly generate formatted results when presenting data.

String expansion considerations

PowerShell expands strings when an assignment is executed. It doesn't reevaluate those strings when the variable is used later.

There's a way to force a string to be expanded if you need to do it—by calling $Execution -Context.InvokeCommand.ExpandString('a is $a'). This method will return a new string with all the variables expanded.

HERE-STRING LITERALS

Getting back to the discussion of literal string notation, there's one more form of string literal, called a *here-string*. A here-string is used to embed large chunks of text inline in a script as illustrated in figure 2.2. This can be powerful when you're generating output for another program. Here's an example that assigns a here-string to the variable $a:

```
PS> $a = @"
One is "1"
Two is '2'
Three is $(2+1)
The date is "$(Get-Date)"
"@
PS> $a
One is "1"
Two is '2'
Three is 3
The date is "06/09/2017 14:54:10"
```

On line 1, the here-string is assigned to the variable $a. The contents of the here-string start on line 2, which has a string containing double quotes. Line 3 has a string with single quotes. Line 4 has an embedded expression, and line 5 calls the Get-Date cmdlet in a subexpression to embed the current date into the string. When you look at the output of the variable shown in lines 9–12, you see the quotes are all preserved and the expansions are shown in place.

NOTE Here's a note for C# users. There's a lexical element in C# that looks a lot like PowerShell here-strings. In practice, the C# feature is most like PowerShell's single-quoted strings. In PowerShell, a here-string begins at the end of the line and the terminating sequence must be at the beginning of the line that terminates the here-string. In C#, the string terminates at the first closing quote that isn't doubled up.

Here-strings start with @<quote><newline> and end with <newline><quote>@. The <new-lines> are important because the here-string quote sequences won't be treated as quotes without them. The content of the here-string is all the lines between the beginning and ending quotes but not the lines the quotes are on. Because of the fancy opening and closing quote sequences, other special characters (such as quotes that would cause problems in regular strings) are fine here. This makes it easy to generate string data without having quoting errors.

Here-strings come in single- and double-quoted versions like regular strings, with the significant difference being that variables and subexpressions aren't expanded in the single-quoted variant. The single-quoted version is best for embedding large blocks of literal text where you don't want to deal with individually quoting $ everywhere. You'll see how useful this can be when we look at the Add-Type cmdlet in chapter 7.

That should be enough about strings for now. Let's move on to numbers and numeric literals.

2.2.2 Numbers and numeric literals

As mentioned earlier, PowerShell supports all the basic .NET numeric types and performs conversions to and from the different types as needed. Table 2.3 lists these numeric types.

Table 2.3   Numeric literals

Example numeric literal	.NET full type name	Short type name
1 0x1FE4	System.Int32	[int]
10000000000	System.Int64	[long]
1.1 1e3	System.Double	[double]
There's no single-precision numeric literal but you can use a cast: [float] 1.3	System.Single	[single] or [float]
1d 1.123d	System.Decimal	[decimal]

In general, you don't specify a numeric literal as having a particular type; the system will figure out the best way to represent the number. By default, an integer will be used. If the literal is too large for a 32-bit integer, a 64-bit integer will be used instead. If it's still too big or if it contains a decimal point, a System.Double will be used. The one case where you want to tell the system that you're requesting a specific type is with the System.Decimal type. These are specified by placing the letter *d* at the end of the number with no intervening space, as shown in table 2.3.

MULTIPLIER SUFFIXES

Plain numbers are fine for most applications, but in the system administration world, there are many special values you want to be able to conveniently represent, namely, those powers of two—kilobytes, megabytes, gigabytes, terabytes, and petabytes. (Terabyte and petabyte suffixes aren't available in PowerShell v1.)

PowerShell provides a set of *multiplier suffixes* for common sizes to help with this, as listed in table 2.4. These suffixes allow you to easily express common large numbers.

Table 2.4   Numeric multiplier suffixes supported in PowerShell. Suffixes marked v2+ are available only in PowerShell v2 or later. GB, TB, and PB also support non-integer values using the System.Double .NET type

Multiplier suffix	Multiplication factor	Example	Equivalent value	.NET type
kb or KB	1024	1KB	1024	System.Int32
kb or KB	1024	2.2KB	2252.8	System.Double
mb or MB	1024*1024	1MB	1048576	System.Int32
mb or MB	1024*1024	2.2MB	2306867.2	System.Double
gb or GB	1024*1024*1024	1GB	1073741824	System.Int32
tb or TB (v2+)	1024*1024*1024* 1024	1TB	1099511627776	System.Int64
pb or PB (v2+)	1024*1024*1024* 1024*1024	1PB	1125899906842624	System.Int64

NOTE Yes, the PowerShell team is aware that these notations aren't consistent with the ISO/IEC recommendations (kilobyte, and so on). Because the point of this notation is convenience and most IT people are more comfortable with KB than with Ki, they choose to err on the side of comfort over conformance in this one case.

HEXADECIMAL LITERALS

The last item we'll cover in this section is hexadecimal literals. When working with computers, it's obviously useful to be able to specify hex literals. PowerShell uses the same notation as C, C#, and so on—preceding the number with the sequence 0x and allowing the letters A–F as the extra digits. As always, the notation is case-insensitive, as shown in the following examples:

```
PS> 0x10
16

PS> 0xDeadBeef
-559038737
```

Now that we've covered the basic literals, strings, and numbers, let's move on to the literals that let you express complex configuration data, inline in your script.

2.3 Collections: dictionaries and hashtables

Perhaps the most flexible data type in PowerShell is the *hashtable*. This data type lets you map a set of keys to a set of values. For example, you may have a hashtable that maps "red" to 1, "green" to 2, and "yellow" to 4.

> **NOTE** A *dictionary* is the general term for a data structure that maps keys to values. In the .NET world, this takes the form of an interface (System .Collections.IDictionary) that describes how a collection should do this mapping. A hashtable is a specific implementation of that interface. Although the PowerShell hashtable literal syntax only creates instances of System .Collections.Hashtable, scripts that you write will work properly with any object that implements IDictionary.

2.3.1 Creating and inspecting hashtables

In PowerShell, you use hash literals to create a hashtable inline in a script. Here's a simple example:

```
PS> $user = @{ FirstName = 'John'; LastName = 'Smith';
PhoneNumber = '555-1212' }
PS> $user

Key                      Value
---                      -----
LastName                 Smith
FirstName                John
PhoneNumber              555-1212
```

This example created a hashtable that contains three key-value pairs. The hashtable starts with the token @{ and ends with }. Inside the delimiters, you define a set of key-value pairs where the key and value are separated by an equals sign (=). Formally, the syntax for a hash literal is

```
<hashLiteral> = '@{' <keyExpression> '=' <pipeline> [ <separator>
    <keyExpression> '=' <pipeline> ] * '}'
```

Hashtable definitions

We showed you this code to create a hashtable:

```
$user = @{ FirstName = 'John'; LastName = 'Smith';
PhoneNumber = '555-1212' }
$user
```

This is a shorthand way of creating a hashtable that we use at the command line that we've also adopted throughout the book to save space. You could create the hashtable like this:

```
$user = @{
FirstName = 'John'
LastName = 'Smith'
PhoneNumber = '555-1212'
}
```

Each member of the key-value pair of the hashtable has its own line. There's no need to use a semicolon (;) between key-value pairs.

The semicolons in the original code aren't part of the hashtable syntax; they're generic line breaks used to enable the definition to be expressed on one line.

Now that you've created a hashtable, let's see how you can use it. PowerShell allows you to access members in a hashtable in two ways: through property notation and through array notation. Here's what the property notation looks like:

```
PS> $user.firstname
John
```

This notation lets you treat a hashtable like an object and is intended to facilitate the use of hashtables as a kind of lightweight data record. Now let's look at using the array notation:

```
PS> $user['firstname']
John

PS> $user['firstname','lastname']
John
Smith
```

Property notation works pretty much the way you'd expect; you specify a property name and get the corresponding value back. Array notation is more interesting. In the second command in the example, you provided two keys and got two values back.

The underlying object for PowerShell hashtables is the .NET type, `System.Collections.Hashtable`. The `keys` property will give you a list of the keys in the hashtable:

```
$user.keys
```

In the array access notation, you can use keys to get a list of all the values in the table:

```
$user[$user.keys]
```

> **NOTE** A more efficient way to get all the values from a hashtable is to use the Values property. The point of this example is to demonstrate how you can use multiple indexes to retrieve the values based on a subset of the keys.

The keys property didn't return the keys in alphabetical order. This is because of the way hashtables work—keys are randomly distributed in the table to speed up access. If you need to get the values in alphabetical order use Sort-Object to perform the ordering.

> **NOTE** The hashtable keys mechanism expects strings, not objects, as keys, so always ensure you convert any sorted keys to strings before using.

A digression: sorting, enumerating, and hashtables

Let's digress and address a question that sometimes comes up when people, especially .NET programmers, first encounter hashtables in PowerShell. The question is: Are hashtables collections or scalar objects? From the .NET perspective, they're enumerable collections like arrays except they contain a collection of key-value pairs. But—and this is important—*PowerShell treats hashtables like scalar objects*. It does this because, in scripting languages, hashtables are commonly used as on-the-fly structures or data records, meaning you don't have to predefine the fields in a record; you make them up as you go. If PowerShell treated hashtables as enumerable collections by default, this wouldn't be possible, because every time you passed one of these "records" into a pipeline, it would be broken up into a stream of individual key-value pairs and the integrity of the original table would be lost.

This causes the most problems for people when they use hashtables in the foreach statement. In a .NET language like C#, the foreach statement iterates over all the pairs. In PowerShell, the foreach loop will run only once because the hashtable isn't considered an enumerable, at least not by default. If you want to iterate over the pairs, you'll have to call the GetEnumerator() method yourself:

```
PS> $h = @{a=1; b=2; c=3}
PS> foreach ($pair in $h.GetEnumerator()) {
    $pair.key + " is " + $pair.value
}

a is 1
b is 2
c is 3
```

In each iteration, the next pair is assigned to $pair and processing continues.

A significant part of the reason this behavior confuses people is when PowerShell displays a hashtable, it uses enumeration to list the key-value pairs as part of the presentation. The result is there's no visible difference between when you call Get-Enumerator() in the foreach loop and when you don't. This is desirable in the sense

(Continued)

that it's a good way to present a hashtable and doesn't require effort from the user to do this. On the other hand, it masks the details of what's going on. As always, it's difficult to serve all audiences perfectly.

Another aspect of the hashtable collection question is people want to be able to "sort" a hashtable the way you'd sort a list of numbers. In the case of a hashtable, this usually means that the user wants to be able to control the order in which keys will be retrieved from the hashtable. Unfortunately, this can't work because the keys are stored in random order.

2.3.2   Ordered hashtables

We stated earlier that a hashtable's keys were distributed randomly to speed up access. This causes much anguish among some users when they use a hashtable to supply the properties and values to be used when creating a new object in PowerShell.

In PowerShell v3 a resolution to this anguish was introduced in the form of an ordered hashtable. This is created in much the same way as an ordinary hashtable except you add the [ordered] cast:

```
PS> $usero = [ordered]@{ FirstName = 'John'; LastName = 'Smith';
  PhoneNumber = '555-1212' }
PS> $usero
```

```
Name                          Value
----                          -----
FirstName                     John
LastName                      Smith
PhoneNumber                   555-1212
```

The underlying .NET type for an ordered hashtable is `System.Collections.Specialized.OrderedDictionary` as opposed to the standard hashtable, which is `System.Collections.Hashtable`. The two .NET types are similar, though not identical, as you'd expect. You use an ordered hashtable in the same way as an ordinary hashtable.

The most important difference is the order of the keys is preserved in the ordered hashtable. But there's one "gotcha" with the way this was implemented. The `OrderedDictionary` type has two ways of retrieving elements from the collection: by key or by the numerical index of the element. In practice, this means you get some unfortunate effects when using integers as keys. The first problem occurs when assigning elements to the hashtable. First, you'll create an ordered dictionary:

```
PS> $oh = [ordered] @{ }
```

Then add an element where the key is the integer 5 and the value is the string "five":

```
PS> $oh[5] = 'five'
Specified argument was out of the range of valid values.
```

```
Parameter name: index
At line:1 char:1
+ $oh[5] = 'five'
+ ~~~~~~~~~~~~~~~
    + CategoryInfo          : OperationStopped: (:) [],
  ArgumentOutOfRangeException
    + FullyQualifiedErrorId : System.ArgumentOutOfRangeException
```

This results in an error message because the OrderedCollection interprets the key 5 as an index into the collection. Because there's no element 5, it fails. There's a (somewhat awkward) workaround where you cast 5 to [object]—it's still a number but now the runtime will use key-based lookup instead of numeric index lookup:

```
PS> $oh[[object] 5] = 'five'
```

Now the assignment succeeds but you have to do the same trick to retrieve the element by key:

```
PS> $oh[[object] 5]
five
```

If you pass a number without the explicit cast, it will look up using the element index. The correct element index for the key 5 is 0:

```
PS> $oh[0]
five
```

Hopefully you won't encounter this problem but it's handy to understand what's going on.

2.3.3 *Modifying and manipulating hashtables*

Next let's look at adding, changing, and removing elements in the hashtable. First let's add the date and the city where the user lives to the $user table:

```
PS> $user.date = Get-Date
PS> $user['city'] = 'Seattle'
PS> $user
Name                         Value
----                         -----
date                         09/06/2017 15:18:12
city                         Seattle
PhoneNumber                  555-1212
FirstName                    John
LastName                     Smith
```

A simple assignment using either the property or array accessor notation allows you to add, or modify, an element to a hashtable. If you want to remove an element from the table use the remove() method:

```
PS> $user.remove("city")
```

If you want to create an empty hashtable, use @{ } with no member specifications between the braces. This creates an empty table you can then add members to incrementally:

```
PS> $newHashTable = @{}
PS> $newHashTable
PS> $newHashTable.one = 1
PS> $newHashTable.two = 2
PS> $newHashTable

Key                       Value
---                       -----
two                       2
one                       1
```

This technique can also be used for an ordered hashtable.

2.3.4 *Hashtables as reference types*

Hashtables are reference types. As an example, create a hashtable, assign it to a variable $foo, as shown in the top part of figure 2.3. Then assign $foo to another variable, $bar; you'll have two variables that point to, or *reference*, the same object, as shown in the bottom part of figure 2.3.

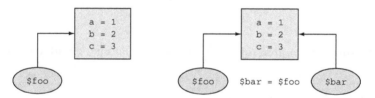

Figure 2.3   Hashtable as a reference type

Consequently, any changes made to one variable will affect the other, because they're pointing to the same object. Let's try this out. Create a new hashtable and assign it to $foo:

```
PS> $foo = @{
  a = 1
  b = 2
  c = 3
}
PS> $foo.a
1
```

Now assign $foo to $bar and verify it matches $foo as you'd expect:

```
PS> $bar = $foo
PS> $bar.a
1
```

Next assign a new value to the element a in $foo:

```
PS> $foo.a = "Hi there"
PS> $foo.a
Hi there
```

And see what happens to $bar:

```
PS> $bar.a
Hi there
```

The change made to $foo has been reflected in $bar.

Now if you want to make a copy of the hashtable instead of copying the reference, you can use the Clone() method on the object:

```
PS> $foo=@{a=1; b=2; c=3}
PS> $bar = $foo.Clone()
```

Change the a member in the table:

```
PS> $foo.a = "Hello"
```

and verify the hashtable in $foo has changed:

```
PS> $foo.a
Hello
```

but the hashtable in $bar hasn't:

```
PS> $bar.a
1
```

because it's a copy, not a reference. This technique can be useful if you're creating a number of tables that are mostly the same. You can create a "template" table, make copies, and then change the pieces you need to.

There's still more to know about hashtables and how they work with operators, but we'll cover that in chapters 3 and 4. For now, let's move on to the next data type.

2.4   *Collections: arrays and sequences*

In the previous section we talked about hashtables and hash literals. Now let's talk about the PowerShell syntax for arrays and array literals. Most programming languages have some kind of array literal notation similar to the PowerShell hash literal notation, where there's a beginning character sequence followed by a list of values, followed by a closing character sequence. Here's how array literals are defined in PowerShell: *They're not. There's no array literal notation in PowerShell.*

Yes, you read that correctly. There's no notation for an array literal in PowerShell. How exactly does this work? How do you define an inline array in a PowerShell script? Here's the answer: Instead of having array literals, there's a set of operations that creates collections as needed. In fact, collections of objects are created and discarded transparently throughout PowerShell. If you need an array, one will be created for you. If you need a singleton (or scalar) value, the collection will be unwrapped as needed.

> **NOTE** Since PowerShell v3, any object is treated as a pseudo-array and has a Count property. This is to remove issues where pipelines could return one, or many, objects. The single object case would cause errors in code designed for a collection of many objects.

2.4.1   *Collecting pipeline output as an array*

The most common operation resulting in an array in PowerShell is collecting the output from a pipeline. When you run a pipeline that emits a sequence of objects and assign that output to a variable, it automatically collects the elements into an array, specifically into a .NET object of type [object[]].

But what about building a simple array in an expression? The simplest way to do this is to use the comma operator (,). See chapter 4 for more information about using the comma operator. When you assign that sequence to a variable, it's stored as an array. Assign these three numbers to a variable, $a, and look at the result type:

```
PS> $a = 1,2,3
PS> $a.GetType().FullName
System.Object[]
```

As in the pipeline case, the result is stored in an array of type [object[]].

2.4.2   *Array indexing*

Let's explore some of the operations that can be performed on arrays. As is commonly the case, getting and setting elements of the array (array indexing) is done with [] brackets. The length of an array can be retrieved with the Length property.

> **NOTE** Arrays in PowerShell are origin-zero—the first element in the array is at index 0, not index 1.

As with hashtables, changes are made to an array by assigning new values to indexes in the array. The following example assigns new values to the first and third elements in $a:

```
PS> $a[0] = 3.1415
PS> $a[2] = 'Hi there'
```

Simple assignment updates the element at the specified index.

2.4.3   *Polymorphism in arrays*

Another important thing to note from the previous example is arrays are *polymorphic* by default. By polymorphic we mean you can store any type of object in an array. When you created the array, you assigned only integers to it. In the subsequent examples, you assigned a floating-point number and a string. The original array was capable of storing any kind of object. In formal terms, PowerShell arrays are polymorphic by default (though it's possible to create type-constrained arrays).

Attempts to assign outside the bounds of an array will result in a range error. This is because PowerShell arrays are based on .NET arrays and their size is fixed. You can add elements through array concatenation using the plus (+) or plus-equals (+=) operators. Now add two more elements to the array from the previous example:

```
PS> $a += 22,33
PS> $a.length
5
PS> $a[4]
33
```

So, the length of the array in $a is now 5. The addition operation did add elements. Here's how this works:

1 PowerShell creates a new array large enough to hold the total number of elements.
2 It copies the contents of the original array into the new one.
3 It copies the new elements into the end of the array.

You didn't add any elements to the original array after all. Instead, you created a new, larger one.

2.4.4 Arrays as reference types

This copying behavior has some interesting consequences. You can explore this further by first creating a simple array and looking at the value using string expansion:

```
PS> $a=1,2,3
PS> "$a"
1 2 3
```

Now assign $a to a new variable, $b, and check that $a and $b have the same elements:

```
PS> $b = $a
PS> "$b"
1 2 3
```

Changing the first element in $a also causes $b to change:

```
PS> $a[0] = 'Changed'
PS> "$a"
Changed 2 3

PS> "$b"
Changed 2 3
```

As with hashtables, array assignment is done by reference. When you assigned $a to $b, you got a copy of the reference to the array instead of a copy of contents of the array. Add a new element to $b:

```
PS> $b += 4
PS> "$b"
Changed 2 3 4
```

$b is now four elements long. Because of the way array concatenation works, $b contains a copy of the contents of the array instead of a reference. If you change $a now, it won't affect $b. Conversely, changing $b will have no effect on $a.

To reiterate, arrays in PowerShell are reference types, not value types. When you assign them to a variable, you get another reference to the array, not another copy of the array.

2.4.5   *Singleton arrays and empty arrays*

You saw how to use the comma operator to build up an array containing more than one element. You can also use the comma operator as a prefix operator to create an array containing only one element. For example:

```
PS> (, 1).length
1
```

This code creates an array containing a single element, 1.

Empty arrays are created through a special form of subexpression notation that uses the @ symbol instead of the $ sign to start the expression. Here's what it looks like:

```
PS> @().length
0
```

This notation is more general—it takes the result of the expression it encloses and ensures it's always returned as an array. If the expression returns $null or a scalar value, it will be wrapped in a one-element array. Given this behavior, the other solution to creating an array with one element is

```
PS> @(1)
1
PS> @(1).length
1
```

You place the value you want in the array in @(...) and you get an array back.

Use this notation when you don't know whether the command you're calling is going to return an array. By executing the command in this way, you're guaranteed to get an array back. Note if what you're returning is already an array, it won't be wrapped in a new array. Compare this to the use of the comma operator:

```
PS> (1,2,3).Length
3
```

```
PS> ( , (1,2,3) ).Length
1

PS> ( @( 1,2,3 ) ).Length
3
```

Line 1 created a regular array of length 3. Next, on line 2, you apply the prefix opera-tor to the array and then get the length. The result now is only 1. This is because the unary comma operator always wraps its arguments in a new array. On line 3, you use the @(...) notation and then get the length. This time it remains 3. The @(...) sequence doesn't wrap unless the object isn't an array.

Now let's look at the last type of literal: the *type literal*. Because object types are so important in PowerShell, you need to be able to express types in a script.

2.5   *Type literals*

In earlier sections you saw a number of things that looked like [type]. These are the *type literals*. In PowerShell, you use type literals:

- To specify a particular type
- As operators in a *cast* (converting an object from one type to another)
- As a part of a *type-constrained* variable declaration
- As an object itself

Here's an example of a cast using a type literal:

```
PS> $i = [int] '123'
```

In this example, you're casting or converting a string into an instance of .NET type System.Int32. You could use the longer .NET type name to accomplish the same thing:

```
PS> $i = [System.Int32] '123'
```

Now let's look at something a bit more sophisticated. If you wanted to make this into an array of integers, you'd do this:

```
PS> $i = [int[]] '123'
```

In this example, you're not only casting the basic type, you're also changing it from a *scalar object* to an array. This *breaks* the general type converter rule that no more than one conversion will be performed in a single step but converting a scalar into an array is so common it's supported directly.

> **NOTE** In PowerShell v1 you had to use a two-step process: $i = [int[]][object[]] '123'.

2.5.1   *Type name aliases*

Obviously, the shorter type name (or *type alias*, as it's known) is more convenient. The number of type aliases has grown to 93 in PowerShell v5.1. You can view the list like this:

```
PS> $tna = [psobject].Assembly.
GetType('System.Management.Automation.TypeAccelerators')::Get
PS> $tna.GetEnumerator() | Sort-Object Key
```

Anything in the `System.Management.Automation` namespace is specific to PowerShell. The other types are .NET types and are covered in the MSDN documentation.

> **Type resolution**
>
> When PowerShell resolves a type name, it first checks the type name alias table; then it checks to see whether a type exists with a full name that matches the string specified. Finally, it prepends the type with `System` and checks to see whether a type exists that matches the new string. This means things that are in the `System` namespace look like they might be aliased.

2.5.2   *Generic type literals*

There's a special kind of type in .NET called a *generic type*, which lets you say something like "a list of strings" instead of "a list" (compare with the standard types described in section 2.1). And although you could do this without generics, you'd have to create a specific type for the type of list. With generics, you create one generic list type (hence the name) and then *parameterize* it with the type it can contain.

> **NOTE**   Generic type literal support was added in v2. In v1 it was possible to express a type literal, but it was a painful process.

This example shows the type literal for a generic list (`System.Collections.Generic.List`) of integers:

```
PS> [system.collections.generic.list[int]] | Format-Table -Autosize

IsPublic IsSerial Name    BaseType
-------- -------- ----    --------
True     True     List`1  System.Object
```

If you look at the type literal, it's easy to see how the collection element type is expressed: `[int]`. This is a nested type literal where the type parameter is enclosed in nested [] brackets. Create an instance of this type:

```
PS> $l = New-Object System.Collections.Generic.List[int]
```

then add some elements to it:

```
PS> $l.add(1)
PS> $l.add(2)
```

Trying to add something that isn't an integer will cause an error because the value can't be converted into an integer.

Now let's look at a type that requires more than one type parameter. For example, a generic dictionary requires two type parameters: the type of the keys and the type of the values. Here's what this looks like:

```
PS> [system.collections.generic.dictionary[string,int]] |
Format-Table -Autosize

IsPublic IsSerial Name          BaseType
-------- -------- ----          --------
True     True     Dictionary`2  System.Object
```

The two type parameters are separated by a comma inside the [] brackets.

Now let's take a trip into the too-much-information zone and look in detail at the process PowerShell uses to perform all these type conversions. This is a "spinach" section—you may not like it, but it's good for you.

The primary uses for type literals are in performing type conversions and invoking *static methods*. We'll look at both uses in the next two sections.

2.5.3 *Accessing static members with type literals*

As mentioned, a common use for type literals is for accessing static methods on .NET classes. You can use the Get-Member cmdlet to look at the members on an object. To view the static members, use the -Static flag:

```
PS> [string] | Get-Member -Static
```

This code will display all the static members in the .NET System.String class. If you want to call one of these methods, you need to use the :: operator. Let's use the Join() method to join an array of strings. First create the array:

```
PS> $s = 'one','two','three'
```

then use the Join() method to join all the pieces into a single string with plus signs in between:

```
PS> [string]::Join(' + ', $s)
one + two + three
```

Another good example of the power of static methods is the [math] class from the .NET Framework. This class, [System.Math], is a pure static class, meaning you can't create an instance of it—you can only use the static methods it provides. It contains a lot of methods and properties, such as useful constants like Pi and e as static properties and all the trigonometric functions as static methods.

As we've said, types in PowerShell provide tremendous power and breadth of capabilities. In many cases, before rolling your own solution it's worth browsing the MSDN documentation on the .NET libraries to see if there's something you can use to solve your problems. Now that you've seen the types, let's look at how PowerShell does type conversions.

2.6   Type conversions

Automatic type conversion is the "secret sauce" that allows a strongly typed language like PowerShell to behave like a typeless command-line shell. Without a comprehensive type-conversion system to map the output of one command to the input type required by another command, PowerShell would be nearly impossible to use as a shell.

In the next few sections we'll go through an overview of how the type-conversion system works. Then we'll look at the conversion algorithm in detail. Finally, we'll explore special conversion rules that apply only when binding cmdlet parameters.

2.6.1   How type conversion works

Type conversions are used any time an attempt is made to use an object of one type in a context that requires another type (such as adding a string to a number). Examples include:

- Converting a string input to a cmdlet parameter to a number as required by the cmdlet
- Casting operations in the shell

In PowerShell, you use types to accomplish many things that you'd do with methods or functions in other languages. You use type literals as operators to convert (or cast) one type of object to another. Here's a simple example:

```
PS> [int] '0x25'
37
```

In this example, a string representing a hexadecimal number is converted into a number by using a cast operation. A token specifying the name of a type in brackets can be used as a unary operator that will try to convert its argument into the desired type. These type cast operations can be composed (several casts can be chained together):

```
PS> [int] [char]'a'
97
```

Notice you first cast the string into a char and then into an int. This is necessary because the simple conversion would try to parse the entire string as a number. This only works for a string containing exactly one character. If you want to convert an entire string, you need to use array types. Here's what that looks like:

```
PS> [int[]] [char[]] 'Hello world'
```

The string was split into an array of characters, then that array of characters was converted into an array of integers. If you wanted to see those numbers in hex, you'd have to use the -f format operator and a format-specifier string:

```
PS> "0x{0:x}" -f [int] [char] 'a'
0x61
```

If you want to make a roundtrip—string to char to int to char to string—you can do this:

```
PS> [string][char][int] ("0x{0:x}" -f [int] [char] 'a')
a
```

When PowerShell converts arrays to strings, it takes each array element, converts that element into a string, and then concatenates all the pieces together. Because this would be an unreadable mess, it inserts a separator between each element. That separator is specified using the $OFS variable (see the about_Automatic_Variables help file) which defaults to a single space. It can be set to anything you want, even the empty string.

> **NOTE** Variable expansion in strings goes through the same mechanism as the type converter, so you'll get the same result.

2.6.2 *PowerShell's type-conversion algorithm*

In this section we'll cover the steps in the conversion process in painful detail—much more than you'll generally need to know in your day-to-day work. But if you want to be an expert on PowerShell, this stuff is for you. In general, the PowerShell type conversions are separated into two major buckets.

> **NOTE** Type conversion is one of the areas of the PowerShell project that grew organically. The team sat down, wrote a slew of specifications, threw them out, and ended up doing something completely different. This is one of the joys of this type of work. Nice, clean theory falls apart when you put it in front of real people. The type-conversion algorithm as it exists today is the result of feedback from many of the early adopters both inside Microsoft as well as outside. The PowerShell community helped tremendously in this area.

POWERSHELL LANGUAGE STANDARD CONVERSIONS
These standard built-in conversions performed by the engine itself. They're always processed first and can't be overridden. This set of conversions is largely guided by the historical behavior of shell and scripting languages, and isn't part of the normal .NET type-conversion system.

.NET-BASED CUSTOM CONVERTERS

.NET-based custom converters use (and abuse in some cases) existing .NET mechanisms for doing type conversion.

Table 2.5 lists the set of built-in language conversions that PowerShell uses. The conversion process always starts with an object of a particular type and tries to produce a representation of that object in the requested target type. The conversions are applied in the order shown in table 2.5. Only one conversion is applied at a time. The PowerShell engine doesn't automatically chain conversions.

Table 2.5   PowerShell language standard conversions

Converting from	To target type	Result description
`$null`	`[string]`	`''`(empty string)
	`[char]`	`'0'` (string containing a single character 0)
	Any kind of number	The object corresponding to 0 for the corresponding numeric type
	`[bool]`	`$false`
	`[PSObject]`	`$null`
	Any other type of object	`$null`
Derived class	Base class	The original object is returned unchanged.
Anything	`[void]`	The object is discarded.
Anything	`[string]`	The PowerShell internal string converter is used.
Anything	`[xml]`	The original object is first converted into a string and then into an XML document object.
Array of type `[X]`	Array of type `[Y]`	PowerShell creates a new array of the target type, then copies and converts each element in the source array into an instance for the target array type.
Non-array (singleton) object	Array of type `[Y]`	Creates an array containing one element and then places the singleton object into the array, converting if necessary.
`System.Collections.IDictionary`	`[Hashtable]`	A new instance of `System.Collections.Hashtable` is created, and then the members of the source `IDictionary` are copied into the new object.
`[string]`	`[char[]]`	Converts the string to an array of characters.
`[string]`	`[regex]`	Constructs a new instance of a .NET regular expression object.
`[string]`	Number	Converts the string into a number using the smallest representation available that can accurately represent that number. If the string isn't purely convertible (only contains numeric information), then an error is raised.

Table 2.5 PowerShell language standard conversions *(continued)*

Converting from	To target type	Result description
`[int]`	`System.Enum`	Converts the integer to the corresponding enumeration member if it exists. If it doesn't, a conversion error is generated.

If none of the built-in PowerShell language-specific conversions could be applied successfully, then the .NET custom converters are tried. Again, these converters are tried in order until a candidate is found that will produce the required target type. This candidate conversion is applied. If the candidate conversion throws an exception (a matching converter is found but it fails during the conversion process), no further attempt to convert this object will be made, and the overall conversion process will be considered to have failed.

> **NOTE** Developing an understanding of these conversions depends on a fair knowledge of the .NET type conversion mechanisms. You'll need to refer to additional documentation if you want to understand everything in table 2.6. With the .NET docs, you can see exactly what steps are being applied in the type-conversion process.

Custom converters are executed in the order described in table 2.6.

Table 2.6 Custom type conversions

Converter type	Description
`PSTypeConverter`	A `PSTypeConverter` can be associated with a particular type using `TypeConverterAttribute` or the `<TypeConverter>` tag in the types .ps1xml file. If the value to convert has a `PSTypeConverter` that can convert to the target type, then it's called. If the target type has a `PSTypeConverter` that can convert from values to convert, then it's called.
	The `PSTypeConverter` allows a single type converter to work for a number of different classes. For example, an `enum` type converter can convert a string to any `enum` (there doesn't need to be separate type to convert each enum). Refer to the PowerShell SDK documentation from MSDN for complete details on this converter.
`TypeConverter`	This is a Common Language Runtime (CLR) defined type that can be associated with a particular type using the `TypeConverterAttribute` or the `<TypeConverter>` tag in the types file. If the value to convert has a `TypeConverter` that can convert to the target type, then it's called. If the target type has a `TypeConverter` that can convert from the source value, then it's called.
	The CLR `TypeConverter` doesn't allow a single type converter to work for a number of different classes. Refer to the PowerShell SDK documentation and the Microsoft .NET Framework documentation for details on the `TypeConverter` class.

Table 2.6 Custom type conversions *(continued)*

Converter type	Description
Parse() method	If the value to convert is a string and the target type has a `Parse()` method, then that `Parse()` method is called. `Parse()` is a well-known method name in the CLR world and is commonly implemented to allow conversion of strings to other types.
Constructors	If the target type has a constructor that takes a single parameter matching the type of the value to convert, then this constructor is used to create a new object of the desired type.
Implicit cast operator	If the value to convert has an implicit cast operator that converts to the target type, then it's called. Conversely, if the target type has an implicit cast operator that converts from value to convert's type, then that's called.
Explicit cast operator	If the value to convert has an explicit cast operator that converts to the target type, then it's called. Alternatively, if the target type has an explicit cast operator that converts from value to convert's type, then that's called.
IConvertable	`System.Convert.ChangeType` is then called.

This section covered the set of type conversions that PowerShell will apply in expressions. In the parameter binder are a few extra steps that are applied first.

2.6.3 *Special type conversions in parameter binding*

In this section we'll go over the extra type-conversion rules that are used in parameter binding that haven't already been covered. If these steps are tried and aren't successful, the parameter binder goes on to call the normal PowerShell type-converter code.

NOTE If at any time failure occurs during the type conversion, an exception will be thrown.

Here are the extra steps:

1 If there's no argument for the parameter, the parameter type must be either a [bool] or the special PowerShell type SwitchParameter; otherwise, a parameter binding exception is thrown. If the parameter type is a [bool], it's set to true. If the parameter type is a SwitchParameter, it's set to SwitchParameter.Present.

2 If the argument value is null and the parameter type is [bool], it's set to false. If the argument value is null and the parameter type is SwitchParameter, it's set to SwitchParameter.Present. Null can be bound to any other type, so it passes through.

3 If the argument type is the same as the parameter type, the argument value is used without any type conversion.

4 If the parameter type is [object], the current argument value is used without any coercion.

5 If the parameter type is a [bool], use the PowerShell Boolean IsTrue() method to determine whether the argument value should set the parameter to true or false.

6 If the parameter type is a collection, the argument type must be encoded into the appropriate collection type. You'll encode a scalar argument type or a collection argument type to a target collection parameter type. You won't encode a collection argument type into a scalar parameter type (unless that type is `System.Object` or `PSObject`).

7 If the argument type is a scalar, create a collection of the parameter type (currently only arrays and `IList` are supported) of length 1 and set the argument value as the only value in the collection. If needed, the argument type is converted to the element type for the collection using the same type-coercion process this section describes.

8 If the argument type is a collection, create a collection of the parameter type with length equal to the number of values contained in the argument value. Each value is then coerced to the appropriate element type for the new collection using the recursive application of this algorithm.

9 If none of these steps worked, use the conversions in table 2.5. If those fail, then the overall parameter binding attempt fails.

Once again, this is a level of detail that you don't often need to consider, but it's useful to know it's available when you need it.

SCRIPTBLOCK PARAMETERS

And finally, there's one last aspect of the parameter binder type converter to cover: a feature called *scriptblock parameters.*

First, a preview of things to come. PowerShell has something called a *scriptblock* which is a fragment of code that you can pass around as an object itself. This is a powerful concept, and we'll cover scriptblocks in great detail in later chapters, but for now we're going to look at them in the context of parameter binding.

Here's how scriptblock parameters work. Normally, when you pipe two cmdlets together, the second cmdlet receives values directly from the first. Scriptblock parameters (you could also call them *computed parameters*) allow you to insert a piece of script to perform a calculation or transformation in the middle of the pipelined operation. This calculation can do pretty much anything you want because a scriptblock can contain any element of PowerShell script.

Here's an example of how this works. You want to take a collection of XML files and rename them as text files. You could write a loop to do the processing, but scriptblock parameters greatly simplify this task. To rename each file, use the `Rename-Item` cmdlet. This cmdlet takes two parameters: the current filename and the new name. Use a scriptblock parameter as an argument to the `-NewName` parameter to generate the new filename. This scriptblock will use the `-replace` operator to replace the .xml file extension with the desired .txt. Here's the command line that performs this task:

```
PS> Get-ChildItem -Path *.xml |
Rename-Item -Path {$_.Name} `
-NewName {$_.Name -replace '\.xml$', '.txt'} -Whatif
```

The original path for -Path is the current name of the file. The -NewName parameter is the filename with the extension replaced. The -WhatIf parameter will let you see what the command will do before moving anything. Once you're happy that the correct operations are being performed, remove the -WhatIf and the renaming will proceed.

Scriptblock parameters can be used with any pipelined parameter as long as the type of that parameter isn't [object] or [scriptblock]. In these cases, the scriptblock is passed as the parameter instead of using it to calculate a new value. You'll see why this is important when we look at the Where-Object and ForEach-Object cmdlets.

You now know everything you need to know about how types work on PowerShell. Well, not quite everything. In the next two chapters, we'll discuss how the PowerShell operators build on this basic type foundation. But for now, we're through!

2.7   *Summary*

- PowerShell is built on the .NET type system and can extend those types as required.
- PowerShell has a set of basic types for working with strings and numbers.
- PowerShell supports advanced types such as hashtables and arrays.
- Type literals can be used in type casts and as a way to call static methods.
- Generic type literals greatly simplify working with generic types.
- PowerShell automatically manages a large number of type conversions.
- Scriptblock parameters allow you to calculate new values for pipelined parameters instead of having to write a loop to do this (we'll look at scriptblocks in detail in chapter 7).

We've mentioned operators a few times in this chapter—they're how PowerShell performs a number of actions. Chapter 3 will introduce the basic operators used in PowerShell.

Operators and expressions

This chapter covers
- Arithmetic operators
- Assignment operators
- Comparison operators
- Pattern matching and text manipulation
- Logical and bitwise operators

> *Operators, Mr. Rico! Millions of them!*
>
> —*Robert A. Heinlein,* Starship Troopers *(paraphrased)*

The goal of PowerShell is to enable you to get real work done. As in any language, expressions consist of operators and objects. The operators perform their operations on objects, giving you (hopefully) useful results. This chapter covers the set of basic operators in PowerShell and how they're used in expressions. Without operators PowerShell can't perform comparisons, arithmetic, logical operations, or a host of other activities. The operators we're going to cover in this chapter are shown in figure 3.1.

> **NOTE** Operators are normally classed as unary if they take a single operand and binary if they take two. The operators in this chapter are all binary. We'll look at unary operators in chapter 4.

Arithmetic operators

```
+  -  *  /  %
```

Assignment operators

```
=  +=  -=  *=  /=  %=
```

Comparison operators

```
-eq  -ne  -gt  -ge  -lt  -le
-ieq -ine -igt -ige -ilt -ile
-ceq -cne -cgt -cge -clt -cle
```

Containment operators

```
-contains  -notcontains   -in  -notin
-icontains -inotcontains  -iin -inotin
-ccontains -cnotcontains  -cin -cnotin
```

Pattern-matching and text-manipulation operators

```
-like  -notlike  -match  -notmatch  -replace  -split
-ilike -inotlike -imatch -inotmatch -ireplace -isplit
-clike -cnotlike -cmatch -cnotmatch -creplace -csplit
                        -join
```

Logical and bitwise operators

```
-and  -or  -not  -xor  -shl
-band -nor -bnot -bxor -shr
```

Figure 3.1   Broad groups of operators we'll cover in this chapter

As you'll see, PowerShell has lots of operators. PowerShell operators are typically more powerful than the corresponding operators in conventional languages such as C# or Java. If you invest the time to learn what the PowerShell operators are and how they work, in a single line of code you'll be able to accomplish tasks that would normally take a significant amount of programming.

One of the characteristics that makes PowerShell operators so powerful is they're *polymorphic*. This means they work on more than one type of object. Although this is generally true in other object-based languages, in those languages the type of the object defines the behavior of the operator.

NOTE   If you're a C# or Visual Basic user, here's something you might want to know. In "conventional" .NET languages, the operator symbols are mapped to a specific method name on a class called op_<operatorName>. For example, in C#, the plus operator (+) maps to the method op_Addition(). Although PowerShell is a .NET language, it takes a different approach that's more consistent with dynamic scripting languages, as you'll see in the following sections.

In PowerShell, the interpreter primarily defines the behavior of the operators, at least for common data types: strings, numbers, hashtables, and arrays. Type-based polymorphic methods are only used as a backup. This allows PowerShell to provide more consistent behavior over this range of common objects and higher-level behaviors than are provided by the objects themselves, especially when dealing with collections. We'll cover these special behaviors in the sections for each class of operator. Now let's get going and start looking at the operators. PowerShell has help files that describe all operators by groups. You can view a list of the available help files that relate to operators:

```
PS> Get-Help operator
```

3.1   *Arithmetic operators*

First we'll cover the basic arithmetic operators shown in figure 3.2.

Arithmetic operators

Figure 3.2   Arithmetic operators in PowerShell that will be covered in this section

We touched on the polymorphic behavior of these operators briefly in chapter 2, where we discussed type conversions. The operators themselves are listed with examples in table 3.1.

Table 3.1   Basic arithmetic operators in PowerShell

Operator	Description	Example	Result
+	Add two values	2 + 4	6
		'Hi ' + 'there'	'Hi there'
		1,2,3 + 4,5,6	1,2,3,4,5,6
*	Multiply two values	2 * 4	8
		'a' * 3	'aaa'
		1,2 * 2	1,2,1,2
-	Subtract one value from another	6 - 2	4
/	Divide two values	6 / 2	3
		7 / 4	1.75
%	Return the remainder from a division operation (modulus)	7 % 4	3

In terms of behavior, the most interesting operators are + and *. We'll cover them in detail in the next two sections.

3.1.1 Addition operator

As mentioned earlier, PowerShell defines the behavior of the + and * operators for numbers, strings, arrays, and hashtables:

- Adding or multiplying two numbers produces a numeric result following the numeric widening rules.
- Adding two strings performs string concatenation, resulting in a new string.
- Adding two arrays joins the two arrays (array concatenation), producing a new array.
- Adding two hashtables creates a new hashtable with combined elements.

The interesting part occurs when you mix operand types. In this situation, the type of the *left* operand determines how the operation will proceed, as shown in table 3.2.

Table 3.2   Result of addition operations

Left operand	Right operand	Result
Number	Anything	PowerShell will convert the right operand to a number.
String	Anything	PowerShell will convert the right operand to a string and append to the left operand (string concatenation).
Array or collection	Scalar	PowerShell will add the right operand to a collection.
Array or collection	Array or other enumerable collection	PowerShell will append the right operand to a collection.

If any of the conversions described in table 3.2 fail, an error will be thrown.

NOTE The "left-hand" rule for arithmetic operators: the type of the left operand determines the type of the overall operation. This is an important rule to remember.

At this point, it's probably a good idea to reiterate how array concatenation is done in PowerShell. Because the underlying .NET array objects are of fixed size (as discussed in chapter 2), concatenation is accomplished by creating a new array of type [object[]] and copying the elements from the operands into this new array. In the process of creating the new array, any type constraint on the original arrays will be lost. If the left operand is [int[]]—an array of type [int]—and you add a non-numeric string to it, a new array will be created that will be of type [object[]], which can hold any type of object. Modifying an array in this manner is common practice when storing data from a number of sources in your script prior to output.

Let's look at an example. First create an integer array:

```
PS> $a = [int[]] (1,2,3,4)
```

Now assign an integer and then a string that can be converted to an integer:

```
PS> $a[0] = 10
PS> $a[0] = '0xabc'
```

Both work fine. Finally, try assigning a non-numeric string to the array element:

```
PS> $a[0] = 'hello'
Cannot convert value "hello" to type "System.Int32".
Error: "Input string was not in a correct format."
At line:1 char:1
+ $a[0] = 'hello'
+ ~~~~~~~~~~~~~~~
    + CategoryInfo          : InvalidArgument: (:) [], RuntimeException
    + FullyQualifiedErrorId : InvalidCastFromStringToInteger
```

This fails, as you might expect. An array of type [int[]] can hold only integers, and 'hello' can't be converted into an integer! So far, so good. Now let's do an array concatenation:

```
PS> $a = $a + 'hello'
```

And now try the assignment that failed previously:

```
PS> $a[0] = 'hello'
```

This time the assignment succeeds without error. What happened here? Let's look at the type of the array:

```
PS> $a.GetType().FullName
System.Object[]
```

When the new, larger array was created to hold the combined elements, it was created as type [object[]], which isn't type constrained. It can hold any type of object, so the assignment proceeded without error.

Finally, let's see how addition works with hashtables. Similar to arrays, addition of hashtables creates a new hashtable and copies the elements of the original tables into the new one. The left elements are copied first; then the elements from the right operand are copied. (This only works if both operands are hashtables.) If any collisions take place—if the keys of any of the elements in the right operand match the keys of any element in the left operand—then an error will occur saying the key already exists in the hashtable. (This was an implementation decision; the PowerShell team could've had the new element overwrite the old one, but the consensus was generating an error message is usually the better thing to do.)

Now that we've finished with addition, let's move on to the multiplication operator.

3.1.2   *Multiplication operator*

As with addition, PowerShell defines multiplication behavior for numbers, strings, and arrays. (PowerShell doesn't do anything special for hashtables for multiplication.) Multiplying numbers works as expected and follows the widening rules discussed in chapter 2. In fact, the only legal right operand for multiplication is a number.

If the operand on the left is a string, then that string is repeated the number of times specified in the right operand. Let's try this out. Multiply the string "abc" by 3:

```
PS> 'abc' * 3
abcabcabc
```

Try multiplying by 0:

```
PS> 'abc' * 0
```

The result appears to be nothing—but which "nothing"—spaces, empty string, or null? Here's how to check:

1 Check the type of the result using (`'abc' * 0`).GetType().FullName, which tells you it's a string.
2 Check the length using (`'abc' * 0`).Length.

Because the length is 0, you can tell it's in fact an empty string.

Now let's look at how multiplication works with arrays. As with strings, multiplication applied to an array repeats the array. Let's look at some examples. First create an array with three elements:

```
PS> $a=1,2,3
PS> $a.Length
3
```

and multiply it by 2:

```
PS> $a = $a * 2
PS> $a.Length
6
```

The length of the new array is 6. Looking at the contents of the array (using variable expansion in strings to save space), you see it's "1 2 3 1 2 3"—the original array doubled.

As with addition, first a new larger array is created during multiplication, and then the component elements are copied into it. This has the same issue that addition had, where the new array is created without type constraints. Even if the original array could hold only numbers, the new array can hold any type of object.

3.1.3 *Subtraction, division, and the modulus operators*

Addition and multiplication are the most interesting of the arithmetic operators in terms of polymorphic behavior, but let's go over the remaining operators. Subtraction, division, and the modulus (%) operators are *only defined for numbers by PowerShell*. (Modulus returns the remainder from a division operation.) Again, as with all numeric computations, the widening rules for numbers are obeyed. For basic scalar types like strings and numbers, these operations are only defined for numbers, so if either operand is a number (not merely the left operand), an attempt will be made to convert the other operand into a number as well.

> **NOTE** Here's an important characteristic about how division works in PowerShell that you should keep in mind. Integer division underflows into floating point (technically System.Double). This means 5 divided by 4 in PowerShell results in 1.25 instead of 1, as it would in C#. If you want to round the decimal part to the nearest integer, cast the result into [int]. You also need to be aware that PowerShell uses what's called "Banker's rounding" when converting floating-point numbers into integers. Banker's rounding rounds 0.5 up sometimes and down sometimes. The convention is to round to the nearest even number, so that both 1.5 and 2.5 round to 2, and both 3.5 and 4.5 round to 4.

If neither operand is a number, you might expect an error, but in PowerShell v5 this will work because the strings can be converted to numbers:

```
PS> '123' / '4'
30.75
```

In earlier versions of PowerShell, the operation is undefined and you'll get an error:

```
PS> '123' / '4'
Method invocation failed because [System.String] doesn't contain
a method named 'op_Division'.
At line:1 char:8
+ '123' /  <<<< '4'
```

Take note of this particular error message, though. PowerShell has no built-in definition for this operation, so as a last step it looks to see whether the type of the left operand defines a method for performing the operation. In fact, PowerShell looks for the op_<operation> methods on the left operand if the operation isn't one of those defined by PowerShell itself. This allows the operators to work on types such as System.Datetime (the .NET representation of dates) even though there's no special support for these types in PowerShell.

Okay, now that you know all about arithmetic operators and operations in PowerShell, you need to have a way to save the results of these operations. Variable assignment is the answer, so we'll look at assignment and the assignment operators next.

3.2 *Assignment operators*

In this section we'll cover the assignment operators, which are shown in figure 3.3 and listed with examples in table 3.3. You'll use these extensively when setting and modifying the values of variables.

Assignment operators

Figure 3.3   PowerShell assignment operators

As you can see, along with simple assignment, PowerShell supports the compound operators that are found in C-based languages. These compound operators retrieve, update, and reassign a variable's value all in one step. The result is a much more concise notation for expressing this type of operation.

In table 3.3, for each of the compound assignment operators, the third column shows the equivalent decomposed operation.

Table 3.3   PowerShell assignment operators

Operator	Example	Equivalent	Description
=	$a = 3		Sets the variable to the specified value.
+=	$a += 2	$a = $a + 2	Performs the addition operation in the existing value, and then assigns the result back to the variable.
-=	$a -= 13	$a = $a - 13	Performs the subtraction operation in the existing value, and then assigns the result back to the variable.
*=	$a *= 3	$a = $a * 3	Multiplies the value of a variable by the specified value or appends to the existing value.
/=	$a /= 3	$a = $a / 3	Divides the value of a variable by the specified value.
%=	$a %= 3	$a = $a % 3	Divides the value of a variable by the specified value and assigns the remainder (modulus) to the variable.

The arithmetic parts of the compound arithmetic/assignment operators follow all the rules for the arithmetic operators described in the previous section. The formal syntax for an assignment expression looks like this:

```
<lvalueList> <assignmentOperator> <pipeline>
<lvalueList> := <lvalue> [ , <lvalue> ] *
<lvalue> := <variable> | <propertyReference> | <arrayReference>
```

One interesting thing to note from this syntax is that multiple assignments are allowed. For example, the expression

```
PS> $a,$b,$c = 1,2,3,4
```

is a perfectly legal statement. It says, "Assign 1 to $a, assign 2 to $b, and assign the remaining elements 3 and 4 of the list to $c." Multiple assignments can be used to greatly simplify certain types of operations, as you'll see in the next section.

3.2.1 Multiple assignments

Multiple assignments work only with the basic assignment operator. You can't use it with any of the compound operators. But it can be used with any type of assignable expression such as an array element or property reference. Here's a quick example where multiple assignments are particularly useful. The canonical pattern for swapping two variables in conventional languages is

```
PS> $temp = $a
PS> $a = $b
PS> $b = $temp
```

This takes three lines of code and requires you to use a temporary variable. Here's how to do it using multiple assignments in PowerShell:

```
PS> $a,$b = $b,$a
```

It's simple and clean—only one line of code with no temporary variables to worry about. So far, you've seen that using multiple assignments can simplify basic operations such as swapping values. But when combined with some of PowerShell's other features, it lets you do much more interesting things than that. You'll see this in the next section.

3.2.2 Multiple assignments with type qualifiers

This is all interesting, but let's look at a more practical example. Say you're given a text file containing some data that you want to parse into a form you can work with. First let's look at the data file:

```
quiet 0 25
normal 26 50
loud 51 75
noisy 76 100
```

This file contains a set of sound-level descriptions. The format is a string describing the level, followed by two numbers describing the upper and lower bounds for these levels out of a possible 100. You want to read this information into a data structure so you can use it to categorize a list of sounds later on. Here's the fragment of PowerShell code needed to do this:

```
PS> $data = Get-Content -Path data.txt | foreach {
    $e=@{}
    $e.level, [int] $e.lower, [int] $e.upper = -split $_
    $e
}
```

You start by using the Get-Content cmdlet to write the data into a pipeline. Each line of the file is sent to the ForEach-Object cmdlet to be processed. The first thing you do in the body of the ForEach-Object cmdlet is initialize a hashtable in $e to hold the result. You take each line stored in the $_ variable and apply the -split operator to it. This splits the string into an array at each space character in the string. (We cover the -split operator in detail later in this chapter.) Then you assign the split string to three elements of the hashtable: $e.level, $e.lower, and $e.upper.

But there's one more thing you want to do. The array being assigned is all strings. For the upper and lower bounds, you want numbers, not strings. To do this, add a cast before the assignable element. This causes the value being assigned to first be converted to the target type. The end result is the upper and lower fields in the hashtable are assigned numbers instead of strings. Finally, note the result of the pipeline is being assigned to the variable $data, so you can use it later on.

Let's look at the result of this execution. Because there were four lines in the file, there should be four elements in the target array:

```
PS> $data.Length
4
```

You see there are. Now let's see if the value stored in the first element of the array is what you expect: it should be the "quiet" level:

```
PS> $data[0]
Key                           Value
---                           -----
upper                         25
level                         quiet
lower                         0
```

You can use the GetType() method to look at the types, and you can see the level description field is a string and the two bounds fields are integers, as expected.

In this last example, you've seen how array assignment can be used to perform sophisticated tasks in only a few lines of code. By now, you should have a good sense of the utility of assignments in processing data in PowerShell. There's one last point to cover about assignment expressions, which we'll discuss in the next section.

3.2.3 *Assignment operations as value expressions*

The last thing you need to know about assignment operators is they're expressions. This means you can use them anywhere you'd use any other kind of expression. This lets you initialize multiple variables at once. Let's initialize $a, $b, and $c to the number 3:

```
PS> $a = $b = $c = 3
```

What exactly happened? Well, it's the equivalent of the following expression:

```
PS> $a = ( $b = ( $c = 3 ) )
```

$c is assigned 3. The expression ($c = 3) returns the value 3, which is in turn assigned to $b, and the result of that assignment (also 3) is finally assigned to $a, so once again, all three variables end up with the same value.

> **NOTE** The three variables are totally independent—not references to the same object.

Now, because you can "intercept" the expressions with parentheses, you can perform additional operations on the values returned from the assignment statements before this value is bound in the outer assignment. Here's an example that does this:

```
PS> $a = ( $b = ( $c = 3 ) + 1 ) + 1
```

In this expression, $c gets the value 3. The result of this assignment is returned, and 1 is added to that value, yielding 4, which is then assigned to $b. The result of this second assignment also has 1 added to it, so $a is finally assigned 5.

Now you understand assignment and arithmetic operators. But a language isn't much good if you can't compare things, so let's move on to the comparison operators.

3.3   *Comparison operators*

In this section we'll cover what the comparison operators are in PowerShell and how they work. These operators are shown in figure 3.4. They come into their own when used in the flow-control statements you'll see in chapter 5.

Comparison operators

```
-eq  -ne  -gt  -ge -lt  -le
-ieq -ine -igt -ige -ilt -ile
-ceq -cne -cgt -cge -clt -cle
```

Figure 3.4   The comparison operators in PowerShell. The operators beginning with "c" are case-sensitive; all others are case-insensitive.

We'll cover how case sensitivity factors into comparisons and how the operators work for scalar values and for collections of values. The ability of these operators to work on collections eliminates the need to write looping code in a lot of scenarios.

PowerShell has a sizable number of comparison operators, in large part because there are case-sensitive and case-insensitive versions of all the operators. These are listed with examples in table 3.4.

Table 3.4   PowerShell comparison operators

Operator	Description	Example	Result
-eq, -ceq, -ieq	Equals	5 -eq 5	$true
-ne, -cne, -ine	Not equals	5 -ne 5	$false
-gt, -cgt, -igt	Greater than	5 -gt 3	$true
-ge, -cge, -ige	Greater than or equal to	5 -ge 3	$true

Table 3.4   PowerShell comparison operators *(continued)*

Operator	Description	Example	Result
-lt, –clt, –ilt	Less than	5 –lt 3	$false
-le, –cle, –ile	Less than or equal to	5 –le 3	$false

In table 3.4, you can see for each operator there's a base or unqualified operator form, such as -eq and its two variants, -ceq and -ieq. The "c" variant is case-sensitive, and the "i" variant is case-insensitive. This raises the question: What's the behavior for the base operators with respect to case? The answer is the unqualified operators are case-insensitive. All three variants are provided to allow script authors to make their intention clear—that they meant a particular behavior rather than accepting the default.

> **Design decisions**
>
> Let's talk about the most contentious design decision in the PowerShell language. And the winner is: Why the heck doesn't PowerShell use the conventional symbols for comparison like >, >=, <, <=, ==, and !=? The answer is the > and < characters are used for output redirection. Because PowerShell is a shell and all shell languages in the last 30 years have used > and < for I/O redirection, people expected that PowerShell would do the same. During the first public beta of PowerShell, this topic generated discussions that went on for months. The PowerShell team looked at a variety of alternatives, such as modal parsing where sometimes > meant greater than and sometimes it meant redirection. They looked at alternative character sequences for the operators like :> or ->, either for redirection or comparison. They did usability tests and held focus groups, and in the end, settled on what they had started with.
>
> The redirection operators are > and <, and the comparison operators are taken from the UNIX test(1) command. It's generally believed that, because these operators have a 30-year pedigree, they're adequate and appropriate to use in PowerShell. (It's also expected that people will continue to complain about this decision, though hopefully not for 30 more years.)

Now that you're clear on the case-sensitivity issue, let's move on to discuss the semantics of the comparison operators. We'll begin by describing their operation on scalar data types; then in the subsequent section we'll describe how they work with collections of objects.

3.3.1   *Scalar comparisons*

In this section we'll explore how the comparison operators work with scalar objects. In particular, we'll cover their polymorphic behavior with scalar data types.

BASIC COMPARISON RULES

As with the assignment operators, the behavior of the comparison operators is significantly affected by the type of the *left* operand. If you're comparing a number and a string, the string will be converted into a number and a numerical comparison will be done. If the left operand is a string, the right operand will be converted to a string, and the results compared as strings.

TYPE CONVERSIONS AND COMPARISONS

As with any PowerShell operator that involves numbers, when comparisons are done in a numeric context, the widening rules are applied. This produced somewhat unexpected results in early versions of PowerShell. Here's an example that illustrates this. In the first part of the example, you use a cast to convert the string "123" into a number. Once you're doing the conversion in a numeric context, the numbers get widened to double because the right operand is a double; and because 123.4 is larger than 123, the -lt operator returns True:

```
PS> [int]'123' -lt 123.4
True
```

Now try it using a string as the right operand. The cast forces the left operand to be numeric, but the right operand is not yet numeric. It's converted to the numeric type of the left operand, which is [int], not [double]. This means the value is truncated and the comparison now returns False:

```
PS> [int] "123" -lt "123.4"
False
```

> **NOTE** This behavior has been corrected in later versions of PowerShell (definitely by v5.1) so expect the previous code to return True.

Finally, if you force the context to be [double] explicitly, the comparison again returns True:

```
PS> [double] "123" -lt "123.4"
True
```

Although all these rules seem complicated (and, speaking as the guy [Bruce] who implemented them, they are), the results are generally what you'd intuitively expect. This satisfies the principle of *least astonishment.* Most of the time you don't need to worry about the specifics and can let the system take care of the conversions. It's only when things don't work as expected that you need to understand the details of the conversion process. To help you debug cases where this happens, PowerShell provides a type-conversion tracing mechanism to help you track down the problems. (Chapter 6 describes how to use this debugging feature.) You can always apply a set of casts to override the implicit behavior and force the results you want.

3.3.2 *Comparisons and case sensitivity*

Next let's look at the "i" and "c" versions of the comparison operators—the case-sensitive and case-insensitive versions. Obviously, case sensitivity only applies to strings. All the comparison operators have both versions. For example, the -eq operator has the following variants:

```
PS> 'abc' -eq 'ABC'
True

PS> 'abc' -ieq 'ABC'
True

PS> 'abc' -ceq 'ABC'
False
```

The default case -eq is case-insensitive, as is the explicitly case-insensitive operator -ieq, so in the example, strings "abc" and "ABC" compare as equal. The -ceq operator is case-sensitive, so with this operator, strings "abc" and "ABC" compare as not equal.

The final item to discuss with scalar comparisons is how things that aren't strings and numbers are compared. In this case, the .NET comparison mechanisms are used:

1 If the object implements the .NET IComparable interface, then that will be used.
2 If not, and if the object on the *left* side has an Equals() method that can take an object of the type of the right operand, this is used.
3 If there's no direct mechanism for comparing the two, an attempt will be made to convert the right operand into an instance of the type of the left operand, and then PowerShell will try to compare the resulting objects. This is how things such as [DateTime] objects are compared.

Not all objects are directly comparable. For example, there's no direct way to compare a System.DateTime object to a System.Diagnostics.Process object—a type conversion error is the result. This is where a human has to intervene. The obvious field on a Process object to compare is the StartTime of the process. Use the property notation to do this:

```
PS> [DateTime]'1/1/2017' -gt (Get-Process powershell*)[0].StartTime
False

PS> [DateTime]'1/1/2018' -gt (Get-Process powershell*)[0].StartTime
True
```

In this expression, you're looking to see whether the *first* element in the list of Process objects had a start time greater than the beginning of this year (no), and whether it had a start time from before the beginning of next year (obviously true). You can use this approach to find all the processes on a computer that started today:

```
PS> Get-Process | where {$_.starttime -ge [DateTime]::today}
```

The Get-Process cmdlet returns a list of all the processes on this computer, and the Where-Object cmdlet selects those processes where the StartTime property of the process is greater than or equal to today.

> **NOTE** The `where` command used in the previous example is an alias for the
> `Where-Object` cmdlet, which is described in chapter 6.

This completes our discussion of the behavior of the comparison operators with scalar data. We paid a lot of attention to the role types play in comparisons, but so far, we've avoided discussing collection types—lists, arrays, and so on. We'll get to that next.

3.3.3 *Using comparison operators with collections*

In this section we'll focus on the behavior of the comparison operators when they're used with collections of objects.

BASIC COMPARISON OPERATIONS INVOLVING COLLECTIONS

Here's the basic behavior. If the *left* operand is an array or collection, the comparison operation will return the elements of that collection that match the right operand. This works with strings as well. When processing the array, the scalar comparison rules are used to compare each element. In the next example, the left operand is an array containing a mix of numbers and strings, and the right operand is the string '2':

```
PS> 1,'2',3,2,'1' -eq '2'
2
2
```

It returns the two '2's. Let's look at more examples where you have leading zeros in the operands:

```
PS> 1,'02',3,02,'1' -eq '2'
2

PS> 1,'02',3,02,'1' -eq 2
2
```

When the elements are compared as numbers, they match. When compared as strings, they don't match because of the leading zero.

CONTAINMENT OPERATORS

All of the comparison operators we've discussed so far return the matching elements from the collection. Although this is extremely useful, there are times when you want to find out whether or not an element is there. This is what the `-contains`, `-notcontains`, `-in` and `-notin` operators, shown in figure 3.5, are for.

Containment operators

```
-contains  -notcontains  -in   -notin
-icontains -inotcontains -iin  -inotin
-ccontains -cnotcontains -cin  -cnotin
```

Figure 3.5 The PowerShell containment operators. Those on the bottom row are case-sensitive and the others are case-insensitive.

These operators return `$true` if the set contains the element you're looking for instead of returning the matching elements. They're listed in table 3.5 with examples.

Table 3.5 PowerShell containment operators

Operator	Description	Example	Result

`-contains`
`-ccontains`
`-icontains`
	The collection on the left contains the value specified on the right.	`1,2,3 -contains 2`	`$true`

`-notcontains`
`-cnotcontains`
`-inotcontains`
	The collection on the left doesn't contain the value specified on the right.	`1,2,3 -notcontains 2`	`$false`

`-in`
`-cin`
`-iin`
	The value specified on the left is in the collection on the right.	`2 -in 1,2,3`	`$true`

`-notin`
`-cnotin`
`-inotin`
	The value specified on the left isn't in the collection on the right.	`2 -notin 1,2,3`	`$false`

The `-contains` operator works like this:

```
PS> 1,'02',3,02,'1' -contains '02'
True

PS> 1,'02',3,02,'1' -notcontains '02'
False
```

Now, instead of returning 02 and 2, you return a single Boolean value. Because all values in PowerShell can be converted into a Boolean value, this doesn't seem as if it would particularly matter, and usually it doesn't. The one case where it does matter is if the matching set of elements is something that's false. This even includes Booleans. The concept is easier to understand with an example:

```
PS> $false,$true -eq $false
False

PS> $false,$true -contains $false
True
```

In the first command, `-eq` searches the list for `$false`, finds it, and then returns the matching value. But because the matching value was literally `$false`, a successful match looks as if it failed. When you use the `-contains` operator in the expression, you get the result you'd expect, which is `$true`. The other way to work around this issue is to use the `@( ... )` construction and the `count` property:

```
PS> @($false,$true -eq $false).count
1
```

The @(...) sequence forces the result to be an array and then takes the count of the results. If there are no matches the count will be zero, which is equivalent to $false. If there are matches the count will be nonzero, equivalent to $true. There can also be some performance advantages to -contains, because it stops looking on the first match instead of checking every element in the list.

> **NOTE** The @(...) construction is described in detail in chapter 4.

It may seem odd to have both a -contains operator and an -in operator. They both appear to do the same thing but from opposite directions. The -in operator was introduced in PowerShell v3:

```
PS> 1,2,3 -contains 2
True

PS> 2 -in 1,2,3
True
```

The -in operator simplifies syntax in certain situations but comes into its own when using the simplified filter syntax in Where-Object:

```
PS> $names = 'powershell', 'powershell_ise'
PS> Get-Process | where Name -in $names
```

The simplified Where-Object syntax takes the form

```
<property> <operator> <value>
```

You can't fit the -contains operator into that pattern as it expects the array to be tested first, so you have to revert to the full syntax of

```
PS> Get-Process | where {$names -contains $_.Name}
```

This isn't as compact or as intuitive as the simplified syntax.

In this section, we covered all the basic comparison operators. We addressed the issue of case sensitivity in comparisons, and we covered the polymorphic behavior of these operations. Now let's move on to look at PowerShell's operators for working with text. One of the hallmark features of dynamic languages is great support for text manipulation and pattern matching. In the next section we'll cover how PowerShell incorporates these features into the language.

3.4 *Pattern matching and text manipulation*

In this section we'll explore the pattern-matching and text-manipulation operators in PowerShell (see figure 3.6).

Pattern-matching and text-manipulation operators

```
-like  -notlike  -match  -notmatch  -replace  -split
-ilike -inotlike -imatch -inotmatch -ireplace -isplit
-clike -cnotlike -cmatch -cnotmatch -creplace -csplit
                        -join
```

Figure 3.6   The pattern-matching and text-manipulation operators in PowerShell. All the operators that use patterns (everything except `-join`) have case-sensitive ("c" prefix) and case-insensitive forms.

Beyond the basic comparison operators, PowerShell has a number of pattern-matching operators. These operators work on strings, allowing you to search through text, extract pieces of it, and edit or create new strings. The other text-manipulation operators allow you to break strings apart into pieces or add individual pieces back together into a single string.

We'll start with the pattern-matching operators. PowerShell supports two built-in types of patterns: *wildcard expressions* and *regular expressions*. Each of these pattern types is useful in distinct domains. We'll cover the operation and applications of both types of patterns along with the operators that use them.

3.4.1   *Wildcard patterns and the -like operator*

You usually find wildcard patterns in a shell for matching filenames. For example, the command

```
PS> Get-ChildItem -Path *.txt
```

finds all the files ending in .txt. In this example, the * matches any sequence of characters. Wildcard patterns also allow you to specify character ranges. In the next example, the pattern

```
PS> Get-ChildItem -Path [fm]*.txt
```

will return all the files that start with either the letter "*f*" or "*m*" that have a .txt extension. Finally, you can use the question mark (?) to match any single character.

The wildcard pattern-matching operators are listed in table 3.6, which includes simple examples of how each one works.

Table 3.6   PowerShell wildcard pattern-matching operators

Operator	Description	Example	Result
-like, -clike, -ilike	Do a wildcard pattern match.	'one' -like 'o*'	$true
-notlike, -cnotlike, -inotlike	Do a wildcard pattern match; true if the pattern doesn't match.	'one' -notlike 'o*'	$false

You can see from the table that there are several variations on the basic -like operator. These variations include case-sensitive and case-insensitive versions of the operator, as well as variants that return true if the target doesn't match the pattern. Table 3.7 summarizes the special characters that can be used in PowerShell wildcard patterns.

Table 3.7 Special characters in PowerShell wildcard patterns

Wildcard	Description	Example	Matches	Doesn't match
*	Matches zero or more characters anywhere in the string.	a*	a aa abc ab	bc babc
?	Matches any single character.	a?c	abc aXc	a~ ab
[<char>-<char>]	Matches a sequential range of characters.	a[b-d]c	abc acc adc	aac aec afc abbc
[<char><char>…]	Matches any one character from a set of characters.	a[bc]c	abc acc	a ab Ac adc

Although wildcard patterns are simple, their matching capabilities are limited, so PowerShell also provides a set of operators that use regular expressions.

3.4.2 *Regular expressions*

Regular expressions (regexes) are conceptually (if not syntactically) a superset of wildcard expressions. By this, we mean you can express the same patterns in regular expressions that you can in wildcard expressions, but with slightly different syntax.

NOTE In PowerShell, wildcard patterns are translated internally into the corresponding regular expressions under the covers.

With regular expressions, instead of using * to match any sequence of characters as you would in wildcard patterns, you use .*; and, instead of using ? to match any single character, you use the dot (.).

Although regular expressions are similar to wildcard patterns, they're much more powerful and allow you to do sophisticated text manipulation with small amounts of script. The PowerShell operators -match, -replace, and -split work with regular expressions.

3.4.3 *The -match operator*

The -match and -replace operators are shown in table 3.8 along with a description and some examples.

Table 3.8 PowerShell regular expression -match and -replace operators. Note the case-sensitive and case-insensitive versions of each operator.

Operator	Description	Example	Result
-match -cmatch -imatch	Do a pattern match using regexes.	'Hello' -match '[jkl]'	$true
-notmatch -cnotmatch -inotmatch	Do a regex pattern match; return true if the pattern doesn't match.	'Hello' -notmatch '[jkl]'	$false
-replace -creplace	Do a regex substitution on the left string and return the modified string.	'Hello' -replace 'ello','i'	'Hi'
-ireplace	Delete the portion of the string matching the regex.	'abcde' -replace 'bcd'	'ae'

The -match operator is similar to the -like operator in that it matches a pattern and returns a result. Along with that result, though, it sets the $matches variable. This variable contains the portions of the string that are matched by individual parts of the regular expressions. The only way to clearly explain this is with an example:

```
PS> 'abcdef' -match '(a)(((b)(c))de)f'
True

PS> $matches

Key                      Value
---                      -----
5                        c
4                        b
3                        bc
2                        bcde
1                        a
0                        abcdef
```

Here, the string on the left of the -match operator is matched against the pattern on the right. In the pattern string, you can see a number of components, each of which is a submatch. We'll get to why this is important in the next section. The result of this expression was true, which means the match succeeded. It also means $matches should be set and contains a hashtable where the keys of the hashtable are indexes that correspond to parts of the pattern that matched. The values are the substrings of the target string that matched. There's always a default element that represents the entire string that matched.

You have the outermost match in index 0, which matches the whole string. Next you have a top-level match at the beginning of the pattern that matches "a" at index 1. At index 2, you have the complete string matched by the next top-level part, which is "bcde". Index 3 is the first nested match in that top-level match, which is "bc". This match also has two nested matches: b at element 4 and c at element 5.

MATCHING USING NAMED CAPTURES

Calculating these indexes is fine if the pattern is simple. If it's complex, as in the previous example, it's hard to figure out what goes where—and even if you do, when you look at what you've written a month later, you'll have to figure it out all over again. The .NET regular expression library provides a way to solve this problem by using named captures. You specify a named capture by placing the sequence ?<name> immediately inside the parentheses that indicate the match group. This allows you to reference the capture by name instead of by number, making complex expressions easier to deal with. Here's what this looks like:

```
PS> 'abcdef' -match '(?<o1>a)(?<o2>((?<e3>b)(?<e4>c))de)f'
True

PS> $matches

Key                          Value
---                          -----
o1                           a
e3                           b
e4                           c
o2                           bcde
1                            bc
0                            abcdef
```

Now let's look at a more realistic example.

PARSING COMMAND OUTPUT USING REGULAR EXPRESSIONS

Existing utilities for Windows produce text output, so you have to parse the text to extract information. (As you may remember, avoiding this kind of parsing was one of the reasons PowerShell was created. But it still needs to interoperate with the rest of the world.) For example, the net.exe utility can return information about your computer configuration. The second line of this output contains the name of the computer. Your task is to extract the name and domain for this computer from that string. One way to do this is to calculate the offsets and then extract substrings from the output. This is tedious and error-prone (because the offsets might change). Here's how to do it using the $matches variable. First let's look at the form of this string:

```
PS> (net config workstation)[1]
Full Computer name           brucepay64.redmond.corp.microsoft.com
```

It begins with a well-known pattern, Full Computer name, so start by matching against that to make sure there are no errors. You'll see there's a space before the name, and the name itself is separated by a period. You're pretty safe in ignoring the intervening characters, so here's the pattern you'll use:

```
PS> $p='^Full Computer.* (?<computer>[^.]+)\.(?<domain>[^.]+)'
```

You check the string at the beginning, and then allow any sequence of characters that ends with a space, followed by two fields that are terminated by a dot. Notice that we don't say that the fields can contain *any* character. Instead, they can contain anything but a period. This is because regular expressions are greedy—they match the longest possible pattern, and because the period is any character, the match won't stop at the period. Now go ahead and apply this pattern:

```
PS> (net config workstation)[1] -match $p
True
```

It matches, so you know that the output string was well formed. Now let's look at what you captured from the string:

```
PS> $matches.computer
brucepay64
```

```
PS> $matches.domain
redmond
```

You see that you've extracted the computer name and domain as desired. This approach is significantly more robust than using exact indexing because

- You checked with a guard string instead of assuming that the string at index 1 was correct.
- You didn't care about where in the line the data appeared, only that it followed a basic well-formed pattern.

With a pattern-based approach, output format can vary significantly, and this pattern would still retrieve the correct data. By using techniques like this, you can write more change-tolerant scripts than you'd otherwise do.

The `-match` operator lets you match text. Now let's look at how to go about making changes to text. This is what the `-replace` operator is for, so we'll explore that next.

3.4.4   *The -replace operator*

The `-replace` operator allows you to do regular expression–based text substitution on a string or collection of strings. For example:

```
PS> '1,2,3,4' -replace '\s*,\s*','+'
1+2+3+4
```

What this has done is replace every instance of a comma surrounded by zero or more spaces with a + sign. A common task is replacing text within a file:

```
PS> ${c:old.txt} -replace 'is (red|blue)','was $1' > new.txt
```

The pattern to replace: `'is (red|blue)'`—the parentheses establish a submatch. Now look at the replacement string. It contains `'$1'`, which might be assumed to be a PowerShell variable. But because the string is in single quotes, it won't be expanded. Instead, the regular expression engine uses this notation to allow submatches to be referenced in the replacement expression. This allows PowerShell to intelligently replace `"is"` with `"was"`:

```
PS> 'The car is red' -replace 'is (red|blue)','was $1'
The car was red
```

The pattern matches `"is red"` but you only want to replace `"is"`. These substitutions make this possible. The complete set of substitution character sequences is shown in table 3.9.

Finally, what happens if the pattern doesn't match? Let's try it:

```
PS> 'My bike is yellow' -replace 'is (red|blue)','was $1'
My bike is yellow
```

You see if the pattern isn't matched, the string is returned as is.

Table 3.9 Character sequences for doing substitutions in the replacement pattern for `-replace` operator

Character sequence	Description
`$number`	Substitutes the last submatch matched by group number.
`${name}`	Substitutes the last submatch matched by a named capture of the form (?<name>).
`$$`	Substitutes a single `"$"` literal.
`$&`	Substitutes a copy of the entire match itself.
`` $` ``	Substitutes all the text from the argument string before the matching portion.
`$'`	Substitutes all the text of the argument string after the matching portion.
`$+`	Substitutes the last submatch captured.
`$_`	Substitutes the entire argument string.

You can use regular expression substitutions and PowerShell variable expansion at the same time by escaping the `'$'` before the substitution with a backtick (`` ` ``). The result looks like this:

```
PS> $a = 'really'
PS> 'The car is red' -replace 'is (red|blue)',"was $a `$1"
The car was really red
```

In the output string the word "red" was preserved using the regular expression substitution mechanism and the word "really" was added by expanding the $a variable.

NOTE You need to double quote (`"`) the replacement string as shown because you're performing variable substitution.

Alternatively, you may want to remove the matching parts. You can do this using `-replace` by omitting the replacement string:

```
PS> 'The quick brown fox' -replace 'quick'
The  brown fox
```

In this example, the word "quick" was removed from the sentence.

Here's one final point we should make clear. The `-replace` operator doesn't *change* strings—it returns a new string with the necessary edits applied.

Up to this point, all the operations we've looked at have involved transformations on a single string. Now let's look at how to take strings apart and put them back together using two more string operators: `-split` and `-join`. This will complete your knowledge of the set of operators PowerShell provides for manipulating strings.

3.4.5   *The -join operator*

PowerShell has two operators for working with collections and strings: `-split` and `-join`. These operators allow you to join the elements of a collection into a single string or split strings into a collection of substrings. We'll look at the `-join` operator first because it's the simpler of the two. This operator can be used both as a unary operator and a binary operator.

The unary form of the `-join` operator allows you to concatenate a collection of strings into a single string with no separator between each item in the resulting string. Here's a simple example. First assign an array of numbers to the variable `$in`:

```
PS> $in = 1,2,3
```

Now use the `-join` operator on this variable and assign the result to a new variable, `$out`:

```
PS> $out = -join $in
PS> $out
123
```

Checking the type of the result

```
PS> $out.GetType().FullName
System.String
```

you see it's a string. The `-join` operator first converted each array element into a string and then joined the results into a single larger string.

Next, let's do something a bit more sophisticated. Say you want to reverse a string. Unfortunately, the .NET `[string]` type has no built-in reverse operator, but the `[array]` type does have a static method for reversing arrays. This method takes an array as input and sorts it in place. To use this, you need to do two conversions: from a string to an array of characters, and from an array of characters back to a string. From chapter 2, you know you can use a cast to convert a string into a character array. The array's `Reverse()` method is used to reverse the contents of the array in place:

```
PS> $ca = [char[]] 'abcd'
PS> [array]::Reverse($ca)
```

Use a unary `-join` to convert the character array back into a string:

```
PS> $ra = -join $ca
PS> $ra
dcba
```

Now let's look at one potential gotcha using the unary form of the operator. Let's redo the join of string "1,2,3" again, but without using a variable to hold the value. Here's what that looks like:

```
PS> -join 1,2,3
1
2
3
```

Surprise! Instead of joining the array members into a single string, it returned the same array. This is because unary operators have higher precedence than binary operators and, in PowerShell, the comma is a binary operator. As a result, the expression is parsed like

```
PS> (-join 1),2,3
1
2
3
```

To use the unary `-join` operator in a more complex expression, then, make sure you put parentheses around the argument expression:

```
PS> -join (1,2,3)
123
```

When parentheses are used, the result of the expression is as expected. Next let's look at the (much more useful) binary form. The obvious difference with this operator is you can specify the string to use as an element separator instead of always using the default of nothing between the joined strings. Place an array to join into a variable called $numbers and put the joined result into a variable called $exp:

```
PS> $numbers = 1,2,3
PS> $exp = $numbers -join '+'
```

Look at the contents of $exp:

```
PS> $exp
1+2+3
```

It contains the numbers with a plus sign between each number. Because this is a valid PowerShell expression, you can pass the resulting string to the Invoke-Expression cmdlet for evaluation. The result is 6. This works on any operator. Let's use the range operator (see chapter 4) and the multiply operator to calculate the factorial of 10. Here's what the code looks like:

```
PS> $fact = Invoke-Expression (1..10 -join '*')
```

This code is evaluating 1*2*3 and so on up to 10, with the result

```
PS> $fact
3628800
```

Although this is a simple way to calculate factorials, it's not efficient. Later on, you'll see more efficient ways of writing this type of expression. For now, let's look at a more practical example and do some work with a file. Let's use a here-string to generate a test file on disk:

```
PS> @'
line1
line2
line3
'@ > out.txt
```

Now use the Get-Content cmdlet to read that file into a variable, $text:

```
PS> $text = Get-Content -Path out.txt
```

The Get-Content cmdlet returns the contents of a file as an array of strings—in fact it's an [object] array, which you should be used to by now. Although this is exactly what you want most of the time, sometimes you want the entire file as a single string. The Get-Content cmdlet (prior to PowerShell v3) has no parameter for doing this, so you'll have to take the array of strings and turn it back into a single string. You can do this with the binary -join operator if you specify the line separator as the string to use when joining the array elements. On Windows, the line separator is two characters: carriage return (`r) and a line feed (`n). In a single string, this is expressed as "`r`n". Now you can use this separator string in a -join expression:

```
PS> $single = $text -join "`r`n"
```

In PowerShell v3 (and later) you can use the -Raw parameter on Get-Content to achieve the same result:

```
PS> $single2 = Get-Content -Path out.txt -Raw
```

Now that you know how to put things together, we'll show you how to take them apart with -split.

3.4.6   *The -split operator*

The `-split` operator performs the opposite operation to `-join`: it splits strings into a collection of smaller strings. Again, this operator can be used in both binary and unary forms.

In its unary form, this operator will split a string on *whitespace* boundaries, where whitespace is any number of spaces, tabs, or newlines. You saw this in an example earlier in this chapter.

The binary form of the operator is much more, ahem, sophisticated. It allows you to specify the pattern to match on, the type of matching to do, and the number of elements to return, as well as match type-specific options. Most of the time you need to specify an argument string and split pattern and let the rest of the options use their default values. Let's look at the basic application of this operator. First, split a string on a character other than whitespace:

```
PS> 'a:b:c:d:e' -split ':'
```

This is pretty straightforward. The string is split into five elements at the : character. But sometimes you don't want all the matches. The `-split` operator allows you to limit the number of elements to return. Do so by specifying an integer after the match pattern:

```
PS> 'a:b:c:d:e' -split ':',3
a
b
c:d:e
```

In this case, you only asked for three elements to be returned. Notice the third element is the entire remaining string. If you specify a split count number less than or equal to 0, then all the splits take place.

By default, `-split` uses regular expressions like `-match` and `-replace`. But if the string you're trying to split contains one of the many characters that have special meaning in regular expressions, things become a bit more difficult because you'll have to escape these characters in the split pattern. This can be inconvenient and error-prone, so `-split` allows you to choose *simple matching* through an option known as `SimpleMatch`. When you specify `SimpleMatch`, instead of treating the split pattern as a regular expression, it's handled as a simple literal string that must be matched. For example, say you want to split on *:

```
PS> 'a*b*c' -split '*'
```

This results in a regular expression parsing error. Now try it again with `SimpleMatch`:

```
PS> 'a*b*c' -split '*',0,'SimpleMatch'
a
b
c
```

This time it worked properly. This option is particularly handy when you aren't using literal split strings but instead are getting them from a script argument or input file. In those cases, it's much simpler to use `SimpleMatch` instead of escaping all the special regular expression characters.

-SPLIT OPERATOR OPTIONS

The last element in the `-split` operator syntax is the match options string. These options are shown in table 3.10. Multiple options can be specified in a string with commas between them, like `RegexMatch,IgnoreCase,MultiLine` or `SimpleMatch,IgnoreCase`.

Table 3.10   Match options for the `-split` operator

Option	Description	Applies to
IgnoreCase	Allows you to override default case-sensitive behavior when using the `-csplit` variant of the operator.	RegexMatch, SimpleMatch
CultureInvariant	Disables any culture-specific matching behavior (what constitutes uppercase, for example) when matching the separator strings.	RegexMatch
IgnorePatternWhitespace	Ignores unescaped whitespace and comments embedded in the pattern. This allows for commenting complex patterns.	RegexMatch
MultiLine	Treats a string as though it's composed of multiple lines. A line begins at a newline character and will be matched by the ^ pattern.	RegexMatch
SingleLine	This option, which is the default, tells the pattern matcher to treat the entire string as a single line. Newlines in the string aren't considered the beginning of a line.	RegexMatch
ExplicitCapture	This option specifies that the only valid captures are explicitly named or numbered ones of the form `(?<name>…)`. This allows unnamed parentheses to act as noncapturing groups without the syntactic clumsiness of the expression `(?:…)`. See section 4.4.3 on how captures work.	RegexMatch

We won't cover the options here. In practice, you aren't likely to need most of them.

USING SCRIPTBLOCKS WITH THE -SPLIT OPERATOR

As powerful as regular expressions are, sometimes you may need to split a string in a way that isn't convenient or easy to handle with regular expressions. To deal with these cases, PowerShell allows you to pass a scriptblock to the operator. The scriptblock is used as a *predicate function* that determines whether there's a match. Here's an example. First set up a string to split. This string contains a list of colors that you want to split into pairs, two colors per pair:

```
PS> $colors = "Black,Brown,Red,Orange,Yellow," +
"Green,Blue,Violet,Gray,White"
```

Next, initialize a countervariable that will be used by the scriptblock. You're using an array here because you need to be able to modify the contents of this variable. Because the scriptblock is executed in its own scope, you must pass it an array so it can modify the value:

```
PS> $count=@(0)
```

And now split the string. The scriptblock, in braces in the example, splits the string on every other comma:

```
PS> $colors -split {$_ -eq ',' -and ++$count[0] % 2 -eq 0 }
Black,Brown
Red,Orange
Yellow,Green
Blue,Violet
Gray,White
```

This gives you the color pairs you were looking for.

Whew! So that's it for the pattern-matching and text-manipulation operators. In this section, we covered the two types of pattern-matching operators—wildcard patterns and regular expressions. All quite spiffy, but let's come back down to Earth now and cover the last of the basic operators in the PowerShell language. These are the logical operators (-and, -or, -xor, -not) and their bitwise equivalents (-band, -bor, -bnot).

3.5 Logical and bitwise operators

PowerShell has logical operators -and, -or, -xor, and -not for combining simpler comparisons into more complex expressions. The logical operators convert their operands into Boolean values and then perform the logical operation.

PowerShell also provides corresponding bitwise operators for doing binary operations on integer values. These operators can be used to test and mask bit fields. Both of these sets of operators are shown in figure 3.7.

```
Logical and bitwise operators

 -and  -or  -not  -xor  -shl
 -band -nor -bnot -bxor -shr
```

Figure 3.7 Logical and bitwise operators available in PowerShell

Table 3.11 lists these operators with examples showing how each can be used.

Table 3.11   Logical and bitwise operators

Operator	Description	Example	Result
-and	Do a logical and of the left and right values.	0xff -and $false	$false
-or	Do a logical or of the left and right values.	$false -or 0x55	$true
-xor	Do a logical exclusive-or of the left and right values.	$false -xor $true $true -xor $true	$true $false
-not	Do the logical complement of the argument value.	-not $true	$false
-band	Do a binary and of the bits in the values on the left and right sides.	0xff -band 0x55	85 (0x55)
-bor	Do a binary or of the bits in the values on the left and right sides.	0x55 -bor 0xaa	255 (0xff)
-bxor	Do a binary exclusive-or of the left and right values.	0x55 -bxor 0xaa 0x55 -bxor 0xa5	255 (0xff) 240 (0xf0)
-bnot	Do the bitwise complement of the argument value.	-bnot 0xff	-256(0x ffffff00)
-shl	All bits are moved *n* places to the left where *n* is the right operand. A zero is inserted in the one's place.	100 -shl 4	1600
-shr	All bits are moved *n* places to the right where *n* is the right operand.	100 -shr 4	6

As with most languages based on C/C++, the PowerShell logical operators are *short-circuit* operators—they only do as much work as they need to. With the -and operator, if the left operand evaluates to $false, then the right operand expression isn't executed. With the -or operator, if the left operand evaluates to $true, then the right operand isn't evaluated.

> **NOTE**   In PowerShell v1, the bitwise operators were limited in that they only supported 32-bit integers ([int]). 64-bit integers ([long]) are supported in PowerShell v2, and later. If the arguments to the operators are neither [int] nor [long], PowerShell will attempt to convert them into [long] and then perform the operation.

3.6   *Where() and ForEach() methods*

PowerShell v4 introduced two new operators for working with collections. While their syntax is identical to method invocation syntax, they're called "operators" because they aren't implemented as methods on the target object. The Where() and ForEach() methods work in a similar manner to the Where-Object and ForEach-Object cmdlets. We're including them with the operators because of the way they're used.

3.6.1 *Where() method*

The `Where()` method provides a way to filter collections using a condensed syntax. In
all cases, using the `Where()` method is faster (up to ten times faster) than using `Where-Object`, but consumes more memory. This is because the cmdlet goes through the parameter binder, which is complex. The method binder is much simpler and therefore faster.
But the `foreach` loop is still the fastest way to iterate over a collection. The syntax will
be more familiar to programmers than administrators so we'll explain it with examples.

Consider a standard use of `Where-Object`:

```
PS> Get-Process | where Handles -gt 1000
```

The collection of processes is filtered and only those processes with more than 1,000
handles are returned. You can use the `Where()` method to achieve the same result:

```
PS> (Get-Process).where({$_.Handles -gt 1000})
PS> (Get-Process).where({$psitem.Handles -gt 1000})
```

You must use either `$_` or `$psitem` with the property on which you're filtering. The `()`
are optional but we recommend you use them to make the syntax more obvious when
you come to review it, or when you're writing for others to use. We'll use the `()` in the
rest of this section to make the syntax more obvious but as an example of not using
them you can write the previous two examples as:

```
PS> (Get-Process).where{$_.Handles -gt 1000}
PS> (Get-Process).where{$psitem.Handles -gt 1000}
```

> **NOTE** Bruce made a change to the parser in PowerShell v4 to allow any
> method that takes a single scriptblock as an argument to be written without
> parentheses around the scriptblock literal. The change was made for these
> methods but works with any method. Also note these methods were added
> to simplify node selection in the Desired State Configuration (DSC) node
> statement (see chapter 18).

Qualifiers can be applied to display the first or last member of the collection:

```
PS> (Get-Process).where({$_.Handles -gt 1000}, 'First')
PS> (Get-Process).where({$_.Handles -gt 1000}, 'Last')
```

This can be extended to the first or last *n* members:

```
PS> (Get-Process).where({$_.Handles -gt 1000}, 'First', 3)
PS> (Get-Process).where({$_.Handles -gt 1000}, 'Last', 3)
```

There's an option to split the results:

```
PS> $proc = (Get-Process).where({$_.Handles -gt 1000}, 'Split')
```

`$proc` is a collection—the first member contains the processes that match the filter and
the second member those that don't.

> **NOTE**   The collection, $proc, is an instance of [System.Collections.Object
> -Model.Collection`1[PSObject]. The fact that it's a collection matters because
> you can add members to a collection but not to an array. A secondary aspect is,
> because it's always the same type, you can write additional extension methods
> on this type to do Linq-like collection operations on the result of the type.

You can further filter the results using Until and SkipUntil:

```
PS> (Get-Process | sort Handles).where({$_.Handles -gt 1000}, 'Until')
```

Using Until will display all results until you reach results that match the filter defined
in the scriptblock. If you want to display only the results that match the filter then use
SkipUntil:

```
PS> (Get-Process | sort Handles).where({$_.Handles -gt 1000}, 'SkipUntil')
```

If you don't sort the members of the collection, SkipUntil will display everything after
the first match irrespective of whether it matches the filter.

3.6.2   *ForEach() method*

The ForEach() method is a bit simpler than the Where() method you've just seen.
Again, demonstrating the use of this method is best achieved by some examples. First,
create an array of integers:

```
PS> $data = 1,2,3,4,5
```

You can execute a scriptblock within the ForEach() method:

```
PS> ($data).ForEach({$_ * 2})
PS> $data.ForEach({$_ * 2})
```

When the data is already an array you don't need to wrap it in (). If you need to change
the type of the objects in the collection, use this approach:

```
PS> $data | Get-Member
PS> $data.ForEach([double]) | Get-Member
```

Values for a particular property can be displayed as follows:

```
PS> (Get-Process).foreach('Name')
```

If the objects within the collection have methods, they can be invoked:

```
PS> (Get-Process -Name notepad).foreach('Name')
PS> (Get-Process -Name notepad).foreach('Kill')
```

You can also pass arguments into the method if required.

3.7   *Summary*

- PowerShell operators are *polymorphic* with special behaviors defined by Power-Shell for the basic types: numbers, strings, arrays, and hashtables. For other object types, the op_ methods are invoked.

- The behavior of most of the binary operators is determined by the type of the operand on the *left*.

- PowerShell uses widening when working with numeric types. For any arithmetic operation, the type of the result will be the narrowest .NET numeric type that can properly represent the result. Integer division will underflow into floating point if the result of the operation isn't an integer. Casts can be used to force an integer result.

- There are two types of pattern-matching operations in PowerShell: wildcard patterns (usually used for matching filenames) and regular expressions.

- Because the comparison and pattern-matching operators work on collections, in many cases you don't need a looping statement to search through collections.

- Regular expressions are powerful and can be used to do complex text manipulations with little code. PowerShell uses the .NET regular expression classes to implement the regular expression operators in the language.

- PowerShell has two operators for converting between strings and collections: -split and -join.

- PowerShell has built-in operators for working with binary values: -band, -bor, -bxor, and -bnot.

- The Where() and ForEach() methods on collections can be used to filter the members of the collection and invoke methods.

We're not done yet! In the next chapter, we'll finish our discussion of operators and expressions. Stay tuned!

Advanced operators
and variables

4

This chapter covers
- Operators for working with types
- Unary operators
- Grouping and subexpressions
- Array, property, and method operators
- The format and redirection operators
- Working with variables

> *The greatest challenge to any thinker is stating the problem in a way*
> *that will allow a solution.*
>
> —*Bertrand Russell*

The previous chapter covered the basic operators in PowerShell, and in this chapter, we'll continue our discussion of operators by looking at the advanced ones, which include things that some people don't think of as operators at all. We'll break the operators into related groups, as shown in figure 4.1.

In this chapter, we'll look at how to work with types, properties, and methods, and how to use these operators to build complex data structures. PowerShell is an automation engine for the Windows environment, and whatever you're doing, you'll need to manipulate data of some sort—for instance, *Windows Management Instrumentation* (WMI) query results, Active Directory user data, or data retrieved from a web service. Irrespective of the data source you'll need the operators in this, and the previous chapter, to enable your processing of that data into the format *you* need to solve *your* problem.

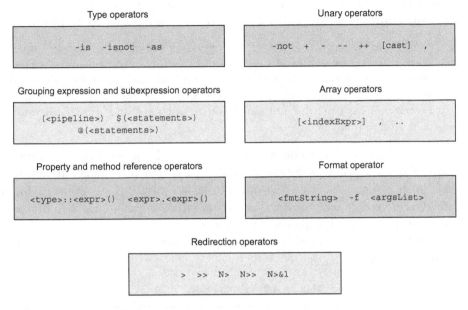

Figure 4.1 The broad groups of operators we cover in this chapter

The chapter concludes with a detailed discussion of how variables work in PowerShell and how you can use them with operators to accomplish significant tasks.

4.1 *Operators for working with types*

The type of an object is fundamental to determining the sorts of operations you can perform on that object. PowerShell provides a set of operators that can work with types, as shown in figure 4.2. They're also listed in table 4.1 with examples and more description.

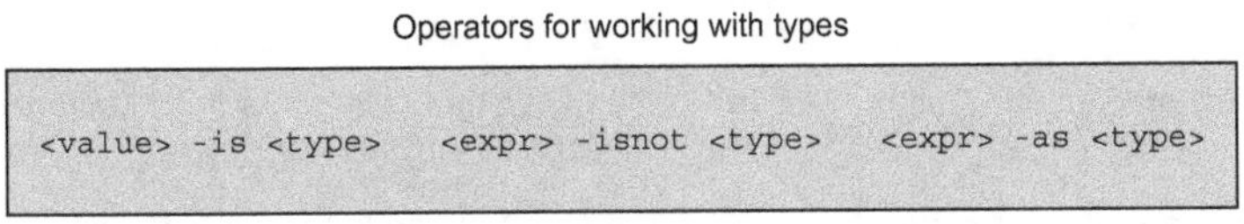

Operators for working with types

```
<value> -is <type>    <expr> -isnot <type>    <expr> -as <type>
```

Figure 4.2 The binary operators for working with types

You can test whether an object is of a particular type using the `-is` operator, which returns true if the object on the left is of the type specified on the right. By "is," we mean the left object is either of the type specified on the right side or is derived from that type.

The -isnot operator returns true if the left expression is not of the type specified on the right. The right operand must be represented as a type or a string that names a type. This means you can use either a type literal such as [int] or the literal string "int". The -as operator will try to convert the left operand into the type specified by the right operand. Again, either a type literal or a string naming a type can be used.

NOTE The PowerShell -is and -as operators are directly modeled on the corresponding operators in C#. But PowerShell's version of -as uses Power-Shell's more aggressive approach to casting. For example, C# won't cast the string "123" into the number 123, whereas the PowerShell operator will. The PowerShell -as operator will also work on any type, and the C# operator is restricted to reference types.

The -as operator is more flexible than a cast—you can use a runtime expression to specify the type, whereas the cast is fixed at parse time. One final difference between a regular cast and using the -as operator is, in a cast, if the conversion doesn't succeed an error is generated. With the -as operator if the cast fails, then the expression returns $null instead of generating an error.

Table 4.1 provides several more examples of how to use the type operators Power-Shell provides.

Table 4.1 PowerShell operators for working with types

Operator	Example	Results	Description
-is	$true -is [bool]	$true	True if the type on the left matches the type of the object on the right.
	$true -is [object]	$true	This is always True—everything is an object except $null.
	$true -is [ValueType]	$true	The left side is an instance of a .NET value type such as an integer or floating-point number.
	'hi' -is [ValueType]	$false	A string is not a value type; it's a reference type so this expression returns False.
	'hi' -is [object]	$true	A string is still an object.
	12 -is [int]	$true	12 is an integer.
	12 -is 'int'	$true	The right side of the operator can be either a type literal or a string naming a type.
-isnot	$true -isnot [string]	$true	The object on the left is not of the type specified on the right.
	$null -isnot [object]	$true	The null value is the only thing that isn't an object.
-as	'123' -as [int]	123	Takes the left side and converts it to the type specified on the right.
	123 -as 'string'	'123'	Turns the left side into an instance of the type named by the string on the right.

In practice, most of the time the automatic type-conversion mechanism will be all you need, and explicit casts will take care of the majority of the remaining cases. Why have these operators? They're mostly used in scripting. If you want to have a script that behaves differently based on whether it's passed a string or a number, for example, you'll need to use the -is operator to select which operation to perform.

4.2 Unary operators

Now let's look at the unary operators, which take only one argument. These operators are shown in figure 4.3 and listed with examples in table 4.2.

```
Unary operators including increment and decrement operators

-not <value>   + <value>   - <value>   [cast] <value>   , <value>
        --<assignableExpr>   <assignableExpr>--
        ++<assignableExpr>   <assignableExpr>++
```

Figure 4.3   Various unary operators

You've seen most of these operators in previous sections. The unary + and - operators do what you'd expect for numbers. Applying them to any other type results in an error.

The use of the type casts as unary operators was discussed at length in chapter 2, so we won't go into it again. The interesting operators in this section are the increment and decrement operators. They match the behavior of the equivalent operators in the C programming language with both the prefix and postfix forms of the operators.

These operators are special in that they take an *assignable expression* as an argument. An assignable expression is, well, anything that can be assigned to it. This includes variables, array elements, and object properties. These operators retrieve the current value of the assignable expression, increment (add 1) or decrement (subtract 1) that value, and then assign it back to the assignable expression. As with the unary + and - operators, the increment (++) and decrement (--) operators are only defined for variables containing numbers. Applying the increment and decrement operators to a variable containing anything other than a number results in an error.

Table 4.2   PowerShell unary operators

Operator	Example	Results	Description
-	- (2+2)	-4	Negation. Tries to convert its argument to a number, and then negates the result.
+	+ '123'	123	Unary plus. Tries to convert its argument to a number and returns the result. This is effectively a cast to a number.
--	--$a; $a--	Depends on the current value of the variable	Pre- and post-decrement operator. Converts the content of the variable to a number, and then tries to subtract one from that value. The prefix version returns the new value; the postfix version returns the original value.

Table 4.2   PowerShell unary operators *(continued)*

Operator	Example	Results	Description
++	++$a; $a++	Depends on the current value of the variable	Pre- and post-increment operator. Converts the variable to a number, and then adds 1 to the result. The prefix version returns the new value; the postfix version returns the original value.
[<type>]	[int] '0x123'	291	Type cast. Converts the argument into an instance of the type specified by the cast.
,	, (1+2)	One-element array containing the value of the expression	Unary comma operator. Creates a new one-element array of type [object[]] and stores the operand in it.

The other thing that's special about these operators is they result in *voidable statements*. This means the output of these expressions, when used as statements, is discarded instead of writing into the output pipe. Expression types that result in voidable statements include assignment expressions and the increment/decrement operators. As is the case in languages like C# or Java, when the increment and decrement operators are used in an expression, they return a value, but when they're used as a standalone statement, they return nothing.

> **NOTE** Early in the development of PowerShell, there were no "voidable" statements. Unfortunately, this meant people kept finding strange values appearing in their output leading to the PowerShell team receiving many complaints. Until they came up with the voidable statement concept, it was thought they'd have to remove ++ and --. Fortunately, they got it to work properly. It's funny how sometimes you need to do something complicated to make the user's experience simple.

Generally, this behavior does what you want and so it won't affect how you use PowerShell other than to make it work as you expect. But sometimes you would like the output to be kept. In those situations, here's a trick you can use: if the expression is enclosed in parentheses, the result will be returned instead of discarded:

```
PS> $1 = 1
PS> foreach ($s in "one","two","three")
{ "$(($1++)): $s" }

1: one
2: two
3: three
```

So far, we've been careful to say only some expressions result in voidable statements. For other statement types, you'll have to explicitly discard the output of the statement, manually turning a regular statement into a voidable one. The way to do this is through an explicit cast using the [void] type literal, as in

```
PS> [void] $(Write-Output "discard me")
```

The statement with a value you want to discard is enclosed in a *subexpression*, and the whole thing is cast to void. Wait, what's a subexpression? We'll look at them next.

4.3 Grouping and subexpressions

So far you've seen a variety of situations where collections of expressions or statements have been grouped together. You've even used these grouping constructs in string expansions. These operators are shown in figure 4.4.

Grouping expression and subexpression operators

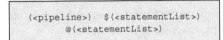

```
(<pipeline>)   $(<statementList>)
       @(<statementList>)
```

Figure 4.4   PowerShell operators for grouping expressions and statements

Now let's look at them in more detail. Table 4.3 provides more details and some examples.

Table 4.3   Expression and statement grouping operators

Operator	Example	Results	Description
(...)	(2 + 2) * 3 (Get-Date).DayOfWeek	12 Returns the current weekday	Parentheses group expression operations and may contain either a simple expression or a simple pipeline. They may not contain statements like while loops.
$(...)	$($p = "a*"; Get-Process $p)	Returns the process objects for all processes starting with the letter a	Subexpressions group collections of statements as opposed to being limited to a single expression. If the contained statements return a single value, that value will be returned as a scalar. If the statements return more than one value, they'll be accumulated in an array.
@(...)	@(dir c:\; dir d:\)	Returns an array containing the FileInfo objects in the root of the C: and D: drives	The array subexpression operator groups collections of statements in the same manner as the regular subexpression operator, but with the additional behavior that the result will always be returned as an array.

The first grouping notation is the simple parenthetical notation. As in most languages, the conventional use for this notation is to control the order of operations. In PowerShell, parentheses also have another use. Looking at the syntax specification shown in figure 4.4 for parenthetical expressions illustrates this:

```
( <pipeline> )
```

From the syntax, you can see pipelines are allowed between simple parentheses. This allows you to use a command or pipeline as a value in an expression. For example, to obtain a count of the number of files in a directory, you can use the Get-ChildItem cmdlet in parentheses and then use the Count property to get the number of objects returned:

```
PS> (Get-ChildItem).count
46
```

> **NOTE** People familiar with other languages tend to assume the expression (1,2,3,4) is an array literal in PowerShell. In fact, as you learned in chapter 2, this isn't the case. The comma operator, discussed in the next section, allows you to easily construct arrays in PowerShell, but there are no array literals as such in the language. All the parentheses do is control the order of operations. There's nothing special about them otherwise. In fact, the precedence of the comma operator is such that you typically never need parentheses for this purpose. More on that later.

Now let's move on to the next set of grouping constructs: the subexpressions.

4.3.1   *Subexpressions $(...)*

There are two forms of the subexpression construct:

```
$( <statementList> )
@( <statementList> )
```

The syntactic difference between a subexpression (either form) and a simple paren-thetical expression is you can have any list of statements in a subexpression instead of being restricted to a single pipeline. This means you can have any PowerShell language element in these grouping constructs, including loop statements. It also means you can have several statements in the group. Let's look at an example that counts the number of elements in the Fibonacci sequence below 100:

```
PS> $($c=$p=1; while ($c -lt 100) {$c; $c,$p=($c+$p),$c}).count
10
```

By enclosing the statements in $(<statement>), you can retrieve the result of the enclosed collection of statements as an array.

> **NOTE** Languages like Python have a special notation for generating collections of objects called *"List Comprehensions."* In PowerShell, because collections occur naturally as a consequence of the shell pipeline model there's no need for this extra syntax. When statements returning multiple objects are used as a value, they'll automatically be collected into an array.

Another difference between the subexpression construct and simple parentheses is how voidable statements are treated. First initialize $a to 0; then use a post-increment expression in parentheses and assign it to the variable $x:

```
PS> $a=0
PS> $x=($a++)
```

Checking the value of $x, you see it's 0, as expected, and $a is now 1. Now do a second assignment, this time with the expression in $(...):

```
PS> $x=$($a++)
```

Checking the value, you see it's $null:

```
PS> $x
PS> $x -eq $null
True
```

This is because the result of the post-increment operation was discarded, so the expression returned nothing.

4.3.2   *Array subexpressions @(...)*

Now let's take a look at the difference between the array subexpression @(...) and the regular subexpression. The difference is, in the case of the array subexpression, the result is always returned as an array; this is a fairly small but useful difference. In effect, it's shorthand for

```
[object[]] $( ... )
```

This shorthand exists because in many cases you don't know if a pipeline operation is going to return a single element or a collection. Rather than writing complex checks, you can use this construction and be assured the result will always be a collection. If the pipeline returns an array, no new array is created and the original value is returned as is. If the pipeline returns a scalar value, that value will be wrapped in a new one-element array. It's important to understand how this is different from the behavior of the comma operator, which *always* wraps its argument value in a new one-element array. Doing something like @(@(1)) doesn't give you a one-element array containing a second one-element array containing a number. The expressions

```
PS> @(1)
PS> @(@(1))
PS> @(@(@(1)))
```

all return the same value. On the other hand,

```
PS> ,1
```

nests to one level, and

```
PS> ,,1
```

nests to two levels, and so forth.

> **NOTE**   How to figure out what the pipeline returns is the single hardest thing to explain in the PowerShell language. The problem is people get confused; they see @(12) returns a one-element array containing the number 12. Because of prior experience with other languages, they expect @(@(12)) should therefore produce a nested array, an array of one element containing an array of one element, which is the integer 12. As mentioned previously, this is *not* the case. Rather, @(@(12)) returns exactly the same thing as @(12). If you think of rewriting this expression as [object[]]$([object[]] $(12)), then it's clear why this is the case—casting an array into an array of the same type has no effect; it's already the correct type, so you get the original array.

Here's an example of where this feature is useful: a pipeline expression that sorts some strings and then returns the first element in the sorted collection. Start by sorting an array of three elements:

```
PS> $('bbb','aaa','ccc' | sort )[0]
aaa
```

This returns "aaa", as you'd expect. Now do it with two elements:

```
PS> $('bbb','aaa' | sort )[0]
aaa
```

Still "aaa", so everything makes sense. Now try it with one element:

```
PS> $('aaa' | sort )[0]
a
```

Wait a minute—*what happened here?* Well, what happened is you sorted one element, and in a pipeline, you can't tell if the commands in the pipeline mean to return a single object (a scalar) or an array containing a single object. The default behavior in PowerShell is to assume that if you return one element, you intended to return a scalar. In this case, the scalar is the string "aaa", and index 0 of this array is the letter *a*, which is what the example returns.

This is where you use the array subexpression notation because it ensures you always get what you want. You know you want the pipeline to return an array, and by using this notation, you can enforce the correct behavior. Here are the same three examples again, but this time using the array subexpression:

```
PS> @('bbb','aaa','ccc' | sort )[0]
aaa

PS> @('bbb','aaa' | sort )[0]
aaa
```

```
PS> @('aaa' | sort )[0]
aaa
```

This time, all three commands return "aaa" as intended. Why have this notation? Why not use the casts? Well, here's what it looks like using the cast notation:

```
PS> ( [object[]] ('aaa' | sort ))[0]
aaa
```

Because of the way precedence works, you need an extra set of parentheses to get the ordering right, which makes the whole expression harder to write. In the end, the array subexpression notation is easy to use, although it's a bit difficult to grasp at first. The advantage is you have to learn something only once, but you get to use it over and over again.

Let's move on to the other operations PowerShell provides for dealing with collections and arrays of objects. The ability to manipulate collections of objects effectively is the heart of any automation system. Let's see what PowerShell has to offer here.

4.4   Array operators

Arrays or collections of objects occur naturally in many of the operations that you execute. An operation such as getting a directory listing in the file system results in a collection of objects. Getting the set of processes running on a machine or a list of services configured on a server both result in collections of objects. Not surprisingly, PowerShell has a set of operators and operations for working with arrays and collections. These operators are shown in figure 4.5.

Array operators

```
<indexValue>[<indexExpression>]
<value1>,  <value2>,   <value3>
   <lowerBound>..<upperBound>
```

Figure 4.5   PowerShell array operators

We'll go over these operators in the following sections.

4.4.1   Comma operator

You've seen many examples using the comma operator to build arrays. We covered this topic in some detail in chapter 2, but there are a couple of things we still need to cover. This means when you're building an array with expressions, you need to wrap those expressions in parentheses as this example illustrates:

```
PS> 1,2,1+2
1
2
1
2
```

The result is an array of the four elements, 1,2,1,2, because the expression was parsed as (1,2,1)+2, building an array of three elements and then appending a fourth. You have to use parentheses to get the desired effect:

```
PS> 1,2,(1+2)
1
2
3
```

> **NOTE**   The comma operator has higher precedence than any other operator except type casts and property and array references. This is worth emphasizing because it's important to keep in mind when writing expressions. If you don't remember this, you'll produce some strange, and incorrect, results.

The next thing we'll look at is nested arrays. Because a PowerShell array can hold any type of object, obviously it can also hold another array. Your task will be to build the tree structure shown in figure 4.6.

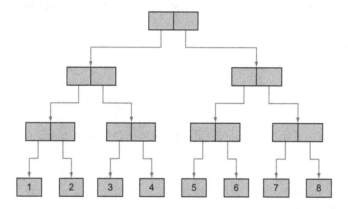

Figure 4.6   A binary tree (arrays of arrays of arrays)

This data structure starts with an array of two elements. These two elements are also both arrays of two elements, and they, in turn, contain arrays of two numbers. Let's see how to go about constructing something like this.

There are a couple of ways you can approach this. First, you can build nested arrays one piece at a time using assignments. Alternatively, you can nest the comma operator within parentheses. Starting with last things first, here's how to build a nested array structure using commas and parentheses. The result is concise:

```
PS> $a = (((1,2),(3,4)),((5,6),(7,8)))
```

And here's the same construction using intermediate variables and assignments. It's rather less concise but hopefully easier to understand.

```
PS> $t1 = 1,2
PS> $t2 = 3,4
```

```
PS> $t3 = 5,6
PS> $t4 = 7,8
PS> $t1_1 = $t1,$t2
PS> $t1_2 = $t3,$t4
PS> $a = $t1_1, $t1_2
```

In either case, what you've done is build a data structure that looks like the tree shown in figure 4.6.

NOTE In Perl and PHP, you have to do something special to get reference semantics with arrays. In PowerShell, arrays are always reference types, so no special notation is needed.

Let's verify the shape of this data structure. First, use the length property to verify that $a holds an array of two elements:

```
PS> $a.Length
2
```

Next, check the length of the array stored in the first element of that array:

```
PS> $a[0].Length
2
```

It's also two elements long, as is the array stored in the second element:

```
PS> $a[1].Length
2
```

Now let's look two levels down. This is done by indexing the result of an index as follows:

```
PS> $a[1][0].Length
2
```

Note that $a[0][0] isn't the same as $a[0,0], which is either a subset of the elements in the array called a *slice* if $a is one-dimensional, or a *single index* if the array is two-dimensional. You can compose index operations as deeply as you need to. This example retrieves the second element of the first element of the second element stored in $a:

```
PS> $a[1][0][1]
6
```

NOTE Remember that in .NET, and therefore PowerShell, array element indexing starts at zero for the first element.

To see exactly what's going on here, look at figure 4.7. In this figure, the dotted lines show the path followed to get to the value 6.

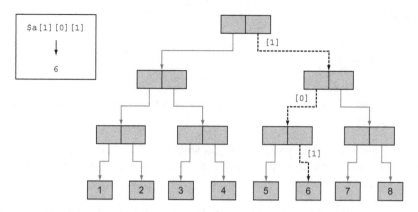

Figure 4.7   Indexing through a binary tree with the expression `$a[1][0][1]`

These examples show how you can construct arbitrarily complex data structures in PowerShell. Although this isn't something you'll need to use frequently, the capability is there if you need it. In section 4.4.3, when we discuss array slices, you'll see an example using nested arrays to index multidimensional arrays.

4.4.2   *Range operator*

The next operator we'll discuss is the range operator (`..`). This operator is effectively a shortcut for generating a sequential array of numbers. For example, the expression

```
1..5
```

is equivalent to

```
1,2,3,4,5
```

although it's somewhat more efficient than using the commas. The syntax for the range operator is

```
<valueExpression> .. <valueExpression>
```

It has higher precedence than all the binary operators except for the comma operator. This means expressions like

```
PS> 1..3+4..6
```

work, but the following gives you a syntax error:

```
PS> 1+3..4+6
```

It's an error because the expression is being parsed like

```
1 + (3..4) + 6
```

This is because the range operator has higher precedence than the addition operator.

In a range operator expression, the left and right operands represent bounds, but either the left or the right can be the upper bound. If the left operand is greater than the right operand, a descending sequence is generated. The boundaries can also be negative.

The upper and lower bounds *must* resolve to integers after applying the usual type conversions. A string that looks like a number will automatically be converted into a number, and a floating-point value will automatically be converted to an integer using the Banker's rounding algorithm described in chapter 3.

The range operator is most commonly used with the `foreach` loop because it allows you to easily loop a specific number of times or over a specific range of numbers. This is done so often that the PowerShell engine treats it in a special way. A range like `1..10mb` doesn't generate a 10 MB array—it treats the range endpoints as the lower and upper bounds of the loop, making it efficient. (The `foreach` loop is described in detail in the next chapter.)

> **NOTE** In PowerShell v1, the range operator was limited to an upper bound of 40 KB to avoid accidentally creating arrays that were too large. In practice, this was never a problem, so this limit was removed in version 2 with one exception. In restricted language mode, this limit is still enforced.

The other place where the range operator gets used frequently is with array slices, which you'll learn about next.

4.4.3 *Array indexing and slicing*

Most people don't think of indexing into an array as involving operators or that `[ ]` is an operator, but in fact, that's exactly what it is. It has a left operand and a right operand (the "right" operand is inside the brackets). The syntax for an array indexing expression is

```
<valueExpression> [ <valueExpression> ]
```

There are a couple of things to note here. First, this is one of the few areas where you can't directly use a pipeline. That's because brackets don't (and can't) delimit a pipeline as they're used in pipeline arguments as wildcard patterns. If you want to use a pipeline as an index expression, you have to use parentheses or the subexpression notation.

The second thing to note is spaces *aren't* allowed between the last character of the expression being indexed and the opening bracket. This is necessary to distinguish array expressions on the command line from wildcard patterns.

From the syntax, you can see array indexing works on more than variables; it can be applied to any expression that returns a value. Because the precedence of the square brackets is high (meaning they get evaluated before most other operators), you usually have to put the expression in parentheses. If you don't, you'll get an error. For example:

```
PS> (1,2,3)[0]
1
```

Here you retrieved the first element in the collection, which is at index 0. (Like all .NET-based languages, indexes start at 0 in PowerShell.) PowerShell also supports negative indexes, which index from the end of the array. Let's try it out:

```
PS> (1,2,3)[-1]
3

PS> (1,2,3)[-2]
2
```

Specifying –1 retrieves the last element in the array, –2 retrieves the second-to-last element, and so on. In fact, negative indexes are exactly equivalent to taking the length of the array and subtracting the index from the array. In effect, negative indexing is shorthand for $array.Length - $index.

ARRAY SLICES

You've seen how to get individual elements out of an array. You can get sequences of elements out of arrays as well. Extracting these sequences is called *array slicing*, and the results are *array slices*, as illustrated in figure 4.8.

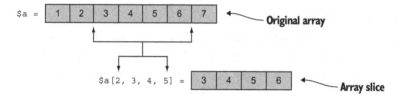

Figure 4.8   How an array slice is generated from the original array

Slicing is done by specifying an array of indexes instead of a single index. The corresponding element for each index is extracted from the original array and returned as a new array that's a slice of the original. From the command line, this operation looks like this:

```
PS> $a = 1,2,3,4,5,6,7
PS> $indexes = 2,3,4,5
PS> $a[$indexes]
3
4
5
6
```

This example used a variable storing the array 2,3,4,5 to get the corresponding elements out of the array in $a. Now let's process the values that are stored in the $indexes variable. You'll use the ForEach-Object cmdlet to process each element of the array and assign the results back to the array:

```
PS> $indexes = 2,3,4,5 | foreach {$_-1}
```

You want to adjust for the fact that arrays start at index 0, so subtract 1 from each index element. Now when you do the indexing

```
PS> $a[$indexes]
2
3
4
5
```

you get the elements that correspond to the original index value—2 returns 2, and so on. But do you need to use the intermediate variable? You have to wrap the expression in brackets so it will be treated as a single value:

```
PS> $a[(2,3,4,5 | foreach {$_-1})]
2
3
4
5
```

4.4.4 Using the range operator with arrays

There's one other tool in the indexing toolkit: the range operator discussed in the previous section. This operator is a convenient way to get slices of arrays. Say you have an array of ten elements, with values 0–9. To get the first four elements of an array, you can use the range operator as follows:

```
PS> $a = 0..9
PS> $a[0..3]
```

By taking advantage of the way negative indexing works, you can get the last four elements of the array by doing this:

```
PS> $a[-4..-1]
```

You can even use ranges to reverse an array. To do this, you need to know the length of the array, which you can get through the length property. You can see this in the following example, which casts the result of the expression to a string so it will be displayed on one line:

```
PS> [string] $a[ ($a.Length-1) .. 0]
9 8 7 6 5 4 3 2 1 0
```

> **NOTE**   This isn't an efficient way of reversing the array. Using the `Reverse` static member on the `[array]` class is more efficient.

In PowerShell, slicing works for retrieving elements of an array, but you *can't* use it for assignments. You get an error if you try. For example, to replace the slice `[2,3,4]` with a single value 12, here's what you have to do:

```
PS> $a = $a[0,1] + 12 + $a[5 .. 9]
PS> "$a"
0 1 12 5 6 7 8 9
```

You have to take the array slices before and after the desired values and then concatenate all three pieces together to produce a new array.

4.4.5   *Working with multidimensional arrays*

So far we've covered one-dimensional arrays as well as arrays of arrays (which are also called *jagged arrays*). The reason for the term *jagged* is shown in figure 4.9.

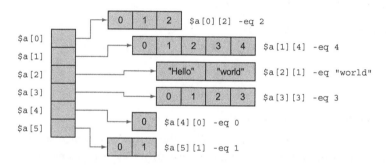

Figure 4.9   An example of a jagged array in the variable `$a`. Each member of `$a` is also an array but they're all of different lengths—hence the term jagged.

In figure 4.9, `$a` is an array of arrays as you've seen before, but each of the member arrays is a different length. Instead of having a regular structure, you have a jagged one because the counts are uneven.

Now that you understand what a jagged array is, we'll move on to multidimensional arrays. PowerShell needs to support multidimensional arrays because .NET allows for arrays to be multidimensional and PowerShell is built on top of .NET. Figure 4.10 shows a two-dimensional array.

As shown in figure 4.10, PowerShell indexes into multidimensional arrays by looking at the type of the array and mapping the set of indexes onto the number of dimensions, or *rank*, the array has. If you specify two indexes and the array is one-dimensional, you'll get two elements back. If the array is two-dimensional, you'll get one element back. Let's try this.

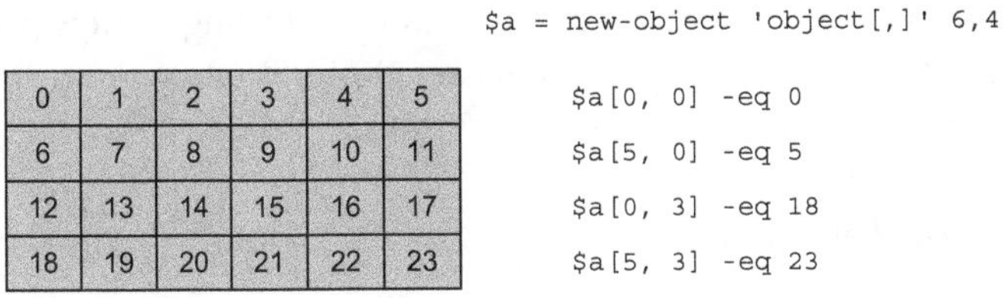

```
$a = new-object 'object[,]' 6,4
```

0	1	2	3	4	5
6	7	8	9	10	11
12	13	14	15	16	17
18	19	20	21	22	23

```
$a[0, 0] -eq 0
$a[5, 0] -eq 5
$a[0, 3] -eq 18
$a[5, 3] -eq 23
```

Figure 4.10 A two-dimensional 6 x 4 array of numbers

Construct a multidimensional array using the `New-Object` cmdlet:

```
PS> $2d = New-Object -TypeName 'object[,]' -ArgumentList 2,2
```

This statement created a 2 x 2 array of objects. Look at the dimensions of the array by retrieving the `Rank` property from the object:

```
PS> $2d.Rank
2
```

Now set the value in the array to particular values. Do this by indexing into the array:

```
PS> $2d[0,0] = "a"
PS> $2d[1,0] = 'b'
PS> $2d[0,1] = 'c'
PS> $2d[1,1] = 'd'
PS> $2d[1,1]
d
```

This appears to imply that slices don't work in multidimensional arrays, but in fact they do when you use nested arrays of indexes and wrap the expression by using the comma operator in parentheses:

```
PS> $2d[ (0,0) , (1,0) ]
a
b
```

This example retrieved the elements of the array at indexes (0,0) and (1,0). And, as in the case of one-dimensional arrays, you can use variables for indexing. You can even use a variable containing a pair of index arrays:

```
PS> $one = 0,0
PS> $two = 1,0
PS> $pair = $one,$two
PS> $2d[ $pair ]
a
b
```

This covers pretty much everything you need to know about arrays. Now let's move on to properties and methods. As you'll remember from chapter 1, properties and methods are the attributes of an object that let you inspect and manipulate that object.

Because PowerShell is an object-based shell, a good understanding of how properties and methods work is necessary if you want to master PowerShell. We're going to be spending a fair bit of time on these features, so let's get started.

4.5   *Property and method operators*

As you've seen in many examples so far, the property reference operator in PowerShell is the dot (.). As was the case with array indexing, this is properly considered an operator in PowerShell with left and right operand expressions. This operator, along with the static member operator : :, is shown in figure 4.11.

Property and method reference operators

```
<typeValue>::<memberNameExpr>   <typeValue>::<memberNameExpr>(<arguments>)
    <value>.<memberNameExpr>    <value>.<memberNameExpr>(<arguments>)
```

Figure 4.11   Property and method operators in PowerShell

NOTE When we say *property* here, we're talking about any kind of data member on an object, regardless of the underlying CLR representation (or implementation) of the member. If you don't know what this means, good—because it doesn't matter. But some people like to know all the details of what's going on.

First let's look back at the basics. Everything in PowerShell is an object (even scripts and functions). Objects have properties (data) and methods (code). To get at both, you use the dot operator. To get the length of a string, you use the length property:

```
PS> 'Hello world!'.Length
12
```

In a similar fashion, you can get the length of an array:

```
PS> (1,2,3,4,5).Length
5
```

As was the case with the left bracket in array indexing, spaces aren't permitted between the left operand and the dot. This is necessary to make sure that arguments to cmdlets aren't mistaken for property reference operations.

4.5.1   *Dot operator*

What's special about the dot operator? Well, just as the left operand can be an expression, so can the right operand. The right operand is evaluated, which results in a value. That value is then used as the name of the property on the left operand to retrieve the values of the property. This series of steps is illustrated in figure 4.12.

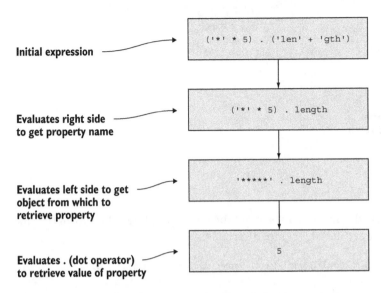

Initial expression

```
('*' * 5) . ('len' + 'gth')
```

Evaluates right side to get property name

```
('*' * 5) . length
```

Evaluates left side to get object from which to retrieve property

```
'*****' . length
```

Evaluates . (dot operator) to retrieve value of property

```
5
```

Figure 4.12   The steps performed to retrieve a calculated property from an object

Let's look at an example of how this process can be used with variables. First define a variable to hold the name of the property you want to retrieve:

```
PS> $prop = 'length'
```

Now, use that variable in an expression to retrieve the property:

```
PS> 'Hello world'.$prop
11
```

This mechanism gives you that magic "one more level of indirection" computer science people are so fond of. Let's expand on this. To get a list of all the properties on an object, use the Get-Member (or gm) cmdlet on an object. This example uses Get-ChildItem to get a FileInfo object to work with:

```
PS> Get-ChildItem -Path c:\windows\*.dll | Get-Member -type property
```

You only need the name, so you can use the Name property on these objects:

```
PS> Get-ChildItem -Path c:\windows\*.dll |
Get-Member -type property |
select Name

Name
----
Attributes
CreationTime
```

```
CreationTimeUtc
Directory
DirectoryName
Exists
Extension
FullName
IsReadOnly
LastAccessTime
LastAccessTimeUtc
LastWriteTime
LastWriteTimeUtc
Length
Name
```

Next, you'll use this list of names to get the corresponding values from the first .dll file in the list. First get the object into a variable:

```
PS> $obj = @(Get-ChildItem -Path $env:windir\system32\*.dll)[0]
```

And get the list of names; for brevity's sake, get the properties that start with the letter *l*:

```
PS> $names = $obj | Get-Member -Type property l* | foreach {$_.name}
```

> **NOTE** In PowerShell v3 and later, to extract a property from a pipeline, you can use foreach <name>. For example, the command dir | foreach fullname would return the full path name for all the files in the current directory.

Finally, use the list of names to print out the value:

```
PS> $names | foreach { "$_ = $($obj.$_)" }
LastAccessTime = 07/16/2016 12:42:05
LastAccessTimeUtc = 07/16/2016 11:42:05
LastWriteTime = 07/16/2016 12:42:05
LastWriteTimeUtc = 07/16/2016 11:42:05
Length = 34816
```

FALLBACK DOT OPERATOR

In section 2.1.3 we introduced the concept of a fallback operator, where if the object itself doesn't have a property and that object is a collection, PowerShell will check the contained objects to see if that member exists and return a collection of those values.

> **NOTE** It's effectively the equivalent of the foreach <name> mentioned in the preceding note, but it's much faster. On the down side, to use it with commands, you have to write the expression in parentheses. And as an expression, it doesn't stream.

Here's the example we just looked at, but rewritten with the fallback dot:

```
PS> $names = ( $obj | Get-Member -Type property l*).name
```

Because you have the names in a variable, which is an expression, rather than the foreach cmdlet, you could use the foreach fallback operator (but remember there can be no space between the h and the "{"), which looks like this:

```
PS> $names.foreach{ "$_ = $($obj.$_)" }
LastAccessTime = 07/16/2016 12:42:05
LastAccessTimeUtc = 07/16/2016 11:42:05
LastWriteTime = 07/16/2016 12:42:05
LastWriteTimeUtc = 07/16/2016 11:42:05
Length = 34816
```

You get the same output. But wait, you say foreach doesn't look like a property, and you'd be correct. It's a method that we'll look at in more detail in the next section.

USING METHODS

Let's look at using methods. The method call syntax is

```
<valueExpression> . <methodName> ( <argument> , <argument> , ... )
```

As always, spaces aren't allowed before or after the dot or before the opening parenthesis. Here's a basic example:

```
PS> 'Hello world!'.Substring(0,5)
Hello
```

This example uses the Substring method to extract the first six characters from the left operand string (the 6th is the space). As you can see, the syntax for method invocations in PowerShell matches what you see in pretty much every other language that has methods. Contrast this with how commands are called. In method calls, arguments in the argument list are separated by commas, and the whole list is enclosed in parentheses. With commands, the arguments are separated with spaces and the command ends at the end of a line or at a command terminator, such as the semicolon or the pipe symbol.

Empirically, a programmer-style syntax for programmer-style activities like method invocations and a shell-style syntax for shell-style activities like command invocation seem to work best. This approach is not without some small issues. First, if you want to pass an expression to a method, you have to wrap that array in parentheses so the array comma operator isn't confused with the argument separator commas. Second, if you want to use the output of a command as an argument, you have to wrap the command in parentheses. Here's an example:

```
PS> [string]::join('+',(1,2,3))
1+2+3
```

This example uses the [string]::Join static method to create a string out of the array 1,2,3 with a plus sign between each one. Now let's do the same thing with the output of a command. The handle count for the PowerShell processes will be output and joined into a string, again separated with the plus sign (with spaces on either side this time):

```
PS> [string]::join(' + ', (Get-Process p* | foreach{$_.handles}))
752 + 699
```

You might have noticed the use of the double-colon operator (::) in these examples. We briefly discussed this operator in chapter 3 as part of our discussion of types in PowerShell. In the next section, we'll look at it in more detail.

4.5.2 *Static methods and the double-colon operator*

The :: operator is the static member accessor. Whereas the dot operator retrieved instance members, the double-colon operator accesses static members (properties as well as methods) on a class, as is the case with the join method in the example at the end of the last section. The left operand to the static member accessor is required to be a type—either a type literal or an expression returning a type, as you see here:

```
PS> $t = [string]
PS> $t::join('+',(1,2,3))
1+2+3
```

The language design team chose to use a separate operator for accessing static methods because of the way static methods are accessed. Here's the problem. If you had a type MyModule with a static property called Module, then the expression

```
[MyModule].Module
```

is ambiguous. That's because there's also an instance member Module on the System .Type instance representing the type MyModule. Now you can't tell if the "Module" instance member on System.Type or the "Module" static member on MyModule should be retrieved. By using the double-colon operator, you remove this ambiguity.

> **NOTE** Other languages get around this ambiguity by using the typeof() operator. Using typeof() in this example, typeof(MyModule).Module retrieves the instance property on the Type object and MyModule.Module retrieves the static property implemented by the MyModule class.

USING NAMESPACES IN POWERSHELL V5 AND LATER

One of the problems with using type names anywhere is how long they can be—for example, [System.Windows.Forms.Form]. Most languages deal with that through some sort of using statement and, with PowerShell v5, that's also finally true for PowerShell!

> **NOTE** And it only took ten years for it to be added. Bruce apologizes.

The syntax for the using namespace statement is as follows:

```
using namespace <namespace>
```

This will make all the types defined in that namespace directly available to scripts. A related use of using is to load assemblies, which look like:

```
using assembly <assembly>
```

We used both of these statements in the example at the beginning of chapter 1:

```
using assembly  System.Windows.Forms
using namespace System.Windows.Forms
$form = [Form] @{
    Text = 'My First Form'
}
$button = [Button] @{
    Text = 'Push Me!'
    Dock = 'Fill'
}
$button.add_Click{
    $form.Close()
}
$form.Controls.Add($button)
$form.ShowDialog()
```

This fragment of script loads the Windows Forms assembly into memory and then makes all the types defined in the namespace System.Windows.Forms available.

Here are a couple of important points to remember about the using statement. First, it has to be the first non-comment statement in a script or module. This is because, with using, types are resolved at compile time instead of runtime. This is a good thing because it helps you catch your errors sooner. Second, you have to have the assembly containing the reference type namespace loaded before you can run your script. Because a lot of things are loaded by PowerShell by default this isn't that much of a problem. This is what using assembly <...> is intended for. By specifying both statements as shown in the example, everything will work fine.

> **NOTE** There was a bug in how using assembly worked; instead of scanning the assembly before it's loaded, it defers loading it until runtime. This, unfortunately, makes it exactly useless for its intended purpose. Hopefully that bug will be fixed by the time you read this, but if not and you see a "type not found" error, at least you'll know why.

So far, so good with methods. You know how to call them "statically" where you know the name of the method to call beforehand. But PowerShell is a dynamic language, so one might expect that there's a way to call them using a name discovered at runtime. This is the topic of the next section.

4.5.3 *Indirect method invocation*

Earlier we talked about how you could do indirect property references by using a variable on the right side of the dot operator. You can do the same thing with methods, but it's a bit more complicated. The obvious approach

```
$x.$y(2)
```

doesn't work. What happens is $x.$y returns an object that lists the *overloads* for that method that's the different forms of the method that you can use:

```
PS> 'abc'.substring

OverloadDefinitions
-------------------
string Substring(int startIndex)
string Substring(int startIndex, int length)
```

Now that you have this information object, what else can you do with it? The thing you most probably want to do is invoke it, and the way to do that is to use the Invoke method on the method information object:

```
PS> 'abc'.substring.Invoke(1)
bc
```

This also works for static methods. First assign the name of the operation to invoke to a variable:

```
 PS> $method = 'sin'
```

look at the information about that method:

```
PS> [math]::$method

OverloadDefinitions
-------------------
static double Sin(double a)
```

and finally, invoke it:

```
PS> [math]::$method.Invoke(3.14)
0.00159265291648683
```

Although it's an advanced technique, the ability to invoke properties and methods indirectly turns out to be powerful because it means the behavior of your script can be configured at runtime. You'll learn how this can be used when we talk about script-blocks in chapter 7.

    This finishes our discussion of properties and methods. You may have noticed in some of the examples so far, you've had to do some fairly complicated things to display the results in the way you want. Clearly, on occasion you'll need a better way to present output, and that's the purpose of the format operator, covered in the next section.

4.6 *Format operator*

Most of the time, PowerShell's built-in formatting and output system will take care of presenting your results, but sometimes you need more explicit control over the formatting of your output. You may also want to format text strings in a specific way, like displaying numbers in hexadecimal format. PowerShell allows you to do these things with the format operator, shown in figure 4.13.

Format operator

```
<formatSpecificationString> -f <argumentList>
```

Figure 4.13 The format operator lets you control the formatting of your output.

The format operator (`-f`) is a binary operator that takes a format string as its left operand and an array of values to format as its right operand. Here's an example:

```
PS> '{2} {1} {0}' -f 1,2,3
3 2 1
```

In the format string, the values enclosed in braces correspond to the index of the element in the right operand array. The element is converted into a string and then displayed. Along with reordering, when the elements are displayed, you can control how they're laid out.

NOTE For people familiar with the Python language, the PowerShell format operator is modeled on the Python `%` operator but uses `-f` because `%` isn't used in PowerShell formatting directives.

Here are more examples:

```
PS> '|{0,10}| 0x{1:x}|{2,-10}|' -f 10,20,30
|        10| 0x14|30        |
```

Here, the first format specifier element (`,10`) tells the system to pad the text out to ten characters. The next element is printed with the specifier `:x`, telling the system to display the number as a hexadecimal value. The final display specification has a field width specifier, but this time it's a negative value, indicating that the field should be padded to the right instead of to the left.

The `-f` operator is shorthand for calling the .NET `Format` method on the `System.String` class. The key benefit of the `-f` operator is it's a lot shorter to type. This is useful when you're typing on the command line. The underlying `Format()` method has a rich set of specifiers. The basic syntax of these specifiers is

```
{<index>[,<alignment>][:<formatString>]}
```

Some examples of using format specifiers are shown in table 4.4.

Table 4.4   Examples of using format specifiers

Format specifier	Description	Example	Output
{0}	Displays a particular element	'{0} {1}' -f 'a','b'	a b
{0:x}	Displays a number in hexadecimal	'Ox{0:x}' -f 181342	0x2c45e
{0:X}	Displays a number in hexadecimal with the letters in uppercase	'Ox{0:X}' -f 181342	0x2C45E
{0:d*n*}	Displays a decimal number left-justified, padded with zeros	'{0:d8}' -f 3	00000003
{0:p}	Displays a number as a percentage	'{0:p}' -f .123	12.30%
{0:C}	Displays a number as currency (based on your cultural settings). C can be upper or lower case.	'{0:c}' -f 12.34	$12.34
{0,*n*}	Displays with field width *n*, left-aligned	'|{0,5}|' -f 'hi'	| hi|
{0,-*n*)	Displays with field width *n*, right-aligned	'|{0,-5}|' -f 'hi'	|hi |
{0:hh} {0:mm}	Displays the hours and minutes from a DateTime value	'{0:hh}:{0:mm}' -f (Get-Date)	01:34

There are many more things you can do with formatting. Refer to the Microsoft MSDN documentation for the full details of the options.

Now that you know how to format strings, let's look at how you can direct your output to files with the redirection operators.

4.7   *Redirection and redirection operators*

All modern shell languages have input and output redirection operators, and PowerShell is no different. The redirection operators supported in PowerShell are shown in figure 4.14.

Redirection operators

```
<pipeline> > <outputFile>    <pipeline> >> <outputFile>
<pipeline> 2> <errorFile>    <pipeline> 2>> <errorFile>
              <pipeline> 2>&1
```

Figure 4.14   Redirection operators that are available in PowerShell

You can use the redirection operators to send particular types of output to a file. The type of data to be output is identified as follows:

- * = All output
- 1 = Success output
- 2 = Errors
- 3 = Warning messages

- 4 = Verbose output
- 5 = Debug messages
- 6 = Information messages

The All, Warning, Verbose, and Debug redirection operators were introduced in Power-Shell v3. The Information redirection operator was introduced in PowerShell v5.

NOTE The Input redirection operator, <, isn't implemented in PowerShell. Using this operator in an expression will result in a syntax error.

The redirection operators allow you to control where output and other data objects are written (including discarding them, if that's what you want to do). The following example saves the output of the Get-Date cmdlet to a file called out.txt:

```
PS> Get-Date > out.txt
```

Now let's see what happens when you redirect the error output from a cmdlet. You'll let the output be displayed normally:

```
PS> Get-ChildItem out.txt,nosuchfile 2> err.txt

    Directory: C:\Test

Mode                LastWriteTime         Length Name
----                -------------         ------ ----
-a----        16/05/2016     16:40          22278 out.txt
```

Obviously, no error was displayed on the console. Let's see what was written to the error file:

```
PS> Get-Content err.txt
Get-ChildItem : Cannot find path 'C:\Test\nosuchfile' because it does not
  exist.
At line:1 char:1
+ Get-ChildItem out.txt,nosuchfile 2> err.txt
+ ~~~~~~~~~~~~~~~~~~~~~~~~~~~~~~~~~~~~~~~~~~~~~
+ CategoryInfo          : ObjectNotFound: (C:\test\nosuchfile:String)
[Get-ChildItem], ItemNotFoundException
+ FullyQualifiedErrorId : PathNotFound,Microsoft.PowerShell.Commands.
  GetChildItemCommand
```

You see the full error message that would've been displayed on the console. The > operator will overwrite any previous contents of the file. Use >> (or *n*>>) to append to the chosen output file.

The next operator to discuss is the stream combiner, *n*>&1. This operator causes the appropriate data objects to be routed into the output stream instead of going to their dedicated stream. For example, if you want to get all the output and error records from a script to go to the same file, you'd use

```
PS> myScript > output.txt 2>&1
```

or

```
PS> myScript 2>&1 > output.txt
```

The order doesn't matter. Now all the error records will appear inline with the output records in the file. This technique also works with assignment:

```
PS> $a = myScript  2>&1
```

This code causes all the output and error objects from myScript to be placed in $a. You can then separate the errors by checking for their type with the -is operator, but it would be easier to separate them upfront. This is another place where you can use the grouping constructs. The following construction allows you to capture the output objects in $output and the error objects in $error:

```
PS> $error = $( $output = myScript ) 2>&1
```

You'd use this idiom when you wanted to take additional action on the error objects. For example, you might be deleting a set of files in a directory. Some of the deletions might fail. These will be recorded in $error, allowing you to take additional actions after the deletion operation has completed.

Sometimes you want to discard output or errors. In PowerShell, you do this by redirecting to $null. If you don't care about the output from myScript, then you'd write

```
PS> myScript > $null
```

and to discard the errors, you'd write

```
PS> myScript 2> $null
```

The last thing to mention for I/O redirection is, under the covers, redirection is done using the Out-File cmdlet. In fact,

```
PS> myScript > file.txt
```

is syntactic sugar for

```
PS> myScript | Out-File -Path file.txt
```

In some cases, you'll want to use Out-File directly because it gives you more control over the way the output is written using the -Encoding parameter, which lets you specify the encoding (such as ASCII, Unicode, UTF8, and so on). The -Width parameter tells the cmdlet how wide you want the output formatted. The full details for this cmdlet are available by running the command

```
PS> Get-Help Out-File -Full
```

at the PowerShell command line.

Earlier in this section we talked about assignment as being a kind of output redirection. This analogy is even more significant than we alluded to. We'll go into details in the next section, when we finally cover variables themselves.

4.8 Working with variables

In many of the examples so far, you've used variables. Now let's look at the details of PowerShell variables. First, PowerShell variables aren't declared; they're created as needed on first assignment. There also isn't any such thing as an uninitialized variable. If you reference a variable that doesn't yet exist, the system will return the value `$null` (although it won't create a variable).

> **NOTE** `$null`, like `$true` and `$false`, is a special constant variable that's defined by the system. You can't change the value of these variables.

You can tell whether a variable exists by using the `Test-Path` cmdlet:

```
PS> Test-Path variable:NoSuchVariable
False
```

This works because variables are exposed through the PowerShell unified drive names. Just as files and the registry are available through virtual drives, so are PowerShell variables. You can get a list of all the variables that currently exist by using:

```
PS> Get-ChildItem variable:/
```

The results will vary depending on the version of PowerShell you're running.

How do you create a variable? Let's find out.

4.8.1 Creating variables

A number of variables are defined by the system: `$true`, `$false`, and `$null` are the ones you've seen so far.

> **NOTE** Run the command `Get-Help about_Automatic_Variables` to get a list including detailed descriptions of all the automatic variables.

Unlike many other languages, in PowerShell, you don't have to declare variables. You create variables by assigning to the variable name as shown in the following:

```
PS> Test-Path variable:myNewVariable
False

PS> $myNewVariable = 'i exist'
PS> Test-Path variable:myNewVariable
True
```

TYPE-CONSTRAINED VARIABLES

By default, a PowerShell variable can hold any type of object. If you want to add a type-constraint attribute to a variable, you use the cast notation on the left of the variable. Let's add a type constraint to the variable $var:

```
PS> [int] $var = 2
```

Looking at the result, you see the number 2:

```
PS> $var
2
```

That's fine. What happens if you try to assign a string to the variable?

```
PS> $var = '0123'
PS> $var
123
```

First, there was no error. Second, by looking at the output of the variable, you can see the string "0123" was converted into the number 123. This is why we say the variable has a type attribute. Unlike strongly typed languages where a variable can only be assigned an object of the correct type, PowerShell will allow you to assign any object as long as it's convertible to the target type using the rules described in chapter 2. If the type isn't convertible, you'll get a runtime type-conversion error.

ATTRIBUTE-CONSTRAINED VARIABLES

PowerShell has always supported type-constrained variables like you saw in the previous section. PowerShell v5 also introduced the capability to use more sophisticated constraints—the same constraints used in cmdlets and advanced functions—expressed using attributes. An attribute looks like a type but contains a possibly empty parenthetical expression. Some examples are [Parameter()] and [ValidateLength(0,5)]. Here's an example showing how to use the [ValidateRange()] attribute on a variable. The goal is to restrict the length of the string that could be assigned to a variable. This can be enforced by adding the constraint as follows:

```
PS> [ValidateLength(0,5)] [string] $cv = ''
```

This says the string must be between zero and five characters long. Try it by assigning the string "12345" to the variable:

```
PS> $cv = '12345'
```

The assignment quietly succeeds. Now try it again with a string one character longer:

```
PS> $cv = '123456'
The variable cannot be validated because the value 123456
is not a valid value for the cv variable.
At line:1 char:1
```

```
+ $cv = '123456'
+ ~~~~~~~~~~~~~~~
    + CategoryInfo          : MetadataError: (:) [],
  ValidationMetadataException
    + FullyQualifiedErrorId : ValidateSetFailure
```

This time it fails as expected.

> **NOTE** At best, the default error message in this example would have to be described as "suboptimal." On the up side, because it's a built-in message, it's localized, which means it's readable everywhere. On the down side, that makes it incomprehensible in all languages. This isn't to say the overall feature is useless. This type of declarative checking can replace a lot of custom validation code and less code leads to smaller programs and fewer errors. Remember to catch the exception (see the try statement in chapter 14) and provide useful error messages to your users.

4.8.2 *Variable name syntax*

But wait—so far, we've totally ignored the rules for variable names! Obviously, you need to know what characters are legal in a variable name. We've delayed talking about this because PowerShell is, as you might expect, much more flexible than most languages when it comes to naming variables. In fact, a variable name can contain literally any character you want, as long as you follow a couple of simple rules. There are two notations for variables. The simple notation starts with a dollar sign followed by a sequence of characters, which can include letters, numbers, the underscore, and the colon:

```
PS> $_i_am_variable_number_2 = 2
```

The colon in a variable name is used as a drive separator—more on that in a minute, but first we'll look at the alternate notation for variables. This notation, which requires enclosing the variable name in braces, allows you to use any character in a variable name, including spaces. Here's an example of what that would look like:

```
PS> ${This is a variable name}
```

You can use any character you want in the braces. Even the close brace is allowed if you escape it by writing `} as in ${a`}}.

Earlier, we said the colon character was special in a variable name. This is used to delimit the *drive or namespace qualifier* that the system uses to locate the variable. For example, to access PowerShell global variables, you use the global namespace qualifier:

```
PS> $global:var = 13
PS> $global:var
13
```

This example sets the variable var in the global context to the value 13. You can also use the namespace notation to access variables at other scopes. This is called a *scope modifier.* Scopes will be covered in chapter 6, so we won't say anything more about them here.

Along with the scope modifiers, the namespace notation lets you get at any of the resources surfaced in PowerShell as drives. For example, to get at the environment variables, you use the `env` namespace:

```
PS> $env:SystemRoot
C:\WINDOWS
```

In this example, you retrieved the contents of the `SystemRoot` environment variable. You can use these variables directly in paths. Many of the namespace providers are also available through the variable notation (but you usually have to wrap the path in braces):

```
PS> ${c:old.txt} -replace 'is (red|blue)','was $1' > new.txt
```

The initial construct should now start to make sense. The sequence `${c:old.txt}` is a variable that references the file system provider through the C: drive and retrieves the contexts of the file named old.txt. With this simple notation, you read the contents of a file. No open/read/close—you treat the file itself as an atomic value.

> **NOTE** Using variable notation to access a file can be startling at first, but it's a logical consequence of the unified view model in PowerShell. Because things like variables and functions are available as drives, things such as drives are also available using the variable notation. In effect, this is an application of the Model-View-Controller (MVC) pattern. Each type of data store (file system, variables, environment, and so forth) is a model. The PowerShell provider infrastructure acts as the controller, and there are (by default) two views: the file system navigation view and the variable view. The user is free to choose and use the view most suitable to the task at hand. For the technical minded, the provider must implement the `IContentCmdletProvider` interface for this technique to work.

You can also write to a file using the namespace variable notation. Here's that example rewritten to use variable assignment instead of a redirection operator (remember, earlier we said assignment can be considered a form of redirection in PowerShell):

```
PS> ${c:new.txt} = ${c:old.txt} -replace 'is (red|blue)','was $1'
```

You can even do an in-place update of a file by using the same variable on both sides of the assignment operator. To update the file old.txt instead of making a copy, use

```
PS> ${c:old.txt} = ${c:old.txt} -replace 'is (red|blue)','was $1'
```

All you did was change the name in the variable reference from new.txt to old.txt. This won't work if you use the redirection operator, because the output file is opened before the input file is read. That would have the unfortunate effect of truncating the previous contents of the output file. In the assignment case, the file is read atomically—all at once, processed, and then written atomically. This allows for "in-place" edits because the file is buffered entirely in memory instead of in a temporary file. To do this with redirection, you'd have to save the output to a temporary file and then rename the temporary file so it replaces the original. Now let's leverage this feature along with multiple assignments to swap two files, f1.txt and f2.txt:

```
PS> ${c:f1.txt},${c:f2.txt} = ${c:f2.txt},${c:f1.txt}
```

Issues with using variables to read files

All these examples using variables to read and write files cause the entire contents of files to be loaded into memory as a collection of strings. On modern computers, it's possible to handle very large files this way, but doing this is memory-intensive and, depending on what you're doing, may not be the most efficient solution. Also, in the case of huge files (like Big Data) you'll eventually run out of memory and fail. Keep this in mind when using these techniques.

When accessing a file using the variable namespace notation, PowerShell assumes that it's working with a text file. Because the notation doesn't provide a mechanism for specifying the encoding, you can't use this technique on binary files. You'll have to use the `Get-Content -Raw` and `Set-Content` cmdlets instead.

When the file system provider reads the file, it returns the file as an array of strings. This provides a simple way to get the length of a file:

```
PS> ${c:file.txt}.Length
```

4.8.3 Working with variable cmdlets

You can also work with variables using the variable cmdlets, which let you do a couple of things you can't do directly from the language.

INDIRECTLY SETTING A VARIABLE

Sometimes it's useful to be able to get or set a variable when you won't know the name of that variable until runtime. For example, you might want to initialize a set of variables from a .csv file. You can't do this using the variable syntax in the language because the name of the variable to set is resolved at parse time. First you need a .csv file:

```
PS> Get-Content variables.csv
"Name", "Value"
"srcHost",  "machine1"
"srcPath",  "c:\data\source\mailbox.pst"
"destHost", "machine2"
"destPath", "d:\backup"
```

As you can see, the .csv file is a text file with rows of values separated by commas, hence CSV, or comma-separated values. The choice of `Name` and `Value` was deliberate because these are the names of the parameters on the Set-Variable cmdlet. This cmdlet takes input from the pipeline by property name and value so you can't pipe the output of Import-CSV directly into Set-Variable:

```
PS> Import-Csv .\variables.csv | foreach {Set-Variable -Name $_.Name -Value
    $_.Value}
```

It's as simple as that. If you wanted to see the full details, you could specify the -Verbose parameter to the cmdlets, and it would display each variable as it was set. You can use the parameters on the cmdlet to directly set a variable:

```
PS> Set-Variable -Name srcHost -Value machine3
PS> $srcHost
machine3
```

Now let's see what else you can do with the cmdlets.

GETTING AND SETTING VARIABLE OPTIONS

If there's a cmdlet to set a variable, there should also be a cmdlet to get variables—the Get-Variable cmdlet:

```
PS> Get-Variable -ValueOnly srcHost
machine3
```

Notice this example specified the -ValueOnly parameter. What happens if you don't do that? If -ValueOnly isn't specified, Get-Variable returns the [PSVariable] object that PowerShell uses to represent this object. You can see the Name and Value properties on this object, but there are a lot of other properties as well. Let's explore the Options property. This property allows you to set options on the variable including things like ReadOnly and Constant. The variables you've created so far are still changeable:

```
PS> $srcHost = 'machine9'
PS> $srcHost
machine9
```

But if you're using them to configure the environment, you may not want them to be. To address this, you can set the ReadOnly option using Set-Variable and the -Option parameter:

```
PS> Set-Variable -Option ReadOnly -Name srcHost -Value machine1
PS> $srcHost = 'machine4'
Cannot overwrite variable srcHost because it is read-only
or constant.
At line:1 char:1
+ $srcHost = 'machine4'
+ ~~~~~~~~~~~~~~~~~~~~~
    + CategoryInfo          : WriteError:
(srcHost:String) [], SessionStateUnauthorizedAccessException
    + FullyQualifiedErrorId : VariableNotWritable
```

Now when you try to change the value of this variable, you get an error. The variable is unchanged. If you can't change it, how about removing it? Try the remove command:

```
PS> Remove-Variable srcHost
Remove-Variable : Cannot remove variable srcHost because it is constant or
    read-only. If the variable is read-only,try the operation again specifying
    the Force option.
At line:1 char:1
+ Remove-Variable srcHost
+ ~~~~~~~~~~~~~~~~~~~~~~~~
    + CategoryInfo          : WriteError: (srcHost:String) [Remove-Variable],
    SessionStateUnauthorizedAccessException
    + FullyQualifiedErrorId : VariableNotRemovable,Microsoft.PowerShell.
    Commands.RemoveVariableCommand
```

This failed with the expected error. But you can still force the removal of a read-only variable by using the -Force parameter on Remove-Variable:

```
PS> Remove-Variable -Force srcHost
```

When you specify -Force, the variable is removed and there's no error. If you don't want the value to be changed, you can use the Constant option:

```
PS> Set-Variable -Option Constant -Name srcHost -Value machine1
```

When this option is specified, even using -Force will fail if you try to remove the variable.

USING PSVARIABLE OBJECTS AS REFERENCES

And now for one last trick. You've looked at how to use the name of a variable to access it indirectly. You can bypass the name-lookup process and use the variable reference directly. Let's see how this works. To use a PSVariable object as a reference, first you have to get one. Earlier you saw how to do this with Get-Variable (or its alias gv):

```
PS> $ref = Get-Variable -Name destHost
```

Now that you have a reference, you can use the reference to get the variable's name:

```
PS> $ref.Name
destHost
```

or its value:

```
PS> $ref.Value
machine2
```

Having the reference also allows you to set the variable's value:

```
PS> $ref.Value = 'machine12'
```

When you check the variable using the language syntax, you see the change:

```
PS> $destHost
machine12
```

VARIABLE NAMES VS. VARIABLE VALUES

Here's a tip to keep in mind if you're trying to do these tricks. You need to keep variable *name* and variable *value* firmly separated in your thinking. Remember that $ isn't part of the variable's name. It's part of a token in the PowerShell language indicating that whatever follows the $ is the name of a variable.

The correct way to use the variable cmdlets is to use the variable name without the leading $.

4.8.4   *Splatting a variable*

The last topic that we're going to touch on in this chapter is something called *variable splatting*, which affects how argument variables are passed to commands. Splatting turns each value in a collection into individual arguments. If you have an array with three elements in it, those elements will be passed as three individual arguments. If you have a hashtable, each name-value pair becomes a named parameter–argument pair for the command.

To do this, when referencing the variable that you want to pass to the command, you use @ instead of $ as the prefix to the variable. Here's an example to show how this works. First you need a command to work with—you'll define a function (see chapter 6) that takes three arguments:

```
PS> function s {param ($x, $y, $z)  "x=$x, y=$y, z=$z" }
```

This function uses string expansion to display the value of each of its parameters. Now create an array to pass into this command:

```
PS> $list = 1,2,3
```

The variable $list contains three integers. Pass this using the normal variable notation:

```
PS> s $list
x=1 2 3, y=, z=
```

From the output, you can see all three values in the argument were assigned to the $x parameter. The other two parameters didn't get assigned anything. Next, splat the variable by calling the function with @list instead of $list:

```
PS> s @list
x=1, y=2, z=3
```

This time the output shows each parameter was assigned one member of the array in the variable. What happens if there are more elements than there are variables? Let's try it. First add some elements to the $list variable:

```
PS> $list += 5,6,7
```

Now the variable contains seven elements. Pass this to the function:

```
PS> s @list
x=1, y=2, z=3
```

It appears the last four arguments have vanished. In fact, what has happened is they're assigned to the special variable $args. Let's redefine the function to show this:

```
PS> function s {param ($x, $y, $z)  "$x,$y,$z args=$args" }
```

Print out the three formal arguments $x, $, and $z along with the special $args variable. When you run the new function

```
PS> s @list
1,2,3 args=5 6 7
```

you see the missing arguments have ended up in $args. The most important use of splatting is for enabling one command to effectively call another. Variable parameters and how they're bound are covered in much more detail in chapter 6.

Now that you understand how an array of values can be splatted, let's look at how you work with named parameters. In the previous example, you could have used the explicit names of the parameters to pass things in instead of relying on position. For example, you can use the names to explicitly pass in values for -x and -y, in the reverse order:

```
PS> s -y first -x second
second,first, args=
```

You see second is in the first (x) position and first is in the second (y) position. How can you use splatting to do this? Well, parameters and their values are name-value pairs, and in PowerShell, the way to work with name-value pairs is with hashtables. Let's try this out. First create a hashtable with the values you want:

```
PS> $h = @{x='second'; y='first'}
```

Now splat the hashtable the same way you splatted the variable containing an array:

```
PS> s @h
second,first, args=
```

As before, the x parameter gets the value second, and the y parameter gets the value first. The next question you should have is: What happens if you also want to explicitly pass in -z? Try it:

```
PS> s -z third  @h 1 2 3
second,first,third args=1 2 3
```

It works exactly the way you want. If you specify the parameter both in the hashtable and explicitly on the command line, you'll get an error.

Splatting

By now we're sure you're wondering why this technique is it called *splatting*. Here's the reasoning behind this term. Think of a rock hitting a car windshield. A rock is a solid object that remains intact after it bounces off your car. Next, think of a bug hitting the windshield instead of a rock. Splat! The contents of the bug are distributed over the windshield rather than remaining as a single object. This is what splatting does to a variable argument. It distributes the members of the argument collection as individual arguments instead of remaining a single intact argument. The other rational behind this term is that in Ruby, the operator is *, which is what the aforementioned insect looks like post impact. PowerShell can't use * because it would be confused with the wildcard character. Instead it uses @ because splatting involves arrays and PowerShell uses @ for many array operations. We submit that this is the most visceral mnemonic in the programming language field (at least that we're aware of).

That's all we're going to say about variables here. In chapter 6, we'll return to variables and talk about how variables are defined in functions and how they're scoped in the PowerShell language. We'll also look at splatting again when we cover how commands can call other commands.

4.9   Summary

- The type operators allow you to write scripts that have *polymorphic* behavior. By using these operators to examine the types of objects, you can decide how to process different types of objects. You can also use the operators to dynamically convert from one type of object to another.
- The prefix and postfix operators ++ and -- are a convenient way of incrementing and decrementing variables.
- The subexpression operator $(...) allows you to use arbitrary PowerShell script code anywhere that you can use a value expression. The array subexpression operator @(...) also guarantees that the result of an expression will always be an array.
- PowerShell arrays support both *jagged* arrays—arrays that contain or reference other arrays—and multidimensional arrays. Array slicing is supported, both for

one-dimensional and multidimensional arrays when retrieving values. It isn't supported when assigning to an array index.

- Use the comma operator (,) to build arrays and complex nested data structures such as jagged arrays.

- Use the dot operator (.) for accessing instance members and the double-colon (::) operator for accessing static members. We looked at how to indirectly invoke both properties and methods using these operators.

- The `using namespace` and `using assembly` operators can make it much easier to work directly with .NET types as well as PowerShell classes (see chapter 19).

- The format operator `-f` can be used to perform complex formatting tasks when the default formatting doesn't produce the desired results. The formatting sequences are the same as the sequences used by the `System.String.Format()` method in the .NET framework.

- The PowerShell redirection operators allow you to control where the output and error objects are written. They also allow you to easily discard these objects if so desired by redirecting to `$null`. The redirection operators are "syntactic sugar" for the `Out-File` cmdlet. Using the cmdlet directly allows you to control things such as what file encoding will be used when writing to a file.

- PowerShell variable namespaces let you access a variety of Windows data stores, including environment variables and the file system, using the variable notation.

- It's possible to use the variable cmdlets to set options on variables and do indirect variable accesses using either the variable name or a `PSVariable` object.

- PowerShell uses *splatting* to allow you to take collections of values, either arrays or hashtables, and distribute the members of these collections as individual arguments to a command.

You can perform a lot of tasks using only operators and variables, but to get the most from PowerShell you need to dig further into the language. You'll start that in the next chapter when we introduce the various flow control statements.

Flow control in scripts 5

This chapter covers

- Conditional, looping, and switch statements
- Labels, break, and continue
- Flow control with cmdlets
- Statements as values
- Performance issues

*I may not have gone where I intended to go, but I think I have ended up where I
needed to be.*

—*Douglas Adams,* The Long Dark Tea-Time of the Soul

Previous chapters showed how you can solve surprisingly complex problems in
PowerShell using only commands and operators. Sooner or later, though, if you
want to write significant programs or scripts, you must add custom looping or
branch logic to your solution. Conditional statements enable your code to branch,
dependent on tests you create. Loops execute a block of code one or more times
depending on criteria you set—making your code shorter and more easily maintained. In this chapter, we'll cover PowerShell's take on the traditional programming constructs that all languages possess.

Flow-control behavior in PowerShell

As always, behavioral differences exist with the PowerShell flow-control statements (if, switch, and loop statements) of which new users should be aware. The most obvious difference is PowerShell typically allows the use of pipelines in places where other programming languages only allow simple expressions. This makes the Power-Shell switch statement both a looping construct and a conditional statement—which is why it gets its own group.

The PowerShell flow-control statements and cmdlets are listed in figure 5.1, arranged in groups. Each of the flow-control statements described in this chapter has a corresponding about* help file with additional examples.

Conditional statements

```
If ( <expr> ) { <statements> }
If ( <expr> ) { <statements> } else { <statements> }
If ( <expr> ) { <statements> } elseIf ( <expr> ) { <statements> } else { <statements> }
```

Loop statements

```
while ( <expr> ) { <statements> }
do { <statements> } while ( <expr> )
do { <statements> } until ( <expr> )
for ( <expr>; <expr>; <expr> ){ <statements> }
foreach ($var in <pipeline> ) { <statements> }
```

Break and continue statements

```
break       break <label>
continue    continue <label>
```

The switch statement

```
switch ( <expr> ) { <pattern1> { <statements> } <pattern2> { <statements> } }
switch ( <expr> ) { <pattern1> { <statements> } default { <statements> } }
```

Flow-control cmdlets

```
... | Foreach-Object <scriptblock>
... | Foreach-Object -Begin <scriptblock> -Process <scriptblock> -End <scriptblock>
... | Foreach-Object <operational statement>
... | Where-Object <scriptblock>
... | Where-Object <property> <operator> <value>
```

Figure 5.1 PowerShell flow-control statements

This is also the first time we've dealt with keywords in PowerShell. *Keywords* are part of the core PowerShell language, which means they can't be redefined or aliased. Keywords are case-insensitive, though by convention are written in lowercase in Power-Shell scripts.

NOTE A full list of keywords can be found in the `about_Language_Keywords` help file. You should also view the `about_Reserved_Words` file for words that have special meaning in PowerShell and so shouldn't be used as variable names.

Keywords are also *context-sensitive*, which means they're only treated as keywords in a statement context—usually as the first word in a statement. This is important because it lets you have both a `foreach` loop statement and a `foreach` filter cmdlet, as you'll see later in this chapter. Let's begin our discussion with the conditional statement.

5.1 *Conditional statement*

PowerShell has one main conditional statement: the `if` statement, shown in figure 5.2.

Conditional statements

```
If ( <expr> ) { <statements> }
If ( <expr> ) { <statements> } else { <statements> }
If ( <expr> ) { <statements> } elseIf ( <expr> ) { <statements> } else { <statements> }
```

Figure 5.2 The syntax of the PowerShell conditional statement

This statement lets a script decide whether an action should be performed by evaluating a conditional expression and then selecting the path to follow based on the results of that evaluation. The PowerShell `if` statement is similar to the `if` statement found in most programming languages, though `elseif` is used as a single keyword for subsequent clauses.

Let's work through examples that illustrate how the `if` statement works:

```
PS> if ($x -gt 100){
    "It's greater than one hundred"
} elseif ($x -gt 50){
    "It's greater than 50"
} else {
    "It's not very big."
}
```

In this example, if the variable $x holds a value greater than 100, the string "It's greater than one hundred" will be emitted. If $x is greater than 50 but less than 100, it will emit "It's greater than 50"; otherwise, you'll get "It's not very big." You can have zero or more `elseif` clauses to test different things. The `elseif` and `else` parts are optional, as is the case in other languages.

NOTE `elseif` is a single keyword with no spaces allowed between the words.

The braces are mandatory around the statement lists, even when you have only a single statement, or even no statements, in the list. Leaving out the {} generates a syntax error.

Grammar lessons

The PowerShell grammar technically could support leaving out the braces. In fact, the PowerShell team did enable this feature at one point, but when people tried it out, it resulted in a lot of errors, and the code was harder to read and maintain. The problem is a newline or a semicolon is required to terminate a command. This leads to the situation where you write something like

```
if ($x -gt 3) write x is $x while ($x--) $x
```

and discover, because you've missed the semicolon before the `while` statement, it writes out the `while` statement instead of executing it. In the end, the cost of typing a couple of additional characters was more than offset by a decreased error rate. For this reason, the language design team decided to make the braces mandatory. The braces make the syntactical associations within the code much more obvious.

In scripts, the syntax of the PowerShell flow-control statements is reasonably freeform with respect to whitespace. But when PowerShell is being used interactively, the `else` or `elseif` keyword *has to be on the same line as the previous closing brace*—otherwise, the interpreter will consider the statement complete and execute it immediately.

The PowerShell `if` statement allows a pipeline in the condition clause:

```
PS> if (( Get-ChildItem *.txt | Select-String -List spam ).Length -eq 3)
{
    'Spam! Spam! Spam!'
}
```

In this case, you search all the text files in the current directory looking for the word "spam." If exactly three files contain this word, then you print out

```
Spam! Spam! Spam!
```

NOTE Yes, these are, in fact, Monty Python references. This is where the Python language got its name. If you're familiar with Python or Perl, you'll occasionally recognize cultural references from those languages in PowerShell examples here and elsewhere. Many of the PowerShell development team members had their first scripting experiences with those languages.

Because you can use pipelines and subexpressions in the conditional part of an `if` statement, you can write quite complex conditional expressions in PowerShell. With subexpressions, you can even use an `if` statement inside the condition part of another `if` statement:

```
PS> $x = 10
PS> if ( $( if ($x -lt 5) { $false } else { $x } ) -gt 20)
    {$false} else {$true}
True
```

```
PS> $x = 25
PS> if ( $( if ($x -lt 5) { $false } else { $x } ) -gt 20)
    { $false } else {$true}
False
```

If looking at this makes your head hurt, welcome to the club—it made ours hurt to write it! Let's dissect this statement and see what it's doing. Let's take the inner `if` statement first:

```
if ($x -lt 5) { $false } else { $x }
```

You can see this statement is straightforward. If `$x` is less than the number 5, it returns false; otherwise, it returns the value of `$x`. What the outer `if` statement is doing is also pretty obvious: if the result of the first (formally inner) statement is greater than 20, it returns `$false`; otherwise it returns `$true`.

Now that you can do branching, let's move on to the looping statements.

5.2   *Looping statements*

Looping is the ability to repeat a set of actions some specific number of times, either based on a count or a condition expression. The PowerShell loop statements cover both of these cases and are shown in figure 5.3.

Loop statements

```
while ( <expr> ) { <statements> }
do { <statements> } while ( <expr> )
do { <statements> } until ( <expr> )
for ( <expr>; <expr>; <expr> ){ <statements> }
foreach ($var in <pipeline> ) { <statements> }
```

Figure 5.3   PowerShell loop statements

5.2.1   *while loop*

The `while` statement is PowerShell's basic looping statement. It executes the commands in the statement list as long as a conditional test evaluates to true. A `while` loop tests at the top of the loop. If your conditional test is false at the start, the loop won't execute.

When you execute a `while` statement, PowerShell evaluates the `<expression>` pipeline section of the statement before entering the `<statements>` section. The output from the pipeline is then converted to either *true* or *false*, following the rules for the Boolean interpretation of values described in chapter 2. As long as this result converts to true, PowerShell reruns the `<statements>` section, executing each statement in the list.

For example, the following `while` statement displays the numbers 1–3:

```
$val = 0
while($val -ne 3)
```

```
{
    $val++
    write-host "The number is $val"
}
```

In this example, the condition ($val isn't equal to 3) is true while $val is 0, 1, and 2. Each time through the loop, $val is incremented by 1 using the unary ++ increment operator ($val++). The last time through the loop, $val is 3. When $val equals 3, the condition statement evaluates to false and the loop exits.

You can accomplish all the basic iterative patterns using the while loop, but PowerShell provides several other looping statements for common cases. Let's look at those next.

5.2.2 *do-while loop*

The other while loop variant in PowerShell is the do-while loop. This is a *bottom-tested* variant of the while loop—it always executes the statement list at least once before checking the condition. The while loop from the previous section becomes

```
$val = 0
do
{
    $val++
    Write-Host "The number is $val"
} while ($val -ne 3)
```

The do-while loop is effectively equivalent to

```
<statementList>
while ( <pipeLine> )
{
        <statementList>
}
```

where the two statement lists are identical. The final variation of the while loop is the do-until statement. It's identical to the do-while loop except that the sense of the test is inverted and the statement will loop *until* the condition is true instead of *while* it's true. Our example becomes

```
$val = 0
do {
    $val++
    Write-Host "The number is $val"
} until ($val -ge 3)
```

In this case, the statement loops until $val is greater than or equal to 3. Notice the difference in the way the condition is written, because it's the termination of the condition, not its continuation.

Having covered the two variations of the while loop, we'll look at the for and foreach loops next.

5.2.3   *for loop*

The for loop is the basic counting loop in PowerShell. It's typically used to step through a collection of objects. It's not used often in PowerShell because there are usually better ways for processing a collection. But the for loop is useful when you need to know explicitly which element in the collection you're working with. The canonical example is

```
PS> for ($i=0; $i -lt 5; $i++) { $i }
```

Notice the three pipelines in the parentheses are general pipelines. Conventionally, the initialization pipeline initializes the loop counter variable, the test pipeline tests this variable against some condition, and the increment pipeline increments the loop counter. But because these are arbitrary pipelines, they can do anything. (Note if initialization and increment pipelines produce output, it's discarded by the interpreter.) Here's an example where the condition test is used to generate a side effect that's then used in the statement list body:

```
PS> for ($i=0; $($y = $i*2; $i -lt 5); $i++) { $y }
0
2
4
6
8
```

In this example, the pipeline to be tested is a subexpression that first sets $y to be twice the current value of $i and then compares $i to 5. In the loop body, you use the value in $y to emit the current loop counter times 2. A more practical example would be initializing two values in the initialization pipeline:

```
PS> for ($($result=@(); $i=0); $i -lt 5; $i++) {$result += $i }
PS> "$result"
0 1 2 3 4
```

Here you use a subexpression in the initialization pipeline to set $result to the empty array and the counter variable $i to 0. Then the loop counts up to 5, adding each value to the result array.

Using the for loop is straightforward, but managing the loop counter becomes annoying because it involves writing more code than other loop structures. The foreach loop, by comparison, lets the loop counter count take care of itself, so let's move on.

5.2.4   *foreach loop*

The whole point of using a scripting language for automation is so you can operate on more than one object at a time. PowerShell provides many ways of operating on collections. Perhaps the most straightforward of these mechanisms is the foreach loop.

> **NOTE** To reiterate, when the word "foreach" is used at the beginning of a statement, it's recognized as the `foreach` keyword. When it appears in the middle of a pipeline, it's treated as the name of a command (`ForEach-Object`). When used as a method name, it's treated as the fallback `.foreach()` method. Of all the looping constructs, the `foreach` construct will be the one you use most often.

This statement is syntactically identical to the C# foreach loop except that you don't, and can't, declare the type of the loop variable. This example loops over all the text files (.txt extension) in the current directory, calculating the total size of all the files:

```
PS> $l = 0; foreach ($f in Get-ChildItem *.txt) { $l += $f.length }
```

First you set the variable that will hold the total length to 0. Then, in the `foreach` loop, you use the `Get-ChildItem` command to get a list of the text files in the current directory. The `foreach` statement assigns elements from this list one at a time to the loop variable `$f` and then executes the statement list with this variable set. At the end of the statement, `$f` will retain the last value that was assigned to it, which is the last value in the list. Compare this example to the `for` loop examples in the previous section. Because you don't have to manually deal with the loop counter and explicit indexing, this example is significantly simpler.

> **NOTE** In C#, the `foreach` loop variable is local to the body of the loop and is undefined outside the loop. This isn't the case in PowerShell; the loop variable is another variable in the current scope. After the loop has finished executing, the variable is still visible and accessible outside the loop and will be set to the last element in the list. If you want to have a locally scoped variable, you can do this with scriptblocks, which are discussed in detail in chapter 7.

EVALUATION ORDER IN THE FOREACH LOOP

It's important to note that a `foreach` loop doesn't stream the results of the pipeline. The pipeline to loop over is run to completion, and only then does the loop body begin executing. Let's take a second to compare this behavior with the way the `ForEach-Object` cmdlet works. Using the `ForEach-Object` cmdlet, this statement would look like

```
PS> Get-ChildItem *.txt | ForEach-Object { $l += $_.length }
```

In the case of the `ForEach-Object`, the statement body is executed as soon as each object is produced. In the `foreach` statement, all the objects are collected before the loop body begins to execute. This has two implications.

First, because in the `foreach` statement case all the objects are gathered at once, you need to have enough memory to hold all these objects. In the `ForEach-Object` case, only one object is read at a time, so less storage is required. From this, you'd think `ForEach-Object` should always be preferred. In the bulk-read case, though, there are some optimizations that the `foreach` statement does which allow it to perform significantly faster than the ForEach-Object cmdlet. The result is a classic speed versus space trade-off. In practice, you rarely need to consider these issues, so use whichever seems most appropriate to the solution at hand.

> **NOTE** The ForEach-Object cmdlet is covered later in this chapter. For Ruby language fans, ForEach-Object is effectively equivalent to the .map() operator.

Second, in the ForEach-Object case, the execution of the pipeline element generating the object is interleaved with the execution of the ForEach-Object cmdlet. The command generates one object at a time and then passes it to foreach for processing before generating the next element. This means the statement list can affect how subsequent pipeline input objects are generated.

> **NOTE** Unlike traditional shells where each command is run in a separate process and can therefore run at the same time, in PowerShell they're alternating—the command on the left runs and produces an object, and then the command on the right runs.

USING THE $FOREACH LOOP ENUMERATOR IN THE FOREACH STATEMENT

Executing the foreach statement also defines a special variable for the duration of the loop. This is the $foreach variable, and it's bound to the *loop enumerator*. An enumerator is a .NET object that captures the current position in a sequence of objects. The foreach statement keeps track of where it is in the collection through the loop enumerator. By manipulating the loop enumerator, you can skip forward in the loop. Here's an example:

```
PS> foreach ($i in 1..10)
{ [void] $foreach.MoveNext(); $i + $foreach.Current }
3
7
11
15
19
```

In this example, the foreach loop iterates over the collection of numbers from 1 to 10. In the body of the loop, the enumerator is used to advance the loop to the next element. It does this by calling the $foreach.MoveNext() method and then retrieving the next value using $foreach.Current. This lets you sum up each pair of numbers—(1,2), (3,4), and so on—as the loop iterates.

> **NOTE** The foreach statement can iterate over anything PowerShell considers enumerable—anything that implements the .NET IEnumerable interface. PowerShell adapts that slightly. There are some classes that implement IEnumerable that PowerShell doesn't consider enumerable including strings and hashtables. Because PowerShell unravels collections freely, you don't want a string to suddenly be turned into a stream of characters or a hashtable to be shredded into a sequence of key-value pairs. Hashtables in particular are com-

monly used as lightweight, typeless objects in the PowerShell environment, so you need to preserve their scalar nature.

The value stored in $foreach is an instance of an object that implements the [System .Collections.IEnumerator] interface. Here's an example that shows how to look at the members that are available on this object:

```
PS> [System.Collections.IEnumerator].Getmembers()|foreach{"$_"}
Boolean MoveNext()
System.Object get_Current()
Void Reset()
System.Object Current
```

The output of this statement shows the Current and MoveNext() members you've used. There's also a Reset() member that will reset the enumerator to the start of the collection.

Finally, you need to know how the foreach statement treats scalar objects. Because of the way pipelines work, you don't know ahead of time if the pipeline will return a collection or a single scalar object. In particular, if the pipeline returns a single object, you can't tell if it's returning a scalar or a collection consisting of one object. You can use the @(...) construction described in chapter 4 to force an array interpretation, but this ambiguity is common enough that the foreach statement takes care of this by itself. A scalar object in the foreach statement is automatically treated as a one-element collection:

```
PS> foreach ($i in "hi") {$i }
hi
```

In this example, the value to iterate over is the scalar string "hi". The loop executes exactly once, printing hi. This usually works great, but null values can cause some problems.

THE FOREACH LOOP AND $NULL

What happens if the value to iterate over is $null? Let's find out:

```
PS> foreach ($i in $null) { "executing" }
```

Nothing happens. This will be a change if you used PowerShell v2 where $null was treated as a scalar value so the loop would run once.

> **NOTE** $null is treated as an empty collection in PowerShell v3 and later. In effect, you can't iterate over any collection that's empty (no elements).

If you pass in an array of nulls

```
PS> foreach ($i in $null, $null, $null) {"hi"}
```

the statement prints hi three times because there were three elements in the array, even though the values of those elements are null.

On that note, let's move on to a slightly different topic and talk about break, continue, and using labeled loops to exit nested loop statements.

5.3 *Labels, break, and continue*

The loops you saw in the previous section performed a structured exit in that they ran until meeting the criteria established for terminating the loop. There are many occasions when you need to perform an unstructured exit from a loop. Your code may be, for example, periodically testing connectivity to a remote machine after it's been rebooted and you want to exit the loop when connectivity is established. In this section, we'll discuss how to do non-structured exits from the various looping statements using the break and continue statements shown in figure 5.4. We'll also cover *labeled loops* and how they work with break and continue.

Break and continue statements

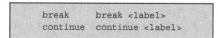

```
break        break <label>
continue     continue <label>
```

Figure 5.4   The PowerShell break and continue statements, which may optionally take a label indicating which loop statement to break to.

Let's look at some simple examples. Here's a while loop that stops counting at 5:

```
PS> $i=0; while ($true) { if ($i++ -ge 5) { break } $i }
```

Notice in this example that the while loop condition is $true. This loop would run forever were it not for the break statement. As soon as $i hits 5, the break statement is executed and the loop terminates. Now let's look at the continue statement. In this example, you have a foreach loop that loops over the numbers from 1 to 10:

```
PS> foreach ($i in 1..10)
{
    if ($i % 2)
    {
        continue
    }
    $i
}

2
4
6
8
10
```

If the number isn't evenly divisible by 2, then the continue statement is executed (remember that 0 will evaluate to $false in the if condition). Where the break statement immediately terminates the loop, the continue statement causes the flow of execution to jump back to the beginning of the loop and move on to the next iteration. The end result is only even numbers are emitted. The continue statement skips the line that would have printed the odd numbers.

So, the basic `break` and `continue` statements can handle flow control in a single loop. But what about nested loops? This is where *labels* come in. Before the initial keyword on any of PowerShell's loop statements, you can add a label naming that statement. Then you can use the `break` and `continue` keywords to jump to that statement. Here's a simple example:

```
:outer while (1)
{
    while(1)
    {
        break outer;
    }
}
```

In this example, without the `break` statement, the loop would repeat forever. Instead, the `break` will take you out of both the inner and outer loops.

> **NOTE** In PowerShell, labeled `break` and `continue` statements have one rather unusual but occasionally useful characteristic: They'll continue to search up the call stack until a matching label is found. This search will even cross script and function call boundaries. This means a break inside a function inside a script can transfer control to an enclosing loop in the calling script. This allows for wide-ranging transfer of control. This will make more sense when you get to chapter 6, where functions are introduced.

One last thing to know about the `break` and `continue` statements: the name of the label to jump to is an expression, not a constant value. You could, for example, use a variable to name the target of the statement. Let's try this out. First set up a variable to hold the target name:

```
PS> $target = 'foo'
```

Now use it in a loop. In this loop, if the least significant bit in the value stored in $i is 1 (yet another way to test for odd numbers), you skip to the next iteration of the loop named by $target:

```
PS> :foo foreach ($i in 1..10) {
  if ($i -band 1) { continue $target } $i
}
```

This produces a list of the even numbers in the range 1..10.

At this point, we've covered all of the basic PowerShell flow-control statements, as well as using labels and `break` and `continue` to do nonlocal flow-control transfers. Now let's move on to the `switch` statement, which in PowerShell combines both looping and branching capabilities.

5.4   *switch statement*

The if statement in section 5.1 is usually used to test a single criterion with flow branching depending on the result. When you need to test multiple criteria it's possible to write multiple if statements (or many elseif statements), but using a switch statement gives you more options for less code. The switch statement, shown in figure 5.5, is the most powerful statement in the PowerShell language: It combines pattern matching, branching, and iteration into a single control structure. This is why it gets its own section.

The switch statement

```
switch ( <expr> ) { <pattern1> { <statements> } <pattern2> { <statements> } }
switch ( <expr> ) { <pattern1> { <statements> } default { <statements> } }
```

Figure 5.5   PowerShell switch **statement syntax**

At the most basic level, the switch statement in PowerShell is a way of selecting an action based on a particular value. But the PowerShell switch statement has a number of additional capabilities. It can be used as a looping construct where it processes a collection of objects instead of a single object. It supports the advanced pattern-matching features that you've seen with the -match and -like operators. (How the pattern is matched depends on the flags specified to the switch statement.) It can be used to efficiently process an entire file in a single statement.

5.4.1   *Basic use of the switch statement*

Let's begin by exploring the basic functions of the switch statement:

```
PS> switch (1) { 1 { 'One' } 2 { 'Two' } }
One
```

The value to switch on is in the parentheses after the switch keyword. In this example, it's the number 1. That value is matched against the pattern in each clause, and *all matching actions are taken.* You'll see how to change this in a second.

In this example, the switch value matches 1, so that clause emits the string "One". If you change the switch value to 2, you get two as the result.

What if you have two clauses that match the switch value?

```
PS> switch (2) { 1 { 'One' } 2 { 'Two' } 2 {'another 2'} }
Two
another 2
```

You can see both actions are executed. As we stated earlier, the switch statement executes all clauses that match the switch value. If you want to stop at the first match, you use the break statement:

```
PS> switch (2) {1 {'One'} 2 {'Two'; break} 2 {'another 2'}}
Two
```

This causes the matching process to stop after the first matching statement was executed. But what happens if no statements match? Well, the statement quietly returns nothing. A default action can be used as a safety net in this case using the default clause:

```
PS> switch (3) { 1 { 'One' } 2 { 'Two' } default {'default'} }
default
```

In this example, when the switch value is 3, no clause matches and the default clause is run. But when there's a match, the default isn't run, as it's not considered a match.

This covers the basic mode of operation. Now let's move on to more advanced features.

5.4.2 Using wildcard patterns with the switch statement

By default, the matching clauses make an equivalence comparison against the object in the clause. If the matching object is a string, the check is done in a case-insensitive way, as you see in the next example:

```
PS> switch ('abc') {'abc' {'one'} 'ABC' {'two'}}
one
two
```

The switch value 'abc' in this example was matched by both 'abc' and 'ABC'. You can change this behavior by specifying the -CaseSensitive option:

```
PS> switch -case ('abc') {'abc' {'one'} 'ABC' {'two'}}
one
```

Now the match occurs only when the case of the elements match.

> **NOTE** We only used -case instead of the full name of -CaseSensitive. Parameters can be abbreviated provided ambiguous resolution to two, or more, parameter names is avoided.

Next, let's discuss the next switch option, -wildcard. When -wildcard is specified, the switch value is converted into a string, and the tests are conducted using the wildcard pattern. This is shown here:

```
PS> switch -wildcard ('abc') {a* {'astar'} *c {'starc'}}
astar
starc
```

In the example, the pattern a* matches anything that begins with the letter "a," and the pattern *c matches anything that ends with the letter "c." Again, all matching clauses are executed.

There's one more element to mention at this point. When a clause is matched, the element that matched is always assigned to the variable $_ before running the clause (you can use $psitem instead of $_ in PowerShell v3 and later). When matching on patterns, it's much more useful to be able to get at the object that matched. If you're matching against filename extensions, for example, you'd want to get at the full filename to do any processing on that file. Here's a basic example that shows how to use $_ in your code:

```
PS> switch -wildcard ('abc') {a* {"a*: $_"} *c {"*c: $_"}}
a*: abc
*c: abc
```

The results show $_ was replaced by the full string of the switch value.

5.4.3 *Using regular expressions with the switch statement*

As we discussed in chapter 3, the wildcard patterns, though useful, have limited capabilities. For more sophisticated pattern matching, you use regular expressions. Regular expressions are available in the switch statement through the -regex flag. Let's rewrite the previous example using regular expressions instead of wildcards:

```
PS> switch -regex ('abc') {^a {"a*: $_"} 'c$' {"*c: $_"}}
a*: abc
*c: abc
```

As you see, $_ is still bound to the entire matching key. But one of the most powerful features of regular expressions is submatches. A submatch, or *capture*, is a portion of the regular expression that's enclosed in parentheses, as discussed in chapter 3 with the -match operator. The $matches variable provides access to the submatches from the switch statement. The next example shows how this works:

```
PS> switch -regex ('abc') {'(^a)(.*$)' {$matches}}
```

Key	Value
2	bc
1	a
0	abc

In the result shown here, $matches[0] is the overall key; $matches[1] is the first submatch, in this case the leading a; and $matches[2] is the remainder of the string. As always, matching is case-insensitive by default, but you can specify the -case option to make it case-sensitive, as shown here:

```
PS> switch -regex ('abc') {'(^A)(.*$)' {$matches}}
```

Key	Value
2	bc
1	a
0	abc

```
PS> switch -regex -case  ('abc') {'(^A)(.*$)' {$matches}}
```

In the first command, you changed the match pattern from a to A, and the match still succeeded because case was ignored. In the second command, you added the -case flag, and this time the match didn't succeed.

What if you need something a bit more sophisticated than a simple pattern match? You may want to split the range of possible values into groups so you'll need to test if the switch value is greater than or less than (or both) particular values. The switch statement lets you handle this by specifying an expression in braces instead of a pattern. In the next example, you specify two expressions that check against the switch value. Again, the switch value is made available through the variable $_:

```
PS> switch (8) {
      {$_ -gt 3} {'greater than three'}
      {$_ -gt 7} {'greater than 7'}
}

greater than three
greater than 7
```

Both clauses fired as they both match. You can use these matching clauses with any of the other three matching modes:

```
PS> switch (8) {
      {$_ -gt 3} {'greater than three'}
             8 {"Was $_"}
}

greater than three
Was 8
```

The first expression, {$_ -gt 3}, evaluated to true, so "greater than three" was printed, and the switch value matched 8 so "Was 8" also printed (where $_ was replaced by the matching value).

Now you have exact matches, pattern matches, conditional matches, and the default clause. But what about the switch value itself? So far, all the examples have been simple scalar values. What happens if you specify a collection of values? This is where the switch statement acts like a form of loop.

NOTE switch works like the other looping statements in that the expression in the parentheses is fully evaluated before it starts iterating over the individual values.

Let's look at another example where you specify an array of values:

```
PS> switch(1,2,3,4,5,6) {
      {$_ % 2} {"Odd $_"; continue}
            4 {'FOUR'}
      default {"Even $_"}
}

Odd 1
Even 2
```

```
Odd 3
FOUR
Odd 5
Even 6
```

In this example, the `switch` value is `1,2,3,4,5,6` (you could use the `range` operator and simplify to `1..6`). The `switch` statement loops over the collection, testing each element against all the clauses. The first clause returns "Odd $_" if the current switch element isn't evenly divisible by 2. The next clause prints out "FOUR" if the value is 4. The default clause prints out "Even $_" if the number is even. Note the use of `continue` in the first clause. This tells the `switch` statement to stop matching any further clauses and move on to the next element in the collection. In this instance, the `switch` statement is working in the same way that the `continue` statement works in the other loops. It skips the remainder of the body of the loop and continues on with the next loop iteration. What happens if you used `break` instead of `continue`?

As with the other loops, `break` doesn't skip the remainder of the current iteration; it terminates the overall loop processing.

Iterating over a fixed collection isn't that interesting. In fact, you can use a pipeline in the switch value, as the next example shows. In this example, you want to count the number of DLLs, text files, and log files in the directory c:\windows. First you initialize the counter variables:

```
PS> $dll=$txt=$log=0
```

Now you run the `switch` statement. This `switch` statement uses wildcard patterns to match the extensions on the filenames. The associated actions increment a variable for each extension type:

```
PS> switch -wildcard (Get-ChildItem c:\windows) {
        *.dll {$dll++}
        *.txt {$txt++}
        *.log {$log++}
}
```

Once you have the totals, display them:

```
PS> "dlls: $dll text files: $txt log files: $log"
dlls: 6 text files: 9 log files: 120
```

Note in this example the pipeline element is being matched against every clause. Because a file can't have more than one extension, this doesn't affect the output, but it does affect performance somewhat.

> **NOTE** It's faster to include a `continue` statement after each clause so the matching process stops as soon as the first match succeeds.

Here's something else we glossed over earlier in our discussion of $_ —it always contains the object that it was matched against. This is important to understand when you're using the pattern-matching modes of the switch statement. The pattern matches create a string representation of the object to match against, but $_ is still bound to the original object. Here's an example that illustrates this point. This is the same as the previous example, but this time, instead of counting the number of files, you want to calculate the total size of all the files having a particular extension. Here are the revised commands:

```
PS> $dll=$txt=$log=0
PS> switch -wildcard (Get-ChildItem c:\windows) {
     *.dll {$dll += $_.length; continue}
     *.txt {$txt += $_.length; continue}
     *.log {$log += $_.length; continue}
}
PS> "dlls: $dll text files: $txt log files: $log"
dlls: 166913 text files: 1866711 log files: 6669437
```

Notice how you're using $_.length to get the length of the matching file object. If $_ were bound to the matching string, you'd be counting the lengths of the filenames instead of the lengths of the files.

5.4.4 *Processing files with the switch statement*

There's one last mode of operation for the switch statement to discuss: the -file option. Instead of specifying an expression to iterate over as the switch value, the -file option allows you to name a file to process. Here's an example that processes the files in your Temp folder. Start by creating the file:

```
PS> Get-ChildItem $env:TEMP -File |
Select-Object -ExpandProperty Name |
Out-File $env:TEMP\files.txt
```

Again, start by initializing the counter variables. Use the -regex and -file options to access and scan the file and check for particular extensions:

```
PS> $lg=$tm=$cr=0
PS> switch -regex -file $env:TEMP\files.txt {
     '\.log$' {$lg++}
     '\.tmp$' {$tm++}
     '\.cvr$' {$cr++}
}
PS> "log:$lg tmp:$tm cvr:$cr"
log:0 tmp:5 cvr:0
```

Now it's possible to do the same thing by using Get-Content or even the file system name trick you learned in chapter 4:

```
PS> $lg=$tm=$cr=0
PS> switch -regex (${c:\temp\files.txt}) {
     '\.log$' {$lg++}
     '\.tmp$' {$tm++}
     '\.cvr$' {$cr++}
}
PS> "log:$lg tmp:$tm cvr:$cr"
```

This code uses ${c:\temp\files.txt} to access the file content instead of -file. Why have the -file option? There are two reasons.

The -file operation reads one line at a time, so it uses less memory than the Get-Content cmdlet, which has to read the entire file into memory before processing. Also, because -file option is part of the PowerShell language, the interpreter can do some optimizations, which gives -file performance advantages.

So, overall, the -file option can potentially give you both speed and space advantages in some cases (the space advantage typically being the more significant, and therefore the more important of the two). When your task involves processing a lot of text files, the -file switch can be a useful tool.

5.4.5 *Using the $switch loop enumerator in the switch statement*

One more point: As the foreach loop used $foreach to hold the loop enumerator, the switch statement uses $switch to hold the switch loop enumerator. This is useful in a common pattern—processing a list of options. Say you have a list of options where the option -b takes an argument and -a, -c, and -d don't. You'll write a switch statement to process a list of these arguments. First set up a list of test options. For convenience, start with a string and then use the -split operator to break it into an array of elements:

```
PS> $options= -split '-a -b Hello -c'
```

Next initialize the set of variables that will correspond to the flags:

```
PS> $a=$c=$d=$false
PS> $b=$null
```

Now you can write your switch statement. The interesting clause is the one that handles -b. This clause uses the enumerator stored in $switch to advance the item being processed to the next element in the list. Use a cast to [void] to discard the return value from the call to $switch.MoveNext()(more on that later). Then use $switch.Current to retrieve the next value and store it in $b. The loop continues processing the remaining arguments in the list, as follows:

```
PS> switch ($options){
    '-a' { $a=$true }
    '-b' { [void] $switch.MoveNext(); $b= $switch.Current }
    '-c' { $c=$true }
    '-d' { $d=$true }
}
```

The last step in this example is to print the arguments in the list to make sure they were all set properly:

```
PS> "a=$a b=$b c=$c d=$d"
a=True b=Hello c=True d=False
```

You see $a and $c are true, $b contains the argument "Hello", and $d is still false because it wasn't in your list of test options. The option list has been processed correctly.

> **NOTE** This isn't a robust example because it's missing all error handling. In a complete example, you'd have a default clause that generated errors for unexpected options. Also, in the clause that processes the argument for -b, rather than discarding the result of MoveNext() it should check the result and generate an error if it returns false. This would indicate that there are no more elements in the collection, so -b would be missing its mandatory argument.

This finishes the last of the flow-control statements in the PowerShell language. In the next section, we'll go over a couple of the cmdlets that let you control the flow of your script in a manner similar to the flow-control statements.

5.5 Flow control using cmdlets

PowerShell's control statements are part of the language proper, but there are also cmdlets, shown in figure 5.6, that can be used to accomplish similar operations.

Flow-control cmdlets

```
... | Foreach-Object <scriptblock>
... | Foreach-Object -Begin <scriptblock> -Process <scriptblock> -End <scriptblock>
... | Foreach-Object <operational statement>
... | Where-Object <scriptblock>
... | Where-Object <property> <operator> <value>
```

Figure 5.6 Flow-control cmdlets

These cmdlets use blocks of PowerShell script enclosed in braces to provide the "body" of the control statement. These pieces of script are called *scriptblocks* and are described in detail in chapter 8. The two most frequent flow-control cmdlets that you'll encounter are ForEach-Object and Where-Object.

5.5.1 ForEach-Object cmdlet

There are two ways to construct a ForEach-Object (aliased as foreach) command. The first, which has always been present in PowerShell, uses a scriptblock to specify the operation. The examples you've seen so far follow this model. In PowerShell v3 it became possible to create an operation statement that specifies a property value or method name. We'll start with the scriptblock version.

FOREACH-OBJECT WITH SCRIPTBLOCK

The ForEach-Object cmdlet operates on each object in a pipeline in much the same way that the foreach statement operates on the set of values that are provided to it. For example, here's a foreach statement that prints the size of each text file in the current directory:

```
PS> foreach ($f in Get-ChildItem *.txt) { $f.length }
```

Using the `ForEach-Object` cmdlet, the same task can be accomplished this way:

```
PS> Get-ChildItem *.txt | foreach-object {$_.length}
```

The results are the same, so what's the difference? One obvious difference is you don't have to create a new variable name to hold the loop value. The automatic variable `$_` is used as the loop variable. In PowerShell v3 and later, `$psitem` can be used as an alternative loop variable.

> **NOTE** Automatic variables are common in scripting languages. These variables aren't directly assigned in scripts. Instead, they're set as the side effect of an operation. Perl inspired the use of `$_` in PowerShell. `$psitem` was introduced to resolve some of the confusion around `$_`. Automatic variables can help reduce the size of a script, but they can also make a script hard to read and difficult to reuse because *your* use of automatics may collide with *ours*. From a design perspective, our approach with automatic variables follows the salt curve. A little salt makes everything taste better. Too much salt makes food inedible. The language design team tried to keep the use of automatics in PowerShell at the "just right" level. This is always a subjective judgment. Some people really like salt.

A subtler difference, as discussed previously, is that the loop is processed one object at a time. In a normal `foreach` loop, the entire list of values is generated before a single value is processed. In the `ForEach-Object` pipeline, each object is generated and then passed to the cmdlet for processing.

You'll end up using the `ForEach-Object` cmdlet a lot in command lines to perform simple transformations on objects. Given the frequency of use, there are two standard aliases for this cmdlet. The first one is (obviously) `foreach`.

> **NOTE** When `foreach` is the first word in a statement, it's a keyword; otherwise it's the name of a command.

Now let's look at the second alias. Even though `foreach` is significantly shorter than `ForEach-Object`, there have still been times when users wanted it to be even shorter.

> **NOTE** Users wanted to get rid of this notation entirely and have `foreach` be implied by an open brace following the pipe symbol. This would have made about half of PowerShell users happy. Unfortunately, the other half was adamant that the implied operation be `Where-Object` instead of `ForEach-Object`.

Where extreme brevity is required, there's a second built-in alias that's the percent sign (`%`). Now readers are saying, "You told us the percent sign is the modulus operator!" Well, that's true, *but only when it's used as a binary operator*. If it appears as the first symbol in a statement, it has no special meaning, so you can use it as an alias for `ForEach-Object`. As with keywords, operators are also context-sensitive.

The % alias results in concise, but hard-to-read, statements such as the following, which prints the numbers from 1 to 5, times 2:

```
PS> 1..5|%{$_*2}
```

Clearly this construction is great for interactive use where brevity is important, but it shouldn't be used when writing scripts.

The last thing to know about the ForEach-Object cmdlet is it can take multiple scriptblocks. If three scriptblocks are specified, the first one is run before any objects are processed, the second is run once for each object, and the last is run after all objects have been processed. This is good for conducting accumulation-type operations. Here's another variation that sums the number of handles used by the service host svchost processes:

```
PS> gps svchost | %{$t=0}{$t+=$_.handles}{$t}
6322
```

The standard alias for Get-Process is gps. This is used to get a list of processes where the process name matches svchost. These process objects are then piped into ForEach -Object, where the handle counts are summed up in $t and then emitted in the last scriptblock. This example uses the % alias to show how concise these expressions can be. In an interactive environment, brevity is important. The full (more readable) version of this code would be

```
PS> Get-Process -Name svchost |
foreach -Begin {$t=0} -Process {$t+=$_.handles} -End {$t}
```

And here's something to keep in mind when using ForEach-Object. The ForEach-Object cmdlet works like all cmdlets: if the output object is a collection, it gets unraveled. One way to suppress this behavior is to use the unary comma operator. For example, in the following, you assign $a an array of two elements, the second of which is a nested array:

```
PS> $a =  1,(2,3)
```

When you run it through ForEach-Object, you'll find that the length of the result is now 3, and the second element in the result is the number 2:

```
PS> $b = $a | foreach { $_ }
PS> $b.length
3
PS> $b[1]
2
```

In effect, the result has been "flattened." But if you use the unary comma operator before the $_ variable, the result has the same structure as the original array:

```
PS> $b = $a | foreach { , $_ }
PS> $b.length
2
```

```
PS> $b[1]
2
3
```

When chaining `foreach` cmdlets, you need to repeat the pattern at each stage:

```
PS> $b = $a | foreach { , $_ } | foreach { , $_ }
```

Why don't you preserve the structure as you pass the elements through instead of unraveling by default? Well, both behaviors are, in fact, useful. Consider the following example, which returns a list of loaded module names:

```
PS> Get-Process | foreach {$_.modules} | sort -unique modulename
```

Here the unraveling is exactly what you want. When we were designing PowerShell, we considered both cases; and in applications, on average, unraveling by default was usually what we needed. Unfortunately, it does present something of a cognitive bump that surprises users learning to use PowerShell.

USING THE RETURN STATEMENT WITH FOREACH-OBJECT

Although the `ForEach-Object` cmdlet looks like a PowerShell statement, remember it's in fact a command, and the body of code it executes is a scriptblock, also known as an *anonymous function.* (By *anonymous,* we mean we haven't given it a name. We cover this in detail in section 10.1.)

The important thing to know is the `return` statement (see chapter 6), when used in the scriptblock argument to `ForEach-Object`, exits only from the `ForEach-Object` scriptblock, not from the function or script that's calling `ForEach-Object`. If you want to return out of a function or script in a `foreach` loop, either use the `foreach` statement where the `return` will work as desired, or use the nonlocal labeled `break` statement discussed earlier in this chapter.

HOW FOREACH-OBJECT PROCESSES ITS ARGUMENTS

Let's talk about how the `ForEach-Object` cmdlet processes its argument scriptblocks. A reader of the first edition of this book observed what he thought was an inconsistency between how the cmdlet is documented and how the following example behaves:

```
$words | ForEach-Object {$h=@{}} {$h[$_] += 1}
```

The help text for the cmdlet (use `help ForEach-Object -Full` to see this text) says that the `-Process` parameter is the only positional parameter in the parameter set for the scriptblock `ForEach-Object` option and that it's in position 1. Therefore, according to the help file, because the `-Begin` parameter isn't positional, the example shouldn't work. This led the reader to assume that either there was an error in the help file or that he misunderstood the idea of positional parameters.

In fact, the help file is correct (because the cmdlet information is extracted from the code), but the way it works is tricky.

If you look at the signature of the -Process parameter, you'll see that, yes, it's positional, but it also takes a collection of scriptblocks and receives all remaining unbound arguments. In the case of

```
PS> Get-ChildItem | foreach {$sum=0} {$sum++} {$sum}
```

the -Process parameter is getting an array of three scriptblocks, whereas -Begin and -End are empty. Now here's the trick. If -Begin is empty and -Process has more than two scriptblocks in the collection, then the first one is treated as the -Begin scriptblock and the second one is treated as the -Process scriptblock. If -Begin is specified but -End isn't and there are two scriptblocks, then the first one is treated as the Process clause and the second one is the End clause. If both -Begin and -End are specified, the remaining arguments will be treated as multiple Process clauses. This allows

```
PS> Get-ChildItem | foreach {$sum=0} {$sum++} {$sum}
PS> Get-ChildItem | foreach -begin {$sum=0} {$sum++} {$sum}
PS> Get-ChildItem | foreach {$sum=0} {$sum++} -end {$sum}
PS> Get-ChildItem | foreach -begin {$sum=0} {$sum++} -end {$sum}
PS> Get-ChildItem | foreach -begin {$sum=0} -process {$sum++} -end {$sum}
```

to work as expected and deliver the same result.

> **NOTE** Using the parameters to explicitly assign scriptblocks to -begin, -process, and -end, as in the last example, is the best practice as it's much easier to understand when you look at the code a long time after writing.

On that note, we're finished with our discussion of ForEach-Object using a scriptblock. Now, it's time to look at the newer option—using an operation statement.

FOREACH-OBJECT WITH OPERATION STATEMENT

PowerShell v3 introduced a more natural language version of ForEach-Object that uses an operational statement rather than a scriptblock. As an example, consider the following:

```
PS> Get-Process | ForEach-Object {$psitem.ProcessName}
```

This displays the process name for each process on the system. Using an operation statement, this becomes

```
PS> Get-Process | ForEach-Object ProcessName
```

or

```
PS> Get-Process | ForEach-Object -MemberName ProcessName
```

if the parameter name is used.

You can only access a single property in this manner. This will fail:

```
PS> Get-Process | ForEach-Object ProcessName, Handles
```

Using methods on the pipeline objects is similar. For instance:

```
PS> 'test', 'strings' | foreach {$_.ToUpper()}
```

can be written as

```
PS> 'test', 'strings' | foreach ToUpper
```

if the method you're using requires arguments:

```
PS> 'test', 'strings' | foreach Replace -ArgumentList 'st', 'AB'
```

As with the property name option, you can only use a single method using this approach.

We'll touch on ForEach-Object again in chapter 7 when we discuss scriptblocks, but for now, let's move on to the other flow-control cmdlet commonly used in PowerShell (which, by the way, also uses scriptblocks—you may detect a theme here).

5.5.2   *Where-Object cmdlet*

The other common flow-control cmdlet is Where-Object which is used to select objects from a stream. The Where-Object cmdlet works in one of two ways. The first way is it takes each pipeline element it receives as input, executes its scriptblock (see!) argument, passing in the current pipeline element as $_, and then, if the scriptblock evaluates to true, the element is written to the pipeline. The second way involves testing an individual property against a given value with a specific operator. We'll come to that version in a minute but first we'll look at using a scriptblock.

As an example, here's yet another way to select even numbers from a sequence of integers:

```
PS> 1..10 | where {-not ($_ -band 1)}
```

The scriptblock enclosed in the braces receives each pipeline element, one after another. If the least significant bit in the element is 1, then the scriptblock returns the logical complement of that value ($false) and that element is discarded. If the least significant bit is 0, the logical complement of that is $true and the element is written to the output pipeline. Notice the common alias for Where-Object is where. And, as with ForEach-Object, because this construction is so commonly used interactively, there's an additional alias, which is the question mark (?). This allows the previous example to be written as

```
PS> 1..10|?{!($_-band 1)}
```

Again, this is brief, but it looks like the cat walked across the keyboard (trust us on this one). Although this is fine for interactive use, don't use it in scripts because it's hard to understand and maintain.

As another, more compelling example of "software by cats," here's a pathological example that combines elements from the last few chapters—type casts, operators, and the flow-control cmdlets—to generate a list of strings of even-numbered letters in the alphabet, where the length of the string matches the ordinal number in the alphabet ("A" is 1, "B" is 2, and so on):

```
PS> 1..26|?{!($_-band 1)}|%{[string][char]([int][char]'A'+$_-1)*$_}
BB
DDDD
...
XXXXXXXXXXXXXXXXXXXXXXXX
ZZZZZZZZZZZZZZZZZZZZZZZZZZ
```

The output is fairly self-explanatory, but the code isn't. Figuring out how this works is left as an exercise to the reader and as a cautionary tale not to foist this sort of rubbish on unsuspecting coworkers. They know where you live.

WHERE-OBJECT AND GET-CONTENT'S -READCOUNT PARAMETER

On occasion, a question comes up about the Get-Content (alias gc) cmdlet and how its -ReadCount parameter works. This can be an issue particularly when using this cmdlet and parameter with Where-Object to filter the output of Get-Content. The issue comes up when the read count is greater than 1. This causes PowerShell to act as if some of the objects returned from Get-Content are being skipped and affects both ForEach-Object and Where-Object. After all, these cmdlets are supposed to process or filter the input one object at a time, and this isn't what appears to be happening.

Here's what's going on. Unfortunately, the -ReadCount parameter has a confusing name. From the PowerShell user's perspective, it has nothing to do with reading. What it does is control the number for records *written* to the next pipeline element, in this case Where-Object or ForEach-Object. The following examples illustrate how this works. In these examples, you'll use a simple text file named test.txt, which contains ten lines of text and the ForEach-Object cmdlet (through its alias %) to count the length of each object being passed down the pipeline. You'll use the @(...) construct to guarantee that you're always treating $_ as an array. Here are the examples with different -ReadCount values:

```
PS> gc test.txt -ReadCount 1 | % { @($_).count } | select -first 1
1
PS> gc test.txt -ReadCount 4 | % { @($_).count } | select -first 1
4
```

When -ReadCount is greater than 1, the variable $_ is set to a *collection* of objects where the object count of that collection is equivalent to the value specified by -ReadCount. In another example, you'll use ForEach-Object to filter the pipeline:

```
PS> gc test.txt -read 5 | ? {$_ -like '*'} | % { $_.count }
5
5
```

You can see the filter result contains two collections of 5 objects each written to the pipeline for a total of 10 objects. Now use `ForEach-Object` and the `if` statement to filter the list:

```
PS> (gc test.txt -read 10 | foreach {if ($_ -match '.') {$_}} |
Measure-Object).count

10
```

This time you see a count of 10 because the value of `$_` in the `ForEach-Object` cmdlet is unraveled when written to the output pipe. And now let's look at one final example using `Where-Object`:

```
PS> (gc test.txt -read 4 | foreach {$_} | where {$_ -like '*'} |
Measure-Object).count

10
```

Here you've inserted one more `ForEach-Object` command between the `gc` and the `Where-Object`, which unravels the collections in `$_` and so you again see a count of 10.

> **NOTE** Here's the annoying thing: From the `Get-Content` developer's perspective, it *is* doing a read of `-ReadCount` objects from the provider. `Get-Content` reads `-ReadCount` objects and then writes them as a single object to the pipeline instead of unraveling them. (This is probably a bug that's turned into a feature.) Anyway, the name makes perfect sense to the developer and absolutely no sense to the user. This is why developers always have to be aware of the user's perspective even if it doesn't precisely match the implementation details.

In summary, whenever `-ReadCount` is set to a value greater than 1, usually for performance reasons, object collections are sent through the pipeline to `Where-Object` instead of individual objects. As a result, you have to take extra steps to deal with unraveling the batched collections of objects.

WHERE-OBJECT SIMPLIFIED

PowerShell v3 introduced a simplified syntax for a single comparison statement. So far, you've seen `Where-Object` used like this:

```
PS> Get-Process | where {$_.Handles -gt 1000}
```

The simplified syntax modifies this to

```
PS> Get-Process | where Handles -gt 1000
```

If you use the parameter names rather than positional parameters, it becomes

```
PS> Get-Process | where -Property Handles -gt -Value 1000
```

The important point is what looks like an operator is a parameter! Table 5.1 compares the two ways of constructing a filter with `Where-Object`.

Table 5.1   Comparison of syntax styles for `Where-Object`

Syntax style	Property		Value	Comment	Multiple comparisons
Old	`$_.Handles`	`-gt`	1000	`-gt` is operator	Yes
New	`Handles`	`-gt`	1000	`-gt` is parameter	No

Remember, you can only use a single comparison in the newer style syntax. If you need to perform multiple comparisons, then revert to the old style.

Just because you can doesn't mean you should

There are many ways of doing things in PowerShell. When writing your code, you shouldn't do something merely because you can. As an example of what we mean, consider

```
PS> Get-Process | where Handles -gt 1000
```

Remember `-gt` isn't an operator, it's a parameter. If you look at the `Where-Object` help file you'll see most of the common operators have been implemented as parameters for this syntax. This means you can do this:

```
PS> Get-Process | where -Property Handles  -Value 1000 -gt
```

The `-Property` and `-Value` parameters are positional parameters, so you could do this:

```
PS> Get-Process | where Handles  1000 -gt
```

Although asking a candidate to explain this would be a great interview question, it isn't the way we'd recommend you write your code as it's more difficult to understand than

```
PS> Get-Process | where Handles -gt 1000
```

Thinking about code maintainability as you write your code will make *your* life easier in the future.

At this point we've covered the two main flow-control cmdlets in detail. Now, let's look at one final feature of the PowerShell language: the ability to use all these statements we've been talking about as expressions that return values.

5.6   *Statements as values*

Let's return to the difference between statements and expressions (see chapter 4). In general, statements don't return values, but if they're used as part of a subexpression (or a function or script as you'll see later on), they do return a result. This is best illustrated with an example. Assume you didn't have the range operator and wanted to generate an array of numbers from 1 to 10. Here's the traditional approach you might use in a language such as C#:

```
PS> $result = New-Object -TypeName System.Collections.ArrayList
PS> for ($i=1; $i -le 10; $i++) { $result.Add($i) }
PS> "$($result.ToArray())"
1 2 3 4 5 6 7 8 9 10
```

First you create an instance of `System.Collections.ArrayList` to hold the result. Then you use a `for` loop to step through the numbers, adding each number to the result's `ArrayList`. Finally, you convert the `ArrayList` to an array and display the result. This is a straightforward approach to creating the array, but requires several steps. Using loops in subexpressions, you can simplify it quite a bit. From PowerShell v2 onward, the ability to assign the output of a flow-control statement has been simplified so you can directly assign the output to a variable. The example you saw earlier can be simplified to

```
PS> $result = for ($i=1; $i -le 10; $i++) {$i}
PS> "$result"
1 2 3 4 5 6 7 8 9 10
```

Used judiciously, the fact that statements can be used as value expressions can simplify your code in many circumstances. By eliminating temporary variables and extra initializations, creating collections is greatly simplified. Conversely, it's entirely possible to use this statement-as-expression capability to produce scripts that are hard to read. You should always keep that in mind when using these features in scripts. The other thing to keep in mind when you use statements is the performance of your scripts. Let's dig into this in a bit more detail.

5.7   *A word about performance*

Now that we've covered loops in PowerShell, this is a good time to talk about performance. PowerShell is an interpreted language, which has performance implications. Tasks with a lot of small repetitive actions can take a long time to execute. Anything with a loop statement can be a performance hotspot for this reason. Identifying these hotspots and rewriting them can have a huge impact on script performance. Let's look at an example.

This script processes a collection of events, extracting events having a specific name and ID and placing them into a new collection. The script looks something like this:

```
$results = @()
for ($i=0; $i -lt $EventList.length ; $i++)
{
    $name = [string] $Events[$i].ProviderName
    $id = [long] $Events[$i].Id
```

```
    if ($name -ne "My-Provider-Name")
    {
        continue
    }
    if ($id -ne 3005) {
        continue
    }
    $results += $Events[$i]
}
```

This script indexes through the collection of events using the `for` statement and then uses the `continue` statement to skip to the next event if the current event doesn't match the desired criteria. If the event does match the criteria, it's appended to the result collection. Although this works correctly, for large collections of events it takes several minutes to execute. Let's look at some ways to speed it up and make it smaller.

First, consider how you're indexing through the collection. This requires a lot of index operations, variable retrievals, and increments that aren't the most efficient operations in an interpreted language like PowerShell. Instead, PowerShell has a number of constructs that let you iterate through a collection automatically. Given that the task is to select events where some condition is true, the `Where-Object` cmdlet is an obvious choice. The second optimization is how the result list is built. The original code manually adds each element to the result array. If you remember our discussion on how array concatenation works, this means the array has to be copied each time an element is added. The alternative approach, as we discussed, is to let the pipeline do the collection for you. With these design changes, the new script looks like this:

```
$BranchCache3005Events = $events | where {
    $_.Id -eq 3005 -and $_.ProviderName -eq "My-Provider-Name"}
```

The revised script is both hundreds of times faster and significantly shorter and clearer.

> **NOTE** The preceding code assumes you've already collected the list of events into the `$events` variable for other purposes. If you're only performing the single action, it's more efficient to make gathering the events list part of the pipeline operation.

The rule for writing efficient PowerShell scripts is to let the system do the work for you. Use `foreach` instead of explicit indexing with `for` if you can. If you ever find yourself doing concatenation in a loop to build up a string or collection, look at using the pipeline instead. You can also take advantage of the fact all PowerShell statements return values, so an even faster (but less obvious or simple) way to do this is to use the `foreach` statement:

```
$BranchCache3005Events = @( foreach ($e in $events) {
    if ($e.Id -eq 3005 -or
        $e.ProviderName -eq "Microsoft-Windows-BranchCacheSMB") {$e}} )
```

The key here is still letting the system implicitly build the result array instead of constructing it manually with +=. Likewise, for string concatenation

```
$s = -join $(  foreach ($i in 1..40kb) { "a" } )
```

is faster than

```
$s = "";  foreach ($i in 1..40kb) { $s += "a" }
```

Following the guidelines, scripts are shorter, faster and frequently simpler and clearer (though not always).

5.8   *Summary*

- PowerShell allows you to use pipelines where other languages only allow expressions.
- There are two ways of handling flow control in PowerShell. The first is to use the language flow-control statements such as `while` and `foreach`. But when performing pipelined operations, the alternative mechanism—the flow-control cmdlets `ForEach-Object` and `Where-Object`—can be more natural and efficient.
- When iterating over collections, keep in mind the trade-offs between the `foreach` statement and the `ForEach-Object` cmdlet.
- Any statement can be used as a value expression when nested in a subexpression, but keep in mind the potential complexity that this kind of nested statement can introduce.
- The PowerShell `switch` statement has powerful pattern-matching capabilities, going well beyond what similar statements in other languages can do. And, along with the pattern matching, it can be used as a looping construct for selecting and processing objects from a collection or lines read from a file.
- The choice of statements and how you use them can have a significant effect on the performance of your scripts. This is something to keep in mind, but remember: worry only about performance if it becomes a problem. Otherwise, try to focus on making things as clear as possible.

You can perform a vast array of work interactively using the variables, operators, and flow-control statements you've seen so far. In the next chapter, we'll introduce functions that enable you to create reusable code.

PowerShell functions

6

This chapter covers

- Fundamentals of PowerShell functions
- Function parameters and return values
- Functions in the pipeline
- Variable scoping

> *Porcupine quills. We've always done it with porcupine quills.*
>
> *—Dilbert*

In this chapter we'll begin looking at how to create reusable commands by combining the features from the previous chapters. Functions and scripts are the two command types that can be written in the PowerShell language. (Cmdlets and external commands are written in a language such as C# that can be compiled.) We'll start with functions because they're simpler. In the next chapter, we'll cover scripts as well as introduce advanced programming features available to both functions and scripts.

NOTE The functions you'll see in this chapter are simple functions. Chapter 7 discusses advanced functions, including how to turn a simple function into an advanced function. These two chapters are the foundation for modules that we discuss in chapters 8 and 9.

Prior programming experience can be both a blessing and a curse when learning to program in PowerShell. Most of the time, what you already know makes it easier. The syntax and most of the concepts will probably be familiar. Unfortunately, *similar* isn't *identical*, and this is where prior experience can trip you up. You'll expect PowerShell to work like your favorite language, and it won't work quite the same way. We'll call out these issues as we encounter them, so put away your porcupine quills and let's get started.

6.1   *Fundamentals of PowerShell functions*

In this section we'll cover the basic concepts and features of PowerShell functions. Functions are the most lightweight form of PowerShell command. They exist in memory only for the duration of a session. When you exit the shell session, the functions are gone. They're also simple enough that you can create useful functions in a single line of code.

> ### Functions and scriptblocks
>
> A function, at its simplest, is defined as follows:
>
> ```
> function <name> {<statement list>}
> ```
>
> A scriptblock, at its simplest, is defined like this:
>
> ```
> {<statement list>}
> ```
>
> In both cases the braces contain a list of PowerShell statements that are executed when the function or scriptblock is invoked. You've seen scriptblocks used with `Where-Object` and `Foreach-Object` or the looping and conditional statements in previous chapters. Scriptblocks are covered in more detail in chapter 10.
>
> Looking at the two, you can describe a function as a named scriptblock or a scriptblock as an anonymous function—we prefer the latter.

We'll start by working through a number of examples showing you how to create simple functions. Take a look at our first example:

```
PS> function hello { 'Hello world' }
```

In this example, `hello` is a function because it's preceded by the `function` keyword. This function should emit the string "Hello world". Execute it to verify this:

```
PS> hello
Hello world
```

Yes, it works exactly as expected. You've created your first command.

Okay, that was easy. Now you know how to write a simple PowerShell function. The syntax is shown in figure 6.1.

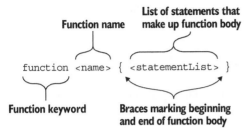

Figure 6.1 **The simplest form of a function definition in PowerShell**

A function that writes only "Hello world" isn't too useful. Let's see how to personalize this function by allowing an argument to be passed in.

6.1.1 *Passing arguments using $args*

The ability to pass values into a function is called *parameterizing* the function. In most languages, this means modifying the function to declare the parameters to process. For simple PowerShell functions, you don't have to do this because there's a default argument array that contains all the values passed to the function. This default array is available in the variable $args. Here's the previous hello example modified to use $args to receive arguments:

```
PS> function hello { "Hello there $args, how are you?" }
PS> hello Bob
Hello there Bob, how are you?
```

String expansion inserts the value stored in $args into the string that's emitted from the hello function. Now let's see what happens with multiple arguments:

```
PS> hello Bob Alice Ted Carol
Hello there Bob Alice Ted Carol, how are you?
```

Following the string expansion rules described in chapter 2, the values stored in $args get interpolated into the output string with each value separated by a space or, more specifically, separated by whatever is stored in the $OFS variable.

NOTE Both $args and $OFS are described in the help file about_Automatic_Variables.

So, let's take one last variation on this example. We'll set $OFS in the function body with the aim of producing a more palatable output:

```
PS> function hello
{
$ofs=","
"Hello there $args and how are you?"
}
```

```
PS> hello Bob Carol Ted Alice
Hello there Bob,Carol,Ted,Alice and how are you?
```

That's better. Now at least you have commas between the names. Let's try it again, with commas between the arguments:

```
PS> hello Bob,Carol,Ted,Alice
Hello there System.Object[] and how are you?
```

This isn't the result you were looking for. What happened? Let's define a new function:

```
PS> function count-args {
    "`$args.count=" + $args.count
    "`$args[0].count=" + $args[0].count
}
```

This function will display the number of arguments passed to it as well as the number of elements in the first argument. First, you use it with three scalar arguments:

```
PS> count-args 1 2 3
$args.count=3
$args[0].count=1
```

As expected, it shows that you passed three arguments. It shows a value of 1 for the Count property on $args[0] because $args[0] is a scalar (the number 1) which has a Count property of 1 by default. Try it with a comma between each of the arguments:

```
PS> Count-Args 1,2,3
$args.count=1
$args[0].count=3
```

Now you see that the function received one argument, which is an array of three elements. Finally, try it with two sets of comma-separated numbers:

```
PS> count-args 1,2,3 4,5,6,7
$args.count=2
$args[0].count=3
```

The results show that the function received two arguments, both of which are arrays. The first argument is an array of three elements and the second is an array with four elements. The comma here works like the binary comma operator in expressions, as discussed in chapter 4.

Two values on the command line with a comma between them will be passed to the command as a single argument. The value of that argument is an array of those elements. This applies to any command, not only functions. Now let's look at a couple of examples where $args enables simple but powerful scenarios.

6.1.2   *Example functions: ql and qs*

$args works straightforwardly and allows you to write pretty slick commands. Here are two functions that aren't in the PowerShell base:

```
PS> function ql { $args }
PS> function qs { "$args" }
```

They may not look like much, but they can significantly streamline a number of tasks. The first function is ql, which stands for *quote list*. This is a Perl-ism. Say you want to build a list of the colors. To do this with the normal comma operator, you'd do the following, which requires lots of quotes and commas:

```
PS> $col = "black","brown","red","orange","yellow","green",
    "blue","violet","gray","white"
```

With the ql function, you could write it this way:

```
PS> $col = ql black brown red orange yellow green blue violet gray white
```

That's much shorter and requires less typing. Remember that elastic syntax concept? When you're trying to fit a complex expression onto one line, things like ql can help. What about the other function, qs? It does approximately the same thing but uses string concatenation to return its arguments as a single string instead of an array:

```
PS> $string = qs This is a     string
PS> $string
This is a string
```

Note that the arguments are concatenated with a single space between them. The original spacing on the command line has been lost, but that usually doesn't matter.

Parameter syntax

Parameters can be passed into a number of PowerShell structures:

- Functions
- Scripts (chapter 7)
- Scriptblocks (chapter 10)

Functions can define their parameters in two ways:

```
function <name> (<parameter list>) {<statement list>}
```

or

```
function <name> {param (<parameter list>) <statement list>}
```

Scripts and scriptblocks use the second format with a param block inside the braces. We'll show the first, simpler way in this chapter and discuss the second method in more detail in the next chapter when we discuss advanced functions. Using a param block is the recommended technique as it gives a consistent approach.

6.2   *Declaring formal parameters for a function*

Using $args works, as you've seen, but a much better way would be to declare function parameters using names instead of indexes into an array. The high-level syntax for this is shown in figure 6.2.

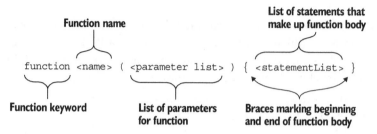

Figure 6.2   **The syntax for defining a function with explicit parameters in PowerShell. The parameter list is optional: you can either have empty parentheses or omit them, as you saw in figure 6.1.**

Here's a simple example of what this looks like in a real function:

```
PS> function subtract ($from, $count) { $from - $count }
```

In this function definition, there are two formal parameters: $from and $count. When the function is called, each argument will be bound to the corresponding formal parameter, either by position or by name. What does that mean? Well, binding by position is obvious:

```
PS> subtract 5 3
2
```

In this case, the first argument, 5, is bound to the first formal parameter, $from, and the second argument is bound to the second parameter, $count. Now let's look at using the parameter names as keywords:

```
PS> subtract -from 5 -count 2
3

PS> subtract -from 4 -count 7
-3
```

If you try to use the same parameter twice, you'll receive an error message that the parameter name can be used only once. You now know that there are two ways to match formal parameters with arguments. Can you mix and match? Let's try it:

```
PS> subtract -from 5 6
-1
```

You see that it did work as you'd expect. `$from` is set to 5, `$count` is set to 6, and you know that 5 minus 6 is –1. Now change which parameter is named:

```
PS> subtract -count 5 6
1
```

Now `$count` is set to 5 and `$from` is set to 6. This may seem a bit odd. Let's dig into the details of how it works next.

6.2.1 *Mixing named and positional parameters*

The rules for binding parameters to named and positional parameters are simple:

- Any named parameters are bound and then removed from the list of parameters that still need to be bound.
- Any remaining parameters are then bound by position.

Now let's go back to the example function:

```
PS> function subtract ($from, $count) { $from - $count }
```

When calling this function, if no named parameters are specified, then `$from` is position 0 and `$count` is position 1.

If you specify `-from`, then `$from` is bound by name and *removed* from the list of things that need to be bound positionally. This means that `$count`, which is normally in position 2, is now in position 1. Got all that? Probably not; we have a hard time following it ourselves.

All you need to think about is whether you're using named parameters or positional ones. Try to avoid mixing and matching if possible. If you do want to mix and match, always put the parameters that you want to specify by name at the end of the parameter list; put them at the end of the `param` statement or the function argument list. That way, they don't affect the order of the parameters you want to bind by position. (In chapter 7, you'll learn a better way to control how parameters are processed.)

Functions as commands

The way functions are called in PowerShell often causes people with prior programming experience to make a common error. They see the word *function* and try to call a PowerShell function the way they would in whatever other language they're used to. Instead of calling it like a command (which is what functions are), they try to call it by doing something like this:

```
subtract(1,2)
```

PowerShell will happily accept this because there's nothing syntactically wrong with it. The problem is that the statement is totally wrong semantically.

(Continued)

Functions (as opposed to methods on objects) in PowerShell are commands like any other commands.

Arguments to commands are separated by spaces. If you want to provide multivalued arguments for a single command, then you must separate those multiple values with commas (more on this later). Also, parentheses are needed only if you want the argument to be evaluated as an expression (see chapter 1 on parsing modes). What this "function call" is doing is passing a single argument, which is an array of two values. And that's wrong. Consider yourself warned. Really. This has tripped up some smart people. If you remember this discussion, then someday, somewhere, you'll be able to lord this bit of trivia over your coworkers, crushing their spirits like—oh—wait— sorry—it's that darned inner voice leaking out again.

So far, all your work has been with type-less parameters, and this has its advantages. It means that your functions can typically work with a wider variety of data types. But sometimes you want to make sure that the parameters are of a particular type (or are at least convertible to that type). Although you could do this the hard way and write a bunch of type-checking code, PowerShell is all about making life easier for the user, so let's talk about a better way to do this by specifying typed parameters.

6.2.2 Adding type constraints to parameters

You don't have to specify types for PowerShell function parameters (most scripting languages don't allow it), but sometimes it can be quite useful. It allows you to catch type mismatches in function calls earlier and provide better error messages. Adding type constraints to parameters is what we'll cover in this section.

To type-constrain a parameter, you provide a type literal before the variable name in the parameter list. Figure 6.3 shows what this looks like.

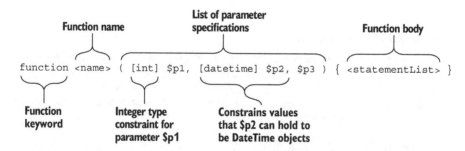

Figure 6.3   How type constraints are added to some of the parameters of a function. Type constraints aren't required for all parameters; in this case, $p3 is left unconstrained.

Let's work through an example. Define a function nadd that takes two parameters that you'll constrain to be integers:

```
PS> function nadd ([int] $x, [int] $y) {$x + $y}
```

Now use this function to add two numbers:

```
PS> nadd 1 2
3
```

Adding 1 and 2 gives 3. No surprise there. Now add two strings:

```
PS> nadd '1' '2'
3
```

The answer is still 3. Because of the type constraints on the parameters, numeric addition is performed even though you passed in two strings. In effect, the type constraints on function parameters are casts and follow the type-conversion rules described in chapter 2. Now let's see what happens when you pass in something that can't be converted to a number:

```
PS> nadd @{a=1;b=2} '2'
nadd : Cannot process argument transformation on parameter 'x'.
Cannot convert the "System.Collections.Hashtable" value of type "System.
    Collections.Hashtable" to type "System.Int32".
At line:1 char:6
+ nadd @{a=1;b=2} '2'
+      ~~~~~~~~~~
    + CategoryInfo          : InvalidData: (:) [nadd],
  ParameterBindingArgumentTransformationException
    + FullyQualifiedErrorId : ParameterArgumentTransformationError,nadd
```

You get an error message mentioning where the function was used and why it failed. Now define another function that doesn't have the type constraints:

```
PS> function add ($x, $y) {$x + $y}
```

Call this function with a hashtable argument:

```
PS> add @{a=1;b=2} '2'
A hash table can only be added to another hash table.
At line:1 char:24
+ function add ($x, $y) {$x + $y}
+                        ~~~~~~~
    + CategoryInfo          : InvalidOperation: (:) [], RuntimeException
    + FullyQualifiedErrorId : AddHashTableToNonHashTable
```

You still get an error, but notice where the error message is reported. Because it happened in the body of the function, the error message is reported in the function itself, not where the function was called as it was in the previous function. It's much more useful for the user of the function to know where the call that failed was rather than knowing where in the function it failed.

PowerShell and overloading

If you're used to traditional object-oriented languages, you might expect to be able to create overloads for a particular function name by specifying different signatures, but overloading isn't supported in PowerShell. If you define function a as

```
function a ([int] $b) { }
```

and later define function a as

```
function a ([string] $b) { }
```

then the new definition will replace the old definition rather than adding a new overload.

You can still use $args to specify a variable number of arguments to a function even when you have a formal parameter list.

6.2.3   *Handling variable numbers of arguments*

By default, any remaining arguments that don't match formal arguments will be captured in $args. The following example function illustrates this:

```
PS> function a ($x, $y) {
  "x is $x"
  "y is $y"
  "args is $args"
}
```

Now let's use it with a single argument:

```
PS> a 1
x is 1
y is
args is
```

The single argument is bound to $x. $y is initialized to $null and $args has zero elements in it. Now try it with two arguments:

```
PS> a 1 2
x is 1
y is 2
args is
```

This time $x and $y are bound, but $args is still empty. Next, try it with three arguments:

```
PS> a 1 2 3
x is 1
```

```
y is 2
args is 3
```

Any and all extra arguments end up in $args.

This automatic handling of excess arguments is useful behavior, but in many cases, you prefer that extra arguments be treated as an error. One way to make sure that no extra arguments are passed to your function is to check whether $args.length is 0 in the function body. If it's not 0, some arguments were passed. This is, however, a bit awkward. In chapter 7, we'll look at a much better way to handle this.

Earlier we mentioned that formal parameters that don't have corresponding arguments are initialized to $null. Although this is a handy default, it would be more useful to have a way of initializing the parameters to specific values.

6.2.4 *Initializing function parameters with default values*

In this section we'll show you how to initialize the values of function parameters. By using initialization, the user of the function doesn't have to specify all possible parameters on the command line. The ones that aren't specified will get the default values. You can reduce typing when using the function if you set default values to match your most common usage pattern. Alternatively, you can set the defaults to safe values that won't cause problems if you forget to use a parameter. The syntax for creating default parameter values is shown in figure 6.4.

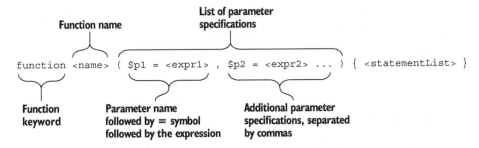

Figure 6.4 The more complex function definition syntax where initializer expressions are provided for each variable. Note that the initializers are constrained to be expressions, but using the subexpression notation you can put anything here.

Let's move right into an example:

```
PS> function add ($x=1, $y=2) { $x + $y }
```

This function initializes the formal parameters $x to 1 and $y to 2 if no parameters are specified. When you use it with no arguments

```
PS> add
3
```

it returns 3. With one argument

```
PS> add 5
7
```

it returns the argument plus 2, which in this case is 7. And finally, with two arguments

```
PS> add 5 5
10
```

it returns the result of adding them. From this example, it's obvious that you can initialize the variable to a constant value. What about something more complex? The initialization sequence as shown in figure 6.4 says that an initializer can be an expression. If you remember from chapter 4, an expression can be a subexpression, which can contain any PowerShell construct. An initializer can do anything: calculate a value, execute a pipeline, reformat your hard drive (*not* recommended), or send out for snacks from Tahiti by carrier pigeon (we've not had much luck with that one, though).

Let's try this feature out. Define a function that returns the day of the week for a particular date:

```
PS> function dow ([datetime] $d = $(Get-Date)) {
    $d.dayofweek
}
```

This function takes one argument, $d, that's constrained to be something that matches a date or time. If no argument is specified, it's initialized to the result of executing the Get-Date cmdlet (which returns today's date). Now let's try it out. First, run it with no arguments:

```
PS> dow
Tuesday
```

It prints out what day today is. Then run it with a specific date:

```
PS> dow 'oct 10, 2017'
Tuesday
```

You see that one of us has a birthday on a Tuesday in 2017. This is a simple example of using a subexpression to initialize a variable.

In most shell languages, you often provide only the name of a parameter without arguments to control a command's behavior—traditionally called *flags* or *switches*. Let's see how this is handled in PowerShell.

6.2.5   *Using switch parameters to define command switches*

In this section we're going to cover how to specify *switch parameters*, but before we do that, let's talk a bit more about parameter processing in general. In all shell environments, commands typically have three kinds of parameters, as shown in table 6.1.

Table 6.1   Typical classifications of parameter types found in all command shells

Parameter type	Description
Switches	Switches are present or absent, such as `Get-ChildItem -Recurse`.
Options	Options take an argument value, such as `Get-ChildItem -Filter *.cs`.
Arguments	These are positional and don't have a name associated with them.

This pattern holds true for most shells, including `cmd.exe` and `Bash`, although the specific details of the syntax may vary. The PowerShell team canonicalized things a bit more because they used formal terms for each of these, as shown in table 6.2.

Table 6.2   Formal names for parameter types in PowerShell

Parameter type	Formal name in PowerShell
Switches	Switch parameters
Options	Parameters
Arguments	Positional parameters

Arguments are positional parameters because they're always associated with a parameter name. But you can leave out the name, and the interpreter will figure out what parameter it is from its position on the command line. For example, in the `Get-ChildItem` command, the `-Path` parameter is a positional parameter with position 0.

Switch parameters are the opposite; you specify the parameter but the argument is left out. The interpreter assigns the parameter a value based on whether the parameter is present or absent. The `-Recurse` parameter for `Get-ChildItem` is a good example. If it's present, you'll get a recursive directory listing starting at the current directory.

So how do you indicate that something should be a switch parameter? PowerShell uses types to control behavior, so a switch parameter is marked with the type `[switch]`. This is illustrated in figure 6.5.

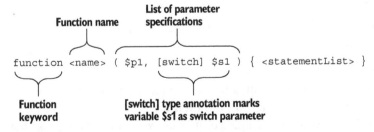

Figure 6.5   Marking a parameter as a switch or flag by adding the `[switch]` type constraint to it

Initializing switches is neither necessary nor recommended because the value of a switch is highly constrained. Here's an example function that uses a switch parameter:

```
PS> function get-soup (
    [switch] $please,
    [string] $soup= 'chicken noodle'
)
{
    if ($please) {
        "Here's your $soup soup"
    }
    else
    {
        'No soup for you!'
    }
}
```

Try out this function:

```
PS> get-soup
No soup for you!

PS> get-soup -please
Here's your chicken noodle soup

PS> get-soup -please tomato
Here's your tomato soup
```

So, if you say "please," you get soup. If not, no soup for you!

Soup or no soup, we're going to move on with our exploration of switch parameters and look at a feature that seems almost contradictory.

SPECIFYING ARGUMENTS TO SWITCH PARAMETERS

By definition, switch parameters don't take arguments, but there's one important scenario where you do need to do exactly this: when you need to pass the value of a switch parameter on one function to a switch parameter on another function. Consider a function foo that has a switch parameter -s. From function bar, you want to call

```
PS> foo
```

sometimes and

```
PS> foo -s
```

other times, and this will be controlled by a switch parameter on the bar function. You could use if statements to handle this, but even if you need to pass only one parameter through this way, you significantly complicate your code. And if you have more than one—well, let's just say it gets ugly quickly. To avoid that, you can use a feature in PowerShell designed with exactly this scenario in mind. Here's how it works. Although switch parameters don't require arguments, they *can* take one if you specify the parameter with a trailing colon:

```
PS> Get-ChildItem -Recurse: $true
```

Here's an example. You'll define a bar function that passes its $x switch parameter to the -s switch parameter on function foo. First, define the foo function:

```
PS> function foo ([switch] $s) { "s is $s" }
PS> foo -s
s is True

PS> foo
s is False
```

Now define function bar, in which we'll call foo as discussed previously:

```
PS> function bar ([switch] $x) { "x is $x"; foo -s: $x }
```

Call bar without passing -x,

```
PS bar
x is False
s is False
```

and you see that $s emitted from foo is false. Now call bar again, but specify -x this time,

```
PS> bar -x
x is True
s is True
```

and you see that specifying -x has caused -s to be set to true as well.

This functions-calling-functions pattern is pretty much the only time you should ever have to pass an argument to a switch function.

> **NOTE** A script author should *never* have to write a function, script, or cmdlet where a switch parameter is initialized to $true because it makes the commands hard to use.

Switch parameters are designed so that they need only be present or absent to get the desired effect. If you have a situation where you're considering initializing a switch to $true, you probably should be using a Boolean parameter instead of a switch parameter.

6.2.6 *Switch parameters vs. Boolean parameters*

Having both Boolean and switch parameters in PowerShell may seem redundant, but they're used to solve two quite different problems. To reiterate, the important difference between the two is that switch parameters don't require an argument. Booleans do. Specifying a switch parameter on the command line is sufficient for PowerShell to know that the parameter should be set to true.

For Boolean parameters (identified with the `[bool]` type accelerator), an argument must be specified each time the parameter is present. This is illustrated in the following example:

```
PS> function tb ([bool] $x) { [bool] $x }
PS> tb
False

PS> tb -x
tb : Missing an argument for parameter 'x'. Specify a parameter of type
    'System.Boolean' and try again.
At line:1 char:4
+ tb -x
+    ~~
    + CategoryInfo          : InvalidArgument: (:) [tb],
   ParameterBindingException
    + FullyQualifiedErrorId : MissingArgument,tb

PS> tb -x $true
True

PS> tb -x $false
False
```

With the tb function, if -x isn't present, the return value is $false. If it's present but no argument is specified, an error occurs. If it's present and a Boolean value is provided as the argument, the return value is the same as the argument.

Boolean type conversions for [bool] parameters

You need to be aware of a characteristic in how Boolean type conversions work for [bool] parameters. The argument to a [bool] parameter must be either a Boolean value ($true, $false, or the result of an expression that returns a Boolean) or a number where 0 is treated as $false and positive non-zero is treated as $true. A negative number generates an error. This is a departure from how objects are converted to Boolean elsewhere in PowerShell. This inconsistency was introduced deliberately because new PowerShell users would try commands like Get-Something -boolParameter false and be surprised when -boolParameter ended up being true, not false. (Remember, non-zero-length strings are considered true everywhere else in the system.) The cognitive dissonance resulting from having "false" evaluate to $true was a stumbling block for some new users. To mitigate this, PowerShell makes passing anything other than a number or a Boolean value an error condition. This seems to be the least inconsistent solution because the new behavior is a proper subset of normal type conversion.

You use Boolean parameters when you're writing a command to change the value of some of the properties on the object passing through the pipeline. This is part of the common Get/Update/Set pattern where you get an object from a store, change some properties on that object, and then pass it to an update command. In this pattern, you want to change the value of the property only if there's a corresponding parameter on the command line.

If the parameter is present, you want to set the property on the pipeline object to be the value passed to the parameter. If the parameter is absent, you don't want to change it. We'll dig into this a bit more in the next section, but first we'll digress to investigate a common configuration management pattern and how you deal with it in PowerShell.

A DIGRESSION: THE GET/UPDATE/SET PATTERN

A lot of management data is contained in database-like remote stores. Microsoft Exchange and Active Directory are two examples. The characteristic usage pattern for working with these stores is:

1. Get a record from the remote store.
2. Modify some property or properties on this object.
3. Send the modified object back to the store where the changes are recorded.

For example, when managing Exchange mailboxes, the mailbox objects are retrieved from the server, modified, and then sent back to the server to update the database. It's an important enough pattern that we're going to work through a somewhat extended example illustrating this approach in PowerShell. The following listing implements a simple database that contains information about familiar characters from the comic strips.

Listing 6.1 The `Get-Character` **function**

```
$characterData = @{                                    Stores character data in
  'Linus' = @{ age = 8; human = $true}                 hashtable of hashtables
  'Lucy' = @{ age = 8; human = $true}
  'Snoopy' = @{ age = 2; human = $true}
}
                                                       Gets data
function Get-Character ($name = '*')                    from table
{
  foreach ($entry in $characterData.GetEnumerator() | Write-Output)
  {
    if ($entry.Key -like $name)
    {                                                  Builds merged
        $properties = @{ 'Name' = $entry.Key } +       hashtable
          $entry.Value
        New-Object PSCustomObject -Property $properties    Emits character
    }                                                      record
  }
}
function Set-Character {                  Processes record,
  process {                               updates character entry
    $characterData[$_.name] =
      @{
        age = $_.age
        human = $_.human
      }
```

```
    }
}
function Update-Character (
  [string] $name = '*',
  [int] $age,
  [bool] $human
)
{
  begin
  {
    if ($PSBoundParameters.'name')
    {
      $name = $PSBoundParameters.name
      [void] $PSBoundParameters.Remove('name')
    }
  }
  process
  {
    if ($_.name -like $name)
    {
      foreach ($p in $PSBoundParameters.GetEnumerator())
      {
        $_.($p.Key) = $p.value          ◁——— Updates properties
      }                                        on object
    }
    $_
  }
}
```

NOTE To make this example work, you need to use a few features that we haven't covered yet: the process keyword used in Update-Character, custom objects, and the $PSBoundParameters automatic variable. We'll cover the process keyword later in this chapter and the $PSBoundParameters variable in chapter 7. This variable is key to making this example work because it lets you see which parameters were specified on the command line. Creating custom objects using the New-Object command is explored in chapter 10. Of these features, only the process keyword is available in PowerShell v1. The others are available only in PowerShell v2 and later.

In this example, the character data is stored in nested hashtables, making it easy to access by name. The Get-Character function retrieves characters from the table and emits custom objects for each character. The Set-Character data reverses this process and uses the inbound records to update the character table. The Update-Character function is where you see the use case for Boolean parameters mentioned in the previous section. Let's apply this code to manage your character database. First, you'll get a listing of all the characters in the table:

```
PS> Get-Character

Name    age human
----    --- -----
Snoopy   2  True
```

```
Lucy      8   True
Linus     8   True
```

Immediately you see that there's a problem with this data. It lists Snoopy as being human even though you know he's a dog (well, at least if you're a *Peanuts* fan). You'll need to use the Update-Character function to fix this:

```
PS> Get-Character |
  Update-Character -name snoopy -human $false |
  Format-Table -AutoSize

Name    age human
----    --- -----
Snoopy    2 False
Lucy      8 True
Linus     8 True
```

Note that you haven't updated the table—you're only looking at how the updated table will look. You can verify the data hasn't changed by calling Get-Character again. Now do the Set part of Get/Update/Set:

```
PS> Get-Character |
  Update-Character -name snoopy -human $false |
  Set-Character
```

Then dump the table to verify that change:

```
PS> Get-Character

Name    age human
----    --- -----
Snoopy    2 False
Lucy      8 True
Linus     8 True
```

Now Snoopy is no longer marked as human. But there's something else you want to check on. You'll dump the records that show the data for characters whose names begin with *L*:

```
PS> Get-Character L*

Name   age human
----   --- -----
Lucy     8 True
Linus    8 True
```

And there's the problem: the table lists Lucy and Linus as being the same age. Because Linus is Lucy's younger brother, you know the current age property must be wrong. Again, you'll use Update-Character piped to Set-Character to update the data, correcting the character's age:

```
PS> Get-Character Linus |
  Update-Character -age 7 |
  Set-Character
```

```
PS> Get-Character | Format-Table -AutoSize

Name    age human
----    --- -----
Snoopy    2 False
Lucy      8 True
Linus     7 True
```

Now the table is correct.

In this extended example, you looked at a common pattern for working with management data—Get/Update/Set—which you're likely to run into many times doing systems management. In the process, we demonstrated the reason for Boolean parameters being distinct from switch parameters: They address two quite different usage patterns.

By now, you've probably had enough discussion on how stuff gets passed into functions. Let's talk about how stuff comes out of functions instead.

6.3   *Returning values from functions*

Now it's time to talk about returning values from functions. We've been doing this all along, but there's something we need to highlight. Because PowerShell is a shell, it doesn't return results—it writes output or *emits objects*. As you've seen, the result of any expression or pipeline is to emit the result object to the caller. At the command line, if you type three expressions separated by semicolons, the results of all three statements are output:

```
PS> 2+2; 9/3; [math]::sqrt(27)
```

Let's put this into a function:

```
PS> function numbers { 2+2; 9/3; [math]::sqrt(27) }
```

Now run that function:

```
PS> numbers
4
3
5.19615242270663
```

Just as when you typed it on the command line, three numbers are output. Now assign the results to a variable:

```
PS> $result = numbers
```

Then check the content of that variable:

```
PS> $result.length
3

PS> $result[0]
4
```

```
PS> $result[1]
3
PS> $result[2]
5.19615242270663
```

From the output, you can see that $result contains an array with three values in it. Here's what happened. As each statement in the function was executed, the result of that statement was captured in an array, which was then was stored in $result. The easiest way to understand this is to imagine variable assignments working like redirection, except the result is stored in a variable instead of in a file.

Let's try something more complex. The goal here is twofold. First, you want to increase your understanding of how function output works. Second, you want to see how to take advantage of this feature to simplify your scripts and improve performance.

Let's redefine the function numbers to use a while loop that generates the numbers 1 to 10:

```
PS> function numbers{
    $i=1
    while ($i -le 10)
    {
        $i
        $i++
    }
}
```

Capture the results in a variable:

```
PS> $result = numbers
```

What ended up in the variable? First, check the type

```
PS> $result.GetType().FullName
System.Object[]
```

and the length

```
PS> $result.length
10
```

The output of the function ended up in an array of elements, even though you never mentioned an array anywhere. The PowerShell runtime will spontaneously create a collection when needed, as discussed in chapter 4.

In a traditional language, you have to initialize a result variable, $result, to hold the array being produced, add each element to the array, and then emit the array. This code is significantly more complex: You have to manage two variables in the function now instead of one. If you were writing in a language that didn't automatically extend the size of the array, it would be even more complicated, because you'd have to add code to resize the array manually. And even though PowerShell will automatically resize the array, it's not efficient compared to capturing the streamed output.

> **NOTE** The point is to make you think about how you can use the facilities that PowerShell offers to improve your code. If you find yourself writing code that explicitly constructs arrays, consider looking at it to see if it can be rewritten to take advantage of streaming instead.

Then again, every silver lining has a cloud. As wonderful as all this automatic collecting of output is, there are potential pitfalls. Sometimes you'll find things in the output collection that you didn't expect and have no idea how they got there. That can be hard (and frustrating) to figure out. In the next section, we'll explore the reasons why this might happen and you'll learn how to go about debugging the problem if you encounter it.

6.3.1   *Debugging problems in function output*

When writing a function, you need to keep in mind something that's specific to shell environments: The result of *all* statements executed will appear in the output of the function. This means that if you add debug message statements that write to the output stream of your function, this debug output will be mixed into the output of the function.

> **NOTE** In text-based shells, the usual way to work around mixing debug information with output is to write the debug messages to the error stream (stderr). This works fine when the error stream is simple text, but in PowerShell, the error stream is composed of error objects. All the extra information in these objects, while great for errors, makes them unpalatable for writing simple debug messages. There are better ways of handling this, as you'll see in chapter 15 when we talk about debugging.

Here's an example function where we've added a couple of debug statements:

```
PS> function my-func ($x) {
    "Getting the date"
    $x = get-date
    "Date was $x, now getting the day"
    $day = $x.day
    "Returning the day"
    $day
}
```

Let's run the function:

```
PS> my-func
Getting the date
Date was 04/07/2017 12:50:47, now getting the day
Returning the day
7
```

You see the debug output as well as the result. That's fine—that's the point of debugging messages. But now let's capture the output of the function into a variable:

```
PS> $x = my-func
```

This time you see no output, which is expected, but neither do you see the debugging messages, and that wasn't expected or desired. If you look at what ended up in $x, you'll see that everything is there: output and debug, all mixed together. This is a trivial example, and we're sure it feels like we're beating the issue to death, but this is the kind of thing that leads to those head-slapping how-could-I-be-so-dumb moments in which you'll be writing a complex script and wonder why the output looks funny. Then you'll remember that debugging statement you forgot to take out. "Duh!" you'll cry. "How could I be so dumb!"

> **NOTE** This issue isn't exclusive to PowerShell. Back before the advent of good debuggers, people would do `printf` debugging (named after the `printf` output function in C). It wasn't uncommon to see stray output in programs because of this. Now, with good debuggers, stray output is pretty infrequent. PowerShell provides debugging features (which we'll cover in chapter 15) that you can use instead of `printf` debugging. In particular, the Integrated Scripting Environment (ISE) included with PowerShell has a built-in graphical debugger for scripts.

Another thing to be careful about is operations that emit objects when you don't expect them to. This is particularly important to keep in mind if you use a lot of .NET methods in your scripts. The problem is that many of these methods return values that you don't need or care about. This isn't an issue with languages like C# because the default behavior in these languages is to discard the result of an expression. In PowerShell, though, the default is to always emit the result of an expression; consequently, these method results unexpectedly appear in your output. You'll most often encounter this problem when using the `System.Collections.ArrayList` class. The `Add()` method on this class helpfully returns the index of the object that was added by the call to `Add()` (we're aware of no real use for this feature—it probably seemed like a good idea at the time). This behavior looks like this:

```
PS> $al = New-Object -TypeName System.Collections.ArrayList
PS> $al.count
0

PS> $al.add(1)
0

PS> $al.add(2)
1
```

Every time you call `Add()`, a number displaying the index of the added element is emitted. Now say you write a function that copies its arguments into an `ArrayList`. This might look like

```
PS> function addArgsToArrayList {
  $al = New-Object -TypeName System.Collections.ArrayList
  $args | foreach { $al.add($_) }
}
```

It's a pretty simple function, but what happens when you run it? Take a look:

```
PS> addArgsToArrayList a b c d
0
1
2
3
```

As you can see, every time you call Add(), a number gets returned. That's not helpful. To make it work properly, you need to discard this undesired output. Let's fix this. Here's the revised function definition:

```
PS> function addArgsToArrayList {
  $al = New-Object -TypeName System.Collections.ArrayList
  $args | foreach { [void] $al.add($_) }
}
```

It looks exactly like the previous one except for the cast to void in the third line. Now let's try it out:

```
PS> addArgsToArrayList a b c d
```

This time you don't see any output, as desired. Keep this tip in mind when working with .NET classes in functions.

6.3.2 *The return statement*

Now that you've debugged and cleaned up your output, let's talk about PowerShell's return statement. Yes, PowerShell does have a return statement, and yes, it's similar to the return statement in other languages. But remember—similar isn't the same.

Remember we talked about how functions in PowerShell are best described as writing output rather than returning results? Why, then, does PowerShell need a return statement? The answer, at this stage, is *flow control.*

> **NOTE** When we discuss PowerShell classes in chapter 19 you'll see that the return statement is required for outputting from methods. This difference can trip people up, so be aware.

Sometimes you want to exit a function early. Without a return statement, you'd have to write complex conditional statements to get the flow of control to reach the end. In effect, the return statement is like the break statement we covered in chapter 5—it "breaks" to the end of the function.

The next question is: Is it possible to "return" a value from a function using the return statement? Yes, it is. This looks like

```
return 2+2
```

which is shorthand for

```
Write-Output (2+2) ; return
```

The `return` statement is included in PowerShell because it's a common pattern that programmers expect to have. Unfortunately, it can sometimes lead to confusion for new users and nonprogrammers. They forget that because PowerShell is a shell, every statement emits values into the output stream. Using the `return` statement can make this somewhat less obvious.

Because of this potential for confusion, you should generally *avoid* using the `return` statement in functions and scripts unless you need it to simplify your logic. Even then, you should probably avoid using it to return a value. The one circumstance where it makes sense is in a "pure" function where you're returning only a single value.

6.4 *Using simple functions in a pipeline*

So far, we've only talked about using functions as standalone statements. But what about using functions in pipelines? After all, PowerShell is all about pipelines, so shouldn't you be able to use functions in pipelines? The answer is yes, with some considerations that need to be taken into account.

> **NOTE** The best way of creating simple functions to use on the pipeline is shown in section 6.4.2. The examples earlier in this section should be thought of as a lead in to that discussion.

The nature of a function is to take a set of inputs, process it, and produce a result. How do you make the stream of objects from the pipeline available in a function? This is accomplished through the `$input` variable. When a function is used in a pipeline, a special variable, `$input`, is available that contains an enumerator that allows you to process through the input collection. Let's see how this works:

```
PS> function sum {
  $total=0;
  foreach ($n in $input) { $total += $n }
  $total
}
```

A function `sum` is defined that takes no arguments but has one implied argument, which is `$input`. It will add each of the elements in `$input` to `$total` and then return `$total`. It will return the sum of all the input objects.

We said that `$input` is an *enumerator*. You may remember our discussion of enumerators from chapter 5 when we talked about the `$foreach` and `$switch` variables. The same principles apply here. You move the enumerator to the next element using the MoveNext() method and get the current element using the Current property. This is important in remoting, as you'll see in chapter 11. Here's the sum function rewritten using the enumerator members directly:

```
PS> function sum2 {
  $total=0
  while ($input.MoveNext()){
   $total += $input.Current
  }
  $total
}
```

Now you need to write a variation of this that works with something other than numbers. This time you'll write a function that has a formal parameter and also processes input. The parameter will be the name of the property on the input object to sum up. Here's the function definition:

```
PS> function sum3 ($p){
  $total=0
  while ($input.MoveNext()){
    $total += $input.Current.$p
  }
  $total
}
```

In line 6 of the function, you can see the expression $input.Current.$p. This expression returns the value of the property named by $p on the current object in the enumeration. Use this function to sum the lengths of the files in the current directory:

```
PS> Get-ChildItem | sum3 length
9111
```

You invoke the function passing in the string "length" as the name of the property to sum. The result is the total of the lengths of all of the files in the current directory.

Remember that $input is an enumerator. That means you can use it only once. When you've read to the end, you can't cycle back and reuse it. If you do need to reuse the contents of $input, then you need to convert the contents to an array. You can't use $input in advanced functions but you'll see alternative approaches in the next chapter.

This shows that it's pretty easy to write functions that you can use in a pipeline, but there's one thing we haven't touched on. Because functions run all at once, they can't do streaming processing. In the previous example, where you piped the output of Get-ChildItem into the function, what happened was that the Get-ChildItem cmdlet ran to completion and the accumulated results from that were passed as a collection to the function. How can you use functions more effectively in a pipeline? That's what we'll cover next.

6.4.1 *Functions with begin, process, and end blocks*

It would be nice if you could write user-defined cmdlets that can initialize some state at the beginning of the pipeline, process each object as it's received, and then do cleanup work at the end of the pipeline. And you can. The full structure of a function cmdlet is shown in figure 6.6.

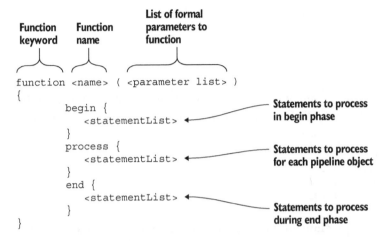

Figure 6.6   **The complete function definition syntax for a function in PowerShell that will have cmdlet-like behavior**

In figure 6.6 you see that you can define a clause for each phase of the cmdlet processing. This is exactly like the phases used in a compiled cmdlet, as mentioned in chapter 1. The begin keyword specifies the clause to run before the first pipeline object is available. The process clause is executed once for each object in the pipeline, and the end clause is run once when all the objects have been processed.

> **NOTE** Using the Filter keyword, instead of function as shown here, you can create a type of function known as a filter. It can be used on the pipeline, running once for each input object coming from the pipeline. You can think of a filter as function with only a process block. Using a function with begin/process/end blocks produces a better solution and is the recommended way to proceed. Filters are a restricted option that was required only in PowerShell v1.

The current pipeline object is available in the process clause in the special variable $_ (or $psitem). As always, an example is the best way to illustrate this:

```
PS> function my-cmdlet ($x) {
  begin {$c=0; "In Begin, c is $c, x is $x"}
  process {$c++; "In Process, c is $c, x is $x, `$_ is $_"}
  end {"In End, c is $c, x is $x"}
}
```

You define all three clauses in this function. Each clause reports what it is and then prints out the values of some variables. The variable $x comes from the command line; the variable $c is defined in the begin clause, incremented in the process clause, and displayed again in the end clause. The process clause also displays the value of the current pipeline object. Now let's run it:

```
PS> 1,2,3 | my-cmdlet 22
In Begin, c is 0, x is 22
In Process, c is 1, x is 22, $_ is 1
In Process, c is 2, x is 22, $_ is 2
In Process, c is 3, x is 22, $_ is 3
In End, c is 3, x is 22
```

As you can see, the argument 22 is available in all three clauses, and the value of $c is also maintained across all three clauses. What happens if there's no pipeline input? Let's try it:

```
PS> my-cmdlet 33
In Begin, c is 0, x is 33
In Process, c is 1, x is 33, $_ is
In End, c is 1, x is 33
```

Even if there's no pipeline input, the process clause is still run exactly once. You don't have to specify all three of the clauses. If you specify only the process clause, you might as well use the filter keyword, because the two are identical.

If you've been following along with the examples in this chapter, by now you'll have created quite a number of functions. Care to guess how to find out what you've defined?

6.5   *Managing function definitions in a session*

Because it's easy to create functions in PowerShell, it also needs to be easy to manage those functions. Rather than provide a custom set of commands (or worse yet, a set of keywords) to manage functions, you can take advantage of the namespace capabilities in PowerShell and use the function drive. Because it's mapped as a drive, you can get a list of functions the same way you get a list of the contents of any other drive. Let's use Get-ChildItem to find out about the mkdir function:

```
PS> Get-ChildItem -Path function:\mkdir

CommandType Name   Version Source
----------- ----   ------- ------
Function    mkdir
```

By using Get-ChildItem on the path function:\mkdir, you can see mkdir exists and is a function. Wildcards can be used, so Get-ChildItem function:\mk* is allowed.

And, if you use Get-ChildItem on the function drive, you'll get a complete list of all functions. Let's do this but get a count of the number of functions:

```
PS> (Get-ChildItem function:\).count
78
```

Our test environment has 78 functions defined. Now let's create a new one:

```
PS> function clippy { "I see you're writing a function." }
```

Now check for the function itself:

```
PS> Get-ChildItem function:\clippy

CommandType Name     Version Source
----------- ----     ------- ------
Function    clippy
```

Running Get-ChildItem on function:clippy doesn't give you the function definition entry for this function in PowerShell v3 and later. You can view the definition:

```
PS> Get-ChildItem function:\clippy |
Format-Table CommandType, Name, Definition -AutoSize -Wrap

CommandType Name   Definition
----------- ----   ----------
   Function clippy "I see you're writing a function."
```

The -Wrap parameter on Format-table will ensure that multiline function definitions are displayed correctly. Try displaying the definition of the sum3 function from section 6.4 to see the difference.

Now that you know how to add functions to your session, let's see how to remove them. You'll remove the clippy function you just created. Because you're removing an item from the function: drive, you'll remove the function the same way you'd remove a file from a file system drive with the Remove-Item command:

```
PS> Remove-Item function:/clippy
```

And make sure it's gone:

```
 PS> (Get-ChildItem function:/).count
78
PS> Get-ChildItem function:clippy
Get-ChildItem : Cannot find path 'clippy' because it does not exist.
At line:1 char:1
+ dir function:\clippy
+ ~~~~~~~~~~~~~~~~~~~~~
    + CategoryInfo          :
    ObjectNotFound: (clippy:String) [Get-ChildItem],
    ItemNotFoundException
    + FullyQualifiedErrorId : PathNotFound,Microsoft.PowerShell.Commands.
  GetChildItemCommand
```

Yes! You've removed clippy from the system.

> **NOTE** Longtime Microsoft Office users will no doubt be feeling an intense burst of satisfaction with this last example. We've all longed to eradicate that annoying paperclip "assistant," and at last we have the pleasure, if in name only.

And, even more amusing, Microsoft Word doesn't even recognize "clippy"—it keeps trying to autocorrect to "clippie." Some unresolved issues, perhaps?

The techniques we've covered in this section allow you to manipulate the functions defined in your current session. As with any drive, you can list the functions, create them, delete them, and rename them. But regardless, all these functions will disappear when the session ends when you exit PowerShell. What about "permanent" functions? How can you define functions that are always available? This is where scripts come in, as you'll see in chapter 7. In the meantime, there's one more topic that impacts how functions work: variable scoping and lifetime. We've ignored it so far, but we do need to cover it in some depth. Let's begin now.

6.6   *Variable scoping in functions*

So far, we've ignored when variables are created, but there are specific rules that cover that. These rules govern when variables come into existence and where they're visible. The set of rules that covers variable lifetime and visibility is called the *scoping rules* of the language.

First, let's introduce some terminology for our discussion. In programming language design, there are two general approaches to scoping—*lexical* and *dynamic.* Most programming languages and many scripting languages are lexically scoped. In a lexically scoped language, it's *where* the name of something is defined that matters. Names are visible in the block they're defined in and in any nested blocks but aren't visible outside the enclosing block unless they're explicitly exported in some way. Because where they're defined controls the visibility for the variable, this is determined at compile time and is therefore called *lexical* (or sometimes *static*) scoping.

Dynamic scoping involves *when* the variable is defined. The visibility of the variable is controlled by the runtime or dynamic behavior of the program, not the compile-time or static behavior (hence the term *dynamic*).

> **NOTE**   For the language folks in the audience, PowerShell uses a variation on traditional dynamic scoping: hygienic dynamic scoping. This has also been called *dynamic scoping with implicit let binding* (if you care). The significant difference is in how assignment is done. In traditional dynamic scoping, if a variable exists in an outer scope, it will be assigned to the current scope. In PowerShell, even if there's an existing variable in an outer scope, a new local variable will be created on first assignment. This guarantees that a function, in the absence of scope modifiers, won't mess up the calling scopes (hence the term *hygienic*).

6.6.1   *Declaring variables*

Ignoring function parameters (which are a form of declaration), PowerShell has no variable declaration statement—a variable simply comes into existence on first assignment. We discussed this in chapter 4, but it's more important now.

NOTE You'll see more developer-orientated semantics when we look at PowerShell classes in chapter 19.

Figure 6.7 shows a diagram of how variable names are resolved in PowerShell.

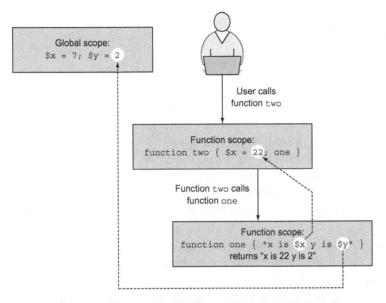

Figure 6.7   How variables are resolved across different scopes. They're resolved first in the local scope, then in the immediate caller's scope, and so on until the global scope is reached. In this case, lookup of $x resolves to 22 in the scope for function one**. Lookup of** $y **resolves to 2 in the global scope, resulting in the output string "x is 22 y is 2".**

Let's look at an example. First, define two simple functions, one and two:

```
PS> function one { "x is $x" }
PS> function two { $x = 22; one }
```

Function one prints out a string displaying the value of $x. Function two sets the variable $x to a particular value and then calls function one. Now let's try them out. Before you work with the functions, set $x to 7 interactively, to help illustrate how scoping works:

```
PS> $x=7
```

Now call function one:

```
PS> one
x is 7
```

As expected, it prints x is 7. Now call function two:

```
PS> two
x is 22
```

Not surprisingly, because two sets $x to 22 before calling one, you see x is 22 returned. What happened to $x? Let's check:

```
PS> $x
7
```

It's still 7! Now call one again:

```
PS> one
x is 7
```

It prints x is 7. What exactly happened here? When you first assigned 7 to $x, you created a new global variable, $x. When you called function one the first time, it looked for a variable $x, found the global definition, and used that to print the message.

When you called function two, it defined a new local variable called $x before calling one. This variable is local—it didn't change the value of the global $x, but it did put a new $x on the scope stack. When it called one, this function searched up the scope stack looking for $x, found the new variable created by function two, and used that to print x is 22.

On return from function two, the scope containing its definition of $x was discarded. The next time you called function one, it found the top-level definition of $x. Now let's compare this to a language that's lexically scoped. We happen to have Python installed on a computer, so from PowerShell, we'll start the Python interpreter:

```
python
Python 2.2.3 (#42, May 30 2003, 18:12:08) [MSC 32 bit (Intel)] on
 win32Type "help", "copyright", "credits" or "license" for more information.
```

Now let's set the global variable x to 7. (Note: even if you aren't familiar with Python, these examples are simple, so you shouldn't have a problem following them.)

```
x=7
```

Now print x to make sure it was properly set:

```
print x
7
```

You see that it is, in fact, 7. Now define a Python function one:

```
def one():
    print "x is " + str(x)
```

And now define another function two that sets x to 22 and then calls one:

```
def two():
    x=22
    one()
```

As with the PowerShell example, one prints x is 7.

```
one()
x is 7
```

Now call two:

```
two()
x is 7
```

Even though two defines x to be 22, when it calls one, one still prints 7. That's because the local variable x isn't lexically visible to one—it will always use the value of the global x, which you can see hasn't changed:

```
print x
7
```

At this point, we hope you have a basic understanding of how variables are looked up in PowerShell. Sometimes, though, you want to be able to override the default lookup behavior. We'll discuss this in the next section.

> **NOTE** UNIX shells used dynamic scoping because they didn't have a choice. Each script is executed in its own process and receives a copy of the parent's environment. Any environment variables that a script defines will then be inherited by any child scripts that it, in turn, calls. The process-based nature of the UNIX shells predetermines how scoping can work. The interesting thing is that these semantics are pretty much what PowerShell uses, even though the PowerShell team wasn't limited by the process boundary. The team tried a number of different schemes, and the only one that was satisfactory was the one that most closely mimicked traditional shell semantics. We suppose this shouldn't be a surprise—it's worked well for several decades now.

6.6.2 *Using variable scope modifiers*

We've now arrived at the subject of variable scope modifiers. In the previous section, we discussed scope and the default PowerShell lookup algorithm. Now you'll see that you can override the default lookup by using a scope modifier. These modifiers look like the namespace qualifiers mentioned in chapter 5. To access a global variable $var, you'd write

```
PS> $global:var
```

Let's revisit the functions from the previous section:

```
PS> function one { "x is $global:x" }
```

This time, in the function one, you'll use the scope modifier to explicitly reference the global $x:

```
PS> function two { $x = 22; one }
```

The definition of function two is unchanged. Now set the global $x to 7 (commands at the top level always set global variables, so you don't need to use the global modifier):

```
PS> $x=7
```

Now run the functions:

```
PS> one
x is 7

PS> two
x is 7
```

This time, because you told one to bypass searching the scope change for $x and go directly to the global variable, calls to both one and two return the same result, x is 7.

When we look at scripts in chapter 8, you'll see additional scoping rules and qualifiers, but for now, you have all you need to work with functions.

In the next chapter, you'll extend your PowerShell programming knowledge to include writing scripts. We'll also look at some of the advanced features in PowerShell.

6.7   *Summary*

- PowerShell programming can be done with either functions or scripts, though in this chapter we focused only on basic functions.
- Functions are created using the function keyword.
- The simplest form of function uses $args to receive parameters automatically.
- More sophisticated parameter handling for functions requires the use of parameter declarations. This can be done by placing the parameter names in parentheses after the name of the function or in the body of the function using the param keyword.
- PowerShell uses dynamic scoping for variables. You can modify how a variable name is resolved by using the scope modifiers in the variable names.
- Functions stream their output. They return the results of every statement executed as though it were written to the output stream. This feature means you almost never have to write your own code to accumulate results.
- Because of the differences between how functions work in PowerShell and how they work in more conventional languages, you may receive some unexpected results when creating your functions, so you picked up some tips on debugging these problems.

- Functions can specify begin, process, and end blocks in the function body.
- The `function:` drive is used to manage the functions defined in your session. This means you use the same commands you use for managing files to manage functions.

Now that you understand the basics, it's time to get more advanced. In the next chapter, we'll apply what you've learned about functions to scripts, see the differences, and show you how to create advanced functions.

Advanced functions
and scripts

7

This chapter covers

- PowerShell scripts
- Writing advanced functions and scripts
- Dynamic parameters
- Default parameters
- Documenting functions and scripts

> *And now for something completely different . . .*
>
> —*Monty Python*

In chapter 6 we introduced the basic elements needed for programming in Power-Shell when we looked at PowerShell functions. In this chapter, we're going to expand your repertoire by introducing PowerShell scripts.

> **NOTE** If you skipped chapter 6, you should probably go back and read it before proceeding. Why? Because all the material we covered on functions also applies to scripts.

Once we're finished with the basics of scripts (which won't take long), we'll move on to PowerShell's advanced production scripting features, which enable you to write full-featured applications complete with proper documentation. By the end of this chapter, you should be well on your way to becoming an expert PowerShell programmer.

7.1 PowerShell scripts

Let's dig into scripts to see what they have in common with functions and what additional features you need to be aware of. We'll begin by looking at the execution policy that controls what scripts can be run. Then you'll see how parameters and the exit statement work in scripts. We'll also spend time on the additional scoping rules that scripts introduce. Finally, you'll learn ways you can apply and manage the scripts you write.

> **NOTE** A PowerShell script is a file with a .ps1 extension that contains Power-Shell commands.

For your first script, we'll re-create the "Hello world" program from chapter 1. You can do it from the command line using redirection to write the script text to a file called hello.ps1:

```
PS> '"Hello world"' > hello.ps1
```

Note the double quotes in the example. You want the script to contain "Hello world" with the quotes intact. Now execute the script:

```
PS> ./hello.ps1
Hello world
```

You see that the file executed and returned the expected phrase.

> **NOTE** In this example, even though hello.ps1 is in the current directory, you had to insert ./ in front of it to run it. That's because PowerShell doesn't execute commands out of the current directory by default. This prevents accidental execution of the wrong command.

7.1.1 Script execution policy

There's a possibility that instead of getting the expected output, you received a nasty error message that looked something like this:

```
PS> ./hello.ps1
The file C:\Documents and Settings\brucepay\hello.ps1 cannot be loaded. The
   file C:\Documents and Settings\brucepay\hello.ps1 is not digitally signed.
   The script will not execute on the system
. Please see "get-help about_signing" for more details.
At line:1 char:11
+ ./hello.ps1 <<<<
```

This PowerShell feature helps prevent running possibly malicious scripts. By default, PowerShell prevents any scripts from running, including your profile (if you have one). The mechanism that controls this is called the *execution policy*. By setting the execution policy, you can control what kind of scripts can be run. You should be aware that the execution policy is not a security feature like an ACL—you can always get around it. Instead, it's a kind of safety belt that helps keep you from possibly doing the wrong thing. For example, the default setting is intended to prevent virus attacks like the infamous ILOVEYOU virus from many years back, where users were being tricked into accidentally executing code mailed to them.

> **NOTE** On client operating systems the default is to block script execution. On Windows Server 2012 R2 and later server operating systems, the default execution policy allows scripts to run locally using the `RemoteSigned` setting.

A scripting tool is no good if you can't script, so there's a cmdlet called `Set -ExecutionPolicy` that you can use to change the execution policy. If you got the error when you tried to execute the script, you should run the following command as Administrator:

```
PS> Set-ExecutionPolicy remotesigned
```

After the command has run successfully, you should be able to run hello.ps1:

```
PS> ./hello.ps1
Hello world
```

> **NOTE** Changing the execution policy to `RemoteSigned` will allow you to execute local scripts that you create yourself while still protecting you from accidentally running scripts from remote sources such as email or a website, unless they're signed (see `about_Signing` for details on how to sign a script). Of course, for this check to work, the mail tool or the web browser used to download the script must set the Zone Identifier stream to indicate where the file came from. Internet Explorer and Microsoft Outlook set this properly. At a minimum, we recommend you use the `RemoteSigned` policy.

If you can't run `Set-ExecutionPolicy` with the necessary administrator privileges but have PowerShell v2 or later, you can use the `-Scope` parameter on the cmdlet to set the execution policy for just the current session (the current process). This looks like

```
Set-ExecutionPolicy -Scope process remotesigned
```

You'll be prompted to confirm this operation. You reply `Y` to tell the system to proceed to make the change. Now when you try to run scripts they'll work—but remember, you changed the execution policy for only this session. The next time you start PowerShell, you'll have to rerun the command.

Okay, now that you have your basic script running, let's start adding functionality to it.

> ## Running elevated
>
> *Running elevated* is a term used on Windows Vista or later that has to do with the User Access Control (UAC) feature added in Vista. It means you're running with administrative privileges. This can be done only when starting a process. Interactively, you can start an elevated PowerShell session by right-clicking the PowerShell icon and selecting Run as Administrator. You then get the UAC prompt asking if you want to allow this action.
>
> If you want to run a single command elevated in a script, you can do so with the `Start-Process` cmdlet and the `-Verb` parameter. For example, you can run `Set-ExecutionPolicy` in an elevated PowerShell session as follows:
>
> ```
> Start-Process -Verb runas -FilePath powershell.exe
> -ArgumentList 'Set-ExecutionPolicy -ExecutionPolicy RemoteSigned'
> ```
>
> When this command is run, you're prompted to allow the action. If you say yes, a new console window appears, the command executes, and the newly created console window closes after the command is complete.

7.1.2 Passing arguments to scripts

Passing those arguments to scripts is pretty much like passing them to basic functions. We'll start with the `$args` variable and look at a modified version of the basic script. Using redirection, this version overwrites the old version of the script:

```
PS> '"Hello $args"' > hello.ps1
```

Run it with an argument:

```
PS> ./hello Bruce
Hello Bruce
```

Great—hello, PowerShell! But if you don't supply an argument

```
PS> ./hello
Hello
```

you get an impersonal greeting.

> **NOTE** You don't have to specify the .ps1 extension when running the script. PowerShell adds this automatically when looking for a script file.

You can take advantage of a here-string to generate a slightly longer script:

```
PS> @'
if ($args) { $name = "$args" } else { $name = "world" }
"Hello $name!"
'@ > hello.ps1
```

This script has two lines. The first sets a local variable $name to the value of $args if it's defined. If it's not defined, it sets $name to world. If you run the script with no arguments, you get the generic greeting:

```
PS> ./hello
Hello world!
```

If you run it with an argument, you get a specific greeting:

```
PS> ./hello Bruce
Hello Bruce!
```

These are the same basic things you did with functions, and they have some limitations. It would be much more useful to have named, typed parameters, as was the case with functions. Obviously, the external definition of parameters isn't going to work with scripts because there's no "external." Consequently, there's only one way to define formal parameters for a script: through the param statement.

> **NOTE**   The internal param statement has become the de facto best practice for functions over the external definition of parameters. The param statement is a comma-delimited list of parameters. Forgetting the comma is a very common typing error!

The param statement must be the first executable line in the script or function. Only comments and empty lines may precede it. Let's visit the "Hello world" example one more time. Again, you'll use a here-string and redirection to create the script. The here-string makes it easy to define a multiline script:

```
PS> @'
param($name="world")
"Hello $name!"
'@ > hello.ps1
```

Here you're adding a second line to the script to declare the script parameter. When you run the script, you find the expected results, first with no arguments

```
PS> ./hello
Hello world!
```

and then with a name argument:

```
PS> ./hello Bruce
Hello Bruce!
```

The script could be written as a single line because there's no need for any kind of separator after the param statement for the script to be valid. Because PowerShell lends itself to one-liner type solutions, this can be handy.

Obviously, scripts must have additional characteristics that you don't find with functions. Let's explore those now.

7.1.3 *Exiting scripts and the exit statement*

As was the case with functions, you can return from scripts simply by getting to the end of the script or by using the `return` statement (section 6.3.2). The `return` statement will let you return from a script but only if it's called from the top level of a script. If you call `return` from a function inside the script, it will return only from that function and not from the script.

But what happens when you want to cause a script to exit from within a function defined in that script? PowerShell has the `exit` statement to do exactly this. So far, you've been using this statement to exit a PowerShell session. But when `exit` is used inside a script, it exits that script. This is true even when called from a function in that script. Here's what that looks like:

```
PS> @'
function callExit { "calling exit from callExit"; exit}
CallExit
"Done my-script"
'@ > my-script.ps1
```

The function `CallExit` defined in this script calls `exit`. The function is called before the line that emits `"Done my-script"`, so you shouldn't see that text emitted. Let's run it:

```
PS> ./my-script.ps1
calling exit from CallExit
```

You see that the script was correctly terminated by the call to `exit` in the function `CallExit`.

The `exit` statement is also how you set the exit code for the PowerShell process when calling `PowerShell.exe` from another program. Here's an example that shows how this works. From within `cmd.exe`, run `PowerShell.exe`, passing it a string to execute. This script will emit the message "Hi there" and then call `exit` with an exit code of 17:

```
C:\>powershell "'Hi there'; exit 17"
Hi there
```

And now you're back at the `cmd.exe` prompt. `cmd.exe` makes the exit code of a program it's run available in the variable `ERRORLEVEL`, so check that variable:

```
C:\> echo %ERRORLEVEL%
17
```

You see that it's 17 as expected.

In the next section, we'll look at another feature of scripts: variable scoping.

7.1.4   *Scopes and scripts*

In chapter 6, we covered the scoping rules for functions. These same general rules also apply to scripts:

- Variables are created when they're first assigned.
- Variable are always created in the current scope, so a variable with the same name in an outer (or global) scope isn't affected.
- In both scripts and functions, you can use the $global:name scope modifier to explicitly modify a global variable.

Now let's see what's added for scripts.

Scripts introduce a new named scope called the *script scope*, indicated by using the $script: scope modifier. This scope modifier is intended to allow functions defined in a script to affect the global state of the script without affecting the overall global state of the interpreter. This is shown in figure 7.1.

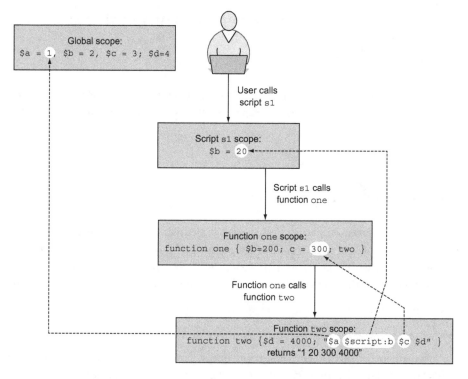

Figure 7.1   How variables are resolved across different scopes when scripts are involved.

Variables prefixed with the $script: modifier resolve in the script scope. Variable references with no scope modifier resolve using the normal lookup rules. In figure 7.1, the user calls script s1, which creates a new script scope. s1 calls function one, which causes a new function scope to be created. one calls function two, creating a second function scope and resulting in a total of four scopes in the scope chain. In function two, $a resolves in the global scope, $script:b resolves in the script scope (skipping the function one scope because of the $script: modifier), $c resolves in the function one scope, and $d resolves in the function two scope ($d is local to two).

Let's look at an example. First, set a global variable $x to 1:

```
PS> $x = 1
```

Then create a script called my-script. In this script, you'll create a function called lfunc. The lfunc function will define a function-scoped variable $x to be 100 and a script-scoped variable $x to be 10. The script itself will run this function and then print the script-scoped variable $x. Use a here-string and redirection to create the script interactively:

```
PS> @'
function lfunc { $x = 100; $script:x = 10 ; "lfunc: x = $x"}
lfunc
"my-script:x = $x"
'@ > my-script.ps1
```

Now run the script:

```
PS> ./my-script.ps1
lfunc: x = 100
my-script:x = 10
```

You see that the function-scoped variable $x was 100; the script-scoped $x was 10

```
PS> "global: x = $x"
global: x = 1
```

and the global $x is still 1.

SIMPLE LIBRARIES: INCLUDING ONE SCRIPT FROM ANOTHER

As you build libraries of useful functions, you need to have a mechanism to include one script inside another (or to run in the global environment) to make these library functions available. PowerShell allows you to do this through a feature called dot-sourcing a script or function.

> **NOTE** The dot-sourcing mechanism (sometimes called *dotting*) was the only way to build libraries in PowerShell v1. In PowerShell v2 and later, dot-sourcing is still used for configuration, but the modules feature (chapters 8 and 9) is the recommended way to create script libraries.

So far in our discussions, you've usually focused on the results of a function and wanted all the local variables when the script or function exits. This is why scripts and functions get their own scope. But sometimes you do care about all the intermediate by-products. This is typically the case when you want to create a library of functions or variable definitions. In this situation, you want the script to run in the current scope.

So how do you dot-source a script? By putting a dot or period in front of the name when you execute it. Note that there has to be a space between the dot and the name; otherwise, it will be considered part of the name. Let's look at an example. First, create a script that sets $x to 22

```
PS> @'
"Setting x to 22"
$x = 22
'@ > my-script.ps1
```

and test it. Set $x to a known value and then run the script as you would normally. Checking $x, you see that it is (correctly) unchanged. Now dot-source the script:

```
PS> . ./my-script
Setting x to 22

PS> $x
22
```

This time, $x is changed. What follows the . isn't limited to a simple filename; it could be a variable or expression.

The last thing to note is that dot-sourcing works for both scripts and functions. Define a function to show this:

```
Ps> function set-x ($x) {$x = $x}
PS . set-x 3
Ps> $x
3
```

In this example, you've defined the function set-x and dotted it, passing in the value 3. The result is that the global variable $x is set to 3. This covers how scoping works with scripts and functions. When we look at modules in chapter 8, you'll see another variation on scoping.

Now that you know how to build simple script libraries, we'll show you how to manage all these scripts you're writing.

7.1.5 *Managing your scripts*

Earlier we looked at managing functions using the function drive. Because scripts live in the file system, there's no need to have a special drive for them—the file system drives are sufficient. But this does require that you understand how scripts are found in the file system. Like most shells, PowerShell uses the PATH environment variable to find scripts. You can look at the contents of this variable using the environment variable provider $ENV:PATH.

NOTE The results may be easier to read if you use $env:Path -split ';'.

The other thing to know (and we mentioned it previously but people still forget it) is that PowerShell doesn't run scripts out of the current directory (at least not by default).

If you want to run a script out of the current directory, you can either add that directory to the path or prefix your command with ./, as in ./mycmd.ps1 or simply ./mycmd. The script search algorithm will look for a command with the .ps1 extension if there isn't one on the command. A common approach is to have a scripts directory where all your personal scripts are placed and a network share for when multiple users need to access the same scripts. Scripts are just text, so using a version control system like RCS or Subversion will work well for managing your scripts.

Now let's look at one more variation on scripting. So far, you've been running PowerShell scripts only from within a PowerShell console. There are times when you need to run a PowerShell script from a non-PowerShell application like cmd.exe or when creating shortcuts that launch PowerShell scripts because PowerShell.exe isn't the default file association for a .ps1 file (security strikes again—this prevents accidental execution of scripts).

7.1.6 *Running PowerShell scripts from other applications*

Let's look at what's involved in using PowerShell.exe to run a script and go over a few issues that exist.

Here's something that can trip people up when using PowerShell.exe to execute a script. The PowerShell interpreter has two parameters that let you run PowerShell code when PowerShell is started. These parameters are -Command and -File, as shown in figure 7.2.

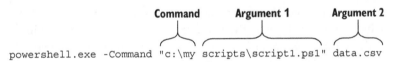

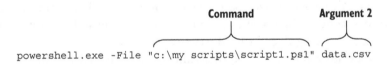

Figure 7.2 How the command line is processed when using the -Command parameter (top) versus the -File parameter (bottom). With -Command, the first argument is parsed into two tokens. With -File, the entire first argument is treated as the name of a script to run.

If you use the -Command parameter, the arguments to PowerShell.exe are accumulated and then treated as a script to execute. This is important to remember when you try to run a script using PowerShell from cmd.exe using this parameter. Here's the problem people run into: Because the arguments to PowerShell.exe are a script to execute, not the name of a file to run, if the path to that script has a space in it, you'll get an error because PowerShell treats the spaces as delimiters. Consider a script called my script .ps1. When you try to run this

```
powershell "./my script.ps1"
```

PowerShell will complain about my being an unrecognized command. It treats my as a command name and script.ps1 as an argument to that command. To execute a script with a space in the name, you need to do the same thing you'd do at the PowerShell command prompt: put the name in quotes and use the call (&) operator:

```
powershell.exe "& './my script.ps1'"
```

Now the script will be run properly. This is one of the areas where having two types of quotes comes in handy. Also note that you still have to use the relative path to find the script even if it's in the current directory.

To address this problem PowerShell.exe now has a second parameter that makes this easier: the -File parameter. This parameter takes the first argument after the parameter as the name of the file to run, and the remaining arguments are passed to the script. The example now simplifies to

```
powershell -File "my script.ps1"
```

This is clearly much simpler than the v1 example.

There's one more advantage to using -File. When you run a script using -Command, the exit keyword will exit the script but not the PowerShell session (though usually it looks like it did). This is because the arguments to -Command are treated the same way commands typed interactively into PowerShell work. You wouldn't want a script you're running to cause your session to exit accidentally. If you use -File instead of –Command, calling exit in the script will cause the PowerShell.exe process to exit. This is because -File treats the entire contents of the script as the command to execute instead of executing a command that names the script file.

Now let's see why this is important. It matters if you're depending on the exit code of the PowerShell process to decide some condition in the calling script. If you use -Command, the exit code of the script is set, but the process will still exit with 0. If you use -File, PowerShell.exe will exit with the correct exit code.

This concludes our coverage of the basic information needed to run PowerShell scripts. If you've used other scripting languages, little of what you've seen so far should seem unfamiliar. In the next few sections we're going to look at features that are rather more advanced.

7.2   *Writing advanced functions and scripts*

The scripts and functions you've seen so far don't have all the features of compiled cmdlets. You need a way to write production-quality scripts complete with integrated help and so on. In this section, we'll introduce features that enable your commands, written in the PowerShell language, to have all the capabilities available to cmdlets. We'll be using functions for all the examples just for simplicity's sake. Everything in the rest of this chapter that applies to functions applies equally to scripts.

All these new features are enabled by adding *metadata* to the function or script parameters. Metadata is information about information, and you use it in PowerShell to declaratively control the behavior of functions and scripts. What this means is that you're telling PowerShell *what* you want to do but not *how* to do it; for example, you can tell a parameter that it can accept values only from a predefined set. When you run the function, the value for that parameter will be checked to determine if it's a member of the set. If it is a member, the function runs. If it isn't a member of the approved set of values, an error is thrown. All you do is define the metadata—the set of approved values—and PowerShell takes care of the checking and subsequent actions.

> **NOTE** One of the most frequent mistakes we see people make is creating code to perform the actions they can get the metadata to perform. Don't reinvent the wheel. Use your time to develop code that benefits your organization.

We're ready to dive in now, but first a warning. There's a lot of material here, and some of it is a bit complex, so taking your time and experimenting with the features is recommended.

> **NOTE** This stuff is much more complex than the PowerShell team wanted. Could it have been simpler? Maybe, but the team hasn't figured out a way to do it yet. The upside of the way these features are implemented is that they match how things are done in compiled cmdlets. This way, the time invested in learning this material will be of benefit if you want to learn to write cmdlets at some point. And at the same time, if you know how to write cmdlets, then all this stuff will be pretty familiar.

7.2.1   *Specifying script and function attributes*

In this section, we'll look at the features you can control through metadata attributes on the function or script definition (as opposed to on parameters, which we'll get to in a minute). Figure 7.3 shows how the metadata attributes are used when defining a function, including attributes that affect the function as well as individual parameters on that function.

Notice that there are two places where the attributes can be added to functions: to the function itself and to the individual parameters. With scripts, the metadata attribute has to appear before the `param` statement, though the `param` has to be the first non-comment line. The metadata attributes are considered part of the `param` statement.

The `CmdletBinding` attribute is used to add metadata to the function, specifying behaviors that apply to all parameters and the return type of the function, for instance. The attribute syntax where the attribute names are enclosed in brackets is similar to the way you specify types. This is because attributes are implemented using .NET types. The important distinction is that an attribute must have parentheses after the name. As you can see in figure 7.3, you can place properties on the attribute in the parentheses. But even if you're specifying no attributes, the parentheses must still be there so the interpreter can distinguish between a type literal and an attribute. Now let's look at the most important attribute: `CmdletBinding`.

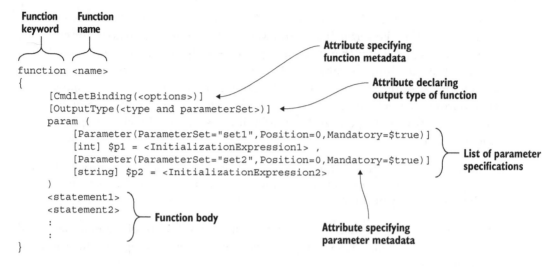

Figure 7.3 Attributes that apply to the entire function appear before the `param` statement, and attributes for an individual parameter appear before the parameter declaration.

7.2.2 The CmdletBinding attribute

The CmdletBinding attribute is used to specify properties that apply to the whole function or script. You also get a number of common parameters such as -Debug and -Verbose added to your function for no extra work!

Implicit metadata

The CmdletBinding attribute adds the common parameters to a function. Let's start with a simple function:

```
PS> function x {1+1}
PS> Get-Command x -Syntax
x
```

Using [CmdletBinding()] explicitly creates an advanced function:

```
PS> function x {[CmdletBinding()] param() 1+1}
PS> Get-Command x -Syntax
x [<CommonParameters>]
```

You can implicitly create an advanced function by using the Parameter attribute:

```
PS> function x {param([Parameter()][int]$x) $x+1}
PS> Get-Command x -Syntax
x [[-x] <int>] [<CommonParameters>]
```

This is legal PowerShell and documented in the about_Functions_Advanced_Parameters help file: "All attributes are optional. But if you omit the CmdletBinding attribute,

> **(Continued)**
>
> then to be recognized as an advanced function, the function must include the `Parameter` attribute."
>
> The implicit approach works, but we recommend that you use the explicit approach and the `CmdletBinding` attribute.

Simply having the attribute in the definition changes how excess parameters are handled. If the function is defined without this attribute, the arguments for which there are no formal parameters are simply added to the `$args` variable. As discussed earlier, although this can be useful, it's usually better to generate an error for this situation.

You can check for this case and see if `$args.Count` is greater than 0, but it's easier to handle this declaratively by adding the metadata attribute, as shown here:

```
PS> function x {[CmdletBinding()] param($a, $b)
"a=$a b=$b args=$args"}
```

When you run the command with extra arguments

```
PS> x 1 2 3 4
x : A positional parameter cannot be found that accepts argument '3'.
At line:1 char:1
+ x 1 2 3 4
+ ~~~~~~~~~
    + CategoryInfo          : InvalidArgument: (:) [x],
  ParameterBindingException
    + FullyQualifiedErrorId : PositionalParameterNotFound,x
```

the system catches this and generates the error message. You get standard, complete, and consistent error messages that are already set up to display in many languages with minimal effort on your part!

Now let's look at the properties that can be specified for the `CmdletBinding` attribute. These properties are shown in table 7.1.

Table 7.1 Properties available on the `CmdletBinding` attribute

Name	Possible values
ConfirmImpact	Low, Medium, High, None
DefaultParameterSetName	Name of default parameter set defined in function
HelpURI	URI of online help for function
SupportPaging	$true, $false
SupportsShouldProcess	$true, $false
PositionalBinding	$true, $false

We'll describe what each of these properties does and how to use them in the next few subsections.

THE CONFIRMIMPACT PROPERTY

Not all commands have the same consequences, and sometimes you need to ask the user to confirm an action. You have a way to indicate this with this property. The ConfirmImpact property specifies when the action of the function should be confirmed by calling the ShouldProcess() method.

The call to the ShouldProcess() method displays a confirmation prompt only when the ConfirmImpact argument is equal to or greater than the value of the $Confirm-Preference preference variable. (The default value of the argument is Medium.) Obviously, this property should be used only when SupportsShouldProcess is also specified.

THE DEFAULTPARAMETERSETNAME PROPERTY

The DefaultParameterSetName property specifies the name of the parameter set that the runtime will use if it can't figure out the parameter set from the specified parameters. We'll look at this a bit more when we cover the parameter metadata in section 7.2.4.

THE HELPURI PROPERTY

The HelpURI property specifies the internet address (Uniform Resource Identifier (URI)) of the online version of the help file associated with the function. The online help is used when the -Online parameter is used with Get-Help. The address must include the http or https part of the URI. This value is returned by Get-Command:

```
PS> Get-Command Get-Service  | Format-List help*
HelpUri  : http://go.microsoft.com/fwlink/?LinkID=113332
HelpFile : Microsoft.PowerShell.Commands.Management.dll-Help.xml
```

If a URI is specified, an external help file or comment-based help will override the value supplied through the HelpUri property of CmdletBinding.

THE SUPPORTSPAGING PROPERTY

The SupportsPaging property adds three parameters to the function, as shown in table 7.2.

Table 7.2   Parameters added to a function by the SupportsPaging property

Name	Purpose
First	Gets first *n* objects only.
Skip	Ignores first *n* objects and then gets remaining objects.
IncludeTotalCount	Reports number of objects in the data set, followed by objects. Unknown total count is returned if number of objects can't be determined.

The use of this property is best demonstrated by an example:

```
function test-paging {
    [CmdletBinding(SupportsPaging=$true)]
    param()

    $firstnumber =
    [math]::Min($pscmdlet.PagingParameters.Skip, 20)

    $lastnumber =
    [math]::Min($pscmdlet.PagingParameters.First +
    $firstnumber -1, 20)

    if ($pscmdlet.PagingParameters.IncludeTotalCount){
        $totalcountaccuracy = 1.0

        $totalcount =
        $pscmdlet.PagingParameters.NewTotalCount(20,
        $totalcountaccuracy)

        Write-Output $totalcount
    }
    $firstnumber..$lastnumber | Write-Output
}
```

The function will return a collection of consecutive numbers. The first number in the collection is a minimum of 20 and the value of the Skip parameter, which defaults to 0. The last number is the minimum of 20 and the sum of the value of the First parameter plus the value of the first number in the collection minus 1.

If the IncludeTotalCount parameter is used, the NewTotalCount method is invoked. The $totalcountaccuracy variable determines the accuracy of the count:

- Accuracy = 1 implies the exact number of results are known.
- Accuracy > 0 but < 1 implies the count of the items is only an estimate. The accuracy of the estimate improves as the value approaches 1.
- Accuracy = 0 implies the number of items is unknown.

Sample results of using the test-paging function are shown in table 7.3.

Table 7.3 Results of using test-paging function

Test	Result
test-paging	Displays 0–20
test-paging -Skip 5	Displays 5–20
test-paging -First 5	Displays 0–4
test-paging -First 5 -Skip 2	Displays 2–6
test-paging -First 5 -Skip 2 -IncludeTotalCount	Displays Total count:20 and numbers 2–6

THE SUPPORTSSHOULDPROCESS PROPERTY

When the SupportsShouldProcess property is set to true, it tells the runtime to enable the -Confirm and -WhatIf standard parameters. The function uses the ShouldProcess() method to ask the user for feedback before proceeding with the operation or to show what the operation might have done to the system. The $PSCmdlet variable is an automatic variable that provides the callback mechanisms which the function needs to make the expected calls. We'll cover the $PSCmdlet variable in more detail at the end of this section.

Let's write an example function that shows how it all works. The purpose of this function is to allow the user to stop processes on the system. Because stopping the wrong process could have undesirable consequences, you want to be able to use the -Confirm and -WhatIf parameters.

This function uses the Win32_Process WMI class to get objects representing processes on the system. (See chapter 16 for more information about WMI.) You filter the set of processes using the Where-Object cmdlet and then call the Terminate() method on the process object.

Obviously this is a potentially destructive operation, so you want to call the Should-Process() method before proceeding with the action (you saw this behavior with the Set-ExecutionPolicy cmdlet). You call this method passing two [string] arguments. The first argument is used to tell the user what object you're going to operate on. The second argument describes the operation to be performed—an operation caption. If this method returns true, you call Terminate() to end the process. Let's try it. First, define the function:

```
function Stop-ProcessUsingWMI
{
    [CmdletBinding(SupportsShouldProcess=$True)]
    param(
      [parameter(mandatory=$true)] [regex] $pattern
    )
    foreach ($process in Get-WmiObject Win32_Process |
        where { $_.Name -match $pattern })
    {
        if ($PSCmdlet.ShouldProcess(
            "process $($process.Name) " +
            " (id: $($process.ProcessId))" ,
            "Stop Process"))
        {
            $process.Terminate()
        }
    }
}
```

Next, start a Notepad process:

```
PS> notepad
```

Now call `Stop-ProcessUsingWMI`, specifying the `-WhatIf` parameter:

```
PS> Stop-ProcessUsingWMI notepad -Whatif
What if: Performing operation "Stop Process" on Target
"process notepad.exe  (id: 6748)".
```

You see a description of the operation that would be performed. The `-WhatIf` option was only supposed to show what it would have done, but not do it, so you'll use `Get -Process` to verify that the command is still running:

```
Get-Process notepad | Format-Table name,id -auto

Name     Id
----     --
notepad 6748
```

Let's perform the operation again but this time use the `-Confirm` flag. This requests that you be prompted for confirmation before executing the operation. When you get the prompt, you'll respond y to continue with the operation:

```
PS> Stop-ProcessUsingWMI notepad -Confirm

Confirm
Are you sure you want to perform this action?
Performing operation "Stop Process" on Target
"process notepad.exe  (id: 6748)".
[Y] Yes  [A] Yes to All  [N] No  [L] No to All
[S] Suspend[?] Help (default is "Y"): y
```

And the operation was performed. Use `Get-Process` to confirm that the Notepad process no longer exists—you'll get an error saying the process can't be found.

Using the `ShouldProcess` mechanism in your scripts and functions when they'll perform destructive operations is a scripting best practice. Although it requires a bit of effort on the script author's part, it adds tremendous value for the script user.

THE $PSCMDLET VARIABLE

As mentioned earlier, the `$PSCmdlet` variable gives the script or function author the necessary callbacks and properties needed to be able to take advantage of all the advanced function features. As well as being able to call `ShouldProcess()`, you get access to the parameter set name through the `$PSCmdlet.ParameterSetName` property. It allows you to halt a pipeline containing this command by calling the `$PSCmdlet .ThrowTerminatingError()` method. It makes all the features available to compiled cmdlet writers available to script and function authors. Refer to the PowerShell SDK documentation to get complete details on the features available through `$PSCmdlet`.

THE POSITIONALBINDING PROPERTY

The `PositionalBinding` property determines whether parameters are positional by default. Its default value is `$true`, so PowerShell will always assign position numbers to the function's parameters in the order in which they are declared in the `param` statement of the function. If you don't want your function to use positional parameters, set the property's value to `$false`. If an individual parameter has a `Position` argument, that value will take precedence over the setting in the `PositionalBinding` property.

This completes our discussion of the `CmdletBinding` attribute and the properties that apply to the function or script as a whole. Next, we'll explore the other attribute that can be applied to a function or script: `OutputType`.

7.2.3   *The OutputType attribute*

The `OutputType` attribute allows you to declare the expected return type of a function or script. Like the `CmdletBinding` attribute, this attribute applies to the whole function. It doesn't affect the output type and isn't checked by the runtime at any point. What it does do is allow you to document the expected return type in such a way that tools such as editors can use it to do things like provide IntelliSense for the next cmdlet to add to a pipeline. In this scenario, the editor would show the list of cmdlets that take the previous output type as an input.

Specifying the return type sounds like it should be easy, but functions may return more than one type. In fact, some cmdlets, like `Where-Object`, can return any type because they return only what they were passed. A more common and manageable case occurs when you have different types of objects being returned when different parameters sets are used, as shown here.

```
Listing 7.1   Testing output type
```

```
function Test-OutputType
  {
    [CmdletBinding(DefaultParameterSetName = '1nt')]
    [OutputType('asInt', [int])]
    [OutputType('asString', [string])]
    [OutputType('asDouble', ([double], [single]))]
    [OutputType('lie', [int])]
    param (
      [parameter(ParameterSetName='asInt')] [switch] $asInt,
      [parameter(ParameterSetName='asString')] [switch] $asString,
      [parameter(ParameterSetName='asDouble')] [switch] $asDouble,
      [parameter(ParameterSetName='lie')] [switch] $lie
    )
  Write-Host "Parameter set: $($PSCmdlet.ParameterSetName)"
  switch ($PSCmdlet.ParameterSetName) {
      'asInt' { 1 ; break }
      'asString' { '1' ; break }
      'asDouble' { 1.0 ; break }
      'lie' { 'Hello there'; break } }
  }
```

Now let's try out some of the different switches:

```
PS> (Test-OutputType -asString).GetType().FullName
Parameter set: asString
System.String
```

```
PS> (Test-OutputType -asInt).GetType().FullName
Parameter set: asInt
System.Int32
```

Okay—everything is as expected; in each case the correct type was returned. Now use the -lie parameter:

```
PS> (Test-OutputType -lie).GetType().FullName
Parameter set: lie
System.String
```

Even though you specified the OutputType to be [int], the function returned a string. As we said, the attribute is only documentation—it doesn't enforce the type.

NOTE The return type in PowerShell class methods is normative (enforced). We'll cover this in greater detail in chapter 19.

You can discover the output types using the OutputType property produced by Get-Command:

```
PS> (Get-Command Test-OutputType).OutputType
```

```
Name                             Type
----                             ----
asInt
int                              System.Int32
asString
string                           System.String
asDouble
System.Double System.Single System.Double
lie
int                              System.Int32
```

The Name property shows the parameter set name, if appropriate, and then the name and type of the OutputType. There will be one set of entries per OutputType defined in the function.

This also works for cmdlets:

```
PS> (Get-Command Get-Service).OutputType | Format-List
```

```
Name  : System.ServiceProcess.ServiceController
Type  : System.ServiceProcess.ServiceController
```

At this point, you might be saying, "Why bother to specify this?" The answer is that good scripts will last beyond any individual release of PowerShell.

NOTE One of us has scripts written over 10 years ago when PowerShell v1 was still in beta and known as Monad!

This information is somewhat useful now and will probably be much more useful in the future. As a best practice, it's strongly recommended that this information be included in scripts that you want to share with others.

Something we skipped over in the `OutputType` example was the `Parameter` attribute. We used it but didn't talk about what it does. We'll remedy that in the next section.

7.2.4 Specifying parameter attributes

We specify additional information on parameters using the `Parameter` attribute. This information is used to control how the parameter is processed. The attribute is placed before the parameter definition, as shown in figure 7.4.

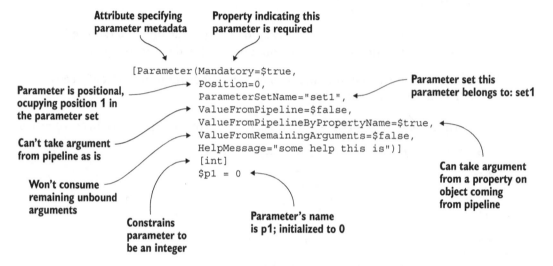

Figure 7.4 This figure shows how the `Parameter` attribute is used when declaring a variable. The attribute must appear before that variable name and its optional initializer expression. The figure includes all the properties that can be set on the parameter.

As was the case with the `CmdletBinding` attribute, specific behaviors are controlled through a set of properties provided as arguments to the attribute. Although figure 7.4 shows all the properties that can be specified, you only have to provide the ones you want to set to something other than the default value.

NOTE A common error is to provide all of the properties and give them their default values. This is a waste of your time and will most likely introduce typing mistakes.

Let's look at an example and then go through each of the properties.

The following example shows a parameter declaration that defines the `-Path` parameter. Say you want the parameter to have the following characteristics:

- It's mandatory; that is, the user must specify it or an error is generated.
- It takes input from the pipeline.
- It requires its argument to be convertible to an array of strings.

The parameter declaration needed to do all that looks like this:

```
param (
    [parameter(Mandatory=$true,
     ValueFromPipeline=$true)]
    [string[]] $Parameter
)
```

The result is fairly simple because you need to specify only the things you want to change. All other properties keep their default values. In the next few sections, we'll look at each of the possible properties, what each does, and how it can be used.

THE MANDATORY PROPERTY

By default, all function and script parameters are optional, which means that the caller of the command doesn't have to specify them. If you want to require that the parameter be specified, set the `Mandatory` property in the `Parameter` attribute to `$true`; if the property is absent or set to `$false`, the parameter is optional.

> **NOTE** We see a lot of functions where people write `Mandatory=$false` on all their parameters. This is not needed and is a waste of effort. Also, default values are ignored when the parameter is made mandatory. You can use `Mandatory` without the value but we recommend the full syntax for clarity.

The following example shows the declaration of a parameter that's required when the function is run:

```
function Test-Mandatory
{
    param ( [Parameter(Mandatory=$true)] $myParam)
    $myParam
}
```

Now run this function without a parameter:

```
PS> Test-Mandatory

cmdlet Test-Mandatory at command pipeline position 1
Supply values for the following parameters:
myParam: HELLO THERE
HELLO THERE
```

The PowerShell runtime notices that a mandatory parameter wasn't specified on the command line, so it prompts the user to specify it, which we do. Now the function can run to completion.

THE POSITION PROPERTY

You saw earlier in this chapter that all parameters are both positional and named by default. When using advanced parameter specification metadata, either adding the `CmdletBinding` attribute to the whole function or specifying an individual `Parameter` attribute, parameters remain positional by default, until you specify a position for at least one of them.

Once you start formally specifying positions, all parameters default to non-positional unless the Position property for that parameter is set. The following example shows a function with two parameters, neither one having Position set:

```
function Test-Position
{
  param (
    [parameter()] $p1 = 'p1 unset',
    $p2 = 'p2 unset'
  )
  "p1 = '$p1' p2='$p2'"
}
```

Now when you run it with positional parameters

```
PS> Test-Position one two
p1 = 'one' p2='two'
```

the arguments are bound by position and there's no error.

Replace

```
[parameter()] $p1 = 'p1 unset',
```

with

```
[parameter(Position=0)] $p1 = 'p1 unset',
```

and run it again with two positional parameters:

```
PS> Test-Position one two
Test-Position : A positional parameter cannot be found that accepts argument
    'two'.
At line:1 char:1
+ Test-Position one two
+ ~~~~~~~~~~~~~~~~~~~~~~
    + CategoryInfo          : InvalidArgument: (:) [Test-Position],
  ParameterBindingException
    + FullyQualifiedErrorId : PositionalParameterNotFound,Test-Position
```

This time you get an error. Although there's a second parameter, it's no longer positional. If you run the function again specifying the second parameter by name,

```
PS> Test-Position one  -p2 two
p1 = 'one' p2='two'
```

it all works.

THE PARAMETERSETNAME PROPERTY

The `ParameterSetName` property allows you to specify the parameter set or sets that a parameter belongs to. If no parameter set is specified, the parameter belongs to all the parameter sets defined by the function. The following listing shows the parameter declaration of two parameters that belong to two different parameter sets.

Listing 7.2   Testing parameter sets

```
function Test-ParameterSets
{
  param (
    [parameter(ParameterSetName='s1')] $p1='p1 unset',
    [parameter(ParameterSetName='s2')] $p2='p2 unset',
    [parameter(ParameterSetName='s1')]
    [parameter(ParameterSetName='s2',Mandatory=$true)]
     $p3='p3 unset',
     $p4='p4 unset'
  )
  'Parameter set = ' + $PSCmdlet.ParameterSetName
  "p1=$p1 p2=$p2 p3=$p3 p4=$p4"
}
```

You can view the parameter sets available on a command—cmdlet, function, or script:

```
PS> Get-Command Test-ParameterSets -Syntax

Test-ParameterSets [-p1 <Object>] [-p3 <Object>]
[-p4 <Object>] [<CommonParameters>]

Test-ParameterSets -p3 <Object> [-p2 <Object>]
[-p4 <Object>] [<CommonParameters>]
```

Notice the difference in the way -p3 is shown between the parameter sets. The lack of [] in the second parameter set indicates that it's mandatory. Modifying the parameter behavior between parameter sets like this is a common question on forums.

> **NOTE**   The ability to modify the parameter behavior by parameter set is very powerful, but as with all options the more complicated you make things, the harder they are to maintain.

Let's try it. First, call the function, specifying -p1 and -p4:

```
PS> Test-ParameterSets -p1 one -p4 four
Parameter set = s1
p1=one p2= p3=p3 unset p4=four
```

The parameter binder resolves to parameter set s1, where the -p3 parameter isn't mandatory. Next specify -p1, -p3, and -p4:

```
PS> Test-ParameterSets -p1 one -p3 three -p4 four
Parameter set = s1
p1=one p2=p2 unset p3=three p4=four
```

You still resolve to parameter set s1 but this time -p3 is bound. Now let's look at the other parameter set. Because you're specifying -p2 instead of -p1, the second parameter set, s2, is used, as you can see in the output:

```
PS> Test-ParameterSets -p2 two -p3 three
Parameter set = s2
p1=p1 unset p2=two p3=three p4=p4 unset
```

Now in parameter set s2, the parameter -p3 is mandatory. Try running the function without specifying it:

```
PS> Test-ParameterSets -p2 two

cmdlet Test-ParameterSets at command pipeline position 1
Supply values for the following parameters:
p3: THREE
Parameter set = s2
p1=p1 unset p2=two p3=THREE p4=p4 unset
```

The runtime will prompt for the missing parameter. You provide the missing value at the prompt, and the function completes successfully.

Let's verify that the parameter -p4 is allowed in both parameter sets. You run the following command specifying -p4:

```
PS> Test-ParameterSets -p2 two -p3 three -p4 four
Parameter set = s2
p1=p1 unset p2=two p3=three p4=four
```

This works properly. Now try specifying all four of the parameters in the same command; this shouldn't work because -p1 and -p2 are in different parameter sets, so the parameter binder can't resolve to a single parameter set:

```
PS> Test-ParameterSets -p1 one -p2 two -p3 three `
 -p4 four
Test-ParameterSets : Parameter set cannot be resolved using the specified
  named parameters.
At line:1 char:1
+ Test-ParameterSets -p1 one -p2 two -p3 three -p4 four
+ ~~~~~~~~~~~~~~~~~~~~~~~~~~~~~~~~~~~~~~~~~~~~~~~~~~~~~~~
    + CategoryInfo          : InvalidArgument: (:)
  [Test-ParameterSets], ParameterBindingException
    + FullyQualifiedErrorId : AmbiguousParameterSet,Test-ParameterSets
```

As expected, the system responds with an error.

THE VALUEFROMPIPELINE PROPERTY

You saw earlier how to use $_ in the process block to handle pipeline objects. This approach works but makes it difficult to handle both pipeline and command-line bindings.

The `ValueFromPipeline` property enables parameters to take values from the command line and the pipeline. Here's an example:

```
function Test-ValueFromPipeline
{
    param([Parameter(ValueFromPipeline = $true)] $x)
    process { $x }
}
```

Now try it with the command line

```
PS> Test-ValueFromPipeline 123
123
```

and it works properly. Now try a pipelined value:

```
PS> 123 | Test-ValueFromPipeline
123
```

This also works properly. And because you're using the process block, you can handle a collection of values as well as single values.

The `ValueFromPipeline` property allows you to tell the runtime to bind the entire object to the parameter. But sometimes you only want a property on the object. This is what the `ValueFromPipelineByPropertyName` attribute is for, as you'll see next.

THE VALUEFROMPIPELINEBYPROPERTYNAME PROPERTY

Whereas `ValueFromPipeline` caused the entire pipeline object to be bound to the parameter, the `ValueFromPipelineByPropertyName` property tells the runtime to use a property on the object instead of the whole object when binding the parameter. The name of the property to use comes from the parameter name. Let's modify the previous example to illustrate this:

```
function Test-ValueFromPipelineByPropertyName
{
 param(
  [Parameter(ValueFromPipelineByPropertyName=$true)]
  $DayOfWeek
 )
 process { $DayOfWeek }
}
```

This function has one parameter, named `DayOfWeek`, that's bound from the pipeline by property name. Notice that you haven't added a type constraint to this property, so any type of value will work. Let's use the `Get-Date` cmdlet to emit an object with a `DayOfWeek` property:

```
PS> Get-Date | Test-ValueFromPipelineByPropertyName
Saturday
```

This returns `Saturday` (the day we wrote this), so binding from the pipeline works fine. What happens when you bind from the command line?

```
PS> Test-ValueFromPipelineByPropertyName (Get-Date)
15 April 2017 21:23:03
```

This time you get the entire `DateTime` object. Normal command-line binding isn't affected by the attribute. To get the same result, you have to extract the property yourself:

```
PS> Test-ValueFromPipelineByPropertyName `
  ((Get-Date).DayOfWeek)
Saturday
```

That takes care of the single-value case. For multiple objects, each inbound pipeline object is bound to the parameter by property name one at a time. Next, we'll show how to handle variable numbers of arguments when using command metadata.

THE VALUEFROMREMAININGARGUMENTS PROPERTY

You saw earlier that when you didn't use any of the metadata annotations, excess arguments ended up in the `$args` variable. But once you add the metadata, the presence of excess arguments results in an error. Because it's sometimes useful to allow a variable number of parameters, PowerShell provides the `ValueFromRemaining-Arguments` property, which tells the runtime to bind all excess arguments to this parameter. The following example shows a function with two parameters. The first argument goes into the `-First` parameter and the remaining arguments are bound to `-Rest`:

```
function vfraExample
{
  param (
    $First,
    [parameter(ValueFromRemainingArguments=$true)]
    $Rest
  )
  "First is $first rest is $rest"
}
```

Let's run the function with four arguments:

```
PS> vfraExample 1 2 3 4
First is 1 rest is 2 3 4
```

The first ends up in `$first` with the remaining placed in `$rest`. Now try using `-Rest` as a named parameter:

```
PS> vfraExample 1 -Rest 2 3 4
vfraExample : A positional parameter cannot be found that accepts argument
  '3'.
At line:1 char:1
+ vfraExample 1 -Rest 2 3 4
```

```
+ ~~~~~~~~~~~~~~~~~~~~~~~~~
    + CategoryInfo          : InvalidArgument: (:)
[vfraExample], ParameterBindingException
    + FullyQualifiedErrorId : PositionalParameterNotFound,vfraExample
```

This fails. When the parameter is specified by name, it won't receive the excess arguments and you'll get an error. If you use the parameter by name, you'll have to pass the remaining arguments explicitly as a list, as shown here:

```
PS> vfraExample 1 -Rest 2,3,4
First is 1 rest is 2 3 4
```

THE HELPMESSAGE PROPERTY

The HelpMessage property allows you to attach a short help message to the parameter. This message is displayed *only* when prompting for a missing mandatory parameter.

First, you need a function that has a mandatory parameter so the runtime will prompt if you don't supply it. Also, make it an array so you can specify more than one object when prompted. Here's the function:

```
function helpMessageExample
{
  param (
    [parameter(Mandatory=$true,
        HelpMessage='An array of path names.')]
    [string[]]
    $Path
  )
  "Path: $path"
}
```

Now run it with no arguments so the system will prompt for the missing value:

```
PS> helpMessageExample

cmdlet helpMessageExample at command pipeline position 1
Supply values for the following parameters:
(Type !? for Help.)
Path[0]: !?
An array of path names.
Path[0]: foo
Path[1]: bar
Path[2]:
Path: foo bar
```

When prompted, you can enter !? to see the help message, giving you more information about the type of thing you're supposed to enter.

> **NOTE** A common error is that users forget that the parameters in the param() block are a comma-separated list. Forgetting the comma after the parameter definition is easy to do and can cause you to lose a lot of time tracking down the error. You've been warned.

And with that, we're finished with our discussion of the `Parameter` attribute and its properties. But we're not finished with parameter attributes quite yet. The next thing to look at is the `Alias` attribute. This is a pretty simple feature, but it has a couple of important uses.

7.2.5   *Creating parameter aliases with the Alias attribute*

The `Alias` attribute allows you to specify alternate names for a parameter. It's typically used to add a well-defined shortcut for that parameter. If you'll recall our parameter discussion in chapter 1, we said that you only have to specify enough of a parameter name to uniquely identify it. Unfortunately, if you add a new parameter to a command that has the same prefix as an existing parameter, you now need a longer prefix to distinguish the name.

Any scripts that used the old short prefix would fail because they'd be unable to distinguish which parameter to use. This is where the `Alias` attribute comes in. It can be used to add distinctive and mnemonic short forms for parameters.

Let's look at an example. The following function defines a single parameter: -ComputerName. You'll give this parameter an alias: -CN. Here's the function definition:

```
function Test-ParameterAlias
{
    param (
        [alias('CN')]
        $ComputerName
    )
    "The computer name is $ComputerName"
}
```

These options all work as expected:

```
PS> Test-ParameterAlias -ComputerName foo
PS> Test-ParameterAlias -CN foo
PS> Test-ParameterAlias -com foo
```

Next, create a new version of the command. Add a new parameter: -Compare. Here's the new function definition:

```
function Test-ParameterAlias
{
    param (
        [alias('CN')]
        $ComputerName,
        [switch] $Compare
    )
    "The computer name is $ComputerName,
     compare=$compare"
}
```

Try running the command with the parameter prefix -Com again:

```
PS> Test-ParameterAlias -Com foo
Test-ParameterAlias : Parameter cannot be processed because the parameter
    name 'com' is ambiguous. Possible matches include: -ComputerName -Compare.
```

```
At line:1 char:21
+ Test-ParameterAlias -com foo
+                     ~~~~
    + CategoryInfo          : InvalidArgument: (:) [Test-ParameterAlias],
   ParameterBindingException
    + FullyQualifiedErrorId : AmbiguousParameter,
Test-ParameterAlias
```

This time you get an error because -Com could refer to either parameter. But if you use the -CN alias

```
PS> Test-ParameterAlias -CN foo
The computer name is foo,
    compare=False
```

it works.

Another scenario where you might add an alias is when you're also using the Value-FromPipelineByPropertyName property on the Parameter attribute. There are a number of places where the objects you're working with have similar parameters with different names. For example, the file system objects returned by Get-ChildItem have a Name property, whereas the objects returned by Get-Process have a ProcessName property. If you wanted to create a function that worked with both of these types, you could have a parameter named Name with an alias ProcessName. How about also working with services? The objects returned from Get-Service have a ServiceName property. No problem—just add another alias for ServiceName. In practice, there's no limit to the number of aliases that can be assigned to a parameter.

Now let's look at the last type of parameter metadata: the validation attributes that let you constrain the parameter values in much more interesting ways than just by type.

7.2.6 *Parameter validation attributes*

The last class of parameter attributes we'll cover are the parameter validation attributes. You already know how to add a type constraint to a parameter where you require that the argument be of a particular type. The parameter validation attributes allow you to specify additional constraints on the argument to a parameter. The available parameter validation attributes are shown in figure 7.5.

In many cases these constraints seem like trivial functions (and mostly they are), but they're valuable for a couple of reasons:

- *They declare the parameter contract.* This means that by inspecting the parameter declaration, you can see what constraints are present. This also means that other tools can work with this information as well to drive IntelliSense-like features.
- *You don't have to write any error-handling code.* By specifying the attribute, you're declaring the constraint, and the runtime takes care of doing the work of checking the value for you. Because the PowerShell runtime does the check, it can generate standardized error messages, translated into whatever language the user's environment is configured for. It's a nifty feature.

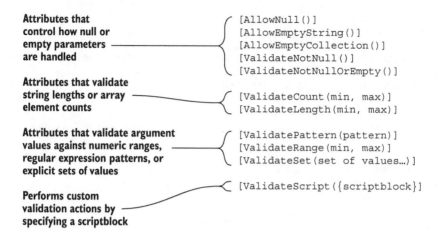

Attributes that control how null or empty parameters are handled
```
[AllowNull()]
[AllowEmptyString()]
[AllowEmptyCollection()]
[ValidateNotNull()]
[ValidateNotNullOrEmpty()]
```

Attributes that validate string lengths or array element counts
```
[ValidateCount(min, max)]
[ValidateLength(min, max)]
```

Attributes that validate argument values against numeric ranges, regular expression patterns, or explicit sets of values
```
[ValidatePattern(pattern)]
[ValidateRange(min, max)]
[ValidateSet(set of values…)]
```

Performs custom validation actions by specifying a scriptblock
```
[ValidateScript({scriptblock})]
```

Figure 7.5   The validation attributes can be applied to script and function parameters to specify additional parameter checks to perform when binding arguments.

> **NOTE**   A very common error is for users to write line after line of code, testing and validating their input parameters. Don't! Use these validation attributes instead.

The other interesting thing is that the set of attributes isn't fixed; a .NET programmer can create new attributes by deriving from the existing base classes. Although this isn't yet possible in the PowerShell language, you do have ValidateScript, which lets you do similar things. We'll get to that once we cover the other available attributes.

VALIDATION ATTRIBUTE: ALLOWNULL

The AllowNull attribute should make sense only if the associated parameter is marked as mandatory. This is because, by default, mandatory parameters don't allow you to pass $null to them. If this attribute is specified, the check is suppressed and $null can be passed to the parameter. For example:

```
function allowNullExample
{
  param
  (
    [parameter(Mandatory=$true)]
    [AllowNull()]
    $objectToTest
  )
  $objectToTest -eq $null
}
```

VALIDATION ATTRIBUTE: ALLOWEMPTYSTRING

The AllowEmptyString attribute is a variation on the AllowNull attribute. Mandatory parameters won't permit empty strings to be passed either. You should specify this attribute if, for some unknown reason, you want to allow your function or script to deal with empty strings in mandatory parameters.

> **NOTE** It's hard to think of a good case where you want to allow $null or an empty argument to be passed to a function. If you do this but don't have correct code in your function or script implementation, your users may find themselves having to debug NullReference exceptions—not a nice thing to do to your users.

VALIDATION ATTRIBUTE: ALLOWEMPTYCOLLECTION

This is the last variation on the attributes that are used with mandatory parameters to disable some of the default checks. The AllowEmptyCollection attribute allows an empty collection as the argument of a mandatory parameter.

> **NOTE** In cases that follow an error is thrown if the validation attempt fails. This has the benefit of preventing any processing by the function.

VALIDATION ATTRIBUTE: VALIDATENOTNULL

The ValidateNotNull attribute is the opposite of AllowNull. This attribute turns on the check for $null if the parameter isn't mandatory:

```
function validateNotNullExample
{
  param
  (
    [ValidateNotNull()]
    $objectToTest
  )
  $objectToTest -eq $null
}
```

VALIDATION ATTRIBUTE: VALIDATENOTNULLOREMPTY

The ValidateNotNullOrEmpty attribute specifies that the argument of the parameter isn't permitted to be set to $null, an empty string, or an empty array.

VALIDATION ATTRIBUTE: VALIDATECOUNT

The ValidateCount attribute specifies the minimum and maximum numbers of values that can be passed to an array parameter. The runtime generates an error if the number of elements in the argument is outside the range. In the following example, one parameter, $pair, requires exactly two values:

```
function validateCountExample
{
  param (
    [int[]] [ValidateCount(2,2)] $pair
  )
  "pair: $pair"
}
```

Try the function with one argument:

```
PS> validateCountExample 1
validateCountExample : Cannot validate argument on parameter 'pair'. The
   number of provided arguments (1) is fewer than the minimum number of
   allowed arguments (2). Provide more than 2 arguments, and then try
the command again.
At line:1 char:22
+ validateCountExample 1
+                      ~
    + CategoryInfo          : InvalidData: (:) [validateCountExample],
    ParameterBindingValidationException
    + FullyQualifiedErrorId : ParameterArgumentValidationError,validateCount
    Example
```

You get the expected error. Next, pass in a pair of numbers:

```
PS> validateCountExample 1,2
pair: 1 2
```

That works. Finally, pass in three numbers:

```
PS> validateCountExample 1,2,3
validateCountExample : Cannot validate argument on parameter 'pair'. The
   number of provided arguments, (3), exceeds the maximum number of allowed
arguments (2). Provide fewer than 2 arguments, and then try the command
   again.
At line:1 char:22
+ validateCountExample 1,2,3
+                      ~~~~~
    + CategoryInfo          : InvalidData: (:) [validateCountExample],
    ParameterBindingValidationException
    + FullyQualifiedErrorId : ParameterArgumentValidationError,validateCount
    Example
```

Again, you get an error.

VALIDATION ATTRIBUTE: VALIDATELENGTH

The ValidateLength attribute can be used only with strings or arrays of strings. It allows you to specify the minimum and maximum lengths of the argument strings. If the argument is an array of strings, each element of the array will be checked. In the following example, the specified user names must have 8 to 10 characters:

```
function validateLengthExample
{
  param (
    [string][ValidateLength(8,10)] $username
  )
  $userName
}
```

VALIDATION ATTRIBUTE: VALIDATEPATTERN

The `ValidatePattern` attribute allows you to specify a regular expression to use to validate the argument string. For example, the `$hostName` parameter in the following function must start with a letter from *a* to *z* followed by one to seven digits:

```
function validatePatternExample
{
  param (
    [ValidatePattern('^[a-z][0-9]{1,7}$')]
    [string] $hostName
  )
  $hostName
}
```

Try it with a valid string:

```
PS> validatePatternExample b123
b123
```

It returns the argument with no error. Now try an invalid argument that has too many numbers:

```
PS> validatePatternExample c123456789
validatePatternExample : Cannot validate argument on parameter 'hostName'.
  The argument "c123456789" does not match the "^[a-z][0-9]{1,7}$" pattern.
  Supply an argument that matches "^[a-z][0-9]{1,7}$" and try the command
  again.
At line:1 char:24
+ validatePatternExample c123456789
+                        ~~~~~~~~~~
    + CategoryInfo          : InvalidData: (:) [validatePatternExample],
  ParameterBindingValidationException
    + FullyQualifiedErrorId : ParameterArgumentValidationError,validatePatte
  rnExample
```

You get an error as expected. Unfortunately, the error message isn't completely helpful—all it reports is the pattern that failed but not why it failed or what the intent of the pattern was. This limits the usefulness of this attribute somewhat.

VALIDATION ATTRIBUTE: VALIDATERANGE

The `ValidateRange` attribute allows you to constrain the range of a numeric argument. This means that instead of saying the argument must be an integer, you can say that it must be an integer in the range 1 through 10, as shown here:

```
function validateRangeExample
{
  param (
    [int[]][ValidateRange(1,10)] $count
  )
  $count
}
```

As you saw with the `ValidateLength` attribute for strings, this attribute can be applied to a collection, in which case it will validate each member of the collection. If a member is outside the range

```
PS> validateRangeExample 1,2,3,22,4
validateRangeExample : Cannot validate argument on parameter 'count'. The
   22 argument is greater than the maximum allowed range of 10. Supply an
   argument that is less than or equal to 10 and then try the command again.
At line:1 char:22
+ validateRangeExample 1,2,3,22,4
+                      ~~~~~~~~~~
    + CategoryInfo          : InvalidData: (:) [validateRangeExample],
   ParameterBindingValidationException
    + FullyQualifiedErrorId : ParameterArgumentValidationError,validateRange
   Example
```

it fails, indicating the value that couldn't be processed and why.

VALIDATION ATTRIBUTE: VALIDATESET

The `ValidateSet` attribute ensures that the argument is a member of the specific set of values passed to the attribute. In the following example, the argument to the `$color` parameter can contain only the values red, blue, or green:

```
function validateSetExample
{
  param (
    [ValidateSet('red', 'blue', 'green')]
    [ConsoleColor] $color
  )
  $color
}
```

Try it with a valid argument

```
PS> validateSetExample red
Red
```

and an invalid argument:

```
PS> validateSetExample cyan
validateSetExample : Cannot validate argument on parameter 'color'. The
   argument "Cyan" does not belong to the set "red,blue,green" specified by
   the ValidateSet attribute. Supply an argument that
is in the set and then try the command again.
At line:1 char:20
+ validateSetExample cyan
+                    ~~~~
    + CategoryInfo          : InvalidData: (:) [validateSetExample],
   ParameterBindingValidationException
    + FullyQualifiedErrorId : ParameterArgumentValidationError,validateSet
   Example
```

Note that the error message contains the list of valid values. Notice that you passed an array of arguments to the parameter, but the type of the parameter is `[ConsoleColor]`, not [ConsoleColor[]]—it's not an array parameter. This works because [Console-Color] is a .NET enum type where multiple values can be combined to produce a new value in the set. The PowerShell runtime understands this and combines the arguments to produce a single result.

VALIDATION ATTRIBUTE: VALIDATESCRIPT

As promised, we've saved the best (or at least the most powerful) for last. The Validate-Script attribute allows you to specify a chunk of PowerShell script to use to validate the argument. This means it can do anything. The argument to test is passed in as $_ to the code fragment, which should return $true or $false. In the following example, the attribute is used to verify that the argument is an even number:

```
function validateScriptExample
{
  param (
    [int] [ValidateScript({$_ % 2 -eq 0})] $number
  )
  $number
}
```

This succeeds for 2

```
PS> validateScriptExample 2
2
```

and fails for 3:

```
PS> validateScriptExample 3
validateScriptExample : Cannot validate argument on parameter 'number'. The
  "$_ % 2 -eq 0" validation script for the argument with value "3" did not
return a result of True. Determine why the validation script failed, and then
  try the command again.
At line:1 char:23
+ validateScriptExample 3
+                       ~
  + CategoryInfo          : InvalidData: (:) [validateScriptExample],
  ParameterBindingValidationException
  + FullyQualifiedErrorId : ParameterArgumentValidationError,validateScript
  Example
```

As with the ValidatePattern attribute, the error message doesn't provide the best user experience, limiting the value of this attribute for validation. On the other hand, it can also be used for things like logging and tracing, counting the number of times the parameter was used, and so on simply by taking the appropriate action and then returning $true.

Now that we've covered all the things you can do with explicit parameters, we're going to investigate an alternate mechanism for parameter specification. This alternate mechanism allows you to write scripts and functions that can dynamically adapt their parameter signatures to the environment.

7.3   *Dynamic parameters and dynamicParam*

Explicit or static parameters are defined as part of the source code for a script or function and are fixed when that script or function is compiled. But a script or function can also define parameters at *runtime*. These new parameters are added dynamically based on runtime conditions instead of statically at parse time. This allows you to write functions to *specialize* their interface (that is, their parameters) based on ambient conditions. The best example of this is a cmdlet like Set-Content. When Set-Content is used in a file system drive, it lets you specify file-specific parameters like -Encoding. In other providers where this parameter doesn't make sense, it isn't present in the cmdlet signature. Because these parameters are defined dynamically, they're called (no surprise, we're sure) *dynamic parameters*. Cmdlets have always had this capability, but PowerShell v2 made the facility available for scripts and functions as well.

If you want your scripts and functions to have dynamic parameters, you have to use the dynamicParam keyword. The syntax for this keyword is

```
dynamicParam { <statement-list> }
```

Let's work through the steps needed to implement dynamic parameters.

> **WARNING**   This isn't for the faint of heart, but it's a powerful technique that, when needed, allows you to deliver the best experience for the users of your scripts.

7.3.1   *Steps for adding a dynamic parameter*

In this section, we'll walk you through the steps necessary to define dynamic parameters in a function. First, you'll specify a dynamicParam block in your function. Then, in the body of the dynamicParam block, you'll use an if statement to specify the conditions under which the parameter is to be available. To define the parameters you want to expose, you need to use the New-Object cmdlet to create an instance of the type:

```
System.Management.Automation.RuntimeDefinedParameter
```

You'll use this object to define your dynamic parameter and, at a minimum, you'll have to specify its name. If you need to apply additional attributes, you'll have to use the New-Object cmdlet to create an instance of the type:

```
System.Management.Automation.ParameterAttribute
```

This is used to include the Mandatory, Position, or ValueFromPipeline attributes you saw earlier in this chapter.

In the following example, you define a function with two static parameters—Name
and Path—and an optional dynamic parameter named dp1. dp1 is in the set1 parameter set and has a type: [int]. The dynamic parameter is available only when the value
of the Path parameter begins with HKLM:, indicating that it's being used in the Registry
drive. The complete function is shown in figure 7.6 (the code is available in the book's
download).

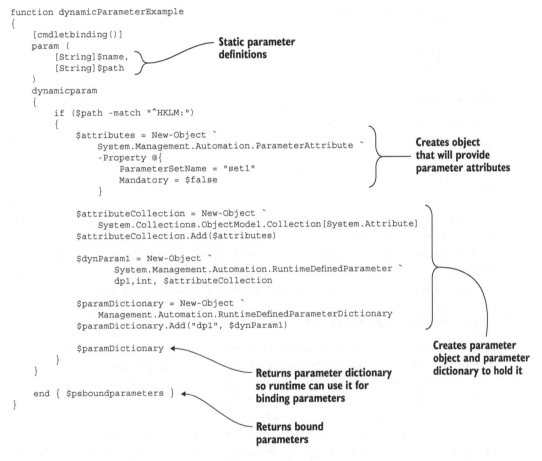

```
function dynamicParameterExample
{
    [cmdletbinding()]
    param (                                          Static parameter
        [String]$name,                               definitions
        [String]$path
    )
    dynamicparam
    {
        if ($path -match "^HKLM:")
        {
            $attributes = New-Object `
                System.Management.Automation.ParameterAttribute `    Creates object
                -Property @{                                         that will provide
                    ParameterSetName = "set1"                        parameter attributes
                    Mandatory = $false
                }

            $attributeCollection = New-Object `
                System.Collections.ObjectModel.Collection[System.Attribute]
            $attributeCollection.Add($attributes)

            $dynParam1 = New-Object `
                System.Management.Automation.RuntimeDefinedParameter `
                dp1,int, $attributeCollection

            $paramDictionary = New-Object `
                Management.Automation.RuntimeDefinedParameterDictionary
            $paramDictionary.Add("dp1", $dynParam1)

            $paramDictionary                         Creates parameter
        }                                            object and parameter
    }                                                dictionary to hold it
    end { $psboundparameters }
}
```

Returns parameter dictionary
so runtime can use it for
binding parameters

Returns bound
parameters

**Figure 7.6 A function that defines dynamic parameters. If the -Path parameter is set to something that
starts with HKML:, an additional parameter, dp1, will be defined for the function.**

This function will return the bound parameters in the end block of the function.

NOTE The variable $PSBoundParameters is an automatic variable which contains
a hashtable with all the parameters that were bound when the command was
invoked. You'll learn more about this variable when we cover proxy commands
in chapter 10.

The presence of the `dynamicParam` block forces you to explicitly use the `end` keyword just like using the `begin` and `process` keywords would. Now run the function. Try the function in the C: drive:

```
PS> dynamicParameterExample -dp1 13 -Path c:\
dynamicParameterExample : A parameter cannot be found that matches parameter
  name 'dp1'.
At line:1 char:29
+ dynamicParameterExample -dp1 <<<<  13 -Path c:\
    + CategoryInfo          : InvalidArgument: (:) [dynami
  cParameterExample], ParameterBindingException
    + FullyQualifiedErrorId : NamedParameterNotFound,dynam
  icParameterExample
```

You get an error saying that no `-dp1` parameter was found. Now try it with `HKLM`:

```
PS> dynamicParameterExample -dp1 13 -Path HKLM:\

Key                        Value
---                        -----
Path                       HKLM:\
dp1                        13
```

This time, the function executes without error and shows you that the dynamic parameter was bound as desired.

As you can see, using dynamic parameters is a fairly complex task. The task is more or less the same in a script or in a compiled language like C#. If you can follow this example, you're well on your way to understanding dynamic parameters in C#.

7.3.2   *When should dynamic parameters be used?*

So when would you use this technique? The most common case is something like the namespace providers mentioned earlier where most of the parameters are the same but certain parameters may only be present based on the path. This allows you to have one command to deal with many similar but slightly different scenarios, which reduces the number of commands a user has to learn.

The other place where dynamic parameters might be used is where you want to base the parameters on some type of dynamic configuration, like the set of columns in a database table. You could write a single cmdlet, called something like `Update-DatabaseTable`, that uses the names and types of the columns to add dynamic parameters for the cmdlet.

This concludes our discussion of dynamic parameters. Next, we'll turn our attention to setting default values.

7.4   *Cmdlet default parameter values*

You've seen that creating default values for functions and scripts is a useful tool. But most parameters on most cmdlets don't have default values. This means that every time you use a cmdlet you have to supply the values to each parameter you use. Wouldn't it be nice if cmdlets had default values?

You can use the $PSDefaultParameterValue preference variable (introduced in PowerShell v3) to create default values for parameters on cmdlets and advanced functions (that use the CmdletBinding attribute) but *not* scripts or simple functions. If the cmdlet or function author has defined default values, you can use $PSDefaultParameterValue to override those values. In addition to defining a single value as a default, you can assign a script block to determine the value to use.

$PSDefaultParameterValue exists only in the PowerShell session in which it's defined. If you want to use the same set of values each time, you should define them in your profile.

The default values stored in $PSDefaultParameterValue are held as a type of hashtable (System.Management.Automation.DefaultParameterDictionary to be specific), meaning you can use standard hashtable techniques to manage default values.

7.4.1 *Creating default values*

You need to supply three things to create a default value:

- The cmdlet (or advanced function) name
- The parameter name
- The value or scriptblock to assign to the parameter

You can set a single default value like this:

```
PS> $PSDefaultParameterValues= @{
'Get-Process:Name'='powershell'}
```

The cmdlet and parameter names are separated by a colon (:). The cmdlet and parameter names are the hashtable key and the default value is the hashtable value. Now, when you use the Get-Process cmdlet, the name parameter is automatically populated with PowerShell:

```
PS> Get-Process

Handles NPM(K)  PM(K)  WS(K) CPU(s)     Id SI ProcessName
------- ------  -----  ----- ------     -- -- -----------
    665     30  66536  82964   1.70  13168 29 powershell
```

If you need to override the default value, you need only to supply a value to the parameter; for instance

```
PS> Get-Process -Name *
```

will return all running processes, and

```
PS> Get-Process -Name winword
```

will return data on the process running winword (MS Word).

If you type another $PSDefaultParameterValues statement, you'll overwrite the current setting:

```
PS> $PSDefaultParameterValues

Name                              Value
----                              -----
Get-Process:Name                  PowerShell

PS> $PSDefaultParameterValues= @{
'Get-Service:Name'='BITS'}

PS> $PSDefaultParameterValues

Name                              Value
----                              -----
Get-Service:Name                  BITS
```

Does that mean you can have only a single default parameter value at a time? No. Remember, we said that $PSDefaultParameterValues was a hashtable and that you can use standard hashtable techniques to manage your default values.

You use the Add() method to define additional default values, supplying the cmdlet parameter names together with the default value as comma-delimited key–value pairs:

```
PS> $PSDefaultParameterValues.Add('Get-Process:Name', 'PowerShell')

PS> $PSDefaultParameterValues.Add('Get-CimInstance:ClassName', 'Win32_
    ComputerSystem')

PS> $PSDefaultParameterValues

Name                              Value
----                              -----
Get-Process:Name                  PowerShell
Get-Service:Name                  BITS
Get-CimInstance:ClassName         Win32_ComputerSystem
```

You can define default values for multiple parameters on a single cmdlet, but remember that each parameter can have only a single default value.

7.4.2 Modifying default values

Needs change, and at some point, you'll need to change your default values. You can remove single entries from $PSDefaultParameterValues:

```
PS> $PSDefaultParameterValues.Remove('Get-CimInstance:ClassName')

PS> $PSDefaultParameterValues

Name                              Value
----                              -----
Get-Process:Name                  PowerShell
Get-Service:Name                  BITS
```

You need to supply the cmdlet:parameter names to define the key of the entry you want to remove.

Alternatively, you may want to change a default value rather than eliminate one:

```
PS> $PSDefaultParameterValues['Get-Service:Name'] = 'LanmanWorkstation'

PS> $PSDefaultParameterValues

Name                         Value
----                         -----
Get-Process:Name             PowerShell
Get-Service:Name             LanmanWorkstation
```

We're working with a hashtable so it's a simple matter of supplying a new value to the appropriate key. You can view the value of a single entry by supplying the key:

```
PS> $PSDefaultParameterValues['Get-Service:Name']
LanmanWorkstation
```

If you have a set of scripts that assume radically different default values and you don't want to supply those values, you can disable the use of default values:

```
PS> $PSDefaultParameterValues.Add('Disabled', $true)
```

or

```
PS> $PSDefaultParameterValues['Disabled']=$true
```

> **NOTE** Default parameters are either all enabled or all disabled. You can't disable some parameters and not others.

Default parameters are re-enabled by setting the `Disabled` entry to $false:

```
PS> $PSDefaultParameterValues['Disabled']=$false
PS> $PSDefaultParameterValues

Name                         Value
----                         -----
Get-Process:Name             PowerShell
Get-Service:Name             LanmanWorkstation
Disabled                     False
```

If you're sure you don't want to disable your default parameters again, you can remove the entry (which also enables your defaults):

```
PS> $PSDefaultParameterValues.Remove('Disabled')
```

You can remove all default values by using

```
PS> $PSDefaultParameterValues.Clear()
```

So far, we've looked at single default values, but we stated earlier that you can use a scriptblock to define the default value depending on the conditions. We'll finish our look at default parameters by discovering how to use scriptblocks.

7.4.3 *Using scriptblocks to determine default value*

If you want your default value to change depending on conditions, then you have to supply a scriptblock to set the value:

```
PS> $PSDefaultParameterValues=@{
'Format-Table:AutoSize'=
{if ($host.Name -eq 'ConsoleHost'){$true}}}
```

The result of this default parameter is that if you use Format-Table in the PowerShell console, the -Autosize parameter is automatically enabled. This isn't the case for other hosts such as the ISE.

Some parameters take a scriptblock as their value. If you need to set a default value for this type of parameter, the scriptblock supplying the default value has to be inside an extra set of braces {} so that the result is treated as a scriptblock:

```
PS> $PSDefaultParameterValues.Add(
'Invoke-Command:ScriptBlock',
{{Get-EventLog -Log Application}})

PS> $PSDefaultParameterValues
```

```
Name                            Value
----                            -----
Format-Table:AutoSize           if ($host.Name -eq
                                'ConsoleHost'){$true}
Invoke-Command:ScriptBlock      {Get-EventLog -Log
                                 Application}
```

This completes our discussion of parameterization of scripts and functions. You now have all the necessary tools to define optimal interfaces or signatures for your scripts and functions. But knowing how to define the signature for a script is only half the battle—at least if you want someone other than yourself to use these scripts. No matter how good the interface is, production scripting still requires documentation for the scripts you're producing. In the next section, we'll explain how to accomplish this.

7.5   *Documenting functions and scripts*

In this section, we'll look at mechanisms you can use to provide documentation for your scripts. The following three features are available:

- Automatic help information generated from the function or script definition
- A special way of processing comments to extract help information from them
- A mechanism for associating external help files with a function or script

The first of these mechanisms is the automatic generation of help text from a function or script definition. When you define a function, the PowerShell help system can generate some help information for that function, as shown in figure 7.7.

As you can see, in figure 7.7, the help subsystem tries to do as much work for you as it can automatically. In the next section, we'll look at the fields that can be automatically generated.

```
non-Administrator 64 bit C:\test                    —    □    ×
PS>  function abc {param([int] $x, $y)}             ^
PS>  Get-Help abc

NAME
     abc

SYNTAX
     abc [[-x] <int>] [[-y] <Object>]


ALIASES
     None


REMARKS
     None


PS>                                                 v
```

Figure 7.7   Automatically generated help information

7.5.1   *Automatically generated help fields*

A certain number of the help fields are generated automatically. These elements are described in table 7.4.

Table 7.4   Automatically generated help fields

Help element	Description
Name	The Name section of the help topic for a function is taken from the name of the function. For a script, it's taken from the name of the script file.
Syntax	The Syntax section of the help topic is generated from the function or script syntax (the parameter definitions). If a parameter has a type attribute associated with it, that type will be displayed as part of the syntax. If you don't specify a parameter type, Object is inserted as the default value.
Aliases	The Aliases section is taken from the information in the alias store.
Parameter list	The Parameter list in the help topic is generated from the function or script syntax and from the descriptions that you add to the parameters. The function parameters appear in the Parameters section in the same order in which they appear in the function or script definition. The spelling and capitalization of parameter names are also taken from the definition.
Common parameters	The common parameters are added to the syntax and parameter list of the help topic, even if they have no effect.
Parameter attribute table	Get-Help generates the table of parameter attributes that appears when you use the -Full or -Parameter parameter of Get-Help. The value of the Required, Position, and Default properties is taken from the function or script definition.
Remarks	The Remarks section of the help topic is automatically generated from the function or script name.

The automatically generated help is minimal. You'll deliver a much better result by adding your own help content.

7.5.2 *Creating manual help content*

Although it's handy to know the command's syntax, knowing what the command does is more useful. This is where the manual documentation mechanisms come in. Power-Shell provides two ways for documenting scripts and functions: inline with special documentation comments or externally in a help file.

Documentation comments (or *doc comments*) are a convention when writing scripts such that these comments can be automatically used to fill in help information. These comments must be placed in particular locations in scripts for them to be processed as doc comments and can contain a number of markup tags for structuring the help information. We'll cover these details in the next section. The final mechanism for providing function/script help uses external files.

External help files are XML files written in the Microsoft Assistance Markup Language (MAML) format.

> **BRUCE NOTE**   MAML is a terrible, terrible thing. The PowerShell team apologizes for foisting it on you, but it was foisted on us. In the future, we're hoping to go with something much simpler like Markdown. A PowerShell module—platyPS—generates PowerShell external help files from Markdown. The module is available from the PowerShell gallery.

Since PowerShell v2, the help file facility can be used with functions and scripts as well as cmdlets. So why have these external files? Because they allow the help content to be translated (localized) into many languages, whereas doc comments only allow help to be written in a single language. Doc comments also require the script file itself to be changed just to fix a typo in the help documentation.

> **NOTE**   Most help files are *not* shipped with PowerShell since version 3.0. You need to download the help files using `Update-Help`. See the about_ Updatable_Help (which does ship with PowerShell). Microsoft will update the help files periodically. The updatable help system enables you to refresh your help files.

As you can see, the help mechanism scales from simple but incomplete up to a full production-level, localizable help system. We won't say anything else about creating external help files but will concentrate on the doc comment mechanism.

7.5.3 *Comment-based help*

Comment-based help is the easiest way to add help for functions and scripts. It works by using special help comment tags in comments associated with a function definition or script. These comments are parsed by the PowerShell interpreter and used to create the help topics. Once this information is available, the `Get-Help` cmdlet returns help objects just like those you get from the help files associated with cmdlets. When you specify the correct tags, doc comments can specify all the help views provided by Get-Help, such as Detailed, Full, Example, and Online, to display function and script help.

Comment-based help is written as a series of comments. These can be single-line comments, where there is a # before each line, but most people use the block comment feature, where the comments are enclosed in <# and #> sequences. All the lines in a doc comment topic must be contiguous. If a doc comment follows a comment that's not part of the help topic, there must be at least one blank line between the last non-help comment line and the beginning of the comment-based help.

For functions, the doc comments can be placed in one of three places:

- At the beginning of the function body, after the open brace.
- At the end of the function body. There must be a blank line between the function's closing brace and the last line of the comment.
- Before the function keyword. In this case, if the comment is to be processed as a doc comment, there can't be more than one blank line between the last line of the comment and the function keyword.

For scripts, the doc comments must be placed as follows:

- At the beginning of the script file, in which case there can be only non-doc comments or blank lines before the first doc comment
- At the end of the script file

There's one other little issue to consider: If the doc comments for a script are at the beginning of a script and the first thing a script contains is a function definition, then should the doc comment apply to the script or the function? This ambiguity is resolved by requiring that there be at least two blank lines between the end of the doc comment for the script and the beginning of the function.

Let's look at an example; you'll use block comments and the .SYNOPSIS and .DESCRIPTION tags to add a definition for the abc function.

NOTE PowerShell added block comments to make it easier to write doc comments. The sequences <# and #> were chosen in part because they look somewhat like XML, which is used for external help files.

Here's what the new function definition looks like:

```
function abc ([int] $x, $y)
{
<#
.SYNOPSIS
This is my abc function
.DESCRIPTION
This function is used to demonstrate writing doc
comments for a function.
#>
}
```

When you run `Get-Help`, you see

```
Get-Help abc

NAME
    abc

SYNOPSIS
    This is my abc function

SYNTAX
    abc [[-x] <Int32>] [[-y] <Object>] [<CommonParameters>]

DESCRIPTION
    This function is used to demonstrate writing doc
    comments for a function.

RELATED LINKS

REMARKS
    To see the examples, type: "get-help abc -examples".
    For more information, type: "get-help abc -detailed".
    For technical information, type: "get-help abc -full".
```

The basic pattern should be obvious by now. Each help section begins with a special tag of the form `.TAGNAME`, followed by the content for that section. The tag must appear on a line by itself to be recognized as a tag but can be preceded or followed by whitespace. The order in which tags appear doesn't matter. Tags are not case-sensitive but by convention they're always written in uppercase. (This makes the structure of the comment easier to follow.)

For a comment block to be processed as a doc comment, it must contain at least one section tag. Most tags can be specified only once per function definition, but there are exceptions. For instance, `.EXAMPLE` can appear many times in the same comment block. The help content for each tag begins on the line after the tag and can span multiple lines.

7.5.4   *Tags used in documentation comments*

You can use a fairly large number of tags when creating doc comments. These tags are shown in table 7.5. They're listed in the order in which they typically appear in output of `Get-Help`.

Table 7.5   Tags that can be used in doc comments

Tag name	Tag content
.SYNOPSIS	A brief description of the function or script. This tag can be used only once in each help topic.
.DESCRIPTION	A detailed description of the function or script.
.PARAMETER	The description of a parameter.
.EXAMPLE	An example showing how to use a command.

Table 7.5   Tags that can be used in doc comments *(continued)*

Tag name	Tag content
`.INPUTS`	The type of object that can be piped into a command.
`.OUTPUTS`	The types of objects the command returns.
`.NOTES`	Additional information about the function or script.
`.LINK`	The name of a related topic.
`.COMPONENT`	The technology or feature that the command is associated with.
`.ROLE`	The user role for this command.
`.FUNCTIONALITY`	The intended use of the function.
`.FORWARDHELPTARGETNAME`	Redirects to the help topic for the specified command.
`.FORWARDHELPCATEGORY`	Specifies the help category of the item in the `.FORWARDHELPTARGETNAME` tag.
`.REMOTEHELPRUNSPACE`	Specifies the name of a variable containing the `PSSession` to use when looking up help for this function. This keyword is used by the `Export-PSSession` cmdlet to find the help topics for the exported commands.
`.EXTERNALHELP`	Specifies the path to an external help file for the command.

Some of these tags require a bit more explanation. This is addressed in the following sections.

.PARAMETER <Parameter-Name> HELP TAG

This is where you add the description for a parameter. The parameter must be named in the argument to the tag. You can include a `.PARAMETER` tag for each parameter in the function or script, and the `.PARAMETER` tags can appear in any order in the comment block. The order in which things are presented is controlled by the parameter definition order, not the help tag order. If you want to change the display order, you have to change the order in which the parameters are defined.

Alternatively, you can specify a parameter description by placing a comment before the parameter definition on the body of the function or script. If you use both a syntax comment and a `.PARAMETER` tag, the description associated with the `.PARAMETER` tag is used, and the syntax comment is ignored.

.LINK HELP TAG

The `.LINK` tag lets you specify the names of one or more related topics. Repeat this tag for each related topic. The resulting content appears in the `Related Links` section of the help topic. The `.LINK` tag argument can also include a URI to an online version of the same help topic. The online version opens when you use the `-Online` parameter of `Get-Help`. The URI must begin with http or https.

.COMPONENT HELP TAG

The .COMPONENT tag describes the technology or feature area the function or script is associated with. For example, the component for Get-Mailbox would be Exchange.

.FORWARDHELPTARGETNAME <COMMAND-NAME> HELP TAG

.FORWARDHELPTARGETNAME redirects to the help topic for the specified command. You can redirect users to any help topic, including help topics for a function, script, cmdlet, or provider.

.FORWARDHELPCATEGORY <CATEGORY> HELP TAG

The .FORWARDHELPCATEGORY tag specifies the help category of the item in ForwardHelp-TargetName. Valid values are Alias, Cmdlet, HelpFile, Function, Provider, General, FAQ, Glossary, ScriptCommand, ExternalScript, Filter, and All. You should use this tag to avoid conflicts when there are commands with the same name.

.REMOTEHELPRUNSPACE <PSSESSION-VARIABLE> HELP TAG

The .REMOTEHELPRUNSPACE tag won't make sense to you until we cover remoting in chapter 11. It's used to specify a *session* that contains the help topic. The argument to the tag is the name of a variable that contains the PSSession to use. This tag is used by the Export-PSSession cmdlet to find the help topics for the exported commands.

.EXTERNALHELP <XML HELP FILE PATH>

The .EXTERNALHELP tag specifies the path to an XML-based help file for the script or function. In versions of Windows from Vista on, if the specified path to the XML file contains UI-culture-specific subdirectories, Get-Help searches the subdirectories recursively for an XML file with the name of the script or function in accordance with the language fallback standards for Windows, just as it does for all other XML-based help topics.

At long last, we're finished with our journey through the advanced function and script features. You now know how to create, declare, constrain, and document your functions. At this point, you're well on your way to becoming a scripting expert.

7.6   *Summary*

- PowerShell programming can be done with either functions or scripts.
- Scripts are pieces of PowerShell script text stored in a file with a .ps1 extension.
- Scripts introduced a new kind of variable scope: the script command and the $script: scope modifier are used to reference variables at the script scope.
- PowerShell has a sophisticated attribution system for annotating parameters.
- Using attributes, you can control a wide variety of argument-binding behaviors.
- You can specify alternate names for parameters using parameter aliases and additional constraints on the values that can be bound using validation attributes.
- $PSDefaultParameterValue can be used to set default values for advanced functions and cmdlets.

- There are comprehensive mechanisms for documenting your scripts and functions.
- You get simple documentation for free just by declaring a function.
- You can add inline documentation with your code using doc comments and provide external help files containing the documentation.

Even though we discussed a lot of material in this chapter, we've covered only part of the story of programming with PowerShell. In chapter 8, you'll learn about modules, which are the best way to distribute your functions, and in chapter 10, we'll dive into the plumbing underlying all of this when we cover scriptblocks, which are the objects underlying the infrastructure for scripts and functions.

Using and authoring modules

> *The value of a telecommunications network is proportional to the square of the*
> *number of connected users of the system.*
>
> *—Robert Metcalfe (Metcalfe's Law)*

A popular meme in the software industry is that the best programmers are lazy—rather than writing new code to solve a problem, they try to reuse existing code. This leverages the work that others have done to debug and document that code. Unfortunately, this kind of reuse happens less often than it should.

> **NOTE** From user studies, the PowerShell team has verified that prior to the introduction of PowerShell, the most common reuse pattern in the IT professional community is copy and paste. A user gets a script from somewhere, copies it, and then modifies it, repeating this process for each

new application. Although this works to a degree and has a low barrier to entry, it doesn't scale well. This approach is slowly changing to thinking about code reuse, but adoption is slow.

The typical excuses for not "indulging their lazy sides" are overconfidence ("I can do a better job," also known as *not invented here syndrome*), underestimating ("It will only take me 10 minutes to do that"), and ignorance ("I didn't know somebody had already implemented that"). There's no longer an excuse for this last point. With modern search engines, it's easy to find things. The introduction of the PowerShell gallery, which we'll cover later, makes finding quality modules much simpler. There are also over 10,000 projects using PowerShell on GitHub (https://github.com/) including open source code from Microsoft. There's an official PowerShell team repository at https://github.com/powershell.

But finding the code is only part of the solution because the code has to be in a form that can be reused. The most common way to facilitate code reuse is to package the code in a *module*. The PowerShell help files define a module:

> *A module is a package that contains Windows PowerShell commands, such as cmdlets, providers, functions, workflows, variables, and aliases.*

Think of a *module* as a library of functionality that's loaded when you need it. In this chapter, we're going to examine how PowerShell facilitates code reuse with its module system. You'll learn how to find existing modules on your system and how to install new ones on the system. Then we'll look at how you can create modules and package your code so that others can use it.

8.1 The role of a module system

In the previous chapter, you organized your code into functions and scripts and used dot-sourcing to load libraries of reusable script code. This is the traditional shell-language approach to code reuse.

PowerShell modules provide a more manageable, production-oriented way to package code. PowerShell modules build on features you've already learned; for example, a PowerShell script module is a PowerShell script with a special extension (.psm1) loaded in a special way. We'll cover all of these details in later sections, but first you need to understand the problem domains that the PowerShell module system was designed to address.

8.1.1 Module roles in PowerShell

Modules serve three roles in PowerShell. These roles are listed in table 8.1.

Table 8.1   The roles modules play in PowerShell

Role	Description
Configuring the environment	Packaging a set of functions to configure the environment is what you usually use dot-sourcing for, but modules allow you to do this in a more controlled way.
Reusing code	Facilitating the creation of reusable libraries is the traditional role of modules in a programming language.
Composing solutions	Modules can be used to create a solution— a domain-specific application. PowerShell modules have the unique characteristic of being nested. In most programming languages, when one module loads another, all the loaded modules are globally visible. In PowerShell, modules nest. If the user loads module A and module A loads module B, then all the user sees is module A (at least by default). Sometimes all you'll do in a module is import some other modules and republish a subset of those modules' members.

The concepts involved in the first role—configuration—were covered when we talked about dot-sourcing files. The second role—facilitating reuse—is, as we said, the traditional role for modules. The third role is unique to PowerShell. Let's look at this third role in more detail.

8.1.2   *Module mashups: composing an application*

One of the unique features that PowerShell modules offer is the idea of a *composite management application.* This is conceptually similar to the idea of a web mashup, which takes an existing service and tweaks it, or adds layers on top of it, to achieve some other, more specific purpose. The notion of management mashups is important as we move into the era of software plus services (or clients plus clouds, if you prefer). Low operating costs make hosted services attractive. The problem is how you manage all these services, in particular when you need to delegate administration responsibility to a slice of the organization.

For example, you might have each department manage its own user resources: mailboxes, customer lists, web portals, and so forth. To do this, you need to slice the management interfaces and republish them as a single coherent management experience. Sounds like magic, doesn't it?

Well, much of it still is, but PowerShell modules can help because they allow you to merge the interfaces of several modules and republish only those parts that need to be exposed. The individual modules being composed are hidden from the user so components can be swapped out as needed without necessarily impacting the end user. This magic is accomplished through module manifests and nested modules. We'll cover nested modules in this chapter, but manifests are a large enough topic that they get their own chapter (chapter 9).

PowerShell v5 takes controlling the functionality you make available to users to a new level with the introduction of Just Enough Administration (JEA). This framework provides, in effect, role-based access to PowerShell functionality at the cmdlet and module level. JEA restricts administrators' access to only those commands they need to perform their jobs. You can use JEA to create controlled access portals, or even self-service portals, in your enterprise.

Now that you know why you want modules, let's look at how you can use them in PowerShell.

8.2 Module basics

In this section, we'll cover the basic information needed to use PowerShell modules. The first thing to know is that the module features in PowerShell are exposed through cmdlets, not language keywords. For example, you can get a list of the module commands using the `Get-Command` command:

```
PS> Get-Command -Noun Module* | Format-Wide -Column 3

Find-Module            Install-Module          Publish-Module
Save-Module            Uninstall-Module        Update-Module
Update-ModuleManifest  Export-ModuleMember     Get-Module
Import-Module          New-Module              New-ModuleManifest
Remove-Module          Test-ModuleManifest
```

Note that in the command name pattern, you use wildcards because there are a couple of different types of module cmdlets. These cmdlets and their descriptions are shown in table 8.2.

Table 8.2 The cmdlets used for working with modules

Module cmdlet	Description
Get-Module	Gets a list of the modules currently loaded in memory
Import-Module	Loads a module into memory and imports the public commands from that module
Remove-Module	Removes a module from memory and removes the imported members
Export-ModuleMember	Specifies the members of a module to export to the user of the module
New-ModuleManifest	Creates a new metadata file for a module directory
Test-ModuleManifest	Runs a series of tests on a module manifest, validating its contents
Update-ModuleManifest	Updates a module manifest file, either modifying content or adding new content
New-Module	Creates a new dynamic module

Each cmdlet has its own help file, as you'd expect. There's also an `about_modules` help topic that describes modules and how they work in PowerShell. You can use this built-in help as a quick reference when working in a PowerShell session.

8.2.1   *Module terminology*

Before we get too far into modules, there are a number of concepts and definitions we should cover. Along with the names of the cmdlets, table 8.2 introduced two new terms—*module member* and *module manifest*—and reintroduced a couple of familiar terms—*import* and *export*—used in the context of modules. These terms and their definitions are shown in table 8.3.

Table 8.3   A glossary of module terminology

Term	Description
Module member	A module member is any function, variable, or alias defined inside a script. Modules can control which members are visible outside the module by using the `Export-ModuleMember` cmdlet.
Module manifest	A module manifest is a PowerShell data file that contains information about the module and controls how the module gets loaded.
Module type	The type of module. Just as PowerShell commands can be implemented by different mechanisms like functions and cmdlets, so modules also have a variety of implementation types. PowerShell has four module types: *script*, *binary*, *cim*, and *manifest*.
Nested module	One module can load another, either procedurally by calling `Import-Module` or by adding the desired module to the `NestedModules` element in the module manifest for that module.
Root module	The root module is the main module file loaded when a module is imported. It's called the root module because it may have associated nested modules.
Imported member	An imported module member is a function, variable, or alias imported from another module.
Exported member	An exported member is a module member that has been marked for export. It's marked to be visible to the caller when the module is imported. If module `foo` imports module `bar` as a nested member, the exported members of `bar` become the imported members in `foo`.

We'll talk more about these concepts in the rest of this chapter. Now we'll introduce another core module concept.

8.2.2   *Modules are single-instance objects*

An important characteristic of modules is that there's only ever one instance of the module in memory. If a second request is made to load the module, the fact that the module is already loaded will be caught and the module won't be reprocessed (at least as long as the module versions match; module versions are covered in chapter 9).

> **NOTE**   You can ensure a module is reloaded by using the `-Force` parameter on `Import-Module`. It's very useful when testing module changes and fixing bugs. Using the force makes you a PowerShell Jedi!

There are a couple of reasons for this behavior. Modules can depend on other modules, so an application may end up referencing a module multiple times, and you don't want to be reloading all the time because it slows things down. The other reason is that you want to allow for private static resources—bits of data that are reused by the functions exported from a module and aren't discarded when those functions are, as is normally the case.

Say we have a module that establishes a connection to a remote computer when the module is loaded. This connection will be used by all the functions exported from that module. If the functions had to reestablish the connection every time they were called, the process would be extremely inefficient. When you store the connection in the module, it will persist across the function calls.

8.3 Working with modules

Enough with the backstory; let's start working with PowerShell modules. You'll begin by seeing which modules are loaded in your session and which are available for loading, then learning how to load additional modules, and understanding how to unload them. (We'll leave *creating* a module until section 8.4.) Let's get started.

8.3.1 Finding modules on the system

The Get-Module cmdlet is used to find modules—either the modules that are currently loaded or the modules that are available to load. The signature for this cmdlet is shown in figure 8.1.

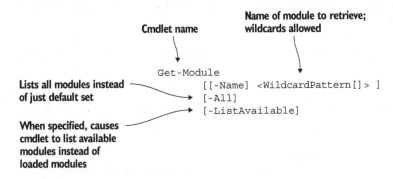

Figure 8.1 The syntax for the Get-Module cmdlet. This cmdlet is used to find modules, either in your session or available to be loaded.

When run with no options, Get-Module lists all the top-level modules loaded in the current session. If -All is specified, both explicitly loaded and nested modules are shown. (We'll explain the difference between *top-level* and *nested* in a minute.) If -ListAvailable is specified, Get-Module lists all the modules available to be loaded based on the current $ENV:PSModulePath setting. If both –ListAvailable and -All are specified, the contents of the module directories are shown, including subdirectories.

Let's try this and see how it works; running Get-Module with no parameters on a new PowerShell v5 session shows three modules installed by default:

```
Microsoft.PowerShell.Management
Microsoft.PowerShell.Utility
PSReadline
```

> **NOTE** The core PowerShell modules were migrated from binary snap-ins to modules in PowerShell v3. Snap-ins have been deprecated since PowerShell v2, and we strongly advise against packaging your functionality as a snap-in.

Let's see what's available for loading on the system. You can use the -ListAvailable parameter on Get-Module to find the system modules that are available. (In this example, the output is filtered using the Where-Object cmdlet so you don't pick up any non-system modules.)

```
PS> Get-Module -ListAvailable | where { $_.path -match "System32" }
```

And you see 74 modules listed on a new Windows 10 machine (PowerShell v5.1). There are other system modules that we'll come to in a minute.

> **NOTE** What you see listed will vary depending on which operating system you're running and which features are installed on the computer. On Windows servers, depending on what server roles are installed (such as Active Directory), you'll see additional modules in this output.

By default, the output shows only the module type, version, name, and exported commands.

The set of properties for a module is much larger than what you saw in the default. Let's look at more properties for the PSWorkflow module:

```
PS> Get-Module -ListAvailable PSWorkflow | Format-List

Name              : PSWorkflow
Path              : C:\WINDOWS\system32\WindowsPowerShell\v1.0\
                    Modules\PSWorkflow\PSWorkflow.psd1
Description       :
ModuleType        : Manifest
Version           : 2.0.0.0
NestedModules     : {Microsoft.Powershell.Workflow.ServiceCore}
ExportedFunctions : New-PSWorkflowSession
ExportedCmdlets   : New-PSWorkflowExecutionOption
ExportedVariables :
ExportedAliases   : nwsn
```

In this output, you see the types of module members that can be exported: functions, cmdlets, variables, and aliases. You also see the module type (Manifest), the module version, and a description (if set). An important property to note is the Path property. This is the path to where the module file lives on disk.

In the next section, you'll see how PowerShell goes about finding modules on the system.

THE $ENV:PSModulePath VARIABLE

As you saw in the output from Get-Module, loadable modules are identified by their path the same as executables. They're loaded in much the same way as executables: A list of directories is searched until a matching module is found. There are a couple of differences, though. Instead of using $ENV:PATH, modules are loaded using a new environment variable: $ENV:PSModulePath. And where the execution path is searched for files, the module path is searched for *subdirectories* containing module files. This arrangement allows a module to include more than one file. By default, the module path is:

```
C:\Users\<user name>\Documents\WindowsPowerShell\Modules
C:\Program Files\WindowsPowerShell\Modules
C:\WINDOWS\system32\WindowsPowerShell\v1.0\Modules\
```

The folder C:\Program Files\WindowsPowerShell\Modules was added to the default module path in PowerShell v4. It was originally intended as the location for modules containing Desired State Configuration (DSC) resources (see chapter 18). Because DSC runs as System, there was no user account to put them in and they had to go somewhere. At the same time, it was clear from the way people were installing things that there should have been a machine-wide place to install modules. The addition of C:\Program Files\WindowsPowerShell\Modules to the default module path solves both of these issues. Modules downloaded from the PowerShell gallery are installed in this location (see section 8.4.4).

In PowerShell v5 a number of other modules are also installed in this location, including PowerShellGet (which manages PowerShell modules) and PackageManagement (which manages software installation packages) .

In the next section, you'll explore the search algorithm in detail.

THE MODULE SEARCH ALGORITHM

The flow chart in figure 8.2 explains the process for locating a module.

As you can see from the number of steps in the algorithm, the search mechanism used in loading a module is sophisticated and a bit complicated. Later on, we'll look at ways to get more information about what's being loaded.

Now that you know which modules are available, you need to be able to load them.

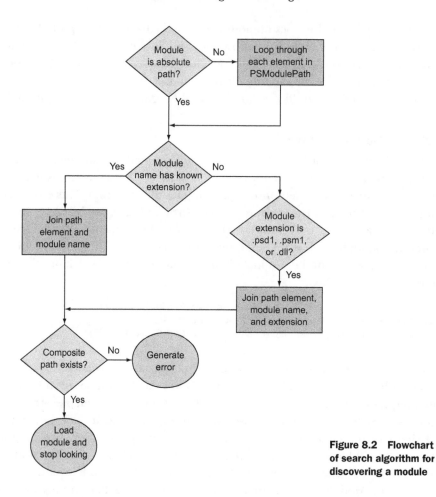

Figure 8.2   Flowchart of search algorithm for discovering a module

8.3.2   Loading a module

Beginning with PowerShell v3, modules that are found on the module path will be auto-loaded. Modules in folders not on the module path can be loaded with `Import-Module`.

MODULE AUTOLOADING

PowerShell v3 introduced the capability of autoloading modules. Any of the following actions will cause the module to be loaded into your session:

- Running a command using a cmdlet from the module
- Using `Get-Command` to get information on a cmdlet in the module
- Using `Get-Help` to read the help information for a cmdlet in the module

As an example, open a new PowerShell session, then run these commands:

```
PS> Get-Module
PS> Get-CimInstance -ClassName Win32_OperatingSystem
PS> Get-Command Get-WinEvent
```

```
PS> Get-Help Start-Transcript
PS> Get-Module
```

You'll see the initial modules loaded by default, as explained in section 8.3.1. Running the additional commands will cause autoloading of these modules, respectively:

```
CimCmdlets
Microsoft.PowerShell.Diagnostics
Microsoft.PowerShell.Host
```

You need to remember a few things about module autoloading:

- Using Get-Command with a wildcard (*) won't load modules—PowerShell assumes you're attempting a discovery action.
- Only modules on the module path defined by $env:PSModulePath can be autoloaded.
- Commands that use PowerShell providers might not load the module.

Module autoloading is useful when you're working interactively. It's frustrating when you forget to load a module and try to use a cmdlet on earlier versions of PowerShell—yes, that is the voice of experience. The fact that your modules now work for you makes life much easier.

Module autoloading issues

Please note that life is not all Skittles and beer with autoloading, mostly because you don't know what you're getting. There's also a significant performance cost to maintaining the command cache. It's great for interactive use but isn't recommended for production scripting. In fact, the new recommendation would be to use the using -module keyword. Because of the way classes work, the dependent module *must* be imported with using -module—otherwise, you won't get type checking.

Some users prefer to maintain control of module loading. You can control autoloading by using the $PSModuleAutoLoadingPreference preference variable. Table 8.4 lists the values this variable can take.

Table 8.4 Possible values of the $PSModuleAutoLoadingPreference variable

Value	Meaning
All	Default. Module autoloading is enabled as described previously.
ModuleQualified	Module is loaded only when the module qualified name of the command is used. Get-Command Get-CimInstance won't trigger autoloading but Get-Command CimCmdlets\Get-CimInstance will.
None	Module autoloading is disabled.

By default, the `$PSModuleAutoLoadingPreference` preference variable is undefined, which means module autoloading is on in all PowerShell sessions.

If you need to import a module manually, you must use the `Import-Module` cmdlet.

USING IMPORT-MODULE

Modules are automatically loaded by default, but there are occasions when you may want to control when they are loaded. If you're developing a module, for example, the module may be stored in a folder off the module path, and you'll need to manually load new versions of the module as you make changes.

The `Import-Module` cmdlet loads modules into your current session. The syntax for this cmdlet is shown in figure 8.3. As you can see, this cmdlet has many parameters, allowing it to address a wide variety of scenarios. We'll look at the basic features of this cmdlet in this section and cover some obscure features in later sections of this chapter.

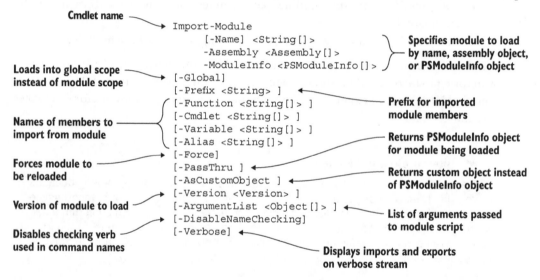

Figure 8.3   The syntax for the `Import-Module` cmdlet. This cmdlet is used to import modules into the current module context or the global context if -Global is specified.

This cmdlet has numerous parameters. We'll cover many of them in the next sections. Some of the more advanced parameters will be covered in chapters 9 and 10.

LOADING A MODULE BY NAME

The most common way to load a module is to specify its name. You saw how to find modules using the `Get-Module` cmdlet in the previous section. One of the modules you discovered was `PSDiagnostics`. Let's use `Import-Module` to load this module now:

```
PS> Import-Module psdiagnostics
```

By default, nothing is output when you load a module. This is as expected and desirable because when you're loading library modules in scripts or in your profile, you don't want chattiness. Unless there's an error, loading a module should be silent.

When you do want to see what was loaded, use `Get-Module`. The output is substantially abbreviated when displayed as a table, so use `Format-List` to see the details of the loaded module as you did when you were exploring the on-disk modules:

```
PS> Get-Module PSDiagnostics | Format-List

Name               : PSDiagnostics
Path               : C:\WINDOWS\system32\WindowsPowerShell\v1.0\
                     Modules\PSDiagnostics\PSDiagnostics.psm1
Description        :
ModuleType         : Script
Version            : 1.0.0.0
NestedModules      : {}
ExportedFunctions  : {Disable-PSTrace, Disable-PSWSManCombinedTrace,
                      Disable-WSManTrace, Enable-PSTrace...}
ExportedCmdlets    :
ExportedVariables  :
ExportedAliases    :
```

Let's examine this output for a minute. The most obvious thing to notice is that the `ExportedFunctions` member in the output is no longer empty. When you load a module, you can finally see all the available exported members. The other thing to notice is that the module type has been changed from `Manifest` to `Script`. Again, the details of the implementation of the module aren't known until after the module has been loaded. We'll cover module manifests and the details on module types in chapter 10.

To see what commands were imported, you can use `Get-Command` with the `-Module` option:

```
PS> Get-Command -Module PSDiagnostics
```

This list matches the list of exports from the module, as you can see with `Get-Module`:

```
PS> (Get-Module psdiag*).exportedfunctions
```

Let's remove this module using the `Remove-Module` cmdlet and look at other ways you can specify which module to load:

```
PS> Remove-Module PSDiagnostics
```

Again, the command completes with no output.

In addition to loading a module by name, you can load it by path, again paralleling the way executables work. Let's do this with the `PSDiagnostics` module. You saw the path in the output of the earlier example. We'll use this path to load the module. Because this is a system module, it's loaded from the PowerShell install directory. This means that you can use the built-in `$PSHOME` variable in the path:

```
PS> Import-Module $PSHOME/modules/PSDiagnostics/PSDiagnostics
```

Call `Get-Module` to verify that it has been loaded.

By loading a module using a full path, you know exactly which file will be processed. This can be useful, for example, when you're developing modules, as you'll see in section 8.4. Let's remove this module again as we move on to the next example:

```
PS> Remove-Module PSDiagnostics
```

TRACING MODULE LOADS WITH -VERBOSE

So far, you've allowed the modules to be loaded without caring about the details of what's happening. This is fine as long as everything works, but remember how complex the module search algorithm was. When you get into more complex scenarios where you're loading multiple modules, it's useful to see what's happening. You can do this by specifying the -Verbose flag:

```
PS> Import-Module PSDiagnostics -Verbose

VERBOSE: Loading module from path
'C:\WINDOWS\system32\WindowsPowerShell\v1.0\Modules\
PSDiagnostics\PSDiagnostics.psd1'.
VERBOSE: Loading module from path
'C:\WINDOWS\system32\WindowsPowerShell\v1.0\Modules\
PSDiagnostics\PSDiagnostics.psm1'.
VERBOSE: Importing function 'Disable-PSTrace'.
VERBOSE: Importing function 'Disable-PSWSManCombinedTrace'.
VERBOSE: Importing function 'Disable-WSManTrace'.
VERBOSE: Importing function 'Enable-PSTrace'.
VERBOSE: Importing function 'Enable-PSWSManCombinedTrace'.
VERBOSE: Importing function 'Enable-WSManTrace'.
VERBOSE: Importing function 'Get-LogProperties'.
VERBOSE: Importing function 'Set-LogProperties'.
VERBOSE: Importing function 'Start-Trace'.
VERBOSE: Importing function 'Stop-Trace'.
```

All the output that begins with VERBOSE: is generated when the -Verbose flag is specified. It shows two things: the path to the module file and a list of all members (in this case, functions) being imported into your session. This is pretty straightforward with a simple scenario, but you'll see that it can become much more complicated when we get to nested modules in section 8.4.6.

IMPORTS AND EXPORTS

Thus far, you've defaulted to loading everything that a module exports into your session. You don't have to do that—and there are cases where you don't *want* to do it. Importing too many commands clutters up your session and makes it hard to find what you're looking for. To avoid this, you can control what gets imported by using the -Function, -Cmdlet, -Alias, and -Variable parameters on Import-Module. As you'd expect, each of these parameters controls a particular type of import from the module. You've seen all the command types previously as well as PowerShell variables. The PSDiagnostics module only exports functions, so you can use that feature to restrict what gets loaded. Say you only wanted to load Enable-PSTrace. Here's what this would look like:

```
PS> Import-Module  PSDiagnostics -Verbose `
 -Function Enable-PSTrace

VERBOSE: Loading module from path
'C:\Windows\system32\WindowsPowerShell\v1.0\Modules\
psdiagnostics\psdiagnostics.psd1'.
VERBOSE: Loading module from path
'C:\Windows\system32\WindowsPowerShell\v1.0\Modules\
psdiagnostics\PSDiagnostics.psm1'.
VERBOSE: Importing function 'Enable-PSTrace'.
```

In the verbose output, you see that only `Enable-PSTrace` was imported into your session. Using `Get-Command -Module PSDiagnostics` confirms that only the required function has been loaded.

Now you know how to avoid creating clutter in your session. But what if it's too late and you already have too much stuff loaded? You'll learn how to fix that next.

8.3.3 *Removing a loaded module*

Because your PowerShell session can be long running, there may be times when you want to remove a module. As you saw earlier, you do this with the `Remove-Module` cmdlet.

> **NOTE** Typically, the only people who remove modules are those who are developing the module in question or those who are working in an application environment that's encapsulating various stages in the process as modules. A typical user rarely needs to remove a module—it's often quicker to start a new PowerShell session. The PowerShell team almost cut this feature because it turns out to be quite hard to do in a sensible way.

The syntax for `Remove-Module` is shown in figure 8.4.

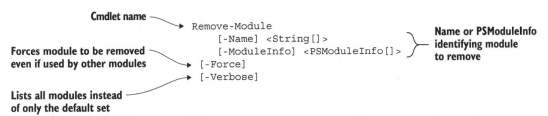

Figure 8.4   The syntax for `Remove-Module`. Note that this command doesn't take wildcards.

When a module is removed, all the modules it loaded as nested modules are also removed from the global module table. This happens *even if the module was explicitly loaded at the global level.*

> **NOTE** Any .NET types that are loaded by the module aren't unloaded by calling `Remove-Module` because .NET doesn't support the removal of types. The types remain in memory until the PowerShell session is closed.

To illustrate, let's look at how the module tables are organized in the environment. This organization is shown in figure 8.5.

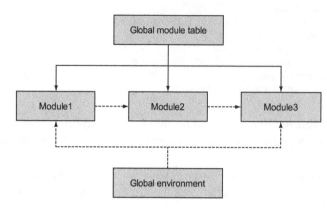

Figure 8.5   How the module tables are organized. The global module table holds a reference to all loaded modules. Each module in turn has a reference to the modules it has loaded.

First, let's talk about the global module table. This master table has references to all the modules that have been loaded either explicitly or implicitly by another module. Anytime a module is loaded, this table is updated. An entry is also made in the environment of the caller. In figure 8.5, Module1 and Module3 are loaded from the global module environment, so there are references from the top-level module table. For example, Module1 loads Module2, causing a reference to be added to the global module table and the private module table for Module1. Module2 loads Module3 as a nested module. Because Module1 has already been loaded from the global environment, no new entry is added to the global module table, but a private reference is added to the module table for Module2.

Now you'll remove Module3 from the global environment. The updated arrangement of modules is shown in figure 8.6.

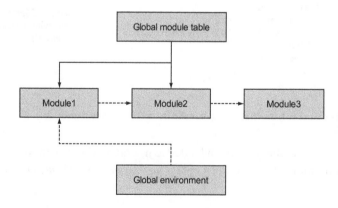

Figure 8.6   How the module tables are organized after Module3 is removed at the top level. The global module table no longer has a reference to Module3, but the local module table for Module2 still has a link to that object.

Next, you'll update Module3 and reload it at the top level. The final arrangement of modules is shown in figure 8.7.

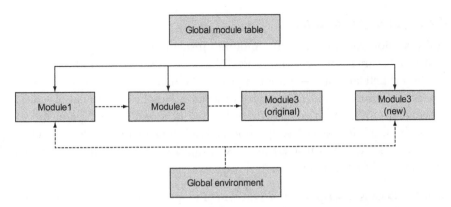

Figure 8.7 How the module tables are organized when the revised Module3 is loaded at the top level. The global module table now has a reference to the new Module3, but the local module table for Module2 still has a link to the original Module3.

In the final arrangement of modules in figure 8.7, two versions of Module3 are loaded into the same session. Although this is extremely complicated, it permits multiple versions of a module to be loaded at the same time in the same session, allowing different modules that depend on different versions of a module to work at the same time. This is a pretty pathological scenario, but the real world isn't always tidy. Eventually you do have to deal with things you'd rather ignore, so it's good to know how.

How exported elements are removed

With an understanding of how modules are removed, you also need to know how the imported members are removed. There are two different flavors of member removal behavior depending on the type of member you're removing. Functions, aliases, and variables have one behavior. Cmdlets imported from binary modules have a slightly different behavior. This is an artifact of the way the members are implemented. Functions, aliases, and variables are data structures that are dynamically allocated and so can be replaced. Cmdlets are backed by .NET classes, which can't be unloaded from a session because .NET doesn't allow the assemblies containing these classes to be unloaded. Because of this, the implementation of the cmdlet table depends on hiding or *shadowing* a command when there's a name collision when importing a name from a module. For the other member types, the current definition of the member is replaced. Why does this matter? It doesn't matter at all until you try to remove a module.

When you remove a module that has imported cmdlets, causing existing cmdlets to be shadowed, the previously shadowed cmdlets become visible again. But when you remove a module that imports colliding functions, aliases, or variables, because the old definitions were overridden instead of shadowed, the definitions are removed.

Okay, this has gotten a bit heavy. Let's move on to something more creative and exciting. In section 8.4, you'll finally start writing your own modules.

8.4   *Writing script modules*

In this section you'll start writing modules instead of only using them. For now, we'll limit our coverage to script modules. That's because script modules are written in the PowerShell language—something you're familiar with by now. In section 8.5, we'll expand our coverage to include binary modules, which requires dabbling in C#.

When showing you how to write script modules, we'll also explain in more detail how script modules work. A script module is a file that contains PowerShell script text with a .psm1 extension instead of a .ps1 extension. A PowerShell script module is a script with a different extension.

> **NOTE**   Because a script module is a form of script, it obeys execution policy like a script. Before you can load a script module, you'll need to change the execution policy to be RemoteSigned as a minimum, as described in section 7.1.1.

Is it as simple as that? Well, almost. Let's walk through an example where you convert a script into a module and see what changes during the process.

8.4.1   *A quick review of scripts*

You're going to write a short script to work with in this conversion exercise. This script is indented to implement a simple counter. You get the next number from the counter by calling Get-Count and you reset the sequence using the Reset-Count command. The script is shown in this listing.

Listing 8.1   Counter.ps1 script

```
$script:count = 0
$script:increment = 1
                                    ❶  Getting
function Get-Count                      a counter
{
    return $script:count += $increment
}

function Reset-Count
{                                   ❷  Resetting a
    $script:count=0                     counter
    setIncrement 1
}

function setIncrement ($x)
{                                   ❸  Helper
    $script:increment = $x              function
}
```

As you can see, this script defines the two functions we mentioned, Get-Count ❶ and Reset-Count ❷. But it also defines a number of other things that aren't part of the specification: a helper function, setIncrement ❸, and two script-level variables, $count and $increment. These variables hold the state of the counter. Obviously, running the script won't be useful as the commands are defined at the script scope and are removed when the script exits. Instead, you'll dot-source the script to load the script members into your environment:

```
PS> . .\counter.ps1
```

This creates the elements without showing anything (which is what you want a library to do in most cases). Now manually verify that you got what you intended:

```
PS> Get-Command *-count

CommandType     Name                        Version     Source
-----------     ----                        -------     ------
Function        Get-Count
Function        Reset-Count
```

The functions are there so you can try them out. Start with Get-Count:

```
PS> Get-Count
1
PS> Get-Count
2
```

Each call to Get-Count returns the next number in the sequence. Now use the Reset -Count command and call Get-Count to verify that the count has been reset:

```
PS> Reset-Count
PS> Get-Count
1
```

But what about the other private members in the script? Using Get-Command you see that the setIncrement function is also visible:

```
PS> Get-Command setIncrement

CommandType     Name                        Version     Source
-----------     ----                        -------     ------
Function        setIncrement
```

And you can even call it directly:

```
PS> setIncrement 7
PS> Get-Count
8
PS> Get-Count
15
```

Because this function was supposed to be a private implementation detail, the fact that it's publicly visible isn't desirable. Likewise, you can also get at the state variables you created:

```
PS> Get-Variable count, increment

Name                        Value
----                        -----
```

```
count                           15
increment                        7
```

The problem with this is clear: $count isn't a unique name, so the chance of it colliding with a similarly named variable from another script is high. This lack of isolation between scripts makes using dot-sourcing a fragile way to build libraries.

Finally, try to remove this script, emulating what you've been doing with Remove -Module. This turns out to be quite complicated. You end up having to write a command that looks like this:

```
PS> Remove-Item -Verbose  variable:count,
variable:increment,function:Reset-Count,
function:Get-Count,function:setIncrement

VERBOSE: Performing operation "Remove Item"
        on Target "Item: count".
VERBOSE: Performing operation "Remove Item"
        on Target "Item: increment".
VERBOSE: Performing operation "Remove Item"
        on Target "Item: Reset-Count".
VERBOSE: Performing operation "Remove Item"
        on Target "Item: Get-Count".
VERBOSE: Performing operation "Remove Item"
        on Target "Item: setIncrement".
```

This is necessary because there's no implicit grouping of all the members created by a script.

Finding function definitions

The path to the file where a function was defined is attached to the scriptblock of the function. For the counter example we've been discussing, the path might look like this:

```
PS> ${function:Get-Count}.File
C:\TestScripts\counter.ps1
```

This File property makes it easier to figure out where things came from in your environment when you have to debug it. For example, all the functions that were defined in your profile will have the path to your profile in them, functions that were defined in the system profile will have the system profile path, and so on. This fixes only part of the problem—managing functions—and doesn't deal with variables and aliases.

At this point, it's clear that although it's possible to build libraries using dot-sourcing, there are a number of problems with this approach. Private implementation details leak into the public namespace, and the members of a dot-sourced script lose any sort of grouping that allows you to manage them as a whole.

> **NOTE** Building libraries of functionality in this manner isn't a recommended best practice.

Let's turn this script into a module and see how that fixes the problem.

8.4.2 *Turning a script into a module*

Now let's turn the counter script into a module. Do this by changing the extension on the module from .ps1 to .psm1 (where the *m* stands for *module*):

```
PS> copy .\counter.ps1 .\counter.psm1 -Force -Verbose

VERBOSE: Performing the operation "Copy File"
on target "Item: C:\TestScripts\counter.ps1
Destination: C:\TestScripts\counter.psm1".
```

You're using the -Force parameter here to make the example work all the time. Try loading the renamed file. The module wasn't run. The default action is to open the file in the editor associated with the extension (Notepad.exe by default). This is because module files aren't commands and can't be run. Instead, you need to use the Import -Module command to load this module:

```
PS> Import-Module .\counter.psm1
```

Now that you've loaded a module, you can try the Get-Module command and see something useful:

```
PS> Get-Module counter

ModuleType Version  Name    ExportedCommands
---------- -------  ----    ----------------
Script     0.0      counter {Get-Count, Reset-Count, setIncrement}
```

Again, let's use the Format-List cmdlet to see the object in more detail:

```
PS> Get-Module counter | Format-List

Name              : counter
Path              : C:\TestScripts\counter.psm1
Description       :
ModuleType        : Script
Version           : 0.0
NestedModules     : {}
ExportedFunctions : {Get-Count, Reset-Count, setIncrement}
ExportedCmdlets   :
ExportedVariables :
ExportedAliases   :
```

An important thing to notice is that the Path property stores the full path to where the module was loaded from. The module type is script and the version is 0.0—the default for a script module. (When we look at manifests in chapter 9, you'll see how to change this.) The most important things to notice are the export lists. You see that all the functions defined in the script module are being exported but no variables are. To verify this, use Get-Command to look for all the functions defined by the script:

```
PS> Get-Command -Module counter

CommandType Name            Version Source
----------- ----            ------- ------
Function    Get-Count       0.0     counter
Function    Reset-Count     0.0     counter
Function    setIncrement    0.0     counter
```

You can immediately see one of the benefits of using modules: You can work with sets of related elements as a unit. (More on this in a bit.) Now that you've loaded the functions, you have to run them to make sure they work:

```
PS> Get-Count
1
PS> Get-Count
2
PS> Get-Count
3
```

As before, you see that Get-Count returns the next element in the sequence. Now let's check on the variables used by Get-Count. These were a big problem when you dotted the script:

```
PS> $count
PS> $increment
```

Neither exists. Try assigning a value to $count and see whether it makes a difference:

```
PS> $count = 100
PS> Get-Count
4
```

As desired, it has no effect on Get-Count. Try Reset-Count and verify that it works:

```
PS> Reset-Count
PS> Get-Count
1
```

And it does. Now let's look at another issue you had to deal with when using script libraries: how to remove the imported elements. With modules, you can remove the module:

```
PS> Remove-Module counter
```

This will remove the module from the session along with all imported members, so if you try to run Get-Count now, you get an error:

```
PS> Get-Count
Get-Count : The term 'Get-Count' is not recognized as the name of
a cmdlet, function, script file, or operable program. Check the
spelling of the name, or if a path was included, verify that the
```

```
path is correct and try again.
At line:1 char:1
+ Get-Count
+ ~~~~~~~~~
    + CategoryInfo          : ObjectNotFound: (Get-Count:String) [],
  CommandNotFoundException
    + FullyQualifiedErrorId : CommandNotFoundException
```

In the next section, we'll look at ways to get more fine-grained control over the things that modules export.

8.4.3 *Controlling member visibility with Export-ModuleMember*

Let's recap what you saw in the last example. You converted a script to a module by changing the file extension. When you imported the module, all the functions you'd defined were visible by default, but nothing else was. This is the default behavior in a module when you don't do anything to control member visibility. Because script libraries written for v1 typically depended on this behavior, renaming them with a .psm1 extension may be all that's needed to turn them into modules.

Although this approach is simple, it's not too flexible. For complex scenarios, you need to be able to control exactly what gets exported; for example, you may need to use a number of helper functions in your module that you don't want to make public. You do this with the Export-ModuleMember cmdlet. This cmdlet lets you declare exactly which commands and variables are exported from the module. We'll start by reviewing how it works with functions.

CONTROLLING WHICH FUNCTIONS ARE EXPORTED

First, we'll look at how you can hide the functions you want to be private in a module. Take a look at another variation of the counter module.

Listing 8.2   Counter module

```
$script:count = 0
$script:increment = 1

function Get-Count
{
    return $script:count += $increment
}

function Reset-Count
{
    $script:count=0
    setIncrement 1
}

function setIncrement ($x)
{
    $script:increment = $x
}

Export-ModuleMember *-Count          Controlling
                                      function export
```

The only difference between this version and the previous one is the last line, which uses the `Export-ModuleMember` cmdlet. This line says "Export all functions matching the pattern *-Count." Save the module as counter1.psm1. Now import the module:

```
PS> Import-Module .\counter1.psm1
```

You verify that the Get- and Reset-Count commands are there by using

```
PS> Get-Command *-Count
```

But the `setIncrement` command isn't, because it wasn't explicitly exported:

```
PS> Get-Command setIncrement
Get-Command : The term 'setIncrement' is not recognized as the
name of a cmdlet, function, script file, or operable program.
Check the spelling of the name, or if a path was included,
verify that the path is correct and try again.
At line:1 char:1
+ Get-Command setIncrement
+ ~~~~~~~~~~~~~~~~~~~~~~~~~
    + CategoryInfo          : ObjectNotFound:
(setIncrement:String) [Get-Command],
CommandNotFoundException
    + FullyQualifiedErrorId : CommandNotFoundException,
Microsoft.PowerShell.Commands.GetCommandCommand
```

Remove the module to clean up after yourself:

```
Ps> Remove-Module counter1
```

Function export rules

Here's the rule to remember: If there are no calls to `Export-ModuleMember` in a script module, all functions are exported by default and all other member types are private. If there's at least one call to `Export-ModuleMember`, whatever the cmdlet does overrides the default. This means PowerShell doesn't know exactly what set of functions will be exported until the script has run to completion.

We'll look further into function exporting in a minute, but first let's finish up with variables and aliases.

CONTROLLING WHAT VARIABLES AND ALIASES ARE EXPORTED

Although functions are exported by default, variables and aliases aren't. Again, to change the default set of exports, use the `Export-ModuleMember` cmdlet. Let's look at a third variation on the counter module.

Listing 8.3 Exporting variables

```
$script:count = 0
$script:increment = 1
function Get-Count { return $script:count += $increment }      ┐ Defining
                                                               │ alias
function Reset-Count { $script:count=0;  setIncrement 1 }
New-Alias -Name reset -Value Reset-Count              ◄────────┘
                                                               ┐ Controlling
function setIncrement ($x) {  $script:increment = $x }         │ export

Export-ModuleMember -Function *-Count -Variable increment -Alias reset  ◄──┘
```

This time, there are two changes to the script. First, you're defining an alias for the
Reset-Count function. Second, you're using Export-ModuleMember to explicitly control
all of the exports: functions, variables, and aliases. Now, if the member doesn't appear
in a call to Export-ModuleMember, it won't be exported.

NOTE Use a new PowerShell session for this example to ensure all variables
from previous examples are eliminated.

Let's import the updated module

```
PS> Import-Module .\counter2.psm1
```

and verify the contents. Check that the *-Count commands are loaded with

```
PS> Get-Command *-Count
```

What about setIncrement? You weren't supposed to export it, so there should be an
error when you try calling the following:

```
PS> setIncrement 10
setIncrement : The term 'setIncrement' is not recognized as the
name of a cmdlet, function, script file, or operable program.
Check the spelling of the name, or if a path was included,
verify that the path is correct and try again.
At line:1 char:1
+ setIncrement 10
+ ~~~~~~~~~~~~
    + CategoryInfo          : ObjectNotFound:
(setIncrement:String) [], CommandNotFoundException
    + FullyQualifiedErrorId : CommandNotFoundException
```

And there is. The function wasn't exported from the module, so it can't be imported
by the module loaded. Finally, check to see if your variables were exported properly by
trying to display their contents:

```
PS> $count
PS> $increment
1
```

You can see that the `$count` variable wasn't exported because nothing was displayed. The `$increment` variable was exported, so the value was output.

Next, check to see if the `reset` alias was exported:

```
PS> Get-Alias reset

CommandType     Name                          Version   Source
-----------     ----                          -------   ------
Alias           reset -> Reset-Count          0.0       counter2
```

Test the alias by using `Get-Count` a number of times; then use `reset`.

WHEN MODULE EXPORTS ARE CALCULATED

Now let's return to something we mentioned earlier: The set of module members to export is not known until runtime. The `Export-ModuleMember` cmdlet doesn't export the function; it adds it to a list of members to export. Once execution of the module body is completed, the PowerShell runtime looks at the accumulated lists of exports and exports those functions. The export algorithm is shown in figure 8.8.

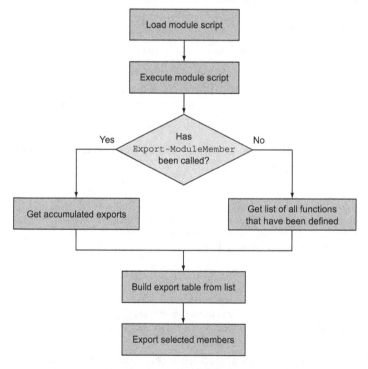

Figure 8.8   The order of the steps when processing a module manifest. At any point prior to the next-to-the-last step, if an error occurs, module processing will stop and an error will be thrown.

As shown in figure 8.8, PowerShell loads and executes the module file. As execution proceeds, the module code defines functions and may or may not call `Export-ModuleMember`.

If it does call `Export-ModuleMember`, then the specified members to export are added to the exports list. When execution has completed, control returns to the module loader, which checks to see if anything was put into the export list. If there were no calls to `Export-ModuleMember`, then this list is empty. In that case, the loader finds all the functions defined in the module's scope and exports them. If there was at least one call to `Export -ModuleMember`, then the module loader uses the export list to control what gets exported.

So far, you've been loading the module using the path to the module file. This is a good approach for development, but eventually you'll need to put it into production. In the next section you'll learn how.

8.4.4 *Installing a module*

As of PowerShell v5 you have two broad categories of module availability. The first category, manual installation, has been available since modules were introduced in Power-Shell v2. Manual installation encompasses modules you write yourself and those you may explicitly copy or download from other sources. The second category, automatic installation, was introduced with PowerShell v5 and the PowerShell Gallery—a public gallery of modules you can reuse. Access to the gallery is done through (surprise!) a module called PowerShellGet. The PowerShellGet module includes commands to find and install modules from the PowerShell Gallery. You can also add public or private repositories to the search path.

MANUAL INSTALL

A manual module installation is simple to perform. All you have to do is create a subdirectory of one of the directories in the module path and copy the module file, or files, into that folder—the proverbial Xcopy install that people like to talk about.

> **NOTE** Installing your modules into `$pshome\Modules` is not recommended. Updates and changes to PowerShell may overwrite the contents of that folder obliterating your module. You did have another copy, didn't you?

Let's look at the first element of the default module path:

```
PS> ($ENV:PSModulePath -split ';')[0]
C:\Users\brucepay\Documents\WindowsPowerShell\Modules
```

The Modules directory in `Documents\WindowsPowerShell` is the user's personal module repository.

> **NOTE** You can create a separate folder for your own modules and add it to the module path in your profile.

You're going to install the counter module in it so you don't have to load it using the full path anymore—in fact, autoloading removes the need to manually load the module. Let's get the repository path into a variable so it's easier to use:

```
PS> $mm = ($ENV:PSModulePath -split ';')[0]
```

Next, create the module directory:

```
PS> New-Item -Path $mm/Counter2 -ItemType Directory

    Directory: C:\Users\brucepay\Documents\WindowsPowerShell\Modules

Mode                LastWriteTime         Length Name
----                -------------         ------ ----
d-----         22/04/2017     11:11              Counter2
```

Install the module by copying it into the directory just created:

```
PS> Copy-Item -Path .\counter2.psm1 -Destination $mm\Counter2
```

Now try it out. Use the -ListAvailable option on Get-Module to see if the module lookup algorithm will find it:

```
PS> Get-Module -ListAvailable Counter2 | Format-List name, path

Name : Counter2
Path : C:\Users\brucepay\Documents\WindowsPowerShell\
       Modules\Counter2\Counter2.psm1
```

And it does. This means you should be able to load it by name:

```
PS> Import-Module -Verbose counter2
VERBOSE: Loading module from path 'C:\Users\brucepay\Documents\
   WindowsPowerShell\Modules
\Counter2\Counter2.psm1'.
VERBOSE: Importing function 'Get-Count'.
VERBOSE: Importing function 'Reset-Count'.
VERBOSE: Importing variable 'increment'.
VERBOSE: Importing alias 'reset'.
```

It works. Installing a module is as simple as copying a file. Try removing the module and then using the Get-Count function to test autoloading.

MODULE FOLDERS

You may be wondering why you have to put in into a directory—it's only a single file. In chapter 9, you'll see that a production module is more than a single .psm1 file; for example, the DNSClient module (introduced with Windows 8) has a number of files:

```
Mode         LastWriteTime  Length Name
----         -------------  ------ ----
d----- 03/11/2016     13:16        en-US
-a---- 18/03/2017     20:58   1705 DnsClient.psd1
-a---- 18/03/2017     20:58  17850 DnsClientPSProvider.Format.ps1xml
-a---- 18/03/2017     20:58   4788 DnsClientPSProvider.Types.ps1xml
-a---- 04/03/2017     11:35    391 DnsClient_5696d5ef-fa2d-4997-94f1-
   0bc13daa2ac5_HelpInfo.xml
-a---- 18/03/2017     20:58  61640 DnsCmdlets.Format.ps1xml
-a---- 18/03/2017     20:58  22151 DnsCmdlets.Types.ps1xml
-a---- 18/03/2017     20:58  20344 DnsConfig.Format.ps1xml
```

```
-a----  18/03/2017     20:58     1100 DnsConfig.Types.ps1xml
-a----  18/03/2017     20:58    39424 dnslookup.dll
-a----  18/03/2017     20:58     4504 MSFT_DnsClient.cdxml
-a----  18/03/2017     20:58     4130 MSFT_DnsClientCache.cdxml
-a----  18/03/2017     20:58     1306 MSFT_DnsClientGlobalSetting.cdxml
-a----  18/03/2017     20:58     3613 MSFT_DnsClientServerAddress.cdxml
-a----  18/03/2017     20:58     5188 PS_DnsClientNRPTGlobal_v1.0.0.cdxml
-a----  18/03/2017     20:58     1704 PS_DnsClientNrptPolicy_v1.0.0.cdxml
-a----  18/03/2017     20:58    18650 PS_DnsClientNRPTRule_v1.0.0.cdxml
```

This is why modules are stored in a directory—it allows all the module resources to be gathered in one place, making it easy to distribute a multifile module. Zip it up and send it out.

> **NOTE** Downloading and installing a zipped module on Windows Vista or later requires extra steps because files downloaded using Internet Explorer are blocked by default. PowerShell honors this blocking attribute, so you won't be able to load the module until you unblock it. The most effective way to do this is to unblock the zip file before unzipping it. Then, when you unzip it, all the extracted files will also be unblocked. To unblock a file, use `Unblock-File -Path ./myfile.zip`. If you have a number of files to unblock, then use `Get-ChildItem -Path c:\mypath\* | Unblock-File`.

PowerShell v5 introduced the ability to have multiple versions of a module installed into the same folder; you use subfolders to separate the versions:

```
PS> Get-ChildItem  `
-Path 'C:\Program Files\WindowsPowerShell\Modules\Pester'

    Directory: C:\Program Files\WindowsPowerShell\Modules\Pester

Mode              LastWriteTime         Length Name
----              -------------         ------ ----
d-----       18/03/2017     21:03              3.4.0
d-----       20/03/2017     13:57              4.0.2
```

Using `Import-Module` or accessing the module via autoloading will automatically load the latest version of the module available on your system:

```
PS> Get-Module -ListAvailable Pester

    Directory: C:\Program Files\WindowsPowerShell\Modules

ModuleType Version Name    ExportedCommands
---------- ------- ----    ----------------
Script     4.0.2   Pester  {Describe, Context, It, Should...}
Script     3.4.0   Pester  {Describe, Context, It, Should...}
```

If you need to import a specific version of the module, you'll use the `-RequiredVersion` parameter:

```
PS> Import-Module -Name Pester -RequiredVersion 3.4.0
```

> **NOTE**   You can use the `-MinimumVersion` parameter to specify a version number. `Import-Module` will only import a version that's greater than or equal to the specified version.

Installing a module manually is okay if (a) you found the module in the first place, and (b) you want to install it only once. It is still, however, a bit fiddly, including the "find the module" bit, so PowerShell v5 introduced the PowerShell Gallery—a public, searchable module repository along with a set of commands to make it easy to find, download, and install modules.

POWERSHELLGET

The commands in the PowerShellGet module manage finding, installing, updating, and potentially uninstalling modules, scripts, and DSC resources (find only) on your system. The modules are stored in a central repository, which provides a central distribution point for your code. PowerShellGet provides you with a number of commands:

```
PS> Get-Command -Module PowerShellGet | Format-Wide -Column 3
```

```
Find-Command            Find-DscResource        Find-Module
Find-RoleCapability     Find-Script             Get-InstalledModule
Get-InstalledScript     Get-PSRepository        Install-Module
Install-Script          New-ScriptFileInfo      Publish-Module
Publish-Script          Register-PSRepository   Save-Module
Save-Script             Set-PSRepository        Test-ScriptFileInfo
Uninstall-Module        Uninstall-Script        Unregister-PSRepository
Update-Module           Update-ModuleManifest   Update-Script
Update-ScriptFileInfo
```

The `Find-*` commands enable you to search repositories in various ways, as shown in table 8.5.

Table 8.5   PowerShellGet search targets

Command	Search target
Find-Command	Searches modules in registered repositories for PowerShell commands such as cmdlets, aliases, functions, and workflows.
Find-DscResource	Finds DSC resources contained in modules that match the specified criteria from registered repositories.
Find-Module	Finds modules from the online gallery that match the specified criteria.
Find-RoleCapability	Finds PowerShell role capabilities in modules. PowerShell role capabilities define which commands, applications, and so on are available to a user at a Just Enough Administration endpoint.
Find-Script	Finds a specified script in registered repositories.

Once you've found the module, you can install it using `Install-Module`.

NuGet

The `PowerShellGet` and `PackageManagement` modules use the `Nuget` package management software as used in Microsoft Visual Studio or Chocolatey. The NuGet package manager is open source software licensed under the Apache 2 License. This means you can take the code, modify it, and redistribute it freely, as long as you adhere to the terms of the license. But this software is not installed as part of the Windows operating system or by a PowerShell update. Instead, you'll have to download and install it yourself. Fortunately, this is easy.

If you attempt to use the PowerShellGet or the PackageManagement module without NuGet installed, you'll be prompted to download and install the file nuget-anycpu.exe to C:\Users\<user>\AppData\Local\PackageManagement\ProviderAssemblies.

When prompted, accept the request to install NuGet, and then wait for the install to complete before proceeding.

The default repository in PowerShell v5 for PowerShellGet is the PowerShell gallery that Microsoft manages:

```
PS> Get-PSRepository | Format-List
```

```
Name                       : PSGallery
SourceLocation             : https://www.powershellgallery.com/api/v2/
Trusted                    : False
Registered                 : True
InstallationPolicy         : Untrusted
PackageManagementProvider  : NuGet
PublishLocation            : https://www.powershellgallery.com/
                             api/v2/package/
ScriptSourceLocation       : https://www.powershellgallery.com
                             /api/v2/items/psscript/
ScriptPublishLocation      : https://www.powershellgallery.com
                             /api/v2/package/
ProviderOptions            : {}
```

Note two things: First, the default repository is internet-based, so any software obtained from the gallery should be thoroughly tested in your environment before production use. Second, the gallery is untrusted by default, which means that you'll be prompted before installation of a module.

PowerShell repositories

The PowerShell gallery is managed by Microsoft, and a number of tests are performed on any published code to ensure the modules adhere to best practice and hopefully eliminate any malicious code.

It's still your responsibility to test any code you download!

> **(Continued)**
>
> Many organizations don't want to publish their code to an online repository that's available to the general public. In this case, you need to set up an internal repository and set that as the default. PowerShellGet works happily with multiple repositories. You can download from the PowerShell gallery, test, and then upload to your internal repository so that you always have a consistent known version in use.

Once you've discovered the available repositories, you can view the available modules:

```
PS> Find-Module -Repository PSGallery
```

At the time of writing, over 1700 modules were available, so we won't list them all. If you don't supply the repository name, `Find-Module` will scan all available repositories. If you supply a module name, `Find-Module` will scan for only that one:

```
PS> Find-Module -Repository PSGallery -Name Pscx

Version Name Repository Description
------- ---- ---------- -----------
3.2.2   Pscx PSGallery  PowerShell Community Extensions...
```

Once you've found your module, installing is simple:

```
PS> Install-Module -Name Pscx

Untrusted repository.
You are installing the modules from an untrusted repository. If you trust
this repository, change its InstallationPolicy value by running the Set-
PSRepository cmdlet. Are you sure you want to install the modules from
'PSGallery'?
[Y] Yes  [A] Yes to All  [N] No  [L] No to All  [S] Suspend  [?] Help
   (default is "N"): Y
```

As we said earlier you'll be prompted because the PowerShell gallery is an untrusted source. All module sources, even the official PowerShell gallery, are marked untrusted by default. This is an aspect of the secure-by-default philosophy used in PowerShell. You can test the module's availability:

```
PS> Get-Module -ListAvailable pscx

    Directory: C:\Program Files\WindowsPowerShell\Modules

ModuleType Version Name ExportedCommands
---------- ------- ---- ----------------
Script     3.2.2   Pscx {Add-PathVariable, Clear-MSMQueue...}
```

If you later decide you don't need the module, you can uninstall it using `Uninstall -Module`.

> **NOTE** Modules managed through PowerShellGet will always install in Program Files. We don't recommend moving PowerShellGet-managed modules from this location.

If the module author provides an update, you can download that with (you guessed it) `Update-Module`. One interesting point with `Update-Module` is that it will install the new version side by side with the old one, as described earlier. PowerShell will automatically use the new version and effectively ignore any older versions.

TESTING MODULES FROM AN ONLINE REPOSITORY

The recommended way to test modules from the gallery is to use `Save-Module` to download the module to some place that *isn't* in PSModulePath. Now you can safely inspect it:

```
PS> Save-Module -Name Timezone -Repository PSGallery -Path C:\testmodule
```

You can view the download:

```
PS> Get-ChildItem -Path C:\testmodule\ -Recurse

    Directory: C:\testmodule

Mode                LastWriteTime         Length Name
----                -------------         ------ ----
d-----        27/06/2016     17:17                Timezone

    Directory: C:\testmodule\Timezone

Mode                LastWriteTime         Length Name
----                -------------         ------ ----
d-----        27/06/2016     17:17                1.2.2

    Directory: C:\testmodule\Timezone\1.2.2

Mode                LastWriteTime         Length Name
----                -------------         ------ ----
-a----        02/06/2016     23:27           3149 Timezone.Help.Tests.ps1
-a----        02/06/2016     23:27           8336 Timezone.psd1
-a----        02/06/2016     23:27           7173 Timezone.psm1
-a----        02/06/2016     23:27           5924 Timezone.Tests.ps1
```

Notice that the module is downloaded into a folder with the module name and is versioned. You can inspect the code in the module and run tests to determine its applicability and safety in your environment.

If you need to load the same module onto many machines, it may be simpler to download once and then copy to the machines. But you won't get access to the other module management tools such as update and uninstall. A better approach may be to create your own internal repository and target that for the installations.

In all the exercises so far, you've depended on the module-scoping semantics to make things work. Now is a good time to develop your understanding of exactly how these new scoping rules operate. In the next section, we'll look at how function and variable names are resolved when using modules.

8.4.5   *How scopes work in script modules*

In section 7.4, we covered how scripts introduced script-specific scoping rules. As you've seen, modules also introduce new scoping rules. The primary goal of these module-specific rules is to insulate modules from accidental contamination picked up from the caller's environment. This insulating property makes module behavior more predictable, and that, in turn, makes modules more reusable.

To accomplish this isolation, each module gets its own scope chain. As with the default scope chain, the module scope chain eventually ends at the global scope (which means that module and default scope chains share the same global variables). Walking up the module scope chain, right before you reach the global scope, you'll encounter a new distinguished scope: the *module scope*. This scope is somewhat similar to the script scope except it's created only once per loaded module and is used to share and preserve the state of that module. A diagram of all of these pieces is shown in figure 8.9.

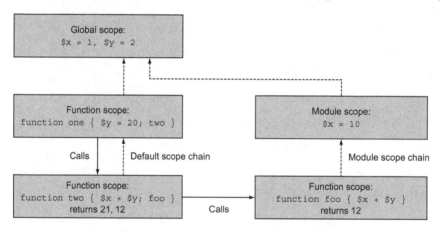

Figure 8.9   How variables are resolved in a module context. Function one **calls** two, **and** two **calls the module function** foo. **Functions** one **and** two **look up variables in the default scope. The module function** foo **uses the module scope chain.**

Let's spend some time walking through figure 8.9. In the diagram, you see boxes indicating three functions. The two on the left (one and two) are defined in the default scope and will use the default scope chain to look up variables. The function shown on the right (foo) is defined inside a module and so uses the module scope chain. Now let's call function one. This function sets a local variable, $y, to 20 then calls function two.

In the body of two, you're adding $x and $y together. This means that you have to look up the variables to get their values. The dashed lines in figure 8.9 show the order in which the scopes will be checked. Following the default scope path, the first instance of a variable named $y is found in the local scope of function one and has a value of 20. Next, you follow the scope path to find $x, and you don't find it until you hit the global scope, where it resolves to 1. Now you can add them, yielding the value 21.

Function two then calls the module function foo. This function also adds $x and $y, but this time you'll use the module scope chain to look up the variables. You travel up the module chain and don't find the defined variable $y until you hit the global scope, where its value is 2. When you look up $x, you find that it was set to 10 in the module scope. You add 2 and 10 and get 12. This shows how local variables defined in the caller's scope can't have an impact on the module's behavior. The module's operations are insulated from the caller's environment.

At this point, we've covered most of the important details of what happens when a module is loaded into the global environment. But modules can be loaded into other modules too. This is where reuse can kick in—modules building on modules delivering more and more functionality. You'll see how this works in the next section when we introduce nested modules.

8.4.6 *Nested modules*

In this section, we'll cover what happens when modules import other modules. Because Import-Module is a regular cmdlet, it can be called from anywhere. When it's called from inside another module, the result is a *nested module*. A nested module is only directly visible to the calling module. This is much easier to show than to explain. Let's look at a module called usesCount.psm1.

Listing 8.4   usesCount.psm1

```
Import-Module .\counter2.psm1

function CountUp ($x)
{
    while ($x-- -gt 0) { Get-Count }
}
```

This module imports the counter2 module created earlier and then defines a single function, countUp. Import this module:

```
PS> Import-Module .\usesCount.psm1
```

Now call Get-Module to see what's loaded:

```
PS> Get-Module

ModuleType Version     Name       ExportedCommands
---------- -------     ----       ----------------
Script     0.0         usesCount  {CountUp, Get-Count, Reset-Count, reset}
<default modules removed for brevity>
```

The first thing to notice in this output is that the nested module isn't shown. This is by design—you don't want to expose module implementation details by default. The other thing to notice is that there are more commands in the ExportedCommands list than merely CountUp. Let's use Format-List to see all the information about the module:

```
PS> Get-Module usesCount | Format-List

Name              : usesCount
Path              : C:\TestScripts\usesCount.psm1
Description       :
ModuleType        : Script
Version           : 0.0
NestedModules     : {counter2}
ExportedFunctions : {CountUp, Get-Count, Reset-Count}
ExportedCmdlets   :
ExportedVariables :
ExportedAliases   : reset
```

This shows you that three functions were exported from this module even though the module itself defined only one. This is because the functions that are being imported from the nested module are exported from the root module, usesCount. Remember, all defined functions in a module are exported by default. This includes function definitions that were imported from a nested module as well as those defined in the module body.

Although nested modules are hidden by default, there's a way to see all the modules that are loaded, including nested modules. You use the -All flag on Get-Module:

```
PS> Get-Module -All

ModuleType Version    Name       ExportedCommands
---------- -------    ----       ----------------
Script     0.0        counter2   {Get-Count, Reset-Count, reset}
Script     0.0        usesCount  {CountUp, Get-Count, Reset-Count, reset}
<output truncated for brevity>
```

Using this flag, you see both of the modules that are loaded. Let's look at some of the commands that were imported. First, look at the function that came from the root module:

```
PS> Get-Command countup | Format-List -Force -Property Module*

ModuleName : usesCount
Module     : usesCount
```

There's a lot of information available, but the properties that are most interesting for this discussion are ModuleName and Module. ModuleName names the module that this function was exported from; the Module property points to the module that *defined* this function. For top-level modules, the defining and exporting modules are the same; for nested modules, they aren't. From the ModuleName property, you see that this function was exported from module usesCount. Now let's look at one of the functions that was imported from the nested module and then re-exported:

```
PS> Get-Command Get-Count | Format-List -Force -Property Module*

ModuleName : usesCount
Module     : usesCount
```

From the output, you see that the module name for the function shows the top-level module name, not the name of the module where the function was defined. This makes sense because they're both exported from the same module. But they were defined in separate files. Knowing where a function is defined is critical to debugging, as you'll learn in chapter 15. The way to see where a function was defined is to look at the `File` property on the scriptblock that makes up the body of the function:

```
PS> ${function:CountUp}.File
C:\TestScripts\usesCount.psm1

PS> ${function:Get-Count}.File
C:\TestScripts\counter2.psm1
```

This is a fairly easy way to see where the module came from, once you know how.

IMPORT INTO THE GLOBAL ENVIRONMENT WITH -GLOBAL

When one module loads another, by default it becomes a nested module. This is usually what you want, but perhaps you want to write a module that manipulates modules. In this scenario, you need to be able to import the module into a context other than your own. Although there isn't a way to import directly into an arbitrary context, the `-Global` flag on `Import-Module` allows you to import into the global context. Let's work on a variation of the usesCount module to see how this works. The modified script module is shown next.

Listing 8.5 usesCount2.psm1

```
Import-Module -Global .\counter2.psm1
function CountUp ($x)
{
    while ($x-- -gt 0) { Get-Count }
}
```

The significant difference in this version is the use of the `-Global` parameter on `Import-Module`. First, import the module:

```
PS> Import-Module .\usesCount2.psm1
```

Then look at the modules that are loaded:

```
PS> Get-Module

ModuleType Version    Name         ExportedCommands
---------- -------    ----         ----------------
Script     0.0        counter2     {Get-Count, Reset-Count, reset}
Script     0.0        usesCount2   CountUp
<output truncated for brevity>
```

This time you see that both modules are loaded at the top level instead of one being nested inside another. Also, the `ExportedCommand` property for usesCount2 doesn't report the functions defined in counter2 as being exported from usesCount2. When you use Get-Command to look at functions from each of the modules, the functions defined in counter2 are shown as being in the correct module, as is the case for the CountUp functions. In effect, you've written a module that manipulates modules.

IMPORT WITH -SCOPE PARAMETER

Prior to PowerShell v4 you could load a module into the global scope (by using the -Global parameter) or into the current module scope, which is the default action. The introduction of the -Scope parameter in PowerShell v4 gives you more flexibility. The parameter has two options: -Scope Global (same as -Global) and -Scope Local.

Importing a module into the local scope means importing into the scope of the caller. If you do Import-Module -Scope Local inside a script, the exported functions will be visible only to the script. If you do -Scope Local inside a function, then the exported commands are visible only in that function's scope. In both cases, the exported commands get cleaned up when the function or script exits. This makes it much easier to work with different versions of the same module in a script by importing them into the scopes of different functions.

Let's see how that works in practice. Create a folder called ScopeTest—preferably not on your PSModulePath so it doesn't autoload. Create subfolders 1.0.0 and 1.1.0 inside ScopeTest. Each will hold a different version of a module.

Create the module using this code:

```
function Hello {
    Write-Host 'Hello World'
}
```

Save into the 1.0.0 folder as ScopeTest.psm1. Create a module manifest file ScopeTest.psd1. Ensure the module version is set to 1.0.0 in the manifest.

> **NOTE** Manifest files are covered in chapter 9. The sample code for the book supplies copies of the code discussed in this section if you don't want to skip ahead.

Now copy the contents of the 1.0.0 folder to 1.1.0. Change the version number in the manifest file to 1.1.0 and change 'Hello World' to 'Hello Universe' in the .psm1 file.

You now have two versions of the module. You can use this script to test the -Scope parameter:

```
function fscope {
  Import-Module C:\testmodule\ScopeTest -RequiredVersion 1.1.0 `
-Scope Local -Force
  Write-Information "`n In function" -InformationAction Continue
  hello
}

Write-Information "`n In Script" -InformationAction Continue
Import-Module C:\testmodule\ScopeTest -RequiredVersion 1.0.0 `
-Scope Global -Force
hello
```

```
Write-Information "`n Moving to function" -InformationAction Continue
fscope

Write-Information "`n Back in Script and Finish" `
-InformationAction Continue
hello
```

When you run the script you should see these results:

```
PS> C:\testmodule\ScopeTest\ScopeTest.ps1

 In Script
Hello World

 Moving to function

 In function
Hello Universe

 Back in Script and Finish
Hello World
```

The script loads the 1.0.0 version of the module into the global scope and executes the `hello` function. The `fscope` function is called, which loads the 1.1.0 version of the module into the local scope and executes the `hello` function—giving the result `'Hello Universe'`. After exiting the `fscope` function, the call to `hello` gives the original result of `'Hello World'` again.

> **NOTE** It's worth experimenting with the `-Scope` parameter to ensure you understand its action. For instance, change the `-Scope` value to Global in the `fscope` function and observe the results.

This completes our coverage of script modules, which are the type of module most people are likely to write. The next module type we'll look at is binary modules, which everyone uses but are usually created by programmers (because they're written in languages that must be compiled in an assembly or DLL file).

8.5 *Binary modules*

This section explores how binary modules operate in PowerShell. Binary modules contain the classes that define cmdlets and providers. Unlike script modules, binary modules are written in compiled languages like C# or Visual Basic. They're used to deliver much of the packaged functionality in the PowerShell distribution. From a technical perspective, a binary module is a .NET assembly (a DLL) compiled against the PowerShell libraries.

Programming topics aren't the focus of the book, but we'll spend time looking at how binary modules are written and compiled. This implies that you'll have to do some C# programming to produce a module to work with. In the following sections, we'll look at how to create and load binary modules, how they interact with script modules, and any issues you need to be aware of when working with them.

PowerShell snap-ins

PowerShell snap-ins were the only way to add binary cmdlets to PowerShell v1. You had to register the DLL containing the snap-in before you could load it into PowerShell.

Snap-ins were deprecated in PowerShell v2 when modules were introduced. Modules are the recommended way to extend PowerShell.

The only thing you need to know about snap-ins is that you shouldn't use them.

8.5.1   Creating a binary module

The first thing you'll need for our experiments is a module to work with, so in this section you'll learn how to create that module. Remember that binary modules are written in a language like C#, so you'll do a bit of non-PowerShell programming. A simple binary module is shown next.

Listing 8.6   A binary module

```
$source = @"
using System.Management.Automation;

[Cmdlet("Write", "InputObject")]
public class MyWriteInputObjectCmdlet : Cmdlet
{
    [Parameter]
    public string Parameter1;                                         ❶ Parameter
                                                                          attributes
    [Parameter(Mandatory = true, ValueFromPipeline=true)]
    public string InputObject;

    protected override void ProcessRecord()
    {
        if (Parameter1 != null)
                WriteObject(Parameter1 +  ":" +  InputObject);
            else
                WriteObject(InputObject);
    }
}                                                                    Add-Type ❷
"@
Add-Type -TypeDefinition $source -OutputAssembly examplemodule.dll
```

If you were paying attention in the previous chapter, this should be pretty comprehensible. You should certainly recognize the [Parameter()] attributes ❶ from advanced functions. Before you can use this C# code as a module, you need to compile it. PowerShell has a handy, powerful cmdlet called Add-Type, ❷ designed to make this kind of thing easy. Here you'll use it to compile the source code into the output assembly Example-Module.dll. Save listing 8.6 as examplemodule.ps1 and run it.

Once the module DLL has been created, you can load it the same way you loaded a script module, using `Import-Module`:

```
PS> Import-Module ./examplemodule.dll
```

As before, you'll use `Get-Module` to look at the module information object for `-ExampleModule`:

```
PS> Get-Module -Name examplemodule | Format-List

Name               : examplemodule
Path               : C:\TestScripts\examplemodule.dll
Description        :
ModuleType         : Binary
Version            : 0.0.0.0
NestedModules      : {}
ExportedFunctions  :
ExportedCmdlets    : Write-InputObject
ExportedVariables  :
ExportedAliases    :
```

You see the name and path as expected. The module type is binary, and it's exporting a single cmdlet, `Write-InputObject`. Now try this new cmdlet:

```
PS> 1,2,3 | Write-InputObject -Parameter1 'Number'
Number:1
Number:2
Number:3
```

It's all working fine.

Other than the implementation of a binary module, there's not much difference in behavior when using it. Well, there's one major difference: Binary modules are implemented as .NET assemblies, and .NET assemblies can't be unloaded from a session (it's a .NET thing, not a PowerShell thing); therefore, binary modules can't be unloaded from a session. This means that you can't update a binary module once it's been loaded. You can't even update the assembly on disk because the file is locked when the assembly is loaded. If you rerun the examplemodule.ps1 script you used to build the assembly earlier, you'll get a set of rather intimidating error messages. If you need to make changes, you'll have to close PowerShell and open a new session to perform the compilation.

As we said, as long as the binary module is loaded into any PowerShell session, it can't be updated. This can be annoying when you're developing a binary module, but in a production environment it isn't likely to be a problem—at least until you need to service a binary module to fix a bug. This is one area where script modules do have an advantage: they're much easier to update dynamically than binary modules.

A way to get aspects of both module types is to combine binary and script module files in a single module directory. You'll learn how this all works next.

8.5.2   *Nesting binary modules in script modules*

In section 8.4.6, we explored the idea of nested modules, where one script module is imported into another. This nesting concept also works with binary modules so script modules can import binary modules. One consequence is that it means that script modules may also export cmdlets even though they can't define them. The way nested modules work, the calling module can filter the exports of the nested module. This means you can use a script module to filter the members exported from a binary module. Let's see how this works. In the process of doing this, we'll introduce a couple of Import-Module features that you haven't seen so far.

For this example, the next listing contains a script module that loads the binary module created in the previous section.

Listing 8.7   Wrapping a binary module in a script module—WrapBinaryModule.psm1

```
param (
    [bool] $showCmdlet          ①  Defining
)                                   parameter

Import-Module $PSScriptRoot\ExampleModule.dll -Verbose    ②  Importing
                                                              module

function wof                    ③  Defining
{                                   function
    param ($o = "Hi there")
    Write-InputObject -InputObject $o
}
                                ④  Determining
if ($showCmdlet)                    exports
{
    Export-ModuleMember -Cmdlet Write-InputObject
}
else
{
    Export-ModuleMember -Function wof
}
```

There are a number of interesting things to see in this module. Right at the beginning, you see a param statement ① defining a parameter for the module. As this implies, script modules can be parameterized. The values to bind to the module's parameters are passed using the -ArgumentList parameter on Import-Module. This parameter is used to pass a list of argument values, which means that module parameters can only be positional.

The other new feature can be seen in the call to Import-Module, ② where you're loading the binary module. The path to the binary module is specified using the $PSScriptRoot (or $PSModuleRoot introduced in PowerShell v5) automatic variable. This variable was introduced in PowerShell v2 and contains the path to the directory from which the script module was loaded. In the script, the call to Import-Module specifies the -Verbose parameter so you can see this path.

In the body of the module, you define a function, wof. ❸ This function uses the imported cmdlet to write an object to the output stream.

The module ends with an if statement ❹ that uses the $showCmdlet module parameter to decide whether the function or the cmdlet should be exported from the module. Let's load the module without specifying any arguments and see what happens:

```
PS> Import-Module .\WrapBinaryModule.psm1 -Verbose
VERBOSE: Loading module from path 'C:\TestScripts\WrapBinaryModule.psm1'.
VERBOSE: Importing cmdlet 'Write-InputObject'.
VERBOSE: Importing function 'wof'.
```

From the -Verbose output, you can see that the binary module has been loaded and the location it has been loaded from. Now use Get-Module to get information about the loaded module:

```
PS> Get-Module WrapBinaryModule |
Format-List Name, ExportedFunctions, ExportedCmdlets

Name              : WrapBinaryModule
ExportedFunctions : {[wof, wof]}
ExportedCmdlets   : {}
```

From the output, you see that the function was exported, but no cmdlets were. Now try this function:

```
PS> wof 123
123
```

It works, so everything is as intended. This is an important pattern to be aware of. Using this pattern, you can use a script module to wrap a cmdlet but leave the cmdlet itself hidden. This allows you to customize the command experience even though you may not be able to change the cmdlet itself.

Let's reverse the scenario. You'll reload the script module (using the -Force flag to make sure the script gets processed again), but this time you'll pass in an argument to the script:

```
PS> Import-Module .\WrapBinaryModule.psm1 -Force `
  -ArgumentList $true -Verbose
VERBOSE: Removing the imported "wof" function.
VERBOSE: Loading module from path 'C:\TestScripts\WrapBinaryModule.psm1'.
VERBOSE: Importing cmdlet 'Write-InputObject'.
VERBOSE: Importing cmdlet 'Write-InputObject'.
```

Because the binary module is already loaded, you see the importing message. Remember, you can't update a binary module in your session once it's been loaded. The point here is to use script modules to give you at least a partial workaround for this scenario—in this case, controlling the visibility of the cmdlet. Once again, call Get-Module to see what was imported:

```
PS> Get-Module WrapBinaryModule |
    Format-List Name, ExportedFunctions, ExportedCmdlets

Name               : WrapBinaryModule
ExportedFunctions : {}
ExportedCmdlets    : {[Write-InputObject, Write-InputObject]}
```

This time you see the cmdlet but not the function as intended. Even though you couldn't change the binary module, you could still control what it exported.

> **NOTE** There are limits to this—you can't export more cmdlets; you can only filter the existing imports. You also can't rename the cmdlet itself, though you could proxy it through a function if you wanted to change its name. See section 10.5.2 for a description of how to create command proxies.

So far, all of our work with modules has been pretty much ad hoc—we're making stuff up as we go along. The modules have none of the metadata (description, author information, copyright, and so on) needed in a production environment for figuring out things like which modules need to be patched. In the next chapter, we'll address this and see how module manifests are used to fill in the missing pieces.

CDXML modules

There are three basic types of module:

- Script modules covered in section 8.4
- Binary modules that are covered in this section
- CDXML modules

CDXML modules are based on WMI classes. The base implementation provides a `Get-` cmdlet that retrieves the same information as if the class had been used with `Get-CimInstance` or `Get-WmiObject`. Any methods available on the WMI class can be used to create cmdlets performing the same task.

A CDXML module is an XML file. It's treated as a PowerShell module in terms of being located in a subfolder off the module path. The file has a .CDXML extension. Many of the modules delivered with Windows 8 and later are created using CDXML techniques.

PowerShell uses the cmdlets-over-objects technology introduced in PowerShell v3 to create functions from the XML file when the module is loaded. You can view the function in the PowerShell function drive.

CDXML modules are treated in a similar manner to script modules, so we won't cover them in any detail. We suggest *PowerShell and WMI* by Richard Siddaway (Manning, 2012) as a good reference.

8.6   *Summary*

- Modules are discovered, both in memory and on disk, using the `Get-Module` cmdlet.
- Modules are loaded with `Import-Module` and removed from memory with `Remove -Module`.
- PowerShell uses the `$ENV:PSModulePath` environment variable to search the file system for modules to load when an unqualified module name is specified.
- Modules on the module path are autoloaded.
- A fully qualified path name can be used to load a module directly without going through the search process.
- There are three basic types of modules: script modules, which are written using the PowerShell language; binary modules, which are written in a compiled language; and CDXML modules, which are based on WMI classes.
- No registration process is needed to make a module available for use—you need to be able to read the file somehow.
- Script modules are another form of script (with a .psm1 extension); they obey the Execution Policy setting like regular scripts.
- Script modules execute in their own isolated environment, called the *module context*. A script module also has access to the global environment, which is shared across all modules.
- The commands in the PowerShellGet module enable you to find, download, and manage modules from online repositories. The default repository is the PSGallery.

The focus in this chapter was on how to construct simple ad hoc modules. In the next chapter, we introduce *module manifests*—a mechanism to add production metadata to our modules as well as provide a way to deal with multifile modules.

Module manifests and metadata

This chapter covers

- Module folder structure
- Module manifest structure and elements
- Advanced module operations
- Publishing a module

*The world is my world: this is manifest in the fact that the limits of language (of that
language which alone I understand) mean the limits of my world.*

—*Ludwig Wittgenstein,* Tractatus Logico-Philosophicus

In chapter 8, we introduced PowerShell modules and covered the basics needed for
using and writing modules. The code in your module isn't the full story. There needs to
be a way to attach production-oriented metadata to your modules—it's the difference
between ad hoc and production scripting. *Module manifests* enable you to annotate
and organize the pieces in more complex, multifile modules. You can think of them as
a set of instructions to be implemented when the module is loaded. The instructions
tell PowerShell which cmdlets, variables, and aliases to load and which will remain private. Like bookkeeping and inventory management, manifests are complicated and a
bit boring but absolutely necessary when doing production scripting.

A *manifest* is a file in the module containing a set of metadata about the module, and instructions on how to load the module are the subject of this chapter.

We'll start with a discussion of the layout of a module's directory structure. Then we'll introduce the manifest and look at its contents. We'll explore the tools provided for authoring and testing manifests and walk through each manifest element, describing its purpose and how to use it. You'll learn advanced module techniques, including how to manipulate metadata from within a module, control the module access mode, and set up actions to take when a module is removed.

9.1 Module folder structure

A module in the module path ($ENV:PSModulePath) is a directory containing a collection of files. One of the files in the module directory is the module manifest. This file usually has the same name as the directory and has a .psd1 extension. You can see an example of this structure by looking at the contents of the system module directory. This directory contains modules that are installed with Windows and are visible in the directory $PSHome/Modules. The structure of some of the modules in this directory is shown in figure 9.1.

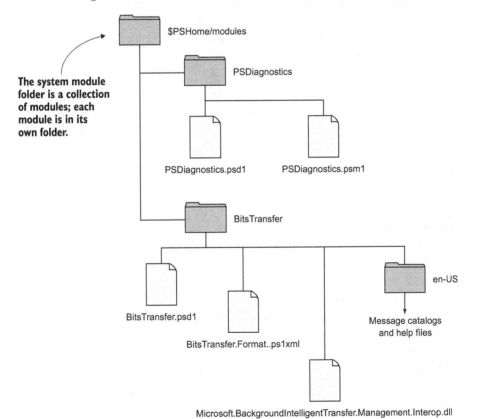

Figure 9.1 The layout of the system modules that ship with Windows. Each module is stored in its own folder, with a .psd1 file containing the module manifest. The PSDiagnostics folder contains the PSDiagnostics module. The BitsTransfer folder contains the BitsTransfer module.

In figure 9.1, you see that two modules are stored in the system module directory. These modules are directories containing the files that make up the module contents. Each folder contains a .psd1 file that's the manifest for the module.

> **NOTE** In addition to the files shown in figure 9.1 you may see a filename of the form BitsTransfer_8fa5064b-8479-4c5c-86ea-0d311fe48875_HelpInfo.xml. These files are created by the updatable help system. Ignore them.

The first module directory, PSDiagnostics, contains two files: the manifest file and a script module that defines the commands for this module. Notice that the directory, manifest, and script files all have the same name.

> **NOTE** The directory and manifest must have the same name—otherwise, the module won't load. A single script file should have the same name by convention. If there isn't a manifest, the script file must have the same name as the directory.

The second module is the BitsTransfer module. The structure of this module folder is a little more complicated. In addition to the manifest, it contains a format file, an interop DLL, and a subdirectory, en-US. This subdirectory is used to hold the message catalogs that allow for localized messages.

> **NOTE** The previous description is true for system modules, but you'll find that the overall module structure in PowerShell v5 has changed to allow multiple versions of a module to be installed. The folder structure becomes *ModuleName/ version/module contents*. We'll discuss this further when we introduce publishing to the PowerShell gallery.

We'll go over how all these elements are used when we discuss the contents of module manifests in the next section.

9.2   *Module manifest structure*

As you saw in the previous section, a module manifest is stored in a file with a .psd1 extension. This extension indicates that it's a PowerShell data file, which is a type of script that's limited in the things it can contain. We'll talk about these restrictions in section 9.6, but for now, you need to know that it's a text file containing PowerShell scripts.

This script code must return a hashtable containing a predetermined set of keys when executed by the system. These keys define the manifest elements for the module. Because these manifest files are fairly long and somewhat complex, PowerShell provides a cmdlet, `New-ModuleManifest`, to help create a manifest. Run this command so you'll have an example manifest to work with:

```
PS> New-ModuleManifest testManifest.psd1
```

> **NOTE** In PowerShell v2 all of the parameters on `New-ModuleManifest` were mandatory, so you would be prompted for every unspecified parameter even

if you weren't going to use it. This was changed in PowerShell v3, and only the -Path parameter is mandatory, and so that's the only parameter for which you'll be prompted. If in doubt, use Show-Command to drive the use of New-ModuleManifest.

The generated file will contain comments for each element, describing what the element is used for. The manifest file you've created is shown in the following listing. Note the values that are automatically added for a number of items, including Module-Version, GUID, Author, and Copyright.

Listing 9.1 testmanifest.psd1

```
#
# Module manifest for module 'testManifest'
#
# Generated by: Richard
#
# Generated on: 23/04/2017
#

@{

# Script module or binary module file associated with this manifest.
# RootModule = ''

# Version number of this module.
ModuleVersion = '1.0'

# Supported PSEditions
# CompatiblePSEditions = @()

# ID used to uniquely identify this module
GUID = '75d7e8c4-5d7e-49bc-a5f6-45554be47ca6'

# Author of this module
Author = 'Richard'

# Company or vendor of this module
CompanyName = 'Unknown'

# Copyright statement for this module
Copyright = '(c) 2017 Richard. All rights reserved.'

# Description of the functionality provided by this module
# Description = ''

# Minimum version of the Windows PowerShell engine required by this module
# PowerShellVersion = ''

# Name of the Windows PowerShell host required by this module
# PowerShellHostName = ''

# Minimum version of the Windows PowerShell host required by this module
# PowerShellHostVersion = ''

# Minimum version of Microsoft .NET Framework required by this module. This
   prerequisite is valid for the PowerShell Desktop edition only.
# DotNetFrameworkVersion = ''
```

```
# Minimum version of the common language runtime (CLR) required by this
  module. This prerequisite is valid for the PowerShell Desktop edition
  only.
# CLRVersion = ''

# Processor architecture (None, X86, Amd64) required by this module
# ProcessorArchitecture = ''

# Modules that must be imported into the global environment prior to
  importing this module
# RequiredModules = @()

# Assemblies that must be loaded prior to importing this module
# RequiredAssemblies = @()

# Script files (.ps1) that are run in the caller's environment prior to
  importing this module.
# ScriptsToProcess = @()

# Type files (.ps1xml) to be loaded when importing this module
# TypesToProcess = @()

# Format files (.ps1xml) to be loaded when importing this module
# FormatsToProcess = @()

# Modules to import as nested modules of the module specified in RootModule/
  ModuleToProcess
# NestedModules = @()

# Functions to export from this module, for best performance, do not use
  wildcards and do not delete the entry, use an empty array if there are no
  functions to export.
FunctionsToExport = @()

# Cmdlets to export from this module, for best performance, do not use
  wildcards and do not delete the entry, use an empty array if there are no
  cmdlets to export.
CmdletsToExport = @()

# Variables to export from this module
VariablesToExport = '*'

# Aliases to export from this module, for best performance, do not use
  wildcards and do not delete the entry, use an empty array if there are no
  aliases to export.
AliasesToExport = @()

# DSC resources to export from this module
# DscResourcesToExport = @()

# List of all modules packaged with this module
# ModuleList = @()

# List of all files packaged with this module
# FileList = @()

# Private data to pass to the module specified in RootModule/ModuleToProcess.
  This may also contain a PSData hashtable with additional module metadata
  used by PowerShell.
PrivateData = @{
```

```
    PSData = @{

        # Tags applied to this module. These help with module discovery in
    online galleries.
        # Tags = @()

        # A URL to the license for this module.
        # LicenseUri = ''

        # A URL to the main website for this project.
        # ProjectUri = ''

        # A URL to an icon representing this module.
        # IconUri = ''

        # ReleaseNotes of this module
        # ReleaseNotes = ''

    } # End of PSData hashtable

} # End of PrivateData hashtable

# HelpInfo URI of this module
# HelpInfoURI = ''

# Default prefix for commands exported from this module. Override the default
  prefix using Import-Module -Prefix.
# DefaultCommandPrefix = ''

}
```

Remember we said it was long and complex? In fact, it's complex enough that Power-Shell also includes a cmdlet to test a manifest. This cmdlet is called (surprise) `Test -ModuleManifest`. You'll use it to test the manifest you've generated to make sure it's valid (though it would be surprising if it weren't—after all, you created it):

```
PS> Test-ModuleManifest testManifest.psd1

ModuleType Version    Name            ExportedCommands
---------- -------    ----            ----------------
Manifest   1.0        testmanifest
```

If the test is successful, the module information object is returned.

ModuleManifest—PrivateData

Originally the `PrivateData` could be any type you wanted. In PowerShell v5 it was changed so that only hashtables are allowed. This allows multiple manifest extensions to be added as long as they're distinct.

The PSData hashtable was added to the module manifest in PowerShell v5. The contents of PSData are used to supply information for PowerShell repositories such as the online PowerShell Gallery.

Section 9.7 explains the use of the PSData section when we discuss publishing modules to a gallery.

Now that you know it's valid, you can import it. Normally a module doesn't emit anything, but in this case, you want to see it immediately. Specify `-PassThru` (which will cause the module information object to be written to the output pipe)

```
PS> Import-Module .\testManifest.psd1 -PassThru | Format-List

Name                : testmanifest
Path                : C:\test1\testmanifest.psd1
Description         :
ModuleType          : Manifest
Version             : 1.0
NestedModules       : {}
ExportedFunctions   :
ExportedCmdlets     :
ExportedVariables   :
ExportedAliases     :
```

and you see your essentially empty module.

The `New-ModuleManifest` cmdlet creates a manifest that contains all the allowed fields, but most of the fields aren't required. The only field that's required is the module version.

In practice, it's always best to use `New-ModuleManifest` to generate a complete manifest for your modules even if you aren't going to use all the fields immediately. Once you've generated the manifest, you can easily add data to it over time using your favorite text editor.

You can update an existing module manifest using `Update-ModuleManifest`. This cmdlet was introduced in PowerShell v5 as part of the PowerShellGet module.

Language restrictions in a manifest

Because the manifest is a PowerShell data file, its contents are restricted to a small subset of PowerShell language features. This subset includes the basic PowerShell data types (`numbers`, `strings`, `hashtables`, and so on), the `if` statement, and the arithmetic and comparison operators. Things like assignment statements, function definitions, and loop statements aren't allowed.

With only these elements, you'd be limited to using static values for element definitions. This means you wouldn't be able to accommodate variations in system configuration—things like paths to system directories, software installation directories, and drive letters. To allow you to handle these situations, manifests are permitted to read (but *not* write) the `$ENV:` environment provider and can use the `Join-Path` cmdlet to construct paths at runtime. This allows manifest elements to be written in such a way that system differences can be handled.

In the next few sections, we'll go over the contents of the manifest. To make our exploration a bit more manageable, we've divided the manifest elements into three broad categories: production, construction, and content elements. We'll cover each of these areas and the elements they contain, starting with the production elements.

9.3 Production manifest elements

In this section we'll explore the elements that make up the production metadata. These elements are used to add things like copyright information and version numbers. The fields in the module for this are shown in table 9.1. The use of some of the elements is pretty obvious: `Author`, `CompanyName`, `Copyright`, and so forth. We won't cover them beyond the comments in the table. The remaining elements will be covered in the subsections that follow.

Table 9.1 The manifest elements in a module manifest file that contain production-oriented metadata

Manifest element	Type	Default value	Description
ModuleVersion	String	1.0	The version number of this module. This string must be in a form that can be converted into an instance of [System.Version].
GUID	String	Autogenerated	ID used to uniquely identify this module.
Author	String	None	The name of the module creator.
CompanyName	String	Unknown	The company, if any, that produced this module.
Copyright	String	(c) Year Author. All rights reserved.	The copyright declaration for this module with the copyright year and name of the copyright holder.
Description	String	' '	The description of this module. Because this description may be used when searching for a module, it should be a reasonable description, mentioning the purpose of the module and technology area to which it relates.
PowerShellVersion	String	' '	Minimum version of the Windows PowerShell engine required by this module.
PowerShell-HostName	String	' '	Name of the Windows PowerShell host application required by this module. The default PowerShell hosts are ConsoleHost and Windows PowerShell ISE Host. Use $host to discover PowerShell host names.
PowerShellHost-Version	String	' '	Minimum version of the Windows PowerShell host required by this module.
DotNetFramework-Version	String	' '	Minimum version of the .NET Framework required by this module.
CLRVersion	String	' '	Minimum version of the CLR required.

Table 9.1   The manifest elements in a module manifest file that contain production-oriented metadata (continued)

Manifest element	Type	Default value	Description
Processor-Architecture	`String`	`' '`	The processor architecture this module requires. It may be `' '`, `None`, `X86`, `Amd64`, or `IA64`.
RequiredModules	`[object[]]`	`@()`	Modules that must be imported into the global environment prior to importing this module.

In the next few sections, you'll see how the elements in this table are used to make modules more production worthy. We'll begin with an important topic: *module identity*.

9.3.1   *Module identity*

For modules to be shared and serviced (patched) effectively, there needs to be a strong notion of identity that allows you to uniquely identify a module. It can't only be the module name. The name of the module comes from the manifest filename, and there's no guarantee somebody else won't give their module the same name as yours. To guarantee that you can always identify a module regardless of path changes, renames, and so on, the manifest contains a globally unique identifier (GUID). The algorithm used to generate GUIDs is guaranteed to produce a globally unique number. Once you know the GUID for a module, you can always identify it, even if the file gets renamed.

Another important aspect of module identity is the version number. Versioning is what allows you to determine if the module has been patched properly. The `Module -Version` element in the manifest is used to hold the module's version. This element uses the type `System.Version` to represent the version of a module internally. In the manifest file, the element should be assigned a string that can be converted into an instance of `System.Version`. This string must have the form of #.#.#.#—for example, 1.0.0.0. When you use the `-Version` parameter on `Import-Module`, it will search the path in `$ENV:PSModulePath`, looking for the first module whose name matches the requested name and whose module version is equal to or greater than the required version.

9.3.2   *Runtime dependencies*

The remainder of the production elements in the manifest relate to identifying environmental dependencies—what needs to be in the environment for the module to work properly. For many script modules, most of these elements can be left in their default state. Let's go through these elements and what they're used for.

The `CLRVersion` and `DotNetFrameworkVersion` identify dependencies based on what version of the CLR (or .NET) is installed on the system. Why do you need two elements? Because the CLR runtime and the framework (all of the libraries) can and do vary independently; for example, the CLR 3.0 runtime version was 2.0, and the framework version was 3.0.

When adding the dependencies to the manifest, you should specify the minimum highest version required. This depends on the higher revisions being backward compatible with earlier versions and is a fairly safe assumption for the CLR.

Expressing a dependency on the processor architecture isn't likely to be common, but it's possible to have a module that uses .NET interoperation or COM and, as a consequence, has some processor architecture-specific dependency.

The next set of dependencies is on PowerShell itself. The `PowerShellVersion` is pretty straightforward. It specifies the minimum version of PowerShell needed by this module. The `PowerShellHostName` and `ModuleVersion` are only slightly more complex. They allow you to place a dependency on the application that's hosting the PowerShell runtime rather than on the runtime itself. For example, you can have a module that adds custom elements to the PowerShell ISE. This module clearly has a dependency on the name of the host. To find out the name of the string to place here, in the host look at the `Name` property on the object in `$host`.

Once you know which host you're depending on, you also need the version number, which is available through the `Version` property on `$host`.

The final type of dependency is on the modules that are already loaded into the system. This is done through the `RequiredModules` manifest element. In PowerShell v2 this element only checked to see if the listed modules were loaded in memory. This has changed so that from PowerShell v3 onward the required modules are loaded if not already present in memory. Whereas the other elements you've seen so far are either simple strings or strings that can be converted into a version number, this element can take either a module name string or a hashtable containing two or three elements. These hashtable elements allow you to precisely specify the module you're dependent on because they include the module name, the version number, and the GUID of the module that must be loaded (although the GUID is optional).

This covers all the production elements in the manifest. Now that you know you have the right module (Identity) and that it will work in your environment (Dependencies), let's look at the manifest elements that control what happens when the module is loaded. Load-time behavior is controlled by a set of manifest elements that contain entries that are used to construct the in-memory representation of the module.

9.4   *Construction manifest elements*

The construction metadata in this module includes the fields that tell the engine what to load as part of this module. These fields are listed in table 9.2.

Table 9.2 Module manifest elements that contain data used in constructing the module

Manifest element	Type	Default value	Description
`RootModule`	`string`	`' '`	Script module or binary module file associated with this manifest
`RequiredAssemblies`	`[string[]]`	`@()`	Assemblies that must be loaded prior to importing this module
`ScriptsToProcess`	`[string[]]`	`@()`	Script files (.ps1) that are run in the caller's environment prior to importing this module
`TypesToProcess`	`[string[]]`	`@()`	Type files (.ps1xml) to be loaded when importing this module
`FormatsToProcess`	`[string[]]`	`@()`	Format files (.ps1xml) to be loaded when importing this module
`NestedModules`	`[string[]]`	`@()`	Modules to import as nested modules of the module specified in `ModuleToProcess`
`FunctionsToExport`	`String`	`"*"`	Functions to export from this module
`CmdletsToExport`	`String`	`"*"`	Cmdlets to export from this module
`VariablesToExport`	`String`	`"*"`	Variables to export from this module
`AliasesToExport`	`String`	`"*"`	Aliases to export from this module
`DscResourcesToExport`	`[string[]]`	`@()`	DSC resources to export from this module

NOTE In PowerShell v2 `RootModule` was known as `ModuleToProcess`. Both names still work in a manifest, though `RootModule` is recommended because it matches with the latest parameters. `RootModule` is a better description because it supplies the base module with everything else being loaded as submodules. `ModuleToProcess` is an alias for the `RootModule` parameter on `New-ModuleManifest`. If you need backward compatibility to PowerShell 2.0, be sure to use `ModuleToProcess`.

There are two subcategories in the construction elements: "things to load" and "things to export." The relevant code from listing 9.1 is repeated here:

```
@{
# Script module or binary module file associated with this manifest.
# RootModule = ''

# Assemblies that must be loaded prior to importing this module
# RequiredAssemblies = @()

# Script files (.ps1) that are run in the caller's environment prior to
   importing this module.
# ScriptsToProcess = @()

# Type files (.ps1xml) to be loaded when importing this module
# TypesToProcess = @()
```

```
# Format files (.ps1xml) to be loaded when importing this module
# FormatsToProcess = @()

# Modules to import as nested modules of the module specified in RootModule/
   ModuleToProcess
# NestedModules = @()

# Functions to export from this module
FunctionsToExport = '*'

# Cmdlets to export from this module
CmdletsToExport = '*'

# Variables to export from this module
VariablesToExport = '*'

# Aliases to export from this module
AliasesToExport = '*'

# DSC resources to export from this module
# DscResourcesToExport = @()
}
```

We'll start with loading because you can't export anything until something has been loaded. As mentioned previously, none of the fields is required. If they aren't there, then PowerShell assumes the default value for each field, as shown in the table.

9.4.1 *The loader manifest elements*

The next few sections cover each of these manifest elements in the order in which you're most likely to use them when creating a manifest. This isn't the order in which they're processed when the module is loaded. We'll cover the load order as a separate topic in section 9.4.2.

ROOTMODULE MANIFEST ELEMENT

The first loader element we'll discuss is RootModule. It's the most commonly used manifest element and identifies the main, or *root*, active module to load. By *active*, we mean that the file defines executable elements, instead of merely providing metadata definitions. The type of the module file specified in this member will determine the final module type. If no file is specified as the RootModule, then the type shown in the module information object will be Manifest. If it's a script or binary module, it will be the respective module type. Other types will raise errors. The combinations are shown in table 9.3.

Table 9.3 Module types as determined by the RootModule member

Contents of RootModule	Final module type
empty	Manifest
Script module (.psm1 file)	Script
CDXML module (.cdxml file)	Cim

Table 9.3   Module types as determined by the `RootModule` member *(continued)*

Contents of `RootModule`	Final module type
Binary module (.dll, .exe)	`Binary`
A workflow module (.xaml file)	`Workflow`
Module manifest (.psd1 file)	Error—not permitted
Script file	Error—not permitted

PowerShell discoverability

One of the great things about PowerShell is that you can investigate the inner workings using PowerShell itself. As an example, you can discover the available module types like this:

```
PS> [System.Management.Automation.ModuleType].GetFields().Name
value__
Script
Binary
Manifest
Cim
Workflow
```

You could look at the MSDN documentation for the `ModuleType` enumeration at http://mng.bz/5JkY.

But that's not as much fun.

If a script, cdxml, workflow, or binary module is specified in the `RootModule` element, the type of the loaded module will be `Script`, `CIM`, `Workflow`, or `Binary`, respectively, as shown in the `ModuleType` property displayed by `Get-Module`.

> **NOTE** A CIM module is created from a CIM (WMI) class. The module definition is a .cdxml (cmdlet definition XML) file. Details on creating .cdxml modules can be found in *PowerShell and WMI* by Richard Siddaway (Manning, 2012) or *PowerShell in Depth* by Don Jones, et al., (Manning, second edition, 2015).

What it can't be, however, is another manifest module or script file. The reason for this constraint is that the job of a manifest is to add metadata to a script or binary module. If the main module is another manifest, you'd have to deal with colliding metadata. For example, one manifest may declare that the module is version 1.0.0.0, but the second module says it's version 1.2.0.0. There's no way to reconcile this type of collision, so it's not allowed. As a result, PowerShell won't look for a .psd1 file when searching for the module to process. It's expected that production modules will use `RootModule` to identify a single main module.

NESTEDMODULES MANIFEST ELEMENT

The `NestedModules` are loaded before the `RootModule` is loaded. Although the net effect is equivalent to having the main module call `Import-Module`, there are two advantages to this approach. First, it's easy to see what the module is going to lod before loading the module. Second, if there's a problem with loading the nested modules, the main module won't have been loaded and won't have to deal with the load failures.

REQUIREDASSEMBLIES MANIFEST ELEMENT

The `RequiredAssemblies` field loads the assemblies listed in the element if they aren't already loaded. Figure 9.2 shows the steps taken when trying to find the assembly to load.

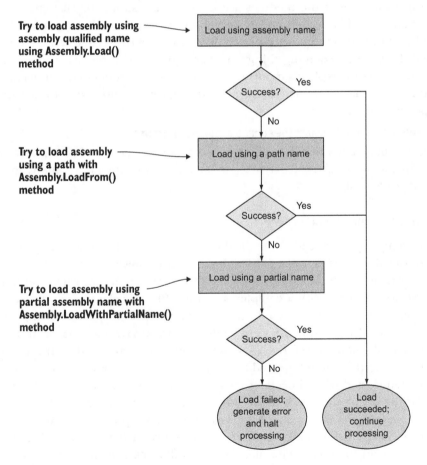

Figure 9.2 The steps taken when trying to load an assembly from the
`RequiredAssemblies` **module**

NOTE   The LoadWithPartialName() method shown in figure 9.2 is deprecated but is unlikely to be removed because PowerShell and many people still rely on this method. The CorePowerShell for Nano server option in Windows Server 2016 uses an alternative mechanism because there isn't a GAC in CoreCLR.

If one of the steps results in a successful load, PowerShell will proceed to the next step in loading a module. If it fails, the entire module loading process is considered a failure.

SCRIPTSTOPROCESS MANIFEST ELEMENT

Now let's talk about ScriptsToProcess and scripts in general. Something we didn't discuss earlier is that NestedModules can also refer to script files. These script files are run in the root module's context—equivalent to dot-sourcing them into the root module script. The scripts listed in ScriptToProcess do something quite different. These scripts are run in the caller's environment, not the module environment, and are run before any of the modules are loaded. This allows for custom setup and environment validation logic. We talked about how version checks work—the first module with a version number equal to or greater than the requested version number will be loaded, assuming things are backward compatible. This might not be true, but there's no explicit support for this level of dependency checking currently. If you're in a situation where you have to do this, you can use a script referenced in ScriptsToProcess.

TYPESTOPROCESS AND FORMATSTOPROCESS MANIFEST ELEMENTS

The last of the loaded manifest elements are TypesToProcess and FormatsToProcess. These are files with a .ps1xml extension that contain formatting instructions and additional type metadata.

9.4.2   *Module component load order*

Module components are loaded into the PowerShell environment using a fixed sequence of steps called the *module load order*. This load order is shown in figure 9.3.

The order in which these steps are taken can be of significance when you're trying to construct a module with a complex structure. In particular, there's an issue load order that causes problems when using binary modules with types and format files.

Because types and format files are loaded before ModuleToProcess is, if the types and format files contain references to any of the .NET types in the binary module, an error saying that the referenced types can't be found because the module's DLL hasn't been loaded yet will occur. To work around this, you need to make sure the DLL for the binary module is loaded first. You do so by adding the DLL to the list of RequiredAssemblies. Because RequiredAssemblies is processed before the types and format file entries, there won't be a problem resolving the types. Then, when it's time to load the binary module, the DLL will already be loaded and will need to be scanned to find the cmdlets and providers. This resolves the problem with effectively no performance impact and only a small increase of complexity for the module owner.

At this point, we've covered all the major module manifest topics. There are the content manifest elements left to look at before we're finished.

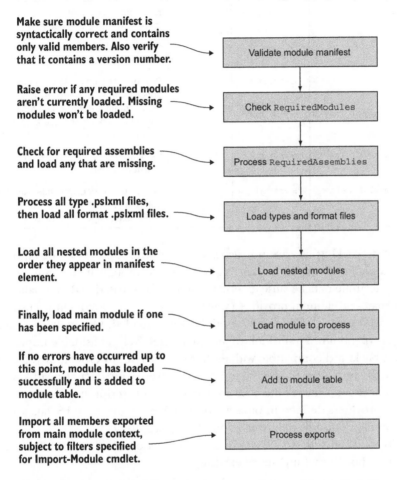

Make sure module manifest is syntactically correct and contains only valid members. Also verify that it contains a version number. → Validate module manifest

Raise error if any required modules aren't currently loaded. Missing modules won't be loaded. → Check `RequiredModules`

Check for required assemblies and load any that are missing. → Process `RequiredAssemblies`

Process all type .ps1xml files, then load all format .ps1xml files. → Load types and format files

Load all nested modules in the order they appear in manifest element. → Load nested modules

Finally, load main module if one has been specified. → Load module to process

If no errors have occurred up to this point, module has loaded successfully and is added to module table. → Add to module table

Import all members exported from main module context, subject to filters specified for Import-Module cmdlet. → Process exports

Figure 9.3 The ordering of the steps when processing a module manifest. If an error occurs at any point prior to the next-to-last step, module processing will stop, and an error will be thrown.

9.5 Content manifest elements

The content manifest elements mainly list the component files that make up a module. Two lists are provided: a list of all loadable module files and a separate list for any other files (data files, icons, audio clips, and so on) that are part of the module. The location of the external help and a default prefix for exported commands can also be specified. These elements are shown in table 9.4.

Table 9.4 Module manifest elements used to list the module's contents

Manifest element	Type	Default value	Description
ModuleList	[string[]]	@()	Non-normative list of all modules packaged with this module.
FileList	[string[]]	@()	Non-normative list of all files packaged with this module.
PrivateData	[hastable]	@{}	Private data to pass to the module specified in RootModule. This may also contain a PSData hashtable with additional module metadata used by PowerShell.
HelpInfoURI	[string]	' '	HelpInfo URI of this module. This points to external help.
DefaultCommandPrefix	[string]	' '	Default prefix for commands exported from this module. Override the default prefix using Import-Module -Prefix.

Note that these packing lists are not *normative*—they aren't processed or enforced by PowerShell, and filing them is optional. As a best practice, though, it's recommended that they contain accurate data because external tools may be created to do the validation.

The PrivateData element provides a way for module writers to include custom data in manifests and make it available to modules when loaded. Originally, PrivateData could be any type, but in PowerShell v5 its type is effectively a hashtable implemented such that it's backward compatible with earlier versions of PowerShell. If you're using PrivateData for your own purposes, you should insert your data as a subkey of the hashtable. The system makes the data available to both script and binary modules, including to providers defined in binary modules. We'll look at the PSData section in section 9.7 when we discuss publishing a module to a gallery.

And we're finished with manifests! In the next section, we'll explore features that are less tedious but (hopefully) more exciting.

9.6 Advanced module operations

In this section, you'll learn sophisticated things you can do with modules. These features are not intended for typical day-to-day use, but they allow for some sophisticated scripting. As always, if you aren't only scripting for yourself, have pity on the person who will have to maintain your code and avoid "stunt scripting."

9.6.1 The PSModuleInfo object

PowerShell modules, like everything in PowerShell, are objects you can work with directly. The type of the object used to reference modules is System.Management.Automation.PSModuleInfo.

You've been looking at these objects all along—this is what Get-Module returns—but you've been using them only to get basic information about a module. In practice, there are a lot of other things that can be done once you have a PSModuleObject. In this section, we'll look at what can be done (and try to explain why you'd do these things).

INVOCATION IN THE MODULE CONTEXT

In our discussion about module scopes, we introduced the concept of a module-level scope, which is used to isolate the private variables and functions. When you execute code where function and variable lookup is done in a module scope, we call this *executing in the module context.* This is what happens anytime you execute a function that has been exported from a module. But you can also cause arbitrary code to be executed in the module context even though it wasn't defined in that context. In effect, you're *pushing* code into the module context. This is done with a PSModuleInfo object using the call operator &.

> **NOTE** Yes, this ability to inject code into a module context violates all the principles of isolation and information hiding. And from a language perspective, this is a bit terrifying, but people do it all the time when debugging. One of the nice things about dynamic languages is that you're effectively running the debugger attached all the time.

To try this out, you'll need a module object to play with. Let's load the counter module we looked at in section 8.4.1. This module has private state in the form of the two variables—$count and $increment—and one public function, Get-Count. Now import it

```
PS> Import-Module .\counter.psm1
```

and use Get-Module to get the module reference:

```
PS> $m = Get-Module counter
```

You could have done this in one step with the -PassThru parameter, as you saw earlier, but we're using two steps here to illustrate that these techniques can be done with any in-memory module. Now run the Get-Count function, and it returns 1, as it should right after the module is first loaded:

```
PS> Get-Count
1
```

Now set a global variable, $count, using the Set-Variable command (again, we're using the command instead of assignment to set the variable for illustration purposes):

```
PS> Set-Variable -Name count -Value 33
```

When you run Get-Count again, it returns 2 because the $count variable it uses exists in the module context:

```
PS> Get-Count
2
```

So far, nothing much to see. Now let's do something a bit fancier. Let's see what the current value of $count in the module context is. You can do this by invoking Get -Variable in the module context with the call operator:

```
PS> & $m Get-Variable count
```

```
Name                          Value
----                          -----
count                         2
```

You see the value is 2. Great. Now you can inspect the private inner state of a module to see what's going on. Next, let's alter that state. You'll execute the same Set-Variable command as before but inside the module this time:

```
PS> & $m Set-Variable -Name count -Value 33
```

Call Get-Count to verify that you have made a change:

```
PS> Get-Count
34
```

The call to Get-Count returns 34, so you've successfully changed the value of the variable it uses in its operation.

Okay, you know how to get and set state in the module, so let's try altering the code. First, look at the body of the Get-Count function:

```
PS> & $m Get-Item function:Get-Count
```

```
CommandType Name        Version Source
----------- ----        ------- ------
Function    Get-Count   0.0     counter
```

Now redefine the function in the module. Instead of adding the increment, add the increment times 2:

```
PS> & $m {
    function script:Get-Count
    {
        return $script:count += $increment * 2
    }
}
```

Although you've redefined the function in the module, you have to reimport the module in order to get the new definition into your function table:

```
PS> Import-Module .\counter.psm1
```

Now you can call the function again to make sure you're getting what you expected:

```
PS> Get-Count
36
```

```
PS> Get-Count
38
```

Yes, `Get-Count` is now incrementing by 2 instead of 1.

All these tweaks on the module affect only the module in memory. The module file on disk isn't changed! If you use the `-Force` parameter on `Import-Module`, you'll force the system to reload the file from disk, reinitializing everything to the way it was:

```
PS> Import-Module .\counter.psml -Force
```

Verify this by running `Get-Count`:

```
PS> Get-Count
1
```

Again, this is one of the characteristics of dynamic languages: the ability of programs to modify themselves in a profound way at runtime and then restore the original state. In the next section we'll look at how to use properties on the `PSModuleInfo` to access the members of a module without importing them.

ACCESSING MODULES EXPORTS USING THE `PSMODULEINFO` OBJECT

The exported members of a module are discoverable through properties on the `PSModuleInfo` object that represents the module. This gives you a way to look at the exported members without having to import them into your environment. For example, the list of exported functions is available in the `ExportedFunctions` member. These properties are hashtables, indexed by the name of the exported member. Let's look at what you can do using these properties.

As always, you need a module to work with. In this case, you'll use a dynamic module, which we'll cover in more detail in chapter 10. Dynamic modules don't require a file on disk, which makes them easy to use for experiments. You'll create a dynamic module and save the `PSModuleInfo` object in a variable called `$m`:

```
PS> $m = New-Module {
  function foo {"In foo x is $x"}
  $x=2
  Export-ModuleMember -func foo -var x
}
```

Now you can use the export lists on the `PSModuleInfo` object to see what was exported:

```
PS> $m | Format-List exported*

ExportedFunctions    : {[foo, foo]}
ExportedCmdlets      : {}
ExportedCommands     : {[foo, foo]}
ExportedVariables    : {[x, System.Management.Automation.PSVariable]}
ExportedAliases      : {}
ExportedWorkflows    : {}
ExportedDscResources : {}
ExportedFormatFiles  : {}
ExportedTypeFiles    : {}
```

In the output, you see that one function and one variable were exported. You also see that the function turns up in the `ExportedCommands` member. Modules can export more than one type of command—functions, aliases, or cmdlets—and this property exists to provide a convenient way to see all commands regardless of type.

> **NOTE** By implementing the exported member properties as hashtables, you can access and manipulate the state of the module in a fairly convenient way. The downside is that the default output for the exported members is a bit strange, especially for functions where you see things like [foo, foo]. These tables map the name of a command to the `CommandInfo` object for that command. When the contents of the table are displayed, both the key and the value are displayed as strings, and because the presentation of a `CommandInfo` object as a string is the name of the object, you see the name twice.

Let's use the `ExportedFunctions` property to see how the function foo is easier to write:

```
PS> $m.ExportedFunctions.foo

CommandType Name Version Source
----------- ---- ------- ------
Function    foo  0.0     __DynamicModule_7263f1…
```

The value returned from the expression is a `CommandInfo` object.

> **NOTE** The value of source is `_DynamicModule_` followed by a GUID, so you'll see a different value each time you try this code.

This means that you can use the call operator, `&`, to invoke this function:

```
PS> & $m.ExportedFunctions.foo
In foo x is 2
```

You can also use the `PSModuleInfo` object to change the value of the exported variable $x:

```
PS> $m.ExportedVariables.x.value = 3
```

Call the function again to validate this change:

```
PS> & $m.ExportedFunctions.foo
In foo x is 3
```

The return value from the call is the updated value as expected. Next, we'll look at some of the methods on `PSModuleInfo` objects.

9.6.2   *Using the PSModuleInfo methods*

The call operator isn't the only way to use the module information object. The object itself has a number of methods that can be useful. Look at some of them:

```
PS> [psmoduleinfo].GetMethods() |
Select-String -notmatch '(get_|set_)'
```

```
System.Management.Automation.ScriptBlock NewBoundScriptBlock(
  System.Management.Automation.ScriptBlock)
System.Object Invoke(System.Management.Automation.ScriptBlock,
  System.Object[])
System.Management.Automation.PSObject AsCustomObject()
<output truncated for brevity>
```

We'll cover the first two listed, `Invoke()` and `NewBoundScriptBlock()`, and save `AsCustom-Object()` for chapter 10.

THE INVOKE() METHOD

This method is a .NET programmer way of doing what you did earlier with the call operator. Assuming you still have the counter module loaded (load it if you don't), let's use this method to reset the count and change the increment to 5. First, get the module information object:

```
PS> $m = Get-Module counter
```

Now invoke a scriptblock in the module context using this method:

```
PS> $m.Invoke({$script:count = 0; $script:increment = 5})
```

The corresponding invocation using the call operator would be as follows:

```
PS> & $m {$script:count = 0; $script:increment = 5}
```

This is scripter-friendly, but either way, let's try to verify the result:

```
PS> Get-Count
5

PS> Get-Count
10
```

The count was reset, and `Get-Count` now increments by 5 instead of 1. Next, let's look at a way to attach modules to a scriptblock.

THE NEWBOUNDSCRIPTBLOCK() METHOD

In this topic, we're jumping ahead a bit because we won't cover scriptblocks in depth until chapter 10. A module-bound scriptblock is a piece of code—a scriptblock—that has the module context to use attached to it. Normally an unbound scriptblock is executed in the caller's context, but once a scriptblock is bound to a module, it always executes in the module context. In fact, that's how exported functions work—they're implicitly bound to the module that defined them.

Let's use this mechanism to define a scriptblock that will execute in the context of the counter module. First, you need to get the module (again). You could use `Get-Module` as before, but now that you know that exported functions are bound to a module, you can use the `Module` property on an exported command to get the module information object. Do so with `Get-Count`:

```
PS> $gcc = Get-Command Get-Count
```

Now you can get the module for this command:

```
PS> $gcc.Module

ModuleType Version Name     ExportedCommands
---------- ------- ----     ----------------
Script     0.0     counter  {Get-Count, Reset-Count, setIncrement}
```

Next, you need to define the scriptblock you're going to bind. Do this and place the scriptblock into a variable:

```
PS> $sb = {param($incr) $script:increment = $incr}
```

This scriptblock takes a single parameter, which it uses to set the module-level `$increment` variable. Now you'll bind it to the target module. Note that this doesn't bind the module to the original scriptblock; instead, it creates a new scriptblock with the module attached:

```
PS> $setIncrement = $gcc.Module.NewBoundScriptblock( $sb )
```

Now test using the scriptblock to set the increment. Invoke the scriptblock with the call operator passing in an increment of 10:

```
PS> & $setIncrement 10
```

And verify that the increment has been changed:

```
PS> Get-Count
20
PS> Get-Count
30
```

Okay, good. But if you want to use this mechanism frequently, it would be useful to have a named function. You can do this by assigning the scriptblock to `Set-Increment` in the `function:` drive:

```
PS> ${function:Set-CountIncrement} = $setIncrement
```

Let's test the function:

```
PS> Set-CountIncrement 100
PS> Get-Count
130

PS> Get-Count
230
```

And now the increment is 100 per the argument to the `Set-CountIncrement`. Now use `Get-Command` to look at the function you've defined:

```
PS> Get-Command Set-CountIncrement | Format-Table name, module

Name                              Module
----                              ------
Set-CountIncrement                counter
```

Similar to `Get-Count`, it's listed as being associated with the counter module. Now that you've introduced the idea of a function being dynamically attached to a module, you should learn about the context where a function gets evaluated—which we'll cover in the next section.

9.6.3 *The defining module vs. the calling module*

In this section we'll go into greater detail about how the execution context for a module is established. We covered module scoping in section 8.4.4. By providing you with a deeper understanding of the details of how this works, we're setting the stage for some of the more advanced topics we'll cover in chapter 10.

Commands always have two module contexts: the context where they were defined and the context where they were called from. This is a somewhat subtle concept that will be explained through the examples in this section. Before PowerShell had modules, this wasn't terribly interesting except for getting filename and line number information for where the function was called and where it was defined. With modules, this distinction becomes more significant. Among other things, the module where the command was defined contains the module-specific resources like the manifest `PrivateData` element mentioned in section 9.5. For functions, the ability to access the two contexts allows the function to access the caller's variables instead of the module variables.

ACCESSING THE DEFINING MODULE

The module that a function was defined in can be retrieved by using the expression `$MyInvocation.MyCommand.Module`. Similarly, the module a cmdlet was defined in is available through the instance property `this.MyInvocation.MyCommand.Module`. If the function is defined in the global scope (or top level), the module field will be `$null`. Let's try that. First, define a function at the top level:

```
PS> function Test-ModuleContext {
    $MyInvocation.MyCommand.Module
}
```

Then run it, formatting the result as a list showing the module name and `PrivateData` fields:

```
PS> Test-ModuleContext | select name,privatedata
```

Nothing was output because the defining module at the top level is always $null. Now let's define the function inside a module. Use a here-string to create a .psm1 file:

```
PS> @'
function Test-ModuleContext {
    $MyInvocation.MyCommand.Module
}
'@ > TestModuleContext.psm1
```

Now load the file and run the same test command as you did previously:

```
PS> Import-Module ./TestModuleContext.psm1
PS> Test-ModuleContext | Format-List name, privatedata

Name        : TestModuleContext
PrivateData :
```

This time the result of the function was not $null—you see the module name, and the PrivateData field is empty because there was no module manifest to provide this data. You can remedy this by creating a module manifest to go along with the .psm1 file. This abbreviated manifest defines the minimum—the module version, the module to process, and a hashtable for PrivateData:

```
PS> @'
  @{
    ModuleVersion = '1.0.0.0'
    ModuleToProcess = 'TestModuleContext.psm1'
    PrivateData = @{a = 1; b = 2 }
  }
'@ > TestModuleContext.psd1
```

Load the module using the manifest and -Force to make sure everything gets updated:

```
PS> Import-Module -Force ./TestModuleContext.psd1
```

Then run the test command:

```
PS> Test-ModuleContext | Format-List name, privatedata

Name        : TestModuleContext
PrivateData : {a, b}
```

You see that the PrivateData field is now also filled in.

ACCESSING THE CALLING MODULE

The module that a function was called from can be retrieved by using the expression $PSCmdlet.SessionState.Module. Similarly, the module a cmdlet is called from is available through this.SessionState.Module. In either case, if the command is being invoked from the top level, this value will be $null because there is no "global module."

NOTE It's unfortunate that the PowerShell team didn't get a chance to wrap the global session state in a module before PowerShell v2 shipped. This means that this kind of code has to be special case for the module being $null some of the time.

WORKING WITH BOTH CONTEXTS

Now let's look at a tricky scenario where you access both contexts at once. This is something that's rarely necessary but when needed is absolutely required.

In functions and script modules, accessing the module session is trivial because unqualified variables are resolved in the module context by default. To access the caller's context, you need to use the caller's session state, available as a property on $PS-Cmdlet. Let's update the Test-ModuleContext module to access a variable, $testv, both in the caller's context and the module context. Here's the module definition:

```
PS> @'
 $testv = 123
 function Test-ModuleContext {
     [CmdletBinding()] param()
     "module testv is $testv"
     $ctestv = $PSCmdlet.SessionState.PSVariable.Get("testv").Value;
     "caller's testv is $ctestv"
}
'@ > TestModuleContext.psm1
```

This defines your test function, specifying that the cmdlet binding be used so you can access $PSCmdlet. The module body also defines a module-scoped variable, $testv. The test function will emit the value of this variable and then use the expression

```
$PSCmdlet.SessionState.PSVariable.Get("testv").Value
```

to get the value of the caller's $testv variable. Next, load the module:

```
PS> Import-Module -Force ./TestModuleContext.psm1
```

Now define a global $testv:

```
PS> $testv = '456'
```

Next, run the command:

```
PS> Test-ModuleContext
module testv is 123
caller's testv is 456
```

And you see the module $testv was correctly displayed as 123 and the caller's variable is the global value 456. Now wait a minute, you say, you could've done this much more easily by specifying $global:testv. That's true if you were only interested in accessing variables at the global level. But sometimes you want to get the local variable in the caller's dynamic scope. Let's try this. Define a new function, `nested`, that will set a local `$testv`:

```
PS> function nested {
  $testv = "789"
  Test-ModuleContext
}
```

This function-scoped `$testv` variable is the caller's variable you want to access, so you should get 789 instead of the global value 456:

```
PS> nested
module testv is 123
caller's testv is 789
```

It works. The module `$testv` was returned as 123, and the caller's `$testv` returned the value of the function-scoped variable instead of the global variable.

When would you need this functionality? If you want to write a function that manipulates the caller's scope—say something like the `Set-Variable` cmdlet implemented as a function—then you'd need this capability. The other time you might need to do this is when you want to access the value of locally scoped configuration variables, such as `$OFS`.

9.6.4   *Setting module properties from inside a script module*

We've talked at length about how manifests are required to set metadata on a module, but there's a way for the script module to do some of this itself during the module load operation. To do that it needs to have access to its own `PSModuleInfo` object during the load. This can be retrieved using the rather awkward expression

```
$MyInvocation.MyCommand.ScriptBlock.Module
```

But once you have the `PSModuleInfo` object, the rest is easy. Try it out by setting the `Description` property on your own module.

SETTING THE MODULE DESCRIPTION

In this example, you'll set the `Description` property for a module from within the module itself. You'll create a module file in the current directory called setdescription.psm1:

```
PS> @'
$mInfo = $MyInvocation.MyCommand.ScriptBlock.Module
$mInfo.Description = "My Module's Description on $(Get-Date)"
'@ > setdescription.psm1
```

On the first line of the module, you copy the reference to the `PSModuleInfo` object into a variable, `$mInfo`. On the second line, you assign a value to the `Description` property on that object. Import the module:

```
PS> Import-Module .\setdescription.psm1
```

Then call `Get-Module`, piping into `Format-List` so you can see only the module name and its description:

```
PS> Get-Module setdescription | Format-List name, description

Name        : setdescription
Description : My Module's Description on 04/23/2017 20:01:10
```

And there you go. You've dynamically set the `Description` property on your module.

Along with being able to set this type of metadata entry on the `PSModuleInfo` object, there are a couple of behaviors you can control as well. You'll see how this works in the next two sections.

9.6.5 *Controlling when modules can be unloaded*

The module `AccessMode` feature allows you to restrict when a module can be unloaded. There are two flavors of restriction: *static* and *constant*. A *static module* is a module that can't be removed unless the `-Force` option is used on the `Remove-Module` cmdlet. A *constant module* can never be unloaded and will remain in memory until the session that loaded it ends. This model parallels the pattern for making variables and functions constant.

To make a module either static or constant, you need to set the `AccessMode` property on the module's `PSModuleInfo` object to the appropriate setting. Set it to `ReadOnly` for static modules and `Constant` for constant modules. You can't do this through the metadata in the module manifest. The appropriate code has to be in the module script file. Let's see how this is done. Here's an example script module called readonly.psm1 that makes itself `ReadOnly` by having these lines at the top of the module:

```
PS> @'
$mInfo = $MyInvocation.MyCommand.ScriptBlock.Module
$mInfo.AccessMode = 'readonly'
'@ > readonly.psm1
```

The first line of the module is the same as the example in the previous section and retrieves the `PSModuleInfo` object. The next line sets the `AccessMode` to readonly. Now load this module and verify the behavior:

```
PS> Import-Module .\readonly.psm1
PS> Get-Module readonly

ModuleType Version Name     ExportedCommands
---------- ------- ----     ----------------
Script     0.0     readonly
```

You've verified that it's been loaded, so now try to remove it:

```
PS> Remove-Module readonly
Remove-Module : Unable to remove the module 'readonly' because it is read-
   only. Add the Force parameter to your command to remove read-only modules.
```

```
At line:1 char:1
+ Remove-Module readonly
+ ~~~~~~~~~~~~~~~~~~~~~~~
    + CategoryInfo          : PermissionDenied: (readonly:PSModuleInfo)
   [Remove-Module], InvalidOperationException
    + FullyQualifiedErrorId : Modules_ModuleIsReadOnly,Microsoft.PowerShell.
   Commands.RemoveModuleCommand
```

When you try to remove the module, you get an error stating that -Force must be used to remove it. Do that:

```
PS> Remove-Module readonly -Force
```

This time you don't get an error. You can verify that the module has been removed by calling Get-Module. Nothing is returned, confirming that the module has been removed. The same approach is used to mark a module as constant.

And now, the final feature we're going to cover: how to run an action when a module is unloaded.

9.6.6 *Running an action when a module is removed*

Sometimes you need to clean up when a module is unloaded. If the module establishes a persistent connection to a server, when the module is unloaded you'll want that connection to be closed. An example of this pattern occurs when using *implicit remoting*. The PSModuleInfo object provides a way to do this through its OnRemove property.

To set up an action to execute when a module is unloaded, assign a scriptblock defining the action to the OnRemove property on the module's PSModuleInfo object. Here's an example that shows how this is done (save as onremove.psm1):

```
PS> @'
$mInfo = $MyInvocation.MyCommand.ScriptBlock.Module
$mInfo.OnRemove = {
      Write-Host "I was removed on $(Get-Date)"
}
'@ > onremove.psm1
```

You get the PSModuleInfo object in the first line, and then you assign a scriptblock that displays a message to the OnRemove property. (Note that you have to call Write-Host if you want to see the message because the output of the scriptblock is ignored.) Let's try it out. Import the module:

```
PS> Import-Module .\onremove.psm1
```

then remove it:

```
PS> Remove-Module onremove
I was removed on 04/23/2017 20:09:09
```

And the message from the scriptblock is printed, confirming that the `OnRemove` action was executed.

Once you have your module working the way you want, you need to be able to make it available to other people. You can provide a zip file containing the module files, but PowerShell v5 supplies a better option: publishing to a PowerShell gallery.

9.7   *Publishing a module to a PowerShell Gallery*

A PowerShell gallery (also known as a *repository*) is a place from which you can download modules. We showed you how to install modules from the PowerShell gallery in chapter 8. To recap, you can find available repositories:

```
PS> Get-PSRepository

Name        InstallationPolicy SourceLocation
----        ------------------ --------------
PSGallery   Untrusted          https://www.powershellgallery.com/api/v2/
```

You can find modules within the gallery:

```
PS>  Find-Module -Name A*tools -Repository PSGallery

Version    Name              Repository Description
-------    ----              ---------- -----------
1.0.1.16   ActiveDirectoryTools PSGallery  Custom tools...
1.30.1.28  ACLReportTools    PSGallery  Provides Cmd...
1.0        AzureStorageTools PSGallery  Azure storag...
2016.5.7.3 ARTools           PSGallery  PowerShell m...
```

Having found the module, you can install it:

```
PS> Install-Module -Name ARTools -Repository PSGallery
```

Alternatively, you can save the module for further inspection and testing:

```
PS> Save-Module -Name ARTools -Repository PSGallery -Path C:\testscripts
```

But this raises a question. How do modules get into the repository?

You can publish modules to a repository using `Publish-Module`. The module has to have a manifest, and the PSData items should be completed. We'll discuss how to generate the correct items in the module manifest and the requirements your module has to meet to enable publishing to the PowerShell gallery.

Modules change as features are added or modified. Those changes need to be published to the gallery.

A private PowerShell gallery

The public PowerShell gallery is just that: public. Many organizations don't allow the installation of software from public sites or want their users to be able to install only approved modules.

The answer is to create a private PowerShell gallery internal to your organization. You can control who can publish modules, and if modules from the public gallery are required you can download them, test them, and then publish to your internal gallery for your users to access.

The PowerShell team has published the code to create and configure a private Power-Shell gallery at https://github.com/powershell/psprivategallery. We'll be using this for the publishing examples so that we don't add our examples to the public gallery.

When you create a private gallery, you have to register it on each machine from which you want to access the gallery:

```
PS> Register-PSRepository -Name PSPrivateGallery `
-SourceLocation 'http://w16gly:8080/api/v2/' `
-InstallationPolicy Trusted
```

The source location will change depending on the machine on which you installed the private gallery

Let's work through publishing a module. The first thing we need is a module.

9.7.1   *A module to publish*

In chapter 8 we created a module, shown in listing 8.2. We'll reuse that module as our example.

Listing 9.2   Counter module

```
$script:count = 0
$script:increment = 1

function Get-Count
{
    return $script:count += $increment
}

function Reset-Count
{
    $script:count=0
    setIncrement 1
}

function setIncrement ($x)
{
    $script:increment = $x
}

Export-ModuleMember *-Count
```

The module is a simple incrementing counter, as discussed in chapter 8. It exports two functions: `Get-Count` and `Reset-Count`.

You need to meet a number of requirements to be able to publish to the PowerShell gallery:

- You need to be a registered user to publish modules to the gallery. You don't need to be registered to download modules.
- You must have a module manifest preferably created using `New-ModuleManifest` and tested with `Test-ModuleManifest`.
- The module manifest should contain a `LicenseURI`, `HelpInfoURI`, and `ProjectURI`. These fields are found in the `PSData` section of the module manifest.
- The module should be scanned with an antivirus scanner before being published.
- `PSScriptAnalyzer` (available from the PowerShell gallery) should be used to scan the module. All errors must be corrected because the gallery also uses `PSScriptAnalyzer` and a module with errors will be unlisted.
- You should follow the appropriate guidelines, published on MSDN, for modules and DSC resources.

NOTE It's becoming accepted best practice in the PowerShell community that Pester-based tests should be included with modules published to the public PowerShell gallery.

Once your module is complete, you should generate a module manifest using `New -ModuleManifest`.

9.7.2 *PSData Packaging elements*

Within the `PrivateData` element you have the option to complete the PSData hashtable. This hashtable provides data for module discovery in online repositories such as the PowerShell Gallery. An example, from the Pester module (installed in Windows 10 or available from the PowerShell Gallery), is here.

Listing 9.3 PSData entries from the Pester module

```
PSData = @{
  # The primary categorization of this module
    (from the TechNet Gallery tech tree).
     Category = "Scripting Techniques"

  # Keyword tags to help users find this module
    via navigations and search.
  Tags = @('powershell','unit testing','bdd','tdd','mocking')

  # The web address of an icon which can be used
    in galleries to represent this module
  IconUri = "http://pesterbdd.com/images/Pester.png"

  # The web address of this module's project or
    support homepage.
  ProjectUri = "https://github.com/Pester/Pester"
```

```
# The web address of this module's license.
  Points to a page that's embeddable and linkable.
LicenseUri = "http://www.apache.org/licenses/LICENSE-2.0.html"

# Release notes for this particular version of the module
# ReleaseNotes = False

# If true, the LicenseUrl points to an end-user license
  (not just a source license) which requires the user
  agreement before use.
# RequireLicenseAcceptance = ""

  # Indicates this is a pre-release/testing version of the module.
IsPrerelease = 'False'
}
```

If you compare this to listing 9.1 you'll see that a number of elements have been added, including `ReleaseNotes` and `RequireLicenseAcceptance`. You can add whatever metadata you need into this section of the manifest.

You can generate the standard PSData entries using `New-ModuleManifest`:

```
PS> $path = "$HOME\Documents\WindowsPowerShell\Modules"
PS> $module = "Counter\1.0.0"
PS> New-ModuleManifest -Path "$path\$module\Counter.psd1" `
-RootModule Counter.psm1 -CompanyName 'PowerShell in Action' `
-Description 'Test module' `
-Author 'Bruce and Richard' -Guid ([System.Guid]::NewGuid()) `
-Copyright 'Bruce and Richard 2017' -ModuleVersion 1.0.0 `
-Tags 'PowerShell', 'Example', 'Counters' `
-ProjectUri 'http://BRproject.com' `
-LicenseUri 'http://BRproject.com/License.html' `
-IconUri 'http://BRproject.com/Counter.png' `
-ReleaseNotes 'http://BRproject.com/ReleaseNotes.html'
```

Running this code produces the following PSData block (comments removed for brevity):

```
    PSData = @{
        Tags = 'PowerShell', 'Example', 'Counters'
        LicenseUri = 'http://brproject.com/License.html'
        ProjectUri = 'http://brproject.com/'
        IconUri = 'http://brproject.com/Counter.png'
        ReleaseNotes = 'http://BRproject.com/ReleaseNotes.html'
    }
```

NOTE   The examples given are fictitious, so please don't try accessing the URIs.

Let's examine the PSData elements in more detail.

TAGS

Tags are used to aid the user when searching for modules in the gallery. For instance, you may be looking for modules that provide functionality for managing Active Directory, as shown in figure 9.4.

```
Administrator 64 bit C:\MyData\SkyDrive\Data\scripts                         —    □    ×
PS>  Find-Module -Tag 'Active Directory' | select Version, Name, Tags

Version Name                   Tags
------- ----                   ----
1.2.2   StaleHosts             {PSModule, active, directory, activedirectory...}
1.0     PSLDAPQueryLogging {LDAP, ActiveDirectory, Active, Directory...}


PS>  Find-Module -Tag 'ActiveDirectory' | select Version, Name, Tags

Version    Name             Tags
-------    ----             ----
2.15       DSInternals      {ActiveDirectory, Security, PSModule}
1.0.1.16   ActiveDirectoryTools  {PSModule, AD, ActiveDirectory}
1.1.147.0  AzureADPreview   {Azure, ActiveDirectory, AzureAD, AD...}
1.0.0.7    ActiveDirectoryStig   {PSModule, ActiveDirectory, AD, DISA...}
1.2.2      StaleHosts       {PSModule, active, directory, activedirectory...}
1.0        ADMirror         {PSModule, ActiveDirectory, GroupPolicy, Testing...}
0.0.0.17   ESAE             {PSModule, RedForest, ESAE, ActiveDirectory...}
1.1        CertificatePS    {Certificate, Domain, Tools, ActiveDirectory...}
1.0        PSLDAPQueryLogging    {LDAP, ActiveDirectory, Active, Directory...}
1.0.6.0    gpowmi           {GroupPolicy, ActiveDirectory, WMI, WMIFilter...}
0.0.0.7    ADConfiguration  {DSC, ActiveDirectory, class, WMF5...}
1.0.0      Spizzi.ActiveDirectory {PSModule, ActiveDirectory}


PS>
```

Figure 9.4 Searching for modules in the PowerShell gallery using tags

Figure 9.4 shows that the results will vary depending on the exact value input to the `Tag` parameter. The syntax for `Find-Module` shows that the `Tag` parameter accepts an array of strings so you can search on multiple tags simultaneously:

```
PS> Find-Module -Tag 'Active Directory', 'ActiveDirectory', 'Active',
    'Directory', 'AD'
```

As a module writer, you need to use sufficient tags to ensure that your module will be found. `Find-Module` treats tags in a *case-insensitive* manner, so you don't need to worry about case issues.

Gallery users should ensure they use a variety of tags so they find the correct modules. There are hundreds of modules in the PowerShell gallery at the time of writing; this number will only increase, so using tags will make your gallery use more efficient.

LICENSEURI

Publishing your module to the PowerShell gallery implies that you want other people to access and use the module. Some of the modules in the gallery are commercial—for instance, the ISEsteroids module—in which case you need to pay to obtain the license. The vast majority are free to use.

A license isn't necessary, but if you want to adopt the standards of the open source community, then using one of the open source licenses is a good idea. The Pester module in listing 9.3 uses the Apache open source license, for example. Information on other licensing options can be discovered at https://opensource.org/licenses. Most PowerShell modules in the gallery don't have a license defined.

PROJECTURI

The PowerShell gallery is the place to publish your finished code. While your module is in development, it's not suitable for publishing. The recommendation is that if you want other people to be able to work on the module, you create a project on the GitHub site: https://github.com. You'll find many PowerShell projects on GitHub, including some from the PowerShell team.

ICONURI

The IconURI entry enables you to define an icon for your module. Many, if not most, module authors don't define an icon.

RELEASENOTES

Release notes are the information you supply to your users describing the features, including those that are new to that version of your module. You could include an About file to perform the same task or store the information online in the project.

If your module changes frequently, you should include release notes to keep the users up to date with changes. Now that you have a module and a module manifest, it's time to publish the module.

9.7.3   *Publishing a module*

We stated earlier in this section that we'd be using a private gallery to demonstrate publishing modules. When you create a private gallery, you can state which modules, if any, you want downloaded from the public gallery. We populated our gallery with three modules:

```
PS> Find-Module -Repository PSPrivateGallery
Version     Name            Type    Repository        Description
-------     ----            ----    ----------        -----------
2016.5.7.3  ARTools         Module  PSPrivateGallery  PowerShell...
2.6         Authenticode    Module  PSPrivateGallery  Function w...
1.6.0       PSScriptAnalyzer Module PSPrivateGallery  PSScriptAn...
```

Publishing the module requires you to supply the module name, the repository to which you'll publish it, and the NuGet API key assigned to your user account:

```
PS> Publish-Module -Name Counter -Repository PSPrivateGallery `
-NuGetApiKey 'c34d0782-b5ad-4b45-9165-a168b7f0436f'

WARNING: This module 'C:\Users\Richard\AppData\Local\Temp\791442835\
    Counter\Counter.psd1' has exported functions. As a best practice, include
    exported functions in the module manifest file(.psd1). You can run
    Update-ModuleManifest -FunctionsToExport to update the manifest with
    ExportedFunctions field.
```

NOTE   When you create an account on the public PowerShell gallery, a NuGet API key is assigned and is stored in your profile. This key is unique to you and

shouldn't be shared. The private gallery lists the key in the ./ Configuration\
PSPrivateGalleryPublishEnvironment.psd1 file.

Your private gallery now contains four modules:

```
PS> Find-Module -Repository PSPrivateGallery

Version     Name            Type    Repository       Description
-------     ----            ----    ----------       -----------
2016.5.7.3  ARTools         Module  PSPrivateGallery PowerShell...
2.6         Authenticode    Module  PSPrivateGallery Function w...
1.6.0       PSScriptAnalyzer Module PSPrivateGallery PSScriptAn...
1.0.0       Counter         Module  PSPrivateGallery Test module
```

The module can now be downloaded to other machines in your environment. You'll
have noticed the warning message about best practice being to use the module manifest file to control the functions that are exported rather than the module file. Let's
update the module to correct that issue.

9.7.4 *Publishing module updates*

When you update the module to move the control of the exported functions into the
module manifest, you should also modify the module version. This needs to be performed manually if you've created a set of folders under the module folder for each
version. The module file (.psm1) in listing 9.2 can be modified by removing the last line.

The module manifest file can be modified using `Update-Module`:

```
PS> $path = "$HOME\Documents\WindowsPowerShell\Modules"
PS> $module = "Counter\1.0.1"
PS> Update-ModuleManifest -Path "$path\$module\Counter.psd1" `
-FunctionsToExport 'Get-Count', 'Reset-Count'
```

The module can now be republished:

```
PS> Publish-Module -Name Counter -Repository PSprivateGallery `
-RequiredVersion 1.0.1 `
-NuGetApiKey 'c34d0782-b5ad-4b45-9165-a168b7f0436f'
```

This time you also give the version you require to be published. The gallery contains
both versions of the module:

```
PS> Find-Module -Repository PSPrivateGallery -Name Counter -AllVersions

Version Name    Type   Repository       Description
------- ----    ----   ----------       -----------
1.0.1   Counter Module PSPrivateGallery Test module
1.0.0   Counter Module PSPrivateGallery Test module
```

It may take a few minutes for the new version of the module to become the default
version shown by `Find-Module`. You can always use the `-RequiredVersion` parameter on
`Install-Module` to control the version you install.

And with that, we're finished with modules ... well, mostly finished. We'll cover a few even more advanced techniques in chapter 10.

9.8 Summary

- Production modules are stored in a directory containing the module manifest and content.
- The metadata or information about a module is contained in a .psd1 file, usually with the same name as the module directory.
- The easiest way to create a module manifest is to use the `New-ModuleManifest` cmdlet.
- `Test-ModuleManifest` is provided to test an existing module for issues.
- A manifest lets you define three types of information for your module: production, construction, and content.
- Production metadata defines things like version number and dependencies.
- Construction elements control how a module is constructed, including specifying any nested modules.
- Content manifest elements deal with other types of content in the module.
- Modules in memory are represented by a `PSModuleInfo` object.
- The `PSModuleInfo` object for a module can be retrieved using `Get-Module` or by using the `Module` property on a scriptblock for that function.
- Using the `PSModuleInfo` object for a module, you can inject code into the module, where it will be executed in the module context. This allows you to manipulate the state of a module without having to reload it. This feature is primarily intended for diagnostic and debugging purposes.
- From within a script module, you can use the `PSModuleInfo` object to directly set some metadata elements like the module description.
- `PSModuleInfo` object has an `AccessMode` field that controls the ability to update or remove a module from the session. This field is set to `ReadWrite` by default but can be set to `Static`, requiring the use of the `-Force` parameter (to update it) or `Constant` (which means it can't be removed from the session). A `Constant` module remains in the session until the session ends.
- To set up an action to be taken when a module is removed, you can assign a scriptblock to the `OnRemove` property on the `PSModuleInfo` object for that module.
- The `PSData` section in the module manifest is used for module discovery in online PowerShell repositories.
- `Publish-Module` is used to publish a module to a PowerShell repository. `Publish-Script` performs the same action for scripts.

In the next chapter, we'll look at some more advanced programming topics that build on what you've learned. These advanced topics will not only introduce some powerful new ways of using PowerShell, they'll also engender a deep understanding of how PowerShell works.

Metaprogramming with scriptblocks and dynamic code

This chapter covers
- Scriptblocks
- Creating and managing objects
- Creating code dynamically
- Steppable pipelines

> *Philosophy have I digested, The whole of Law and Medicine, From each its secrets I have wrested, Theology, alas, thrown in. Poor fool, with all this sweated lore, I stand no wiser than I was before.*
>
> —*Johann Wolfgang Goethe*, Faust

> *Greek letters are cool ...*
>
> —*Not actually a quote from* Beavis and Butthead

Chapters 6 through 9 covered the basic elements of programming in PowerShell and introduced modules as a way of aggregating your code into reusable pieces. In this chapter, we'll take things to the next level and talk about *metaprogramming*, the term used to describe the activity of writing programs that create or manipulate other programs. If you're not already familiar with this concept, you may be asking why you should care. In most environments, if the designer makes a mistake, the user is stuck with the result. This isn't true in PowerShell. Metaprogramming lets you poke into the heart of the system and make things work the way you need them to.

Here's an analogy that should give you the full picture: Imagine buying a computer that was welded shut. You can run all the existing programs and even install new programs. But a case that's welded shut doesn't allow for hardware upgrades.

Traditional programming languages are much like that welded computer. You can extend what they do by adding libraries, but you can't extend the core capabilities of the language. You can't, for example, add a new type of looping statement. In a language that supports metaprogramming, you can undertake such activities as adding new control structures. This is how the `Where-Object` and `ForEach-Object` cmdlets are implemented. They use the metaprogramming features in PowerShell to add what appear to be new language elements. You can even create your own variations of these commands.

We'll begin our investigation with a detailed discussion of PowerShell scriptblocks, which are at the center of most of the metaprogramming techniques. This discussion takes up the first part of this chapter and lays the groundwork for the rest of what we'll discuss. With that material as context, we'll look at how and where scriptblocks are used in PowerShell. We'll look at the role scriptblocks play in the creation of custom objects and types and how they can be used to extend the PowerShell language. We'll cover techniques like proxy functions, dynamic modules, and custom objects—all of which are examples of applied metaprogramming. Then we'll move on, and you'll see how you can use similar techniques with static languages like C# from within your scripts. But first you need to understand scriptblocks themselves.

10.1   *Scriptblock basics*

In PowerShell, the key to metaprogramming is the scriptblock. This is a block of script code that exists as an object reference but doesn't require a name. The `Where-Object` and `ForEach-Object` cmdlets rely on scriptblocks for their implementation. In the example

```
PS> 1..10 | foreach-object { $_ * 2 }
```

the expression in braces—`{ $_ * 2 }`—is a scriptblock. It's a piece of code that's passed to the `ForEach-Object` cmdlet and is called by the cmdlet as needed. A number of cmdlets take scriptblocks as parameters, including `Invoke-Command` and `Start-Job`, which you'll meet in chapters 11 and 13 respectively.

That's all a scriptblock is—a piece of script in braces—but it's the key to all the advanced programming features in PowerShell.

> **NOTE** What we call scriptblocks in PowerShell are called *anonymous functions* or sometimes lambda expressions in other languages. The term *lambda* comes from the lambda calculus developed by Alonzo Church and Stephen Cole

Kleene in the 1930s. A number of languages, including Python and dialects of LISP, still use lambda as a language keyword. In designing the PowerShell language, the PowerShell team felt that calling a spade a spade (and a scriptblock a scriptblock) was more straightforward (the coolness of using Greek letters aside).

We've said that scriptblocks are anonymous functions, and functions are one of the types of commands in PowerShell. But wait! You invoke a command by specifying its name. If scriptblocks are anonymous, they have no names—so how can you invoke them? This necessitates one more diversion before we dig into scriptblocks. Let's talk about how commands can be executed.

10.1.1 *Invoking commands*

The way to execute a command is to type its name followed by a set of arguments, but sometimes you can't type the command name as is. For example, you might have a command with a space in the name. You can't type the command because the space would cause part of the command name to be treated as an argument. And you can't put it in quotes, because this turns it into a string value. You have to use the call operator, &. If, for instance, you have a command called my command, you'd invoke this command by typing:

```
& 'my command'
```

The interpreter sees the call operator and uses the value of the next argument to look up the command to run. This process of looking up the command is called *command discovery*. The result of this command discovery operation is an object of type System .Management.Automation.CommandInfo, which tells the interpreter what command to execute. There are different subtypes of CommandInfo for each of the types of Power-Shell commands.

10.1.2 *Getting CommandInfo objects*

You've used the Get-Command cmdlet before as a way to attain information about a command. This is useful as a kind of lightweight help, but in addition to displaying information, the object returned by Get-Command can be used with the call operator to invoke that command. This is significant. This extra degree of flexibility, invoking a command indirectly, is the first step on the road to metaprogramming.

Let's try this out. First, get the CommandInfo object for the Get-Date command:

```
PS> $d = Get-Command Get-Date
PS> $d.CommandType
Cmdlet

PS> $d.Name
Get-Date
```

As you can see from this example, the name `Get-Date` resolves to a cmdlet with the name `Get-Date`. Now run this command using the `CommandInfo` object with the call operator:

```
PS> & $d

24 April 2017 15:35:22
```

It's as simple as that. Why should you care about this? Because it's a way of getting a link to a specific command in the environment. Say you defined a function `Get-Date`:

```
PS> function Get-Date {'Hi there'}
PS> Get-Date
Hi there
```

Your new `Get-Date` command outputs a string. Because PowerShell looks for functions before it looks for cmdlets, this new function definition hides the `Get-Date` cmdlet. Even using `&` with the string "Get-Date" still runs the function:

```
PS> & 'Get-Date'
Hi there
```

Because you created a second definition for `Get-Date` (the function), now if you use `Get-Command` you'll see only the function. How do you select the cmdlet `Get-Date`?

```
PS> Get-Command Get-Date

CommandType Name      Version Source
----------- ----      ------- ------
Function    Get-Date
```

> **NOTE** If you use `Get-Command Get-Date -CommandType All`, you'll see the function and the cmdlet. This matches the behavior of PowerShell v2, where both commands would be shown.

One way is to find the `CommandInfo` object based on the type of the command:

```
PS> Get-Command -CommandType cmdlet Get-Date

CommandType Name      Version Source
----------- ----      ------- ------
Cmdlet      Get-Date 3.1.0.0 Microsoft.PowerShell.Utility
```

Now put the result of this command into a variable

```
PS> $ci = Get-command -CommandType cmdlet Get-Date
```

and then run it using the call operator:

```
PS> & $ci

24 April 2017 15:37:12
```

The Get-Date cmdlet runs as expected. Another way to select which command to run, because Get-Command returns a collection of objects, is to index into the collection to get the right object:

```
PS> &(Get-Command Get-Date -CommandType All)[1]

24 April 2017 15:37:54
```

Here you use the result of the index operation directly with the call operator to run the desired command. The index is 1 because we're accessing the second element. The Get-Date function is the first element in the collection, and the Get-Date cmdlet is the second element.

This is all interesting, but what does it have to do with scriptblocks? We've demonstrated that you can invoke a command through an object reference instead of by name. This was the problem we set out to work around. Scriptblocks are functions that don't have names, so as you might expect, the way to call a scriptblock is to use the call operator. Here's what that looks like:

```
PS> & {param($x,$y) $x+$y} 2 5
7
```

In this example, the scriptblock is

```
{param($x,$y) $x+$y}
```

This example used the call operator to invoke it with two arguments, 2 and 5, so the call returns 7. This is how you can execute a function if it doesn't have a name. As long as you have access to the scriptblock, you can call it.

10.1.3 *The scriptblock literal*

What you've been writing to create scriptblocks is called a *scriptblock literal*—a chunk of legitimate PowerShell script surrounded by braces. The syntax for this literal is shown in figure 10.1.

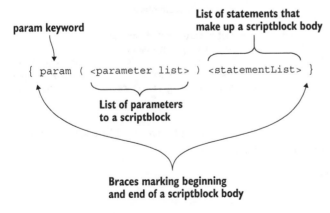

Figure 10.1 Defining a simple scriptblock. Note that the param statement is optional, so a minimal scriptblock has only the braces.

The definition of a scriptblock looks more or less like the definition of a function, except the `function` keyword and function name are missing. If the `param` statement isn't present, the scriptblock will get its arguments through `$args`, exactly as a function would.

Param vs. lambda

The `param` statement in PowerShell corresponds to the lambda keyword in other languages. For example, the PowerShell expression

```
& {param($x,$y) $x+$y} 2 5
```

is equivalent to the LISP expression

```
(lambda (x y) (+ x y)) 2 5
```

or the Python expression

```
(lambda x,y: x+y)(2,5)
```

Also note that, unlike Python lambdas, PowerShell scriptblocks can contain any collection of legal PowerShell statements.

Scriptblocks, like regular functions or scripts, can also behave like cmdlets—they can have one or all of the `begin`, `process`, or `end` clauses that you can have in a function or script. Figure 10.2 shows the most general form of the scriptblock syntax, with all three clauses.

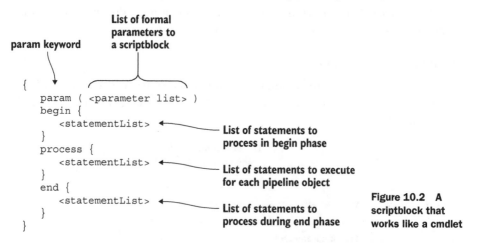

Figure 10.2   A scriptblock that works like a cmdlet

As was the case with a regular function, you don't have to define all the clauses. Here's an example that uses only the `process` clause:

```
PS> 1..5 |&{process{$_ * 2}}
2
4
```

```
6
8
10
```

A scriptblock written this way works like the filters you saw in chapter 6. It also works like the ForEach-Object cmdlet:

```
PS> 1..5 |ForEach-Object {$_ * 2}
```

The ForEach-Object cmdlet is effectively a shortcut for the more complex scriptblock construction.

As we've been going along, we keep talking about how scriptblocks are anonymous functions. This is a good time to see how scriptblocks and named functions are related.

10.1.4 *Defining functions at runtime*

In earlier sections, we said that scriptblocks are functions without names. The opposite is also true—functions are scriptblocks *with* names. What then, exactly, is the relationship between the two? In chapter 6, you learned how to manage the functions in your PowerShell session using the function: drive. To get a list of functions, you could use Get-ChildItem on that drive. You could also delete or rename functions. But we didn't cover the whole story. In fact, the function: drive is, in effect, a set of variables containing scriptblocks. Let's explore this further. First, let's define our favorite function, foo:

```
PS> function foo {2+2}
PS> foo
4
```

You can use the Get-ChildItem cmdlet to get the command information from the function provider:

```
PS> Get-ChildItem function:foo

CommandType Name Version Source
----------- ---- ------- ------
Function    foo
```

Now use Get-Member to get more information about the object that was returned:

```
PS> Get-ChildItem function:foo | Get-Member sc*

   TypeName: System.Management.Automation.FunctionInfo

Name        MemberType Definition
----        ---------- ----------
ScriptBlock Property   scriptblock ScriptBlock {get;}
```

The object that comes back to you is a FunctionInfo object. This is the subclass of CommandInfo that's used to represent a function. As you see, one of the properties on the object is the scriptblock that makes up the body of the function. Retrieve that member:

```
PS> (Get-ChildItem function:foo).ScriptBlock
2+2
```

The scriptblock, when displayed as a string, shows the source code for the scriptblock. Another, simpler way to get back the scriptblock that defines a function is to use the variable syntax:

```
PS> $function:foo.GetType().Fullname
System.Management.Automation.ScriptBlock
```

Now here's the interesting part. Change the definition of this function by assigning a new scriptblock to the function:

```
PS> $function:foo = {'Bye!'}
```

When you run the function again

```
PS> foo
Bye!
```

you see that it's changed. The `function` keyword is, in effect, shorthand for assigning a scriptblock to a name in the function provider.

   Now that you know how to manipulate scriptblocks and functions, let's take this one step further. Objects encapsulate data and code—we spent a lot of time on data in the earlier chapters, and now we have a way of manipulating code too. This means you're ready to take the next step and see how you can use data and scriptblocks to build your own objects.

10.2   *Building and manipulating objects*

Let's kick our scripting up a notch and look at ways to build custom objects. Up to this point in the chapter we've been talking about scriptblocks as standalone functions. Now it's time to talk about how to use scriptblocks to build objects.

> **NOTE**   We're not talking about PowerShell classes here—that topic gets its own chapter (chapter 19). In this section, we're going to look at building typeless objects—objects that have no specific type or class associated with them. Both typed and untyped objects are useful when organizing the data in a PowerShell program. Also, looking at untyped objects will give you an inside look at how objects work in general.

At their core, objects are a binding of data and behaviors. These behaviors are implemented by blocks of script. You needed to know how to build the blocks of code, scriptblocks, before we could talk about building objects. With a good understanding of scriptblocks, we can now discuss manipulating and building objects in PowerShell.

In chapter 2, we talked extensively about types. Now we're concerned with objects—*instances* of types. A type is the pattern or template that describes an object, and an object is an instance of that pattern. In statically typed languages such as C#, once an object is instantiated, its interfaces can't be changed. With dynamic languages such as PowerShell (or Ruby or Python), this isn't true. Dynamic languages allow you to alter the set of members available at runtime.

> **NOTE** As of C# 4.0, the language is no longer purely statically typed. C# 4.0 introduced a new `dynamic` keyword, allowing you to write programs that have dynamic types. In general, though, this feature doesn't get much use because most of the other features in C# (for example, LINQ) work only with typed objects. Where the `dynamic` keyword is useful is in allowing C# to interoperate more effectively with dynamic languages like PowerShell.

In the rest of this section, we'll explore manipulating objects and types in PowerShell. We'll start with a discussion of how to examine existing members, followed by a look at the types of members available on an object. Then we'll cover all the ways to add members to an object, and finally we'll look at the plumbing of the PowerShell type system to give you a sense of the flexibility of the overall system and how it facilitates your goal of writing programs to manipulate programs.

10.2.1 Looking at members

An object's interface is defined by the set of public members it exposes. Public members are the public fields, properties, and methods of the class. As always, the easiest way to look at those members is with the `Get-Member` cmdlet. For example, the members defined on an integer can be viewed like this:

```
PS> 12 | Get-Member
```

Note that this doesn't show you all the members on an `[int]`. It shows you only the instance members. You can also use `Get-Member` to look at the static members:

```
PS> 12 | Get-Member -Static

   TypeName: System.Int32

Name            MemberType Definition
----            ---------- ----------
Equals          Method     static System.Boolean Equals(Objec...
Parse           Method     static System.Int32 Parse(String s...
ReferenceEquals Method     static System.Boolean ReferenceEqu...
TryParse        Method     static System.Boolean TryParse(Str...
MaxValue        Property   static System.Int32 MaxValue {get;}
MinValue        Property   static System.Int32 MinValue {get;}
```

You'll use this mechanism to look at the members you'll be adding to objects in the next couple of sections.

10.2.2 *Defining synthetic members*

One of the most powerful features in the PowerShell environment is the ability to extend existing object types and instances. This allows PowerShell to perform adaptation across a variety of types of data. By *adaptation*, we mean overlaying a common set of interfaces onto existing data sources. This may be as simple as unifying the name of the property that counts a collection to be the string "count" across all countable objects, or as complex as taking a string containing some XML data and being able to treat that string as an object with a set of properties and attributes.

This *isn't* the same as subclassing or creating derived types as you would in PowerShell classes. With classes, if you want to extend a new type, you can do so only by creating an entirely new type. In dynamic languages such as PowerShell, you can add members to existing types and objects. This sounds odd from the point of view of conventional object-oriented programming, because types and member definitions are so tightly tied together. In PowerShell, it's possible to have objects that don't have any type at all.

> **NOTE** If you're a JavaScript user, this won't be surprising. The object-oriented mechanisms in JavaScript use a mechanism called a *prototype*. Prototype-based systems don't have types as discrete objects. Instead, you get an object that has the set of members you want your object to have and use it as the prototype for your new object.

Because the members you'll be adding to objects aren't natively part of the object's definition, they're called *synthetic members*. Synthetic members are used extensively throughout PowerShell for adaptation and extension. Let's look at an example. First, we'll examine the synthetic properties on an object returned by `Get-ChildItem` from the file system:

```
PS> Get-ChildItem $profile | Get-Member ps*

    TypeName: System.IO.FileInfo

Name            MemberType   Definition
----            ----------   ----------
PSChildName     NoteProperty System.String PSChildName=Microsof...
PSDrive         NoteProperty System.Management.Automation.PSDri...
PSIsContainer   NoteProperty System.Boolean PSIsContainer=False
PSParentPath    NoteProperty System.String PSParentPath=Microso...
PSPath          NoteProperty System.String PSPath=Microsoft.Pow...
PSProvider      NoteProperty System.Management.Automation.Provi...
```

Now let's get the same information from the Registry:

```
PS> Get-ChildItem hklm:\software | Get-Member ps*

    TypeName: Microsoft.Win32.RegistryKey

Name            MemberType   Definition
----            ----------   ----------
PSChildName     NoteProperty System.String PSChildName=Adobe
```

```
PSDrive        NoteProperty System.Management.Automation.PSDri...
PSIsContainer  NoteProperty System.Boolean PSIsContainer=True
PSParentPath   NoteProperty System.String PSParentPath=Microso...
PSPath         NoteProperty System.String PSPath=Microsoft.Pow...
PSProvider     NoteProperty System.Management.Automation.Provi...
```

You can see the same set of `PS*` properties with the PowerShell (PS) prefix on the object, even though they're completely different types. Take a look at these properties. They allow you to work with these two different objects in the same way. This means you can always tell whether an object might have children by looking at the `PSIs-Container` property, regardless of the type of the underlying object. And you can always get the path to the object through the `PSPath` property. We call this type of adaptation *object normalization.* By adding this set of synthetic properties to all objects returned from the provider infrastructure, you make it possible to write scripts that are independent of the type of object that the provider surfaces. This makes the scripts both simpler and more reusable. In the next section, we'll start looking at ways of creating synthetic members.

10.2.3 *Using Add-Member to extend objects*

The `Add-Member` cmdlet is the easiest way to add a new member to an object instance, either a static .NET object type or a custom synthetic object. It can be used to add any type of member supported by the PowerShell type system.

> **NOTE** The `-Force` parameter of `Add-Member` can be used to add a new member even if it has the same name as an existing custom member. You can't use `-Force` to replace a standard member of a type.

The list of possible member types that can be added with `Add-Member` is shown in table 10.1. You'll work through examples showing how to use these members. You'll use an instance of the string "Hi there" to do this. For convenience, store it in a variable `$s`:

```
PS> $s = 'Hi there'
```

Now let's go over how you add these member types to an object instance.

Table 10.1 Member types that can be added with `Add-Member`

Member type	Description
AliasProperty	An alias property provides an alternate name for an existing property. If there's an existing `Length` property, then you might alias this to `Count`.
CodeProperty	A property that maps to a static method on a .NET class.
Property	A native property on the object—a property that exists on the underlying object that's surfaced directly to the user. For example, there might be a native property `Length` that you choose to also make available through an extended alias member.

Table 10.1   Member types that can be added with `Add-Member` ***(continued)***

Member type	Description
NoteProperty	A data-only member on the object (equivalent to a .NET field).
ScriptProperty	A property whose value is determined by a piece of PowerShell script.
Properties	The collection of properties exposed by this object.
PropertySet	A named group of properties.
Method	A native method on the underlying object. For example, the `SubString()` method on the class `System.String` shows up as a method.
CodeMethod	A method that is mapped to a static method on a .NET class.
ScriptMethod	A method implemented in a PowerShell script.
ParameterizedProperty	A property that takes both arguments and a value to assign. This is typically used for things like indexers and might look like `$collection.item(2,3) = "hello"`. This sets the element at 2,3 in the collection to the value `"hello"`.
PSVariableProperty	A property that's backed by a variable. This type of member is available only in PowerShell v2 and later. It has an advantage over note properties because it can be type constrained.

ADDING ALIASPROPERTY MEMBERS

The first type of synthetic member you'll add is called an alias property. This property, whose name is (surprise) `AliasProperty`, allows you to provide a new name for an existing property. Let's work with the `Length` property on a string:

```
PS> $s.Length
8
```

As you can see, this string has a length of 8. Let's say that you want to add an alias size for `Length` because you'll be working with a set of objects that all have a size property:

```
PS> $s = Add-Member -InputObject $s -MemberType AliasProperty `
-Name size -Value length -PassThru
```

When you first add a synthetic member to an object, you're creating a new object (but not a new type). This new object wraps the original object in an instance of `System.Management.Automation.PSObject`. Just as `System.Object` is the root of the type system in .NET, `PSObject` is the root of the synthetic type system in PowerShell. For this reason, you assign the result of the `Add-Member` call back to the original variable. To do that, you have to add the `-PassThru` parameter to the command because, by default, the `Add-Member` cmdlet doesn't emit anything.

Let's look at the new member you've added using `Get-Member`:

```
PS> $s | Get-Member size

   TypeName: System.String

Name MemberType     Definition
---- ----------     ----------
size AliasProperty  size = length
```

You can see that the `size` member is there and is an alias property that maps `size` to `Length`. Also, you need to note that the object's type is still `System.String`. The fact that it's wrapped in a `PSObject` is pretty much invisible from the script user's view, though you can test for it, as shown in the next example. Using the `-is` operator, you can test to see whether the object you're dealing with is wrapped in a `PSObject`:

```
PS> $s -is [PSObject]
True

PS> $s -is [string]
True
```

The result of the first command in the example shows that `$s` does contain a `PSObject`, and the second line shows that the object in `$s` is still considered a string, even though it's also a `PSObject`.

The question now is, after all that explanation, did you create this aliased member? The answer is yes:

```
PS> $s.size
8

PS> $s.Length
8
```

Both the `size` and `length` members return the value 8.

ADDING NOTEPROPERTY MEMBERS

Now let's add a *note property*, a way of attaching a new piece of data (a note) to an existing object, rather like putting a sticky note on your monitor. Again, you'll use the same string in `$s`. Let's add a note property called `Description`::

```
PS> $s = Add-Member -InputObject $s -MemberType NoteProperty `
-Name Description -Value 'A string' -Passthru

PS> $s.Description
A string
```

You've added a `Description` property to the object with the value `A string`. And to prove that this property isn't present on all strings, try

```
PS> 'Hi there'.Description
```

and you'll see that the property returns nothing.

The note property is a settable property, so you can change it with an assignment like any other settable property:

```
PS> $s.Description = 'A greeting'
PS> $s.Description
A greeting
```

In this example, you change the value in the note property to A greeting. Note properties allow you to attach arbitrary data to an object. They aren't type constrained, so they can hold any type.

> **NOTE** Sooner or later, if you're working through all the examples in this chapter, something will fail because one example collides with another. If that happens, start a new PowerShell session and keep going. If you're using the ISE, you can switch to a new tab by pressing Ctrl-T. This will allow you to flip back and forth between sessions to compare things.

Next, set the Description property to a [datetime] object:

```
PS> $s.Description = Get-Date
PS> $s.Description

24 April 2017 16:23:40
```

But the value stored in the object is still a [datetime] object, not a string. As such, you can get the DayOfWeek property out of the description property:

```
PS> $s.Description.DayOfWeek
Monday

PS> $s.Description.GetType().FullName
System.DateTime
```

ADDING SCRIPTMETHOD MEMBERS

Both of the synthetic members you've added so far have been pure data properties; no code was involved. Now we'll look at adding members that execute code. We'll start with ScriptMethods, because they're the easiest. You'll add a method that returns the string that it's associated with, reversed.

First, let's find an easy way to reverse a string. If you examine [string], you'll see that there is (unfortunately) no reverse method on the string class. There is, though, a static reverse method on [array] that you can use. This method takes an array and, because it's void, it must (obviously) reverse the array in place. This tells you two things: you need to turn the string into an array (of characters) and then save it in a variable so it can be reversed in place. Converting the string to an array of characters is simple—you can use a cast:

```
PS> $a = [char[]] $s
```

Casting a string into the type [char[]] (array of characters) produces a new object that's the array of individual characters in the original string. To verify this:

```
PS> $a.GetType().FullName
System.Char[]

PS> "$a"
H i   t h e r e
```

You see that the type of the new object is [char[]] and it does contain the expected characters. Now reverse it using the [array]::reverse() static method:

```
PS> [array]::reverse($a)
PS> "$a"
e r e h t   i H
```

When you look at the contents of the array, you see that the array has been reversed. But it's still an array of characters. The final step is to turn this back into a string. To do that, you'll use the unary -join operator:

```
PS> $ns = -join $a
PS> $ns
ereht iH

PS> $ns.GetType().FullName
System.String
```

At this point you've reversed the string in $ns. But the goal of this effort was to attach this as a method to the string object itself. To do so, you need to construct a scriptblock to use as the body of the ScriptMethod.

Listing 10.1   Scriptblock to perform string reversal

```
$sb = {
    $a = [char[]] $this
    [array]::reverse($a)
    -join $a
}
```

This example introduces a new "magic" variable, which is defined only for scriptblocks that are used as methods or properties: the $this variable. $this holds the reference to the object that the ScriptMethod member was called from. Now let's bind this scriptblock to the object as a ScriptMethod using Add-Member:

```
PS> Add-Member -InputObject $s -MemberType ScriptMethod `
-Name Reverse -Value $sb
```

Try it out:

```
PS> $s. Reverse()
ereht iH
```

You get the reversed string as desired.

ADDING SCRIPTPROPERTY MEMBERS

The next type of member we'll look at is the `ScriptProperty` which has up to two methods associated with it—a getter and (optionally) a setter, like a .NET property. These methods are expressed using two scriptblocks. As was the case with the `ScriptMethod`, the referenced object is available in the `$this` member. And, in the case of the setter, the value being assigned is available in `$args[0]`.

Here's an example. You're going to add a `ScriptProperty` member, desc, to `$s` that will provide an alternate way to get at the description `NoteProperty` you added earlier, with one difference: you're only going to allow values to be assigned that are already strings. An attempt to assign something that isn't a string will result in an error. The property definition is shown next.

> **Listing 10.2   Adding a `ScriptProperty`**

```
Add-Member -InputObject $s -MemberType ScriptProperty `
-Name Desc -Value `
  {$this.Description} `
  {
    $t = $args[0]
    if ($t -isnot [string]) {
      throw 'this property only takes strings'
    }
    $this.Description = $t
  }
```

The first scriptblock

```
{$this.Description}
```

is the code that will be executed when getting the property's value. All it does is return the value stored in the description `NoteProperty`. Because the setter needs to do additional work, its scriptblock is more complex:

```
{
    $t = $args[0]
    if ($t -isnot [string])
    {
        throw 'this property only takes strings'
    }
    $this.Description = $t
}
```

First, it saves the value to be assigned into a local variable, `$t`. Next, it checks whether this variable is of the correct type. If not, it throws an exception, failing the assignment.

Let's try out this property. First, directly set the note property to the string "Old description":

```
PS> $s.Description = 'Old description'
```

Now use the `ScriptProperty` getter to retrieve this value:

```
PS> $s.Desc
Old description
```

You see that it's changed as expected. Next, use the `ScriptProperty` to change the description:

```
PS> $s.desc = 'New description'
```

Verify the change by checking both the `NoteProperty` and the `ScriptProperty`:

```
PS> $s.Description
New description

PS> $s.desc
New description
```

Yes, it's been changed. Now try assigning a `[datetime]` object to the property as you did with the description `NoteProperty` previously:

```
PS> $s.desc = Get-Date
Exception setting "Desc": "this property only takes strings"
At line:1 char:1
+ $s.desc = Get-Date
+ ~~~~~~~~~~~~~~~~~~~
    + CategoryInfo          : NotSpecified: (:) [],
  SetValueInvocationException
    + FullyQualifiedErrorId : ScriptSetValueRuntimeException
```

The assignment failed. Using `ScriptProperty` members is a way to do validation and transformation in properties on objects.

> **NOTE** The idea of adding properties to synthetic objects may seem like an academic exercise, but it turns out to be useful. In particular, it's incredibly useful when you need to adapt existing utilities so that they work effectively in the PowerShell environment.

10.2.4 *Adding note properties with New-Object*

The most common case for adding members is when creating a synthetic object with a set of note properties. A *synthetic* object, also known as a *custom* object, is one you create to solve a specific problem instead of using a standard .NET object. This is equivalent to creating records in other languages. In many cases, hashtables are sufficient for record-like scenarios. Creating objects has some advantages: The formatting system treats objects in a more sophisticated way, and assigning to a member that doesn't exist is treated as an error, whereas assigning to a member that doesn't exist in a hashtable creates a new member.

This is a common enough scenario that there's special support for this in Power-Shell with a parameter on the `New-Object` cmdlet: `-Property`. This parameter takes a hashtable and sets each member on the object being created that corresponds to the member in the hashtable. If the member doesn't exist, then a note property is added. If the object being created is a PSCustomObject, then you end up with a pure synthetic object. Here's an example of how this works:

```
PS> $obj = New-Object PSCustomObject -Property @{a=1; b=2; c=3}
```

In this example, you create a new object with three properties: a, b, and c.

> **NOTE** You can use PSObject or PSCustomObject in this case and arrive at the same result. PSObject creates an object of type PSCustomObject.

Using Get-Member you can see that they're all of type NoteProperty:

```
PS> $obj | Get-Member

    TypeName: System.Management.Automation.PSCustomObject

Name         MemberType    Definition
----         ----------    ----------
Equals       Method        bool Equals(System.Object obj)
GetHashCode  Method        int GetHashCode()
GetType      Method        type GetType()
ToString     Method        string ToString()
a            NoteProperty  System.Int32 a=1
b            NoteProperty  System.Int32 b=2
c            NoteProperty  System.Int32 c=3
```

Also notice that the type of the object returned is System.Management.Automation.PSCustomObject, which isn't a type you've seen before. This type of object is used as the base for all pure synthetic objects. Because the properties you added are note properties, you can change their values:

```
PS> $obj.a = 5
PS> $obj | Format-Table
c b a
- - -
3 2 5
```

Property order

In the previous example you used a hashtable to create the object:

```
$obj = New-Object PSCustomObject -Property @{a=1; b=2; c=3}
```

If you want to preserve the order of the properties, use an ordered hashtable:

```
PS> $props = [ordered]@{
  x = 1
  y = 2
  z = 3
  }
```

(Continued)
```
PS> $objo = New-Object PSCustomObject -Property $props
PS> $objo | Format-Table
```

This results in the following:

```
x y z
- - -
1 2 3
```

But if you try to assign to a nonexistent property,

```
PS> $obj.d = 10
Exception setting "d": "The property 'd' cannot be found
on this object. Verify that the property exists and can be set."
At line:1 char:1
+ $obj.d = 10
+ ~~~~~~~~~~~
    + CategoryInfo          : NotSpecified: (:) [],
  SetValueInvocationException
    + FullyQualifiedErrorId : ExceptionWhenSetting
```

you get an error. This can help catch runtime bugs in your code and is one reason to favor synthetic objects over hashtables.

Now, although the `New-Object` cmdlet is easy to use, PowerShell v4 and above have a much slicker way to do this—you can cast a hashtable into a `PSCustomObject`. For example:

```
PS> $co = [PSCustomObject] @{ a=1; b=2; c=3 }
```

Now we'll use `Get-Member` to look at what we've created:

```
PS> $co | Get-Member

    TypeName: System.Management.Automation.PSCustomObject
Name        MemberType   Definition
----        ----------   ----------
Equals      Method       bool Equals(System.Object obj)
GetHashCode Method       int GetHashCode()
GetType     Method       type GetType()
ToString    Method       string ToString()
a           NoteProperty int a=1
b           NoteProperty int b=2
c           NoteProperty int c=3
```

Okay, you say, this saves a bit of typing, but what does it add? Well, a type can be used in places where you can't (easily) use a command. For example, you can use

PSCustomObject as a constraint on a function parameter. A function defined this way would look like this:

```
PS> function ToPSco { param( [PSCustomObject] $x) $x }
PS> $co = ToPSco @{ a=1; b=2; c=3 }
```

Let's see what we've created:

```
PS> $co

Name                              Value
----                              -----
c                                 3
b                                 2
a                                 1
```

You can see that all the note properties have been added as expected. Casting to PSObject, like calling New-Object -Property, is a quick way of creating and attaching note properties to a pure custom object.

So far, we've either been adding members to existing objects or creating purely custom objects. There's one more scenario we need to cover: creating objects that have a subset of the properties on the original object. The easiest way to do this is to use the Select-Object cmdlet. We'll look at how this cmdlet lets you build "subset" objects next.

10.3   *Using the Select-Object cmdlet*

Now that you know how to attach members using Add-Member and create objects with New-Object, let's explore other ways to build synthetic objects. The Select-Object cmdlet, which is used to select a subset of properties on an object, creates a PSCustom -Object to hold these properties.

The Select-Object cmdlet is also a way to select elements from a stream of objects. You can select a range of objects:

```
PS> 1..10 | Select-Object -First 3
```

Here you select the first three elements.

> **NOTE**   PowerShell v3 changed the action of the -First parameter on Select-Object. It now sends a message up the pipeline telling earlier commands to stop processing data. This speeds the response of the pipeline and optimizes performance when you know how many objects you need to deal with.

But, much more interesting for this discussion, it's a way to select fields from an object:

```
PS> Get-ChildItem | Select-Object name,length

Name     Length
----     ------
a.txt    98
b.txt    42
c.txt    102
d.txt    66
```

At first, this looks a lot like `Format-Table`. Let's use `Get-Member` to see how different it is:

```
PS> Get-ChildItem | Select-Object name,length | Get-Member

    TypeName: Selected.System.IO.FileInfo

Name         MemberType   Definition
----         ----------   ----------
Equals       Method       System.Boolean Equals(Object obj)
GetHashCode  Method       System.Int32 GetHashCode()
GetType      Method       System.Type GetType()
ToString     Method       System.String ToString()
Length       NoteProperty System.Int64 Length=98
Name         NoteProperty System.String Name=a.txt
```

Wait! We said that `Select-Object` creates a `PSCustomObject` synthetic object. It does, but PowerShell's type system ensures the original type isn't forgotten. You can see the underlying type:

```
PS> (Get-ChildItem .\a.txt | Select name, length ).PSTypeNames
Selected.System.IO.FileInfo
System.Management.Automation.PSCustomObject
System.Object
```

As was the case with the objects returned from `New-Object -Property`, the type of the object is `System.Management.Automation.PSCustomObject`. The original type of `System.IO.FileInfo` is prepended with `Selected` to show that it's a synthetic version of the original object. That new name is injected as the first name in the object's `PSTypeNames` property.

Even though it's a synthetic object, it's still a first-class citizen in the PowerShell environment. You can sort these objects

```
PS> Get-ChildItem | Select-Object Name,Length | sort Length

Name  Length
----  ------
b.txt 42
d.txt 66
a.txt 98
c.txt 102
```

or do anything else that you can do with a regular object.

But there's more to using `Select-Object` than selecting from the existing set of members. Say you want to add a new field, minute, to these objects. This will be a calculated field as follows:

```
PS> Get-ChildItem | foreach {$_.LastWriteTime.Minute}
5
51
56
54
```

It will be the minute at which the file was last written. You attach this field by passing a specially constructed hashtable describing the member to `Select-Object`. This hashtable has to have two members: name and expression (which can be shortened to *n* and *e* for brevity). The name is the name to call the property, and the expression is the scriptblock used to calculate the value of the field. The definition will look like this:

```
@{Name="minute";Expression={$_.LastWriteTime.Minute}}
```

Let's use it in the pipeline:

```
PS> Get-ChildItem | Select-Object Name,Length,
  @{Name="Minute";Expression={$_.LastWriteTime.Minute}}

Name    Length  Minute
----    ------  ------
a.txt       98      55
b.txt       42      51
c.txt      102      56
d.txt       66      54
```

As intended, the result has three fields, including the synthetic `minute` property you specified with the hashtable. Use `Get-Member` to see what the object looks like. You'll see that there are now three `NoteProperty` members on the objects that were output:

```
Length      NoteProperty long Length=98
Minute      NoteProperty System.Int32 Minute=55
Name        NoteProperty string Name=a.txt
```

For the last few sections, we've been focusing on individual functions (scriptblocks) and object members. Let's switch gears a bit and look at how modules fit into all of this. In chapters 8 and 9, we talked only about modules that were loaded from disk, but there's also a way to create modules dynamically.

10.4   *Dynamic modules*

Dynamic modules are created in memory at runtime rather than being loaded from disk. Dynamic modules relate to regular modules in much the same way as functions are related to scripts. You use a dynamic module rather than a regular, static module when you want to achieve one of the following: encapsulate local state in scripts, implement a dynamic equivalent of the closure feature found in other languages, or simplify the way you create custom objects.

10.4.1   *Dynamic script modules*

Just as there were two basic types of on-disk modules—script modules and binary modules—there are also two types of dynamic modules: the dynamic script module and the dynamic closure.

Let's start by creating a dynamic script module. To create a dynamic module, use the `New-Module` cmdlet which takes a scriptblock as an argument. This scriptblock is executed to define the module's contents. Here's what it looks like:

```
PS> $dm = New-Module {
    $c=0
    function Get-NextCount
        { $script:c++; $script:c }}
```

Other than how they're created; the contents of the module look pretty much like the on-disk modules you created in chapter 8. This is by design and means that all the concepts you learned for on-disk modules also apply to dynamic modules. As we discussed in the previous chapter, if there's no call to `Export-ModuleMember`, all the functions defined in the module are exported and the other types of module members aren't. Verify this by calling the function you defined,

```
PS> Get-NextCount
1
```

which works properly. And, because it wasn't exported, there's no variable $c (try typing the variable) or at least not one related to this dynamic module. Now try to use `Get-Module` to look at the module information, and you don't see anything. What happened? Well, dynamic modules are objects like everything else in PowerShell. The `New-Module` cmdlet has created a new module object but hasn't added it to the module table. This is why you assigned the output of the cmdlet to a variable—so you'd have a reference to the module object. Let's look at that object:

```
PS> $dm | Format-List

Name              : __DynamicModule_5809fa0b-4b24-4a03-a796-0450145fd1a1
Path              : C:\files\5809fa0b-4b24-4a03-a796-0450145fd1a1
Description       :
ModuleType        : Script
Version           : 0.0
NestedModules     : {}
ExportedFunctions : Get-NextCount
ExportedCmdlets   :
ExportedVariables :
ExportedAliases   :
```

The interesting fields are the name and path fields. Because no file is associated with the module, you had to make up a unique path for that object using the current folder (test by examining contents of $pwd). Likewise, you didn't specify a name, so the runtime made one up for you. Why did it do these things? It did this because, although a dynamic module isn't registered by default, it can be added to the module table by piping it to `Import-Module`. Let's give it a try:

```
PS> $dm | Import-Module
```

Now check the module table:

```
PS> Get-Module

ModuleType Version    Name                     ExportedCommands
---------- -------    ----                     ----------------
Script     0.0        __DynamicModule_5809fa0b... Get-NextCount
```

There it is, ugly name and all. You can give a dynamic module a specific name using the -Name parameter on the New-Module cmdlet. First, clean up from the last example

```
PS> Get-Module -Name *dynamic* | Remove-Module
```

and define a new dynamic module, with the same body as last time:

```
PS> New-Module -Name Dynamic1 {
    $c=0
    function Get-NextCount
        { $script:c++; $script:c }} |
    Import-Module
```

Rather than saving the result to a variable, you pipe it directly to Import-Module. Now look at the result:

```
PS> Get-Module

ModuleType Version    Name       ExportedCommands
---------- -------    ----       ----------------
Script     0.0        Dynamic1   Get-NextCount
```

This time the module is registered in the table with a much more reasonable name.

When would you use dynamic modules? When you need to create a function or functions that have persistent resources that you don't want to expose at the global level. This is the same scenario as the on-disk case, but this way you can package the module or modules to load into a single script file.

There's also another way the dynamic module feature is used: to implement the idea of closures in PowerShell. Let's move on and see how that works.

10.4.2 *Closures in PowerShell*

PowerShell uses dynamic modules to create dynamic closures. A *closure* in computer science terms (at least as defined in Wikipedia) is "a function that is evaluated in an environment containing one or more bound variables." A *bound variable* is, for our purposes, a variable that exists and has a value. The *environment* in our case is the dynamic module. The *function* is a scriptblock. In effect, a closure is the inverse of an object. An object is data with methods (functions) attached to that data, and a closure is a function with data attached to that method.

It may be easier to understand closures by starting with the problem they solve. We'll use this function:

```
PS> function add([int]$x) { return { param([int]$y) return $y + $x } }
```

The results are shown in figure 10.3.

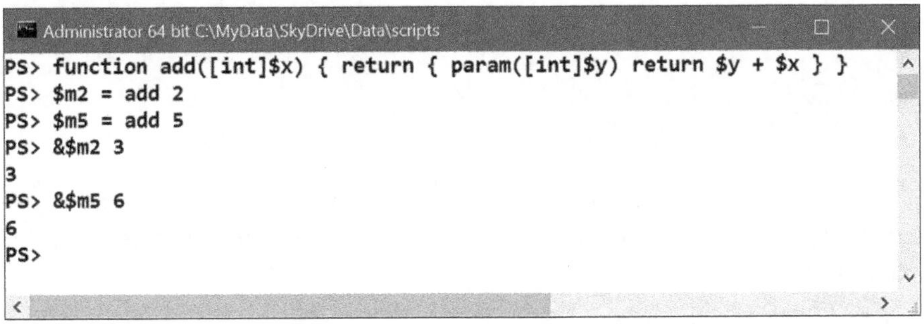

```
Administrator 64 bit C:\MyData\SkyDrive\Data\scripts                    —    □    ×
PS> function add([int]$x) { return { param([int]$y) return $y + $x } }
PS> $m2 = add 2
PS> $m5 = add 5
PS> &$m2 3
3
PS> &$m5 6
6
PS>
```

Figure 10.3 Problem with function variables. Unexpected results from using the function.

The results of using the function are 3 and 6 when intuitively you'd expect 5 and 11. The reason for the discrepancy is that $x isn't defined in the local scope, so the scriptblock doesn't have a value for it—it's effectively 0. Closures overcome this problem.

We'll start with a simpler example; you'll use closures to create a set of counter functions, similar to what you did in chapter 8. The advantage closures give you over plain functions is that you can change what increment to use after the counter function has been defined. The basic function is here.

Listing 10.3 Basic closure in PowerShell

```
function New-Counter
{
    param
    (
        [int]$increment = 1
    )

    $count=0;
    {
        $script:count += $increment
        $count
    }.GetNewClosure()
}
```

There's nothing here you haven't seen so far—you create a variable and then a scriptblock that increments that variable—except for returning the result of the call to the GetNewClosure() method. Let's try this function to see what it does. First, create a counter:

```
PS> $c1 = New-Counter
PS> $c1.GetType().FullName
System.Management.Automation.ScriptBlock
```

Looking at the type of the object returned, you see that it's a scriptblock, so you use the & operator to invoke it:

```
PS> & $c1
1

PS> & $c1
2
```

The scriptblock works as you'd expect a counter to work. Each invocation returns the next number in the sequence. Now create a second counter, but this time set the increment to 2:

```
PS> $c2 = New-Counter 2
```

Invoke the second counter scriptblock:

```
PS> & $c2
2

PS> & $c2
4

PS> & $c2
6
```

It counts up by 2. But what about the first counter?

```
PS> & $c1
3

PS> & $c1
4
```

The first counter continues to increment by 1, unaffected by the second counter. The key thing to notice is that each counter instance has its own copies of the $count and $increment variables. When a new closure is created, a new dynamic module is created, and then all the variables in the caller's scope are copied into this new module.

Here are more examples of working with closures to give you an idea of how flexible the mechanism is. First, you'll create a new closure using a param block to set the bound variable $x. This is the same as the previous example, except that you're using a scriptblock to establish the environment for the closure instead of a named function:

```
PS> $c = & {param ($x) {$x+$x}.GetNewClosure()} 3.1415
```

Now evaluate the newly created closed scriptblock:

```
PS> & $c
6.283
```

This evaluation returns the value of the parameter added to itself. Because closures are implemented using dynamic modules, you can use the same mechanisms you saw in chapter 8 for manipulating a module's state to manipulate the state of a closure. You can do this by accessing the module object attached to the scriptblock. You'll use this object to reset the module variable $x by evaluating `Set-Variable` in the closure's module context:

```
PS> & $c.Module Set-Variable -Name x -Value 'Abc'
```

Now evaluate the scriptblock to verify that it's been changed:

```
PS> & $c
AbcAbc
```

Next, create another scriptblock closed over the same module as the first one. You can do this by using the `NewBoundScriptBlock()` method on the module to create a new scriptblock attached to the module associated with the original scriptblock:

```
PS> $c2 = $c.Module.NewBoundScriptBlock({"x is $x"})
```

Execute the new scriptblock to verify that it's using the same $x:

```
PS> & $c2
x is Abc
```

Now use $c2.module to update the shared variable:

```
PS> & $c2.module Set-Variable -Name x -Value 123
PS> & $c2
x is 123
```

and verify that it's also changed for the original closed scriptblock:

```
PS> & $c
246
```

Finally, create a named function from the scriptblock using the function provider

```
PS> $function:myfunc = $c
```

and verify that calling the function by name works:

```
PS> myfunc
246
```

Set the closed variable yet again, but use $c2 to access the module this time:

```
PS> & $c2.Module Set-Variable -Name x -Value 3
```

and verify that it's changed when you call the named function:

```
PS> myfunc
6
```

These examples should give you an idea of how all of these pieces—scriptblocks, modules, closures, and functions—are related. This is how modules work. When a module is loaded, the exported functions are closures bound to the module object that was created. These closures are assigned to the names for the functions to import. A fairly small set of types and concepts allows you to achieve advanced programming scenarios. In the next section, we'll go back to looking at objects and see how dynamic modules make it easier to create custom object instances.

10.4.3 *Creating custom objects from modules*

There's one more thing you can do with dynamic modules: provide a simpler way to build custom objects. This is a logical step because modules have private data and public members like objects. As modules, they're intended to address a different type of problem than objects, but given the similarity between objects and modules, it would make sense to be able to construct an object from a dynamic module. This is done using the -AsCustomObject parameter on New-Module. You'll use this mechanism to create a point object from a module.

Listing 10.4   New-Point function

```
function New-Point
{
    New-Module -ArgumentList $args -AsCustomObject {
        param (
            [int] $x = 0,
            [int] $y = 0
        )
        function ToString()
        {
            "($x, $y)"
        }
        Export-ModuleMember -Function ToString -Variable x,y
    }
}
```

Now let's try it. Begin by defining two points, $p1 and $p2:

```
PS> $p1 = New-Point 1 1
PS> $p2 = New-Point 2 3
```

You'll use string expansion to display these objects, which will call the ToString() method you exported from the module:

```
PS> "p1 is $p1"
p1 is (1, 1)

PS> "p2 is $p2"
p2 is (2, 3)
```

Now try to assign a string to the X member on one of the points:

```
PS> $p1.X = 'Hi'
Cannot convert value "Hi" to type "System.Int32".
Error: "Input string was not in a correct format."
At line:1 char:1
+ $p1.X = 'Hi'
+ ~~~~~~~~~~~~~
    + CategoryInfo          : MetadataError: (:) [],
  ArgumentTransformationMetadataException
    + FullyQualifiedErrorId : RuntimeException
```

This results in an error because the exported variable is a special type of note property that's backed by the variable. Because it's backed by the variable, any constraints on the variable also apply to the note property, allowing you to create strongly typed members on a synthetic object.

So far, we've covered scriptblocks, modules, and closures in PowerShell. Although these features are somewhat exotic, they're found in most modern (or modernized) languages, including Java, JavaScript, Visual Basic, C#, and Python. In the next section, we're going to cover a related feature that's unique to PowerShell: *steppable pipelines*. Normally once a pipeline starts, it runs to completion. With a steppable pipeline, you can cause the pipeline to process one object at a time (with some limitations). This is a concrete form of metaprogramming, where one script has precise control over the sequence of operations in another.

10.5 Steppable pipelines

Steppable pipelines existed in PowerShell v1 but weren't exposed to the end user. In v2 this feature was made available to the end user. The core use of this feature is to allow one command to wrap, or *proxy*, other commands. In this section, we'll begin with a look at how the feature works and then explore a useful example showing its value.

10.5.1 How steppable pipelines work

The central concept in PowerShell programs is the pipeline, which processes a sequence of objects, one at a time. In chapter 1, we illustrated this with a diagram of the pipeline processor. Let's take another look (see figure 10.4).

Each object is processed completely (ignoring things like sorting) before processing begins on the next one, but the pipeline itself has to process all objects in one go. There are times when it's useful to be able to start a pipeline and then feed it objects as needed. This is what a steppable pipeline lets you do. You can create a pipeline, start it (so all the `begin` clauses are executed), and then pass objects to it for processing one at a time. Let's see how to do this.

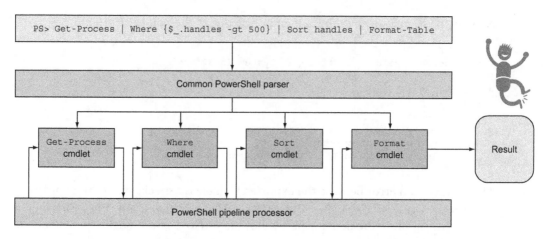

Figure 10.4 Objects flow through a pipeline one at a time. A common parser constructs each of the command objects and then starts the pipeline processor, stepping each object through all stages of the pipeline.

To get a steppable pipeline object, you need to have some object representation of a pipeline. The obvious way to do this is with a scriptblock object, and that's exactly how it works. First, create a scriptblock with exactly one pipeline in it:

```
PS> $sb = { Select-Object name, length }
```

The "one pipeline" part is important—a steppable pipeline maps to a single pipeline, so the scriptblock used to create it must have only a single pipeline. Now get a steppable pipeline object:

```
PS> $sp = $sb.GetSteppablePipeline()
```

Let's look at the type of object you got back and see what its members are:

```
PS> $sp | Get-Member

        TypeName: System.Management.Automation.SteppablePipeline

Name         MemberType  Definition
----         ----------  ----------
Begin        Method      void Begin(bool expectInpu…
Dispose      Method      void Dispose(), void IDisp…
End          Method      array End()
Equals       Method      bool Equals(System.Object obj)
GetHashCode  Method      int GetHashCode()
GetType      Method      type GetType()
Process      Method      array Process(System.Object input…
ToString     Method      string ToString()
```

In this list of members, you can see that there are methods that correspond to the clauses in a function: Begin(), Process(), and End(). These do what you'd expect: Begin() runs all the begin clauses in all of the commands in the pipeline, Process() runs all the process clauses, and End() runs all the end clauses. Let's try running this pipeline. When you call Begin() you have to pass a Boolean value telling the runtime whether to expect input. If there's no input, the pipeline will run to completion in a single step. You do want to pass input objects to the pipeline, so call Begin() with $true:

```
PS> $sp.Begin($true)
```

You need to get some data objects to pass through the pipeline—you'll get a list of DLLs in the PowerShell install directory:

```
PS> $dlls = Get-ChildItem -Path $pshome -Filter *.dll
```

Now loop through this list, passing each element to the steppable pipeline:

```
PS> foreach ($dll in $dlls) { $sp.Process($dll) }

Name              Length
----              ------
PSEvents.dll       56320
pspluginwkr.dll   174592
pwrshmsg.dll        3072
pwrshsip.dll       29696
```

and you see that each element is processed through the pipeline. Finally, call the End() and Dispose() methods to clean up the pipeline:

```
PS> $sp.End()
PS> $sp.Dispose()
```

What happens if you don't call them? If you don't call End(), you may not get all of the output from the pipeline. If you're stepping a pipeline containing the Sort-Object cmdlet, it doesn't return its output until the end clause. And if you don't call Dispose(), then any resources held by cmdlets in the pipeline may not be cleaned up in a timely manner (for example, files may not be closed or other resources may not be released).

Now that you have an idea of how steppable pipelines work, let's look at how you can use them.

10.5.2 *Creating a proxy command with steppable pipelines*

In chapter 1, we discussed how the result of all of the things we type at the command line are streamed through Out-Default to display them on the screen. Out-Default uses steppable pipelines to run the formatter cmdlets to do its rendering and then calls Out-Host to display the formatted output. Let's see how you can add a frequently requested feature to the interactive experience using a proxy for Out-Default.

A commonly requested feature for interactive use is to capture the result of the last output object so it can be made available to the next pipeline. First, you enter a command that displays a result:

```
PS> 2+2
4
```

You want to use that result in the next command you type, so it should be available in a variable called $last. This would let you do subsequent calculations like this:

```
PS> $last+3
7

PS> $last*7
49
```

That would be a nice feature, but it hasn't made it into the product. Fortunately, with steppable pipelines and proxy functions, you can add this feature yourself. The trick is to wrap the Out-Default cmdlet in a proxy function.

Listing 10.5   Wrapper for the Out-Default cmdlet

```
function Out-Default
{
    [CmdletBinding(ConfirmImpact='Medium')]
    param(
        [Parameter(ValueFromPipeline=$true)] `
        [System.Management.Automation.PSObject] $InputObject
    )

    begin
    {
        $wrappedCmdlet = $ExecutionContext.InvokeCommand.GetCmdlet(
          'Out-Default')
        $sb = { & $wrappedCmdlet @PSBoundParameters }
        $__sp = $sb.GetSteppablePipeline()
        $__sp.Begin($pscmdlet)
    }
    process
    {
        $do_process = $true
        if ($_ -is [System.Management.Automation.ErrorRecord])
        {
            if ($_.Exception -is
              [System.Management.Automation.CommandNotFoundException])
            {
                $__command = $_.Exception.CommandName
                if (Test-Path -Path $__command -PathType container)
                {
                    Set-Location $__command
                    $do_process = $false
                }
                elseif ($__command -match
                  '^http://|\.(com|org|net|edu)$')
                {
                    if ($matches[0] -ne 'http://')
                    {
                        $__command = 'HTTP://' + $__command
                    }
```

① Create steppable pipeline wrapping Out-Default

② Check for command-not-found exceptions

③ If directory, cd there; if URL, open browser

```
                        [System.Diagnostics.Process]::Start($__command)
                        $do_process = $false
                    }
                }
            }
            if ($do_process)                    ┌──◄
            {                                    │    Capture last
                                               ④ │    output object
                $global:LAST = $_;
                $__sp.Process($_)
            }
        }
    }
    end
    {
        $__sp.End()
    }
}
```

As mentioned in section 10.1.3, because functions are resolved before cmdlets, when the PowerShell host calls `Out-Default` to display output, it will call your function first. Now you could collect all the output from the command the user typed and display it all at once, but that doesn't provide a good experience. Instead, you'll create a steppable pipeline that runs the `Out-Default` cmdlet inside the `Out-Default` function ❶. Every time the function receives an object, this object will be passed to the steppable pipeline to be rendered immediately. In the process of passing this object along, you can also assign it to the global `$LAST` variable.

When you start the steppable pipeline, rather than passing in a Boolean, you pass in the `$PSCmdlet` object (see chapter 7) for the function. This allows the steppable pipeline to write directly into the function's output and error streams so the function doesn't have to deal with any output from the pipeline. The next thing to notice is that this function does a couple of other useful things besides capturing the last output object. If the last command typed resulted in a "command not found" exception ❷, then you check to see if the command was a path to a directory. If so, you set the current location to that directory ❸. This allows you to type

```
PS> c:\mydir\mysubdir
```

instead of

```
PS> cd c:\mydir\mysubdir
```

The other thing you check is to see if the command looks like a URL. If it does, then try to open it in the browser. ❹ This lets you open a web page by typing the URL. Both of these are minor conveniences, but along with the `$LAST` variable, they make interactive use of PowerShell a more pleasant experience. This example should give you a sense of the flexibility that steppable pipelines provide.

NOTE Run the function and try the examples given at the start of this section.

We began this chapter with scriptblocks, moved from there to synthetic objects, then on to dynamic modules and closures, and finally to steppable pipelines. Now we're going to circle back to the type system and look at it in more detail. We've covered the nice ways to add members to objects and build synthetic objects, so let's dig into the plumbing of the PowerShell type system. In the next section, we'll look at what's happening under the covers.

10.6 *A closer look at the type-system plumbing*

Earlier in this chapter, we said that the core of the PowerShell type system was the PSObject type. This type is used to wrap other objects, providing adaptation and inspection capabilities as well as a place to attach synthetic members. You've used Get-Member to explore objects and the Add-Member, New-Object, and Select-Object cmdlets to extend and create objects. You can do all this directly by using the PSObject class itself. But there's one thing you can't do without understanding PSObject: wrap or shadow an existing property. In this technique, the synthetic property calls the base property that it's hiding. (Don't worry, this is less esoteric than it sounds. A simple example will clarify what we're talking about here.)

> **NOTE** If you've done much object-oriented programming, this concept is similar to creating an override to a virtual method that calls the overridden method on the base class. The difference here is that it's all instance-based; no new type is involved.

Let's look at PSObject in more detail. First, let's examine the properties on this object:

```
PS> [psobject].GetProperties() | foreach Name
BaseObject
Members
Properties
Methods
ImmediateBaseObject
TypeNames
```

From the list, you see some obvious candidates of interest. But how do you get at these members, given that the whole point of PSObject is to be invisible? The answer is that there's a special property attached to all objects in PowerShell called (surprise) PSObject. Let's look at this. First, you need a test object to work on. Use Get-Item to retrieve the DirectoryInfo object for the C: drive:

```
PS> $f = Get-Item c:\
PS> $f

    Directory:

Mode                 LastWriteTime         Length Name
----                 -------------         ------ ----
d--hs-        25/04/2017     14:38                C:\
```

Now let's look at the PSObject member attached to this object:

```
PS> $f.psobject
```

```
BaseObject          : C:\
Members             : {string PSPath=Microsoft.PowerShell.Core\
                        FileSystem::C:\, string PSParentPath=,
                        string PSChildName=C:\, PSDriveInfo PSDrive=C...}
Properties          : {string PSPath=Microsoft.PowerShell.Core\
                        FileSystem::C:\, string PSParentPath=,
                        string PSChildName=C:\, PSDriveInfo PSDrive=C...}
Methods             : {string get_Name(), System.IO.DirectoryInfo
                        get_Parent(), System.IO.DirectoryInfo
                        CreateSubdirectory(string path),
                        System.IO.DirectoryInfo
                        CreateSubdirectory(string path,
                        System.Security.AccessControl.DirectorySecurity
                        directorySecurity), void Create(),
                        void Create(System.Security.AccessControl.
                        DirectorySecurity directorySecurity)...}
ImmediateBaseObject : C:\
TypeNames           : {System.IO.DirectoryInfo,
                        System.IO.FileSystemInfo,
                        System.MarshalByRefObject, System.Object}
```

Right away you see a wealth of information: all the properties you saw on the PSObject type, populated with all kinds of interesting data. First, let's look at the TypeNames member:

```
PS> $f.psobject.TypeNames
System.IO.DirectoryInfo
System.IO.FileSystemInfo
System.MarshalByRefObject
System.Object
```

This member contains the names of all the types in the inheritance hierarchy for a DirectoryInfo object. (These types are all documented in the .NET class library documentation that's part of the MSDN collection. See http://msdn.microsoft.com for more information.)

We'll look at the Properties member next. This collection contains all the properties defined by this type. Let's get information about all the properties that contain the pattern "name":

```
PS> $f.psobject.Properties | where {$_.name -match 'name'}
```

```
MemberType      : NoteProperty
IsSettable      : True
IsGettable      : True
Value           : C:\
TypeNameOfValue : System.String
Name            : PSChildName
IsInstance      : True
```

```
GetterScript      : $this.Name
SetterScript      :
MemberType        : ScriptProperty
IsSettable        : False
IsGettable        : True
Value             : C:\
TypeNameOfValue   : System.Object
Name              : BaseName
IsInstance        : False

MemberType        : Property
Value             : C:\
IsSettable        : False
IsGettable        : True
TypeNameOfValue   : System.String
Name              : Name
IsInstance        : True

MemberType        : Property
Value             : C:\
IsSettable        : False
IsGettable        : True
TypeNameOfValue   : System.String
Name              : FullName
IsInstance        : True
```

You've seen these properties before; this is the same information that would be returned from Get-Member. This is exactly what Get-Member does—it uses the PSObject properties to get this information.

10.6.1 *Adding a property*

Now let's add a new member to this object. You could use Add-Member (and typically you would), but we're talking about the plumbing here, so we'll do it the hard way. First, you need to create the NoteProperty object that you want to add. Do this with the New-Object cmdlet:

```
PS> $np = New-Object `
  -TypeName System.Management.Automation.PSNoteProperty `
  -ArgumentList hi, 'Hello there'
```

Next, add it to the member collection:

```
PS> $f.PSObject.Members.add($np)
```

and you're finished (so it wasn't that hard after all). The hi member has been added to this object, so try it out:

```
PS> $f.hi
Hello there
```

All of the normal members are still there. Now look at the member in the member collection:

```
PS> $f.PSObject.Members | where {$_.name -match '^hi'}

MemberType        : NoteProperty
IsSettable        : True
IsGettable        : True
Value             : Hello there
TypeNameOfValue   : System.String
Name              : hi
IsInstance        : True
```

Notice the `Value` member on the object. Because you can get at the member, you can also set the member

```
PS> ($f.PSObject.Members | where {
  $_.name -match '^hi'}).value = 'Goodbye!'
PS> $f.hi
Goodbye!
```

which is equivalent to setting the property directly on `$f`:

```
PS> $f.hi = 'Hello again!'
PS> $f.PSObject.Members | where {$_.name -match '^hi'}

MemberType        : NoteProperty
IsSettable        : True
IsGettable        : True
Value             : Hello again!
TypeNameOfValue   : System.String
Name              : hi
IsInstance        : True
```

The `Value` member on the note property is `Hello again!`

In section 10.4.3 you saw a different type of note property used when constructing objects out of modules. This type of note property is backed by a variable. You can also create an instance of this type of property. But first you need a variable to use to back the property value:

```
PS> [int] $VariableProperty = 0
```

Now create the `PSVariableProperty` object, passing in the variable to bind:

```
PS> $vp = New-Object `
    -TypeName System.Management.Automation.PSVariableProperty `
    -ArgumentList (Get-Variable VariableProperty)
```

Note that the name of the property and the name of the variable will be the same. Add the property

```
PS> $f.psobject.members.add($vp)
```

and verify that it can be read and written:

```
PS> $f.VariableProperty
0

PS> $f.VariableProperty = 7
PS> $f.VariableProperty
7
```

You can read and write integers, but the backing variable was constrained to be an integer. Let's verify that the constraint was preserved by trying to assign a string to it:

```
PS> $f.VariableProperty = 'Hi'
Cannot convert value "Hi" to type "System.Int32".
Error: "Input string was not in a correct format."
At line:1 char:1
+ $f.VariableProperty = 'Hi'
+ ~~~~~~~~~~~~~~~~~~~~~~~~~~~
    + CategoryInfo          : MetadataError: (:) [],
  ArgumentTransformationMetadataException
    + FullyQualifiedErrorId : RuntimeException
```

You get the error like you saw in section 10.4.3 when you exported a constrained variable from a module as a property.

10.6.2 *Shadowing an existing property*

There's one last item to cover in our discussion of the plumbing: the mechanism that allows you to bypass the adapted members and lets you get at the raw object underneath. This is accomplished through another special member on PSObject called PSBase. This member allows you to get at the object directly, bypassing all the synthetic member lookup. It also makes it possible to create a synthetic member to adapt an existing member. We can clarify this with an example. Say you want to change the name property on a DirectoryInfo object to always return the name in uppercase. Here's what it looks like unadapted:

```
PS> $f = Get-Item c:\windows
PS> $f.name
windows
```

To do this, create a new PSProperty object called Name that will shadow the existing property:

```
PS> $n=New-Object -TypeName Management.Automation.PSScriptProperty `
    -ArgumentList name,{$this.psbase.name.ToUpper()}
```

In the body of the scriptblock for this PSProperty, you'll use $this.psbase to get at the name property on the base object (if you accessed the name property directly, you'd be calling yourself). You apply the ToUpper() method on the string returned by name to acquire the desired result. Now add the member to the object's member collection

```
PS> $f.psobject.members.add($n)
```

and try it out:

```
PS> $f.name
WINDOWS
```

When you access the `name` property on this object, the synthetic member you created gets called instead of the base member, so the name is returned in uppercase. The base object's `name` property is unchanged and can be retrieved through `psbase.name`:

```
PS> $f.psbase.name
windows
```

Although this isn't a technique that you'll typically use on a regular basis, it allows you to do some pretty sophisticated work. You could use it to add validation logic, for example, and prevent a property from being set to an undesired value. You could also use it to log accesses to a property to gather information about how your script or application is being used.

With a solid understanding of the plumbing, you're ready to use everything you've learned and do some applied metaprogramming. In the next section, you'll learn how to write a domain-specific extension to PowerShell.

10.7   Extending the PowerShell language

In the previous section, you learned how to add members to existing objects one at a time, but sometimes you'll want to construct new types rather than extend the existing types. In this section, we'll explain how to do that and also how to use scripting techniques to add the ability to create objects to the PowerShell language.

10.7.1 Little languages

The idea of *little languages*—small, domain-specific languages—has been around for a long time. This was one of the powerful ideas that made the UNIX environment so attractive. Many of the tools that were the roots for today's dynamic languages came from this environment.

In effect, all programs are exercises in building their own languages. You create the nouns (objects) and verbs (methods or functions) in this language. These patterns are true for all languages that support data abstraction. Dynamic languages go further because they allow you to extend how the nouns, verbs, and modifiers are composed in the language. For example, in a language such as C#, it would be difficult to add a new looping construct. In PowerShell, this is minor. To illustrate how easy it is, let's define a new looping keyword called `loop`. This construct will repeat the body of the loop for the number of times the first argument specifies. You can add this keyword by defining a function that takes a number and scriptblock. Here's the definition:

```
PS> function loop ([int] $i, [scriptblock] $b) {
     while ($i-- -gt 0) { . $b }
     }
```

Try it out:

```
PS> loop 3 { 'Hello World' }
Hello world
Hello world
Hello world
```

In a few lines of code, you've added a new flow-control statement to the PowerShell language that looks pretty much like any of the existing flow-control statements. The only problem is that the opening brace has to be on the same line as the command—otherwise, it will be treated as two statements.

> **NOTE** As of version 4, PowerShell does have a way to create real language extensions where everything doesn't have to be on the same line. This is how the language extensions for PowerShell DSC were implemented. Unfortunately, these capabilities are only exposed in the form of rather hard-to-use APIs. Although there are a number of community examples demonstrating how to use these APIs, we're not going to cover them in this book because they're still subject to change. (Microsoft may change the APIs as part of the process of properly exposing them.)

Now let's change gears a bit to talk more about types.

10.7.2 Type extension

You might have noticed that all the examples we've looked at so far involve adding members to instances. But what about adding members to types? Having to explicitly add members to every object you encounter would be pretty tedious, no matter how clever you are.

> **NOTE** Nope—still not talking about classes. Wait for chapter 19. Patience is a virtue (or so they tell us).

You need some way to extend types instead of individual instances. As you might expect, PowerShell lets you do exactly this. In the following sections, we'll introduce the mechanisms that PowerShell provides which let you extend types.

Type extension is performed in PowerShell through a set of XML configuration files. These files are usually loaded at startup time, but they can be extended after the shell has started. In this section, you'll learn how to take advantage of these features.

Let's look at an example. Consider an array of numbers. It's fairly common to sum up a collection of numbers; unfortunately, there's no Sum() method on the Array class:

```
PS> (1,2,3,4).Sum()
Method invocation failed because [System.Int32] does not contain a method
    named 'Sum'.
At line:1 char:1
+ (1,2,3,4).sum()
+ ~~~~~~~~~~~~~~~
    + CategoryInfo          : InvalidOperation: (:) [], RuntimeException
    + FullyQualifiedErrorId : MethodNotFound
```

Using the techniques, we've discussed, you could add such a method to this array:

```
PS> $a = (1,2,3,4)
PS> $a = Add-Member -PassThru -in $a scriptmethod sum {
    $r=0
  foreach ($e in $this) {$r += $e}
  $r
}
```

and finally use it:

```
PS> $a.sum()
10
```

But this would be painful to do for every instance of an array. What you need is a way to attach new members to a type, rather than through an instance. PowerShell does this through type configuration files. These configuration files are stored in the installation directory for PowerShell and loaded at startup. The installation directory path for PowerShell is stored in the $PSHome variable, so it's easy to find these files. They have the word *type* in their names and have an extension of .ps1xml:

```
PS> Get-ChildItem $pshome/*type*.ps1xml
```

You don't want to update the default installed types files because when you install updates for PowerShell, they'll likely be overwritten and your changes will be lost. Instead, create your own custom types file containing the specification of the new member for System.Array. Once you've created the file, you can use the Update -TypeData cmdlet to load it. The definition for the Sum() method extension you want to add to System.Array is shown next.

Listing 10.6 Type file for Sum() method extension

```
<Types>
   <Type>
        <Name>System.Array</Name>
        <Members>
            <ScriptMethod>
                <Name>Sum</Name>
                <Script>
                    $r=$null
                    foreach ($e in $this) {$r += $e}
                    $r
                </Script>
            </ScriptMethod>
        </Members>
    </Type>
</Types>
```

This definition is saved to a file called SumMethod.ps1xml. Now load the file and update the type system definitions:

```
PS> Update-TypeData SumMethod.ps1xml
```

If the file loads successfully, you won't see any output. You can now try out the `Sum()` function:

```
PS> (1,2,3,4,5).Sum()
15
```

It works. And because of the way the script was written, it will work on any type that can be added. Let's add strings:

```
PS> ('abc','def','ghi').Sum()
abcdefghi
```

You can even use it to add hashtables:

```
PS> (@{a=1},@{b=2},@{c=3}).Sum()

Name Value
---- -----
c    3
a    1
b    2
```

You can see that the result is the composition of all three of the original hashtables. You can even use it to put a string back together:

```
PS> ([char[]] 'hal' | foreach{[char]([int]$_+1)}).Sum()
ibm
```

Here you break the original string into an array of characters, add 1 to each character, and then use the `Sum()` method to add them all back into a string.

You should take time to examine the set of type configuration files that are part of the default PowerShell installation. Examining these files is a good way to see what you can accomplish using these tools.

> **WARNING** Make sure you don't make any changes to these files because bad things will happen to your PowerShell implementation.

Starting with PowerShell v3 you can modify types dynamically in a script. Instead of creating a type data file, you can imperatively extend a type with `Update-TypeData`. The dynamically modified type data is available only in the session in which you apply it—exactly the same as if you used a types file. You can also remove modified type data (dynamic or from a type file) using `Remove-TypeData`.

Let's use the example from this section, but this time we'll perform the update dynamically. Save this listing as dynamictypes.ps1.

Listing 10.7   Updating type data dynamically

```
Update-TypeData -TypeName System.Array -MemberName Sum `
-MemberType ScriptMethod -Value {
  $r=$null
```

```
    foreach ($e in $this) {$r += $e}
    $r
} -Force
```
❶ **Defining dynamic type data**

```
"`nSum array of numbers:"
(1,2,3,4,5).Sum()
```
❷ **Summing an array**

```
"`nSum array of strings:"
("abc","def","ghi").Sum()
```

```
"`nSum array of hashtables:"
(@{a=1},@{b=2},@{c=3}).Sum()
```

```
"`nPut string back together:"
([char[]] "hal" | foreach{[char]([int]$_+1)}).Sum()
```

```
Remove-TypeData -TypeName System.Array
```
❸ **Removing dynamic type data**

```
"`nSum array of numbers:"
(1,2,3,4,5).Sum()
```

When defining dynamic types ❶ you need to supply `Update-TypeData` with several pieces of information:

- Type to be modified
- Name of the new member
- Type of the new member
- Value or code used to define the new member

If you compare listing 10.7 with listing 10.6, you'll see the very same data in both. When you modify types dynamically, you should use the `-Force` parameter. This doesn't turn you into a Jedi knight but it ensures that the modification of the type will be applied even if you've already performed the action. It's useful when developing and testing or if you need to rerun the script in the same session multiple times.

The same summations ❷ are perfomed as in the previous discussion on using type files—namely, summing arrays of numbers, strings, and hashtables and putting a string back together. The results are shown in figure 10.5.

You can remove the modified type data ❸ using `Remove-TypeData`. You'll remove all type modifications for that particular type. If you then try to use the `Sum()` method on an array, you'll receive a Method Invocation error because the method doesn't exist. As a further exercise in dynamically modifying types, we'll leave it to you to add a method to `System.String` to reverse the string. (Hint: see the `ScriptMethod` in section 10.2.3.)

We've covered an enormous amount of material so far in this chapter, introducing ideas that are new to a lot of users. If you've hung on to this point, congratulations! There are only a few more topics to complete your knowledge of metaprogramming with PowerShell. Scriptblocks, dynamic modules, and closures can be passed around, invoked, and assigned at runtime, but the body of these blocks is still defined at compile

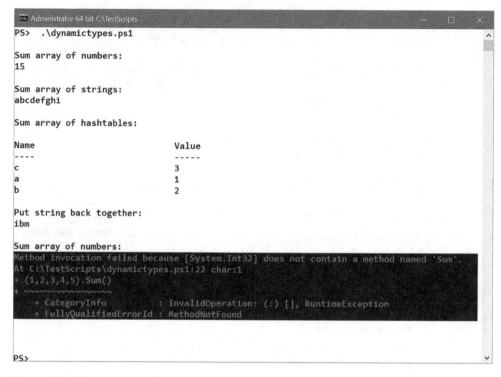

Figure 10.5   Running a script that dynamically updates types

time. In the next section we'll expand our repertoire of techniques by looking at ways to dynamically create code.

10.8 Building script code at runtime

This final section presents the mechanisms that PowerShell provides for compiling script code and creating scriptblocks at runtime. To say that you're compiling when PowerShell is an interpreted language may sound odd, but that's what creating a scriptblock is: a piece of script text is compiled into an executable object. In addition, PowerShell provides mechanisms for directly executing a string, bypassing the need to first build a scriptblock. In the next few sections we'll look at how each of these features works.

10.8.1 The Invoke-Expression cmdlet

The Invoke-Expression cmdlet is a way to execute an arbitrary string as a piece of code. It takes the string, compiles it, and then immediately executes it in the current scope. Here's an example:

```
PS> Invoke-Expression -Command '$a=2+2; $a'
4
```

In this example, the script passed to the cmdlet assigned the result of 2+2 to $a and wrote $a to the output stream. Because this expression was evaluated in the current context, it should also have affected the value of $a in the global scope:

```
PS> $a
4
```

You see that it did. Now invoke another expression:

```
PS> Invoke-Expression '$a++'
PS> $a
5
```

Evaluating this expression changes the value of $a to 5. There are no limits on what you can evaluate with `Invoke-Expression`. It can take any arbitrary piece of script code.

> **WARNING**   Danger! Danger! Danger! If you ever find yourself using the `Invoke -Expression` cmdlet (or the corresponding APIs) in production code, you're almost certainly wrong. With all of the other features covered in this chapter, there's little need to ever use this cmdlet. Certainly, you should never call it on unvalidated user input. Incorrect use of this cmdlet can and has led to code-injection attacks and other security issues in the wild. You have been warned. We will now return you to your regularly scheduled section.

Here's an example where you build a string with several statements in it and execute it:

```
PS> $expr = '$a=10;'
PS> $expr += 'while ($a--) { $a }'
PS> $expr += '"A is now $a"'
PS> [string](Invoke-Expression $expr)
9 8 7 6 5 4 3 2 1 0 A is now -1
```

The first three commands in this example build a string to execute. The first line initializes the variable $a, the second adds a `while` loop that decrements and outputs $a, and the third line outputs a string telling you the final value of $a. Note the double quoting in the last script fragment. Without the nested double quotes, it would try to execute the first word in the string instead of emitting the whole string.

10.8.2   *The ExecutionContext variable*

One of the predefined variables (also called automatic variables) provided by the PowerShell engine is `$ExecutionContext`. This variable is another way to get at various facilities provided by the PowerShell engine. It's intended to mimic the interfaces available to the cmdlet author. The services that matter most to us in this chapter are those provided through the `InvokeCommand` member. Let's look at what this member can do for us:

```
PS> $ExecutionContext.InvokeCommand | Get-Member

   TypeName: System.Management.Automation.
      CommandInvocationIntrinsics
```

```
Name                         MemberType Definition
----                         ---------- ----------
Equals                       Method     bool Equals(System...
ExpandString                 Method     string ExpandStrin...
GetCmdlet                    Method     System.Management...
GetCmdletByTypeName          Method     System.Management...
GetCmdlets                   Method     System.Collections...
GetCommand                   Method     System.Management...
GetCommandName               Method     System.Collections...
GetCommands                  Method     System.Collections...
GetHashCode                  Method     int GetHashCode()
GetType                      Method     type GetType()
InvokeScript                 Method     System.Collections...
NewScriptBlock               Method     scriptblock NewScr...
ToString                     Method     string ToString()
CommandNotFoundAction        Property   System.EventHandle...
HasErrors                    Property   bool HasErrors {ge...
PostCommandLookupAction      Property   System.EventHandle...
PreCommandLookupAction       Property   System.EventHandle...
```

The interesting methods in this list are ExpandString(), InvokeScript(), and New-ScriptBlock(). These methods are covered in the next few sections.

10.8.3 *The ExpandString() method*

The ExpandString() method lets you perform the same kind of variable interpolation that the PowerShell runtime does in scripts. Here's an example. First, set $a to a known quantity:

```
PS> $a = 13
```

Next, create a variable $str that will display the value of $a:

```
PS> $str='a is $a'
```

Because the variable was assigned using single quotes, no string expansion took place. You can verify this by displaying the string:

```
PS> $str
a is $a
```

Now call the ExpandString() method, passing in $str:

```
PS> $ExecutionContext.InvokeCommand.ExpandString($str)
a is 13
```

It returns the string with the variable expanded into its value. An obvious use for this API is templating. If you have a text file containing PowerShell variables and subexpressions, you can cause those variables to be expanded on the file by doing

```
PS> $ExecutionContext.InvokeCommand.ExpandString((Get-Content templatefile.txt))
```

The only downside to this technique is that you need to know what variables are in the file so you can make sure they're all set properly before expanding the template.

10.8.4 The InvokeScript() method

InvokeScript() does the same thing that the Invoke-Expression cmdlet does (in fact, the cmdlet calls the method). It takes its argument and evaluates it like a script. Call this method passing in the string "2+2"

```
PS> $ExecutionContext.InvokeCommand.InvokeScript('2+2')
4
```

and it will return 4.

10.8.5 Mechanisms for creating scriptblocks

The NewScriptBlock() method, like InvokeScript(), takes a string, but instead of executing it, it returns a scriptblock object that represents the compiled script. Let's use this method to turn the string '1..4 | foreach {$_ * 2}' into a scriptblock:

```
PS> $sb = $ExecutionContext.InvokeCommand.NewScriptBlock(
'1..4 | foreach {$_ * 2}')
```

You save this scriptblock into a variable, so let's look at it. Because the ToString() on a scriptblock is the code of the scriptblock, you see the code that makes up the body of the scriptblock:

```
PS> $sb
1..4 | foreach {$_ * 2}
```

Now execute the scriptblock using the & call operator:

```
PS>  & $sb
2
4
6
8
```

The scriptblock executes, printing out the even numbers from 2 to 8.

There's a simpler way of doing this by using a static method on the ScriptBlock class. Here's how to use this static factory class:

```
PS> $sb = [scriptblock]::Create('1..4 | foreach {$_ * 2}')
PS> & $sb
2
4
6
8
```

Using the [ScriptBlock] type accelerator, the newer mechanism is significantly simpler than the rather long expression in the earlier example.

> **NOTE**   Many people have asked why the PowerShell team doesn't allow you to cast a string to a scriptblock. The reason is that they want to make the system resilient against code-injection attacks by minimizing the number of places where executable code can be injected into the system. They particularly want code creation to be an explicit act. Casts are more easily hidden, leading to accidental code injections, particularly when the system may prompt for a string. You don't want those user-provided strings to be converted into code without some kind of check. See the warning at the beginning of this section for more details.

10.8.6   Creating functions using the function: drive

The final way to create a scriptblock is a side effect of creating elements in the `function:` drive. Earlier you saw that it's possible to create a named function by assigning a scriptblock to a name in the `function:` drive:

```
PS> $function:foo = {'Hello there'}
PS> foo
Hello there
```

You could also use the `Set-Item` or `New-Item` cmdlet to do this. For example:

```
PS>  New-Item function:foo -Value {'Hi!'}
New-Item : The item at path 'foo' already exists.
At line:1 char:1
+ New-Item function:foo -value {'Hi!'}
+ ~~~~~~~~~~~~~~~~~~~~~~~~~~~~~~~~~~~~~
    + CategoryInfo          : InvalidArgument: (:)
[New-Item], PSArgumentException
    + FullyQualifiedErrorId : Argument,Microsoft.PowerShell.Commands.
  NewItemCommand
```

You receive an error because the function already exists, so use the `-Force` parameter to overwrite the existing definition:

```
PS> New-Item function:foo -Value { 'Hi!' } -Force

CommandType Name Version Source
----------- ---- ------- ------
Function    foo
```

`New-Item` returns the item created, so you can see that the function has been changed. But that's using scriptblocks. What happens if you pass in strings? The interpreter will compile these strings into scriptblocks and then assign the scriptblocks to the name. Here's an example where the body of the function is determined by the expanded string:

```
PS> $x=5
PS> $y=6
PS> $function:foo = "$x*$y"
```

```
PS> foo
30

PS> $function:foo
5*6
```

The variables $x and $y expand into the numbers 5 and 6 in the string, so the resulting scriptblock is

```
{5*6}
```

Now define another function using foo, but add more text to the function:

```
PS> New-Item function:bar -Value "$function:foo*3"

CommandType Name Version Source
----------- ---- ------- ------
Function    bar

PS> bar
90
```

In the expanded string, `$function:foo` expands into "5*6", so the new function bar is assigned a scriptblock `{5*6*3}`.

This finishes our discussion of the techniques PowerShell provides for compiling script code at runtime. In the next section, we'll look at how to embed static languages like C# and Visual Basic in your scripts. This ability to embed fragments of C# or Visual Basic vastly increases what can be done directly with scripts, but at the cost of some increase in complexity.

10.9 *Compiling code with Add-Type*

In the previous section, we covered techniques for compiling script code at runtime. In this section, you'll learn how to inline code written in static languages into your scripts. The key to doing this is the Add-Type cmdlet. With the Add-Type cmdlet, you can embed code fragments written in compiled languages like C# or Visual Basic in your scripts and then compile that code when the scripts are loaded.

> **NOTE** The need for the Add-Type cmdlet is significantly reduced now that you can create your own classes right in PowerShell, but there are some situations, like interoperating with the operating system, where you still need to use a compiled language like C#.

A particularly interesting application of this technique is that you can create dynamic binary modules. This combines some of the best aspects of script modules with binary modules.

Add-Type can also be used to dynamically load existing .NET assemblies at runtime. Finally, this cmdlet can be used to simplify writing scripts that compile static language code into libraries or executables.

10.9.1 *Defining a new .NET class: C#*

Let's jump into an example where you'll dynamically add a new .NET class at runtime using C#. You'll write the code for this class using C#.

NOTE Creating a class can also be done directly in PowerShell v5, as you'll see in chapter 19. The example in listing 10.8 provides a technique for older versions of PowerShell.

It's a simple class, so even if you aren't a C# programmer, you should be able to understand the code.

Listing 10.8 Creating a class using C#

```
Add-Type @'
using System;

public static class Example1
{
    public static string Reverse(string s)
    {
        Char[] sc = s.ToCharArray();
        Array.Reverse(sc);
        return new string(sc);
    }
}
'@
```

This command should run with no errors. Once it's run, use the new type that you've added:

```
PS> [example1]::Reverse('hello there')
ereht olleh
```

And there you go. You now have a new method for reversing strings. You could also have saved the file externally and then loaded it at runtime.

10.9.2 *Defining a new enum at runtime*

An enum type in .NET is a way of creating a fixed set of name-value constants. The ability to define these types is missing from PowerShell prior to version 5.0 (see chapter 19), but you can work around this by using Add-Type. You'll define an enum that can be used to specify a coffee order. You'll constrain the types of coffee orders you'll allow to Latte, Mocha, Americano, Cappuccino, or Espresso. First, set a variable to the list of drink types:

```
PS> $beverages = 'Latte, Mocha, Americano, Cappuccino, Espresso'
```

Pass a string to Add-Type that contains the fragment of C# needed to define an enum type:

```
PS> Add-Type "public enum BeverageType { $beverages }"
```

It should be easy to see what's going on. You're defining a public type called Beverage-Type using the list of drinks in $beverages. Now that you have the type defined, you can use it in a function to create new drink orders:

```
PS> function New-DrinkOrder ([BeverageType] $beverage)
  {
    "A $beverage was ordered"
  }
```

This function uses the enum to constrain the type of the argument to the function and then return a string showing what was ordered. Use the function to order a latte:

```
PS> New-DrinkOrder latte
A Latte was ordered
```

And the order goes through. Notice that the casing of the drink name matches what was in the DrinkOrder enum definition, not what was in the argument. This is because the argument contains an instance of the DrinkOrder type and not the original string. Let's try to order something other than a coffee and see what happens:

```
PS> New-DrinkOrder coke
New-DrinkOrder : Cannot process argument transformation on parameter
   'beverage'. Cannot convert value "coke" to type "BeverageType".
Error: "Unable to match the identifier name coke to a valid enumerator name.
   Specify one of the following enumerator names and try again:
Latte, Mocha, Americano, Cappuccino, Espresso"
At line:1 char:16
+ New-DrinkOrder coke
+                ~~~~
    + CategoryInfo          : InvalidData: (:) [New-DrinkOrder],
   ParameterBindingArgumentTransformationException
    + FullyQualifiedErrorId : ParameterArgumentTransformationError,
New-DrinkOrder
```

This results in a somewhat verbose but helpful error message telling you why the order failed and what the valid drink types are. That's all well and good, but the customer wants a Coke. Modify the enum definition to include Coke in the list of beverages:

```
PS> $beverages += ", Coke"
```

And call Add-Type again:

```
PS> Add-Type "public enum BeverageType { $beverages }"
Add-Type : Cannot add type. The type name 'BeverageType' already exists.
At line:1 char:1
+ Add-Type "public enum BeverageType { $beverages }"
+ ~~~~~~~~~~~~~~~~~~~~~~~~~~~~~~~~~~~~~~~~~~~~~~~~~~~~
    + CategoryInfo          : InvalidOperation: (BeverageType:String)
[Add-Type], Exception    + FullyQualifiedErrorId : TYPE_ALREADY_
   EXISTS,Microsoft.PowerShell.Commands.AddTypeCommand
```

This time it fails. Remember what we said about static types: once they're defined, they can't be changed. This is something to consider when using Add-Type to inline static code in a script. Static type definitions mean that the script isn't as easy to update as a normal PowerShell-only script. Now let's look at how Add-Type can be combined with dynamic modules.

10.9.3 *Dynamic binary modules*

Like dynamic script modules, a dynamic binary module is constructed in memory rather than loaded from disk. This is where Add-Type comes in. The content of a binary module is defined by a compiled assembly, not script text, and Add-Type lets you build these in-memory assemblies. This script constructs a binary module.

Listing 10.9   The ExampleModuleScript

```
$code = @'
using System.Management.Automation;          ⬅──┐  Contains
                                              ❶  cmdlet code
[Cmdlet("Write", "InputObject")]
public class MyWriteInputObjectCmdlet : Cmdlet
{
    [Parameter()]
    public string Parameter1;

    [Parameter(Mandatory = true, ValueFromPipeline=true)]
    public string InputObject;

    protected override void ProcessRecord()
    {
        if (Parameter1 != null)
                WriteObject(Parameter1 +  ":" +  InputObject);
            else
                WriteObject(InputObject);
    }                                    ❷  Compiles code
}                                           in memory
'@
$bin = Add-Type $code -PassThru         ⬅──   ❸  Gets assembly
$bin.Assembly | Import-Module           ⬅──┘     ref from type
```

This script packages the C# code for a cmdlet into a here-string ❶. It then uses Add-Type to produce the required in-memory assembly ❷, which it passes to Import -Module ❸. The one wrinkle in this approach is the fact that Add-Type returns type objects, not assemblies. Fortunately, this is easy to work around: The type object makes its containing assembly available through the Assembly property. Let's try out the script. First, load it:

```
PS>./ExampleModuleScript
```

then check to see if the module has been created:

```
PS> Get-Module

ModuleType Version    Name                   ExportedCommands
---------- -------    ----                   ----------------
Binary     0.0.0.0    dynamic_code_module... Write-InputObject
```

and there it is. Next, get the `CommandInfo` object for the new cmdlet:

```
PS> $cmd = Get-Command Write-InputObject
PS> $cmd | Format-List

Name              : Write-InputObject
CommandType       : Cmdlet
Definition        :
                    Write-InputObject -InputObject <string>
                    [-Parameter1 <string>] [<CommonParameters>]
Path              :
AssemblyInfo      :
DLL               :
HelpFile          : -Help.xml
ParameterSets     : {-InputObject <string> [-Parameter1 <string>]
                    [<CommonParameters>]}
ImplementingType  : MyWriteInputObjectCmdlet
Verb              : Write
Noun              : InputObject
```

Notice that the `Path`, `DLL`, and `AssemblyInfo` fields for this command are empty. Because the assembly for a dynamic binary module is in-memory only, these items are empty. They need an assembly that was loaded from disk in order to be defined.

Dynamic binary modules make it possible to get the advantages of a script module (being able to read the script) along with the advantages of compiled code (speed and static type checking). The only disadvantage to the user compared with regular binary modules is that the load time may be a bit longer.

10.10 Summary

- Metaprogramming is a set of powerful techniques that cracks open the Power-Shell runtime.
- Metaprogramming allows you to extend the runtime with new keywords and control structures.
- You can directly add properties and methods to objects in PowerShell to adapt or extend objects logically in specific problem domains.
- The fundamental unit of PowerShell code, including the content of all functions, scripts, and modules, is the scriptblock.
- Scriptblocks let you define methods that can be added to objects as script methods.
- Scriptblocks don't necessarily need to be named, and they can be used in many situations, including as the content of variables.

- Scriptblocks are the key to all of the metaprogramming features in PowerShell; they're also an everyday feature that users work with all the time when they use the ForEach-Object and Where-Object cmdlets.

- The call operator & allows you to invoke commands indirectly, by reference rather than by name (a scriptblock is a reference). This also works with the CommandInfo objects returned from Get-Command.

- When using the Update-TypeData cmdlet, you can load type configuration files that allow you to extend a type instead of a single instance of that type.

- PowerShell supports the use of little language, or domain-specific language techniques, to extend the core language. This allows you to more naturally specify solutions for problems in a particular domain.

- You can employ a variety of techniques for compiling and executing code at runtime. You can use the Invoke-Expression cmdlet, engine invocation intrinsics on the $ExecutionContext variable, or the CreateScriptBlock() static method on the [scriptblock] type.

- Dynamic modules allow you to do local isolation in a script. They also underlie the implementation of closures in PowerShell and provide a simpler way to create custom objects.

- The Add-Type cmdlet lets you work with compiled languages from within PowerShell.

- Add-Type provides a means to embed code in these languages directly in your scripts. This ability adds significant power to the environment at some cost in complexity.

- Add-Type also makes it possible to create dynamic binary modules, allowing you to combine some of the benefits of both static and dynamic coding techniques.

This finishes our look at modules and metaprogramming. In the next chapter, we'll move on to examine the techniques you can use to work with remote machines.

11

PowerShell remoting

This chapter covers
- Commands with built-in remoting
- PowerShell remoting subsystem
- Using PowerShell remoting
- Remoting sessions, persistent connections, and implicit remoting
- Remoting considerations and custom remoting sessions

In a day when you don't come across any problems, you can be sure that you are traveling in the wrong path.

—*Swami Vivekananda*

PowerShell is a tool intended for enterprise and cloud management but if it can't manage distributed systems it isn't useful. Fortunately, PowerShell has a comprehensive built-in remoting subsystem. This facility allows you to handle most remoting tasks in any kind of configuration you might encounter.

In this chapter, we're going to cover the features of remoting and how you can apply them. We'll use an example showing how to combine the features to solve a nontrivial problem: monitoring multiple remote machines. We'll then look at some of the configuration considerations you need to be aware of when using Power-Shell remoting.

Let's start with a quick overview of PowerShell remoting.

11.1 PowerShell remoting overview

The ultimate goal for remoting is to be able to execute a command on a remote computer. There are two ways to approach this. First, you could have each command do its own remoting. In this scenario, the command is still executed locally but uses system-level networking capabilities like DCOM to perform remote operations. A number of commands do this, which we'll cover in the next section. The negative aspect of this approach is that each command has to implement and manage its own remoting and authentication mechanisms.

PowerShell includes a second, more general solution, allowing you to send a command (or pipeline of commands or even a script) to the target machine for execution and then retrieve the results. With this approach, you only have to implement the remoting mechanism once and then it can be used with any command. This second solution is the one we'll spend most of our time discussing. But first let's look at the commands that implement their own remoting.

11.1.1 Commands with built-in remoting

A number of commands in PowerShell have a -ComputerName parameter, which allows you to specify the target machine to access. You can discover (some of) these cmdlets by running either of these commands:

```
PS> Get-Help * -Parameter ComputerName
PS> Get-Command -ParameterName ComputerName
```

> **CIM sessions**
>
> Common Information Model (CIM) sessions (see chapter 16) are closely related to PowerShell remoting—they enable more efficient access to WMI classes on remote machines. The cmdlets capable of using CIM sessions can be discovered in a similar way:
>
> ```
> PS> Get-Command -ParameterName Cimsession
> ```

For a new PowerShell v5.1 session on Windows 10, the majority of the cmdlets are listed in table 11.1.

> **NOTE** The number of cmdlets you see will depend on the modules you have on your machine. You won't necessarily see identical results from the two commands given earlier because Get-Help is dependent on analyzing the help files.

Table 11.1   Cmdlets with built-in remoting capability

Add-Computer	Clear-EventLog	Connect-PSSession
Enter-PSSession	Get-EventLog	Get-HotFix
Get-Process	Get-Service	Get-WmiObject
Invoke-Command	Invoke-WmiMethod	Limit-EventLog
New-EventLog	New-PSSession	Receive-Job
Receive-PSSession	Register-WmiEvent	Remove-Computer
Remove-EventLog	Remove-PSSession	Remove-WmiObject
Rename-Computer	Restart-Computer	Send-MailMessage
Set-DscLocalConfigurationManager	Set-Service	Set-WmiInstance
Show-EventLog	Start-DscConfiguration	Stop-Computer
Test-Connection	Write-EventLog	

NOTE We've deliberately excluded the `*WSMan*` cmdlets from table 11.1. The `*WSMan*` cmdlets are effectively deprecated and have been replaced by the `*-CIM*` cmdlets (see chapter 16).

These commands do their own remoting because either the underlying infrastructure already supports remoting or they address scenarios that are of particular importance to system management. You need to supply only one or more computer names to use them against a remote target:

```
PS> Get-Service -Name BITS -ComputerName W16TGT01, W16DSC02

 Status Name DisplayName
 ------ ---- -----------
Stopped BITS Background Intelligent Transfer Service
Stopped BITS Background Intelligent Transfer Service
```

You don't get any indication of which result belongs to which machine by default. In this case, you need to include the `MachineName` property in the output:

```
PS> Get-Service -Name BITS -ComputerName W16TGT01, W16DSC02 |
select Status, Name, MachineName

Status Name MachineName
 ------ ---- -----------
Stopped BITS W16DSC02
Stopped BITS W16TGT01
```

Self-remoting is performed using DCOM and RPC. These protocols will be blocked by default by firewalls. Also, the set of commands that do self-remoting is quite small, so the remaining commands must rely on the PowerShell remoting subsystem to access remote computers. We'll start looking at that in the next section.

11.1.2 *The PowerShell remoting subsystem*

You've seen a few brief examples of how remoting works in previous chapters. You may remember that all those examples used the same basic cmdlet: `Invoke-Command`. This cmdlet allows you to remotely invoke a scriptblock on another computer and is the building block for most of the features in remoting. The partial syntax for this command is shown in figure 11.1.

```
Invoke-Command [[-ComputerName] <string[]>] [-ScriptBlock] <scriptblock>
[-Credential <pscredential>] [-Port <int>] [-UseSSL]
[-ConfigurationName <string>] [-ApplicationName <string>]
[-ThrottleLimit <int>] [-AsJob] [-InDisconnectedSession]
[-SessionName <string[]>] [-HideComputerName] [-JobName <string>]
[-SessionOption <PSSessionOption>]
[-Authentication <AuthenticationMechanism>] [-EnableNetworkAccess]
[-InputObject <psobject>] [-ArgumentList <Object[]>]
[-CertificateThumbprint <string>] [<CommonParameters>]
[-VMId] <guid[]> -VMName <string[]> -ContainerId <string[]>
[[-ConnectionUri] <uri[]>]
```

Figure 11.1   Partial syntax for the `Invoke-Command` cmdlet, which is the core of PowerShell's remoting capabilities. This cmdlet is used to execute commands and scripts on one or more computers. It can be used synchronously or asynchronously as a job. The `VMId`, `VMName`, and `ContainerId` parameters were introduced with PowerShell 5.1 and are valid only on Windows 10 and Windows Server 2016 (or later).

The `Invoke-Command` cmdlet is used to invoke a scriptblock on one or more computers. You do so by specifying a computer name (or list of names) for the machines on which you want to execute the command. For each name in the list, the remoting subsystem will take care of all the details needed to open the connection to that computer, execute the command, retrieve the results, and then shut down the connection. If you're going to run the command on a large set of computers, `Invoke-Command` will also take care of all resource management details, such as limiting the number of concurrent remote connections. Our previous example becomes this:

```
PS>  Invoke-Command -ScriptBlock {Get-Service -Name BITS} `
-ComputerName W16TGT01, W16DSC02

Status  Name DisplayName                                 PSComputerName
------  ---- -----------                                 --------------
Stopped BITS Background Intelligent Transfer Service W16DSC02
Stopped BITS Background Intelligent Transfer Service W16TGT01
```

Note that you now get the computer name that the result refers to in the output.

This is a simple but powerful model if you need to execute only a single command or script on the target machine. But if you want to execute a series of commands on the target, the overhead of setting up and taking down a connection for each command becomes expensive. PowerShell remoting addresses this situation by allowing you to create a persistent connection to the remote computer called a *session*. You do so by using the `New-PSSession` cmdlet.

Both of the scenarios we've discussed so far involve what is called *noninteractive remoting* because you're only sending commands to the remote machines and then waiting for the results. You don't interact with the remote commands while they're executing.

Another standard pattern in remoting occurs when you want to set up an *interactive session* where every command you type is sent transparently to the remote computer. This is the style of remoting implemented by tools like Remote Desktop, Telnet, or SSH (Secure Shell).

> **NOTE** The PowerShell team has announced that SSH support will be built into PowerShell. Basic terminal support will be available with Windows Server 2016. Full SSH integration with the PowerShell Remoting Protocol will be introduced at a later date. Appendix A demonstrates SSH-based remoting between Linux and Windows machines using PowerShell v6.

PowerShell allows you to start an interactive session using the `Enter-PSSession` cmdlet. Use `Exit-PSSession` to close the session when you've finished working. If you enter a remote session created by `New-PSSession`, then using `Exit-PSSession` will suspend the session without closing the remote connection. Because the connection isn't closed, you can later reenter the session with all session data preserved by using `Enter-PSSession` again. An example of an interactive session is given in figure 11.2.

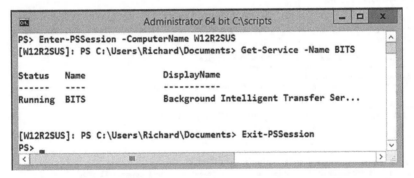

Figure 11.2   Interactive remoting session to the computer W12R2SUS. Notice how the PowerShell prompt changes to incorporate the remote machine name when you enter the session.

These cmdlets—`Invoke-Command`, `New-PSSession`, and `Enter-PSSession`—are the basic remoting tools you'll be using. But before you can use them, you need to make sure remoting is enabled, so we'll look at that next.

11.1.3 Enabling remoting

At this point we have some good news and some bad news for you. The good news is that for Windows Server 2012 and later (including Windows Server 2012 R2 virtual machines running in Azure IaaS), PowerShell remoting is enabled by default. The bad news is that for earlier versions of Window Server and for all versions of the Windows client operating system, PowerShell remoting is turned off by default and has to be enabled.

NOTE You have to turn on PowerShell remoting for a machine to receive and execute remote administration commands. You don't need to turn on remoting to send commands, though you will need to turn it on at least temporarily to change client-side settings such as the `TrustedHosts` list on the local machine.

You enable remoting using the `Enable-PSRemoting` cmdlet. To run this command, you must have administrator privileges on the machine you're going to enable. You need to do the following:

- Start the PowerShell session with elevated privileges (Run As Administrator).
- Ensure that none of the network connections on the machine has a network profile of `Public`. Use `Get-NetConnectionProfile | Set-NetConnectionProfile -NetworkCategory Private` to set the network profile.

By default, `Enable-PSRemoting` runs silently with no output and no input required. You can use the `-Verbose` and `-Confirm` parameters to see what's happening, as shown in figure 11.3.

```
Administrator 64 bit C:\MyData\SkyDrive\Data\scripts                          —   □   ×
PS> Enable-PSRemoting -Verbose -Confirm

WinRM Quick Configuration
Running command "Set-WSManQuickConfig" to enable remote management of this computer by using the Windows Remote
Management (WinRM) service.
 This includes:
    1. Starting or restarting (if already started) the WinRM service
    2. Setting the WinRM service startup type to Automatic
    3. Creating a listener to accept requests on any IP address
    4. Enabling Windows Firewall inbound rule exceptions for WS-Management traffic (for http only).

Do you want to continue?
[Y] Yes  [A] Yes to All  [N] No  [L] No to All  [S] Suspend  [?] Help (default is "Y"): y


Confirm
Are you sure you want to perform this action?
Performing the operation "Set-PSSessionConfiguration" on target "Name: microsoft.powershell SDDL:
O:NSG:BAD:P(A;;GA;;;IU)(A;;GA;;;BA)(A;;GA;;;RM)S:P(AU;FA;GA;;;WD)(AU;SA;GXGW;;;WD). This lets selected users remotely
run Windows PowerShell commands on this computer.".
[Y] Yes  [A] Yes to All  [N] No  [L] No to All  [S] Suspend  [?] Help (default is "Y"): y

Confirm
Are you sure you want to perform this action?
Performing the operation "Set-PSSessionConfiguration" on target "Name: microsoft.powershell.workflow SDDL:
O:NSG:BAD:P(A;;GA;;;BA)(A;;GA;;;RM)S:P(AU;FA;GA;;;WD)(AU;SA;GXGW;;;WD). This lets selected users remotely run Windows
PowerShell commands on this computer.".
[Y] Yes  [A] Yes to All  [N] No  [L] No to All  [S] Suspend  [?] Help (default is "Y"): y

Confirm
Are you sure you want to perform this action?
Performing the operation "Set-PSSessionConfiguration" on target "Name: microsoft.powershell32 SDDL:
O:NSG:BAD:P(A;;GA;;;IU)(A;;GA;;;BA)(A;;GA;;;RM)S:P(AU;FA;GA;;;WD)(AU;SA;GXGW;;;WD). This lets selected users remotely
run Windows PowerShell commands on this computer.".
[Y] Yes  [A] Yes to All  [N] No  [L] No to All  [S] Suspend  [?] Help (default is "Y"): y
PS>
```

Figure 11.3   Enabling PowerShell remoting on a machine

The `Enable-PSRemoting` command performs all the configuration steps needed to allow users with local administrator privileges to remote to this computer in a domain environment. In a non-domain or workgroup environment, as well as for non-admin users, additional steps are required for remoting to work.

11.1.4 Additional setup steps for workgroup environments

If you're working in a workgroup environment—for example, at home—you must take a few additional steps before you can connect to a remote machine. With no domain controller available to handle the various aspects of security and identity, you have to manually configure the names of the computers you trust. If you want to connect to the computer `computerItrust`, then you have to add it to the list of trusted computers (or `TrustedHosts` list).

You can do this via the `WSMan:` drive, as shown in table 11.2. Note that you need to be running as administrator to be able to use the `WSMan:` provider. Once you've completed these steps, you're ready to start playing with some examples.

Table 11.2   Additional steps needed to enable remote access to a computer in a workgroup environment

Step	Command	Description
1	`cd wsman:\localhost\client`	cd'ing into the client configuration node in the `WSMan:` drive allows you to access the WS-MAN configuration for this computer using the provider cmdlets.
2	`$old = (Get-Item .\` `TrustedHosts).Value`	You'll want to update the current value of the `Trusted-Hosts` item, so you get it and save the value in a variable.
3	`$old += ',computerItrust'`	The value of `TrustedHosts` is a string containing a comma-separated list of the computers considered trustworthy. You add the new computer name to the end of this list, prefixed with a comma. (If you're comfortable with implicitly trusting any host, then set this string to `*`, which matches any hostname.)
4	`Set-Item .\TrustedHosts` `$old`	Once you've verified that the updated contents of the variable are correct, you assign it back to the `TrustedHosts` item, which updates the configuration.

A note on security

The computers in the `TrustedHosts` list are implicitly trusted by the *local* computer when you add their names to this list. It's *not* an incoming security feature like a firewall. The identity of these computers won't be authenticated when you connect to them. Because the connection process requires sending *credential information* to these machines, you need to be sure that you can trust these computers. Also, be aware that the `TrustedHosts` list on a machine applies to everyone who uses that computer, not only the user who changed the setting.

> **(Continued)**
>
> That said, unless you allow random people to install computers on your internal network, this shouldn't introduce substantial risk most of the time. If you're comfortable with knowing which machines you'll be connecting to, you can put * in the `Trusted-Hosts` list, indicating that you're implicitly trusting any computer you might be connecting to. As always, security is a principle tempered with pragmatics.

An alternative way of validating the identity of the target computer is to use HTTPS when connecting to that computer. This works because, in order to establish an HTTPS connection, the target server must have a valid certificate installed where the name in the certificate matches the server name. As long as the certificate is signed by a trusted certificate authority you know that the server is the one it claims to be. Unfortunately, this process does require that you have a valid certificate, issued by either a commercial or local CA. This is an entirely reasonable requirement in an enterprise environment but may not always be practical in smaller or informal environments.

11.1.5 *Authenticating the connecting user*

In the previous section, you saw how the client verifies the identity of the target computer. Now we'll explore the converse of this—how the target computer verifies the identity of the connecting user. PowerShell remoting supports a wide variety of ways of authenticating a user, including NTLM and Kerberos. Each mechanism has its advantages and disadvantages. The authentication mechanism also has an important impact on how data is transmitted between the client and the server. Depending on how you authenticate to the server, the data passed between the client and server may or may not be encrypted. Encryption is extremely important in that it protects the contents of your communications with the server against tampering and preserves privacy. If encryption isn't being used, you need to ensure the physical security of your network. No untrusted access to the network can be permitted in this scenario. The possible types of authentication are shown in table 11.3.

Table 11.3   Possible types of authentication available for PowerShell remoting

Auth type	Description	Encrypted payload
Default	Use the authentication method specified by the WS-Management Protocol.	Depends on what was specified.
Basic	Use Basic Authentication, part of HTTP, where the username and password are sent unencrypted to the target server or proxy.	No. Use HTTPS to encrypt the connection.
Digest	Use Digest Authentication, which is also part of HTTP. This mechanism supersedes Basic Authentication and encrypts the credentials.	Yes.

Table 11.3   Possible types of authentication available for PowerShell remoting *(continued)*

Auth type	Description	Encrypted payload
Kerberos	The client computer and the server mutually authenticate using the Kerberos network authentication protocol.	Yes.
Negotiate	Negotiate is a challenge-response scheme that negotiates with the server or proxy to determine the scheme to use for authentication. For example, negotiation is used to determine whether the Kerberos protocol or NTLM is used.	Yes.
CredSSP	Use Credential Security Service Provider (CredSSP) authentication, which allows the user to delegate credentials. This mechanism, introduced with Windows Vista, is designed to support the second-hop scenario, where commands that run on one remote computer need to hop to another computer to do something.	Yes.

For all the authentication types except Basic, the payload of the messages you send is encrypted directly by the remoting protocol. If Basic authentication is chosen, you have to use encryption at a lower layer—for example, by using HTTPS instead of HTTP.

11.1.6 *Enabling remoting in the enterprise*

Remote administration is most likely to be performed against the servers in your environment. As you've seen, the newer versions of Windows Server have PowerShell remoting enabled by default. If you have older servers, you don't want to have to enable remoting on them individually because you may be dealing with tens, hundreds, or thousands of machines. Obviously, you can't use PowerShell remoting to turn on remoting, so you need another way to push configuration out to a collection of machines. This is exactly what Group Policy is designed for. You can use Group Policy to enable and configure remoting as part of the machine policy that gets pushed out.

PowerShell depends on the WinRM (Windows Remote Management) service for its operation. Your Group Policy needs to:

- Ensure the WinRM service will start automatically and is started.
- Configure WinRM to accept remoting requests.
- Configure Windows Firewall to allow remoting requests.

Instructions on creating a suitable Group Policy are available at http://mng.bz/3aHW.

11.2   *Applying PowerShell remoting*

With remoting services enabled, you can start to use them to get your work done. In this section, we're going to look at ways you can apply remoting to solve management problems. We'll start with some simple remoting examples. Next, we'll work with more complex examples where we introduce concurrent operations. Then you'll apply the principles you've learned to solve a specific problem: how to implement a multi-machine configuration monitor. You'll work through this problem in a series of steps, adding more capabilities to your solution, resulting in a simple but fairly complete configuration monitor. Let's start with the most basic examples.

11.2.1 *Basic remoting examples*

Building on our "Hello world" example from chapter 1, the most basic example of remoting is

```
Invoke-Command -ComputerName Servername -ScriptBlock {'Hello world'}
```

The first thing to notice is that Invoke-Command takes a scriptblock to specify the actions. This pattern should be familiar by now—you've seen it with ForEach-Object and Where-Object many times. The Invoke-Command does operate a bit differently, though. It's designed to make remote execution as transparent as possible. For example, if you want to sort objects, the local command looks like this:

```
PS> 1..3 | sort -Descending
```

Now if you want to do the sorting on the remote machine, you'd do this:

```
PS> 1..3 |
Invoke-Command -ComputerName localhost -ScriptBlock {sort -Descending}
```

You're splitting the pipeline across local and remote parts, and the scriptblock is used to demarcate which part of the pipeline should be executed remotely.

> **NOTE** Localhost is used to set a remote session to your local machine for testing purposes. You could use the machine name if preferred or $ENV:COMPUTERNAME.

This works the other way as well:

```
PS> Invoke-Command -ComputerName localhost -ScriptBlock { 1..3 } |
sort -Descending
```

Here you're generating the numbers on the remote computer and sorting them locally. Scriptblocks can contain more than one statement. This implies that the semantics need to change a bit. Whereas in the simple pipeline case streaming input into the remote command was transparent, when the remote command contains more than one statement, you have to be explicit and use the $input variable to indicate where you want the input to go. That looks like the following:

```
PS> 1..3 | Invoke-Command -ComputerName localhost -ScriptBlock {
  'First'
  $input | sort -Descending
  'Last'
}
First
3
```

```
2
1
Last
```

The scriptblock argument to `Invoke-Command` in this case contains three statements. The first emits the string `'First'`, the second does the sort on the input, and the third emits the string `'Last'`.

What happens if you don't specify input? Nothing is emitted between `'First'` and `'Last'`. Because `$input` wasn't specified, the input objects were never processed. You'll need to keep this in mind when you start to build a monitoring solution.

Now let's look at how concurrency—multiple operations occurring at the same time—impacts your scripts.

11.2.2 *Adding concurrency to the examples*

In chapter 1, we talked about how each object passed completely through all states of a pipeline, one by one. This behavior changes with remoting because the local and remote commands run in separate processes that are executing concurrently. This means you now have two threads of execution—local and remote—and that can have an effect on the order in which things are executed. Consider the following statement:

```
PS> 1..3 | foreach { Write-Host $_ -ForegroundColor green;
$_; Start-Sleep 5 } | Write-Host

1
1
2
2
3
3
```

This statement sends a series of numbers down the pipeline. In the body of the `foreach` scriptblock, the value of the current pipeline object is written to the screen (in green) and then passed to the next state in the pipeline. This last stage also writes the object to the screen (in standard color). Given that you know each object is processed completely by all stages of the pipeline, the order of the output is as expected. The first number is passed to `foreach`, where it's displayed and then passed to `Write-Output`, where it's displayed again, so you see the sequence 1, 1, 2, 2, 3, 3.

> **NOTE** `Start-Sleep` is used to build sufficient pauses into the execution so that you can see what's happening. Run the code without `Start-Sleep` to see the difference.

Now let's run this command again using `Invoke-Command` in the final stage:

```
PS> 1..3 | foreach {
  Write-Host -ForegroundColor green  $_
  $_; Start-Sleep 5 } |
    Invoke-Command -ComputerName localhost -ScriptBlock { Write-Host }
```

```
1
2
1
3
2
3
```

The order has changed—you see 1 and 2 from the local process in green on a color display, then you see 1 from the remote process (in your normal foreground text color), and so on. The local and remote pipelines are executing at the same time, which is what's causing the changes to the ordering. Predicting the order of the output is made more complicated by the use of buffering and timeouts in the remoting protocol.

You used the `Start-Sleep` command in these examples to force these visible differences. If you take out this command, you'll get a different pattern:

```
PS> 1..3 | foreach { Write-Host $_ -ForegroundColor green ; $_ } |
  Invoke-Command -ComputerName localhost -ScriptBlock { Write-Host }

1
2
3
1
2
3
```

This time, all the local objects are displayed (in green) and then passed to the remoting layer, where they're buffered until they can be delivered to the remote connection. This way, the local side can process all objects before the remote side starts to operate. Concurrent operation and buffering make it appear a bit unpredictable, but if you didn't have the `Write-Host`s in place, it would be unnoticeable. The important thing to understand is that objects being sent to the remote end will be processed concurrently with the local execution. That means the remoting infrastructure doesn't have to buffer everything sent from the local end before starting execution.

Up to now, you've been passing only simple commands to the remote end. But because `Invoke-Command` takes a scriptblock, you can, in practice, send pretty much any valid PowerShell script. You'll take advantage of this fact in the next section when you start to build your multi-machine monitor.

> **NOTE** Why does remoting require scriptblocks? Two reasons: Scriptblocks are always compiled locally so you'll catch syntax errors as soon as the script is loaded, and using scriptblocks limits vulnerability to code injection attacks by validating the script before sending it.

11.2.3 *Solving a real problem: multi-machine monitoring*

In this section, you're going to build a solution for a real management problem: multi-machine monitoring. With this solution, you're going to gather some basic health information from the remote host. The goal is to use this information to determine when a server may have problems such as out of memory, out of disk, or reduced performance due to a high faulting rate. You'll gather the data on the remote host and return it as a hashtable so you can look at it locally.

Your requirements are as follows:

- Collect the amount of free space on the C: drive from the `Get-PSDrive` command.
- Collect the page fault rate retrieved using CIM (WMI).
- Collect the processes consuming the most CPU from `Get-Process` with a pipeline.
- Collect the processes that have the largest working set, also from `Get-Process`.
- Ensure the list of computers you monitor aren't hardcoded into the script; the computers to monitor will be listed in a file.
- Monitor each computer on specific days with the results stored in the file.
- Apply a throttle limit to control how many simultaneous machines are monitored.
- Parameterize the script for ease of use.

This listing shows a solution to the problem using the techniques you've learned so far in the book.

Listing 11.1   Parameterized monitoring script

```
param (
    [string] $serverFile = 'servers.txt',          ❶ Define
    [int] $throttleLimit = 10,                         parameters
    [int] $numProcesses = 5
)

$gatherInformation ={                         ❷ Create
    param ([int] $procLimit = 5)                 scriptblock
    @{
        Date = Get-Date
        FreeSpace = (Get-PSDrive c).Free
        PageFaults = (Get-WmiObject `
            Win32_PerfRawData_PerfOS_Memory).PageFaultsPersec
        TopCPU = Get-Process |
                Sort-Object CPU -Descending |
                Select-Object -First $procLimit
        TopWS = Get-Process |
                Sort-Object WS -Descending |
                Select-Object -First $procLimit
    }
}
                                              ❸ Get servers
$servers = Import-CSV $serverfile |              to monitor
    Where-Object { $_.Day -eq (Get-Date).DayOfWeek } |
    foreach { $_.Name }

Invoke-Command -ThrottleLimit $throttleLimit -ComputerName $servers `
        -ScriptBlock $gatherInformation `
        -ArgumentList $numProcesses          ❹ Perform
                                                 monitoring
```

The first two parameters ❶ are obvious: $ServerFile is the name of the file containing the list of servers to check, and $throttleLimit is the throttle limit (number of simultaneous connections the monitoring script makes to remote machines). The default throttle limit for Invoke-Command is 32. We're deliberately lowering that to ensure we don't overload the local machine.

The third parameter, $numProcesses, controls the number of process objects to include in the TopCPU and TopWS entries in the table returned from the remote host. Although you could in theory trim the list that gets returned locally, you can't add to it, so you need to evaluate this parameter on the remote end to get full control. That means it has to be a parameter to the remote command. This is another reason scriptblocks are useful. You can add parameters to the scriptblock that's executed on the remote end.

The scriptblock to be passed to the remote machines is defined ❷. Notice the parameter on the scriptblock that's executed on the remote end. That's how the number of processes to return is passed to the remote server.

The list of servers is derived from the input file ❸. The contents of servers.txt would look something like this:

```
Name,Day
W16DSC01,Monday
W16TGT01,Tuesday
W16PWA01,Wednesday
W16DSC02,Saturday
W16CN01,Thursday
W16AS01,Friday
```

When you load the servers, you'll do some processing on this list to determine the current day of the week and decide which servers need monitoring.

The final step ❹ is to use Invoke-Command to send the scriptblock to the appropriate servers. Figure 11.4 shows the script in action.

```
Administrator 64 bit C:\scripts\PIA3e                            —    □    ×

PS> .\serverhealth.ps1 -serverFile .\servers.txt -numProcesses 3 | ft -a -Wrap

Name         Value
----         -----
Date         06/05/2017 12:25:19
TopWS        {System.Diagnostics.Process (wsmprovhost),
             System.Diagnostics.Process (MsMpEng), System.Diagnostics.Process
             (WmiPrvSE)}
PageFaults   1773729
FreeSpace    120929492992
TopCPU       {System.Diagnostics.Process (MsMpEng), System.Diagnostics.Process
             (svchost), System.Diagnostics.Process (System)}


PS>
```

Figure 11.4   Listing 11.1 in action

Listing 11.1 was saved as serverhealth.ps1. We decided we needed only the top three processes rather than the default five. The data is returned as a hashtable. Notice that the process data is embedded as objects. You'd need to perform further processing locally if you wanted to drill down into the process objects.

The result is that, with a small amount of code, you've created a flexible framework for an agentless distributed health monitoring system. With this system, you can run this health model on *any* machine without having to worry about whether the script is installed on that machine or whether the machine has the correct version of the script. It's always available and always the right version because the infrastructure is pushing it out to the target machines. You can even have different files of server names if required.

> **NOTE** What we're doing here isn't what most people would call monitoring, which usually implies a continual semi-real-time mechanism for noticing a problem and then generating an alert. This system is certainly not real time, and it's a pull model, not a push. This solution is more appropriate for configuration analysis.

You now have an idea of how to use remoting to execute a command on a remote server. This is a powerful mechanism, but sometimes you need to send more than one command to a server; for example, you might want to run multiple data-gathering scripts, one after the other, on the same machine. Because there's a significant overhead in setting up each remote connection, you don't want to create a new connection for every script you execute. Instead, you want to be able to establish a persistent connection to a machine, run all the scripts, and then shut down the connection.

11.3   *PowerShell remoting sessions and persistent connections*

In the previous section, you learned how to run individual scriptblocks on remote machines. From the user's point of view, the `Invoke-Command` operation is simple, but under the covers the system has to do a lot of work creating, using, and deleting the connection, which makes creating a new connection each time a costly proposition. Also, you can't maintain any state—things like variable settings or function definitions—on the remote host.

To address these issues, in this section we'll show you how to create persistent connections called *sessions* that will give you much better performance when you want to perform a series of interactions with the remote host as well as allow you to maintain remote state. In the simplest terms, a *session* is the environment where PowerShell commands are executed. This is true even when you run the console host, PowerShell.exe. The console host program creates a local session that it uses to execute the commands you type. This session remains alive until you exit the program. When you use remoting to connect to another computer, you're also creating one remote session for every local session you remote from until explicitly closed. An instance of `wsmprovhost.exe` per connecting session will run on the remote host as long as that session is open.

Each session contains all the things you work with in PowerShell—all the variables, all the functions that are defined, and the history of the commands you typed—and each session is independent of any other session. If you want to work with these sessions, you need a way to manipulate them. You do this in the usual way: through objects and cmdlets. PowerShell represents sessions as objects that are of type PSSession.

By default, every time you connect to a remote computer by name with Invoke -Command, a new PSSession object is created to represent the connection to that remote machine. If you're going to run more than one command on a computer, you need a way to create persistent connections to that computer. You can do this with New -PSSession; the syntax for this cmdlet is shown in figure 11.5.

```
New-PSSession [[-ComputerName] <string[]>] [-Credential <pscredential>]
[-Name <string[]>] [-EnableNetworkAccess] [-Port <int>] [-UseSSL]
[-ConfigurationName <string>] [-ApplicationName <string>]
[-ThrottleLimit <int>] [-SessionOption <PSSessionOption>]
[-Authentication <AuthenticationMechanism>]
[-CertificateThumbprint <string>] [<CommonParameters>]
```

Figure 11.5   The syntax for the New-PSSession cmdlet. This cmdlet is used to create persistent connections to a remote computer.

This command has many of the same parameters that you saw in Invoke-Command. The difference is that, for New-PSSession, these parameters are used to configure the persistent session instead of the transient sessions you saw being created by Invoke -Command. The PSSession object returned from New-PSSession can then be used to specify the destination for the remote command instead of the computer name.

The lifetime of the session begins with the call to New-PSSession and persists until it's explicitly destroyed by the call to Remove-PSSession. Let's look at an example that illustrates how much of a performance difference sessions can make. You'll run Get -Date five times using Invoke-Command and see how long it takes using Measure-Command (which measures command execution time).

First, execute the test without sessions:

```
PS> Measure-Command { 1..5 |
foreach { Invoke-Command W16TGT01 {Get-Date} } } |
Format-Table -AutoSize TotalSeconds

TotalSeconds
------------
   4.7129865
```

The result from Measure-Command shows that each operation appears to be taking a little under one second. Modify the example to create a session at the beginning and then reuse it in each call to Invoke-Command:

```
PS> Measure-Command {
  $s = New-PSSession W16TGT01
  1..5 |
```

```
  foreach { Invoke-Command $s {Get-Date} }
    Remove-PSSession $s
} |
Format-Table -AutoSize TotalSeconds

TotalSeconds
------------
   0.8096949
```

This output shows that it's taking about one-sixth the time as the first command. Increasing the number of remote invocations from 5 to 50 results in an execution time of 1.4997587 seconds. Clearly, for this simple example, the time to set up and break down the connection totally dominates the execution time. Other factors affect real scenarios, such as network performance, the size of the script, and the amount of information being transmitted. Still, it's obvious that when multiple interactions are required, using a session will result in substantially better performance.

The downside is that persistent sessions will monopolize your machine's limited resources, so if you forget to close a session, you may soon hit the limits set (max user connections, max connections per server). Cleaning up unrequired sessions is definitely in your best interest. The two most expensive penalties with remoting are setting up the session and serializing the return data. Filtering on the remote machine to reduce the amount of data to be returned can also significantly improve performance.

11.3.1 *Additional session attributes*

This section describes some PSSession attributes that can have an impact on the way you write your scripts.

SESSIONS AND HOSTS

The host application running your scripts can impact the portability of your scripts if you become dependent on specific features of that host. (This is why PowerShell module manifests include the PowerShellHostName and PowerShellHostVersion elements.) Dependency on specific host functionality is a consideration with remote execution because the remote host implementation is used instead of the normal interactive host. This is necessary to manage the extra characteristics of the remote or job environments. This host shows up as a process named wsmprovhost corresponding to the executable wsmprovhost.exe. This host supports only a subset of the features available in the normal interactive PowerShell hosts.

SESSION ISOLATION

Another point is the fact that each session is configured independently when it's created, and once it's constructed, it has its own copy of the engine properties, execution policy, function definitions, and so on. This independent session environment exists for the duration of the session and isn't affected by changes made in other sessions. This principle is called *isolation*—each session is isolated from, and therefore not affected by, any other session.

ONLY ONE COMMAND RUNS AT A TIME

A final characteristic of a session instance is that you can run only one command (or command pipeline) in a session at one time. If you try to run more than one command at a time, a "session busy" error will be raised. But there's some limited command queuing: if there's a request to run a second command synchronously (one at a time), the command will wait up to four minutes for the first command to be completed before generating the "session busy" error. But if a second command is requested to run asynchronously—without waiting—the busy error will be generated immediately.

With some knowledge of the characteristics and limitations of PowerShell sessions, you can start to look at how to use them.

11.3.2 *Using the New-PSSession cmdlet*

In this section, you'll learn how to use the New-PSSession cmdlet. Let's start with an example. First, you'll create a PSSession on the local machine by specifying localhost as the target computer:

```
PS> $s = New-PSSession -ComputerName localhost
```

> **NOTE** By default a user must be running with elevated privileges to create a session on the local machine. You'll see how to change the default setting later.

You now have a PSSession object in the $s variable that you can use to execute remote commands. Earlier we said each session runs in its own process. You can confirm this by using the $PID session variable to see what the process ID of the session process is. First, run this code in the remote session

```
PS> Invoke-Command -Session $s -ScriptBlock {$PID}
9436
```

and you see that the process ID is 9436. When you get the value in the local session by typing $PID at the command line, as shown here

```
PS> $PID
8528
```

you see that the local process ID is 8528.

> **NOTE** The numbers you see may well be different than those shown here. The important point is that the $PID values are different when running locally and through a remoting session.

Now define a variable in the remote session:

```
PS> Invoke-Command -Session $s -ScriptBlock {$x=1234}
```

With this command, you've set the variable $x in the remote session to 1234. This works in much the same way as it does in the local case—changes to the remote environment are persisted across the invocations. You can define a function and make it reference the $x variable you defined earlier:

```
PS> Invoke-Command -Session $s -ScriptBlock {
  function hi {"Hello there, x is $x"}
}
PS> Invoke-Command -Session $s -ScriptBlock {hi}
Hello there, x is 1234
```

You get the preserved value.

> **NOTE** We've had people ask whether other users on the computer can see the sessions we're creating. As mentioned earlier, this isn't the case. Users have access only to the remote sessions they create and only from the sessions they were created from. There's no way for one session to connect to another session that it didn't itself create. The only aspect of a session that may be visible to another user is the existence of the wsmprovhost process hosting the session.

As you've seen, remote execution is like the local case . . . well, almost. You have to type Invoke-Command every time. If you're executing a lot of interactive commands on a specific machine, this task quickly becomes annoying. PowerShell provides a much better way to accomplish this type of task, as you'll see in the next section.

11.3.3 *Interactive sessions*

In the previous sections, you learned how to issue commands to remote machines using Invoke-Command. This approach is effective but gets annoying for more interactive types of work. To make this scenario easier, you can start an *interactive session* using the Enter-PSSession cmdlet. Once you're in an interactive session, the commands you type are automatically passed to the remote computer and executed without having to use Invoke-Command. Let's try this out. You'll reuse the session you created in the previous section. In that session, you defined the variable $x and the function hi. To enter interactive mode during this session, you'll call Enter-PSSession, passing in the session object, as shown in figure 11.6.

> **NOTE** Only interactive commands are transmitted when you use Enter -PSSession. You can't use it in a script and pass commands to the session.

As soon as you enter interactive mode, you see that the prompt changes: it now displays the name of the machine you're connected to and the current directory.

> **NOTE** The default prompt can be changed in the remote session in the same way it can be changed in the local session. If you have a prompt definition in your profile, you may be wondering why that wasn't used. We'll get to that later when we look at some of the things you need to keep in mind when using remoting.

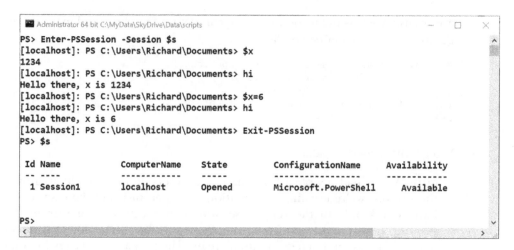

```
Administrator 64 bit C:\MyData\SkyDrive\Data\scripts                    —   □   ✕
PS> Enter-PSSession -Session $s
[localhost]: PS C:\Users\Richard\Documents> $x
1234
[localhost]: PS C:\Users\Richard\Documents> hi
Hello there, x is 1234
[localhost]: PS C:\Users\Richard\Documents> $x=6
[localhost]: PS C:\Users\Richard\Documents> hi
Hello there, x is 6
[localhost]: PS C:\Users\Richard\Documents> Exit-PSSession
PS> $s

 Id Name              ComputerName    State        ConfigurationName      Availability
 -- ----              ------------    -----        -----------------      ------------
  1 Session1          localhost       Opened       Microsoft.PowerShell      Available


PS>
```

Figure 11.6   Using a `PSSession` for interactive remoting

You can see from the code being run in the figure that the value of $x is preserved (1234) and the `hi` function you defined is also available. Changing the value of $x and then rerunning the `hi` function shows the new value displayed in the output.

You can exit an interactive remote session either by using the `exit` keyword or by using the `Exit-PSSession` cmdlet. You see that the prompt changed back and the session still exists. It will persist until explicitly removed with `Remove-PSSession` or the PowerShell instance is closed. You can enter and exit a session as often as you need to as long as it's not removed in the interim.

Another useful feature to consider is the fact that you can have more than one session open at a time. This means you can pop back and forth between multiple computers as needed, which makes dealing with multiple machines convenient.

More differences exist between the pattern where you used `Invoke-Command` for each command and the interactive mode. In the non-interactive `Invoke-Command` case, the remote commands send objects back, where they're formatted on the local machine. In the interactive remoting case, the objects are formatted on the *remote* machine, and simple strings are sent to the local machine to be displayed. Usually this won't matter, but cultural information such as dates and object formatting may be impacted.

Finally, as with the non-interactive remoting case, you can run an interactive session in a temporary session by passing the name of the computer instead of an existing `PSSession`. Using the `PSSession` has the advantage that you can enter and exit the remote session and have the remote state preserved between activities. If the name of the computer is passed in, the connection will be torn down when you exit the session. Because a remote session involves creating a remote host process, forgetting to close your sessions can waste resources. At any point, you can use `Get-PSSession` to get a list of the open sessions you currently have and use `Remove-PSSession` to close them as appropriate.

By now, you should be comfortable with creating and using persistent remote sessions. What we haven't spent much time on yet is how to manage all these connections you're creating.

11.3.4 *Managing PowerShell sessions*

Each PSSession is associated with an underlying Windows process. As such, it consumes significant resources even when no commands are being executed in it. You should delete PSSessions that are no longer needed. This reduces the memory usage and similar drains on the remote system. At the same time, creating new PSSessions also puts a load on the system, consuming additional CPU resources to create each new process. When managing your resource consumption, you need to balance the cost of creating new sessions against the overhead of maintaining multiple sessions. There's no hard-and-fast rule for deciding what this balance should be. In the end, you should decide on an application-by-application basis.

To get a list of the existing PSSessions, you use the Get-PSSession command, and to remove sessions that are no longer needed, you use the Remove-PSSession cmdlet. The Remove-PSSession cmdlet closes the PSSession, which causes the remote process to exit and frees up all the resources it held. Removing the session also frees up local resources like the network connection used to connect to the remote session.

With PowerShell v2 you can view the sessions on the local machine, whereas PowerShell v3 and later enable you to see the sessions on remote as well as local machines. On a local machine, you'll see something like this:

```
PS> Get-PSSession |
Format-List Id, Name, ComputerName, ComputerType, State,
ConfigurationName, Availability

Id                 : 1
Name               : Session1
ComputerName       : W16TGT01
ComputerType       : RemoteMachine
State              : Opened
ConfigurationName  : Microsoft.PowerShell
Availability       : Available
```

The remote machine (use the -ComputerName parameter) may give you results like this:

```
PS> Get-PSSession -ComputerName W16TGT01 |
Format-List Id, Name, ComputerName, ComputerType, State,
ConfigurationName, Availability

Id                 : 1
Name               : Session1
ComputerName       : W16TGT01
ComputerType       : RemoteMachine
State              : Opened
ConfigurationName  : Microsoft.PowerShell
Availability       : Available
```

```
Id                 : 3
Name               : Session1
ComputerName       : W16TGT01
ComputerType       : RemoteMachine
State              : Disconnected
ConfigurationName  : Microsoft.PowerShell
Availability       : Busy
```

In this case, the session with an `Id` of 1 (state is `Opened`) is the session created from your local machine. The session with an `Id` of 3 is another session to the remote machine—in this case, created from a third machine. We know this because we created them. Unfortunately, there's no way to tell who created a session connected to a remote machine or from which machine it was created. Notice that session `Id` 3 is shown with a state of `Disconnected`. This means you aren't connected to it.

> **TIP** The ID number will change every time you access the sessions on the remote machine created by a PowerShell session other than your own. It's worth giving your session distinctive names so that you can easily distinguish between sessions.

On the client end, if you don't explicitly remove the sessions or set timeouts, local sessions will remain open until you end your PowerShell session. But what happens if the client fails for some reason without closing its sessions? If the PowerShell session is closed or the local machine crashes, the remote session will be terminated. If network connectivity is lost or the session times out (the default is two hours), the session may be put into a disconnected state. You can also put a session into a disconnected state manually.

> **NOTE** Commands continue to run in a disconnected session. You can even deliberately create a disconnected session using the `-InDisconnectedSession` parameter of `Invoke-Command`.

The sessions shown earlier in this section have been re-created with distinctive names:

```
PS> Get-PSSession -ComputerName W16TGT01 |
Format-Table Id, Name, ComputerName, State,
Availability -AutoSize

Id Name         ComputerName        State  Availability
-- ----         ------------        -----  ------------
 4 FromW16AS01  W16TGT01           Opened     Available
 5 FromW16DSC01 W16TGT01     Disconnected          Busy
```

`FromW16AS01` is the one from our local machine. That session can be disconnected:

```
PS> Disconnect-PSSession -Name FromW16AS01

Id Name         ComputerName        State  Availability
-- ----         ------------        -----  ------------
 4 FromW16AS01  W16TGT01     Disconnected          None
```

Notice that state changes to `Disconnected` and availability changes to `None`. After closing the PowerShell session that created the session `FromW16AS01` and opening a new PowerShell session, using `Get-PSSession` to test for a session will return nothing as expected—we haven't created any remoting sessions in that PowerShell session.

Now try getting the sessions on the remote server we were working with:

```
PS> Get-PSsession -ComputerName W16TGT01 |
Format-Table Id, Name, ComputerName, State,
Availability -AutoSize

Id Name         ComputerName     State Availability
-- ----         ------------     ----- ------------
 1 FromW16AS01  W16TGT01  Disconnected         None
 2 FromW16DSC01 W16TGT01  Disconnected         Busy
```

You can reconnect to the session—in this case session `FromW16AS01`:

```
PS> Connect-PSSession -ComputerName W16TGT01
Connect-PSSession : Cannot connect PSSession "FromW16DSC01",
either because it is not in the Disconnected state, or it
is not available for connection.
At line:1 char:1
+ Connect-PSSession -ComputerName W16TGT01
+ ~~~~~~~~~~~~~~~~~~~~~~~~~~~~~~~~~~~~~~~~~
    + CategoryInfo          : InvalidOperation: ([PSSession]
  W16TGT01:PSSession) [Connect-PSSession],
RuntimeExcept    ion
    + FullyQualifiedErrorId : PSSessionConnectFailed,Microsoft.PowerShell.
  Commands.ConnectPSSessionCommand

Id Name         ComputerName ComputerType   State  Availability
-- ----         ------------ ------------   -----  ------------
 3 FromW16AS01  W16TGT01     RemoteMachine  Opened Available
```

You can connect to the session `FromW16AS01`, but you can't connect to the session from the third machine because it already has an open connection (hold that thought). Once connected, your session is available for use again:

```
PS> $s = Get-PSSession -Name FromW16AS01
PS> Invoke-Command -Session $s -ScriptBlock `
{Get-CimInstance Win32_OperatingSystem}

SystemDirectory     BuildNumber Version    PSComputerName
---------------     ----------- -------    --------------
C:\Windows\system32 14393       10.0.14393 W16TGT01
<output truncated for brevity>
```

If a session is disconnected from its original host, you can connect to it from either the original host or another machine. After disconnecting the session `FromW16DSC01` from its original host and testing available sessions on the local machine,

```
PS> Get-PSSession -ComputerName W16TGT01 |
Format-Table Id, Name, ComputerName, State,
Availability -AutoSize
```

```
Id Name             ComputerName       State Availability
-- ----             ------------       ----- ------------
 3 FromW16AS01  W16TGT01            Opened    Available
 6 FromW16DSC01 W16TGT01       Disconnected        None
```

you can see that the session `FromW16DSC01` is disconnected and availability is shown as `None`. Connect to it in a similar way as before:

```
PS> Connect-PSSession -Name FromW16DSC01 -ComputerName W16TGT01
PS>  Get-PSSession -ComputerName W16TGT01 |
Format-Table Id, Name, ComputerName, State,
Availability -AutoSize
```

```
Id Name             ComputerName   State Availability
-- ----             ------------   ----- ------------
 3 FromW16AS01  W16TGT01        Opened    Available
 7 FromW16DSC01 W16TGT01        Opened    Available
```

Disconnected sessions created by you on the local or other machine can be reconnected and used as shown. You can even connect to disconnected sessions created by other people as long as you have the credential details they used to create the session originally.

You can also use a PowerShell remoting session for copying files to and from a remote machine.

11.3.5 *Copying files across a PowerShell remoting session*

PowerShell remoting is used to run commands on remote machines, as you saw in earlier sections, and have the results returned to you. In PowerShell v2–v4 you couldn't copy files using a PowerShell remoting session. This changed in PowerShell v5 with the introduction of the `-FromSession` and `-ToSession` parameters on the `Copy-Item` cmdlet. Both of these new parameters take a *single* `PSSession` object as input.

This concept is best described by an example. Start by creating remoting sessions to two machines:

```
PS> $s1 = New-PSSession -ComputerName W16TGT01
PS> $s2 = New-PSSession -ComputerName W16DSC02
```

Now create a file on a remote machine:

```
PS> Invoke-Command -Session $s1 -ScriptBlock {
Get-Process | Out-File -FilePath c:\scripts\proc.txt}
```

You can copy the file from the remote machine to the local machine:

```
PS> Copy-Item -Path c:\scripts\proc.txt -FromSession $s1
```

Check that it arrived and then copy it to the second machine:

```
PS> Copy-Item -Path proc.txt  -Destination C:\Scripts\ -ToSession $s2
```

A simple check confirms that the copy occurred:

```
PS> Invoke-Command -Session $s2 `
-ScriptBlock {Get-ChildItem -Path C:\Scripts\}
```

Everyone looks at the sequence of commands and thinks we can combine the copy steps:

```
PS> Copy-Item -Path c:\scripts\proc.txt  -Destination C:\Scripts\ `
-FromSession $s1  -ToSession $s2
Copy-Item : '-FromSession' and '-ToSession' are mutually exclusive and cannot
  be specified at the same time.
At line:1 char:1
+ Copy-Item -Path c:\scripts\proc.txt  -Destination C:\Scripts\ -FromSe ...
+ ~~~~~~~~~~~~~~~~~~~~~~~~~~~~~~~~~~~~~~~~~~~~~~~~~~~~~~~~~~~~~~~~~~~~~~~~~~~
    + CategoryInfo          : InvalidArgument: (Microsoft.Power...namicParame
   ters:CopyItemDynamicParameters) [Copy-Item],
   ArgumentException
    + FullyQualifiedErrorId : InvalidInput,Microsoft.PowerShell.Commands.
   CopyItemCommand
```

Unfortunately, we can't. The `-FromSession` and `-ToSession` parameters are mutually exclusive.

> **NOTE** This isn't obvious from the help file because the parameters are shown in the same parameter set and their mutual exclusivity isn't mentioned in the text.

You can copy multiple files across a PowerShell remoting session using wildcards to define the files.

11.4 *Implicit remoting*

When doing non-interactive remoting, you have to call `Invoke-Command` every time you want to execute a remote operation. You can avoid this task by using `Enter-PSSession` to set up a remote interactive session. This approach makes remote execution easy but at the cost of making local operations difficult. In this section, we'll look at a mechanism that makes both local and remote command execution easy. This mechanism is called *implicit remoting*.

> **NOTE** For implicit remoting to work, the execution policy on the client machine has to be configured to allow scripts to run, typically by setting it to `RemoteSigned`. This is necessary because implicit remoting generates a temporary module, and PowerShell must be allowed to execute scripts in order to load this module. If execution policy is set to `Restricted` or `AllSigned`, it won't be able to do this. This requirement applies only to the local client machine. A remote server can still use a more restrictive policy. See section 7.1.1 for more information about execution policy.

The goals of implicit remoting are to make the fact that remote operations are occurring invisible to the user and to have all operations look as much like local operations as possible. You can accomplish this goal by generating *local proxy functions* that run the remote commands under the covers. The user calls the local proxy, which takes care of the details involved in making the remote command invocation.

The net effect is that everything looks like a local operation because everything *is* a local operation.

11.4.1 *Using implicit remoting*

To set up the remote proxy functions mentioned in the previous section, use the Import-PSSession cmdlet. The syntax for this cmdlet is shown in figure 11.7.

```
Import-PSSession [-Session] <PSSession> [[-CommandName] <string[]>]
[[-FormatTypeName] <string[]>] [-Prefix <string>] [-DisableNameChecking]
[-AllowClobber] [-ArgumentList <Object[]>]
[-CommandType <CommandTypes>] [-Module <string[]>]
[-FullyQualifiedModule <ModuleSpecification[]>]
[-Certificate <X509Certificate2>] [<CommonParameters>]
```

Figure 11.7   The syntax for the Import-PSSession **cmdlet. This cmdlet is used to create local proxy commands that invoke the corresponding remote command on the target computer.**

Let's explore how this cmdlet works by walking through an example. You'll create a PSSession and then define a function in that session. The goal is to be able to execute this remote function as though it were defined locally. You want to implicitly remote the function. To do that, you call Import-PSSession, which generates a function that you can call locally. This local function does the remote call on your behalf—it acts as your *proxy*.

You'll begin by creating the connection to a remote machine. You may need to get credentials for the remote host.

> **NOTE** In a domain environment, this step is unnecessary as long as your user account has sufficient privileges to access the remote endpoint. But if you want to log on as a different user, credentials will be required.

Establish a session on the remote machine, using credentials if necessary, as shown in figure 11.8.

Next, you'll use Invoke-Command to define a new function on the remote machine. This is the command you'll import:

```
PS> Invoke-Command -Session $s -ScriptBlock {
function Get-Bios {Get-WmiObject Win32_Bios}}
```

The new remote function, called Get-Bios, uses Windows Management Instrumentation (WMI) to retrieve information about the BIOS on the remote machine. Invoke this function through explicit remoting using Invoke-Command so you can see that it

```
■ Administrator 64 bit C:\scripts                                          —   □   ✕
PS> $s = New-PSSession -ComputerName W16TGT01
PS> Invoke-Command -Session $s -ScriptBlock {function Get-Bios {Get-WmiObject Win32_Bios}}
PS> Invoke-Command -Session $s -ScriptBlock {Get-Bios}


SMBIOSBIOSVersion : Hyper-V UEFI Release v1.0
Manufacturer      : Microsoft Corporation
Name              : Hyper-V UEFI Release v1.0
SerialNumber      : 8265-3792-6973-7306-2850-7895-37
Version           : VRTUAL - 1
PSComputerName    : W16TGT01



PS> Import-PSSession -Session $s -CommandName Get-Bios

ModuleType Version    Name                                   ExportedCommands
---------- -------    ----                                   ----------------
Script     1.0        tmp_4qxsxsjw.5m2                       Get-Bios


PS> Get-Bios


SMBIOSBIOSVersion : Hyper-V UEFI Release v1.0
Manufacturer      : Microsoft Corporation
Name              : Hyper-V UEFI Release v1.0
SerialNumber      : 8265-3792-6973-7306-2850-7895-37
Version           : VRTUAL - 1
```

Figure 11.8 Example of implicit remoting

returns a set of information about the BIOS on the remote machine. Now use Import-PSSession to create a local proxy for this command:

```
PS> Import-PSSession -Session $s -CommandName Get-Bios

ModuleType Version    Name                 ExportedCommands
---------- -------    ----                 ----------------
Script     1.0        tmp_4qxsxsjw.5m2     Get-Bios
```

You might recognize the output from this command—it's the same thing you see when you do Get-Module. You now have a local Get-Bios command. Try running it:

```
PS> Get-Bios

SMBIOSBIOSVersion : Hyper-V UEFI Release v1.0
Manufacturer      : Microsoft Corporation
Name              : Hyper-V UEFI Release v1.0
SerialNumber      : 8265-3792-6973-7306-2850-7895-37
Version           : VRTUAL - 1
```

You get the same result you saw when you did the explicit remote invocation but without having to do any extra work to access the remote machine. The proxy command did that for you. This is the goal of implicit remoting: to make the fact that the command is being executed remotely invisible.

NOTE   This is a useful technique because you need to import the Exchange management module into your session if you're administering an Exchange server over a PowerShell remoting session.

Let's see how it all works.

11.4.2 *How implicit remoting works*

When the user requests that a command be imported, a message is sent to the remote computer for processing. The import request processor looks up the command and retrieves the metadata (the `CommandInfo` object) for that command. That metadata is processed to simplify it, removing things like complex type attributes. Only the core remoting types are passed along. This metadata is received by the local machine's proxy function generator. It uses this metadata to generate a function that will implicitly call the remote command.

Let's take a closer look at what the generated proxy looks like. You can see the imported `Get-Bios` command using `Get-Command`:

```
PS> Get-Command Get-Bios

CommandType Name      Version Source
----------- ----      ------- ------
Function    Get-Bios 1.0      tmp_4qxsxsjw.5m2
```

The output shows that you have a local function called `Get-Bios`. You can look at the definition of that function by using the `Definition` property on the `CommandInfo` object returned by `Get-Command`.

Listing 11.2 Definition of the `Get-Bios` proxy function

```
param(
    [switch]${AsJob}
)

Begin {
        try {
            $positionalArguments =
            & $script:NewObject collections.arraylist
            foreach ($parameterName in
                 $PSBoundParameters.BoundPositionally)
            {
                $null = $positionalArguments.Add(
                $PSBoundParameters[$parameterName] )
                $null = $PSBoundParameters.Remove($parameterName)
            }
            $positionalArguments.AddRange($args)
```

```
            $clientSideParameters =
            Get-PSImplicitRemotingClientSideParameters`
            $PSBoundParameters $False

            $scriptCmd = { & $script:InvokeCommand `
                            @clientSideParameters `
                            -HideComputerName `
                            -Session (Get-PSImplicitRemotingSession `
                            -CommandName 'Get-Bios') `
                            -Arg ('Get-Bios', $PSBoundParameters,
                            $positionalArguments) `
                            -Script { param($name, $boundParams,
                            $unboundParams) & $name @boundParams
                            @unboundParams }`
                        }

            $steppablePipeline =
            $scriptCmd.GetSteppablePipeline($myInvocation.CommandOrigin)
            $steppablePipeline.Begin($myInvocation.ExpectingInput,
            $ExecutionContext)
        } catch {
            throw
        }
    }
    Process {
    try {
        $steppablePipeline.Process($_)
    } catch {
        throw
    }
}
    End {
    try {
        $steppablePipeline.End()
    } catch {
        throw
    }
}

    # .ForwardHelpTargetName Get-Bios
    # .ForwardHelpCategory Function
    # .RemoteHelpRunspace PSSession
```

Even though this output has been reformatted a bit to make it more readable, it's a pretty complex function and uses many of the more sophisticated features covered in previous chapters. It uses advanced functions, splatting, scriptblocks, and steppable pipelines. Fortunately, you never have to write these functions yourself.

NOTE You don't have to create proxy functions for this particular scenario, but in section 11.5.2 you saw how this technique can be powerful in extending the PowerShell environment.

The `Import-PSSession` cmdlet does this for you. It will create a proxy function for each command it's importing, which could lead to many commands. As well as generating proxy functions on your behalf, Import-PSSession creates a module to contain these functions.

The module name and path are temporary generated names. This module also defines an OnRemove handler (see chapter 9) to clean up when the module is removed. To see the contents of the module, you can look at the temporary file that was created by using the module's Path property:

```
PS> Get-Content (Get-Command Get-Bios).Module.Path
```

Alternatively, you can save the session to an explicitly named module for reuse with Export-PSSession. You'll save this session as a module called bios:

```
PS> Export-PSSession -OutputModule bios -Session $s `
-type function -CommandName Get-Bios -AllowClobber

        Directory: C:\Users\Richard\Documents\WindowsPowerShell\Modules\bios

Mode                LastWriteTime         Length Name
----                -------------         ------ ----
-a----        08/05/2017     11:51            99 bios.format.ps1xml
-a----        08/05/2017     11:51           528 bios.psd1
-a----        08/05/2017     11:51         11627 bios.psm1
```

Executing this command creates a new module in your user module directory. It creates the script module file (.psm1), the module manifest (.psd1), and a file containing formatting information for the command. You use the -AllowClobber parameter because the export is using the remote session to gather the data. If it finds a command being exported that already exists in the caller's environment, that would be an error. Because Get-Bios already exists, you have to use -AllowClobber.

Import the module into a new PowerShell session—remember to open it with elevated privileges:

```
PS> Import-Module bios
```

It returns right away. It can do this because it hasn't set up the remote connection yet. This will happen the first time you access one of the functions in the module. Run Get-Bios:

```
PS> Get-Bios
Creating a new session for implicit remoting of "Get-Bios" command...
The term 'Get-Bios' is not recognized as the name of a cmdlet, function,
    script file, or operable program. Check the spelling of the name, or if
a path was included, verify that the path is correct and try again.
    + CategoryInfo          : ObjectNotFound: (Get-Bios:String) [],
    CommandNotFoundException
    + FullyQualifiedErrorId : CommandNotFoundException
    + PSComputerName        : W16TGT01
```

When you run this command, you see a message indicating that a new connection is being created. But then you get an error saying the command Get-Bios isn't found.

That's because you're dynamically adding the function to the remote session. When you establish a new session, because you're not adding the function, it isn't there. In the next section, we'll describe how to create remote endpoints that always contain your custom functions. There are a few other issues you need to be aware of when running commands remotely. We'll look at those next.

11.5 Considerations when running commands remotely

When you run commands on multiple computers, you need to be aware, at least to some extent, of how the execution environment can differ on the target machines. For example, the target machine may be running a different version of the operating system or it may have a different processor. There may also be differences in which applications are installed, how files are arranged, or where things are placed in the registry. In this section, we'll look at a number of these issues. Don't be put off by these issues—they're not meant to scare you. They're edge cases you need to be aware of to get the most out of PowerShell remoting.

11.5.1 Remote session startup directory

When a user connects to a remote computer, the system sets the startup directory for the remote session to a specific value. This value will change depending on the version of the operating system on the target machine. If the machine is running Windows Vista, Windows Server 2003 R2, or a later version of Windows, the default starting location for the session is the user's home directory, which is typically C:\Users\<UserName>.

On Windows Server 2003, the user's home directory is also used: C:\Documents\Settings\<UserName>. For Windows XP, the default user's home directory is used: C:\Documents\Settings\Default User.

> **NOTE** Windows Server 2003 and Windows XP are no longer supported by Microsoft and so should be less likely to be found in use with time. But from experience we can say that unsupported operating systems can easily linger for 10 years or more because of a special application that has to run on a particular version of Windows.

The default starting location can be obtained from either the $ENV:HOMEPATH environment or the PowerShell $HOME variable. By using these variables instead of hardcoded paths in your scripts, you can avoid problems related to these differences.

11.5.2 Profiles and remoting

Most PowerShell users eventually create a custom startup script or profile that they use to customize their environment. These customizations typically include defining convenience functions and aliases. Although profiles are a great feature for customizing local interactive sessions, if the convenience commands they define are used in scripts that you want to run remotely, you'll encounter problems. That's because your profiles *aren't* run automatically in remote sessions, and that means the convenience commands defined in the profile aren't available in the remote session. In fact, the $PROFILE variable, which points to the profile file, isn't even populated for remote sessions.

As a best practice, for production scripting you should make sure your scripts never become contaminated with elements defined by your profiles. One way to test this is to run the script from PowerShell.exe with the -NoProfile option, which looks like this:

```
powershell -NoProfile -File myscript.ps1
```

This command will run the script without loading your profile. If the script depends on anything defined in the profile, it will generate errors.

But for remote interactive sessions, it'd be nice to have the same environment everywhere. You can accomplish this by using Invoke-Command with the -FilePath parameter to send your profile file to the remote machine and execute it there. The set of commands you need to accomplish this are:

```
PS> $c = Get-Credential
PS> $s = New-PSSession -Credential $c -ComputerName targetComputer
PS> Invoke-Command -Session $s -FilePath $PROFILE
PS> Enter-PSSession $s
```

First, you get the credential for the target machine (this typically won't be needed in the domain environment). Next, you create a persistent session to the remote computer. Then you use -FilePath on Invoke-Command to execute the profile file in the remote session. With the session properly configured, you can call Enter-PSSession to start your remote interactive session with all your normal customizations.

Alternatively, sometimes you may want to run a profile on the remote machine instead of your local profile. Because $PROFILE isn't populated in your remote session, you'll need to be clever to make this work. The key is that although $PROFILE isn't set, $HOME is. You can use this to compose a path to your profile on the remote computer. The revised list of commands looks like this:

```
PS> $c = Get-Credential
PS> $s = New-PSSession -Credential $ -ComputerName targetComputer
PS> Invoke-Command -Session $s {
  . "$home\Documents\WindowsPowerShell\profile.ps1" }
PS> Enter-PSSession $s
```

This command dot-sources (see section 7.1.4) the profile file in the user's directory on the remote machine into the session.

> **NOTE** This script won't work on XP or Windows Server 2003. Change the script to use "$home\Documents and Setting\WindowsPowerShell\profile.ps1" as the profile path.

In this section, you learned how to cause your profile to be used to configure the remote session environment. Next, we'll examine another area where these variations can cause problems.

11.5.3 *Issues running executables remotely*

PowerShell remoting allows you to execute the same types of commands remotely as you can locally, including external applications or executables. The ability to remotely execute commands like shutdown to restart a remote host or ipconfig to get network settings is critical for system management.

For the most part, console-based commands will work properly because they read and write only to the standard input, output, and error pipes. Commands that won't work are ones that directly call the Windows Console APIs, like console-based editors or text-based menu programs. The reason is that no console object is available in the remote session. Because these applications are rarely used any longer, this fact typically won't have a big impact. But there are some surprises. For example, the net command will work fine most of the time, but if you do something like this (which prompts for a password)

```
PS> net use p: '\\machine1\c$'  /user:machine1\user1 *
Type the password for \\machine1\c$:
```

in a remote session, you'll get an error:

```
[machine1]: > net use p: '\\machine1\c$'  /user:machine1\user1 *
net.exe : System error 86 has occurred.
    + CategoryInfo          : NotSpecified: (System error 86 has
      occurred.:String) [], RemoteException
    + FullyQualifiedErrorId : NativeCommandError

The specified network password is not correct.
Type the password for \\machine1\c$:
[machine1]: >
```

This command prompts for a password and returns an empty string.

The other kind of program that won't work properly is commands that try to open a user interface (also known as "try to pop GUI") on the remote computer. The program starts, but no window will appear. If the command eventually completes, control will be returned to the caller and things will be more or less fine. But if the process is blocked while waiting for the user to provide some input to the invisible GUI, the command will hang and you must stop it manually by pressing Ctrl-C. If the keypress doesn't work, you'll have to use some other mechanism to terminate the process.

One thing we can guarantee is that you'll need to access files—but when you're working remotely, how do you know which files you're using?

11.5.4 *Using files and scripts*

When you enter an interactive PowerShell session and access a file, such as a script or text file, you're obviously using the file on the remote machine. Remember that an interactive session is effectively like running a PowerShell session directly on the machine. But what about when you use Invoke-Command either directly or through a remoting session?

We're going to be running a number of commands to the remote computer (W16TGT01), so we'll create a remoting session:

```
PS> $s = New-PSSession -ComputerName W16TGT01
```

On the W16TGT01 machine, a file exists with these two lines:

```
Write-Host 'Run from W16TGT01'
Write-Host $env:COMPUTERNAME
```

You know that Invoke-Command is used to run commands through a remoting session:

```
PS> Invoke-Command -Session $s -ScriptBlock {C:\Scripts\PiA3e\FileTest.ps1}
Run from W16TGT01
W16TGT01
```

Sometimes you may have a script on your local machine that you need to run on remote machines. One solution would be to copy the script to the remote machines and run it as in the previous example. That would be inefficient if you're dealing with hundreds or thousands of machines.

You can run a local script through a remoting session. Given a script on the local machine

```
Write-Host 'Run from W16AS01'
Write-Host $env:COMPUTERNAME
```

the -FilePath parameter is used to invoke a local script:

```
PS> Invoke-Command -Session $s -FilePath C:\Scripts\PiA3e\FileTest.ps1
Run from W16AS01
W16TGT01
```

Notice that the computer name that's reported is the remote machine rather than the local machine, even though you're running the script from your local disk.

One of the tenets of PowerShell remoting is isolation, but you can access local variables as well as local scripts.

11.5.5 *Using local variables in remote sessions*

When you use a variable in the scriptblock of a command sent to a remote machine, the assumption is that the variable is defined only in the session for the remote machine. For example, define a variable locally:

```
PS> $myvar = 123
```

Now, using the remoting session from the previous section (re-create a session if you closed that session), invoke a command using a variable with the same name:

```
PS> Invoke-Command -Session $s -ScriptBlock {"myvar is $myvar"}
myvar is
```

In the output of the command, you can see that the variable value was not made available in the remote session. In chapters 6 and 7 we discussed scope modifiers and, for instance, how you can use variables from the global scope in your functions by prefixing them with $global:. PowerShell remoting provides a similar (but not identical) mechanism to allow you to use local variables in remote sessions, by using the $using: prefix. Let's try the previous example again, but this time we'll prefix the variable with $using:

```
PS> Invoke-Command -Session $s -ScriptBlock {"myvar is $using:myvar"}
Myvar is 123
```

Here's what's happening: By prefixing the variable name with $using (introduced in PowerShell v3), you're telling PowerShell to *copy* the local value of the variable into the remote session. You're *using* the local variable in the remote session. Where this differs from scope modifiers is that it's one-way only. Changing the variable in the remote session won't change the value of the local value. In fact, if you try to change the value of the $using variable in the remote session, you'll get an error:

```
PS> Invoke-Command -Session $s { $using:myvar = 13 }
At line:1 char:30
+   invoke-command -localhost { $using:myvar = 13 }
+                               ~~~~~~~~~~~~~
The assignment expression is not valid. The input to an assignment operator
    must be an object that is able to accept assignments, such as a variable
    or a property.
    + CategoryInfo          : ParserError: (:) [],
    ParentContainsErrorRecordException
    + FullyQualifiedErrorId : InvalidLeftHandSide
```

Now let's look at more areas where accessing the console can cause problems and how to avoid these problems.

11.5.6 *Reading and writing to the console*

As you saw in the previous section, executables that read and write directly to the console won't work properly. The same considerations apply to scripts that do things like call the System.Console APIs directly themselves. For example, call the [Console]::WriteLine() and [Console]::ReadLine() APIs in a remote session:

```
[machine1]: > [Console]::WriteLine('hi')
[machine1]: >
[machine1]: > [Console]::ReadLine()
[machine1]: >
```

Neither of these calls works properly. When you call the [Console]::WriteLine() API, nothing is displayed, and when you call the [Console]::ReadLine() API, it returns immediately instead of waiting for input.

It's still possible to write interactive scripts, but you have to use the PowerShell host cmdlets and APIs:

```
[machine1]: > Write-Host Hi
Hi
[machine1]: >
[machine1]: > Read-Host "Input"
Input: some input
some input
```

If you use these cmdlets as shown in the example, you can read and write to and from the host, and the remoting subsystem will take care of making everything work.

With console and GUI issues out of the way, let's explore how remoting affects the objects you're passing back and forth.

11.5.7 *Remote output vs. local output*

Much of the power in PowerShell comes from the fact that it passes around objects instead of strings. In this section, you'll learn how remoting affects these objects.

When PowerShell commands are run locally, you're working directly with the live .NET objects, which means that you can use the properties and methods on these objects to manipulate the underlying system state. The same isn't true when you're working with remote objects. Remote objects are *serialized*—converted into a form that can be passed over the remote connection—when they're transmitted between the client and the server, and *deserialized* when received by the client machine.

> **NOTE** The biggest difference you'll find is that the objects returned from a remoting session don't have any of the methods you'd have available from the same object generated locally.

Typically, you can use deserialized objects as you'd use live objects, but you must be aware of their limitations. Another thing to be aware of is that the objects that are returned through remoting will have had properties added that allow you to determine the origin of the command.

POWERSHELL SERIALIZATION

Because you can't guarantee that every computer has the same set of types, the PowerShell team chose to limit the number of types that serialize with *fidelity*, where the remote type is the same type as the local type and the object is fully re-created at the receiving end. To address the restrictions of a bounded set of types, types that aren't serialized with fidelity are serialized as a collection of properties, also called a *property bag*. This property bag has a special property, TypeNames, which records the name of the original type. The serialization code takes each object and adds all its properties to the property bag. Recursively, it looks at values of each the members. If the member value isn't one of the ones supported with fidelity, a new property bag is created, with members of the member's values added to it, and so on. This approach preserves structure if not the type and allows remoting to work uniformly everywhere.

DEFAULT SERIALIZATION DEPTH

The approach we have described allows any object to be encoded and transferred to another system. But there's another thing to consider: objects have members that contain objects that contain members, and so on. The full tree of objects and members can be complex. Transferring all the data makes the system unmanageably slow. This is addressed by introducing the idea of serialization depth. The recursive encoding of members stops when this serialization depth is reached. The default for objects is 1.

The final source of issues when writing portable, remotable scripts has to do with processor architectures and the operating system differences they entail. We'll work through this final set of issues in the next section of this chapter.

11.5.8 *Processor architecture issues*

The last potential source of problems we'll explore is the fact that the target machine may be running on a different processor architecture (64-bit versus 32-bit) than the local machine. If the remote computer is running a 64-bit version of Windows and the remote command is targeting a 32-bit session configuration, such as Microsoft.Power-Shell32, the remoting infrastructure loads a Windows 32-bit process on a Windows 64-bit (WOW64) process, and Windows automatically redirects all references to the $ENV:Windir\System32 directory to the $ENV:WINDIR\SysWOW64 directory. For the most part, everything will still work (that's the point of the redirection), unless you try to invoke an executable in the System32 directory that doesn't have a corresponding equivalent in the SysWOW64 directory.

To find the processor architecture for the session, you can check the value of the $ENV:PROCESSOR_ARCHITECTURE variable. The following command finds the processor architecture of the session in the $s variable. Try this first with the 32-bit configuration:

```
PS> Invoke-Command -ConfigurationName microsoft.powershell32 `
-ComputerName localhost { $ENV:PROCESSOR_ARCHITECTURE }
x86
```

You get the expected x86 result, indicating a 32-bit session, and on the 64-bit configuration

```
PS> Invoke-Command -ConfigurationName microsoft.powershell `
-ComputerName localhost { $ENV:PROCESSOR_ARCHITECTURE }
AMD64
```

you get AMD64, indicating a 64-bit configuration.

This is the last remoting consideration we're going to look at in this chapter. Don't let these issues scare you—remember, they're mostly edge cases. With some attention to detail, the typical script should have no problems working as well remotely as it does locally. The PowerShell remoting system goes to great lengths to facilitate a seamless remote execution experience. But it's always better to have a heads-up on some of the issues so you'll know where to start looking if you run into a problem.

Up to now we've been using the default remoting configuration. In the next section, we'll look at how you can create and configure your own specialized remoting configuration.

11.6   *Building custom remoting services*

So far, we've looked at remoting from the service consumer perspective. It's time for you to take on the role of service creator instead.

The most common remoting scenario for administrators is the one-to-many configuration, in which one client computer connects to a number of remote machines in order to execute remote commands on those machines. This is called the *fan-out* scenario because the connections fan out from a single point, and this is what you've been using in the previous sections.

In enterprises and hosted solution scenarios, you'll find the opposite configuration, where many client computers connect to a single remote computer, such as a file server or a kiosk. This many-to-one arrangement is known as the *fan-in* configuration. This mechanism is used when remote connecting to Exchange servers or Active Directory domain controllers.

Windows PowerShell remoting supports both fan-out and fan-in configurations. In the fan-out configuration, PowerShell remoting connects to the remote machine using the WinRM service running on the target machine. When the client connects to the remote computer, the WS-MAN protocol is used to establish a connection to the WinRM service. The WinRM service then launches a new process (wsmprovhost.exe) that loads a plug-in that hosts the PowerShell engine.

PowerShell remoting protocols

The transport mechanism used in PowerShell remoting consists of a five-layer stack. The stack (from top to bottom) consists of the following:

- *The PowerShell Remoting Protocol (MS-PSRP)*—https://msdn.microsoft.com/en-us/library/dd357801.aspx
- *WS-MAN (implemented by the WinRM service)*—http://mng.bz/DB74 and https://msdn.microsoft.com/en-us/library/cc251395.aspx.
- *Simple Object Access Protocol (SOAP)*—Provides an XML-based messaging framework
- HTTP and HTTPS
- TCP/IP

Creating a new process for each session is fine if there aren't many users connecting to the service. But if several connections are expected, as is the case for a high-volume service, the one-process-per-user model won't scale well. To address this issue, an alternate hosting model, targeted at developers, is available for building custom fan-in applications on top of PowerShell remoting. Instead of using the WinRM service to host WS-MAN and the PowerShell plug-in, Internet Information Services (IIS) is used. In this model, instead of starting each user session in a separate process, all the PowerShell sessions are run in the same process along with the WS-MAN protocol engine.

Having all the sessions running in the same process has certain implications. Because PowerShell lets you get at pretty much everything in a process, multiple users running unrestricted in the same process could interfere with one another. On the other hand, because the host process persists across multiple connections, it's possible to share process-wide resources like database connections between sessions.

Given the lack of session isolation, this approach isn't intended for full-featured general-purpose PowerShell remoting. Instead, it's designed for use with constrained, special-purpose applications using PowerShell remoting. To build these applications, you need two things:

- A way to create a constrained application environment
- A way to connect to PowerShell remoting so the user gets the environment you've created instead of the default PowerShell configuration

We'll start with the second one first and look at how you specify custom remoting endpoints.

11.6.1 *Working with custom configurations*

When connecting to a computer by name through PowerShell remoting, the remoting infrastructure will always connect to the default PowerShell remoting service. In the non-default connection case, you also have to specify the *configuration* on the target computer to connect to. A configuration is made up of three elements:

- The name you use to connect to the endpoint
- A script that will be run to configure the sessions that will run in the endpoint
- An ACL used to control who has access to the endpoint

When using the `Invoke-Command`, `New-PSSession`, or `Enter-PSSession` cmdlets, you can use the `-ConfigurationName` parameter to specify the name of the session configuration you want to connect to. Alternatively, you can override the normal default configuration by setting the `$PSSessionConfigurationName` preference variable to the name of the endpoint you want to connect to.

When you connect to the named endpoint, a PowerShell session will be created, and then the configuration script associated with the endpoint will be executed. This configuration script should define the set of capabilities available when connecting to that endpoint. For example, there may be different endpoints for different types of management tasks—managing a mail server, managing a database server, or managing a web server. For each task, a specific endpoint would be configured to expose the appropriate commands (and constraints) required for performing that task.

11.6.2 *Creating a custom configuration*

Continuing our theme of remote monitoring from section 11.2.3, let's create a configuration that exposes a single custom command, Get-PageFaultRate. This command will return the page fault rate from the target computer.

SESSION CONFIGURATION

Every remoting connection will use one of the named configurations on the remote computer. These configurations set up the environment for the session and determine the set of commands visible to users of that session.

When remoting is initially enabled, a default configuration is created on the system called Microsoft.PowerShell (on 64-bit operating systems, there's also the Microsoft.PowerShell32 endpoint). This endpoint is configured to load the default PowerShell configuration with *all* commands enabled. The security descriptor for this configuration is set so that only members of the local Administrators group can access the endpoint.

You can use the session configuration cmdlets to modify these default session configurations, to create new session configurations, and to change the security descriptors of all the session configurations. These cmdlets are shown in table 11.4.

Table 11.4   The cmdlets for managing the remoting endpoint configurations

Cmdlet	Description
Disable-PSSessionConfiguration	Denies access to the specified session configuration on the local computer by adding an "Everyone AccessDenied" entry to the access control list (ACL) on the configuration
Enable-PSSessionConfiguration	Enables existing session configurations on the local computer to be accessed remotely
Get-PSSessionConfiguration	Gets a list of the existing, registered session configurations on the computer
Register-PSSessionConfiguration	Creates and registers a new session configuration
Set-PSSessionConfiguration	Changes the properties of an existing session configuration
Unregister-PSSessionConfiguration	Deletes the specified registered session configurations from the computer
New-PSSessionConfigurationFile	Creates a PowerShell data language file (see module manifests) with a .pssc extension that defines a session configuration
Test-PSSessionConfigurationFile	Validates the contents of a session configuration file, verifying that the keys and values in the file are all valid (introduced in PowerShell v4).

REGISTERING THE ENDPOINT CONFIGURATION

Endpoints are created using the `Register-PSSessionConfiguration` cmdlet and are customized by registering a startup script. In this example, you'll use a simple startup script that defines a single function, `Get-PageFaultRate`. The script looks like this:

```
PS> @'
function Get-PageFaultRate {
 (Get-WmiObject Win32_PerfRawData_PerfOS_Memory).PageFaultsPersec
}
'@ > Initialize-HMConfiguration.ps1
```

Before you can use this function, you need to register the configuration, specifying the full path to the startup script. Call this new configuration wpia1. From an elevated PowerShell session, run the following command to create the endpoint:

```
PS> Register-PSSessionConfiguration -Name wpia1 `
-StartupScript $pwd/Initialize-HMConfiguration.ps1 -Force

     WSManConfig: Microsoft.WSMan.Management\WSMan::localhost\Plugin

Type            Keys                            Name
----            ----                            ----
Container       {Name=wpia1}                    wpia1
```

The output of the command shows that you've created an endpoint in the WSMan plug-in folder. To confirm this use (see figure 11.9), run the following:

```
PS> dir  wsman:\localhost\plugin
```

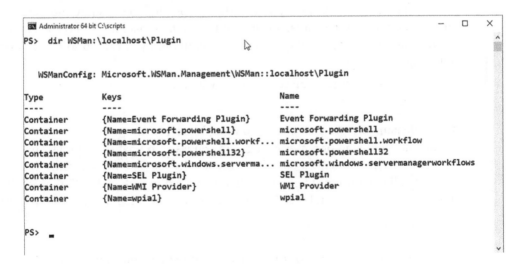

Figure 11.9 Remoting endpoints including the newly created wpia1

This shows a list of all the existing endpoints, including the one you created, `wpia1`. Now test this endpoint with `Invoke-Command` and run the function defined by the startup script:

```
PS> Invoke-Command localhost -ConfigurationName wpia1 {
Get-PageFaultRate }
68200956
```

This code verifies that the endpoint exists and is properly configured. Now clean up by unregistering the endpoint:

```
PS> Unregister-PSSessionConfiguration -Name wpia1 -Force
```

Rerun the `dir` command in figure 11.9 to verify that the endpoint has been removed.

This covers the basic tasks needed to create a custom PowerShell remoting endpoint using a configuration script to *add* additional functionality to the session defaults. Our ultimate goal, though, is to create a custom endpoint with *reduced* functionality, exposing a restricted set of commands to qualified users, so clearly, we aren't finished yet. There are two remaining pieces to look at: controlling individual command visibility, which we'll get to in a while, and controlling overall access to the endpoint, our next topic.

11.6.3 *Access controls and endpoints*

By default, only members of the Administrators group on a computer have permission to use the default session configurations. To allow users who aren't part of the Administrators group to connect to the local computer, you have to give those users Execute permissions on the session configurations for the desired endpoint on the target computer. For example, if you want to enable non-administrators to connect to the default remoting `Microsoft.PowerShell` endpoint, you can do so by running the following command:

```
PS> Set-PSSessionConfiguration Microsoft.PowerShell `
-ShowSecurityDescriptorUI
```

This code launches the dialog box shown in figure 11.10.

You add the name of a user or a group you want to enable to the list, then select the Execute (Invoke) check box. Then dismiss the dialog box by clicking OK. At this point, you'll get a prompt telling you that you need to restart the WinRM service for the change to take effect. Do so by running `Restart-Service winrm` as shown here:

```
PS> Restart-Service winrm
```

Once the service is restarted, the user or group you've enabled can connect to the machine using remoting.

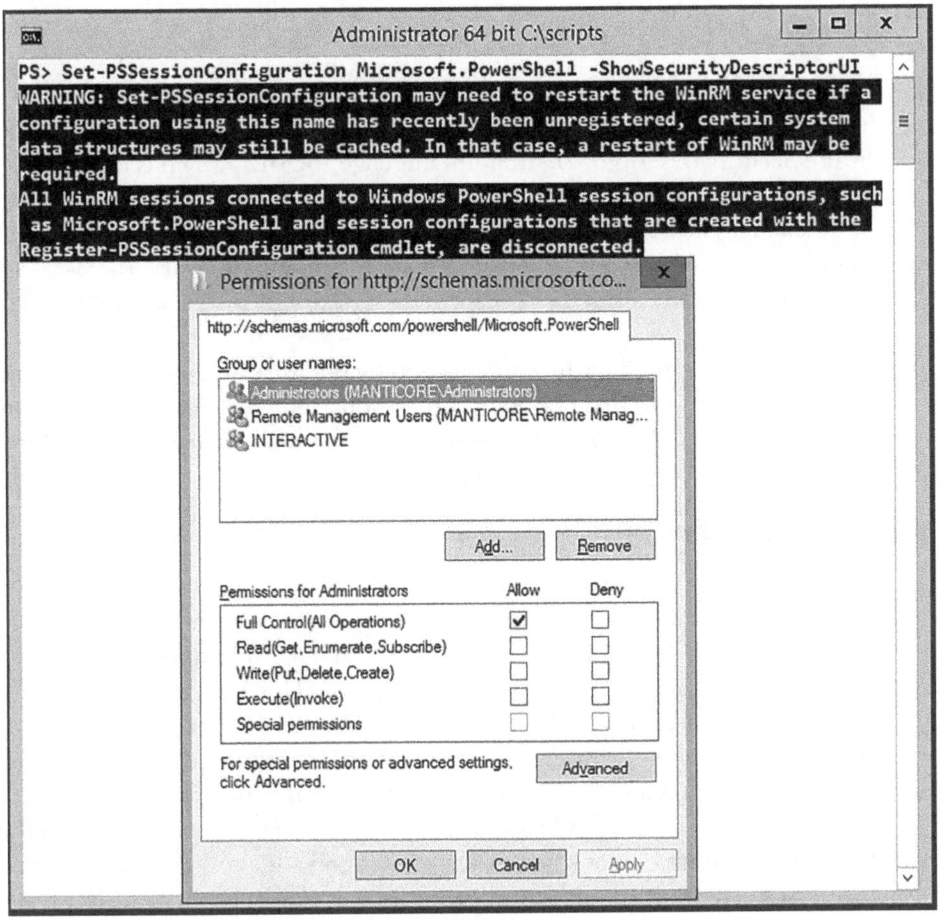

```
Administrator 64 bit C:\scripts                                    _  □  X

PS> Set-PSSessionConfiguration Microsoft.PowerShell -ShowSecurityDescriptorUI
WARNING: Set-PSSessionConfiguration may need to restart the WinRM service if a
configuration using this name has recently been unregistered, certain system
data structures may still be cached. In that case, a restart of WinRM may be
required.
All WinRM sessions connected to Windows PowerShell session configurations, such
 as Microsoft.PowerShell and session configurations that are created with the
Register-PSSessionConfiguration cmdlet, are disconnected.
```

Permissions for http://schemas.microsoft.co...   X

http://schemas.microsoft.com/powershell/Microsoft.PowerShell

Group or user names:

- Administrators (MANTICORE\Administrators)
- Remote Management Users (MANTICORE\Remote Manag...
- INTERACTIVE

[Add...] [Remove]

Permissions for Administrators   Allow   Deny

Full Control(All Operations)	✓	☐
Read(Get,Enumerate,Subscribe)	☐	☐
Write(Put,Delete,Create)	☐	☐
Execute(Invoke)	☐	☐
Special permissions	☐	☐

For special permissions or advanced settings,   [Advanced]
click Advanced.

[OK] [Cancel] [Apply]

Figure 11.10   This dialog box is used to enable the Execute permission on the default remoting configuration. Use this dialog box to allow a user who isn't a member of the Administrators group to connect to this computer using PowerShell remoting.

SETTING SECURITY DESCRIPTORS ON CONFIGURATIONS

When `Enable-PSRemoting` creates the default session configuration, it doesn't create explicit security descriptors for the configurations. Instead, the configurations inherit the security descriptor of the `RootSDDL`. The `RootSDDL` is the security descriptor that controls remote access to the listener, which is secure by default. To see the `RootSDDL` security descriptor, run the `Get-Item` command as shown:

```
PS> Get-Item wsman:\localhost\Service\RootSDDL

      WSManConfig: Microsoft.WSMan.Management\WSMan::localhost\Service

Type          Name    SourceOfValue Value
----          ----    ------------- -----
System.String RootSDDL              O:NSG:BAD:P(A;;GA;;;BA)
```

```
(A;;GR;;;IU)
S:P(AU;FA;GA;;;WD)
AU;SA;GXGW;;;WD)
```

The string format shown in the `Value` output in the example uses the syntax defined by the Security Descriptor Definition Language (SDDL), which is documented in the Windows Data Types specification MS-DTYP in section 2.5.1 at http://mng.bz/QpKC.

To change the `RootSDDL`, use the `Set-Item` cmdlet in the WSMan: drive. To change the security descriptor for an existing session configuration, use the `Set-PSSession-Configuration` cmdlet with the `-SecurityDescriptorSDDL` or `-ShowSecurityDescriptorUI` parameter.

At this point, you know how to create and configure an endpoint and how to control who has access to that endpoint. But in your configuration, all you've done is add new commands to the set of commands you got by default. You haven't addressed the requirement to *constrain* the environment.

11.6.4 *Constraining a PowerShell session*

In section 11.6.2 you saw how to create a new remoting endpoint using `Register-PSSessionConfiguration`, and in the previous section you saw how to control who can access a particular endpoint. In this section, you'll learn how to control, or constrain, what can be done through a particular endpoint. This involves limiting the variables and commands available to the user of the session. You accomplish this by controlling command and variable *visibility*. You're creating a constrained endpoint.

The idea behind a constrained endpoint is that it allows you to provide controlled access to services on a server in a secure manner. This is the mechanism that the hosted Exchange product Outlook.com uses to constrain who gets to manage which sets of mailboxes. The mechanism can also be used in PowerShell Web Access to control access to a server and the commands that can be run on that server.

In PowerShell v2 you had to create a complex script to configure a new endpoint. The script involved manipulating the visibility of cmdlets and variables plus the definition of any new functionality you required.

In PowerShell v3 and later this task became much simpler thanks to the introduction of the `New-PSSessionConfigurationFile` cmdlet; the syntax is shown in figure 11.11.

The only required parameter is the path to the new configuration file:

```
PS> New-PSSessionConfigurationFile -Path .\Defaults.pssc
```

Configuration files are given a .pssc extension. The .pssc file structure is similar to a module manifest; it's a big PowerShell hashtable with name-value pairs. If you examine defaults.pssc (see download) produced by the example, you'll see that you can control a large number of configuration items, including these:

- Execution policy (controls which, if any, scripts can be run)
- Language mode

```
New-PSSessionConfigurationFile [-Path] <string> [-SchemaVersion <version>]
[-Guid <guid>] [-Author <string>] [-CompanyName <string>]
[-Copyright <string>] [-Description <string>]
[-PowerShellVersion <version>] [-SessionType<SessionType>]
[-ModulesToImport <Object[]>] [-Toolkits <string[]>]
[-AssembliesToLoad <string[]>] [-VisibleAliases<string[]>]
[-VisibleCmdlets <Object[]>] [-VisibleFunctions <Object[]>]
[-VisibleProviders <string[]>] [-AliasDefinitions <IDictionary[]>]
[-FunctionDefinitions <IDictionary[]>] [-VariableDefinitions <Object>]
[-RoleDefinitions <IDictionary>] [-EnvironmentVariables <IDictionary>]
[-TypesToProcess <string[]>] [-FormatsToProcess<string[]>]
[-LanguageMode <PSLanguageMode>] [-ExecutionPolicy <ExecutionPolicy>]
[-ScriptsToProcess <string[]>] [<CommonParameters>]
```

Figure 11.11 `New-PSSessionConfigurationFile` **syntax**

- Session type
- PowerShell version
- Existing aliases, cmdlets, functions, and providers that are visible in the endpoint
- New aliases, functions, and variables to create for the endpoint
- Format and type files to load and scripts to process

Language mode for a session configuration controls the types of things that can be executed in a session. The more secure you need the session to be, the more restrictive the language mode session should be. The options are shown in table 11.5.

Table 11.5 Remoting endpoint language options

Option	Meaning
FullLanguage	All PowerShell language elements are permitted.
ConstrainedLanguage	Commands that contain scripts to be evaluated are not allowed. User access is restricted to .NET framework types, objects, or methods. (This is the mode that PowerShell runs in on WinRT devices.)
RestrictedLanguage	Users may run cmdlets and functions. Scriptblocks aren't allowed. Only the following variables are allowed: $PSCulture, $PSUICulture, $True, $False, and $Null. Basic comparison operators are allowed. Assignment statements, property references, and method calls aren't permitted. (This is the language mode used in module manifests, sometimes also called *data language mode* because it can only describe data.)
NoLanguage	Users may run simple pipelines containing cmdlets and functions. No language elements such as scriptblocks, variables, or operators are permitted in the pipeline.

As you progress down the table, the things you can do in the endpoint become more limited until `NoLanguage`, when you're only allowed to run basic pipelines containing cmdlets and functions. The session capabilities are also controllable by restricting the list of cmdlets and functions available to a user. For example, you can restrict the functionality of an endpoint so that a user can only reset their password in Active Directory!

The session type works in conjunction with the language mode. The session type options are listed in table 11.6.

Table 11.6 Session options for remoting endpoints

Option	Meaning	Default language mode
Default	Adds the Microsoft.PowerShell.Core snap-in to the session. This includes the `Import -Module` and `Add-PSSnapin` cmdlets so users can import other modules and snap-ins unless you explicitly prohibit the use of the cmdlets.	FullLanguage
RestrictedRemoteServer	Includes only the following proxy functions: `Exit-PSSession`, `Get-Command`, `Get-FormatData`, `Get-Help`, `Measure-Object`, `Out-Default`, and `Select-Object`. Use `New -PSSessionConfigurationFile` to add modules, functions, scripts, and other features to the session.	NoLanguage
Empty	No modules or snap-ins are added to the session by default. Use `New -PSSessionConfigurationFile` to add modules, functions, scripts, and other features to the session. This option is designed for you to create custom sessions by adding selected commands. If you don't add commands to an empty session, the session is limited to expressions and might not be usable.	NoLanguage

You can explicitly control the visibility of PowerShell elements using the `-Visible*` parameters shown in figure 11.11. This is a "white list" action. If a cmdlet or other element isn't on the list, you won't see it and therefore you won't be able to use it directly.

TIP When using the `-Visible*` parameters, if you don't want to make anything visible for a particular type of command, don't use the parameter. A commented-out default value will be written to the .pssc file.

An example of an extremely constrained endpoint is provided in the following listing.

Listing 11.3   ComplexConstrainedConfiguration.ps1

```
New-PSSessionConfigurationFile `
-Path .\ComplexConstrainedConfiguration.pssc `
-Schema '1.0.0.0' `
```

```
-Author 'Richard' `
-Copyright '(c) PowerShell in Action Third Edition. All rights reserved.' `
-CompanyName 'PowerShell in Action' `
-Description 'Complex Constrained Configuration.' `
-ExecutionPolicy RemoteSigned `
-PowerShellVersion '5.0' `
-LanguageMode NoLanguage `
-SessionType RestrictedRemoteServer `
-FunctionDefinitions @{Name='Get-HealthModel';ScriptBlock={@{
            Date = Get-Date
            FreeSpace = (Get-PSDrive c).Free
            PageFaults = (Get-WmiObject `
            Win32_PerfRawData_PerfOS_Memory).PageFaultsPersec
            TopCPU = Get-Process | Sort-Object -Descending CPU
            TopWS = Get-Process | Sort-Object -Descending WS
    }};Options='None'} `
-VisibleProviders 'FileSystem','Function','Variable'
```

The execution policy is set to RemoteSigned, but in reality, you won't be able to run scripts, as you'll see in a while. Language mode is set to NoLanguage (see table 11.5) and session type to RestrictedRemoteServer (table 11.6). Three providers are made visible, but no modules, cmdlets, aliases, or variables are made available in the session.

A function to get the health of the system is defined and will be created when the endpoint is created. Run the script in listing 11.3 to create a configuration file. The fidelity of a configuration file can be tested:

```
PS> Test-PSSessionConfigurationFile -Path `
.\ComplexConstrainedConfiguration.pssc -Verbose
True
```

In the event of an error in the file, you will see the error only if you use the -Verbose parameter:

```
PS> Test-PSSessionConfigurationFile -Path .\ErrorConfiguration.pssc `
-Verbose

VERBOSE: The member 'LanguageMode' must be a valid enumeration type "System.
  Management.Automation.PSLanguageMode".
Valid enumeration values are "FullLanguage,RestrictedLanguage,NoLanguage,
ConstrainedLanguage". Change the member to the correct type in the file C:\
  MyData\PowerShellinAction3e\Code\Chapter11\ErrorConfiguration.pssc.
False
```

Creating the endpoint is performed with Register-PSSessionConfiguration. In the following example, any existing instances of the endpoint are removed—a useful technique when testing:

```
PS> Unregister-PSSessionConfiguration -Name wpiaccs -Force
PS> Register-PSSessionConfiguration –Path ` .\
  ComplexConstrainedConfiguration.pssc -Name wpiaccs -Force

  WSManConfig: Microsoft.WSMan.Management\WSMan::localhost\Plugin
```

```
Type               Keys                                    Name
----               ----                                    ----
Container          {Name=wpiaccs}                          wpiaccs
```

You can see the new endpoint:

```
PS> dir WSMan:\localhost\Plugin\

    WSManConfig: Microsoft.WSMan.Management\WSMan::localhost\Plugin

Type               Keys                                Name
----               ----                                ----
Container          {Name=Event Forwarding Plugin}      Event Forwarding Plugin
Container          {Name=microsoft.powershell}         microsoft.powershell
Container          {Name=microsoft.powershell.w...     microsoft.powershell.workflow
Container          {Name=microsoft.powershell32}       microsoft.powershell32
Container          {Name=microsoft.windows.serv...     microsoft.windows.server...
Container          {Name=SEL Plugin}                   SEL Plugin
Container          {Name=WMI Provider}                 WMI Provider
Container          {Name=wpiaccs}                       wpiaccs
```

A remoting session can be created to the new endpoint. Notice that you have to give the name of the configuration (endpoint) that you used when performing the registration:

```
PS> $s = New-PSSession -ComputerName localhost -ConfigurationName wpiaccs
```

The session can now be used as normal. Let's start by checking the commands available:

```
PS> Invoke-Command -Session $s -ScriptBlock {Get-Command | select Name}

Name            PSComputerName RunspaceId
----            -------------- ----------
Clear-Host      localhost      0377a4f9-5924-4cb0-83f9-a87f8a335147
Exit-PSSession  localhost      0377a4f9-5924-4cb0-83f9-a87f8a335147
Get-Command     localhost      0377a4f9-5924-4cb0-83f9-a87f8a335147
Get-FormatData  localhost      0377a4f9-5924-4cb0-83f9-a87f8a335147
Get-HealthModel localhost      0377a4f9-5924-4cb0-83f9-a87f8a335147
Get-Help        localhost      0377a4f9-5924-4cb0-83f9-a87f8a335147
Measure-Object  localhost      0377a4f9-5924-4cb0-83f9-a87f8a335147
Out-Default     localhost      0377a4f9-5924-4cb0-83f9-a87f8a335147
Select-Object   localhost      0377a4f9-5924-4cb0-83f9-a87f8a335147
```

NOTE   When you look at this list of commands, you may wonder why some of them are included. For example, Measure-Object seems like a strange thing to have on the list. The reason these commands are included is that they're needed to implement some of the elements of the PowerShell Remoting Protocol. In particular, they're used to help with the command-discovery component described in the PowerShell Remoting Protocol Specification (MS-PSRP) section 3.1.4.5, "Getting Command Metadata."

Compare that with the results on the machine we're using to test the code for this book:

```
PS> Get-Command | Measure-Object | select Count

Count
-----
 2658
```

Our session is constrained! You'll notice that the function we defined, `Get-HealthModel`, is in the list of commands. Let's check that it works:

```
PS> Invoke-Command -Session $s -ScriptBlock {get-healthmodel}

Name                        Value
----                        -----
Date                        08/05/2017 12:57:29
TopWS                       {System.Diagnostics.Proces…
PageFaults                  146394771
FreeSpace                   67302338560
TopCPU                      {System.Diagnostics…
```

The observant reader will have noticed that we used `Get-Date` in the function, but it isn't in the list of commands we obtained from `Get-Command`. Does this mean we can use it directly even though we didn't explicitly make it visible in our configuration definition?

```
PS> Invoke-Command -Session $s -ScriptBlock {Get-Date}
The term 'Get-Date' is not recognized as the name of a cmdlet, function,
script file, or operable program. Check the spelling of the name, or if a
path was included, verify that the path is correct and try again.
```

And the answer is no! This is an important point to understand because it's the key to creating a restricted special-purpose endpoint: an *external* call can only access visible commands, but these commands, because they're defined as part of the configuration, can see all the other commands in the configuration. This means that an externally visible command can call any internal commands in the session. If the user makes an external call to a visible command, that visible command is able to call the private commands.

> **NOTE** All the error messages in this section will be truncated to show only the error text for brevity.

What about using it in a script block or function?

```
PS> Invoke-Command -Session $s -ScriptBlock { & {Get-Date}}
The syntax is not supported by this runspace. This can occur if the runspace
is in no-language mode.

PS> Invoke-Command -Session $s -ScriptBlock {function MyGetDate { [string]
   (Get-Date) }; MyGetDate}
The syntax is not supported by this runspace. This can occur if the runspace
is in no-language mode.
```

If you want to be able to create functions and scriptblocks, you need to be using `Full-Language` mode in your endpoint. What about adding extra modules into the endpoint—modules provide extra functionality? Let's see what modules you have available:

```
PS> Invoke-Command -Session $s -ScriptBlock {Get-Module -ListAvailable}
The term 'Get-Module' is not recognized as the name of a cmdlet, function,
script file, or operable program. Check thespelling of the name, or if a path
was included, verify that the path is correct and try again.
```

You can't see any modules so you can't load them because you don't know what's on the system. You might think about trying to import modules that you know are present, but it will fail. The endpoint is locked down to prevent any further functionality being imported. The function we defined as part of our configuration used variables. Can you use variables in your endpoint?

```
PS> Invoke-Command -Session $s -ScriptBlock {$x =  123; $x}
The syntax is not supported by this runspace. This can occur if the runspace
is in no-language mode.
```

No, they're not allowed. There's still a lot of functionality in legacy commands that you may think to use:

```
PS> Invoke-Command -Session $s -ScriptBlock {ping 127.0.0.1}
The term 'PING.EXE' is not recognized as the name of a cmdlet, function,
script file, or operable program. Check the spelling of the name, or if a
path was included, verify that the path is correct and try again.
```

Notice that the full name of the executable was recognized—but you're not allowed to run it. The final piece of functionality you may try is to run a script. You can try a simple script testch11.ps1 consisting of

```
Get-Service | Sort-Object Status
```

Try this:

```
PS> Invoke-Command -Session $s -ScriptBlock {C:\TestScripts\testch11.ps1}
The term 'C:\TestScripts\testch11.ps1' is not recognized as the name of a
cmdlet, function, script file, or operable program. Check the spelling of the
name, or if a path was included, verify that the path is correct and try again.
```

Again, the endpoint won't allow you to run anything beyond what it's been told is allowed. You do have a constrained remoting session.

> **NOTE**   The example we've used is extreme but was designed to illustrate that you can create an endpoint and control exactly what functionality is exposed.

Step back and think about what you've accomplished here. With a few lines of code, you've defined a secure remote service. From the users' perspective, by using `Import-PSSession` they're able to install the contents of the session to use the services you expose—*by connecting to the service.*

Constrained sessions combined with implicit remoting results in an extremely flexible system, allowing you to create precise service boundaries with little server-side code and *no* client code. Consider how much code would be required to create an equivalent service using alternate technologies!

We'll close the chapter with a new remoting feature introduced with PowerShell v5.

11.7   PowerShell Direct

You normally use the computer name to define the remote machine for PowerShell remoting, whether you're using an interactive session, a persistent session, or `Invoke -Command` in standalone mode (no persistent session). PowerShell v5.1 supplies some new options. You can use a Hyper-V virtual machine name (not necessarily the same as the computer name) or the virtual machine ID (a GUID).

The options to use a virtual machine name or ID apply only under these circumstances:

- The virtual machine must be running on the local host.
- You must be logged on to the Hyper-V host as a Hyper-V administrator.
- You must supply valid credentials for the virtual machine—*not* domain credentials.
- The host operating system must be Windows 10, Windows Server 2016, or later.
- The virtual machine operating system must be Windows 10, Windows Server 2016, or later.

You can use the virtual machine name or ID to connect, but it's usually easier to use the name:

```
PS> Get-VM | where State -eq 'Running' |
select Name, Id

Name      Id
----      --
W16AS01   2a1eabc2-e3cd-495c-a91f-51a1ad43104c
W16DSC01  867c8460-a4fb-4785-9b7c-f27c9351db3c
W16TGT01  be4a5a3f-fc20-49f9-bb0f-b575c85e5734
```

Create a credential for the administrator account on the remote machine and then use the virtual machine name to connect:

```
PS> $cred = Get-Credential -Credential W16TGT01\Administrator
PS> Invoke-Command -VMName W16TGT01 -ScriptBlock {Get-Process} `
-Credential $cred
```

Either of these options will also work:

```
PS> Invoke-Command -VMId be4a5a3f-fc20-49f9-bb0f-b575c85e5734 `
-ScriptBlock {Get-Process} -Credential $cred

PS> Invoke-Command -VMGuid be4a5a3f-fc20-49f9-bb0f-b575c85e5734 `
-ScriptBlock {Get-Process} -Credential $cred
```

NOTE VMGuid is an alias for VMId.

You can create a persistent remoting session:

```
PS>  $s = New-PSSession -VMName W16TGT01 -Credential $cred
PS>  Invoke-Command -Session $s -ScriptBlock {Get-Process}
```

Or you can work interactively:

```
PS>  Enter-PSSession -VMName W16TGT01 -Credential $cred
[W16TGT01]: PS C:\Users\Administrator\Documents>
Use Exit-PSSession to close the interactive session.
```

There are a few things you need to remember when using PowerShell Direct:

- It's only for Hyper-V virtual machines.
- You can ignore network and firewall configurations; you're connecting over the VM bus rather than the network.
- PowerShell must be run with elevated privileges.

And with this, we've come to end of our coverage of the remoting features in PowerShell.

11.8 Summary

- Many PowerShell commands have built-in remoting using a `-ComputerName` parameter.
- Cmdlets with built-in remoting use a variety of connectivity mechanisms including DCOM and RPC.
- `Invoke-Command` uses WS-MAN for remote connectivity.
- You can create an interactive remoting session with `Enter-PSSession`.
- Interactive remoting sessions are closed with `Exit-PSSession`.
- Windows Server 2012 and later enable remoting by default. Azure IAAS virtual machines running Server 2012 R2 or higher also enable PowerShell remoting by default.
- All client operating systems and Windows Server 2008 R2 and earlier need remoting enabled by running `Enable-PSRemoting`.
- Additional configuration may be required in a non-domain environment.
- Users are authenticated using Kerberos in a domain environment when creating remoting sessions.
- Other authentication mechanisms are available for non-domain scenarios.
- `New-PSSession` is used to create a persistent remoting session.
- `Invoke-Command` and interactive sessions can use an existing session created with `New-PSSession`.
- PowerShell sessions can be disconnected and later reconnected. The reconnection can happen on the machine on which the session was created or another machine.

- You can connect to a disconnected session created by another user if you have the correct credential information.
- `Copy-Item` has `-FromSession` and `-ToSession` parameters that enable you to copy files across PowerShell remoting sessions.
- Implicit remoting enables you to import functionality from the remote system into your session. You can save the imported commands as a module.
- Profiles don't run by default in remoting sessions.
- Scripts on the local or remote machine can be run through a remoting session.
- Local variables can be accessed in a remoting session via the `$using` scope modifier.
- Custom endpoints can be created to constrain the functionality available to a user through a specific remoting connection.
- PowerShell Direct enables remoting over the VM bus from a Hyper-V host to a virtual machine on that host.

In the next chapter, we'll look at a feature introduced in PowerShell v3: PowerShell workflows.

PowerShell workflows

12

This chapter covers

- Workflow overview and architecture
- Workflow keywords
- Workflow parameters
- Workflow cmdlets

> *"Hi ho, hi ho. It's off to work we go!"*
>
> —*Snow White and the Seven Dwarfs*

At the beginning of every new release of PowerShell, a planning cycle takes place during which a number of major themes are identified for the release. During the planning cycle for PowerShell v3, one of the key themes was identified as *multi-machine management*—the ability to provision, manage, and monitor a large number of machines in a datacenter. Accomplishing this goal, however, would require changing not only PowerShell but also some related products such as Server Manager.

In Windows 7, which included PowerShell v2 and the first version of Server Manager, the focus was mainly on machine-to-machine management. Server Manager could attach to a remote machine but could manage only one machine at a time. PowerShell was a bit more sophisticated in that it could deal with multiple machines but only if you wanted to do the same thing to each machine.

The key element that was missing was orchestration. In an orchestra, the conductor doesn't play any music. Instead, they direct the orchestra members, each of whom has a specialized role to play and a time to play that role (music). This direction of the orchestra is called, not surprisingly, *orchestration*. A central control point sequences the flow of work to the individual workers. It was clear that workflow management had to become part of the overall management stack to achieve large-scale multi-machine management.

PowerShell workflows were introduced in PowerShell v3. Workflows give you another option when deciding how you'll tackle a task with PowerShell. We'll start with the high-level view of workflows and explain why you need them, their strengths and weaknesses, and the constraints you'll face when using workflows.

> **NOTE** We'll come back to this point a number of times throughout the chapter, but you need to be aware that although workflows look like PowerShell code, they're not PowerShell—they're code written with a PowerShell-like-syntax.

Before we get to the deep technicalities of PowerShell workflows, we need to give you the overview we promised.

12.1 Workflow overview

In this section, we'll give you an overview of when you should consider using workflows. We'll then use the ever-popular "Hello world" approach to create your first workflow. The section closes by looking at the differences between workflows and PowerShell code, followed by the restrictions imposed on your code by using PowerShell.

Workflows introduce a number of keywords that we'll explain. The foreach keyword you've seen already gains new functionality in workflows that we'll demonstrate. Once you have a sound grasp of workflow features and syntax, we'll provide some examples of using workflows. These will include nested workflows, how workflows interact with the PowerShell job engine, and the large set of parameters you can use with workflows. We'll introduce and explain a number of cmdlets for working directly with workflows.

First, though, why should you think about using workflows?

12.1.1 Why use workflows

PowerShell workflows are designed for scenarios where you have processes that meet the following criteria:

- Run for a long time, potentially for days.
- Execute unattended.
- Run in parallel across one or more machines.
- Are interruptible. They can be stopped and restarted through the use of checkpoints, which means the state of the process can be persisted to disk.
- Need to survive a reboot of the system against which the workflow is executing.
- Need to track execution.

So, what kind of task would fit this model? A few real-world examples should help establish when using workflows would be beneficial:

- You need to test hundreds or thousands of servers for the presence of a particular piece of software—a typical compliance issue in many organizations.
- You need to make a series of modifications to the configuration of many servers that involves rebooting the servers in the middle of the process.
- You need to modify the configuration of multiple servers with a process that involves many steps. Capturing the state of the workflow with a series of checkpoints enables you to restart the process from the point of an error rather than from the beginning

By now you are probably thinking, "I can do that already." That's true; there are ways to solve all of these problems without using workflows, but workflows make it easier for you to solve these problems.

There's nothing to stop you solving any of these problems by using non-workflow solutions, but we recommend that you definitely consider using workflows for these three areas:

- You need to interrupt and restart tasks.
- You need to checkpoint the task (persistence).
- You have a mixture of sequential and parallel tasks.

You'll see how workflows solve these problems as we progress through the chapter, but now it's time to discover the architecture of PowerShell workflows.

12.1.2 *Workflow architecture*

In this section, we're going to look at the internal architecture of PowerShell workflow. Having some knowledge of the architecture will help you understand and predict the behavior of a workflow script. Figure 12.1 shows all the pieces of the PowerShell workflow architecture.

This diagram is rather complex, so we'll go through it one piece at a time. On the left side of the picture is a box labelled Main PowerShell runspace. This is your interactive PowerShell session. In workflows, it does only one thing: takes a PowerShell workflow script and translates it into workflow XAML (eXtensible Markup Language). The workflow engine requires this XAML representation in order to execute the workflow. The XAML is then passed to the workflow host component for execution. At this point, the involvement of the main runspace ends (other than to wait for the workflow to finish).

Inside the workflow host, the workflow execution engine is the element that executes the program logic, but there are a couple of other important parts. First is the variable store. The workflow engine has its own way of dealing with variables that's completely separate from the PowerShell runspace variable store. (You'll see why this matters when we get to writing workflows.) The other major component is the persistence

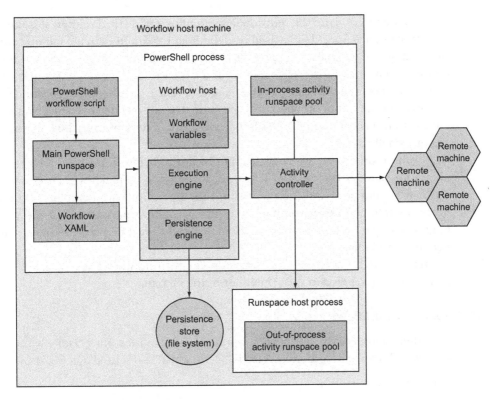

Figure 12.1   PowerShell workflow architecture

store. One of the signature features of a workflow is that it can halt execution, save all state to the persistence, and be resumed at a later time. In the case of a PowerShell workflow, that persistence store is the file system. By default the persistence store is located at $env:LOCALAPPDATA\Microsoft\Windows\PowerShell\WF\PS. This location can be modified by the New-PSWorkflowExecutionOption cmdlet if required.

After receiving the XAML, the workflow execution engine starts processing the steps in the workflow. These individual steps are called *activities*, which include not only imperative actions but also the if statements, loops, and other flow-control statements that make up the workflow. PowerShell workflow exposes PowerShell commands as activities so the workflow engine can run them, but the control statements are specific to the workflow engine. For each PowerShell command, there is a corresponding activity wrapper that will call it. These wrappers are generated using tools that produce a C# wrapper for the command. The C# wrappers for all the commands in a module are compiled into a new binary module with the word *activities* inserted into the name (see table 12.2).

To recap, the workflow engine runs the activity, which in turn runs the command. But as you know, PowerShell commands can run only in runspaces. This is shown on the right side of figure 12.1. PowerShell workflow maintains several pools of runspaces that are used to execute the individual commands. Of particular interest is the out-of-process runspace pool. This is used by default and guarantees that a failing command won't cause the workflow host process to fail. This approach makes the workflow execution significantly more reliable—but at a cost. Running commands out of process adds a lot of overhead because of the need to serialize data between the workflow host process and the out-of-process runspace host. To improve performance, you can also choose to run activities in process but at some risk of destabilizing the engine (usually a pretty small risk).

Also note that these are runspace pools, not individual runspaces, which is what allows for parallel operations. The workflow engine dispatches each command to a runspace in a pool and then waits until the operations are complete. If there are more operations to execute than there are available runspaces, then the workflow engine will queue the remaining commands and they'll be processed as a runspace becomes available.

Okay, enough about architecture; let's start writing workflows. We'll refer to the architecture as needed in the remainder of the chapter.

12.1.3 *Your first workflow*

In earlier chapters we introduced new functionality by creating a "Hello world" example. Workflows are no different. This is "Hello world" presented as a workflow:

```
workflow hello
{
 'Hello World'
}
```

Executing this workflow gives the following output:

```
PS> hello
Hello World
```

If you're thinking, "This looks like a function definition," at this point you're correct. In many cases, workflows look exactly like a function except that the `function` keyword is replaced by the `workflow` keyword. You can see if a function is a workflow by using `Get-Command` on the command name, which in this case gives the following:

```
PS> Get-Command hello

CommandType Name  Version Source
----------- ----  ------- ------
Workflow    hello
```

Let's drill down into our `hello` workflow. A number of interesting features are exposed when you examine the full output from

```
PS> Get-Command hello | Format-List *
```

NOTE Running this command will give you all the information about the workflow, including the XAML representation of the workflow. The resulting output is too large to include in the book, but we've included a copy in the download available from the book's website.

The XAML definition of the workflow is worth examining. If you look through the scriptblock definition you'll see this line:

```
function hello {
```

When a PowerShell workflow is created, the command is persisted as a function. You can test this:

```
PS> Get-ChildItem -Path Function:\hello
CommandType Name   Version Source
----------- ----   ------- ------
Workflow    hello
```

The command type is set as a `Workflow` even though the command is in the function drive. Referring to the architecture, this function is the piece that runs in the main PowerShell runspace. Unlike a regular function, which executes the actions in its body, the job of a workflow function is to pass the XAML definition to the workflow engine, which ultimately does all the execution. This means that the function you defined is quite different than the function that's run in the main runspace. You can view this generated function dispatcher function by running

```
PS> Get-Command hello | select -ExpandProperty Scriptblock
```

Once again, the output of this command is too long to include in the text of the book, but the bulk of the function is a large number of parameter definitions. You can look at these parameters by doing

```
PS> Get-Command hello | select -ExpandProperty Parameters
```

This list of parameters is shown in table 12.1.

Table 12.1 Default workflow parameters

PSParameterCollection	PSComputerName	PSCredential
PSConnectionRetryCount	PSConnectionRetry-IntervalSec	PSRunningTimeoutSec
PSElapsedTimeoutSec	PSPersist	PSAuthentication
PSAuthenticationLevel	PSApplicationName	PSPort
PSUseSSL	PSConfigurationName	PSConnectionURI
PSAllowRedirection	PSSessionOption	PSCertificateThumbprint

Table 12.1 Default workflow parameters (continued)

PSPrivateMetadata	AsJob	JobName
InputObject	ErrorAction	WarningAction
InformationAction	Verbose	Debug
ErrorVariable	WarningVariable	InformationVariable
OutVariable	OutBuffer	PipelineVariable

You should recognize some of the parameters such as Verbose and Debug from Power-Shell functions. Others, such as PSPersist and PSPort, are new workflow-specific parameters that are automatically defined, and available, for every workflow you write without you having to do any extra work!

NOTE The full definition of each of the workflow parameters can be found in the help file about_WorkflowCommonParameters.

We've mentioned the XAML definition corresponding to the workflow function several times. This is the XamlDefinition that was generated for our hello workflow.

Listing 12.1   Xamldefinition of hello workflow

```
<Activity
    x:Class="Microsoft.PowerShell.DynamicActivities.Activity_1303329265"
    xmlns="http://schemas.microsoft.com/netfx/2009/xaml/activities"
    xmlns:sad="clr-namespace:System.Activities.Debugger;assembly=
System.Activities"
    xmlns:local="clr-namespace:Microsoft.PowerShell.DynamicActivities"
    xmlns:mva="clr-namespace:Microsoft.VisualBasic.Activities;assembly=
System.Activities"
    mva:VisualBasic.Settings="Assembly references and imported namespaces
    serialized as XML namespaces"
    xmlns:x="http://schemas.microsoft.com/winfx/2006/xaml"
    xmlns:ns0="clr-namespace:System;assembly=mscorlib"
    xmlns:ns1="clr-namespace:Microsoft.PowerShell.Utility.Activities;
assembly=Microsoft.PowerShell.Utility.Activities"
    xmlns:ns2="clr-namespace:Microsoft.PowerShell.Activities;
assembly=Microsoft.PowerShell.Activities"
    xmlns:ns3="clr-namespace:System.Activities;assembly=System.Activities"
    xmlns:ns4="clr-namespace:System.Management.Automation;
assembly=System.Management.Automation"
    >
    <Sequence>
        <ns2:SetPSWorkflowData>
            <ns2:SetPSWorkflowData.OtherVariableName>Position
            </ns2:SetPSWorkflowData.OtherVariableName>
            <ns2:SetPSWorkflowData.Value>
                <ns3:InArgument x:TypeArguments="ns0:Object">
                    <ns2:PowerShellValue
                     x:TypeArguments="ns0:Object"
```

```
                      Expression="'2:2:hello'" />
                  </ns3:InArgument>
              </ns2:SetPSWorkflowData.Value>
          </ns2:SetPSWorkflowData>
          <ns1:WriteOutput>
              <ns1:WriteOutput.NoEnumerate>[
              System.Management.Automation.SwitchParameter.Present]
              </ns1:WriteOutput.NoEnumerate>
              <ns1:WriteOutput.InputObject>
                  <InArgument x:TypeArguments="ns4:PSObject[]">
                      <ns2:PowerShellValue x:TypeArguments="ns4:PSObject[]"
                      Expression="'Hello World'" />
                  </InArgument>
              </ns1:WriteOutput.InputObject>
          </ns1:WriteOutput>
          <Sequence.Variables>
              <Variable Name="WorkflowCommandName"
               x:TypeArguments="ns0:String" Default = "hello" />
          </Sequence.Variables>
      </Sequence>
  </Activity>
```

The XAML consists of a series of definitions and then, starting at the `<Sequence>` tag, comes the body of the workflow. Reading through the `Sequence` section you'll recognize a number of activities such as `WriteOutput` that correspond to PowerShell commands.

XAML, PowerShell, and workflows

XAML is the language used in Windows Workflow Foundation (WF), which is part of the .NET framework. Although XAML was primarily designed for creating GUIs, it's also used as a common markup across multiple Microsoft products such as Share-Point and Team Foundation Server workflows.

The WF provides an API, a workflow engine, and a designer. Each step in your workflow is modeled as an activity—either from the .NET library or custom-created. Activities are assembled into workflows using the Workflow Designer in Visual Studio.

You can import PowerShell workflows into the Workflow Designer—see http://mng.bz/473s—but the result is not too intelligible because of all of the boilerplate code generated by PowerShell WF. One of the advantages that PowerShell brings to workflow is a much more concise notation for expressing workflows.

(Trivia: Windows Workflow Foundation is abbreviated as WF instead of WWF because WWF conflicted with the World Wildlife Federation trademark. Yes, wildlife, not wrestling.

Now that you've seen under the covers of a PowerShell workflow, how are the various parts generated?

12.1.4 Running a workflow

When you run a PowerShell workflow, the built-in script-to-workflow compiler generates the XAML for you. The user experience is simplified by creating a PowerShell function (with the same parameters) that wraps the XAML. The function's job is to coordinate the execution of the workflow within the PowerShell workflow engine.

A PowerShell workflow is executed as a PowerShell job (see chapter 13), which provides the asynchronous capability of workflows. A job executes in a separate PowerShell process. You can test this by running the code in the following listing.

Listing 12.2 Demonstration of workflow PowerShell processes

```
workflow Invoke-ParallelForEach
{                                                              Define
    foreach -parallel ($i in 1..10)                      ❶   workflow
    {                                                    ❷   Create loop
        InlineScript
        {                                                    Output loop
            "foo: $using:i"                              ❸   counter
        }
        $count = Get-Process -Name PowerShell* |
                Measure-Object |
                Select-Object -ExpandProperty Count
        "Number of PowerShell processes = $count"            Process count
    }                                                    ❹   during execution
}
$startcount = Get-Process -Name PowerShell* |                Initial process
                Measure-Object |                         ❺   count
                Select-Object -ExpandProperty Count
"Number of starting PowerShell processes = $startcount"
Invoke-ParallelForEach
                                                         ❻   Execute workflow
```

> **NOTE** The workflow keywords in listing 12.2 are explained in detail in section 12.2. For now, we'll tell you what they do.

The `workflow` keyword ❶ defines the start of the workflow. A `foreach` statement ❷ creates a loop. The `-parallel` parameter ensures the loop's iterations are run in parallel rather than sequentially. An `InlineScript` ❸ is used to write out the current iteration details and `Get-Process` ❹ is used to determine the number of PowerShell processes in use.

Before the workflow is invoked `Get-Process` is used to determine the initial number of PowerShell processes ❺. The workflow is invoked ❻ and you'll see something like the following:

```
Number of starting PowerShell processes = 2
foo: 9
foo: 6
foo: 10
foo: 7
```

```
foo: 3
Number of PowerShell processes = 7
Number of PowerShell processes = 7
Number of PowerShell processes = 7
foo: 4
foo: 5
foo: 2
Number of PowerShell processes = 7
Number of PowerShell processes = 7
Number of PowerShell processes = 7
foo: 8
foo: 1
Number of PowerShell processes = 7
Number of PowerShell processes = 7
Number of PowerShell processes = 7
Number of PowerShell processes = 7
```

The first thing to note is the output is not sequential. You have a mixture of the iteration number and the number of processes. Also note that the iteration numbers look random.

> **NOTE** This is extremely important to remember. When running tasks in parallel in a workflow, you have no control over the order in which data is returned. If you can't identify where the data comes from, you won't reap the benefit of running the workflow.

The second point to note is the number of PowerShell processes. It immediately jumps from 2 (at the start) to 7, suggesting that the workflow created another 5 processes and used them to perform its tasks. The PowerShell job system will automatically close the sessions that were created. This isn't immediate; there's a slight delay.

We've mentioned that you're not using PowerShell cmdlets when writing workflows; you're using workflow activities. What do we mean by that?

12.1.5 *Cmdlets vs. activities*

When you look at listing 12.2 you see a script written in PowerShell syntax. It uses some cmdlets including `Get-Process`, `Measure-Object`, and `Select-Object`. This all looks familiar, but as you know from your study of the workflow architecture, these aren't cmdlets, and the important phrase in the first sentence of this section is "PowerShell syntax." When you're executing inside a workflow, you're not using the PowerShell runtime (unless you're in an `InlineScript` block) and you're not using cmdlets directly; you're using workflow activities, which are cmdlets with a WF wrapper, as you discovered in the architecture section.

The workflow activities are contained in assemblies (located in the global assembly cache) that correspond to PowerShell modules, as shown in table 12.2.

Table 12.2 PowerShell modules and corresponding activities

PowerShell module	PowerShell activity assembly
n/a	Microsoft.PowerShell.Activities
Microsoft.PowerShell.Core	Microsoft.PowerShell.Core.Activities
Microsoft.PowerShell.Diagnostics	Microsoft.PowerShell.Diagnostics.Activities
Microsoft.PowerShell.Management	Microsoft.PowerShell.Management.Activities
Microsoft.PowerShell.Security	Microsoft.PowerShell.Security.Activities
Microsoft.PowerShell.Utility	Microsoft.PowerShell.Utility.Activities
Microsoft.WSMan.Management	Microsoft.WSMan.Management.Activities

The assembly Microsoft.PowerShell.Activities doesn't have a corresponding cmdlet module because it contains a set of activities that are part of the PowerShell workflow runtime and is loaded when workflows are used.

Each activity has a similar (almost identical) syntax to the corresponding command because the activity wrappers are generated from the cmdlets directly; the properties on the generated activities are a strict superset of the parameters on the command. The difference is in the common parameters. Table 12.3 lists the common parameters found on workflow activities.

Table 12.3 Common activity parameters

AppendOutput	Debug	DisplayName	ErrorAction
Input	MergeError-ToOutput	PSActionRetry-Count	PSActionRetry-IntervalSec
PSActionRunning-TimeoutSec	PSApplication-Name	PSAuthentication	PSCertificate-Thumbprint
PSComputerName	PSConfiguration-Name	PSConnection-RetryCount	PSConnection-RetryIntervalSec
PSConnectionURI	PSCredential	PSDebug	PSDisable-Serialization
PSDisable-Serialization-Preference	PSError	PSPersist	PSPort
PSProgress	PSProgress-Message	PSRemoting-Behavior	PSRequiredModules
PSSessionOption	PSUseSSL	PSVerbose	PSWarning
Result	UseDefaultInput	Verbose	WarningAction

We're not going to explain each parameter, but we do need to make a couple of points:

- `PSActionRetryIntervalSec` relates to retrying actions in the workflow, not network retries.
- `PSRequiredModules` is used by the activity wrapper generator code to tell the WF runtime what module it needs to load in order to run the wrapped command.

In many cases, the parameters match cmdlet parameters you've already seen. Notice that many of them have a `PS` prefix. This can cause confusion where a cmdlet has a `-ComputerName` parameter and the workflow activity has a `-PSComputerName` parameter. The parameters are described in detail in the `about_ActivityCommon-Parameters` help file.

> **NOTE** You've been warned. You will trip over the difference in parameter names at some time when writing workflows.

One important point is that not all cmdlets have corresponding workflow activities. For example, this workflow will work:

```
workflow test1
{
    Get-CimInstance -ClassName Win32_ComputerSystem
}
test1
```

But see what happens if you try to use `Format-Table`:

```
workflow test1
{
    Get-CimInstance -ClassName Win32_ComputerSystem |
    Format-Table Name, Model
}
test1

At line:3 char:5
+     Format-Table Name, Model
+     ~~~~~~~~~~~~~~~~~~~~~~~~~
Cannot call the 'Format-Table' command. Other commands from this module have
  been packaged as workflow activities, but this command was specifically
  excluded. This is likely because the command requires an interactive
  Windows PowerShell session, or has behavior not suited for workflows. To
  run this command anyway, place it within an inline-script
(InlineScript { Format-Table }) where it will be invoked in isolation.
    + CategoryInfo          : ParserError: (:) [], ParseException
    + FullyQualifiedErrorId : CommandActivityExcluded
```

The error message explains why you're getting an error and how you can use the cmdlet in a workflow. Table 12.4 lists the unsupported cmdlet groups.

Table 12.4   Unsupported cmdlet groups

Unsupported cmdlet (group)	Reason
`*Alias`, `*FormatData`, `*History`, `*Location`, `*PSDrive`, `*Transcript`, `*TypeDate`, `*Variable`, `Connect/Disconnect-Wsman`	Change only PowerShell session, so not needed in workflow because each activity runs in its own runspace instance.
`Show-Command`, `Show-ControlPanelItem`, `Get-Credential`, `Show-EventLog`, `Out-Gridview`, `Read-Host`, `Debug-Process`	Workflows don't support interactive cmdlets.
`*BreakPoint`, `Get-PSCallStack`, `Set-PSDebug`	These commands are session-specific, but workflow commands each run in isolation.
`*Transaction`	Workflows don't support transactions.
`Format*`	Workflows are intended to be run in a distributed and asynchronous manner. Excluding the formatting cmdlets ensures a remote scenario isn't broken by accident.
`*PSsession`, `*PSsessionoption`	Remoting controlled by workflow.
`Export-Console`,`Get-ControlPanelItem`, `Out-Default`, `Out-Null`, `Write-Host`, `Export-ModuleMember`, `Add-PSSnapin`, `Get-PSSnapin`, `Remove-PSSnapin`, `Trace-Command`	These are excluded because they affect the current session, excluded because the workflow is non-interactive, excluded because the workflow handles remoting itself, or excluded because they might break the remote asynchronous pattern for workflow.

Some cmdlets, by default, can only be executed locally in workflows, as listed in table 12.5.

Table 12.5   Cmdlets that can only be executed locally in workflows

`Add-Member`	`Compare-Object`	`ConvertFrom-Csv`	`ConvertFrom-Json`
`ConvertFrom-StringData`	`Convert-Path`	`ConvertTo-Csv`	`ConvertTo-Html`
`ConvertTo-Json`	`ConvertTo-Xml`	`ForEach-Object`	`Get-Host`
`Get-Member`	`Get-Random`	`Get-Unique`	`Group-Object`
`Measure-Command`	`Measure-Object`	`New-PSSessionOption`	`New-PSTransportOption`
`New-TimeSpan`	`Out-Default`	`Out-Host`	`Out-Null`
`Out-String`	`Select-Object`	`Sort-Object`	`Update-List`
`Where-Object`	`Write-Debug`	`Write-Error`	`Write-Host`
`Write-Output`	`Write-Progress`	`Write-Verbose`	

If you need to use a cmdlet that doesn't have a matching workflow activity or you want to execute one of the cmdlets from table 12.5 remotely, you have to use an Inline-Script (see section 12.2.3).

12.1.6 *Workflow restrictions*

Given the architectural considerations of the PowerShell workflow runtime, there are a number of restrictions you need to be aware of in PowerShell workflows:

- Language restrictions
- Aliases and positional parameters
- Object serialization and deserialization
- Variable usage

We'll be covering variable usage in section 12.3.1.

LANGUAGE RESTRICTIONS

A number of PowerShell keywords and techniques aren't supported in workflows. Table 12.6 provides a summary.

Table 12.6 PowerShell language and techniques not supported in workflows

Begin, Process, End	Break, Continue	Subexpressions
Multiple assignment	Modify loop variable	Dynamic parameters
Set properties	Dot-sourcing	Advanced parameter validation
Single #requires	Switch statement	Trap statement
Inline help	Setting drive qualified variables	Method invocation on objects
New-Object with -COMobject parameter		

Some of the language restrictions can be overcome by using an InlineScript block, as you'll see later, but the others you need to avoid. They're a restriction imposed by Windows Workflow Foundation, and you'll get an error if you try to use them.

USING ALIASES IN WORKFLOWS

When workflows were first introduced in PowerShell v3 this would have failed:

```
workflow test1
{
    gps powershell*
}
test1
```

The reason for the failure was twofold:

- Aliases weren't allowed.
- Positional parameters weren't allowed.

In addition, in PowerShell v3 you had to use full parameter names. These restrictions were relaxed in PowerShell v4. PowerShell workflows aren't a command-line activity, and its best practice in your scripts to not use aliases, positional parameters, or parameter abbreviations, so we recommend that you adhere to the original restriction.

The objects you receive from a workflow add an additional restriction.

OBJECTS RETURNED FROM WORKFLOWS

Workflows use PowerShell remoting for access to remote machines, so the objects returned to you have been serialized and then deserialized. A deserialized object gives you the properties of the object but not the methods—it's inert. Lots of PowerShell code does something like this:

```
$prc = Get-Process -Name notepad
$prc.Kill()
```

You create an object and then call a method on that object. This approach isn't going to work in your workflows:

```
workflow test2
{
  $prc = Get-Process -Name notepad
  $prc.Kill()
}
```

It will throw an error about method invocation not being supported:

```
At line:4 char:3
+    $prc.Kill()
+    ~~~~~~~~~~~
Method invocation is not supported in a Windows PowerShell Workflow.
To use .NET scripting, place your commands in an inline script:
InlineScript { <commands> }.
    + CategoryInfo          : ParserError: (:) [],
   ParentContainsErrorRecordException
    + FullyQualifiedErrorId : MethodInvocationNotSupported
```

The InlineScript activity is your get-out-of-jail card for a lot of workflow issues—you'll see how it works later and how to perform this technique.

We've spent some time explaining how workflows look like PowerShell, but are different, yet use a PowerShell-like syntax. It's time to dig deeper into workflow syntax and see how to use the workflow keywords.

12.2 *Workflow keywords*

You need to understand a number of keywords in order to get the most out of workflows. These keywords are valid only inside the body of a workflow function. They enable parallel or sequential execution of commands, enable execution of cmdlets that don't have workflow activities, allow embedding pure PowerShell code in workflows, and allow parallel execution inside a foreach loop. Each of these keywords will have a block containing one or more commands.

One of the major reasons for using a workflow is to enable commands to execute in parallel, so we'll start with that.

12.2.1 *Parallel*

By default, the commands within a workflow execute in sequence. Run the following workflow:

```
workflow p1
{
    foreach ($i in 1..4){$i}
    foreach ($j in 4..1){$j}
}
p1
```

You'll see the screen output count up from 1 to 4 and then down from 4 to 1. That's exactly the same output as if you'd run the commands in a function:

```
function f1 {
    foreach ($i in 1..4){$i}
    foreach ($j in 4..1){$j}
}
f1
```

If you need simultaneous execution of commands, you have to use the `parallel` keyword to instruct the workflow to run commands in parallel. The syntax is shown in figure 12.2.

```
workflow <Verb-Noun>
 {
   Parallel
   {
    [<Activity>]
    [<Activity>]
    ...
   }
 }
```

Figure 12.2 Syntax of the `parallel` keyword

Using the `parallel` keyword, our previous example becomes this:

```
workflow p2 {
    parallel {
        foreach ($i in 1..4){$i}
        foreach ($j in 4..1){$j}
    }
}
"$(p2)"
```

This time you'll see a mixture of numbers counting up and counting down, something like this:

```
1 4 2 3 3 2 4 1
```

Parallel execution can be more efficient and can reduce run times:

```
PS> Measure-Command {p1} | Select Milliseconds
PS> Measure-Command {p2} | Select Milliseconds

Milliseconds
------------
         269
         160
```

You can see that the workflow executing commands in parallel finished in a shorter time. This is governed by the hardware where the workflow is running. Also, parallelism is much more effective in the remoting scenario where the real work is done on the remote machine. This is the primary scenario for using it. Simple local parallelism in a workflow isn't terribly useful because there's a lot of overhead in running a workflow.

The ability to execute commands in parallel is great, but as we showed earlier, you have no control over the order in which commands are executed and so you can't predict the order in which the results will be returned. Sometimes you need to be able to control the order in which commands execute.

12.2.2 Sequence

The `sequence` keyword is used to run a set of activities in sequence—in the order in which they are written, which is the default for workflow, so the `sequence` statement is intended to be nested inside `parallel` blocks so that you can execute multiple statements in parallel. An activity in a `sequence` scriptblock will execute only when the preceding activity has completed.

> **NOTE** When you include a `sequence` block in a `parallel` block, you have no control over when the `sequence` block executes within the `parallel` block. You can control the execution only within the `sequence` block.

Figure 12.3 shows alternate syntaxes for using the `sequence` block.

```
workflow <Verb-Noun>              workflow <Verb-Noun>
 {                                 {
   Sequence                          Parallel
   {                                 {
     [<Activity>]                      [<Activity>]
     [<Activity>]                      Sequence
     ...                               {
   }                                     [<Activity>]
 }                                       [<Activity>]
                                         ...
                                       }
                                     }
                                   }
```

Figure 12.3 Alternate syntaxes of a workflow `sequence` block

This needs an example to clarify. Consider this workflow:

```
workflow ps1
{
    parallel {
        foreach ($i in 1..4){$i}
        sequence {
            foreach ($k in 65..68){[char][byte]$k}
            foreach ($k in 87..90){[char][byte]$k}
        }
        foreach ($j in 4..1){$j}
    }
}
"$(ps1)"
```

Executing this workflow will produce the following output:

```
1 A 4 2 B 3 3 C 2 4 D 1 W X Y Z
```

The workflow from section 12.2.1 has been modified by inserting a `sequence` block between the two `foreach` blocks. The workflow will execute the `foreach` blocks and the `sequence` block in parallel. The commands inside the `sequence` block execute in order.

The outputs of the `foreach` blocks and the `sequence` block are intermixed, as you'd expect from parallel execution. The important point is that the output from the `sequence` block is ordered as expected, namely A–D followed by W–Z.

You now know how to execute commands in parallel and force execution to be sequential when required. In the next section, you'll learn about dealing with cmdlets and PowerShell features that aren't supported by workflows.

12.2.3 *InlineScript*

Workflows are written in PowerShell that has new keywords and some language restrictions. How do you incorporate "pure, traditional" PowerShell into a workflow?

This is where `InlineScript` comes to the rescue. An `InlineScript` block can contain any and all valid PowerShell commands irrespective of their being normally supported in workflows.

> **NOTE** In many cases `InlineScript` (or inline functions) are the only practical way to use workflow. Using the workflow activity to get a registry key is ludicrously slow. Workflow is best used to sequence largish blocks of code that you don't want to repeat.

You can use an `InlineScript` block in the main body of the workflow, inside a loop or control statement, or nested inside a parallel or sequential block. The syntax is illustrated in figure 12.4.

An `InlineScript` block has the activity common parameters including `-PSPersist`, but the PowerShell commands inside the `InlineScript` block don't gain any of the activity common parameters or workflow features such as checkpointing.

```
workflow <Verb-Noun>
  {
    InlineScript
    {
      [<Command>]
      [<Command>]
      ...
    }
  }
```

Figure 12.4   Workflow `InlineScript` syntax

Variables defined in a workflow aren't visible to an `InlineScript` block, but the `$using` scope modifier can be used to access those variables; see section 12.3.2.

Using an `InlineScript` block is illustrated here.

Listing 12.3   Using an `InlineScript` block

```
workflow is1
{
    parallel {                                                   ❶ Parallel
        'BootTime from Parallel:'                                   block
        Get-CimInstance -ClassName Win32_OperatingSystem `
        -PSComputerName $env:COMPUTERNAME |
        Select-Object -ExpandProperty LastBootUpTime

                                                                 ❷ InlineScript
        InlineScript {                                              block
            $os = Get-WmiObject -Class Win32_OperatingSystem `
    -ComputerName $env:COMPUTERNAME
            'BootTime from InlineScript: '
             $($os.ConvertToDateTime($os.LastBootUpTime))
        }
    }
}
is1
```

Running the workflow gives these results:

```
BootTime from Parallel:
16 April 2017 22:45:29

BootTime from InlineScript:
16 April 2017 22:45:29
```

The `parallel` block ❶ uses `Get-CimInstance` to retrieve the `Win32_OperatingSystem` WMI class and return the `LastBootUpTime` property. The property is returned as a date as shown in the output (one of the reasons for using the CIM cmdlets rather than the WMI cmdlets). We're using a workflow activity in this block (the `-PSComputerName` parameter).

> **NOTE**   When creating workflows, the PowerShell ISE IntelliSense will work out if you're using a workflow activity or a PowerShell cmdlet and show you the correct parameters.

Conversely, in the `InlineScript` block ❷ we're using a PowerShell cmdlet, `Get -WmiObject`. It also retrieves the `Win32_OperatingSystem` WMI class but has to use the `ConvertToDateTime` method to return the date in a readable format. We deliberately wrapped the method in a subexpression to show PowerShell functionality normally not supported in workflows. We're also using the `-ComputerName` parameter on `Get -WmiObject` as you'd expect.

You've seen workflows that execute in parallel and sequentially, but we haven't looked at iterating over collections yet. Guess what's next!

12.2.4 Foreach -parallel

Loops are an important part of coding; they enable you to repeatedly execute a set of commands with minimal coding effort. We discussed the standard PowerShell looping constructs in chapter 5. Those constructs can also be used in PowerShell workflows.

Listing 12.4 Using loops in workflows

```
workflow fe
{
    'Do loop'
    $i = 1
    $j = @()
    do {
        $j += $i
        $i++
    } while ($i -le 10)
    "$j"

    'While loop'
    $i = 1
    $j = @()
    while ($i -le 10) {
        $j += $i
        $i++
    }
    "$j"

    'For loop'
    $j = @()
    for ($i = 1; $i -le 10; $i++) {
        $j += $i
    }
    "$j"

    'Foreach loop'
    $j = @()
    foreach ($i in 1..10){$j += $i}
    "$j"
}
fe
```

When you execute the workflow, you'll see results like this:

```
Do loop
1 2 3 4 5 6 7 8 9 10
While loop
1 2 3 4 5 6 7 8 9 10
For loop
1 2 3 4 5 6 7 8 9 10
Foreach loop
1 2 3 4 5 6 7 8 9 10
```

You'll immediately notice that each individual loop executes sequentially. You could try to put the loop inside a parallel block, but it wouldn't make any difference.

In the examples in listing 12.4 we're only listing numbers, so parallel versus sequential processing isn't a great issue. If, on the other hand, you're iterating through a collection of computers and needing to perform some actions on them, such as setting a registry key or pulling WMI data, being able to process the loop in parallel would be a significant time saver.

> **NOTE** If all the tasks in your workflow need to access the same set of remote machines, use the -PSComputerName parameter on the workflow, which will force parallel processing across the machines for each command.

The answer is to use foreach with the -parallel parameter, as shown in figure 12.5.

```
Foreach -parallel ($<item> in $<collection>)
  {
    [<Activity1>]
    [<Activity2>]
    ...
  }
```

Figure 12.5 Foreach -parallel **syntax**

As an example consider the following:

```
workflow fep {
    foreach -parallel ($i in 1..10){$i}
}
"$(fep)"
```

This gave the following results when we tested it:

```
10 9 8 7 6 5 4 3 1 2
```

You can see that the results aren't sequential when compared to the results obtained from listing 12.4. The -parallel parameter runs the commands in the script block once, in sequence, for each item in the collection; the parallelization occurs at the item level. The collection must be created, and the variable defined, before the foreach -parallel statement.

This example is more practical:

```
workflow fs {
  $fileshares = Get-FileShare
  foreach -parallel ($fileshare in $fileshares){
    InlineScript {
        Get-Volume -FileShare $using:fileshare |
        Select-Object @{N='Share'; E={$using:fileshare.Name}},
        DriveLetter, FileSystem, HealthStatus,
        @{N='FreePercent';
        E={[math]::Round(($($_.SizeRemaining) / $($_.Size)) * 100, 2)}}
    }
  }
}
fs
```

The collection of file shares on a machine is generated using Get-FileShare. For each file share in the collection, the volume data is retrieved and displayed. The shares are processed in parallel. Note that because the InlineScript activity runs code in a separate runspace (see figure 12.1), as in remoting, the $using: scope modifier is required to access the $fileshare variable. Each share produces results similar to this:

```
Share                 : C$
DriveLetter           : C
FileSystem            : NTFS
HealthStatus          : Healthy
FreePercent           : 39.51
PSComputerName        : localhost
PSSourceJobInstanceId : ac7a4655-397c-483c-be73-6db80e4ae204
```

Notice that the computer name and the job instance identifier are automatically added.

You now have a good understanding of how workflows are constructed and how they work. Let's look at how you use them.

12.3 Using workflows effectively

In this section, we'll look at the parameters available on workflows; this is a separate but overlapping set of parameters to those available on individual activities. We'll then look at using variables in workflows and the scoping issues this introduces, followed by showing you how workflows can be called from other workflows and even nested. We've said that workflows are run as jobs and we'll cover that in chapter 13.

First, you need to know about the parameters available on workflows.

12.3.1 *Workflow parameters*

Workflows have a large number of parameters by default. You saw the list of parameters in section 12.1.2. The default parameters can be split into two sets, as shown by the syntax of a simple workflow:

```
PS> workflow test {'Hello'}
PS> Get-Command test -Syntax

test [<WorkflowCommonParameters>] [<CommonParameters>]
```

The common parameters are those that you also see on functions and cmdlets. These are listed in table 12.7.

Table 12.7 Workflow common parameters

InputObject	ErrorAction	WarningAction	InformationAction
Verbose	Debug	ErrorVariable	WarningVariable
InformationVariable	OutVariable	OutBuffer	PipelineVariable

You've seen these parameters in use throughout the previous chapters. Much more interesting are the parameters that are unique to workflows, as presented in table 12.8.

Table 12.8 Parameters unique to workflows

PSParameterCollection	PSComputerName	PSCredential
PSConnectionRetryCount	PSConnectionRetry- IntervalSec	PSRunningTimeoutSec
PSElapsedTimeoutSec	PSPersist	PSAuthentication
PSAuthenticationLevel	PSApplicationName	PSPort
PSUseSSL	PSConfigurationName	PSConnectionURI
PSAllowRedirection	PSSessionOption	PSCertificateThumbprint
PSPrivateMetadata	AsJob	JobName

> **NOTE** Workflows that are nested three or more levels deep don't support any common parameters.

These parameters are described in the help file about_WorkflowCommonParameters. You should compare the contents of tables 12.7 and 12.8 with table 12.3 (activity common parameters) to see the differences and overlaps.

> **NOTE** Workflow (and activity) common parameters are all optional and named. None of them can be used as a positional parameter. They also don't take input from the pipeline.

We won't describe all these parameters in detail because many overlap with the remoting session parameters you've already seen—which is not surprising because workflows use WS-MAN to communicate with remote machines. Some of the parameters need to be discussed, starting with the way you pass computer names to workflows.

PSCOMPUTERNAME

This parameter specifies a list of computers on which the workflow will be run. You can use the name, IP address, or fully qualified domain name with the same approach as PowerShell remoting; that is, if you use an IP address you have to supply the appropriate credentials and the remote computer must use HTTPS or the IP address must be in the trusted hosts list.

All workflows and activities have -PSComputerName available as a parameter, so where should you put it? As usual, it depends.

If you put it at the workflow level

```
workflow test-remoteaccess {
 Get-WmiObject -Class Win32_ComputerSystem
}
test-remoteaccess -PSComputerName W16TGT01, W16DSC01
```

you'll receive results like these for each machine:

```
Domain              : Manticore.org
Manufacturer        : Microsoft Corporation
Model               : Virtual Machine
Name                : W16TGT01
PrimaryOwnerName    : Windows User
TotalPhysicalMemory : 1116749824
PSComputerName      : localhost
```

Notice that the Get-WmiObject activity has no mention of remote machines. This is one advantage of using -PSComputerName at the workflow level in that you can easily use the same workflow locally and add the -PSComputerName parameter when you need to access remote machines.

Compare this to running Get-WmiObject directly against the local machine:

```
PS> Get-WmiObject -Class Win32_ComputerSystem

Domain              : Manticore.org
Manufacturer        : Microsoft Corporation
Model               : Virtual Machine
Name                : W16AS01
PrimaryOwnerName    : Windows User
TotalPhysicalMemory : 2429566976
```

The workflow adds a PSComputerName property to the output. This is the name of the computer on which you're running the workflow. It is *not* the name of the remote machine even though the workflow has a -PSComputerName parameter! The remote machine name is in the Name property.

NOTE This is one of those confusing points you'll have to remember.

Using -PSComputerName at the workflow level is probably best kept for situations where you have simple data return requirements or you're predominantly performing actions against the remote machine with minimal or no data returned.

When you use the -PSComputerName parameter, it effectively replaces the -Computer-Name parameter on the cmdlet. You don't get free connectivity! You'll also find that you're connecting over the native mechanism used by the cmdlet that corresponds to the workflow activity. If the remote machine doesn't support that particular mode of connectivity, your workflow will fail for that machine.

Moving the -PSComputerName to the activity results in this code:

```
workflow test-remoteaccess {
 param(
  [string[]]$computername
 )
 foreach -parallel ($computer in $computername) {
   Get-WmiObject -Class Win32_ComputerSystem -PSComputerName $computer
 }
}
test-remoteaccess -computername W16TGT01, W16DSC01
```

This workflow defines a parameter that takes a list of computer names. The foreach -parallel statement is used to iterate over the computer names. The computers in the list are processed in parallel, and the commands within the foreach -parallel block are processed sequentially for each computer. You're back to using the native connectivity (DCOM in this case). This approach would be useful when you have a number of activities in your workflow, not all of which need to access a remote machine.

You need to consider one last scenario: running a workflow with an InlineScript block where the cmdlets in the block need to connect to remote machines. The big thing for you to remember in this scenario is that you're running cmdlets, not workflow activities, so you need to use the cmdlet's native parameter -ComputerName.

```
workflow Test-RemoteAccess
{
 param(
  [string[]]$computername
 )
 inlinescript {
  foreach ($computer in $using:computername) {
   Get-WmiObject -Class Win32_ComputerSystem -ComputerName $computer
  }
 }
}
test-remoteaccess -computername W16TGT01, W16DSC01
```

The workflow has a -computername parameter that takes a list of computer names. Within the InlineScript block a foreach loop iterates over the list of computers. You have to define the foreach loop like this:

```
foreach ($computer in $using:computername)
```

The $using modifier enables the loop to access the variable that was defined in a higher scope within the workflow; you'll learn about that in the next section.

You will have to decide, based on what your workflow is doing, how you will pass computer names into the workflow and which parameters you need to use.

PSCONFIGURATIONNAME

This parameter specifies the session configuration used when connecting to remote computers. The default is `Microsoft.PowerShell.Workflow`, as shown in figure 12.6.

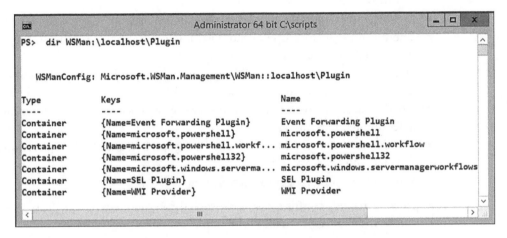

Figure 12.6   Remoting endpoints on a Windows Server 2012 R2 system

The endpoints shown in figure 12.6 are created by default when PowerShell remoting is enabled either explicitly by running `Enable-PSRemoting` or implicitly through installation of Windows Server 2012 (or later). `Microsoft.PowerShell.Workflow` is used by workflows, whereas `Microsoft.PowerShell` and `Microsoft.PowerShell32` are used by PowerShell remoting.

You can drill down further into the endpoint configuration by examining the contents of the InitializationParameters, Resources, and Quotas containers.

The vast majority of the time you can use the default endpoint. If you need to create a new endpoint, you can use the approach outlined in section 11.6.4.

Possibly the most interesting parameter is `-Persist`, but we'll delay talking about that until chapter 13 because we first need to look at using variables in workflows.

12.3.2   *Variables in workflows*

You've seen variables used in various workflows in the earlier sections of this chapter. We've also shown you the $using and $workflow scoping modifiers that are used in workflows. Now it's time to bring this together and show the rules for using variables in workflows. It's not complicated—honest!

Workflows use lexical scoping, so a variable defined inside a block is visible only in that block and nested blocks. This leads to the following restrictions on the use of variables:

- Variables defined in a higher scope are visible to lower workflow scopes but not InlineScript scopes.
- You *can't* have a variable in a lower scope with the same name as a variable in a higher scope—an aspect of lexical scoping caused by the underlying workflow engine.
- If you define or redefine a variable, you can use it in that scope without problems.
- There is no $global scope because workflows *always* run as jobs, so they have a new global context.
- Use the $workflow scope modifier to access, or modify, a variable defined in a higher scope, except in InlineScript blocks.
- Use the $using scope modifier in InlineScript blocks to access, or modify, variables defined in a higher scope.
- Modification of a variable from a higher scope in an InlineScript requires the use of a temporary variable.
- You can't use subexpressions in workflows.

That probably sounds confusing, so let's work through an example of using variables in workflows that'll bring the rules into focus.

Listing 12.5   Using variables in workflows

```
workflow demo-scope
{
    # This is a workflow top-level variable
    $a = 22
    "Initial value of A is: $a"

    # Access $a from Inlinescript (bringing a workflow
    #variable to the PowerShell session) using $using
    inlinescript {"PowerShell variable A is: $a"}
    inlinescript {"Workflow variable A is: $using:a"}

    ## changing a variable value
    $a = InlineScript {$b = $Using:a+5; $b}
    "Workflow variable A after InlineScript change is: $a"

    parallel {
        sequence {
            # Reading a top-level variable
            "Value of A inside parallel is: $a"

            # Updating a top-level variable with
            # $workflow:<variable name>
            $workflow:a = 3
        }
    }
}
```

```
    "Updated value of A is: $a"
}
demo-scope
```

When you run this workflow, you should see this output:

```
Initial value of A is: 22
PowerShell variable A is:
Workflow variable A is: 22
Workflow variable A after InlineScript change is: 27
Value of A inside parallel is: 27
Updated value of A is: 3
```

The workflow starts by defining a variable - $a = 22 and then displaying its value. In an InlineScript if you try to access a variable defined in a higher scope, you get nothing, as shown in the second line of the output. You have to use $using:a to access the variable. If you want to change that variable, you'll have to use a second variable and return it to the original variable:

```
$a = InlineScript {$b = $Using:a+5; $b}
```

The output shows the variable now has a value of 27.

Moving into the parallel block, you can read the variable without any scope issues. If you need to change the variable's value, you can access it via the $workflow scope modifier. The bottom line with variables in workflows is *keep it simple and be careful*.

So far, you've seen single workflows. When using scripts or functions, you can call other scripts or functions (or even nest functions). How do workflows handle this?

12.3.3 *Nested workflows*

Think about how you use your PowerShell scripts and functions; you probably build a number of functions that you reuse and call from other functions and scripts. The whole concept of reusability should permeate your PowerShell code so that you maximize the return from the time and effort you put into developing your code. How can PowerShell functions and PowerShell workflows be used inside other workflows?

The mechanisms available to reuse existing functionality break down into three broad groups:

- PowerShell workflows called from your workflow or nested in your workflow
- PowerShell functions either in the same script file as the workflow or through a PowerShell module
- PowerShell scripts on the local or remote machine

Let's start by looking at how your workflow can interact with other workflows using a practical example from standard Active Directory administration tasks. It's generally regarded as good practice to clean up the accounts in your Active Directory. You would normally look at disabled accounts, expired accounts, and accounts with passwords that never expire. You can make a decision on what to do with each account once you've identified accounts that match your criteria.

To find disabled accounts, run the following:

```
PS> Search-ADAccount -AccountDisabled |
Select-Object -Property DistinguishedName |
Export-Csv -Path c:\ADReports\DisabledAccounts.csv -NoTypeInformation
```

To find expired accounts, do this:

```
PS> Search-ADAccount -AccountExpired |
Select-Object -Property DistinguishedName |
Export-Csv -Path c:\ADReports\ExpiredAccounts.csv -NoTypeInformation
```

To find accounts whose passwords never expire, use this:

```
PS> Search-ADAccount -PasswordNeverExpires |
Select-Object -Property DistinguishedName |
Export-Csv -Path c:\ADReports\PsswdNeverExpireAccounts.csv `
-NoTypeInformation
```

These three simple scripts will be familiar to Active Directory administrators. Using these is more efficient that trying to perform the task by hand, but you have to run them sequentially. Can workflows help you introduce some parallelism?

The most direct approach would be to wrap the scripts into a single workflow:

```
workflow Get-ADReport
{
 parallel {
 Search-ADAccount -AccountDisabled |
 Select-Object -Property DistinguishedName |
 Export-Csv -Path c:\ADReports\DisabledAccounts.csv `
 -NoTypeInformation

 Search-ADAccount -AccountExpired |
 Select-Object -Property DistinguishedName |
 Export-Csv -Path c:\ADReports\ExpiredAccounts.csv `
 -NoTypeInformation

 Search-ADAccount -PasswordNeverExpires |
 Select-Object -Property DistinguishedName |
 Export-Csv -Path c:\ADReports\PsswdNeverExpireAccounts.csv `
 -NoTypeInformation
 }
}
Get-ADReport
```

The three CSV files are produced more or less simultaneously. This is great if this task runs once in a while but not if you need a more granular approach and want to run each search individually. One approach that also has the benefit of making maintenance easier is to move the individual workflows out of the main workflow, like this:

```
workflow get-disabled
{
 Search-ADAccount -AccountDisabled |
 Select-Object -Property DistinguishedName |
 Export-Csv -Path c:\ADReports\DisabledAccounts.csv `
-NoTypeInformation
}

workflow get-expired
{
 Search-ADAccount -AccountExpired |
 Select-Object -Property DistinguishedName |
 Export-Csv -Path c:\ADReports\ExpiredAccounts.csv `
-NoTypeInformation
}

workflow get-passwordneverexpire
{
 Search-ADAccount -PasswordNeverExpires |
 Select-Object -Property DistinguishedName |
 Export-Csv -Path c:\ADReports\PsswdNeverExpireAccounts.csv `
-NoTypeInformation
}

workflow Get-ADReport
{
 parallel {
   get-disabled
   get-expired
   get-passwordneverexpire
   }
}
Get-ADReport
```

You can take this a stage further and separate your workflows into individual files and create a .psm1 file to load them as a module. You can then add further functionality in a granular manner without affecting the bulk of your code.

> **NOTE** In reality, nested workflows can cause problems if you try to nest complicated workflows. The preferred and recommended reuse strategy is to use functions instead of nested workflows.

Functions can be embedded in a workflow or in the script used to create the workflow. In the following workflow, a list of computer names is passed in through the -computerName parameter. A foreach -parallel loop is used to iterate over the list of computers. Test-Connection is used to determine if the remote system is contactable, and if so, the function is called.

In this case, the function is defined outside the workflow. You could as easily have defined it inside the workflow. Similarly, you could put the functions into a separate script and load them and the workflow as part of a module.

The important point is that the workflows or functions you want to call are loaded, or defined, before you want to use them:

```
function get-fcomputersystem {
    param ([string]$fcomputer)
    Get-WmiObject -Class Win32_ComputerSystem -ComputerName $fcomputer
}

workflow get-computersystem
{
    param([string[]]$computerName)

    ## Alternate location for function

    # The contents of the foreach block will be executed in parallel
    foreach -parallel($computer in $computerName) {

        if (Test-Connection -ComputerName $computer -Quiet -Count 1) {
            get-fcomputersystem -fcomputer $computer
        }
        else {
            "$computer unreachable"
        }
    }
}


Get-ComputerSystem -ComputerName $ENV:COMPUTERNAME
```

Scripts are the third and last of the methods you can utilize to reuse existing code. Take the three scripts utilizing `Search-ADAccount` introduced at the top of the section and put each into a script file:

```
get-disabledaccount.ps1
get-expiredaccount.ps1
get-passwordNexpire.ps1
```

You still want these to run in parallel, so you might try this:

```
workflow get-ADReport
{
 parallel {
   c:\adreports\get-disabledaccount.ps1
   c:\adreports\get-expiredaccount.ps1
   c:\adreports\get-passwordNexpire.ps1
 }
}
```

Unfortunately, this won't work and you'll see an error:

```
At line:3 char:4
+    c:\adreports\get-disabledaccount.ps1
+    ~~~~~~~~~~~~~~~~~~~~~~~~~~~~~~~~~~~~~
Cannot find the 'c:\adreports\get-disabledaccount.ps1' command. If this
    command is defined as a workflow, ensure it is defined before the workflow
    that calls it. If it is a command intended to run directly within
    Windows PowerShell (or is not available on this system), place it in an
```

```
InlineScript: 'InlineScript { c:\adreports\get-disabledaccount.ps1 }'
    + CategoryInfo          : ParserError: (:) [], ParseException
    + FullyQualifiedErrorId : CommandNotFound
```

You want the scripts to run using an `InlineScript` block but also ensure parallelism, so run each script separately:

```
workflow get-ADReport {
 parallel {
  inlinescript {c:\adreports\get-disabledaccount.ps1}
  inlinescript {c:\adreports\get-expiredaccount.ps1}
  inlinescript {c:\adreports\get-passwordNexpire.ps1  }
 }
}
```

What about the situation where you want to run a script that exists on a remote system? The answer is to put the scripts in the C:\ADReports folder on the remote machine and run your local workflow as shown here:

```
Get-ADReport -PSComputerName W16TGT01
```

The scripts will run on the remote machine and, because you haven't modified them, that's where the output will be produced.

> **WORKFLOWS AS JOBS** We've said that workflows use the PowerShell job engine a number of times and that workflows are interruptible. We'll look at those two ideas in chapter 13.

You now have a good understanding of workflows and how to use them. The workflows you've seen so far have been scripts. A few cmdlets are also available for working with workflows.

12.4 *Workflow cmdlets*

PowerShell provides you with two workflow modules:

```
PS> Get-Module -ListAvailable *workflow* | Format-Table -AutoSize

    Directory: C:\WINDOWS\system32\WindowsPowerShell\v1.0\Modules

ModuleType Version Name              ExportedCommands
---------- ------- ----              ----------------
Manifest   2.0.0.0 PSWorkflow        {New-PSWorkflowExecutionOption,
                                      New-PSWorkflowSession, nwsn}
Manifest   1.0.0.0 PSWorkflowUtility Invoke-AsWorkflow
```

`New-PSWorkflowExecutionOption` and `New-PSWorkflowSession` from the PSWorkflow module are analogous to the remoting management cmdlets `New-PSSessionOption` and `New-PSSession` respectively. `Invoke-AsWorkflow` is a way to test your code in a workflow without any further modification.

Let's start by looking at the options you have for executing workflows.

12.4.1 Workflow execution options

The syntax for `New-PSWorkflowExecutionOption` is shown in figure 12.7.

```
New-PSWorkflowExecutionOption [-PersistencePath <string>]
[-MaxPersistenceStoreSizeGB <long>] [-PersistWithEncryption]
[-MaxRunningWorkflows <int>] [-AllowedActivity <string[]>]
[-OutOfProcessActivity <string[]>] [-EnableValidation]
[-MaxDisconnectedSessions <int>] [-MaxConnectedSessions <int>]
[-MaxSessionsPerWorkflow <int>] [-MaxSessionsPerRemoteNode <int>]
[-MaxActivityProcesses <int>] [-ActivityProcessIdleTimeoutSec <int>]
[-RemoteNodeSessionIdleTimeoutSec <int>] [-SessionThrottleLimit <int>]
[-WorkflowShutdownTimeoutMSec <int>] [<CommonParameters>]
```

Figure 12.7   Syntax of the `New-PSWorkflowExecutionOption` cmdlet

An object created with `New-PSWorkflowExecutionOption` is used to configure the options for workflow sessions. You'll learn how to create a session for workflows in the next section. The cmdlet common parameters are available on this cmdlet but not the workflow common parameters. Table 12.9 lists the parameters and their meaning.

Table 12.9   `New-PSWorkflowExecutionOption` parameters

Parameter	Meaning
PersistencePath	Path on disk for storing persistence data. Default is $env:LocalAppData\Microsoft\Windows\PowerShell\ WF\PS. Persistence data is created when a workflow is checkpointed or suspended (see chapter 13).
MaxPersistenceStoreSizeGB	Maximum space, in GB, allocated to workflows running in the session. Default is 10 GB. If the size is exceeded, the store is expanded and warnings are displayed.
PersistWithEncryption	Encrypts data in persistence store. Default is false.
MaxRunningWorkflows	Maximum number of running workflows in session. Default is 30.
AllowedActivity	Namespace qualified activities that can be run in the session. Wildcards are allowed. Default is built-in WF activities and activities matching PowerShell core cmdlets.
OutOfProcessActivity	Which allowed activities (specified in AllowedActivity) are run out of process. Default is InlineScript.
EnableValidation	Verifies all workflow activities in session are included in allowed activities list. Default is true.
MaxDisconnectedSessions	Maximum number of remote sessions that are in disconnected state across all remote computers. Default is 100.

Table 12.9 `New-PSWorkflowExecutionOption` **parameters** *(continued)*

Parameter	Meaning
`MaxConnectedSessions`	Maximum number of remote sessions that are in operational state across all remote computers. Default is 100.
`MaxSessionsPerWorkflow`	Maximum number of sessions created to support each workflow. Default is 5.
`MaxSessionsPerRemoteNode`	Maximum number of sessions that can be connected to each remote computer. Default is 5.
`MaxActivityProcesses`	Maximum processes that can be created in a session to support workflow activities. Default is 5.
`ActivityProcessIdleTimeoutSec`	Determines the time before an activity host process is closed once the process becomes idle. Default is 60 seconds.
`RemoteNodeSessionIdleTimeoutSec`	Specifies timeout on an idle session connected to a remote computer. Default is 60 seconds.
`SessionThrottleLimit`	Number of operations created to support all workflows started in a session. Default is 100.
`WorkflowShutdownTimeoutMSec`	Time session is maintained after all workflows are forcibly suspended. Default is 500 seconds.

As an example, we'll modify the code from listing 12.2 to give this:

```
workflow Invoke-ParallelForEach
{
    foreach -parallel ($i in 1..10)
    {
        InlineScript
        {
            "foo: $using:i"
        }
        $count = Get-Process -Name PowerShell* |
                Measure-Object |
                Select-Object -ExpandProperty Count
        "Number of PowerShell processes = $count"
    }
}
```

You can create a new workflow execution option object like this:

```
PS> $wfopt = New-PSWorkflowExecutionOption -MaxSessionsPerWorkflow 20 `
-MaxSessionsPerRemoteNode 20 -MaxActivityProcesses 20
PS> $wfopt
SessionThrottleLimit           : 100
PersistencePath                : C:\Users\Richard\AppData\Local\
                                 Microsoft\Windows\PowerShell\WF\PS
MaxPersistenceStoreSizeGB      : 10
PersistWithEncryption          : False
```

```
MaxRunningWorkflows              : 30
AllowedActivity                  : {PSDefaultActivities}
OutOfProcessActivity             : {InlineScript}
EnableValidation                 : True
MaxDisconnectedSessions          : 1000
MaxConnectedSessions             : 100
MaxSessionsPerWorkflow           : 20
MaxSessionsPerRemoteNode         : 20
MaxActivityProcesses             : 20
ActivityProcessIdleTimeoutSec    : 60
RemoteNodeSessionIdleTimeoutSec  : 60
WorkflowShutdownTimeoutMSec      : 500
```

You can then create a new endpoint:

```
PS> Register-PSSessionConfiguration -Name PiAWorkflows `
-SessionTypeOption $wfopt -SessionType Workflow -Force

WSManConfig: Microsoft.WSMan.Management\WSMan::localhost\Plugin

Type          Keys                          Name
----          ----                          ----
Container     {Name=PiAWorkflows}           PiAWorkflows
```

The workflow endpoints can be explicitly accessed using the -PSConfiguration parameter on your workflow. The default endpoint can be accessed by leaving the parameter off or explicitly providing the endpoint name:

```
PS> Invoke-ParallelForEach `
-PSConfigurationName Microsoft.PowerShell.Workflow
```

If you want to access your new endpoint, then use its name:

```
PS> Invoke-ParallelForEach -PSConfigurationName PiAWorkflows
```

You can modify an endpoint:

```
PS> Set-PSSessionConfiguration -Name PiAWorkFlows `
-SessionTypeOption (New-PSWorkflowExecutionOption `
-SessionThrottleLimit 500) -Force
```

You can review the change:

```
PS> Get-PSSessionConfiguration -Name PiAWorkflows |
select SessionThrottleLimit

SessionThrottleLimit
--------------------
500
```

If you need to remove a workflow endpoint, use this command:

```
PS> UnRegister-PSSessionConfiguration -Name PiAWorkflows –Force
```

NOTE   You can modify the settings on the default workflow endpoint, but they work well in all but the most exceptional cases. If you want to experiment, it's best to create a new endpoint.

You've seen how to use workflows against remote machines using the -PSComputerName parameter. You can also create workflow sessions to remote computers in a similar manner to PowerShell remoting.

12.4.2 Workflow sessions

Workflow sessions are similar to the remoting sessions you saw in chapter 11. You use them to create a permanent connection to the remote machine rather than creating and destroying connections as needed.

Creating a session is similar to PowerShell remoting:

```
PS> $wfs = New-PSWorkflowSession -ComputerName W16TGT01
```

As with PowerShell remoting, the commands you call have to exist on the remote machine or you must supply them to the session. You'll create a scriptblock containing your workflow (including the command to execute the workflow):

```
$sb = {
workflow Invoke-ParallelForEach
{
    foreach -parallel ($i in 1..10)
    {
        InlineScript
        {
            "foo: $using:i"
        }
        $count = Get-Process -Name PowerShell* |
                Measure-Object |
                Select-Object -ExpandProperty Count
        "Number of PowerShell processes = $count"
    }
}
Invoke-ParallelForEach
}
```

The scriptblock is executed through the session:

```
PS> Invoke-Command -Session $wfs -ScriptBlock $sb
```

When the workflow commences, you'll see a warning like this:

```
WARNING: [localhost]:This workflow job cannot be suspended because there are
    no checkpoints (also called persistence points) in the workflow. To make
    the workflow job suspendable, add checkpoints to the workflow.
For more information about how to add checkpoints, see the help topics for
    Windows PowerShell Workflow.
```

When you've finished with your session, its best practice to remove it:

```
PS> Remove-PSSession -Session $wfs
```

Using non-default workflow endpoints remotely

`New-PSWorkflowSession` doesn't give you a way to access any workflow endpoints other than the default one. The `-SessionOption` takes remoting options, not workflow execution options, from `New-PSWorkflowExecutionOption`!

If you need to access a workflow endpoint that you've created, you need to use `New-PSsession` to create the session. In this case we've used the technique from the previous section to create an endpoint called `PiAWorkflows` on a remote machine. A remote session is created to the endpoint:

```
PS> $ts = New-PSSession -ComputerName W16TGT01 `
-ConfigurationName PiAWorkflows
PS> Invoke-Command -Session $ts -ScriptBlock $sb
```

When you run the workflow, you'll see that the number of processes being used has increased. In our test we saw this:

```
Number of PowerShell processes = 11
```

Workflow sessions provide another option when running against remote machines. You can run workflows through standard remoting sessions, in which case they'll use the default workflow endpoint on the remote machine.

PowerShell, and therefore workflow, remoting works against the machine or machines to which you've connected, but if you try to connect to a third machine from your remote machine, you'll hit the double-hop problem.

DOUBLE-HOP PROBLEM

The usual scenario in remote administration is that you're working locally on machine A and connect remotely to machine B to perform one or more tasks. If you try to perform an action on machine C from your session on machine B, you'll receive an error. Let's see what happens. Start with a standard call to a remote machine:

```
PS> Invoke-Command -ScriptBlock {Get-Process lsass} `
-ComputerName W16TGT01
```

This works as expected. Now try accessing another machine from the session on W16TGT01:

```
PS> Invoke-Command -ScriptBlock {
  Invoke-Command -ScriptBlock {
    Get-Process lsass } -ComputerName W16DSC01
} -ComputerName W16TGT01

[W16DSC01] Connecting to remote server W16DSC01 failed with the following
   error message : WinRM cannot process the request. The following error
```

```
with errorcode 0x8009030e occurred while using Kerberos authentication:
A specified logon session does not exist. It may already have been
terminated. Possible causes are:
-The user name or password specified are invalid.
-Kerberos is used when no authentication method and no user name are
specified.
-Kerberos accepts domain user names, but not local user names.
-The Service Principal Name (SPN) for the remote computer name and port
does not exist.
-The client and remote computers are in different domains and there is no
trust between the two domains.
After checking for the above issues, try the following:
 -Check the Event Viewer for events related to authentication.
 -Change the authentication method; add the destination computer to the
WinRM TrustedHosts configuration setting or use HTTPS transport.
Note that computers in the TrustedHosts list might not be authenticated.
  -For more information about WinRM configuration, run the following
command: winrm help config. For more
information, see the about_Remote_Troubleshooting Help topic.
   + CategoryInfo          : OpenError: (W16DSC01:String) [],
PSRemotingTransportException
   + FullyQualifiedErrorId : 1312,PSSessionStateBroken
   + PSComputerName        : W16TGT01
```

This rather long error message boils down to saying that Kerberos authentication failed to connect you to the second machine: your credentials weren't available to the session on machine B (W16TGT01) when it attempted to create a session on machine C (W16DSC01).

One solution to this problem is to use the Credential Security Support Provider (CredSSP), but because that involves sending your password in clear text across the network, this solution isn't acceptable to many organizations. A more acceptable solution is use the RunAs configuration option on a PowerShell remoting session. First, create a credential object on machine B for the account you'll use to connect to machine C:

```
PS> $cred = Get-Credential manticore\richard
```

Then use that credential when you create the remoting endpoint on machine B:

```
PS> Register-PSSessionConfiguration -Name DHsol -RunAsCredential $cred

WARNING: When RunAs is enabled in a Windows PowerShell session configuration,
   the Windows security model cannot enforce a security boundary between
   different user sessions that are created by using this endpoint. Verify
   that the Windows PowerShell runspace configuration is restricted to only
   the necessary set of cmdlets and capabilities.
WARNING: Register-PSSessionConfiguration may need to restart the WinRM
   service if a configuration using this name has recently been unregistered,
   certain system data structures may still be cached. In that case, a
   restart of WinRM may be required.
All WinRM sessions connected to Windows PowerShell session configurations,
   such as Microsoft.PowerShell and session configurations that are created
   with the Register-PSSessionConfiguration cmdlet, are disconnected.
```

Reading the warning that's issued when you create an endpoint with a credential gives you some additional information.

> **NOTE** The credential used for the endpoint is stored as an encrypted secure string on the machine.

You can now use the endpoint and successfully perform a double hop:

```
PS> $tsd = New-PSSession -ComputerName W16TGT01 -ConfigurationName DHsol
PS> Invoke-Command -ScriptBlock {Invoke-Command -ScriptBlock {Get-Process
   lsass } -ComputerName W16DSC01 } -Session $tsd
```

Remote access for workflows works the same way. Use the -RunAsCredential parameter when you create a new workflow endpoint on machine B:

```
PS> Register-PSSessionConfiguration -Name PiAWorkflows `
-RunAsCredential $cred -SessionType Workflow -Force
```

Alternatively, if you have an existing endpoint, you can modify it to add a credential:

```
PS> Set-PSSessionConfiguration -Name PiAWorkflows -RunAsCredential $cred
```

Modify your workflow to access a remote machine by adding the -PSComputerName parameter to the Get-Process activity:

```
$sb = {
workflow Invoke-ParallelForEach
{
    foreach -parallel ($i in 1..10)
    {
        InlineScript
        {
            "foo: $using:i"
        }
        $count = Get-Process -Name PowerShell* -PSComputerName W16DSC01 |
                Measure-Object |
                Select-Object -ExpandProperty Count
        "Number of PowerShell processes = $count"
    }
}
Invoke-ParallelForEach
}
```

Re-create the remote session and run your workflow:

```
PS> $ts = New-PSSession -ComputerName W16TGT01 `
-ConfigurationName PiAWorkflows
PS> Invoke-Command -Session $ts -ScriptBlock $sb
```

Your workflow will now perform the double hop and connect to the third machine. The drawback to this technique is that you need to maintain the credential used on the endpoint. If the password changes, you need to update the endpoint with the new credential. If you need to configure a number of machines in this manner, consider using a service account approach and use an account with a strong password that's changed infrequently.

12.4.3 *Invoking as workflow*

Creating and testing workflows is a nontrivial task, but help is available within Power-Shell through the `Invoke-AsWorkflow` cmdlet in the PSWorkflowUtility module.

The cmdlet runs any command or expression as an inline script in a workflow. You get these benefits of workflows: interruptability, persisting, tracking, and the workflow common parameters. You don't get access to the `parallel` or `foreach -parallel` options.

These examples show how to use the cmdlet:

```
PS> Invoke-AsWorkflow -CommandName Get-Process `
-Parameter @{Name = 'powershell'}

PS> Invoke-AsWorkflow -Expression 'ping 127.0.0.1'
```

This concludes our examination of PowerShell workflows, a powerful tool that in the correct circumstances can be an efficient way to work with multiple remote machines.

12.5 *Summary*

- PowerShell v3 introduced the `workflow` keyword, and although workflows are written with a PowerShell-like syntax, they aren't PowerShell.
- Workflows are excellent when you need to interrupt tasks or have mixture of parallel and sequential tasks.
- Workflows execute as PowerShell jobs.
- You have no control over the order in which data is returned when running tasks in parallel in a workflow.
- Workflows use workflow activities that correspond to PowerShell cmdlets, but not all cmdlets have corresponding activities because they may not make sense in the context of a workflow.
- Workflows and workflow activities have overlapping sets of common parameters.
- A number of PowerShell language options and techniques aren't supported in workflows.
- Workflows run tasks sequentially by default.
- Use the `parallel` block to run commands in parallel.
- Use the `sequence` block to run commands sequentially inside a parallel block.
- An `InlineScript` block can run standard PowerShell commands, including those not supported in workflows.
- `Foreach -parallel` iterates over a collection of objects in parallel.
- The workflow engine allows for nested lexical scope, which PowerShell does not support by default, so the `$workflow:` scope modifier is required to modify a variable defined in a higher scope.

- When using the `InlineScript` activity, you need to use the `$using:` prefix. Note that `$using:` variables are read-only. Workflow-scope variables can't be modified in an `InlineScript` activity.
- You can't use subexpressions in workflows.
- Workflows can be nested and called from other workflows, but it's not recommended that workflows be nested to more than two levels because of the overhead of workflow calling workflow.
- `New-PSWorkflowExecutionOption` can create an object to configure workflow endpoints.
- A new workflow endpoint can be created with `Register-PSSessionConfiguration`.
- `-PSConfigurationName` allows you to specify the workflow endpoint to use.
- Workflow sessions are remoting sessions. Use `Set-PSSessionConfiguration` to modify a workflow endpoint.
- `New-PSWorkflowSession` connects to the default workflow endpoint. `New-PSSession` is used to connect to non-default endpoints, including any end user–created workflow endpoints.
- `Invoke-AsWorkflow` is used to run PowerShell commands and expressions as workflows, providing all the benefits of workflow execution without having to create a workflow to wrap a single command.

In the next chapter, we'll build on what you saw in this chapter when we look at pausing workflows and dig further into PowerShell jobs.

13

PowerShell Jobs

This chapter covers

- Asynchronous processing
- PowerShell jobs
- Job cmdlets
- Job types
- Workflow jobs
- Scheduled jobs

Exit pursued by a bear

—William Shakespeare
Stage directions from The Winter's Tale

So far, most of the techniques we've shown you have been synchronous, meaning you type in the command—be it a cmdlet, script, or function—and wait for the results. The results are back in a few seconds at most, usually far quicker. Synchronous execution is perfect for ad hoc, interactive working, but what about when you're executing a long-running process against many remote machines that could take hours to run? Waiting for those to finish locks you out of further work in that console. You could open additional instances of PowerShell or you could run the tasks asynchronously.

An asynchronous task is one that's started and left to run to completion in the background as you carry on working at other tasks. Asynchronous execution is supplied to PowerShell by using PowerShell jobs.

NOTE   In PowerShell v2, PowerShell jobs depended heavily on PowerShell remoting. Those dependencies were removed in PowerShell v3.

In this chapter, we'll show you how to use PowerShell's job engine to perform tasks asynchronously. We'll start with a look at the types of jobs available in PowerShell and the cmdlets you can use to work with jobs. We'll build on chapter 12 and show how PowerShell jobs are used to manage interruptions to workflows including reboots. We'll close the chapter by looking at how you can combine PowerShell jobs with the scheduler to perform asynchronous tasks without manual intervention—great for those long jobs that run through the middle of the night.

13.1   *Background jobs in PowerShell*

When you run a command in a PowerShell session, the session is effectively blocked until the command completes and returns its results (or fails). You're prevented from running new commands until the command completes. If you change things so that the caller doesn't block, then other commands can run in parallel. This is how PowerShell background jobs work. With background jobs, the arrangement of executing commands and processes is shown in figure 13.1.

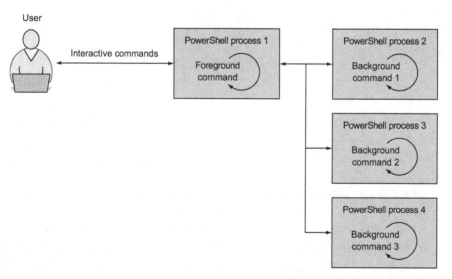

Figure 13.1   The user sends interactive commands to be executed by the foreground loop. Background commands are executed in separate processes; each process has its own command loop. For each background job the user creates, a new instance of PowerShell.exe is run to host the command loop for that job. This means that if there are three background jobs as shown, then four processes are running—three for the background jobs and one for the interactive foreground job.

NOTE Some commands have built-in job support. For example, the WMI commands have an `-AsJob` parameter that allows one or more WMI operations to execute in the background. This type of job doesn't rely on the background-execution mechanism we're describing in this section. Instead, it uses its own implementation of background execution. In the case of WMI jobs, they run in a new process but on a separate thread. The PowerShell job infrastructure was explicitly designed to support this kind of extension. If third parties expose their job abstractions as subclasses of the PowerShell `Job` type, these extension jobs can be managed using the built-in job cmdlets like native PowerShell jobs.

There's more to background jobs than executing multiple things at the same time. Background jobs are designed to be commands that run asynchronously while you continue to do other things at the console. This means there needs to be a way to manage these background jobs—starting and stopping them as well as retrieving the output in a controlled way.

NOTE Background jobs are implemented using processes that are children of your interactive PowerShell process. This means that if you end your PowerShell session, causing the process to exit, this will also cause all the background jobs to be terminated, because child processes are terminated when the parent process exits.

In this section, we'll cover the cmdlets that are used to manage background jobs. We'll look at starting, stopping, and waiting for jobs. We'll explore the `Job` objects used to represent a running job. Finally, you'll learn how to combine remoting with jobs to run jobs on remote machines.

13.1.1 *The job commands*

PowerShell jobs are managed with a set of cmdlets, shown in table 13.1.

Table 13.1 The cmdlets for working with PowerShell jobs

Cmdlet	Description
Start-Job	Used to start background jobs. It takes a scriptblock as the argument representing the job to execute.
Stop-Job	Stops a job based on the JobID.
Get-Job	Returns a list of currently executing jobs associated with the current session.
Wait-Job	Waits for one or more jobs to complete.
Receive-Job	Gets the results for a specific job.
Remove-Job	Removes a job from the job table so the resources can be released.
Debug-Job	Debugs the scriptblock executed by a job. See section 15.6.1.
Suspend-Job	Saves the state and pauses execution of a job—only used with workflow jobs. See section 13.2.
Resume-Job	Restarts a previously suspended job—only used with workflow jobs. See section 13.2.

A background job runs commands asynchronously. It's used to execute long-running commands in a way that the interactive session isn't blocked until that command completes.

NOTE You can use the PowerShell APIs explained in chapter 20 as another way to perform actions asynchronously.

When a synchronous command runs, PowerShell waits until that command has completed before accepting any new commands. When a command is run in the background, instead of blocking, the command returns immediately, emitting an object that represents the new background job.

Although you get back control immediately (a new prompt) with the Job object, you obviously won't get the results of that job even if the job runs quickly. Instead, you use a separate command to get the job's results. You also have commands to stop the job, to wait for the job to be completed, and to delete the job. Let's see how these commands are used.

13.1.2 *Working with the job cmdlets*

You use the Start-Job command to start a background job on a local computer. Let's try this with a simple example that prints a string to the console.

NOTE We're deliberately using simple examples so that the job concepts are stressed rather than the clever code the job is running. In the real world, you wouldn't run most of our examples as jobs.

You'll start a job and then pipe the resulting Job object through Format-List so you can see all of the members on the object:

```
PS> Start-Job -ScriptBlock {'Hi'} | Format-List

HasMoreData     : True
StatusMessage   :
Location        : localhost
Command         : 'Hi'
JobStateInfo    : Running
Finished        : System.Threading.ManualResetEvent
InstanceId      : 7590daa0-de23-4b65-ae4c-6c69970399f1
Id              : 3
Name            : Job3
ChildJobs       : {Job4}
PSBeginTime     : 09/05/2017 10:31:15
PSEndTime       :
PSJobTypeName   : BackgroundJob
Output          : {}
Error           : {}
Progress        : {}
Verbose         : {}
Debug           : {}
Warning         : {}
Information     : {}
State           : Running
```

As with the remoting cmdlets, the command to execute is specified by a scriptblock. When the command runs, you see that an object is returned, containing a wealth of information about the job. We'll look at this object in detail later on. For now, we'll keep looking at the cmdlets. Now that you've started a job, you can use the Get-Job cmdlet to get information about that job:

```
PS> Get-Job | Format-List

HasMoreData    : True
StatusMessage  :
Location       : localhost
Command        : 'Hi'
JobStateInfo   : Completed
Finished       : System.Threading.ManualResetEvent
InstanceId     : 7590daa0-de23-4b65-ae4c-6c69970399f1
Id             : 3
Name           : Job3
ChildJobs      : {Job4}
PSBeginTime    : 09/05/2017 10:31:15
PSEndTime      : 09/05/2017 10:31:15
PSJobTypeName  : BackgroundJob
Output         : {}
Error          : {}
Progress       : {}
Verbose        : {}
Debug          : {}
Warning        : {}
Information    : {}
State          : Completed
```

This cmdlet returned the same Job object that you saw returned from Start-Job. (You can tell it's the same object by looking at the InstanceId, which is a GUID and is guaranteed to be unique for each job.) There's one significant difference in this output: If you look at the State property, you'll see that it has changed from Running to Completed.

The first thing to note is that a job remains in the job table even after it has completed and will remain there until it's explicitly removed using the Remove-Job cmdlet. To get the results of the job, you can use another cmdlet: Receive-Job. This cmdlet will return the results of the command that was executed:

```
PS> Receive-Job -Id 3
Hi
```

This returns the string that was emitted by the scriptblock passed to Start-Job. Using Receive-Job in this manner strips the data from the completed job. If you want to retain the data on the job for future processing, you need to use the -Keep parameter:

```
PS> Start-Job -ScriptBlock {'Hi'}

Id  Name   PSJobTypeName   State     HasMoreData   Location    Command
--  ----   -------------   -----     -----------   --------    -------
5   Job5   BackgroundJob   Running   True          localhost   'Hi'
```

```
PS> Receive-Job -Id 5 -Keep
Hi

PS> Get-Job

Id  Name  PSJobTypeName  State      HasMoreData  Location   Command
--  ----  -------------  -----      -----------  --------   -------
3   Job3  BackgroundJob  Completed  False        localhost  'Hi'
5   Job5  BackgroundJob  Completed  True         localhost  'Hi'
```

Notice the `HasMoreData` property is `False` for job `Id 3` and `True` (you used the `-Keep` parameter) for job `Id 5`.

NOTE Depending on the activity on your system the jobs you run may have a different `Id` and `Name` to those we show.

This isn't an interesting example, so let's try something that will take a bit longer to run. First, define the scriptblock you want to run in the `$jsb` variable:

```
PS> $jsb = {
foreach ($i in 1..10) { Start-Sleep 5; "i is $i" }
}
```

Now start the job. The command is too big to display in the default formatting. The compressed output doesn't matter because the only thing you want at this point is the job's `Id`:

```
PS> Start-Job -ScriptBlock $jsb

Id Name PSJobTypeName State   HasMoreData Location  Command
-- ---- ------------- -----   ----------- --------  -------
9  Job9 BackgroundJob Running True        localhost ...
```

Wait 10 seconds or so and start calling `Receive-Job` with the job's `Id`:

```
PS> Receive-Job 9
i is 1
i is 2
```

The first call returned the first 2 items out of the 10 you're expecting. Wait another 10 seconds and call it again

```
PS> Receive-Job 9
i is 3
i is 4
i is 5
```

and you get another three items. Keep calling it until you get all the items:

```
PS> Receive-Job 9
i is 6
i is 7
```

```
PS> Receive-Job 9
i is 8
i is 9
i is 10

PS> Receive-Job 9
PS>
```

This last call didn't return anything because the job has completed and all items have already been returned. You can verify this by calling `Get-Job`

```
PS> Get-Job 9

Id Name PSJobTypeName State      HasMoreData Location Command
-- ---- ------------- -----      ----------- -------- -------
9  Job9 BackgroundJob Completed False        localhost ...
```

and you see that its state is `Completed`. Because the job is running asynchronously, the number of items that are returned depends on when you call `Receive-Job`.

WAITING FOR JOBS TO COMPLETE

So how do you wait until the job has completed? You could write a loop to keep checking the `State` property, but that would be annoying and inefficient. Instead, you can use the `Wait-Job` cmdlet:

```
PS> $jb = Start-Job $jsb; Wait-Job $jb ; Receive-Job $jb

Id   Name   PSJobTypeName State      HasMoreData Location  Command
--   ----   ------------- -----      ----------- --------  -------
11   Job11  BackgroundJob Completed  True        localhost ...
i is 1
i is 2
i is 3
i is 4
i is 5
i is 6
i is 7
i is 8
i is 9
i is 10
```

In this example, you're capturing the job object emitted by `Start-Job` in the `$jb` variable so you can use it in the subsequent `Wait-Job` and `Receive-Job` commands. Because of the `Wait-Job`, when you call `Receive-Job` you get all the input.

> **NOTE** If you use `Wait-Job`, the PowerShell session is blocked until the job is completed.

Notice that `Wait-Job` returns the object representing the job that has finished. You can use this to simplify the example a bit:

```
PS> Start-Job $jsb | Wait-Job | Receive-Job
i is 1
i is 2
```

```
i is 3
i is 4
i is 5
i is 6
i is 7
i is 8
i is 9
i is 10
```

In this example, `Start-Job` passes the `Job` object to `Wait-Job`. When the job completes, `Wait-Job` passes the `Job` object to `Receive-Job` to get the results. This eliminates the need for an intermediate variable.

REMOVING JOBS

So far, you've been creating jobs but haven't removed any. This means that when you call `Get-Job`, you'll see that there are a number of jobs still in the job table:

```
PS> Get-Job

Id Name  PSJobTypeName State     HasMoreData Location  Command
-- ----  ------------- -----     ----------- --------  -------
3  Job3  BackgroundJob Completed False       localhost 'Hi'
5  Job5  BackgroundJob Completed True        localhost 'Hi'
7  Job7  BackgroundJob Completed False       localhost ...
9  Job9  BackgroundJob Completed False       localhost ...
11 Job11 BackgroundJob Completed False       localhost ...
13 Job13 BackgroundJob Completed False       localhost ...
```

Each time you start a job, it gets added to the job table. You can clean things up using the `Remove-Job` cmdlet. To empty the table, use `Remove-Job` with a wildcard:

```
PS> Remove-Job *
```

or you could use this:

```
PS> Get-Job | Remove-Job
```

Now when you call `Get-Job`, nothing is returned. This is probably not the best way to clean things up. A better solution would be to look for jobs that have completed and have no more data. That would look like the following:

```
function Clear-CompletedJobs {
    Get-Job |
    where { $_.State -eq "Completed" -and -not $_.HasMoreData } |
    Remove-Job
}
```

This function calls `Get-Job` to get the list of all jobs, filters that list based on the `State` and `HasMoreData` properties, and then pipes the filtered list into `Remove-Job`. By doing this, only completed jobs for which all data has been received will be removed. This allows you to clean up the job table without worrying about losing information or getting errors. If you do want to kill all the jobs immediately, you can use the `-Force` parameter on `Remove-Job`.

Running the `Clear-CompletedJobs` function will remove all the jobs in the previous job table except job `Id` `5`. You can remove an individual job:

```
PS> Remove-Job -Id 5
PS> Get-Job
PS>
```

In the next section, we'll look at ways you can apply concurrent jobs to solve problems.

13.1.3 *Working with multiple jobs*

So far, we've looked at simple patterns working with one job at a time, but you can run a number of jobs at the same time. Doing so complicates things—you have to be able to handle the output from multiple jobs, but you get the benefit of running tasks in parallel, which makes you more efficient. Let's look at how to do this.

Listing 13.1 Example of running multiple jobs

```
1..5 | foreach {
    Start-Job -name "job$_" -ScriptBlock {
        param($number)
        $waitTime = Get-Random -Minimum 4 -Maximum 10
        Start-Sleep -Seconds $waitTime
        "Job $number is complete; waited $waitTime"
    } -ArgumentList $_ > $null }

Wait-Job job* | Receive-Job
```

This example starts a number of jobs that will run concurrently, waits for all of them to complete, and then gets all the results. Run the code in listing 13.1 and you'll see results like this:

```
Job 1 is complete; waited 9
Job 2 is complete; waited 5
Job 3 is complete; waited 8
Job 4 is complete; waited 9
Job 5 is complete; waited 7
```

As you can see, all the results are captured, ordered by the job name. Now let's look at a more useful application of this pattern. This listing shows a function that searches multiple directories in parallel looking for a specific pattern.

Listing 13.2 A function that searches a collection of folders in parallel

```
function Search-FilesInParallel
{
    param (
        [parameter(mandatory=$true, position=0)]
            $Pattern,
```

```
        [parameter(mandatory=$true, position=1)]
        [string[]]
            $Path,
        [parameter()]
            $Filter = "*.txt",
        [parameter()]
        [switch]
            $Any
    )

    $jobid = [Guid]::NewGuid().ToString()          ◄─┐ Generate GUID
    $jobs = foreach ($element in $path)               └ to use for job ID.
    {
        Start-Job -name "$Srch{jobid}" -scriptblock {  ◄─┐ Start search job
            param($pattern, $path, $filter, $any)          └ for each path.
            Get-ChildItem -Path $path -Recurse -Filter $filter
                Select-String -list:$any $pattern        ◄─┐ Pass -any switch
        } -ArgumentList $pattern,$element,$filter,$any      └ to Select-String.
    }

    Wait-Job -any:$any $jobs | Receive-Job           ◄─┐ Wait for any
    Remove-Job -force $jobs                             └ or all jobs.
}
```

This function takes a list of folder paths to search, along with a pattern to search for. By default, the function will only search TXT files. It also has a switch, -Any, that controls how the search is performed. If the switch isn't specified, all matches from all folders will be returned. If it's specified, only the first match will be returned and the remaining incomplete jobs will be canceled.

This function seems like a useful tool. Unfortunately, jobs are implemented by creating new processes for each job, and this is an expensive operation—so expensive, in fact, that generally it's much slower than searching all the files serially.

NOTE If the creation of the new process is a significant fraction of your job run time, then you probably don't need to use a job. Keep jobs for long-running tasks.

In practice, PowerShell jobs are a way of dealing with *latency* (the time it takes for an operation to return a result) and not *throughput* (the amount of data that gets processed). This is a good trade-off for remote management tasks when you're talking to many machines more or less at once. The amount of data is frequently not large, and the overall execution time is dominated by the time it takes to connect to a remote machine. With that in mind, let's look at how remoting and jobs work together.

13.1.4 *Starting jobs on remote computers*

PowerShell is designed for administering remote computers, so it follows that you can also create and manage jobs on remote computers.

NOTE To work with remote jobs, remoting must be enabled on the remote machine.

The easiest way to do this is to use the -AsJob parameter on Invoke-Command. Alternatively, the scriptblock passed to Invoke-Command can call Start-Job explicitly. Let's see how this works.

CHILD JOBS AND NESTING

So far we've talked about Job objects as atomic—one Job object per job. In practice, it's a bit more sophisticated than that. There are scenarios when you need to be able to aggregate collections of jobs under a single master, or *executive*, job. We'll get to those situations soon. For now, know that background jobs always consist of a parent job and one or more child jobs.

For jobs started using Start-Job or the -AsJob parameter on Invoke-Command, the parent job is the executive. It doesn't run any commands or return any results.

> **NOTE** The executive does no work—it supervises. All the work is done by the subordinates. That sounds familiar somehow . . . .

This collection of child jobs is stored in the ChildJobs property of the parent Job object. The child Job objects have a name, ID, and instance ID that differ from the parent job so that you can manage the parent and each child job individually or as a single unit.

To see the parent and all the children in a Job, use the Get-Job cmdlet to get the parent Job object and then pipe it to Format-List, which displays the Name and Child-Jobs as properties of the objects. Here's what that looks like:

```
PS> Get-Job | Format-List -Property Name, ChildJobs

Name      : Job3
ChildJobs : {Job4}
```

You can also use a Get-Job command on the child job, as shown in the following command

```
PS> Get-Job -Name Job4

Id Name PSJobTypeName State     HasMoreData Location  Command
-- ---- ------------- -----     ----------- --------  -------
4  Job4               Completed True        localhost 'Hi'
```

and so on until you get to a Job that has no children.

CHILD JOBS WITH INVOKE-COMMAND

Let's look at the scenario where you need to have more than one child job. When Start-Job is used to start a job on a local computer, the job always consists of the executive parent job and a single child job that runs the command. When you use the -AsJob parameter on Invoke-Command to start a job on multiple computers, you have the situation where the job consists of an executive parent job and one child job for each command running on a remote server, as shown in figure 13.2.

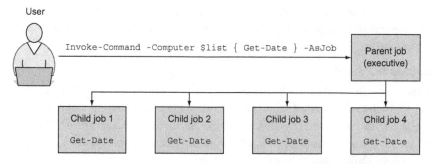

Figure 13.2 The relationship between the executive job and the nested jobs created when `Invoke-Command -AsJob` is used to run commands on multiple remote computers. The user calls `Invoke-Command` to start a job with multiple nested jobs, one for each target node in `$list`.

When you use `Invoke-Command` to explicitly run `Start-Job` on the remote machines, the result is the same as a local command run on each remote computer. The command returns a `Job` object for each computer. The `Job` object consists of an executive parent job and one child job that runs the command.

The parent job represents all the child jobs. When you manage a parent job, you also manage the associated child jobs. For example, if you stop a parent job, all child jobs are also stopped. Similarly, when you get the results of a parent job, you're also getting the results of all child jobs.

Most of the time, you don't need to be concerned with the fact that there are parent and child jobs, but it's possible to manage the child jobs individually. This approach is typically used only when you want to investigate a problem with a job or get the results of only one of a number of child jobs started by using the `-AsJob` parameter of `Invoke-Command`.

The following command uses `Invoke-Command` with `-AsJob` to start background jobs on the local computer and two remote computers. The command saves the job in the `$j` variable:

```
PS> $j = Invoke-Command -ComputerName localhost, W16DC01, W16TGT01 `
-ScriptBlock {Get-Date} -AsJob
```

When you display the `Name` and `ChildJob` properties of the object in `$j`, it shows that the command returned a `Job` object with three child jobs, one for each computer:

```
PS> $j | Format-List Name, ChildJobs

Name      : Job1
ChildJobs : {Job2, Job3, Job4}
```

When you display the parent job, it shows that the overall job was considered to have failed:

```
PS> $j

Id Name PSJobTypeName State  HasMoreData Location          Command
-- ---- ------------- -----  ----------- --------          -------
1  Job1 RemoteJob     Failed True        localhost,W16DC01... Get-Date
```

But on further investigation, when you run `Get-Job` on each of the child jobs, you find that only one of them has failed:

```
PS> Get-Job -Name job2, job3, job4

Id Name PSJobTypeName State      HasMoreData Location  Command
-- ---- ------------- -----      ----------- --------  -------
2  Job2               Failed     False       localhost Get-Date
3  Job3               Completed  True        W16DC01   Get-Date
4  Job4               Completed  True        W16TGT01  Get-Date
```

NOTE The job running on localhost failed because the PowerShell console wasn't running with elevated privileges. Use Run As Administrator to start PowerShell when you want to access the local machine in this manner.

To get the results of all child jobs, use the `Receive-Job` cmdlet to obtain the results of the parent job. But you can also get the results of a particular child job, as shown in the following command:

```
PS> Receive-Job -Id 3 -Keep |
Format-Table PSComputerName, DateTime -AutoSize

PSComputerName DateTime
-------------- --------
W16DC01        09 May 2017 10:50:19
```

In this example, you're using the `-Keep` parameter, which allows you to read, but not remove, output from a job. When you use `-Keep`, the output from the job is retained in the output buffer for that job. You're using it here so that when you do a `Receive-Job` on the executive job, you'll get the output of all jobs in a single collection. In effect, this is a way of peeking at the output of one of the child jobs. By using child jobs, you have much more granular control over the set of activities you have running.

The way you've been working with jobs so far has been much like when you were using `Invoke-Command` and specifying the name of a computer. Each time you contacted the computer, `Invoke-Command` created a new session. You're doing much the same thing when you use `Start-Job`. With `Invoke-Command`, you were able to improve your efficiency by creating sessions. In the next section you'll see how sessions work with jobs.

13.1.5 Running jobs in existing sessions

Each background job runs in its own PowerShell session, paralleling the way each remote command is also executed in its own session. As was the case with remoting, this session can be a temporary one that exists only for the duration of the background job, or it can be run in an existing PSSession. But the way to do this isn't obvious because the `Start-Job` cmdlet doesn't have a `-Session` parameter. Instead, you have to use `Invoke-Command` with the `-Session` and `-AsJob` parameters. Here's what that looks like. First, create a PSSession object:

```
PS> $s = New-PSSession -ComputerName W16DC01
```

Now pass that session object to `Invoke-Command` with `-AsJob` specified:

```
PS> $j = Invoke-Command -Session $s -ScriptBlock {$PID} -AsJob
```

The scriptblock that you're passing in returns the process ID of the session. Use `Receive-Job` to retrieve it:

```
PS> Receive-Job $j
788
```

You can call `Invoke-Command` without `-AsJob` with the same session object and scriptblock:

```
PS> Invoke-Command -Session $s -ScriptBlock {$PID}
788
```

You get the same process ID back, which is expected because the session is persistently associated with the same process.

Start-Job and sessions

Why is there no `-Session` parameter on `Start-Job`? This parameter did exist at one point in the development of PowerShell v2. At that time, jobs and remoting used the same message *transport*. Using the same transport was found to be problematic for a number of reasons:

- It was inefficient for communication with local jobs.
- It required that the remoting service be enabled on the local machine, which has security implications.
- It required users to be running with admin privileges to be able to use the job feature.

To resolve these issues, the existing WS-MAN-based transport used by jobs was replaced with anonymous pipes. This change solved these problems, but it had the unfortunate side effect that jobs could no longer be directly run within `PSSession` instances because the `PSSession` object was tied to WS-MAN remoting.

Keep in mind that when a job is run in an existing `PSSession`, that session can't be used to run additional tasks until the job has completed. This means you have to create multiple `PSSession` objects if you need to run multiple background tasks but want to avoid the overhead of creating new processes for each job. As always, it's up to the script author to decide how best to manage resources for their script.

13.1.6 *Job types*

If you look closely at the output from `Get-Job` in sections 13.1.2 through 13.1.5 you'll see that jobs have a `PSJobTypeName` property. You'll notice that jobs run on the local machine have a `PSJobTypeName` of `BackgroundJob`, whereas jobs run on remote machines have `RemoteJob`.

There are other job types. The full list of job types is shown in table 13.2.

Table 13.2 PowerShell job types

Job Type	Description
BackgroundJob	Job created with `Start-Job`.
RemoteJob	Job created with `-AsJob` parameter of `Invoke-Command`.
PSWorkflowJob	Job created with `-AsJob` parameter of a workflow. See section 13.2.
PSScheduledJob	Job created by a scheduled job trigger. See section 13.3.
CIMJob	Job created with `-AsJob` parameter of a member of a CDXML module.
WMIJob	Job created with `-AsJob` parameter of a WMI cmdlet. Note the CIM cmdlets don't have an `-AsJob` parameter.
PSEventJob	Job created by running `Register-ObjectEvent` and specifying an action with the `-Action` parameter. See section 17.2.3.
ConfigurationJob	Job created by `Start-DSCconfiguration`. Visible only if `-Wait` parameter of `Start-DSCconfiguration` is not used.

Once a job has been created, it's managed by the standard job cmdlets.

Using `-AsJob` with `Get-WmiObject` will return a `WMIJob` type if the target is the local machine or a remote machine:

```
PS> Get-WmiObject -Class Win32_ComputerSystem -AsJob
PS> Get-WmiObject -Class Win32_ComputerSystem -AsJob -ComputerName W16DC01
```

`Get-Job` will always show the job type (`PSJobTypeName`) in the default output:

```
PS> Get-Job

Id Name  PSJobTypeName  State      HasMoreData Location      Command
-- ----  -------------  -----      ----------- --------      -------
1  Job1  RemoteJob      Failed     True        localhost,... Get-Date
5  Job5  RemoteJob      Completed  False       W16DC01       $PID
8  Job8  WmiJob         Completed  True        localhost     Get-Wm...
10 Job10 WmiJob         Completed  True        W16DC01       Get-Wm...
14 Job14 PSWorkflowJob  Completed  True        localhost     hi
```

Unfortunately, `Get-Job` doesn't have a parameter that allows you to filter on job type, so you need to do something like this:

```
Get-Job | where PSJobTypeName -eq 'WmiJob'
```

or use whichever job type you're interested in.

Now that you understand how jobs work, let's look at combining jobs with workflows, as we promised in chapter 12.

13.2   *Workflows as jobs*

We stated at the top of the chapter that workflows could be used in situations where the execution of the process needed to be paused. This pause could include the reboot of a remote machine or even the reboot of the machine on which the workflow is running. Making a workflow pause and then resume is dependent on checkpointing the workflow (persisting the data and execution state to disk) and then reading that data to restart the workflow. Dealing with a reboot is an extension of that approach. The first thing is to understand workflow checkpoints.

13.2.1 *Checkpoints*

The simplest way to checkpoint a workflow is to use the `Checkpoint-Workflow` activity:

```
workflow test-cw1
{
    foreach ($i in 1..10) {$i}
    Checkpoint-Workflow
    foreach ($j in 50..60){$j}
}
test-cw1
```

Running `test-cw1` you'll see the numbers 1–10 and then 50–60 listed with no apparent break. You won't be able to find any persisted data because workflows remove their persisted data on completion—unless they're run as a job, in which case the persisted data is removed when the job is deleted.

> **NOTE** `Checkpoint-Workflow` doesn't have any parameters. You have no control over how the checkpoint is performed or where the data is stored.

`Checkpoint-Workflow` can be used after any activity but not inside an `InlineScript` block. It takes an immediate checkpoint. When using checkpoints make sure of the following:

- The time taken to rerun the section you've checkpointed is longer (preferably a lot longer) than the time it takes to write the checkpoint to disk.
- You take checkpoints after critical steps so the workflow can be resumed rather than restarted.
- You take a checkpoint after steps that aren't *idempotent*
- If your activity is in a pipeline and it's checkpointed, the checkpoint doesn't apply until the pipeline completes.
- Within parallel blocks the checkpoint doesn't apply until the parallel processing has been applied to all items.
- In a sequence block checkpoints are applied after each activity.

You can create a checkpoint in three other ways. The first way is to use the `-PSPersist` workflow parameter:

```
workflow test-cw2 {
    Get-Process
    Get-Service
}
test-cw2 -PSPersist $true
```

In PowerShell v3 -PSPersist was a switch parameter. It's now a Boolean with three possible states:

- *Default*—The -PSPersist parameter is not used. A checkpoint is taken at the beginning and end of the workflow together with any checkpoints explicitly created in the workflow.
- *$true*—Adds a checkpoint to the beginning and end of the workflow and after every activity, in addition to any checkpoints explicitly created in the workflow.
- *$false*—Adds no checkpoints. Only those checkpoints explicitly created in the workflow are taken.

Your second option is to use the -PSPersist activity parameter:

```
workflow test-cw3 {
    Get-Process -PSPersist $true
    Get-Service -PSPersist $true
}
test-cw3
```

When used at the activity level, setting -PSPersist to $true (the parameter was a switch in PowerShell v3) causes a checkpoint to be taken after the activity has completed. A value of $false, or if the parameter isn't present, means a checkpoint won't be taken.

The third option is to use the $PSPersistPreference preference variable:

```
workflow test-cw4 {
    $PSPersistPreference = $true
    Get-Process
    Get-Service
    $PSPersistPreference = $false
}
test-cw4
```

Setting $PSPersistPreference to $true causes a checkpoint to be taken after every activity until it's set back to $false or the workflow ends.

Now that you know how to take checkpoints, how can you use them? You need to run your workflow as a job:

```
workflow test-cw5 {
    foreach ($b in 1..1000) {
        $b
        Checkpoint-Workflow
    }
}
test-cw5 -AsJob
```

The workflow will count from 1 to 1000, taking a checkpoint after each value. Count slowly to five and then shut down PowerShell. That's right! Click the cross in the top-right corner and shut down the console.

Now open another PowerShell console that's running with elevated privileges and use `Get-Job`. You'll find your job has been suspended:

```
PS> Get-Job

Id Name PSJobTypeName State       HasMoreData Location  Command
-- ---- ------------- -----       ----------- --------  -------
5  Job4 PSWorkflowJob Suspended   True        localhost test-cw5
```

You can use `Resume-Job` to restart the workflow. Allow it to run for a few seconds and then stop the workflow job with `Stop-Job`. You can use `Receive-Job` to get the data back from the job. You'll receive the warning shown in figure 13.3 because you've stopped the job before completion.

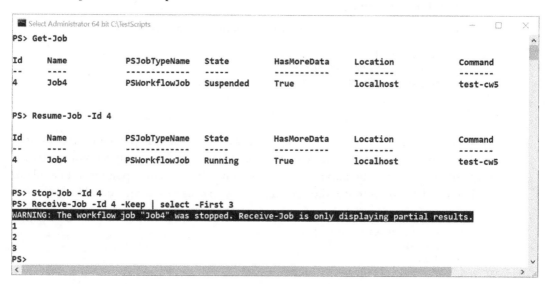

Figure 13.3   Commands to resume a checkpointed workflow

Figure 13.3 illustrates the sequence of commands required to restart a workflow. If you run

```
PS> $count = Receive-Job -Id 4 -Keep
PS> $count.Length
```

you'll be able to check that your results are contiguous—there are no breaks in the number sequence, showing that the data was protected even though the workflow was forcibly stopped.

NOTE   If your workflow has output data prior to being checkpointed, that data won't be present when you use `Receive-Job`.

This is too good a technique to be restricted to inadvertent workflow suspension. You need to be able to force a workflow into suspension as well.

13.2.2 *Suspending workflows*

Deliberately suspending a workflow is a simple matter of using the `Suspend-Workflow` activity:

```
workflow test-ws1 {
    Get-Process
    Suspend-Workflow
    Get-Service
}
test-ws1
```

The process information will be displayed and then the workflow will checkpoint and suspend. You can view the jobs with `Get-Job` and resume the job with `Resume-Job`. The data from the `Get-Service` activity can be viewed using `Receive-Job`. If you don't want to see any results during the running of workflow, run it as a job:

```
workflow test-ws2 {
    Get-Process -PSPersist $true
    Suspend-Workflow
    Get-Service
}
test-ws2 -AsJob -JobName swtest
```

The process data will be saved to disk with the workflow state, and once the workflow job has been resumed and run to completion you can view all your data. Saving the data until execution is complete is a good technique for long-running (overnight?) workflows.

You can use another PowerShell session to resume the job if required, as discussed in the previous section. It's possible to use the `Suspend-Job` cmdlet to force the suspension of a workflow that's running as a job. You'll need to ensure that you've checkpointed the workflow if required so that your data is protected. You'll also need to be able to get progress reports from the job so that you know when to perform the suspension. It's usually easier to suspend the workflow from within the workflow using `Suspend-Workflow`.

NOTE   `Suspend-Job` and `Resume-Job` work only on workflow jobs.

You can also get your workflows to suspend automatically if there's a terminating error within the workflow:

```
workflow test-ws3 {
    Get-Process
    Get-Service
}
test-ws3 -ErrorAction Suspend
```

Any errors that occur in the workflow will cause the workflow to suspend. Again, think about checkpointing to protect your data.

Suspending workflows solves the problem of making workflows interruptible, but we also said that workflows can survive reboots.

13.2.3 *Workflows and reboots*

No, it's not a role-playing game—in this section we'll show you how workflows can survive a reboot. There are two scenarios you need to understand: a reboot on the target remote machine and a reboot on the local machine on which the workflow is executing. Let's start with the easier case where you need to reboot the remote machine you've targeted with your workflow.

A machine can be rebooted using `Restart-Computer`. The following example retrieves the last time a machine was rebooted, forces a reboot, and then waits for the machine to become available before fetching the last boot time again:

```
workflow test-restart {
    Get-CimInstance -ClassName Win32_OperatingSystem |
    Select-Object -ExpandProperty LastBootupTime

    Restart-Computer -Wait

    Get-CimInstance -ClassName Win32_OperatingSystem |
    Select-Object -ExpandProperty LastBootupTime
}
test-restart -PSComputerName W16TGT01
```

The key to pausing the workflow while the remoted machine reboots is the `-Wait` parameter on `Restart-Computer`. Using `-Wait` suppresses the PowerShell prompt and blocks the pipeline until all machines involved in the process have rebooted.

> **Waiting for restart**
>
> The `-Wait` parameter on `Restart-Computer` will cause your code to wait indefinitely for the remote machine to reboot (it has no effect when rebooting the local machine). You can modify the action of `-Wait` with the `-For` parameter, which causes the code to wait for a specific service or feature to be available. Here are your options:
>
> - *Default*—Waits for Windows PowerShell to restart
> - *PowerShell*—Can run commands in a Windows PowerShell remote session on the computer
> - *WMI*—Receives a reply to a Win32_ComputerSystem query for the computer
> - *WinRM*—Can establish a remote session to the computer by using WS-Management
>
> Alternatively, you can opt for a time delay by using the `-TimeOut` parameter, which enables you specify a number of seconds to wait for the remote machine to respond.

Figure 13.4 shows this workflow in progress

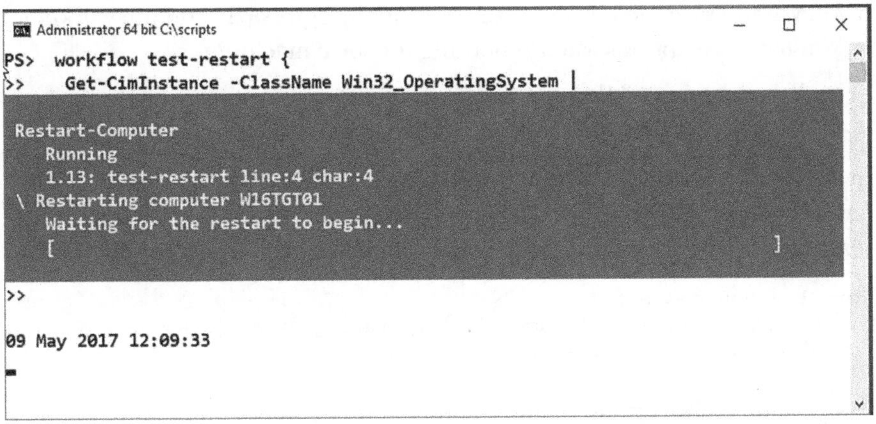

Figure 13.4   Workflow paused while waiting for a remote machine to restart

While `Restart-Computer` is waiting for the remote machine to respond, a progress bar is shown, as can be seen in figure 13.4. The messages on the progress bar indicate the following:

- Waiting for the restart to begin
- Verifying the computer has restarted
- Waiting for WMI connectivity
- Waiting for PowerShell connectivity
- Waiting for WinRM connectivity

These states correspond to the options available on the `-For` parameter of `Restart-Computer`. Figure 13.5 shows the results of the workflow post completion.

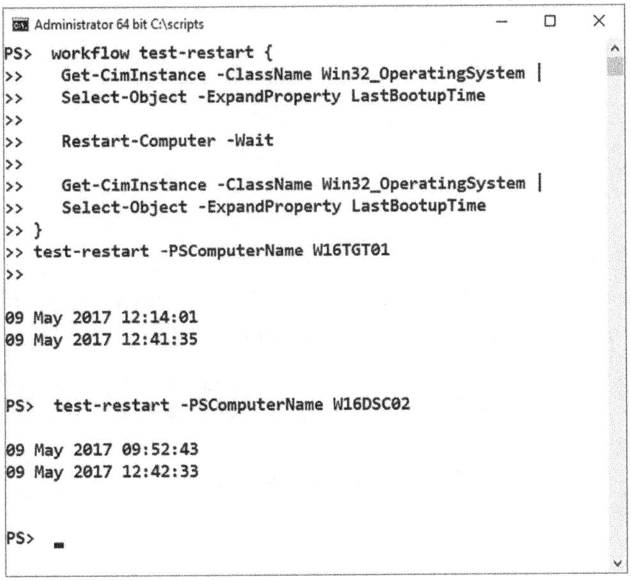

Figure 13.5   Workflow restarting a remote computer

If you want to save the output or suppress the progress bar, run the workflow as a job.

You have two options when rebooting the local machine:

- Resume the workflow manually
- Resume the workflow automatically

In both cases a suspended job is produced when the reboot occurs. This job then has to be resumed either manually or via a scheduled job. Let's start with the manual resumption. The previous workflow is modified to produce this code:

```
workflow test-restart {
    Get-CimInstance -ClassName Win32_OperatingSystem |
    Select-Object -ExpandProperty LastBootupTime

    Restart-Computer
    Suspend-Workflow

    Get-CimInstance -ClassName Win32_OperatingSystem |
    Select-Object -ExpandProperty LastBootupTime
}
```

The `-Wait` parameter has been removed from `Restart-Computer` (it doesn't work when applied to the local machine), and a `Suspend-Workflow` activity is added immediately after the restart command. If you don't force the suspension of the workflow, it will carry through and complete the tasks.

Run the workflow:

```
PS> test-restart -AsJob -JobName boottime
```

Once the machine has rebooted, open an elevated PowerShell console and run

```
PS> Resume-Job -Name boottime
```

When the job has completed, run the following to view the results:

```
PS> Receive-Job -Name boottime

09 May 2017 09:56:44
09 May 2017 14:19:39
```

The more complicated case is to create a situation where the workflow is automatically restarted after the reboot. This involves adding a scheduled task (the documentation says you can use a scheduled job, but that doesn't seem to work) to the script.

Listing 13.3   Automatically resuming workflow on reboot

```
workflow test-restart {
    Get-CimInstance -ClassName Win32_OperatingSystem |     ◁── ❶ Define
    Select-Object -ExpandProperty LastBootupTime               workflow
    Restart-Computer
    Suspend-Workflow
```

```
    Get-CimInstance -ClassName Win32_OperatingSystem |
    Select-Object -ExpandProperty LastBootupTime
}

$actionscript = '-NonInteractive -WindowStyle Normal -NoLogo
➥ -NoProfile -NoExit
➥ -Command "& {Get-Job -Name boottime | Resume-Job}"'

$pstart = "C:\Windows\System32\WindowsPowerShell\v1.0\powershell.exe"   ◄─

Get-ScheduledTask -TaskName ResumeWF |                          ◄─┐   Remove
Unregister-ScheduledTask -Confirm:$false                      ❸   scheduled task

$act = New-ScheduledTaskAction -Execute $pstart `             ◄─┐
-Argument $actionscript                                     ❹   Create task action
$trig = New-ScheduledTaskTrigger -AtLogOn                     ◄─┐

Register-ScheduledTask -TaskName ResumeWF -Action $act `    ◄─┐  ❺   Create trigger
-Trigger $trig -RunLevel Highest                                 │
                                                            Create
                                                            scheduled
test-restart -AsJob -JobName boottime          ◄─┐     Execute   ❻   task
                                               ❼   workflow
```

Create PowerShell startup commands ❷

You'll use the same workflow ❶ as when you performed the workflow resumption manually. The scheduled task will invoke PowerShell ❷ and run the command `Get-Job -Name boottime | Resume-Job`.

Any scheduled tasks of the same name are removed ❸. A task action is created to run the script you created (running PowerShell) ❹, and a job trigger is created ❺ to run the scheduled task at logon.

The scheduled task is registered (created) ❻ using the trigger and actions previously defined. You can then run the workflow ❼ as a job.

Your machine will reboot, and when you log on you'll see a PowerShell console running. After a few seconds, open another PowerShell console and review the jobs. Retrieve the data from the completed workflow job:

```
PS> Receive-Job -Name boottime -Keep

09 May 2017 09:48:42
09 May 2017 14:29:24
```

If you need your workflow to manage reboots, it's much easier if the remote machine is rebooting rather than the local machine. Our recommendation is to ensure you write your workflows in this manner.

The concludes our examination of using jobs with workflows. Our last topic for this chapter looks at how you can use the Windows Scheduler and PowerShell jobs utilizing the scheduled jobs cmdlets.

13.3   *Scheduled jobs*

The ability to execute long-running tasks asynchronously is a great benefit—you don't have to sit and watch them run, for one thing! The PowerShell jobs we've discussed so far have all involved a manual start. Wouldn't it be easier and more convenient if you could schedule jobs to start automatically—in particular, the ones that you run in the middle of the night?

13.3.1   *Creating scheduled jobs*

PowerShell v3 introduced the capability to do that through the `PSScheduledJob` module. The module contains a number of cmdlets:

```
PS> Get-Command -Module PSScheduledJob | Format-Wide -Column 3

Add-JobTrigger          Disable-JobTrigger        Disable-ScheduledJob
Enable-JobTrigger       Enable-ScheduledJob       Get-JobTrigger
Get-ScheduledJob        Get-ScheduledJobOption     New-JobTrigger
New-ScheduledJobOption  Register-ScheduledJob      Remove-JobTrigger
Set-JobTrigger          Set-ScheduledJob          Set-ScheduledJobOption
Unregister-ScheduledJob
```

The cmdlets show three objects involved in working with scheduled jobs:

- Scheduled jobs
- Scheduled job triggers
- Scheduled job options

We'll examine each of these areas in this section.

> **NOTE** Scheduled jobs are different from scheduled tasks. A scheduled job runs a PowerShell job on a trigger activated by the Windows Task Scheduler. A scheduled task runs a script, or command, on activation of a Windows Task Scheduler trigger.

The major difference between scheduled jobs and the jobs discussed in the previous sections is that a scheduled job survives the closure of the PowerShell console, but a regular job doesn't. A scheduled job will continue to exist and run, according to its schedule, until it's disabled or deleted. You can manage the job objects produced by a scheduled job with the standard job cmdlets.

Like with everything in PowerShell, it's easier to explain scheduled jobs with examples. You'll start by creating a simple job that will run a number of times. First, you need a trigger:

```
PS> $t = New-JobTrigger -Once -At "09/05/2017 15:10" `
-RepetitionInterval (New-TimeSpan -Minutes 1) `
-RepetitionDuration (New-TimeSpan -Minutes 10)
```

This trigger will execute on 9 May 2017 at 15:10 (3:10 p.m.). It will repeat execution every minute for 10 minutes. The `-At` parameter specifies the start time. When using `-Once` with `-At` ensure that the start time is in the future.

Many other options are available for setting triggers:

- -AtLogOn—Starts the scheduled job when a specified user, or users, logs on to the machine.
- -AtStartUp—Starts the scheduled job when Windows starts.
- -Daily—Specifies a recurring job that runs every day. You set a number of days between jobs being executed using the -DaysInterval parameter.
- -Weekly—Specifies a job that's run weekly. Use the -DaysOfWeek parameter to control the days it runs—for instance, you may want the job to run only on Saturdays and Sundays. You can specify a number of weeks between executions using -WeeksInterval.

Once you have the trigger defined, you can create the scheduled job:

```
PS> Register-ScheduledJob -Name PiASJ1 -ScriptBlock {Get-Process} `
-Trigger $t -RunNow

Id    Name    JobTriggers    Command       Enabled
--    ----    -----------    -------       -------
1     PiASJ1  1              Get-Process   True
```

You specify the job's name, a scriptblock for the job to execute, and the trigger. You can use the -RunNow parameter of Register-ScheduledJob to run the job once as you register it. This is a useful test to ensure that everything works correctly.

NOTE Set-SetScheduledJob also has a -RunNow parameter for immediate execution of a scheduled job.

Scheduled jobs can be found in the Task Scheduler at Library\Microsoft\Windows\PowerShell\ScheduledJobs.

Your scheduled jobs and their results are stored in $home\AppData\Local\Microsoft\Windows\PowerShell\ScheduledJobs. Look in the <jobname>\Output folder for the results.

By default, the results of 32 instances of each scheduled job are stored. Older jobs will be overwritten as necessary. You can modify the number of saved instances using -MaxResultCount.

You can access the results of your scheduled job using Get-Job:

```
PS> Get-Job -Name PiASJ1 | Format-Table -AutoSize

Id Name   PSJobTypeName  State     HasMoreData Location  Command
-- ----   -------------  -----     ----------- --------  -------
3  PiASJ1 PSScheduledJob Completed True        localhost Get-Process
4  PiASJ1 PSScheduledJob Completed True        localhost Get-Process
5  PiASJ1 PSScheduledJob Completed True        localhost Get-Process
6  PiASJ1 PSScheduledJob Completed True        localhost Get-Process
7  PiASJ1 PSScheduledJob Completed True        localhost Get-Process
8  PiASJ1 PSScheduledJob Completed True        localhost Get-Process
9  PiASJ1 PSScheduledJob Completed True        localhost Get-Process
10 PiASJ1 PSScheduledJob Completed True        localhost Get-Process
11 PiASJ1 PSScheduledJob Completed True        localhost Get-Process
12 PiASJ1 PSScheduledJob Completed True        localhost Get-Process
```

You can access the job's results using `Receive-Job`:

```
PS> Receive-Job -Id 6
```

The `-Keep` parameter hasn't been used, and the results will appear to have been stripped out of the job object. In reality, this isn't the case. The data is still available on disk and can be accessed in *another* PowerShell console. If you use the `-Keep` parameter, you'll be able to repeatedly access the data in the same console.

A scheduled job can be started outside its schedule using `Start-Job`:

```
PS> Start-Job -DefinitionName PiASJ1

Id Name   PSJobTypeName   State   HasMoreData Location  Command
-- ----   -------------   -----   ----------- --------  -------
13 PiASJ1 PSScheduledJob  Running True        localhost Get-Process
```

The job is given a type of scheduled job, but the output isn't persisted to disk and will be lost when the console is closed.

13.3.2 Modifying a scheduled job

Once you've created a scheduled job, you can modify a number of features. Let's start with the trigger.

CHANGING A TRIGGER

A scheduled job can have more than one trigger. You might want to run the scheduled job at 10 a.m. on a Monday and 5 p.m. on a Friday, for instance. To add a trigger to an existing scheduled job, first define the trigger:

```
PS> $t2 = New-JobTrigger -Once -At "09/05/2016 18:30" `
-RepetitionInterval (New-TimeSpan -Minutes 1) `
-RepetitionDuration (New-TimeSpan -Minutes 10)
```

then add the trigger:

```
PS> Add-JobTrigger -Trigger $t2 -Name PiASJ1
```

A scheduled job's triggers can be viewed:

```
PS> Get-JobTrigger -Name PiASJ1

Id Frequency Time                 DaysOfWeek Enabled
-- --------- ----                 ---------- -------
1  Once      09/05/2017 15:10:00             True
2  Once      09/05/2017 18:30:00             True
```

Old triggers can be removed:

```
PS> Remove-JobTrigger -Name PiASJ1 -TriggerId 1
```

SCHEDULED JOB OPTIONS

A number of options are available to you when creating a scheduled job. The default options are listed here:

```
PS> New-ScheduledJobOption
```

```
StartIfOnBatteries      : False
StopIfGoingOnBatteries  : True
WakeToRun               : False
StartIfNotIdle          : True
StopIfGoingOffIdle      : False
RestartOnIdleResume     : False
IdleDuration            : 00:10:00
IdleTimeout             : 01:00:00
ShowInTaskScheduler     : True
RunElevated             : False
RunWithoutNetwork       : True
DoNotAllowDemandStart   : False
MultipleInstancePolicy  : IgnoreNew
JobDefinition           :
```

You can control how the scheduled job behaves if the machine is on, or goes on, battery power. There are a number of options detailing the job's response to the machine being idle or not. You can configure the job to be run with elevated privileges and even hide the job from the Task Scheduler GUI.

RunElevated is probably the most important option. If you use this, you need to also specify the -Credential option in Register-ScheduledJob or Set-ScheduledJob.

13.3.3 *Managing scheduled jobs*

You can view the instances of a scheduled job:

```
PS> Get-job -Name PiASJ1
```

The latest instances can be viewed:

```
PS> Get-job -Name PiASJ1 -Newest 2
```

Jobs executed in a particular time interval can be found:

```
PS> Get-job -Name PiASJ1 -Before "09/05/2017 15:20:00" `
-After "09/05/2017 15:15:00"
```

Individual instances can be removed:

```
PS> Remove-Job -Id 12
```

or you can remove all instances:

```
PS> Remove-Job -Name PiASJ1
```

The scheduled job itself can be removed:

```
PS> Unregister-ScheduledJob -Name PiASJ1
```

This also removes the data stored on disk.

13.4   Summary

- PowerShell jobs run asynchronously.
- A background job runs in a new PowerShell process. Other jobs execute in process but on separate threads.
- Start-Job creates and runs a new background job.
- Use -Keep with Receive-Job to ensure the data remains accessible.
- Wait-Job blocks further interactive processing until the job, or jobs, completes.
- Remove-Job deletes one, many, or all jobs present on the system.
- Jobs are deleted when the PowerShell console is closed.
- You can run jobs on the local and/or remote machines.
- A job consists of a parent job and one or more child jobs. One child job is created per remote machine specified to Invoke-Command when using the -AsJob parameter.
- Multiple job types exist. They are started in different ways but are all managed using the standard job cmdlets.
- Workflow state and data can be explicitly persisted using the Checkpoint-Workflow activity or automatically after each activity using the -PSPersist parameter. Be aware that persisting a workflow is expensive, so this feature should be used when needed rather than enabling it all the time.
- Suspend-Workflow will persist a workflow and halt execution. A suspended job is created that can be resumed at a later time.
- The job cmdlets can be used to manage workflow jobs.
- Resume-Job will restart a suspended workflow job.
- PowerShell workflows can survive a reboot of the remote or local machine.
- A reboot of the local machine while a workflow is executing can be managed manually or automatically using a scheduled task.
- Scheduled jobs are run via the Windows Task Scheduler.
- The results from a scheduled job are stored on disk and are available between PowerShell sessions.
- Scheduled job triggers can be defined on a time basis, user logon, or machine startup.
- The instances of a scheduled job are managed with the standard job cmdlets.
- Job triggers can be added and removed.
- Scheduled job options include running with elevated privileges and hiding from the Task Scheduler.
- Scheduled job instances can be removed singly or in bulk.

Workflows (chapter 12) and jobs (this chapter) provide a strong foundation for performing tasks in a production environment. When writing production code, you need to be able to manage errors that may occur when your code is running—as you'll see in the next chapter.

Errors and exceptions

This chapter covers

- Error handling
- Dealing with terminating errors
- Working with event logs

Progress, far from consisting in change, depends on retentiveness. Those who cannot remember the past are condemned to repeat it.

—*George Santayana,* The Life of Reason

It's always useful to keep in mind that PowerShell isn't merely a shell or scripting language. Its primary purpose is to be an automation tool and perform critical management tasks on a server, such as send software updates, inspect log files, or provision user accounts. You need to be sure that either the task is completed properly or the reason for failure is appropriately recorded.

In this chapter, we'll focus on how PowerShell reports, records, and manages error conditions. Handling of error conditions is one of the areas where PowerShell shines compared to other scripting tools. The support for diagnostic tracing and logging is practically unprecedented in traditional scripting languages. Unfortunately, these features don't come entirely free—there are costs in terms of complexity and execution overhead that aren't there in other environments. All these capabilities are a part of PowerShell as a management tool; Microsoft set a higher bar for PowerShell than has been set for most other language environments.

We'll begin by looking at the error processing subsystem. Errors in PowerShell aren't error codes, strings, or even exceptions as found in languages such as C# and VB.NET. They're rich objects that include almost everything you could think of that might be useful in debugging a problem.

> **NOTE** Some people dislike (okay, despise) the use of the word *rich* in this context. But given the wealth of information that PowerShell error objects contain, rich is the right word.

We'll examine these ErrorRecord objects in detail, along with how they're used by the various PowerShell mechanisms to manage error conditions.

14.1 Error handling

Error handling in PowerShell is structured. PowerShell errors aren't bits of text written to the screen—they're rich objects that contain a wealth of information about where the error occurred and why. There's one aspect to error handling in PowerShell that's unique: the notion of *terminating* versus *nonterminating* errors. This aspect aligns with the streaming model that PowerShell uses to process objects.

Here's a simple example that will help you understand this concept. Think about how removing a list of files from your system should work. You stream this list of files to the cmdlet that will delete the files. But imagine that you can't delete all the files on the list for various reasons. Do you want the command to stop processing as soon as it hits the first element in the list? The answer is probably no. You'd like the cmdlet to do as much work as it can but capture any errors so that you can look at them later. This is the concept of a *nonterminating* error—the error is recorded and the operation continues. There are times when you do want an operation to stop on the first error. These are called *terminating* errors. Sometimes you want an error to be terminating in one situation and nonterminating in another, and PowerShell provides mechanisms that allow you to do that.

> **NOTE** PowerShell is based on .NET, but you need to be aware that in .NET errors are all terminating unless they're handled somewhere in the calling code. PowerShell cmdlets, and advanced functions or scripts, introduce the concept of nonterminating errors, meaning that the error has been managed internally.

Because the architecture supports multiple nonterminating errors being generated by a pipeline, it can't just throw or return an error. Here's where streaming comes into play: nonterminating errors are written to the error stream. By default, these errors are displayed, but there are a number of other ways of working with them. In the next few sections, we'll look at those mechanisms. First, we need to look at the error records themselves.

14.1.1 *ErrorRecords and the error stream*

As we delve into the topic of error handling, we'll first look at capturing error records in a file using redirection, and then you'll learn how to capture error messages in a variable. By capturing these errors instead of merely displaying them, you can go back to analyze and hopefully fix what went wrong.

First, let's review the normal behavior of objects in the pipeline. Output objects flow from cmdlet to cmdlet, but error records are written directly to the default output processor. By default, this is the Out-Default cmdlet, and the error records are displayed:

```
PS> Get-ChildItem -Path nosuchfile
Get-ChildItem : Cannot find path 'C:\test\nosuchfile' because it does not
    exist.
At line:1 char:1
+ Get-ChildItem -Path nosuchfile
+ ~~~~~~~~~~~~~~~~~~~~~~~~~~~~~~~
    + CategoryInfo          : ObjectNotFound: (C:\test\nosuchfile:String)
    [Get-ChildItem], ItemNotFoundException
    + FullyQualifiedErrorId : PathNotFound,Microsoft.PowerShell.Commands.
    GetChildItemCommand
```

These flows are shown in figure 14.1.

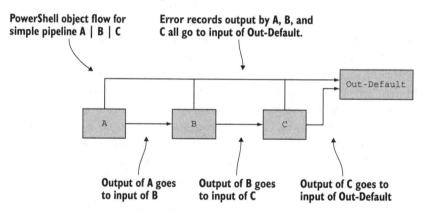

Figure 14.1 This diagram shows the output object and error record routing; then, the simple pipeline A | B | C **is run from a PowerShell host process like PowerShell.exe or PowerShell_ISE.exe. Output objects go to the next command in the pipeline, and error objects go directly to** Out-Default.

In figure 14.1, you see the output objects go from A to B to C and finally to Out-Default. But the error record streams are all merged and go directly to Out-Default.

When you use the redirection operators discussed in chapter 4, you can change flow. For example, you can redirect the error messages to a file:

```
PS> Get-ChildItem -Path nosuchfile 2> err.txt
```

This changes the process to look like what's shown in figure 14.2.

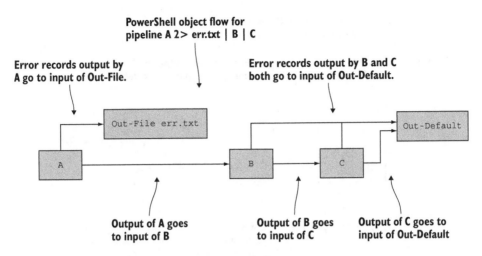

Figure 14.2   Revised pipeline including the use of redirection operators

This approach has the downside that the error message is rendered to displayable text before writing it to the file. When that happens, you lose all the extra information in the objects. Look at what was saved to the file:

```
PS> Get-Content .\err.txt
Get-ChildItem : Cannot find path 'C:\test\nosuchfile' because it does not
   exist.
At line:1 char:1
+ Get-ChildItem -Path nosuchfile 2> err.txt
+ ~~~~~~~~~~~~~~~~~~~~~~~~~~~~~~~~~~~~~~~~~~~
    + CategoryInfo          : ObjectNotFound: (C:\test\nosuchfile:String)
   [Get-ChildItem], ItemNotFoundException
    + FullyQualifiedErrorId : PathNotFound,Microsoft.PowerShell.Commands.
   GetChildItemCommand
```

The error text is there as it would've been displayed on the console, but you've lost all the elements of the object that haven't been displayed. This lost information may be critical to diagnosing the problem. You need a better way to capture this information. The first mechanism we'll look at is capturing the error records by using the stream merge operator 2>&1 and then assigning the result to a variable.

When you add error stream merging to the picture, the flow of objects changes. With stream merging, instead of having all error records going to the default output stream, they're routed into the output stream, and the combined set of objects is passed to the input of the next command. This flow is shown in figure 14.3.

Let's see how this works. First, use the stream merge operator to capture the error stream in a variable by using assignment:

```
PS> $err = Get-ChildItem -Path nosuchfile 2>&1
```

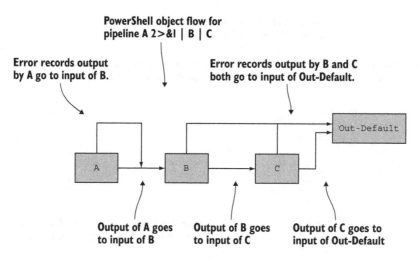

PowerShell object flow for pipeline A 2>&I | B | C

Error records output by A go to input of B.

Error records output by B and C both go to input of Out-Default.

Out-Default

A   B   C

Output of A goes to input of B

Output of B goes to input of C

Output of C goes to input of Out-Default

Figure 14.3   Revised pipeline including the addition of error stream merging

You can use Get-Member to display the properties on the object. Use the -Type parameter on Get-Member to filter the display and only show the properties:

```
PS> $err | Get-Member -Type property
```

Some of the property names are a little tricky to figure out, so further explanation is in order. Table 14.1 lists the important properties, their types, and a description of each.

Table 14.1   ErrorRecord properties and their descriptions

Property name	Property type	Description
CategoryInfo	ErrorCategoryInfo	This string breaks errors into a number of broad categories.
ErrorDetails	ErrorDetails	This may be null. If present, Error-Details can specify additional information, most importantly ErrorDetails. Message, which (if present) is a more exact description and should be displayed instead of Exception.Message.
Exception	System.Exception	This is the underlying .NET exception corresponding to the error that occurred.
FullyQualifiedErrorId	System.String	This identifies the error condition more specifically than either the ErrorCategory or the Exception. Use FullyQualifiedErrorId to filter highly specific error conditions. Note that this is a nonlocalized field, so performing string matches against it will continue to work regardless of language settings.

Table 14.1 `ErrorRecord` **properties and their descriptions** *(continued)*

Property name	Property type	Description
`InvocationInfo`	`InvocationInfo`	This object contains information about where the error occurred—typically the script name and line number.
`TargetObject`	`System.Object`	This is the object that was being operated on when the error occurred. It may be `null`, because not all errors will set this field.

You can look at the values of an error record's properties by piping the error object into `Format-List`. To see all the properties, you must specify `-Property` `*` along with `-Force`. This command tells the formatting subsystem to skip the default presentation and show all properties. The result looks like this:

```
PS> $err | Format-List -Property * -Force

writeErrorStream      : True
PSMessageDetails      :
Exception             : System.Management.Automation.ItemNotFoundException:
                        Cannot find path 'C:\test\nosuchfile' because it
                        does not exist.  at
                        System.Management.Automation.SessionStateInternal.
                        GetChildItems(String path, Boolean recurse,
                        UInt32 depth, CmdletProviderContext context)
                        At  Microsoft.PowerShell.Commands.
                        GetChildItemCommand.ProcessRecord()
TargetObject          : C:\test\nosuchfile
CategoryInfo          : ObjectNotFound: (C:\test\nosuchfile:String)
                        [Get-ChildItem],ItemNotFoundException
                        FullyQualifiedErrorId :
                        PathNotFound,Microsoft.PowerShell.Commands.
                        GetChildItemCommand
ErrorDetails          :
InvocationInfo        : System.Management.Automation.InvocationInfo
ScriptStackTrace      : at <ScriptBlock>, <No file>: line 1
PipelineIterationInfo : {0, 1}
```

In this output, you can see the exception that caused the error was `ItemNotFound-Exception`. The `TargetObject` property contains the full path the cmdlet used to locate the item. This overall error is placed in the broader category of `ObjectNotFound`. There are no additional error details for this object.

Let's look closer at the `InvocationInfo` property. This member provides information about where the error occurred. Here's what it looks like:

```
PS> $err.InvocationInfo

MyCommand             : Get-ChildItem
BoundParameters       : {}
UnboundArguments      : {}
ScriptLineNumber      : 1
```

```
OffsetInLine          : 8
HistoryId             : 8
ScriptName            :
Line                  : $err = Get-ChildItem -Path nosuchfile 2>&1
PositionMessage       : At line:1 char:8
                        + $err = Get-ChildItem -Path nosuchfile 2>&1
                        +        ~~~~~~~~~~~~~~~~~~~~~~~~~~~~~~~~~~~~
PSScriptRoot          :
PSCommandPath         :
InvocationName        : Get-ChildItem
PipelineLength        : 0
PipelinePosition      : 0
ExpectingInput        : False
CommandOrigin         : Internal
DisplayScriptPosition :
```

Because you enter this command on the command line, the script name is empty and the script line number is 1. `OffsetInLine` is the offset in the script line where the error occurred. Other information is also available, such as the number of commands in the pipeline that caused an error, as well as the index of this command in the pipeline. This message also includes the line of script text where the error occurred. Finally, there's the `PositionMessage` property. This property takes all the other information and formats it into what you see in PowerShell errors.

Extracting all the detailed information from an error record is a fairly common occurrence when debugging scripts, so it's worth writing a small helper function to make it easier. The next listing shows a function that will dump out all the properties of an error object and then iterate through any `InnerException` properties on the error record exception to show all the underlying errors that occurred.

Listing 14.1 The `Show-ErrorDetails` function

```
function Show-ErrorDetails
{
    param(
        $ErrorRecord = $Error[0]
    )                                                               ❶ Show depth
                                                                      of nested
    $ErrorRecord | Format-List -Property * -Force                     exception
    $ErrorRecord.InvocationInfo | Format-List -Property *
    $Exception = $ErrorRecord.Exception
    for ($depth = 0; $Exception -ne $null; $depth++)              ❷ Show
    {   "$depth" * 80                                               exception
        $Exception | Format-List -Property * -Force                 properties
        $Exception = $Exception.InnerException
    }                                                            ┐ Link to nest
}                                                                ❸ exceptions
```

This function takes a single parameter that holds the error record to display. By default, it shows the most recent error recorded in `$error`. It begins by showing all the properties in the record followed by the invocation information for the faulting command.

Then it loops, tracing through any nested exceptions ❸, showing each one ❷ proceeded by a separator ❶ line showing the nesting depth of the displayed exception.

There's a lot of information in these objects that can help you figure out where and why an error occurred. The trick is to make sure you have the right error objects available at the right time. It isn't possible to record every error that occurs—it would take up too much space and be impossible to manage. If you limit the set of error objects that are preserved, you want to make sure that you keep those you care about—having the wrong error objects doesn't help. Sometimes you're interested only in certain types of errors or only in errors from specific parts of a script. To address these requirements, PowerShell provides a rich set of tools for capturing and managing errors.

14.1.2 The $error variable and –ErrorVariable parameter

The point of rich error objects is that you can examine them after the error has occurred and possibly take remedial action. To do that, you have to capture them first. In the previous section, we showed you how to redirect the error stream, but the problem with this approach is that you have to think of it beforehand. Because you don't know when errors occur, in practice you'd have to do it all the time. Fortunately, PowerShell performs some of this work for you and automatically "remembers the past," at least as far as errors go. There's a special variable $error that contains a collection of the errors that occurred while the engine was running. This collection is maintained as a circular bounded buffer. As new errors occur, old ones are discarded, as shown in figure 14.4.

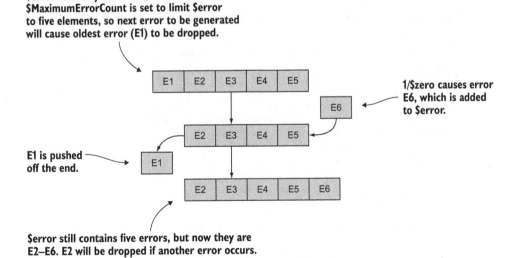

$error currently contains five errors E1–E5.
$MaximumErrorCount is set to limit $error
to five elements, so next error to be generated
will cause oldest error (E1) to be dropped.

1/$zero causes error
E6, which is added
to $error.

E1 is pushed
off the end.

$error still contains five errors, but now they are
E2–E6. E2 will be dropped if another error occurs.

Figure 14.4   How the `$error` **variable handles new errors when** `MaximumErrorCount` **has been reached. The oldest error is dropped, and the new one is added to the end.**

The number of errors that is retained is controlled by the $MaximumErrorCount variable, which can be set to a number from 256 (the default setting) to 32768. The collection in $error is an array (technically an instance of System.Collections.ArrayList) that buffers errors as they occur. The most recent error is always stored in $error[0].

> **NOTE** Although it's tempting to think that you could set $MaximumErrorCount to some large value (32768 is the largest allowed) and never have to worry about capturing errors, in practice this strategy isn't a good idea. Rich error objects also imply fairly large error objects. If you set $MaximumErrorCount to too large a value, you won't have any memory left. In practice, there's usually no reason to set it to anything larger than the default, though you may set it to something smaller if you want to make more space available for other things. Also, even if you have only a few objects, these objects may be large. If you find that this is the case for a particular script, you can change the maximum error count to something small. As an alternative, you could clean out all the entries in $error by calling $error.Clear().

Let's explore using the $error variable. You'll start with the same error as before:

```
PS> Get-ChildItem -Path nosuchfile
Get-ChildItem : Cannot find path 'C:\test\nosuchfile' because it does not
    exist.
At line:1 char:1
+ Get-ChildItem -Path nosuchfile
+ ~~~~~~~~~~~~~~~~~~~~~~~~~~~~~~~~
    + CategoryInfo          : ObjectNotFound: (C:\test\nosuchfile:String)
    [Get-ChildItem], ItemNotFoundException
    + FullyQualifiedErrorId : PathNotFound,Microsoft.PowerShell.Commands.
    GetChildItemCommand
```

You didn't explicitly capture it, but it's available in $error[0] with all the error properties:

```
PS> $error[0]
Get-ChildItem : Cannot find path 'C:\test\nosuchfile' because it does not
    exist.
At line:1 char:1
+ Get-ChildItem -Path nosuchfile
+ ~~~~~~~~~~~~~~~~~~~~~~~~~~~~~~~~
    + CategoryInfo          : ObjectNotFound: (C:\test\nosuchfile:String)
    [Get-ChildItem], ItemNotFoundException
    + FullyQualifiedErrorId : PathNotFound,Microsoft.PowerShell.Commands.
    GetChildItemCommand
```

For example, here's the exception object:

```
PS> $error[0].Exception
Cannot find path 'C:\test\nosuchfile' because it does not exist.
```

and here's the target object that caused the error:

```
PS> $error[0].TargetObject
C:\test\nosuchfile
```

Now let's do something that will cause a second error:

```
PS> 1/0
Attempted to divide by zero.
At line:1 char:1
+ 1/$null
+ ~~~~~~~
    + CategoryInfo          : NotSpecified: (:) [], RuntimeException
    + FullyQualifiedErrorId : RuntimeException
```

Here you have a division-by-zero error.

Let's verify that the second error is in $error[0]. Look at the exception member:

```
PS> $error[0].Exception
Attempted to divide by zero.
```

Yes, it is. You'll also verify that the previous error, "file not found," is now in position 1:

```
PS> $error[1].Exception
Cannot find path 'C:\test\nosuchfile' because it does not exist.
```

Again, yes, it is. As you can see, each new error shuffles the previous error down one element in the array.

> **TIP** The key lesson to take away from this is that when you're going to try to diagnose an error, you should copy it to a "working" variable so it doesn't get accidently shifted out from under you because you made a mistake in one of the commands you're using to examine the error. In particular, you should never depend on the value of $error when writing tests because you may end up looking at the wrong value due to side effects in the test code. In general, you should consider $error as a trace log of errors that have occurred.

The $error variable is a convenient way to capture errors automatically, but there are two problems with it:

- $error captures only a limited number of errors—the default is 256—so important information may fall off the end of the buffer.
- $error contains all the errors that occur, regardless of where they came from or what command generated them, mixed together in a single collection. You'll find it hard to locate the information you need to diagnose a specific problem.

You can work around the first problem by using redirection to capture all the errors, but that still doesn't address mixing all the errors together. To deal with this second issue, when you want to capture all the errors from a specific command, you use a standard parameter available on all commands called -ErrorVariable. This parameter names a variable to use for capturing all the errors that the command generates—the command's error handler performs the action of writing the information to the

variable. Here's an example: this command generates three error objects, because the
files nofuss, nomuss, and nobother don't exist:

```
PS> Get-ChildItem -Path nofuss, nomuss, nobother -ErrorVariable errs
Get-ChildItem : Cannot find path 'C:\test\nofuss' because it does not exist.
At line:1 char:1
+ Get-ChildItem -Path nofuss, nomuss, nobother -ErrorVariable errs
+ ~~~~~~~~~~~~~~~~~~~~~~~~~~~~~~~~~~~~~~~~~~~~~~~~~~~~~~~~~~~~~~~~~~~~
    + CategoryInfo          : ObjectNotFound:
(C:\test\nofuss:String) [Get-ChildItem], ItemNotFoundException
    + FullyQualifiedErrorId : PathNotFound,Microsoft.PowerShell.Commands.
  GetChildItemCommand

Get-ChildItem : Cannot find path 'C:\test\nomuss' because it does not exist.
At line:1 char:1
+ Get-ChildItem -Path nofuss, nomuss, nobother -ErrorVariable errs
+ ~~~~~~~~~~~~~~~~~~~~~~~~~~~~~~~~~~~~~~~~~~~~~~~~~~~~~~~~~~~~~~~~~~~~
    + CategoryInfo          : ObjectNotFound:
(C:\test\nomuss:String) [Get-ChildItem], ItemNotFoundException
    + FullyQualifiedErrorId : PathNotFound,Microsoft.PowerShell.Commands.
  GetChildItemCommand

Get-ChildItem : Cannot find path 'C:\test\nobother' because it does not
  exist.
At line:1 char:1
+ Get-ChildItem -Path nofuss, nomuss, nobother -ErrorVariable errs
+ ~~~~~~~~~~~~~~~~~~~~~~~~~~~~~~~~~~~~~~~~~~~~~~~~~~~~~~~~~~~~~~~~~~~~
    + CategoryInfo          : ObjectNotFound:
(C:\test\nobother:String) [Get-ChildItem], ItemNotFoundException
    + FullyQualifiedErrorId : PathNotFound,Microsoft.PowerShell.Commands.
  GetChildItemCommand
```

In the command, you specified the name of the error variable to place these records
into: errs.

> **NOTE** The argument to -ErrorVariable is the name of the variable with no
> leading $. If errs had been written as $errs, then the errors would've been
> stored in the variable named by the value in $errs, not $errs itself. Also note
> that the -ErrorVariable parameter works like a tee—the objects are captured
> in the variable, but they're also streamed to the error output. If -ErrorAction
> is set to Ignore, the errors won't be captured in the variable.

Let's verify that the errors were captured. First, the number of elements in $err should
be 3:

```
PS> $errs.Count
3
```

It is. Now dump the errors themselves:

```
PS> $errs
Get-ChildItem : Cannot find path 'C:\test\nofuss' because it does not exist.
At line:1 char:1
+ Get-ChildItem -Path nofuss, nomuss, nobother -ErrorVariable errs
```

```
+ ~~~~~~~~~~~~~~~~~~~~~~~~~~~~~~~~~~~~~~~~~~~~~~~~~~~~~~~~~~~~~~~~~
    + CategoryInfo          : ObjectNotFound:
(C:\test\nofuss:String) [Get-ChildItem], ItemNotFoundException
    + FullyQualifiedErrorId : PathNotFound,Microsoft.PowerShell.Commands.
  GetChildItemCommand

Get-ChildItem : Cannot find path 'C:\test\nomuss' because it does not exist.
At line:1 char:1
+ Get-ChildItem -Path nofuss, nomuss, nobother -ErrorVariable errs
+ ~~~~~~~~~~~~~~~~~~~~~~~~~~~~~~~~~~~~~~~~~~~~~~~~~~~~~~~~~~~~~~
    + CategoryInfo          : ObjectNotFound:
(C:\test\nomuss:String) [Get-ChildItem], ItemNotFoundException
    + FullyQualifiedErrorId : PathNotFound,Microsoft.PowerShell.Commands.
  GetChildItemCommand

Get-ChildItem : Cannot find path 'C:\test\nobother' because it does not
  exist.
At line:1 char:1
+ Get-ChildItem -Path nofuss, nomuss, nobother -ErrorVariable errs
+ ~~~~~~~~~~~~~~~~~~~~~~~~~~~~~~~~~~~~~~~~~~~~~~~~~~~~~~~~~~~~~~
    + CategoryInfo          : ObjectNotFound:
(C:\test\nobother:String) [Get-ChildItem], ItemNotFoundException
    + FullyQualifiedErrorId : PathNotFound,Microsoft.PowerShell.Commands.
  GetChildItemCommand
```

They do, in fact, match the original error output.

> **NOTE** The errors should match the original output because they're the same error objects. The -ErrorVariable parameter (alias -ev) captures references to each object written to the error stream. In effect, the same object is in two places at once—well, three if you count the default $error variable.

Because there's no need to see the object twice, you can use redirection to discard the written objects and save only the references stored in the specified variable. Let's rerun the example this way:

```
PS> Get-ChildItem -Path nofuss, nomuss, nobother `
-ErrorVariable errs 2>$null
```

This time nothing is displayed; verify the error count:

```
PS> $errs.Count
3
```

It's 3 again, as intended. Let's check the TargetObject member of the last error object to verify that it's the filename nobother:

```
PS> $errs[2].TargetObject
C:\test\nobother
```

Yes, it is. This example illustrates a more sophisticated way of capturing error objects than merely displaying them. In section 14.1.5, you'll see an even more flexible way to control how errors are redirected.

All of these mechanisms provide useful tools for handling collections of error objects, but sometimes all you care about is that an error occurred at all. A couple of additional status variables, $? and $LASTEXITCODE, enable you to determine whether an error occurred.

14.1.3 *Determining whether a command had an error*

Displaying errors is useful—it lets the user know what happened. But scripts also need to know when an error has occurred so they can react properly. For example, a script shouldn't try to remove a file if the cd into the directory containing the file failed. PowerShell makes this easy by providing two error variables ($? and $LASTEXITCODE) that capture the command status. First, to see if an error occurred when executing a command, a script can check the status of the variable $?, a simple Boolean variable that holds the execution status of the last command.

> **NOTE**   The use of the $? variable is borrowed from the UNIX shells.

The $? variable will be true if the entire operation succeeded and false otherwise. If any of the operations wrote an error object, then $? will be set to false even if the error was discarded using redirection. This is an important point: it means that a script can determine whether an error occurred even if the error isn't displayed. Here are examples showing the use of $?. First, you call Get-Item, passing in items you know exist and don't exist:

```
PS> Get-Item c:, nosuchfile, c:

    Directory: C:\

Mode                LastWriteTime         Length Name
----                -------------         ------ ----
d-----         02/05/2016     14:52                test
Get-Item : Cannot find path 'C:\test\nosuchfile' because it does not exist.
At line:1 char:1
+ Get-Item c:, nosuchfile, c:
+ ~~~~~~~~~~~~~~~~~~~~~~~~~~~~
    + CategoryInfo          : ObjectNotFound:
(C:\test\nosuchfile:String) [Get-Item], ItemNotFoundException
    + FullyQualifiedErrorId : PathNotFound,Microsoft.PowerShell.Commands.
    GetItemCommand

d-----         02/05/2016     14:52                test
```

You get the expected error:

```
PS> $?
False
```

and $? is false. Now try the same command, but this time specify only items that exist:

```
PS> Get-Item c:, c:

    Directory: C:\
```

Mode	LastWriteTime		Length	Name
----	-------------		------	----
d-----	02/05/2016	14:52		test
d-----	02/05/2016	14:52		test

```
PS> $?
True
```

This time there are no errors, and $? is true.

Whereas the $? variable only indicates success or failure, the second error variable $LASTEXITCODE contains the exit code of the last command run. But this applies to only two types of commands: native or external commands and PowerShell scripts (but not functions).

> **NOTE** On Windows, when a process exits it can return a single integer as its exit code. This integer is used to encode a variety of conditions, but the only one we're interested in is whether it's zero or non-zero. This convention is used by almost all programs. If they were successful, then their exit code is zero. If they encountered an error, then the exit code is non-zero.

PowerShell captures the exit code from a script or executable in $LASTEXITCODE, and if that value is non-zero, it sets $? to false. Let's use cmd.exe to demonstrate this. You can tell cmd.exe to execute a single command by passing it the /c option along with the text of the command. In this example, the command you want to run is exit, which takes a value to use as the exit code for the command:

```
PS> cmd /c exit 0
```

You told cmd to exit with code 0. Verify this by checking the values of $? and $LAST-EXITCODE, respectively:

```
PS> $?
True

PS> $LASTEXITCODE
0
```

As expected, the exit code was zero, and consequently $? is true.

> **NOTE** Ensure you access the value of $? first because accessing $LASTEXITCODE will reset $?.

Next, try it with a non-zero value:

```
PS> cmd /c exit 1
PS> $?
False

PS> $LASTEXITCODE
1
```

This time the exit code is 1, so $? is set to false. You can do the same exercises with scripts. First, create a script that exits with a zero exit code:

```
PS> 'exit 0' > invoke-exit.ps1
PS> .\invoke-exit.ps1
PS> $?
True

PS> $LASTEXITCODE
0
```

$LASTEXITCODE is 0, and $? is true. Now try it with a non-zero value:

```
PS> 'exit 25' > invoke-exit.ps1
PS> .\invoke-exit.ps1
PS> $?
False

PS> $LASTEXITCODE
25
```

Now $LASTEXITCODE contains the value the script exited with, which is 25, and $? is set to false.

So far, we've looked at how to capture errors and how to detect when they occur. Next, we'll explore some of the methods PowerShell provides to control what happens when an error is generated.

14.1.4 *Controlling the actions taken on an error*

Earlier, we talked about the differences between terminating and nonterminating errors. Sometimes you want to be able to turn nonterminating errors into terminating ones because the operation you're performing is too critical to tolerate nonterminating errors. Imagine you're setting up a website for a user. You want to reuse a directory that had been previously used for someone else. First, you want to remove all the old files and then install the new user's files. Obviously, you can't start installing the new files until all the old ones are deleted. In this situation, the failure to delete a file, which is normally a nonterminating error, must now be treated as a terminating error. The next step in the process can't begin until the current step is 100% complete.

The way to control whether errors are treated as terminating or nonterminating is by setting the error action policy, which you do by setting the error action preference. This is a mechanism that allows you to control the behavior of the system when an error occurs. There are a number possible settings for this preference as described in table 14.2.

Table 14.2 The supported identifiers and numeric equivalents for `ErrorActionPreference` and the `-ErrorAction` common parameter

Identifier	Numeric value	Descriptions
Continue	2	This is the default preference setting. The error object is written to the output pipe and added to $error, and $? is set to false. Execution then continues at the next script line.
SilentlyContinue	0	When this action preference is set, the error message isn't written to the output pipe before continuing execution. Note that it's still added to $error, and $? is still set to false. Again, execution continues at the next line.
Stop	1	This error action preference wraps a nonterminating error as a terminating error. The error object is then thrown as an exception instead of being written to the output pipe. $error and $? are still updated. Execution does not continue.
Inquire	3	Prompts the user requesting confirmation before continuing with the operation. At the prompt, the user can choose to continue, stop, or suspend the operation.
Ignore	4	Ignores the error and continues processing. Works with the -ErrorAction common parameter but isn't allowed as an option for $ErrorActionPreference.
Suspend	5	Suspends the command for further investigation. Works only with PowerShell workflows.

There are two ways to set the error action preference: by setting the $ErrorAction-Preference variable as in

```
PS> $ErrorActionPreference = 'SilentlyContinue'
```

or by using the -ErrorAction (or -ea) parameter that's available on all cmdlets, advanced functions, and advanced scripts.

Let's see examples of these preferences in action. Here's a simple one. First, run a command that has some nonterminating errors. You'll use the Get-Item cmdlet to get two items that exist and two items that don't exist:

```
PS> Get-Item -Path c:\, nosuchfile, c:\test, c:\nosuchfolder

    Directory:

Mode                LastWriteTime         Length Name
----                -------------         ------ ----
d--hs-        02/05/2016     09:51                C:\
Get-Item : Cannot find path 'C:\test\nosuchfile' because it does not exist.
At line:1 char:1
+ Get-Item -Path c:\, nosuchfile, c:\test, c:\nosuchfolder
+ ~~~~~~~~~~~~~~~~~~~~~~~~~~~~~~~~~~~~~~~~~~~~~~~~~~~~~~~~~~~
    + CategoryInfo          : ObjectNotFound:
(C:\test\nosuchfile:String) [Get-Item], ItemNotFoundException
```

```
     + FullyQualifiedErrorId : PathNotFound,Microsoft.PowerShell.Commands.
  GetItemCommand

  Directory: C:\

Mode                LastWriteTime         Length Name
----                -------------         ------ ----
d-----       02/05/2016      15:48               test
Get-Item : Cannot find path 'C:\nosuchfolder' because it does not exist.
At line:1 char:1
+ Get-Item -Path c:\, nosuchfile, c:\test, c:\nosuchfolder
+ ~~~~~~~~~~~~~~~~~~~~~~~~~~~~~~~~~~~~~~~~~~~~~~~~~~~~~~~~~~~~
    + CategoryInfo          : ObjectNotFound:
(C:\nosuchfolder:String) [Get-Item], ItemNotFoundException
    + FullyQualifiedErrorId : PathNotFound,Microsoft.PowerShell.Commands.
  GetItemCommand
```

When you look at the output, you can see that there are two output objects and two error messages. You can use redirection to discard the error messages, making the code easier to read:

```
PS> Get-Item -Path c:\, nosuchfile, c:\test, c:\nosuchfolder 2> $null

  Directory:

Mode                LastWriteTime         Length Name
----                -------------         ------ ----
d--hs-       02/05/2016      09:51                C:\

  Directory: C:\

Mode                LastWriteTime         Length Name
----                -------------         ------ ----
d-----       02/05/2016      15:48               test
```

Now you only see the output objects because you've sent the error objects to $null. You can use the -ErrorAction parameter to do the same:

```
PS> Get-Item -Path c:\, nosuchfile, c:\test, c:\nosuchfolder `
-ErrorAction SilentlyContinue

  Directory:

Mode                LastWriteTime         Length Name
----                -------------         ------ ----
d--hs-       02/05/2016      09:51                C:\

  Directory: C:\

Mode                LastWriteTime         Length Name
----                -------------         ------ ----
d-----       02/05/2016      15:48               test
```

Again, the error messages aren't displayed, but this time it's because they aren't being written to the console. Instead of being written and discarded the errors will be written to $error. If you use -ErrorAction Ignore, the errors are ignored and discarded with no entry written to $error.

Finally, let's try the Stop preference:

```
PS> Get-Item -Path c:\, nosuchfile, c:\test, c:\nosuchfolder `
-ErrorAction Stop

    Directory:

Mode                LastWriteTime        Length Name
----                -------------        ------ ----
d--hs-        02/05/2016     09:51              C:\
Get-Item : Cannot find path 'C:\test\nosuchfile' because it does not exist.
At line:1 char:1
+ Get-Item -Path c:\, nosuchfile, c:\test, c:\nosuchfolder -ErrorAction ...
+ ~~~~~~~~~~~~~~~~~~~~~~~~~~~~~~~~~~~~~~~~~~~~~~~~~~~~~~~~~~~~~~~~~~~~~~~
    + CategoryInfo          : ObjectNotFound:
(C:\test\nosuchfile:String) [Get-Item], ItemNotFoundException
    + FullyQualifiedErrorId : PathNotFound,Microsoft.PowerShell.Commands.
  GetItemCommand
```

This time, you see only one output message and one error message—the first one. This is because the error is treated as a terminating error and execution stops.

NOTE In earlier versions of PowerShell, the error message contained additional text explaining that execution stopped because of the error action preference setting. This is no longer the case in PowerShell v5.

The -ErrorAction parameter controls the error behavior for exactly one cmdlet. If you want to change the behavior for an entire script or even a whole session, you can do so by setting the $ErrorActionPreference variable. Let's redo the last example but use the variable instead of the parameter:

```
PS> & {
    $ErrorActionPreference = 'Stop'
    Get-Item -Path c:\, nosuchfile, c:\test, c:\nosuchfolder
  }

    Directory:

Mode                LastWriteTime        Length Name
----                -------------        ------ ----
d--hs-        02/05/2016     09:51              C:\
Get-Item : Cannot find path 'C:\test\nosuchfile' because it does not exist.
At line:3 char:1
+ Get-Item -Path c:\, nosuchfile, c:\test, c:\nosuchfolder
+ ~~~~~~~~~~~~~~~~~~~~~~~~~~~~~~~~~~~~~~~~~~~~~~~~~~~~~~~~~~~
    + CategoryInfo          : ObjectNotFound:
(C:\test\nosuchfile:String) [Get-Item], ItemNotFoundException
    + FullyQualifiedErrorId : PathNotFound,Microsoft.PowerShell.Commands.
  GetItemCommand
```

Again, the cmdlet stops at the first error instead of continuing.

NOTE In this example, note the use of the call operator & with a scriptblock containing the scope for the preference setting. Using the pattern & { ...script text... }, you can execute fragments of script code so that any variables set in the enclosed script text are discarded at the end of the scriptblock. Because setting $ErrorActionPreference has such a profound effect on the execution of the script, we're using this technique to isolate the preference setting.

Through the -ErrorActionPreference parameter and the $ErrorActionPreference variable, the script author has good control over when errors are written and when they're terminating. Nonterminating errors can be displayed or discarded at will. But what about terminating errors? How does the script author deal with them? Sometimes you want an error to terminate only part of an operation. For example, you might have a script move a set of files using a series of steps for each move. If one of the steps fails, you want the overall move operation to terminate for that file, but you want to continue processing the rest of the files. To do this, you need a way to manage these terminating errors or exceptions, and that's what we'll discuss next.

14.2   *Dealing with errors that terminate execution*

This section will deal with the ways that PowerShell processes errors that terminate the current flow of execution, also called *terminating errors*. If you have a programming background, you're probably more familiar with terminating errors when they're called by their more conventional name—*exceptions*. Call them what you will; we're going to delve into catching these terminating errors. We'll look at ways to trap or catch these errors and take action as a consequence. In some cases, these may be remedial actions (such as trying to fix the problem) or recording that the errors occurred.

The only way for exceptions to be caught in PowerShell v1 was by using the trap statement, which is somewhat similar to the on error statement in Visual Basic or VBScript. A better approach is the try/catch statement, modeled after the try/catch statement in C#, which was introduced in PowerShell v2.

The trap statement

Accepted best practice within the PowerShell community is to use try/catch rather than trap. We'll cover the trap statement for completeness.

The trap statement can appear anywhere in a block of code. This means that it may be specified after a statement that generates an error and still handle that error. When an exception (terminating error) occurs that isn't otherwise handled, control will be transferred to the body of the trap statement, and the statements in the body are then executed.

You can optionally specify the type of exception to catch, such as division by zero. But this can cause issues because traps don't unwrap the underlying error, so they always

(Continued)

see an `ActionPreferenceStopException` with originally nonterminating errors emitted from cmdlets. If no exception is specified, then it will trap all exceptions.

```
PS> trap { "Got it!" } 1/$null

Got it!
Attempted to divide by zero.
At line:1 char:21
+ trap { "Got it!" } 1/$null
+                    ~~~~~~~~
    + CategoryInfo          : NotSpecified: (:) [], RuntimeException
    + FullyQualifiedErrorId : RuntimeException
```

What happens after a `trap` handler execution has completed depends on how the block finishes. If the body of the `trap` handler block finishes normally, an error object will be written to the error stream, and, depending on the setting of `$ErrorAction-Preference`, either the exception will be rethrown or execution will continue at the statement after the statement that caused the exception.

You can control the interpreter's behavior after you leave the `trap` handler by the `break` and `continue` keywords. Exiting a trap block using `break` is somewhat equivalent to the error action preference `SilentlyContinue`. Using `continue` ensures that the exception is handled and the error doesn't bubble on.

The exception that was trapped is available in the `trap` block in the `$_` variable.

```
PS> $zero = 0
PS> trap { "Got it: $_"; continue } 1/$zero;
Got it: Attempted to divide by zero.
```

After the `trap` statement has completed, control transfers to the next statement in the same scope as the `trap` statement.

14.2.1 *The try/catch/finally statement*

The `trap` statement, although powerful and flexible, ended up being hard to use for many of the traditional script/programming error-handling patterns. To address this, PowerShell v2 introduced the more familiar `try/catch/finally` statement found in other languages. As is the case with all of the other PowerShell flow-control statements, this statement adopts the syntax from C#.

There are three parts to this statement: the `try` block, the `catch` block, and the `finally` block. The `try` block is always required along with at least one of the `catch` or `finally` clauses. If an error occurs in the code in the `try` block resulting in an exception, PowerShell checks to see if there is a `catch` block specified. If there is a `catch` block, then it checks to see if specific exception types are to be caught. If at least one of the specified types matches, then the catch block is executed. If not, then the search continues looking for another catch block that might match.

> **NOTE** This is one place where the PowerShell try/catch statement has some advantages over its C# cousin. In C#, only one exception can be specified per catch clause, so it's more complicated to take the same action for multiple exceptions that don't have a common base class.

If there's a catch block with no exception types specified, this clause will be executed (which tends to be the most common case). And if there's a finally block, the code in the finally block runs. (The finally block always runs whether or not there was an exception.) Here's an example using a catch statement with no exception type specified:

```
PS> try {
    1
    2
    3/$null
    4
    5
}
catch {
    "ERROR: $_"
}
finally {
    'ALL DONE'
}

1
2
ERROR: Attempted to divide by zero.
ALL DONE
```

In this example, the third statement in the try block causes a terminating error. This error is caught and control transfers to the catch block. Then, when the catch block is complete, the finally block is executed. This flow of control is shown in figure 14.5.

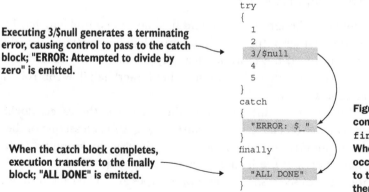

Executing 3/$null generates a terminating error, causing control to pass to the catch block; "ERROR: Attempted to divide by zero" is emitted.

When the catch block completes, execution transfers to the finally block; "ALL DONE" is emitted.

```
try
{
    1
    2
    3/$null
    4
    5
}
catch
{
    "ERROR: $_"
}
finally
{
    "ALL DONE"
}
```

Figure 14.5   The flow of control in a try/catch/ finally statement. When an exception occurs, control transfers to the catch block and then the finally block.

The complete processing logic for the try/catch/finally statement is shown in the flowchart in figure 14.6.

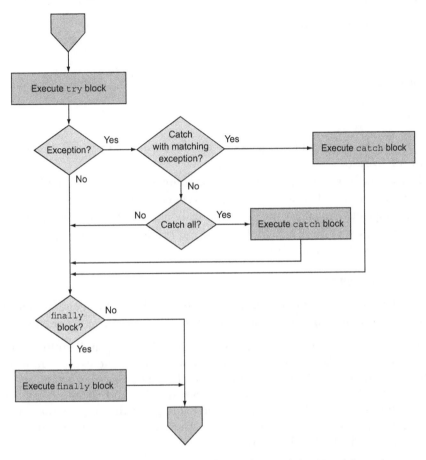

Figure 14.6 The complete logical flow in the `try/catch/finally` **statement**

USING TRY/CATCH IN EXPRESSIONS

An interesting application of the try/catch statement when used in combination with PowerShell's expression-oriented syntax is that it makes it fairly easy to write functions that provide default values if an expression throws an exception. Let's look at using try/catch in a custom div function. We want a function that never throws an exception even when dividing by zero. The function might look like this:

```
function div {
    param
    (
        [int] $x,

        [int] $y
    )
```

```
    try {
        $x/$y
    }
    catch {
        [int]::MaxValue
    }
}
```

Give it a try

```
PS> div 1 0
2147483647
```

and you get the maximum integer value instead of the error you normally get when you divide by zero.

Clearly, exceptions are a powerful error-handling mechanism. With this mechanism, errors are never missed because you forgot to check for a return code. In fact, you have to do the opposite and take action to suppress them instead. Having mastered catching other people's exceptions, let's look at how you can leverage this feature in your own scripts with the `throw` statement.

14.2.2 *The throw statement*

To complete the exception-handling topic, you need a way to generate terminating errors or exceptions. You can accomplish this by using the `throw` statement.

> **NOTE** In the original design, `throw` was supposed to be a cmdlet rather than a keyword in the language. But having a cmdlet throw the exception meant that the thrown exception was subject to the cmdlet's error action policy, and the whole point of `throw` was to bypass this policy and always generate an exception. It wasn't so much a case of the tail wagging the dog as it was staple-gunning the poor beast to the floor. And so, learning from past mistakes, Microsoft made it into a keyword.

The simplest example is to throw nothing:

```
PS> throw
ScriptHalted
At line:1 char:1
+ throw
+ ~~~~~
    + CategoryInfo          :
    OperationStopped: (:) [], RuntimeException
    + FullyQualifiedErrorId : ScriptHalted
```

This approach is convenient for casual scripting. You don't need to create an error object or exception object—the `throw` statement takes care of all of that. Unfortunately, the message you get isn't too informative. If you want to include a meaningful message, you can easily provide your own:

```
PS> throw 'My Message!'
My Message!
```

```
At line:1 char:1
+ throw 'My Message!'
+ ~~~~~~~~~~~~~~~~~~~~
    + CategoryInfo          :
OperationStopped: (My Message!:String) [], RuntimeException
    + FullyQualifiedErrorId : My Message!
```

You see the message in the output. It's also possible to use `throw` to throw `Error-Record` objects or .NET exceptions if you want to use more detailed error handling. Instead of passing a string, you pass these objects.

To complete this chapter, we'll look at the data available in the event log. The event log is the central store for log messages from the system as well as from all the applications, services, and drivers running on that machine. It's a one-stop shop for diagnostic information. You'll see how to access this diagnostic treasure trove using PowerShell.

14.3 PowerShell and the event log

The Windows event log provides a central place where applications and operating system components can record events like the starting and stopping of an operation, progress, and system and application errors. For system administration, having access to the event log is critical. As an admin tool, PowerShell support for the event log is quite important, so that's what we're going to look at in this section.

14.3.1 The EventLog cmdlets

PowerShell v1 had only a single, fairly limited command (`Get-EventLog`) for working with the event log. More sophisticated operations required using the underlying .NET classes. PowerShell v2 filled this gap and now there's a comprehensive set of cmdlets for working with the event log, as shown in table 14.3.

Table 14.3 The PowerShell `EventLog` cmdlets

Cmdlet name	PowerShell version	Description
Get-EventLog	v1, enhanced in v2	Gets the events in an event log, or a list of the event logs, on the local or remote computers
Clear-EventLog	v2	Deletes all entries from specified event logs on the local or remote computers
Write-EventLog	v2	Writes a new event log entry to the specified event log on the local or remote computer
Limit-EventLog	v2	Sets the event log properties that limit the size of the event log and the age of its entries
Show-EventLog	v2	Displays the event logs of the local or a remote computer using the event viewer MMC console
New-EventLog	v2	Creates a new event log and a new event source on a local or remote computer
Remove-EventLog	v2	Deletes an event log or unregisters an event source

Show-EventLog

You may be wondering why PowerShell includes this cmdlet—all it does is launch the event log viewer. The answer is simple: usability. PowerShell is a command-line shell, so you should be able to launch GUI applications from the command line. You can, but there's a small problem: most of the commands you want to run, including GUI commands, have names that aren't obvious. For example, to launch the control panel applet for adding and removing software, you run `appwiz.cpl`. To change the display settings, run `desk.cpl`. These command names, though related to their function, are certainly not obvious to a user. Similarly, the command to start the event viewer is `eventvwr.msc`. In contrast, the `Show-EventLog` cmdlet, which follows the PowerShell naming guidelines, can easily be intuited once you know the rules. The next question is why provide a cmdlet instead of an alias? Because, as well as command naming, a cmdlet provides standard parameter handling, which allows for things like tab completion. By providing a "shim" cmdlet for the existing application, one more small bump is removed from the command-line user's experience.

The `Get-EventLog` cmdlet is what we'll focus our attention on here. This cmdlet allows you to retrieve a list of the available application and system event logs and then look at the content of each of the logs. To get a list of the available logs, run `Get-EventLog -List`. The output will look something like this:

```
PS> Get-EventLog -List

  Max(K) Retain OverflowAction        Entries Log
  ------ ------ --------------        ------- ---
  20,480      0 OverwriteAsNeeded       1,607 Application
  20,480      0 OverwriteAsNeeded           0 HardwareEvents
     512      7 OverwriteOlder              0 Internet Explorer
  20,480      0 OverwriteAsNeeded           0 Key Management Service
     128      0 OverwriteAsNeeded           9 OAlerts
  20,480      0 OverwriteAsNeeded       3,171 Security
  20,480      0 OverwriteAsNeeded       1,927 System
  15,360      0 OverwriteAsNeeded       1,569 Windows PowerShell
```

In addition to the names of the logs, you can see the configuration settings for each log, such as the amount of space the log might take and what happens when the log fills up. You can use the `Limit-EventLog` cmdlet to change these limits for a log:

```
PS> Limit-EventLog -LogName Application -MaximumSize 25mb
```

then verify that the limit has been changed:

```
PS> Get-EventLog -List | where Log -match 'Application'

  Max(K) Retain OverflowAction        Entries Log
  ------ ------ --------------        ------- ---
  25,600      0 OverwriteAsNeeded       1,607 Application
```

As well as listing the available logs, `Get-EventLog` lets you see the events in any log. Because the event logs can be quite large, the cmdlet supports a variety of options to control the amount of data returned. Table 14.4 describes the various `Get-EventLog` filter parameters.

Table 14.4 The types of filters provided by the *Get-EventLog* cmdlet

Filter	Description
Source	The -Source parameter allows you to filter log entries based on the name used to register the event source. This name is usually the name of the application logging the events, but for larger applications, it may be the name of a subcomponent within that application.
Message	The -Message parameter allows the retrieved entries to be filtered based on the event's message text. The specified filter strings may contain wildcard patterns. (Note that because the text of a message is usually translated, the use of the -Message filter may not be portable to different locations.)
InstanceID	The InstanceId for an entry is the message resource identifier for the event. This identifier is used to retrieve the localized text for a message from the resource file for the registered event source. Because this identifier isn't localized, the -InstanceID parameter provides a way to filter events by message that's portable across locales because the message text is localized but the resource ID is always the same value.
EntryType	The entry type (or severity level) is a way of classifying events based on the potential impact of the corresponding event on the system's behavior. The entry types are Information, Warning, Error, and Critical. Two additional event types can occur in the security log: Success Audit and Failure Audit.
UserName	The -UserName parameter filters based on the name of the user on whose behalf the event occurred. Wildcards patterns can be used in arguments to this parameter.
Before	Gets only the events that occur before the specified date and time.
After	Gets only the events that occur after the specified date and time.

Let's see how these parameters are used by working through a few examples. We'll look at the Application log.

Start by listing the newest 10 events in this log:

```
PS> Get-EventLog -LogName Application -Newest 10

Index Time          EntryType    Source   InstanceID Message
----- ----          ---------    ------   ---------- -------
34931 May 09 20:39 Warning      Outlook  1073741851 OAB Downlo...
34930 May 09 20:36 Information  Outlook  1073741851 Starting O...
34929 May 09 20:32 Information  NVWMI    1090519043 runPipeSer...
34928 May 09 20:32 Information  NVWMI    1090519043 runPipeSer...
34927 May 09 20:32 Information  NVWMI    1090519043 runPipeSer...
34926 May 09 20:32 Information  NVWMI    1090519043 NVWMI - Ba...
34925 May 09 20:32 Information  NVWMI    1090519043 runPipeSer...
34924 May 09 20:32 Information  NVWMI    1090519043 runPipeSer...
34923 May 09 20:32 Information  NVWMI    1090519043 NVWMI - Ba...
34922 May 09 20:32 Information  NVWMI    1090519043 runPipeSer...
```

The `-Index` parameter lets you retrieve a specific entry from the log. Use `Format-List` to display additional properties of the entry:

```
PS> Get-EventLog -LogName Application -Index 34931 | Format-List

Index              : 34931
EntryType          : Warning
InstanceId         : 1073741851
Message            : OAB Download Failed. (Result code in event data).
Category           : (0)
CategoryNumber     : 0
ReplacementStrings : {OAB Download Failed. (Result code in event data).}
Source             : Outlook
TimeGenerated      : 09/05/2017 20:39:01
TimeWritten        : 09/05/2017 20:39:01
UserName           :
```

Now retrieve events using this message's `InstanceID`:

```
PS> Get-EventLog -LogName Application -InstanceId 1073741851 -Newest 5

Index Time            EntryType    Source   InstanceID Message
----- ----            ---------    ------   ---------- -------
34932 May 09 20:41 Information Outlook 1073741851 Starting O...
34931 May 09 20:39 Warning     Outlook 1073741851 OAB Downlo...
34930 May 09 20:36 Information Outlook 1073741851 Starting O...
34906 May 09 20:32 Warning     Outlook 1073741851 OAB Downlo...
34904 May 09 20:31 Information Outlook 1073741851 Starting O...
```

You can use `-Before` and `-After` to retrieve messages around a specific date (and time if desired):

```
PS> Get-EventLog -LogName Application -After 'April 30/2017' `
-Before 'May 3/2017'
```

Here you retrieve all the messages between May 1 and May 2 in 2017. You can combine `-Before`, `-Newest`, `-Message`, and `-After` to perform further filtering. For example, to retrieve the last 10 messages on May 2, use this:

```
PS> Get-EventLog -LogName Application -Before 'May 3/2017' -Newest 10
```

or, you can use `-Message` and `-After` to find all messages matching a specific pattern that occurred after a specific date. For this example, use the month and day numbers and let the year default to the current year:

```
PS> Get-EventLog -LogName Application -Message '*Defender*' `
-After 'April 30/2017' |
Format-List UserName, TimeGenerated, EntryType, Message
```

You'll see a number of records of this form:

```
UserName      :
TimeGenerated : 09/05/2017 13:00:07
EntryType     : Information
```

```
Message        : Updated Windows Defender status successfully to
                 SECURITY_PRODUCT_STATE_ON.
```

Why is all this useful? Imagine you see a critical error in an application. This error shows up in the Application log. You suspect that it might be related to either a hardware issue or a bad device driver. Rather than manually poring over hundreds of log entries, you can use the date from the Application log entry to retrieve the events in the System log that occurred shortly before the application.

Digging through the entries, you identify the problem that led to the failure. From this, you get the `Source` and `InstanceID` identifying the problematic entry. You quickly write a script to remediate the problem on this machine but realize that there may be other machines in the organization with similar issues. You put together a list of potentially at-risk machines and pass this list to `Get-EventLog` using the `-Computer-Name` parameter. You also specify the `-Source` and `-InstanceID` parameters of the problematic message. This command will search the event logs of all the at-risk machines, returning a list of event log entries matching the criteria. From this set of events, you can get the names of all the computers that need to be fixed. Finally, you can use PowerShell remoting to run the remediation script on all the machines with the problem.

> **NOTE** Although you need PowerShell remoting to run the remediation script on the target machines, PowerShell remoting isn't used when you use `Get-EventLog` to access a remote computer. `Get-EventLog` uses its own remoting protocol. This means you can use `Get-EventLog` to examine the logs of the target computer to help diagnose what went wrong using its own built-in remoting to connect to that computer. It's not dependent on PowerShell remoting.

The `Get-EventLog` filtering capabilities make this kind of forensic analysis easy. One of the things you might want to analyze is PowerShell itself.

14.3.2 *Examining the PowerShell event log*

When PowerShell is installed, the installation process creates a new event log called Windows PowerShell. As PowerShell executes, it writes a variety of information to this log, which you can see using the `Get-EventLog` cmdlet. Let's use the cmdlet to get the last few records from the PowerShell event log. As always, you can use the tools PowerShell provides to filter and scope the data you want to look at. You'll use an array slice to get the last five records from the log:

```
PS> Get-EventLog -LogName 'Windows PowerShell' | select -Last 5

Index Time          EntryType    Source    InstanceID Message
----- ----          ---------    ------    ---------- -------
    5 Nov 03 11:15  Information   PowerShell       600 Provider "Fi...
    4 Nov 03 11:15  Information   PowerShell       600 Provider "Fu...
    3 Nov 03 11:15  Information   PowerShell       600 Provider "En...
    2 Nov 03 11:15  Information   PowerShell       600 Provider "Al...
    1 Nov 03 11:15  Information   PowerShell       600 Provider "Re...
```

The default presentation of the event records doesn't show much information. Let's look at one event in detail and see what it contains:

```
PS> Get-EventLog -LogName 'Windows PowerShell' |
select -Last 1 | Format-List *
```

First, you get some basic event log elements common to all event log entries:

```
EventID            : 600
MachineName        : brucepayquad
Data               : {}
Index              : 1
```

Next, you see the event category. This isn't the same as the error category discussed earlier. PowerShell event log entries are grouped into several large categories:

```
Category           : Provider Lifecycle
CategoryNumber     : 6
```

Next is the entry type and a message describing the entry. This is followed by a collection of detail elements, which includes things such as the state transition for the engine as well as some of the versioning information you saw on the $host object earlier. This is included in case you have multiple hosts for a particular engine:

```
EntryType          : Information
Message            : Provider "Registry" is Started.

                     Details:
                         ProviderName=Registry
                         NewProviderState=Started

                         SequenceNumber=1

                         HostName=ConsoleHost
                         HostVersion=5.1.14393.0
                         HostId=ee0ff0ec-0be8-49ab-8c47-beed57a906e7
                         HostApplication=C:\Windows\System32\
                         WindowsPowerShell\v1.0\powershell.exe
                         EngineVersion=
                         RunspaceId=
                         PipelineId=
                         CommandName=
                         CommandType=
                         ScriptName=
                         CommandPath=
                         CommandLine=
Source             : PowerShell
```

The following fields specify the replacement strings that are available. These strings are substituted into the log message text:

```
ReplacementStrings : {Registry, Started,        ProviderName=Registry
                        NewProviderState=Started

                        SequenceNumber=1
```

```
HostName=ConsoleHost
HostVersion=5.1.14393.0
HostId=ee0ff0ec-0be8-49ab-8c47-beed57a906e7
HostApplication=C:\Windows\System32\
WindowsPowerShell\v1.0\powershell.exe
EngineVersion=
RunspaceId=
PipelineId=
CommandName=
CommandType=
ScriptName=
CommandPath=
CommandLine=}
```

Finally, you get additional information for identifying the event log entry and when it occurred:

```
InstanceId       : 600
TimeGenerated    : 03/11/2016 11:15:13
TimeWritten      : 03/11/2016 11:15:13
UserName         :
Site             :
Container        :
```

Granted, the output isn't all that interesting, but when you're trying to figure out what went wrong on your systems, being able to see when the PowerShell interpreter was started or stopped could be useful. There are also certain types of internal errors (also known as *bugs*) that may cause a PowerShell session to terminate. These errors also will be logged in the PowerShell event log.

So far, we've looked at the classic event logs that have always been available in Windows. A new type of event log was introduced with Windows Vista; unfortunately, Get-EventLog and the other cmdlets listed in table 14.3 don't work with these logs. You have to use Get-WinEvent.

14.3.3 Get-WinEvent

When working with the new Windows Event Log technology in Windows Vista and later, you have only Get-WinEvent. There are no cmdlets that can perform the other tasks listed in table 14.3.

> **NOTE** Get-WinEvent can also read classic event log backup files (.evt files), so it can be used to analyze any files of that type you may need to access.

In this section, we'll show the differences in the way Get-EventLog and Get-WinEvent filter data from the event logs. We'll start by examining the full list of available event logs:

```
PS> Get-WinEvent -ListLog *
```

You'll see the classic event logs Get-EventLog displays and then a large number of logs, most of them named Microsoft-Windows-<something>. A standard Windows 10 machine has approximately 400 of these logs. You can view a subset of the available logs:

```
PS> Get-WinEvent -ListLog Microsoft-Windows-PowerShell* |
select Logmode, RecordCount, LogName

 LogMode RecordCount LogName
 ------- ----------- -------
 Circular          0 Microsoft-Windows-PowerShell-Des...
   Retain          0 Microsoft-Windows-PowerShell/Admin
 Circular        358 Microsoft-Windows-PowerShell/Operational
```

Get-WinEvent can filter event log data using a hashtable or an XPath query. We'll use the hashtable syntax to re-create the filtering examples we used in section 14.3.1. The first task is to select the newest five entries in the log:

```
PS> Get-WinEvent -LogName Application | select -First 5

   ProviderName: Outlook

TimeCreated            Id LevelDisplayName Message
-----------            -- ---------------- -------
09/05/2017 20:58:00 27 Information      Starting OAB dow...
09/05/2017 20:52:51 27 Warning          OAB Download Fai...
09/05/2017 20:41:43 27 Information      Starting OAB dow...
09/05/2017 20:39:01 27 Warning          OAB Download Fai...
09/05/2017 20:36:47 27 Information      Starting OAB dow...
```

You can select single records by the RecordId property:

```
PS> Get-WinEvent -LogName Application | where RecordId -eq 34935

ProviderName: Outlook

TimeCreated            Id LevelDisplayName Message
-----------            -- ---------------- -------
09/05/2017 20:52:51 27 Warning          OAB Download Fai...
```

Unfortunately, RecordId isn't part of the default output, so you'll have to format your display to include that data if you require access to it.

You can search the event log for events that occur in a specific time period:

```
PS> $start = (Get-Date).AddDays(-2)
PS> $end = (Get-Date).AddDays(-1)
PS> Get-WinEvent -FilterHashtable @{LogName='Application';
 StartTime=$start; EndTime=$end}
```

You'll notice that the ProviderName is supplied as part of the output. The records are displayed in chronological order—youngest first unless the -Oldest parameter is used to reverse the order. It may be advantageous to view the records with all the records from a single provider grouped together, with the individual records in descending time order:

```
PS> Get-WinEvent -FilterHashtable @{LogName='Application';
StartTime=$start; EndTime=$end} |
Sort-Object -Property @{Expression='ProviderName';
Descending=$false},
@{Expression='TimeCreated';Descending=$true}
```

`Sort-Object` will sort the records obtained by `Get-WinEvent` so that the provider names are in alphabetical order and the records for each provider are displayed from youngest to oldest. You can view the records from a single provider:

```
PS> Get-WinEvent -FilterHashtable @{Logname='Application';
   ProviderName='SecurityCenter'; StartTime=$start; EndTime=$end}
```

That's all we're going to cover on event logs in this chapter. From these examples, you can see that the event logs provide a lot of information, much of which can help you manage and maintain your systems. The trick is being able to extract and correlate the information across the various logs, and this is where PowerShell can be very useful.

14.4 Summary

- There are two types of errors in PowerShell: terminating and nonterminating.
- Error records are written directly to default output.
- Error records are rich objects.
- The `$error` variable stores the last 256 errors (by default).
- You can specify a specific variable for errors by using the `-ErrorVariable` parameter.
- `$?` stores a Boolean value indicating execution status of the last command.
- `$LASTEXITCODE` stores the exit code of the last console command or exit statement but isn't affected by cmdlets or .NET code.
- `$ErrorActionPreference` and the `-ErrorAction` parameter can be used to control the action taken if an error occurs.
- Terminating errors and exceptions can be managed by the `trap` statement or the `try`/`catch`/`finally` statements (preferred).
- Use the `throw` statement to generate your own terminating exceptions.
- The `Get-EventLog` cmdlet reads classic event logs.
- `Get-WinEvent` must be used for the new style event logs.

All these error features are great for letting you know something is wrong, but how do you go about fixing the problem? That's the topic of the next chapter.

15

Debugging

This chapter covers

- Creating script instrumentation
- Capturing session output
- The PowerShell debugger
- Command-line debugging
- Debugging PowerShell jobs, runspaces, and remote scripts

> *Big Julie: "I had the numbers taken off for luck, but I remember where the spots formerly were."*
>
> —*Guys and Dolls,* words and music by Frank Loesser

No one writes code that always works correctly the first time it's run. When the worst happens and your code won't run, or deliver the correct results, you need to debug it to find the problem or problems. Start by adding statements that track your code's execution and capture session output and then move on to more advanced techniques using the PowerShell debugger on running code. The techniques we'll show you in this chapter will enable you to find and fix code problems much faster.

Let's start by looking at how you can provide instrumentation for your scripts so they provide you with diagnostic information.

15.1 Script instrumentation

The most basic form of debugging a script is to put statements in it, using the `Write*` cmdlets, that display information about the script's execution. The `Write*` cmdlets separate your debugging output from the rest of the output by displaying the debugging output directly on the console.

> **NOTE** These statements will slow down your code execution because they'll still be parsed even if they aren't run. You may need to remove them in production code if execution speed is of paramount importance.

Checking the code before it runs can catch a number of potential errors as well as help you implement best practices in your coding.

15.1.1 The Write* cmdlets

A number of cmdlets enable you to write out information during the execution of your scripts:

```
PS> Get-Command write* -Module Microsoft.PowerShell.Utility |
Format-Wide -Column 3

Write-Debug          Write-Error          Write-Host
Write-Information    Write-Output         Write-Progress
Write-Verbose        Write-Warning
```

Output streams

The `Write*` cmdlets are closely tied to the output streams of the same name. The `Error`, `Warning`, `Verbose`, and `Progress` streams are targeted at the end user of the script. `Information` targets the operator; `Debug` targets the developer.

`Error` is self-explanatory with the complication of terminating and nonterminating errors. It tracks what went wrong.

`Warning` is for things that might be wrong; for example, not including an `Import-DSCResource` statement for the default resources is a warning. It's used infrequently because most conditions should be treated as errors. The PSDesiredStateConfiguration.psm1 module has a number of `Write-Warning` statements.

`Verbose` is for giving the user more detailed information about the behavior of the operation they requested (example: `Copy-Item -Verbose`). It tracks what's happening in detail.

`Debug` is used by developers to instrument code to make it easier to discover and analyze bugs in their scripts. Unlike `Write-Host`, `Debug` statements can be added to a script and left in place to assist in the debugging process later on or in the field (with, as mentioned, the caveat that they add execution overhead). As an example, the PSDesiredStateConfiguration.psm1 module has lots of `Debug` statements. `Debug`

> *(Continued)*
>
> tracks information that's useful for figuring out why the script misbehaved and for locating bugs.
>
> `Information` is a new stream in PowerShell v5 and is targeted at the operations team rather than the immediate user. It should be used to track operational behavior. For example, in DSC, it would be used to track what state checks are being done and consequently why an operation is being performed. For instance, in DSC, a file was missing so a new file will be created. It's the equivalent of writing to the analytic log.
>
> `Progress` tracks simple progress as a percentage. In many cases, using `Verbose` is more useful than `Progress`, but people like progress bars. A progress bar will slow down execution of your code by a significant amount.
>
> Knowing what's tracked in each stream enables you to target your debugging efforts correctly.

You've seen `Write-Output` in action throughout the book. It does what it says and outputs whatever it's passed to the next step in the pipeline—or if it's at the end of pipeline, to the default output mechanism, usually the screen:

```
PS> 1..3 | foreach {$psitem | Write-Output}
1
2
3
```

You don't need to use this cmdlet because the default action at the end of a pipeline is to display objects on the pipeline. It's useful when you want to force output.

`Write-Progress` isn't considered debugging as such, but it will display a progress bar during execution of one or more commands. Tracking the progress of your code's execution may supply clues if something goes wrong. Run the following in the console and the ISE and observe the results:

```
$max = 10000
1..$max |foreach {
  Write-Progress -Activity Test  -PercentComplete (($psitem/$max)*100)
}
```

Interestingly the code runs much quicker in the ISE.

NOTE   Outputting progress activity will slow down execution of your code.

The `Write-Host` cmdlet is the way that most people start creating script instrumentation:

```
PS> 1..3 | foreach {
    $x = $psitem * 2
    Write-Host -Object "$psitem doubled is: $x"
}
```

```
1 doubled is: 2
2 doubled is: 4
3 doubled is: 6
```

The drawback is that your output from `Write-Host` is mixed in with your code output:

```
PS> 1..3 | foreach {
    $x = $psitem * 2
    Write-Host -Object "$psitem doubled is: $x"

    $y += $x
    $y
}

1 doubled is: 2
2
2 doubled is: 4
6
3 doubled is: 6
12
```

Also, using `Write-Host` is an all-or-nothing proposition—you can't turn it on and off to suit your needs. Ideally, you want to separate the output of your instrumentation, at least visually, and control whether the instrumentation is active. You can use the `-ForegroundColor` and `-BackgroundColor` parameters to control the text colors for `Write-Host`, but there are better approaches.

VERBOSE AND DEBUG

`Write-Verbose` and `Write-Debug` enable you to output information from your script, or function, when you need it. You can turn off the information during normal usage and turn it on when you have a problem. `Debug` is for outputting developer debug information when your code runs, similar to the debug log in the event log. The `Verbose` stream is for giving the end user more information about the operation they requested.

> **NOTE** The `Information` stream is for information about how the operation is proceeding, equivalent to the analytic log in the event log.

Today in DSC, verbose messages are recorded in the analytic log. If the `Information` stream had been around when DSC was started, it would have been using `Information` and not `Verbose`.

You use these two cmdlets together with the `[CmdletBinding()]` attribute that we discussed in chapter 7. Consider this simple function:

```
function fdvtest {
    [CmdletBinding()]
    param(
        [Parameter(ValueFromPipeline=$true)]
        [int]$i,

        [int]$mult=2
    )
```

```
    PROCESS {
        $i * $mult
    }
}
```

The output is

```
PS> 1..3 | fdvtest
2
4
6
```

Look at the function's syntax:

```
PS> Get-Command fdvtest -Syntax

fdvtest [[-i] <int>] [[-mult] <int>] [<CommonParameters>]
```

The CommonParameters include -Verbose and -Debug. Before you can use those parameters and get any sensible output, you need to add the appropriate statements. Let's say you want to see a message before the calculation. You can use Write-Verbose:

```
function fdvtest {
    [CmdletBinding()]
    param(
        [Parameter(ValueFromPipeline=$true)]
        [int]$i,

        [int]$mult=2
    )

    PROCESS {
        Write-Verbose -Message 'Performing multiplication'
        $i * $mult
    }
}
```

Running the function without the -Verbose switch gives you the same output as previously. When you run the function with the -Verbose switch

```
PS> 1..3 | fdvtest -Verbose
VERBOSE: Performing multiplication
2
VERBOSE: Performing multiplication
4
VERBOSE: Performing multiplication
6
```

you get a clearly labeled message that serves to separate your debugging messages from the normal output. The verbose messages are in a different color (defaults are yellow in the console and cyan in the ISE) than the normal output to give further emphasis. Write-Verbose can output messages that enable you to track the progress of your code.

You can control the color for verbose, debug, warning, error, and information messages using Tools > Options in the ISE and then selecting Output Streams on the Colors and Fonts tab. In the console, you can view the colors for the streams using the following:

```
PS> $host.PrivateData

ErrorForegroundColor      : Red
ErrorBackgroundColor      : Black
WarningForegroundColor    : Yellow
WarningBackgroundColor    : Black
DebugForegroundColor      : Yellow
DebugBackgroundColor      : Black
VerboseForegroundColor    : Yellow
VerboseBackgroundColor    : Black
ProgressForegroundColor   : Yellow
ProgressBackgroundColor   : DarkCyan
```

The colors can be modified. If you don't like red for the error color:

```
PS> $host.PrivateData.ErrorForegroundColor = 'Green'
```

Your errors are now shown in green! The console settings are on a session basis, so you need to put the changes into your profile if you want them to be applied to all your console sessions.

Debug messages can also be added to your code:

```
function fdvtest {
    [CmdletBinding()]
    param(
        [Parameter(ValueFromPipeline=$true)]
        [int]$i,

        [int]$mult=2
    )
    BEGIN {
        Write-Debug "`$mult = $mult"
    }

    PROCESS {
        Write-Verbose -Message 'Performing multiplication'
        Write-Debug -Message "`$i = $i"

        $i * $mult
    }
}
```

In this case, a debug message has been added to give the value of the multiplier and the value of $i. When you run the function with the -Debug parameter, you'll see a dialog each time the code reaches a Write-Debug statement, as shown in figure 15.1.

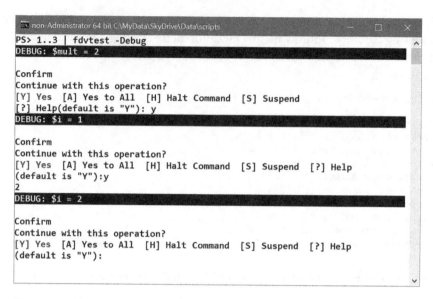

Figure 15.1   Output when using the `-Debug` **functionality**

If you halt or suspend the command, you can step into it and use the standard Power-Shell debugging functionality, which we'll get to soon.

> **NOTE**   When you use the `-Verbose` or `-Debug` switch, it will turn on the appropriate output for all cmdlets in your script or function as well as enabling the appropriate `Write` cmdlet.

ERROR, WARNING, AND INFORMATION

In chapter 4 you saw how to redirect output to the `Error`, `Warning`, and `Information` streams. You can achieve the same thing by using the appropriate `Write` cmdlet. Unlike the `Write-Verbose` and `Write-Debug` cmdlets from the previous section, you don't get a switch to enable the functionality at the script or function level.

When you use `Write-Information` or `Write-Warning`, further processing depends on the value of the appropriate preference variable (or parameter), as shown in table 15.1.

Table 15.1   Cmdlet and preference variable relationships

Category	Cmdlet	Preference variable	Parameter
Information	Write-Information	$InformationPreference	InformationAction
Warning	Write-Warning	$WarningPreference	WarningAction
Error	Write-Error	$ErrorActionPreference	ErrorAction

You can view the current values of the preference variables like this:

```
PS> Get-Item variable:*preference

Name                            Value
----                            -----
ConfirmPreference               High
DebugPreference                 SilentlyContinue
ErrorActionPreference           Continue
ProgressPreference              Continue
VerbosePreference               SilentlyContinue
WarningPreference               Continue
InformationPreference           SilentlyContinue
WhatIfPreference                False
```

Write-Error declares a nonterminating error, which won't stop further processing. As you saw in chapter 14, you can use Throw to declare a terminating error.

> **NOTE** Starting in Windows PowerShell v5, Write-Host is a wrapper for Write-Information. It uses the Information stream instead of writing directly to the host. You can now use Write-Host to emit output to the Information stream, but the $InformationPreference preference variable and InformationAction common parameters don't affect Write-Host messages.

As usual, the easiest way to explain the use of these cmdlets is with an example:

```
1..7 |
foreach {
    switch ($psitem) {
        1 {
            Write-Information -MessageData "Starting. Value is $_" `
            -InformationAction Continue
            Break
        }
        5 {
            Write-Warning -Message "Nearly Finished. Value is $_"
            Break
        }
        7 {
            Write-Error -Message "Value of $_ is too high" `
            -ErrorAction Continue
        }
        default {
            Write-Information -MessageData "Value is $_" `
            -InformationAction Continue
        }
    }
}
```

When you run this code, you'll see this output:

```
Starting. Value is 1
Value is 2
Value is 3
```

```
Value is 4
WARNING: Nearly Finished. Value is 5
Value is 6
    :        <truncated for brevity as repeat of code>
Value of 7 is too high
    + CategoryInfo          : NotSpecified: (:) [Write-Error],
  WriteErrorException
    + FullyQualifiedErrorId : Microsoft.PowerShell.Commands.
  WriteErrorException
```

Notice that the output from `Write-Warning` has a `WARNING:` prefix to draw your attention, but that from `Write-Information` does not. It is in the standard text color.

When you looked at the event logs in chapter 14, you saw that events were logged under the categories of `Information`, `Warning`, and `Error`. If you prefer to have the messages from your code instrumentation written to the event log, you'll use `Write-EventLog`. You can even create your own specific event log, as you'll see next.

15.1.2 *Writing events to the event Log*

You can write your `Information`, `Warning`, and `Error` messages to the console, but that assumes that you'll be watching execution of the script. If you're running the code in the middle of the night, this isn't an optimum solution. Using the event logs enables you to capture the messages for future analysis. It's possible to use one of the existing event logs, but you can create your own:

```
PS> New-EventLog -LogName PiALog -Source Scripts
```

You need to provide a name for the log and an event source. Administrative privileges are required to create event logs. You can have multiple sources per log file, but source names must be unique on the machine—you can't use the same source name for sources writing to two different logs. You can create additional sources:

```
PS> New-EventLog -LogName PiALog -Source Functions
```

You can view the sources associated with an individual log file like this:

```
PS> Get-CimInstance -ClassName Win32_NTEventLogFile `
-Filter "LogFileName='PiALog'" |
select -ExpandProperty Sources

PiALog
Functions
Scripts
```

Now that you have your log file, let's modify the code from the example in the previous section to use your new log:

```
1..7 |
foreach {
    switch ($psitem) {
```

```
    1 {
        Write-EventLog -Message "Starting. Value is $_" `
        -LogName PiALog -Source Scripts -EntryType Information `
        -EventId 1001
        Break
        }
    5 {
        Write-EventLog -Message "Nearly Finished. Value is $_" `
        -LogName PiALog -Source Scripts -EntryType Warning `
        -EventId 1010
        Break
        }
    7 {
        Write-EventLog -Message "Value of $_ is too high" `
        -LogName PiALog -Source Scripts -EntryType Error `
        -EventId 1020
        }
    default {
        Write-EventLog -Message "Value is $_" `
        -LogName PiALog -Source Scripts -EntryType Information `
        -EventId 1002
        }
    }
}
```

When you run this code, you won't see any output. You can view the records written into the event log like so:

```
PS> Get-EventLog -LogName PiALog

Index Time            EntryType    Source  InstanceID Message
----- ----            ---------    ------  ---------- -------
    7 May 10 11:47 Error        Scripts       1020 Value of 7 is too high
    6 May 10 11:47 Information Scripts       1002 Value is 6
    5 May 10 11:47 Warning      Scripts       1010 Nearly Finished. Va…
    4 May 10 11:47 Information Scripts       1002 Value is 4
    3 May 10 11:47 Information Scripts       1002 Value is 3
    2 May 10 11:47 Information Scripts       1002 Value is 2
    1 May 10 11:47 Information Scripts       1001 Starting. Value is 1
```

Using the features described in this section and the previous section, you can instrument your scripts in order to debug their behavior. Although this is a tried-and-true way of debugging, it's reactive, and you can't work with the script while it's running. PowerShell provides other mechanisms to find problems in your scripts. One of these features is strict mode, our next topic.

15.1.3 *Catching errors with strict mode*

PowerShell provides built-in static and runtime checks to help you catch errors in your scripts. Static checks are performed at script load/compile time, and runtime checks are dynamic checks done at runtime.

> **NOTE**   These features are similar to `Option Explicit` in Visual Basic or strict mode in PERL and are named after the PERL feature.

PowerShell v1 could check for undefined variables through the `Set-PSDebug` cmdlet. PowerShell v2 introduced `Set-StrictMode`, which enables a much more comprehensive set of checks. `Set-StrictMode` affects only the current scope and any child scopes, so you can use it in scripts without affecting the global scope and therefore other scripts.

> **NOTE**   Strict mode turns on certain checks in regular scripts and functions. PowerShell classes (see chapter 19) have their own built-in set of strict checks that are always enabled. The checks in classes are intended to support more robust *programming*, as opposed to scripting, in PowerShell. If you're writing large applications in PowerShell, using classes can result in more robust code because of these additional checks.

You can control the checks that are performed by using the `-Version` parameter, which takes 1, 2, or `Latest` as an argument controlling whether v1 or v2 checks are enabled, as shown in table 15.2.

Table 15.2   Strict mode versions

Version	Action
1	Prohibits references to uninitialized variables, except for uninitialized variables in strings
2	As 1, plus:
	▪ Prohibits references to uninitialized variables (including uninitialized variables in strings)
	▪ Prohibits references to nonexistent properties of an object
	▪ Prohibits function calls that use the syntax for calling methods
	▪ Prohibits a variable without a name (`${}`) (PowerShell v5 checks for this with strict mode turned off)
Latest	Selects the latest (strictest) version available

Unless you have a specific need to do otherwise, it's usually recommended to use `Latest` as your version.

CATCHING UNINITIALIZED VARIABLE USE IN STRING EXPANSIONS

Strict mode in v1 caught only references to uninitialized variables in script text. It didn't catch the use of uninitialized variables in string expansions. Strict mode v2 fixes this, and the use of uninitialized variables is caught everywhere. In non-strict mode, for example, when you reference a nonexistent variable, it's treated as being equivalent to `$null`.

Now turn on strict mode v1 and reference a nonexistent variable:

```
PS> Set-StrictMode -Version 1
PS> $nosuchvariable
```

```
The variable '$nosuchvariable' cannot be retrieved because it
has not been set.
At line:1 char:1
+ $nosuchvariable
+ ~~~~~~~~~~~~~~~
    + CategoryInfo          :
    InvalidOperation: (nosuchvariable:String) [], RuntimeException
    + FullyQualifiedErrorId : VariableIsUndefined
```

You get the uninitialized variable message as expected. Now put the string in quotes

```
PS> "$nosuchvariable"
```

and it expands the string with no errors. Turn on strict mode v2 and try the string expansion:

```
PS> Set-StrictMode -Version 2
PS> "$nosuchvariable"
The variable '$nosuchvariable' cannot be retrieved because it
has not been set.
At line:1 char:2
+ "$nosuchvariable"
+  ~~~~~~~~~~~~~~~
    + CategoryInfo          :
    InvalidOperation: (nosuchvariable:String) [], RuntimeException
    + FullyQualifiedErrorId : VariableIsUndefined
```

You also get the uninitialized variable error in the string expansion case.

CATCHING ATTEMPTS TO READ NONEXISTENT PROPERTIES

To have appropriately shell-like behavior, by default PowerShell allows you to try dereferencing nonexistent properties. That means you can do things like display a mixed collection of [System.IO.FileInfo] and [System.IO.DirectoryInfo] objects, including a reference to the Length property that doesn't exist for [System.IO.DirectoryInfo] objects. Imagine how annoying it would be to type dir and get a lot of "property not found" errors. Try running

```
PS> dir | foreach { $_.name + " " + $_.length }
```

in your home directory with strict mode v2 turned on, and you'll see what we mean.

> **NOTE** This applies only to explicit property references in script text. Cmdlets still ignore missing properties even when strict mode v2 is turned on. The interactive environment is pretty much unusable otherwise.

Try a simple example. First, turn off strict mode and then get a [DateTime] object into the variable $date:

```
PS> Set-StrictMode -Off
PS> $date = Get-Date
```

Now reference a nonexistent property

```
PS> $date.nosuchproperty
```

and no error is raised. Now turn on strict mode and try accessing the property:

```
PS> Set-StrictMode -Version Latest
PS> $date.nosuchproperty
The property 'nosuchproperty' cannot be found on this object.
Verify that the property exists.
At line:1 char:1
+ $date.nosuchproperty
+ ~~~~~~~~~~~~~~~~~~~~~
    + CategoryInfo          : NotSpecified: (:) [], PropertyNotFoundException
    + FullyQualifiedErrorId : PropertyNotFoundStrict
```

This time you get an error. As with the variable check, property checks will help catch typos in your script. It would be better if you could catch them at compile time, but then you'd need to know the types of all the expressions. Because PowerShell is dynamically typed, that isn't possible.

> **NOTE** But what about checking against the type constraints on variables, you might ask? Strict mode could include this kind of check, but it can't do a complete check because PowerShell allows extensions on instances as well as types. For example, when you look at a file entry in PowerShell, you see a Mode property. The underlying .NET type [System.IO.FileInfo] doesn't have a property with this name. The Mode property is one of the properties added by the PowerShell runtime. Because these properties can be added at runtime, even for a type-constrained variable, the most you could say is that the member probably won't exist by the time the statement is executed. Only the runtime check is guaranteed to be correct.

CHECKING FOR FUNCTIONS CALLED LIKE METHODS

An extremely common source of errors for experienced programmers is to call functions in the same way you would in other languages or in the same way methods are called in PowerShell. Let's see this in action. Turn off strict mode:

```
PS> Set-StrictMode -Off
```

then define a function that looks like this:

```
PS> function divide ($x,$y) { $x / $y }
```

This function takes two arguments, divides the first by the second, and returns the result. Now let's call it like a method, with parentheses around a function. This is how you'd call a function in a language like C#:

```
PS> divide(9, 3)
Method invocation failed because [System.Object[]]
does not contain a method named 'op_Division'.
```

```
At line:1 char:27
+ function divide ($x,$y) { $x / $y }
+                           ~~~~~~~
    + CategoryInfo          : InvalidOperation:
(op_Division:String) [], RuntimeException
    + FullyQualifiedErrorId : MethodNotFound
```

What happens is that you get a surprising error. You know that numbers can be divided, so why does this fail? By putting the two arguments in parentheses, you're telling the system to pass a single argument, which is an array of two numbers. We talked about this problem in section 6.2.1. Now turn on strict mode and try it again:

```
PS> Set-StrictMode -Version Latest
PS> divide(9, 3)
The function or command was called as if it were a method. Parameters should
  be separated by spaces. For information about parameters, see the about_
  Parameters Help topic.
At line:1 char:1
+ divide(9, 3)
+ ~~~~~~~~~~~~
    + CategoryInfo          : InvalidOperation: (:) [], RuntimeException
    + FullyQualifiedErrorId : StrictModeFunctionCallWithParens
```

This time you get a prescriptive error message explaining exactly what's gone wrong. Follow the instructions, rewriting the function call, removing the parameters, and separating it with spaces instead of a comma, and then try running it again:

```
PS> divide 9 3
3
```

This time it works.

This technique may seem like a trivial, almost silly check, but this issue has caused many problems for many people, including members of the PowerShell team.

APPLYING STRICT MODE TO SCRIPTS

You now know what the checks are—let's talk about when to apply them. In general, it's recommended that new code be written to be strict mode Latest "clean." The code should produce no errors when strict mode Latest is turned on. The temptation is to leave it on all the time.

Unfortunately, this approach can break a lot of script code. Many scripts are written to take advantage of the default property dereference behavior. That means a lot of fixing may be necessary. There are also cases where rewriting the code to not depend on this behavior can be messy—the code would have to either explicitly check for the existence of a property before trying to access it or explicitly trap the exception and ignore it.

> **NOTE**　Our recommendation is to use strict mode when developing but ensure it's turned off in production.

Consider the example at the beginning of the section that addressed catching references to nonexistent properties:

```
PS> dir | foreach { $_.name + " " + $_.length }
```

This code results in an error every time `dir` returns a directory object. To make this work in strict mode `Latest`, you'd have to do something like

```
PS> dir | foreach { $_.name + " " + $(try { $_.length } catch { $null })}
```

where the `try/catch` statement is used to process the error. In this code, if there's no exception, then the value of the property is returned. If there is an exception, the `catch` block returns `$null`. (At least the expression-oriented nature of the PowerShell language simplifies this example instead of requiring intermediate variables and an `if` statement.)

15.1.4 *Static analysis of scripts*

Most of the checks performed in strict mode are applied only at runtime, but there are some other checks you can do statically before you ever run the script. This was made possible in PowerShell v2 by the introduction of the PowerShell tokenizer API, a .NET class that takes the text of a PowerShell script and breaks it down into pieces called *tokens*.

Tokens correspond to the types of elements found in the PowerShell language, which include things like keywords and operators—all the things we talked about in chapters 2 through 8. Unfortunately, this mechanism isn't packaged in a convenient way for scripting. It was designed for the PowerShell ISE, but with a little work it's still usable from a script. First, we'll discuss how to use the API. We'll start by tokenizing a small piece of script text. If you have strict mode turned on, you'll have to turn it off for these examples:

```
PS> Set-StrictMode -Off
```

Put the text you want to tokenize into a variable:

```
PS> $script = "function abc ($x) {dir; $x + 1}"
```

The tokenizer returns two things: the tokens that make up the script and a collection of any errors encountered while parsing the script. Because the API is designed for use from languages that can't return multiple values, you also need to create a variable to hold these errors:

```
PS> $parse_errs = $null
```

Now you're ready to tokenize the script. Do so by calling the static method `Tokenize()` on the `PSParser` class as follows:

```
PS> $tokens = [System.Management.Automation.PSParser]::
Tokenize($script,[ref] $parse_errs)
```

This code will put the list of tokens in the $tokens variable, and any parse errors will be placed into a collection in $parse_errs. Now dump these two variables—$parse_errs to the error stream and $tokens to the output stream:

```
PS> $parse_errs | Write-Error
PS> $tokens | Format-Table -AutoSize Type,Content,StartLine,StartColumn

              Type Content  StartLine StartColumn
              ---- -------  --------- -----------
           Keyword function         1           1
   CommandArgument abc              1          10
        GroupStart (                1          14
          GroupEnd )                1          15
        GroupStart {                1          17
           Command dir              1          18
StatementSeparator ;                1          21
          Operator +                1          24
            Number 1                1          26
          GroupEnd }                1          27
```

Because the text being tokenized is a valid PowerShell script, no errors are generated. You do get a list of all the tokens in the text displayed on the screen. You can see that each token includes the type of the token, the content or text that makes up the token, as well as the start line and column number of the token. You'll now wrap this code into a function to make it easier to call. Name the function Test-Script:

```
function Test-Script {
    param (
        [Object]$script
    )

    $parse_errs = $null
    $tokens = [system.management.automation.psparser]::
    Tokenize($script,[ref] $parse_errs)
    $parse_errs | Write-Error
    $tokens
}
```

Try it on a chunk of invalid script text:

```
PS> Test-Script "function ($x) {$x + }" |
Format-Table -AutoSize Type,Content,StartLine, StartColumn

Test-Script : System.Management.Automation.PSParseError
At line:1 char:1
+ Test-Script "function ($x) {$x + }" |
+ ~~~~~~~~~~~~~~~~~~~~~~~~~~~~~~~~~~~~
    + CategoryInfo          : NotSpecified: (:) [Write-Error],
   WriteErrorException
    + FullyQualifiedErrorId : Microsoft.PowerShell.Commands.
   WriteErrorException,Test-Script

Test-Script : System.Management.Automation.PSParseError
At line:1 char:1
```

```
+ Test-Script "function ($x) {$x + }" |
+ ~~~~~~~~~~~~~~~~~~~~~~~~~~~~~~~~~~~~
    + CategoryInfo          : NotSpecified: (:) [Write-Error],
  WriteErrorException
    + FullyQualifiedErrorId : Microsoft.PowerShell.Commands.
  WriteErrorException,Test-Script

Test-Script : System.Management.Automation.PSParseError
At line:1 char:1
+ Test-Script "function ($x) {$x + }" |
+ ~~~~~~~~~~~~~~~~~~~~~~~~~~~~~~~~~~~~
    + CategoryInfo          : NotSpecified: (:) [Write-Error],
  WriteErrorException
    + FullyQualifiedErrorId : Microsoft.PowerShell.Commands.
  WriteErrorException,Test-Script

Test-Script : System.Management.Automation.PSParseError
At line:1 char:1
+ Test-Script "function ($x) {$x + }" |
+ ~~~~~~~~~~~~~~~~~~~~~~~~~~~~~~~~~~~~
    + CategoryInfo          : NotSpecified: (:) [Write-Error],
  WriteErrorException
    + FullyQualifiedErrorId : Microsoft.PowerShell.Commands.
  WriteErrorException,Test-Script

     Type Content StartLine StartColumn
     ---- ------- --------- -----------
  Keyword function         1           1
GroupStart (               1          10
  GroupEnd )               1          11
GroupStart {               1          13
  Operator +               1          15
  GroupEnd }               1          17
```

Now you see a number of errors. When you run a script that has syntax errors, you get one error before the parsing continues. With the tokenizer API, the parser tries to reset itself and continue. This means that you may be able to deal with more errors at one time, but the reset process doesn't always work and sometimes you get incorrect errors.

NOTE In many cases the first error is the culprit, and correcting that also removes subsequent errors in the report. But it's not always the case, so be prepared for several passes through the process.

The other thing to notice is that in the list of tokens being displayed, some of the tokens in the script, such as the variables, aren't output. Again, this is because when the parser attempts to recover, it can get confused and miss some tokens. That's why when you run a script you get only one error displayed. You know the first error displayed by the tokenizer is correct but aren't sure about the rest. It's simpler, if not more efficient, to deal with one correct error at a time rather than a collection of possible incorrect errors.

Let's rewrite the test function. You're going to do a little work to clean up the errors, but you'll also add a new static check. Because the tokenizer output tells you what tokens are commands, you can use `Get-Command` to see if there are any references to commands that don't exist. This won't always be an error—a script may load a module defining the missing command at runtime—so you need to consider it a warning to investigate instead of an error. Here's what the new script looks like:

```
function Test-Script {
    param (
        [Object]$script
    )

    $parse_errs = $null
    $tokens = [system.management.automation.psparser]::
    Tokenize($script, [ref] $parse_errs)
    foreach ($err in $parse_errs)
    {
        'ERROR on line ' +
        $err.Token.StartLine +
        ': ' + $err.Message +
        "`n"
    }
    foreach ($token in $tokens)
    {
        if ($token.Type -eq 'CommandArgument')
        {
            $gcmerr = Get-Command $token.Content 2>&1
            if (! $? )
            {
                'WARNING on line ' +
                $gcmerr.InvocationInfo.ScriptLineNumber +
                ': ' + $gcmerr.Exception.Message +
                "`n"
            }
        }
    }
}
```

The first part of the script hasn't changed much—you tokenize the string and then display any errors, though in a more compact form. Then you loop through all of the tokens looking for code commands. If you find a command, you check to see if it exists. If not, you display a warning.

Let's try it out. First, define the test script with expected errors and an undefined command:

```
$badScript = @'
for ($a1 in nosuchcommand)
{
    while ( )
    $a2*3
}
'@
```

Now run the test and see what you get:

```
PS> Test-Script $badScript
ERROR on line 1: Unexpected token 'in' in expression or statement.

ERROR on line 3: Missing expression after 'while' in loop.

ERROR on line 3: Missing statement body in while loop.

WARNING on line 17: The term 'nosuchcommand' is not recognized as the name of
a cmdlet, function, script file, or operable program. Check the spelling of
the name, or if a path was included, verify that the path is correct and try
again.
```

In the output you see the expected syntax errors, but you also get a warning for the undefined command. You could do many things to improve this checker, such as looking for variables that are used only once. By using these analysis techniques on the script text, you can find potential problems much sooner than you would if you waited to hit them at runtime.

> **NOTE** We include this section to introduce the basic concept of tokens and the tokenizer. In practice, there are powerful static analysis tools that do far more than what we've looked at in these simple examples. The PSScriptAnalyzer, created by the PowerShell team, provides an extensive set of rules for analyzing your code. There's also a third-party commercial offering tool called ISESteroids, which provides an excellent interactive code analysis experience inside the PowerShell ISE. Both of these tools are available from the PowerShell Gallery. Using these tools is highly recommended.

So far, we've looked at a number of tools and approaches that you can use to learn what's wrong with your scripts. But how do you figure out what's going on when other people are running your (or other people's) scripts in a different environment, possibly at a remote location? To help with this, PowerShell includes a *session transcript* mechanism. You'll learn how this works in the next section.

15.2 *Capturing session output*

When trying to debug what's wrong with someone's script at a remote location, you'll find it extremely helpful to see the output and execution traces from a script run. PowerShell allows you to do this via a mechanism that captures console output in transcript files. This transcript capability is exposed through the Start-Transcript and Stop-Transcript cmdlets.

> **NOTE** Up until PowerShell v5, the implementation of these cmdlets is a feature of the console host (PowerShell.exe) and so is not available in other hosts, including the PowerShell ISE. This changed in PowerShell v5 when the transcript functionality was added to the PowerShell ISE. Other host applications may have similar mechanisms.

15.2.1 *Starting the transcript*

To start a transcript, run Start-Transcript, as shown in the next example. Let's begin by running a command before starting the transcript so you can see what is and is not recorded, as shown in figure 15.2.

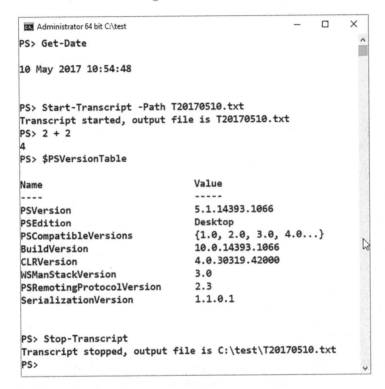

Figure 15.2 Using the transcript cmdlets

Run Get-Date to get the current date and then start the transcript. If you didn't specify a filename for the transcript file, one will be automatically generated for you in your Documents directory. Now run a couple of additional commands and stop the transcript. Again, it conveniently tells you the name of the file containing the transcript:

Now let's see what was captured:

```
PS> Get-Content -Path C:\test\T20170510.txt
**********************
Windows PowerShell transcript start
Start time: 20170510105524
Username: W510W16\Richard
RunAs User: W510W16\Richard
Machine: W510W16 (Microsoft Windows NT 10.0.14393.0)
Host Application: powershell
Process ID: 8732
PSVersion: 5.1.14393.1066
```

```
PSEdition: Desktop
PSCompatibleVersions: 1.0, 2.0, 3.0, 4.0, 5.0, 5.1.14393.1066
BuildVersion: 10.0.14393.1066
CLRVersion: 4.0.30319.42000
WSManStackVersion: 3.0
PSRemotingProtocolVersion: 2.3
SerializationVersion: 1.1.0.1
**********************
Transcript started, output file is T20170510.txt
PS>
PS>2 + 2
4
PS>
PS>$PSVersionTable

Name                              Value
----                              -----
PSVersion                         5.1.14393.1066
PSEdition                         Desktop
PSCompatibleVersions              {1.0, 2.0, 3.0, 4.0...}
BuildVersion                      10.0.14393.1066
CLRVersion                        4.0.30319.42000
WSManStackVersion                 3.0
PSRemotingProtocolVersion         2.3
SerializationVersion              1.1.0.1

PS>
PS>Stop-Transcript
**********************
Windows PowerShell transcript end
End time: 20170510105547
**********************
```

The transcript file includes a header showing you the start time, the name of the user running the script, and the name and OS information about the computer on which the command is run.

You see the filename yet again because it was written out after transcription was turned on and so is captured in the transcript.

After that, you see the output of the commands you ran (including `Stop-Transcript`) and finally a trailer showing the time the transcript stopped.

15.2.2 *What gets captured in the transcript*

It seems obvious that everything should get captured in the transcript file, but that isn't the case in the early versions of PowerShell. The transcript captured everything written through the host APIs. What *didn't* get captured was anything that bypasses these APIs and writes directly to the console. This missing information is most significant when you're running applications like ipconfig.exe. If these commands weren't redirected within PowerShell, then their output went directly to the console and bypassed the host APIs. Instead of running

```
PS> cmd /c echo THIS WONT BE CAPTURED
```

you had to use

```
PS> cmd /c echo THIS WILL BE CAPTURED 2>&1 | Write-Host
```

New in Powershell v5 is the -IncludeInvocationHeader parameter, which adds a time stamp when commands are run. An example is shown in figure 15.3.

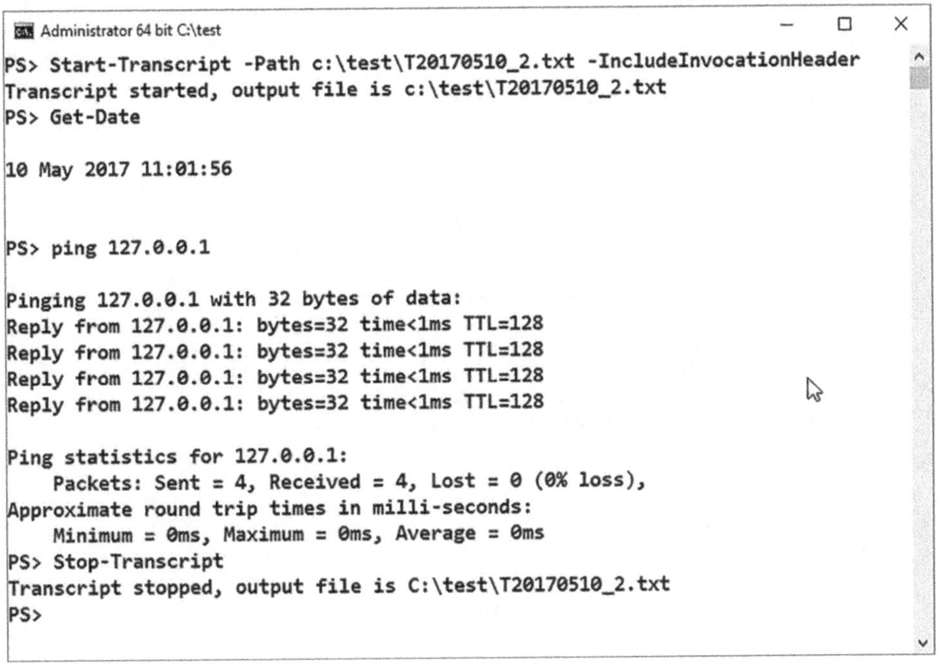

```
Administrator 64 bit C:\test                                    —  □  ×
PS> Start-Transcript -Path c:\test\T20170510_2.txt -IncludeInvocationHeader
Transcript started, output file is c:\test\T20170510_2.txt
PS> Get-Date

10 May 2017 11:01:56


PS> ping 127.0.0.1

Pinging 127.0.0.1 with 32 bytes of data:
Reply from 127.0.0.1: bytes=32 time<1ms TTL=128
Reply from 127.0.0.1: bytes=32 time<1ms TTL=128
Reply from 127.0.0.1: bytes=32 time<1ms TTL=128
Reply from 127.0.0.1: bytes=32 time<1ms TTL=128

Ping statistics for 127.0.0.1:
    Packets: Sent = 4, Received = 4, Lost = 0 (0% loss),
Approximate round trip times in milli-seconds:
    Minimum = 0ms, Maximum = 0ms, Average = 0ms
PS> Stop-Transcript
Transcript stopped, output file is C:\test\T20170510_2.txt
PS>
```

Figure 15.3 Using the -IncludeInvocationHeader **parameter in a transcript**

The transcript file looks like this:

```
**********************
Windows PowerShell transcript start
Start time: 20170510110151
Username: W510W16\Richard
RunAs User: W510W16\Richard
Machine: W510W16 (Microsoft Windows NT 10.0.14393.0)
Host Application: powershell
Process ID: 8732
PSVersion: 5.1.14393.1066
PSEdition: Desktop
PSCompatibleVersions: 1.0, 2.0, 3.0, 4.0, 5.0, 5.1.14393.1066
BuildVersion: 10.0.14393.1066
CLRVersion: 4.0.30319.42000
WSManStackVersion: 3.0
PSRemotingProtocolVersion: 2.3
SerializationVersion: 1.1.0.1
```

```
**********************
Transcript started, output file is c:\test\T20170510_2.txt
PS>
**********************
Command start time: 20170510110156
**********************
PS>Get-Date

10 May 2017 11:01:56

PS>
**********************
Command start time: 20170510110204
**********************
PS>ping 127.0.0.1

Pinging 127.0.0.1 with 32 bytes of data:
Reply from 127.0.0.1: bytes=32 time<1ms TTL=128
Reply from 127.0.0.1: bytes=32 time<1ms TTL=128
Reply from 127.0.0.1: bytes=32 time<1ms TTL=128
Reply from 127.0.0.1: bytes=32 time<1ms TTL=128

Ping statistics for 127.0.0.1:
    Packets: Sent = 4, Received = 4, Lost = 0 (0% loss),
Approximate round trip times in milli-seconds:
    Minimum = 0ms, Maximum = 0ms, Average = 0ms
PS>
**********************
Command start time: 20170510110218
**********************
PS>Stop-Transcript
**********************
Windows PowerShell transcript end
End time: 20170510110218
**********************
```

Using the transcript cmdlets, it's easy to have the remote user capture the output of their session. Have the remote user call Start-Transcript, run their script, and then call Stop-Transcript. This process will produce a transcript file that the user can send to you for examination.

So far, we've looked at ways of capturing information about code that's executing. It's time to go deeper and learn how to interactively debug your code to discover why things aren't working as they should.

15.3 *PowerShell script debugging features*

The PowerShell debugging tools have grown over the versions of PowerShell. PowerShell v1 didn't include a debugger but did have some limited tracing capabilities. Version 2 introduced a much more comprehensive debugger along with graphical debugging support in the ISE. With PowerShell, you can now debug jobs, workflows, and PowerShell runspaces as well as processes.

The debugging tools available are outlined in table 15.3.

Table 15.3 Debugging tools

PowerShell debugger	Debugger connectivity	Tracing
`Get-PSCallStack`	`Debug-Job`	`Get-TraceSource`
`Disable-PSBreakpoint`	`Debug-Process`	`Set-TraceSource`
`Enable-PSBreakpoint`	`Debug-Runspace`	`Trace-Command`
`Get-PSBreakpoint`	`Disable-RunspaceDebug`	
`Remove-PSBreakpoint`	`Enable-RunspaceDebug`	
`Set-PSBreakpoint`	`Get-RunspaceDebug`	
	`Set-PSDebug`	
	`Wait-Debugger`	

We'll start by looking at the limited (but still useful) tracing features carried over from v1. Then you'll learn how to debug from the ISE. You'll see the command-line debugger and the additional capabilities it has to offer, including debugging jobs, workflows, and remote scripts. Finally, we'll look at the command-tracing capabilities.

15.3.1 *The Set-PSDebug cmdlet*

The `Set-PSDebug` cmdlet can be used to set the PowerShell v1 strict mode, although as shown in section 15.1.3 `Set-StrictMode` gives more options. The debugger has subsumed what `Set-PSDebug` does, making the cmdlet effectively redundant. We'll mention the remaining features for completeness but strongly advise you to use the debugger for these actions.

TRACING STATEMENT EXECUTION

You turn on basic script tracing as follows:

```
PS> Set-PSDebug -Trace 1
```

In this trace mode, each statement executed by the interpreter will be displayed on the console. The debugging output is prefixed with the DEBUG: tag and is typically shown in a different color than normal text. Note that the entire script line is displayed. This means that if you have a loop all on one line, you'll see the line repeated.

> **NOTE** This is a good reason, even though PowerShell doesn't require it, to write scripts with one statement per line: it can help with debugging, both when tracing and when using the debugger to set breakpoints.

Basic tracing doesn't show you any function calls or scripts you're executing. You don't see when you enter the function. To get this extra information, you need to turn on full tracing:

```
PS> Set-PSDebug -Trace 2
DEBUG:    1+  >>>> Set-PSDebug -Trace 2
```

NOTE   You only see the DEBUG:.. output if you already have tracing enabled.
Use Set-PSDebug -Trace 0 to turn tracing off.

Now define a function:

```
PS> function foo {"`$args is " + $args}
```

When you execute the function in this mode, you also see the function calls, as shown
in figure 15.4.

```
non-Administrator 64 bit C:\MyData\SkyDrive\Data\scripts    —    □    ×
PS> Set-PSDebug -Trace 2
PS> function foo {"`$args is " + $args}
DEBUG:     1+  >>>> function foo {"`$args is " + $args}
DEBUG:     ! CALL function '<ScriptBlock>'
PS> foreach ($i in 1..3) {foo $i}
DEBUG:     1+ foreach ($i in  >>>> 1..3) {foo $i}
DEBUG:     ! CALL function '<ScriptBlock>'
DEBUG:     ! SET $foreach = 'IEnumerator'.
DEBUG:     1+ foreach ( >>>> $i in 1..3) {foo $i}
DEBUG:     ! SET $i = '1'.
DEBUG:     1+ foreach ($i in 1..3) { >>>> foo $i}
DEBUG:     1+ function foo  >>>> {"`$args is " + $args}
DEBUG:     ! CALL function 'foo'
DEBUG:     1+ function foo { >>>> "`$args is " + $args}
$args is 1
DEBUG:     1+ function foo {"`$args is " + $args >>>> }
DEBUG:     1+ foreach ( >>>> $i in 1..3) {foo $i}
DEBUG:     ! SET $i = '2'.
DEBUG:     1+ foreach ($i in 1..3) { >>>> foo $i}
DEBUG:     1+ function foo  >>>> {"`$args is " + $args}
DEBUG:     ! CALL function 'foo'
DEBUG:     1+ function foo { >>>> "`$args is " + $args}
$args is 2
DEBUG:     1+ function foo {"`$args is " + $args >>>> }
DEBUG:     1+ foreach ( >>>> $i in 1..3) {foo $i}
DEBUG:     ! SET $i = '3'.
DEBUG:     1+ foreach ($i in 1..3) { >>>> foo $i}
DEBUG:     1+ function foo  >>>> {"`$args is " + $args}
DEBUG:     ! CALL function 'foo'
DEBUG:     1+ function foo { >>>> "`$args is " + $args}
$args is 3
DEBUG:     1+ function foo {"`$args is " + $args >>>> }
DEBUG:     1+ foreach ( >>>> $i in 1..3) {foo $i}
DEBUG:     ! SET $foreach = ''.
PS>
```

Figure 15.4   Tracing
function calls

In addition to function calls, full tracing adds to the display by showing variable assignments.
For each iteration in the loop, tracing shows the following:

- Loop iteration
- Function call

- Statement doing the assignment
- Assignment to $x, including the value assigned
- Statement that emits the value

The value displayed is the string representation of the object being assigned, truncated to fit in the display. It depends on the ToString() method defined for that object to decide what to display. For arrays and other collections, it shows you a truncated representation of the elements of the list. Overall, script tracing is pretty effective, but sometimes you still need to add calls to the Write cmdlets, as discussed in section 15.1.1.

Debugging scripts run by other people

The other thing to remember is PowerShell's transcript capability. Transcripts combined with tracing provide a valuable tool to help with debugging scripts that are being run by other people in your organization. By capturing the trace output in a transcript file, you can get a much better idea of what a script is doing in the other user's environment.

Tracing is also valuable in debugging remote scripts where you can't use the ISE debugger, as you'll see later in this chapter.

STEPPING THROUGH STATEMENT EXECUTION

The next debugging feature we'll look at is the mechanism that PowerShell provides for stepping through a script.

> **NOTE** Like the tracing mechanism, this stepping feature is also a carryover from PowerShell v1. It's largely subsumed by the PowerShell debugger, but there are some advanced scenarios, such as debugging dynamically generated code, where it's still quite useful. If you use [ScriptBlock]::Create() to dynamically generate a scriptblock, you can't set a breakpoint because you don't have a line number in a file to use to set the breakpoint. More on this later.

You turn stepping on by calling the Set-PSDebug cmdlet with the -Step parameter:

```
PS> Set-PSDebug -Step
```

> **NOTE** Using -Step automatically sets a Trace level of 1.

Rerun the foreach loop and take a look at the prompt that's displayed:

```
PS> foreach ($i in 1..3) {foo $i}

Continue with this operation?
   1+ foreach ($i in  >>>> 1..3) {foo $i}
[Y] Yes  [A] Yes to All  [N] No  [L] No to All   [S] Suspend  [?] Help
(default is "Y"):
```

The interpreter displays the line to be executed and then asks the user to select Yes, Yes to All, No, or No to All. The default is Yes.

If you answer Yes, that line will be executed and you'll be prompted as to whether you want to execute the next line. If you answer Yes to All, then step mode will be turned off and execution will continue normally. If you answer either No or No to All, the current execution will be stopped and you'll be returned to the command prompt. There's no difference in the behavior between No and No to All.

There's one more option in the stepping list that we haven't talked about: Suspend. This option is interesting enough to cover in its own section.

15.3.2 *Nested prompts and the Suspend operation*

One of the most interesting aspects of dynamic language environments is that a script can recursively call the interpreter. You saw this with the `Invoke-Expression` cmdlet in chapter 10. A variation is to recursively call the interpreter *interactively*. This means you are, in effect, suspending the currently running command and starting a new nested session. This sequence of events is illustrated in figure 15.5.

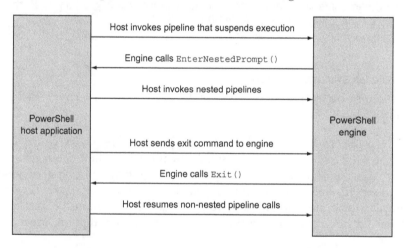

Figure 15.5   Suspending execution and entering a nested prompt requires operations on both the host and engine sides of the session.

In figure 15.5, you see that the user makes a call to the engine using the interfaces provided by the host application. In this case, instead of returning to the caller, the engine calls back to the host indicating that it should enter a nested-prompt mode. While in nested-prompt mode, because the original command pipeline is still active (the engine never returned to the host), the host must now use *nested pipelines* to execute commands. This continues until the engine calls the `Exit()` API, usually in response to a request from the user, and the host can resume the original pipeline.

The net effect of all this is that you can suspend the currently executing PowerShell pipeline and interact with PowerShell at the nested prompt. Why is this interesting?

Because it allows you to examine and modify the state of the suspended session by using the regular PowerShell commands you're used to. Instead of creating a whole new language for debugger operations, you use the same language you're debugging. This feature is the core of all of the debugging capabilities in PowerShell.

There are a couple of ways to enter a nested-prompt session, as you'll see in the next two sections.

SUSPENDING A SCRIPT WHILE IN STEP MODE

The Suspend operation prompt shown during stepping creates a nested interactive session. Let's try it. First, turn on stepping:

```
PS> Set-PSDebug -Step
```

Then run a statement that should loop 10 times, printing out the numbers 1–10:

```
PS> $i=0; while ($i++ -lt 10) { $i }
```

You'll see all the intermediate blather. Keep stepping until the first number is displayed.

At this point, use the Suspend operation to suspend stepping. When prompted, respond by typing s followed by pressing Enter instead of only pressing Enter. This leaves you at the position shown in figure 15.6.

You immediately receive a new prompt. In figure 15.6 the prompt changes from PS> to PS>>.

NOTE The way to tell when you're in nested-prompt mode is to check the $NestedPromptLevel variable. If you're in a nested prompt, this variable will be greater than 0.

```
PS> Set-PSDebug -Step
PS> $i=0; while ($i++ -lt 10) {$i}

Continue with this operation?
   1+ >>>> $i=0; while ($i++ -lt 10) {$i}
[Y] Yes  [A] Yes to All  [N] No  [L] No to All  [S] Suspend  [?] Help (default is "Y"): y
DEBUG:     1+ >>>> $i=0; while ($i++ -lt 10) {$i}

Continue with this operation?
   1+ $i=0; while ( >>>> $i++ -lt 10) {$i}
[Y] Yes  [A] Yes to All  [N] No  [L] No to All  [S] Suspend  [?] Help (default is "Y"): y
DEBUG:     1+ $i=0; while ( >>>> $i++ -lt 10) {$i}

Continue with this operation?
   1+ $i=0; while ($i++ -lt 10) { >>>> $i}
[Y] Yes  [A] Yes to All  [N] No  [L] No to All  [S] Suspend  [?] Help (default is "Y"): y
DEBUG:     1+ $i=0; while ($i++ -lt 10) { >>>> $i}
1

Continue with this operation?
   1+ $i=0; while ( >>>> $i++ -lt 10) {$i}
[Y] Yes  [A] Yes to All  [N] No  [L] No to All  [S] Suspend  [?] Help (default is "Y"): s
PS>>
```

Figure 15.6 Suspending execution of a script

In this nested prompt, you can do anything you'd normally do in PowerShell. In this case, you want to inspect the state of the system. For example, let's check to see what the variable $i is set to:

```
PS> $i
1
```

But you're not limited to inspecting the state of the system: you can change it. Let's make the loop end early by setting the value to something larger than the terminating condition. Set it to 100.

Now exit the nested-prompt session with the normal exit statement. This returns you to the previous level in the interpreter where, because you're stepping, you're prompted to continue. Respond by typing a followed by pressing Enter for [A] Yes to All to get out of step mode. You can turn off debugging and view the value of $i, as shown in figure 15.7.

```
non-Administrator 64 bit C:\MyData\SkyDrive\Data\scripts                    —    □    ×
Continue with this operation?
   1+ $i=0; while ($i++ -lt 10) { >>>> $i}
[Y] Yes  [A] Yes to All  [N] No  [L] No to All  [S] Suspend  [?] Help (default is "Y"): y
DEBUG:      1+ $i=0; while ($i++ -lt 10) { >>>> $i}
1

Continue with this operation?
   1+ $i=0; while ( >>>> $i++ -lt 10) {$i}
[Y] Yes  [A] Yes to All  [N] No  [L] No to All  [S] Suspend  [?] Help (default is "Y"): s
PS>>  $i=100
PS>>  exit

Continue with this operation?
   1+ $i=0; while ( >>>> $i++ -lt 10) {$i}
[Y] Yes  [A] Yes to All  [N] No  [L] No to All  [S] Suspend  [?] Help (default is "Y"): a
DEBUG:      1+ $i=0; while ( >>>> $i++ -lt 10) {$i}
PS>  Set-PSDebug -Off
PS>  $i
101
PS>
```

Figure 15.7   Modify the value of a variable while the script is suspended.

There are two things to notice here: the loop terminates, and the value of $i is 101 (the loop incremented before it terminated).

Prompt

If you don't see the change in prompt shown in figures 15.6 and 15.7, check the prompt function in your profile. It should contain something like this:

```
$(if (Test-Path -Path variable:/PSDebugContext) {'[DBG]: '}
else {''}) + "PS$('>' * ($nestedPromptLevel + 1)) "
```

> **(Continued)**
>
> This sets the prompt to `PS>` for normal use and adds a further `>` for each level of nesting that you enter. If you switch to the debugging prompt (section 15.4.1), the prompt changes to `[DBG]: PS>>`. Another `>` character will be added if you enter a nested prompt while in debug mode.
>
> You can see other options for including in your prompt in the `about_prompts` help file.

Using the Suspend feature, you can stop a script at any point and examine or modify the state of the interpreter. You can even redefine functions in the middle of execution (although you can't change the function that's currently executing). This makes for a powerful debugging technique, but it can be annoying to use stepping all the time. Also, many users forget to end Suspend mode. This is where having a real debugger makes all the difference.

> **PowerShell debugger**
>
> With PowerShell v2, a powerful new debugger was added to the product. It can be used in graphical mode (in the ISE) or can be accessed through the debugging cmdlets. The operations of the graphical debugger are performed through the debugging cmdlets, so our discussion will center on them.

15.4   Command-line debugging

Given the nature of the PowerShell environment, you need to support debugging in a variety of environments. The most effective way to do that is to enable debugging scripts from the command line.

> **NOTE**   The graphical debugger is built on top of the commands we're going to cover in this section. Anything that can be done in the graphical debugger can be done from the command line, but the commands provide a great deal of power that isn't exposed in the graphical debugger.

This makes it possible to use the debugger from the console host as well. As always, these debugging features are surfaced through a set of cmdlets. The cmdlets are listed in table 15.4.

Table 15.4   The PowerShell debugger cmdlets

Cmdlet	Description
Get-PSCallStack	Gets the current call stack
Enable-PSBreakPoint	Enables an existing breakpoint
Disable-PSBreakPoint	Disables a breakpoint without removing it

Table 15.4 The PowerShell debugger cmdlets *(continued)*

Cmdlet	Description
Set-PSBreakPoint	Sets a breakpoint
Get-PSBreakPoint	Gets the list of breakpoints
Remove-PSBreakPoint	Removes an existing breakpoint

Command-line debugging is also important for another reason: There are many more things you can do using these cmdlets, including writing scripts to debug scripts. All the features you've seen in the GUI debugger are available from the command line, but not all the command-line features are available from the GUI. In fact, the GUI debugger surfaces only a portion of the functionality of what can be done with the PowerShell debugger. In the next few sections, we'll dig into these capabilities.

15.4.1 *Working with breakpoint objects*

Let's begin our discussion by looking at how breakpoints are implemented. So far, you've seen a fairly conventional debugger experience, but the introspective nature of PowerShell allows you to do much more when working with breakpoints. As with most everything else, breakpoints in PowerShell are objects (as you'll see in a moment) that you can script against.

Breakpoints have an interesting property, -Action, which holds instances of our old friend, the scriptblock. By specifying actions in scriptblocks, breakpoints can do much more than interrupt execution when the breakpoint is hit. Using scriptblocks allows you to perform arbitrary actions controlling when or even whether the breakpoint fires. Let's see how this works with a simple test script (save as testscript2.ps1):

```
PS> @'
"Starting"
$sum = 0
foreach ($i in 1..10)
{
    $sum += $i
}
"The sum is $sum"
'@ > testscript2.ps1
```

This script loops over the numbers from 1–10, summing them and then printing the result. Now define a breakpoint for this script using the Set-PSBreakPoint command:

```
PS> $firstBP = Set-PSBreakpoint -Script testscript2.ps1 -Line 4 `
 -Action {
     if ($i -gt 3 -and $i -lt 7)
     {
         Write-Host "> DEBUG ACTION: i = $i, sum = $sum"
     }
}
```

This command specifies that a scriptblock will be executed every time you hit line 4 in the test script. In the body of the scriptblock, you're checking to see if the value of $i is greater than 3 and less than 7. If so, you'll display a message. You have to use Write-Host to display this message because the results of the scriptblock aren't displayed. The Set-PSBreakpoint command returns an instance of a breakpoint object. Let's display it as a list so you can see its members:

```
PS> $firstBP | Format-List

Id       : 1
Script   : C:\test\testscript2.ps1
Line     : 4
Column   : 0
Enabled  : True
HitCount : 0
Action   :
                if ($i -gt 3 -and $i -lt 7)
                {
                    Write-Host "> DEBUG ACTION: i = $i, sum = $sum"
                }
```

This code shows the full path to the script and the line in the script that will trigger the action as well as the action itself.

> **NOTE** The Id number may be different in your case depending on other actions you've taken in the console. Id numbers start at zero.

You can use Get-Member to examine the breakpoint object:

```
PS> Get-PSBreakpoint | Get-Member

   TypeName: System.Management.Automation.LineBreakpoint

Name        MemberType Definition
----        ---------- ----------
Equals      Method     bool Equals(System.Object obj)
GetHashCode Method     int GetHashCode()
GetType     Method     type GetType()
ToString    Method     string ToString()
Action      Property   scriptblock Action {get;}
Column      Property   int Column {get;}
Enabled     Property   bool Enabled {get;}
HitCount    Property   int HitCount {get;}
Id          Property   int Id {get;}
Line        Property   int Line {get;}
Script      Property   string Script {get;}
```

In this output, you see some familiar bits of information: the breakpoint ID and the line and script where it applies. The HitCount property records the number of times a breakpoint has been hit. The Action property you've already met.

Run the test script to see how it works:

```
PS> .\testscript2.ps1
Starting
```

```
> DEBUG ACTION: i = 4, sum = 6
> DEBUG ACTION: i = 5, sum = 10
> DEBUG ACTION: i = 6, sum = 15
The sum is 55
```

The output shows the value of $i and $sum as long as $i is between 3 and 7 as intended.

Before we move on to the next example, remove all the breakpoints so they don't confuse the results in the example:

```
PS> Get-PSBreakpoint | Remove-PSBreakpoint
```

Using the HitCount property

The HitCount property is interesting because the scriptblock can control whether or not a script breaks. You may want the script to break only after a certain number of iterations or if a variable has a specific value. Here's an example:

```
Get-PSBreakpoint | Remove-PSBreakpoint

# Write the value each time
$null = Set-PSBreakpoint -line 19 -script example.ps1 -Action {
    Write-Verbose -verbose "The value of num is $num"
}

# Break the fifth time the breakpoint has been encountered
$null = Set-PSBreakpoint -line 19 -script example.ps1 -Action {
    if ($_.HitCount -eq 5)
    {
        break
    }
}

foreach ($num in 1 .. 10)
{
    "Num is $num"
}
"I'm done"
```

The use of break and continue in breakpoint actions makes it possible to create arbitrary conditional breakpoints. This is powerful. Also, if you don't break, then you can do things like trace execution in a fine-grained way. This is much more effective than Set-PSDebug -trace, for example.

This time, instead of only displaying a message, you're going to use the break keyword to break the script under specific conditions. Here's the command to define the new breakpoint:

```
PS> $firstBP = Set-PSBreakpoint -Script testscript2.ps1 -Line 4 `
-Action {
    if ($i -eq 4)
    {
```

```
            Write-Host "> DEBUG ACTION: i = $i, sum = $sum"
            break
        }
    }
}
```

For this breakpoint, you'll fire only the action on line 4 of the test script. In the script-block body, you'll display the message as before and then call `break`, which will break the execution of the script, as shown in figure 15.8.

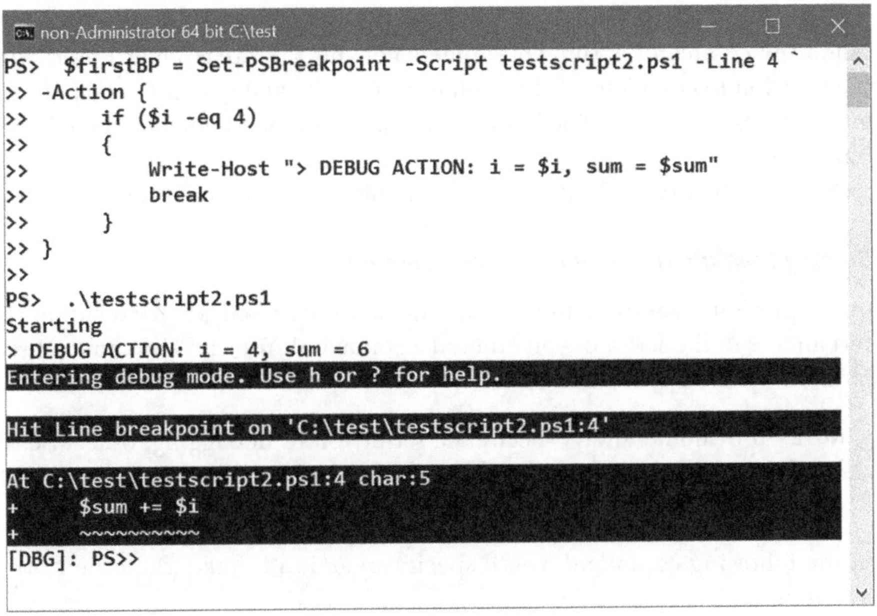

```
non-Administrator 64 bit C:\test                               ─    □    ✕

PS> $firstBP = Set-PSBreakpoint -Script testscript2.ps1 -Line 4 `  ^
>> -Action {
>>      if ($i -eq 4)
>>      {
>>          Write-Host "> DEBUG ACTION: i = $i, sum = $sum"
>>          break
>>      }
>> }
>>
PS> .\testscript2.ps1
Starting
> DEBUG ACTION: i = 4, sum = 6
Entering debug mode. Use h or ? for help.

Hit Line breakpoint on 'C:\test\testscript2.ps1:4'

At C:\test\testscript2.ps1:4 char:5
+     $sum += $i
+     ~~~~~~~~~~~
[DBG]: PS>>                                                         v
```

Figure 15.8   Entering the command-line debugger

You have a number of options available at the break prompt. Type `?` at the break prompt to view them. Use the `c` command to continue execution and complete the script. The completed script displays the sum. Don't forget to clean up the breakpoint.

Now let's move on to the next example.

15.4.2 *Setting breakpoints on commands*

The most common scenario using the debugger involves setting breakpoints on lines in a file, but it's also possible to break on a specific command. Define a simple function

```
PS> function hello { 'Hello world!' }
```

and set a breakpoint on that function:

```
PS> Set-PSBreakpoint -Command hello
```

This time you won't associate an action and you'll allow the default behavior—causing a break in execution—to occur. Execute the function:

```
PS> hello
Hit Command breakpoint on 'hello'

At line:1 char:16
+ function hello { 'Hello world!' }
+                ~
[DBG]: PS>>
```

When the command is run, you immediately hit the breakpoint. Enter c and allow the function to complete. Among other things, the ability to set breakpoints on commands as opposed to specific lines in a script allows you to debug interactively entered functions.

Now let's move on to the final example in this section: setting breakpoints on variables.

15.4.3 *Setting breakpoints on variable assignment*

In the previous examples, the breakpoints were triggered when execution reached a certain line in the script or you entered a command. You can also cause a break when variables are read or written.

> **NOTE** You should always specify the script you're debugging; otherwise, the breakpoint triggers whenever the variable changes with unpredictable and potentially undesired results.

In the following command, you'll specify an action to take when the $sum variable is written:

```
PS> $thirdBP = Set-PSBreakpoint -Script testscript2.ps1 `
-Variable sum -Mode Write -Action {
      if ($sum -gt 10)
      {
          Write-Host "> VARIABLE sum was set to $sum"
      }
  }
```

For this breakpoint, you're using -Mode Write to specify that the breakpoint should trigger only when the variable is written. In practice, you could have omitted this because Write is the default mode (the other modes are Read and ReadWrite). Then in the action scriptblock, you'll use Write-Host as before to display the value of $sum, but only when it's greater than 10. Let's see what this breakpoint looks like:

```
PS> $thirdBP | Format-List

Id         : 2
Variable   : sum
AccessMode : Write
```

```
Enabled    : True
HitCount   : 0
Action     :
                       if ($sum -gt 10)
                       {
                           Write-Host "> VARIABLE sum was set to $sum"
                       }
```

You see the line, variable, and access mode that will trigger the action and the script-block to execute when triggered. Run the test script:

```
PS> .\testscript2.ps1
Starting
> VARIABLE sum was set to 15
> VARIABLE sum was set to 21
> VARIABLE sum was set to 28
> VARIABLE sum was set to 36
> VARIABLE sum was set to 45
> VARIABLE sum was set to 55
The sum is 55
```

You see the output messages from the action scriptblock. One of the nice things is that a variable-based breakpoint isn't tied to a specific line number in the script, so it will continue to work even when you edit the script.

Although these examples are by no means exhaustive, they give you a sense of the capabilities of the PowerShell command-line debugger. You're able to do much more sophisticated debugging from the command line. But even for the command line, there are a number of limitations to the debugging capabilities. We'll look at these limitations in the final part of this section.

15.4.4 *Debugger limitations and issues*

The PowerShell debugger, though powerful, does suffer from a couple of limitations. The dynamic nature of the PowerShell language means that code can be created at any time and you aren't always able to set breakpoints on this code. This is where the techniques you saw earlier in the chapter can help. You can insert the example breakpoint function into dynamic or anonymous code, allowing you to effectively set a breakpoint in that code.

Also, because variables are never declared, it's not possible to specify an instance of a variable via its declaration; you can only select the target variable by name. Scoping a breakpoint to a particular file or command helps with correctly targeting the desired variable.

So far, we've looked at debugging PowerShell scripts on the local machine. Power-Shell v4 and v5 introduced the capability to debug other types of PowerShell commands and scripts running on remote machines.

15.5   *Beyond scripts*

A number of cmdlets enable you to connect to PowerShell commands. They were listed in table 15.3 under the "Debugger connectivity" header. For convenience, they're listed again here:

- `Debug-Job`
- `Debug-Process`
- `Debug-Runspace`
- `Disable-RunspaceDebug`
- `Enable-RunspaceDebug`
- `Get-RunspaceDebug`

This list shows that you now have the capability to debug jobs, processes, and Power-Shell runspaces. In addition, you can debug workflows and scripts running on remote computers. Let's see how these features work.

15.5.1   *Debugging PowerShell jobs*

PowerShell jobs were introduced in chapter 13. A job runs in a separate PowerShell session that's automatically created, used, and removed. Once the job starts, you don't have any visibility inside the job. Now you can use the standard PowerShell debugging techniques to investigate your jobs.

Let's run a simple (never–ending) job:

```
PS> $sb = {
  $i = 0
  while ($true) {
    "My value is $i"
    $i++
    Start-Sleep -Seconds 5
  }
}

PS> Start-Job -Name MyLongJob -ScriptBlock $sb
```

This sets a variable, `$i`, to 0. The code then loops through, listing and incrementing the variable with a five-second pause before running the next iteration of the loop. Figure 15.12 shows this job running in the ISE.

The job starts and displays the standard job information as expected. You can use `Debug-Job` to open the job for debugging. A job can be accessed by `Id`, `Name`, `Instan-ceId`, or a job object. When you start debugging the job, you receive a message showing the line of code at which the job has stopped:

```
PS> Debug-Job -id 3
Stopped at: while ($true) {
[DBG]: [Job4]: PS C:\Users\Richard\Documents>> $i
9
```

The `Debug-Job` cmdlet attaches the ISE (or console) debugger to the job. You can then debug the script running in the job as if it were running interactively in the ISE (or the console). Once you've finished debugging, you can quit the debugger, by using the `quit` command, which will end debugging and stop the job or detach the debugger and allow the job to continue running, as shown in figure 15.9.

Your prompt changes to the debug prompt, and you can apply standard debugging techniques such as investigating the value of variables. You can use the `detach` command to stop debugging and allow the job to continue.

NOTE Don't forget to stop the job and remove it!

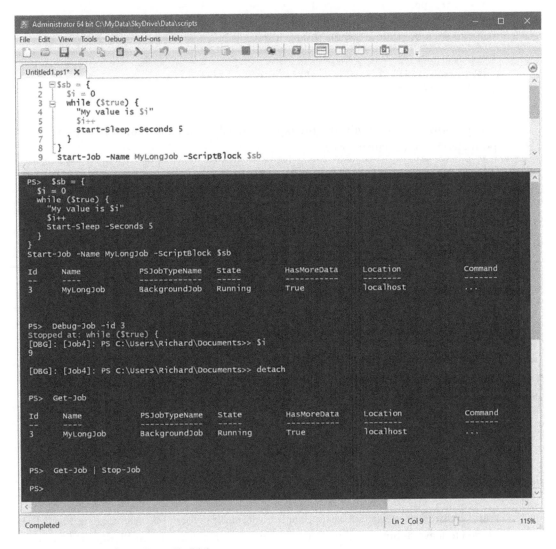

Figure 15.9 **Debugging a PowerShell job**

This is a big step forward, but you don't know where you're going to enter the script that the job is running. In a similar manner to other PowerShell scripts, setting a breakpoint in the script the job is running gives you control of where debugging starts.

If you modify the previous example to be a script:

```
PS> @'
$i = 0
while ($true) {
  "My value is $i"
   $i++
   Start-Sleep -Seconds 5
}
'@ > dbjob.ps1
```

you can set a breakpoint when you create the job:

```
PS> $job = Start-Job -ScriptBlock {
  Set-PSBreakpoint -Script C:\test\dbjob.ps1 -Line 3
  C:\test\dbjob.ps1
}
```

The job will run until it hits the breakpoint. It will then pause with a state of AtBreak-point, as shown in figure 15.10.

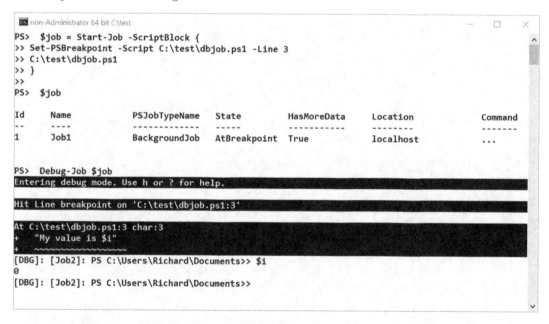

Figure 15.10   Using `Set-PSBreakpoint` **in a PowerShell job**

You'll be presented with a debug prompt and can perform your debugging tasks. Use detach to leave debugging and return to normal job activity. PowerShell workflows that are running as jobs also can be debugged using the techniques in this section.

You may often find yourself running scripts on a remote machine. Debugging in this scenario has been problematic in the past but is now fully supported.

15.5.2 Debugging remote scripts

Debugging of remote scripts through the console was introduced in PowerShell v4. In PowerShell v5 this was extended to include debugging remote scripts through the ISE.

NOTE The ISE (but not the console) can be used to open, edit, and save remote script files.

Put the dbjob.ps1 script from the previous section onto a remote machine. Remember that you can copy files to and from remote machines over PowerShell remoting sessions in PowerShell v5.

Create a remoting session to the machine on which you want to debug the script and enter the session:

```
PS> $s = New-PSSession -ComputerName server01
PS> Enter-PSSession -Session $s
```

You can then open the file for editing:

```
psedit -FileName C:\scripts\dbjob.ps1
```

Figure 15.11 shows this in action.

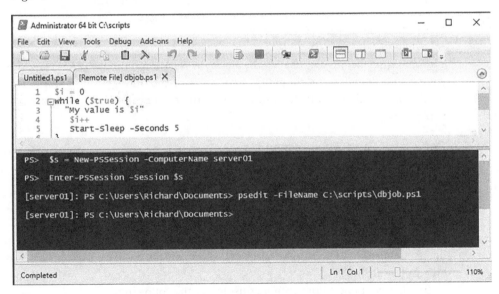

Figure 15.11   Editing and debugging a file on a remote server

Notice the [Remote File] decorator as part of the tab header for the file that's being edited. When you edit a file in this manner, you're accessing it across the remoting session; the file is copied across the session and stored locally in temporary storage. When changes to the file are saved, the file is copied back across the remoting session to the machine it came from.

You can set breakpoints in the file and the debugger will be opened when you run the file from the ISE, as shown in figure 15.12.

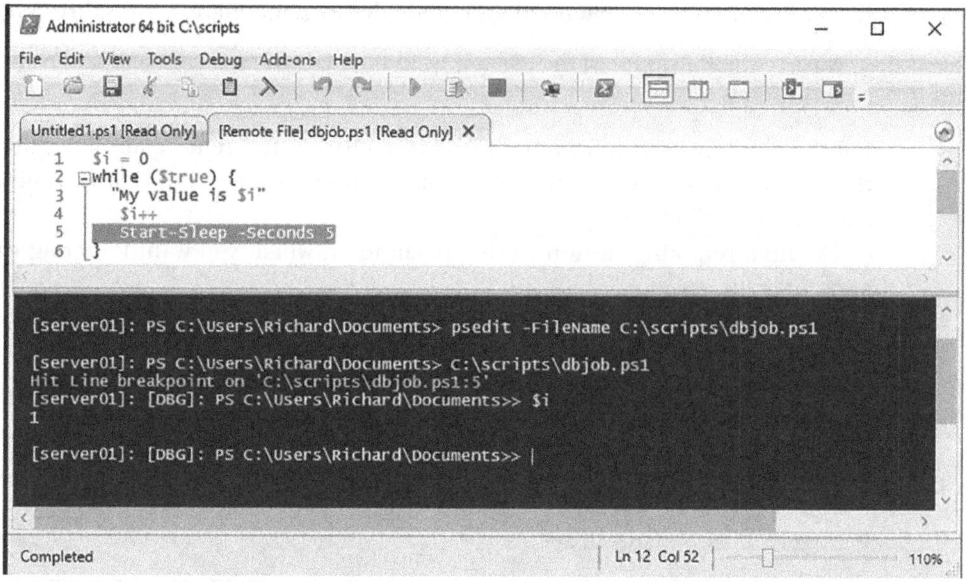

Figure 15.12 Debugging a remote script

The debugger behaves in exactly the same way as when debugging a local script. When you've completed your debugging, type q to exit the debugger and stop script execution. The last debugging technique we want to show you is debugging PowerShell runspaces.

15.5.3 *Debugging PowerShell runspaces*

You saw runspaces in chapter 12 when we discussed PowerShell workflows. We'll cover runspaces from an API viewpoint in chapter 20, but for now think of a runspace as an instance of PowerShell running inside an application. The PowerShell console and the ISE are runspaces you're already familiar with.

Runspaces are useful in cases where you need high-performance parallel processing, so being able to debug the scripts inside a runspace will be useful. This is available only in PowerShell v5.

In a newly opened PowerShell console, try the following:

```
PS> Get-Runspace

Id Name         ComputerName Type  State  Availability
-- ----         ------------ ----  -----  ------------
 1 Runspace1 localhost       Local Opened Busy
```

You'll see the identical result in a newly opened instance of the ISE.

Create and open a new runspace:

```
PS> $rsp = [RunspaceFactory]::CreateRunspace()
PS> $rsp.Open()
```

> **NOTE** RunspaceFactory is a shortcut to System.Management.Automation
> .Runspaces.RunspaceFactory.

Try Get-RunSpace again:

```
PS> Get-Runspace

Id Name       ComputerName Type  State  Availability
-- ----       ------------ ----  -----  ------------
 1 Runspace1  localhost    Local Opened Busy
 2 Runspace2  localhost    Local Opened Available
```

Now you have two runspaces. The original runspace shows as busy—it's the console (or the ISE) that you're using. The new runspace shows as available, so let's get it working:

```
PS> $ps = [powershell]::Create()
PS> $ps.Runspace = $rsp
PS> [void]$ps.AddScript('C:\test\dbjob.ps1')
PS> $as = $ps.BeginInvoke()
```

Create an instance of PowerShell and set its runspace to the new runspace. Add a script to the runspace (it's the same one as in previous examples in this section) and use the BeginInvoke() method to run the script asynchronously.

> **NOTE** PowerShell is a shortcut for System.Management.Automation.PowerShell.

Now that the script is running, you can see that both runspaces are busy:

```
PS> Get-Runspace

Id Name       ComputerName Type  State  Availability
-- ----       ------------ ----  -----  ------------
 1 Runspace1  localhost    Local Opened Busy
 2 Runspace2  localhost    Local Opened Busy
```

You can now attach the debugger to the runspace:

```
PS> Debug-Runspace -Id 2
Debugging Runspace: Runspace2
To end the debugging session type the 'Detach' command at
the debugger prompt, or type 'Ctrl+C' otherwise.

Entering debug mode. Use h or ? for help.

At C:\test\dbjob.ps1:2 char:8
+ while ($true) {
+        ~~~~~
[DBG]: [Process:4244]: [Runspace2]: PS C:\WINDOWS\system32>>
```

You can now perform debugging tasks such as viewing variable contents:

```
[DBG]: [Process:4244]: [Runspace2]: PS C:\WINDOWS\system32>> $i
69
[DBG]: [Process:4244]: [Runspace2]: PS C:\WINDOWS\system32>>
```

Notice that the debug prompt shows you the process and the runspace you're debugging. Use detach to exit the debugger and allow the script to continue. In this case your script is an infinite loop, so it needs to be stopped:

```
PS> $ps.Stop()
PS> Get-Runspace

Id Name          ComputerName Type  State  Availability
-- ----          ------------ ----  -----  ------------
 1 Runspace1 localhost        Local Opened Busy
 2 Runspace2 localhost        Local Opened Available
```

Close and remove the runspace:

```
PS> $rsp.Close()
PS> $rsp.Dispose()
```

If your runspace is hosted in a different process (application), you can use Enter-PSHostProcess to start debugging. On remote systems, enable Enter-PSHostProcess on the remote machine and connect to the process from within a remote PowerShell session. First, identify the PowerShell host to which you want to connect:

```
PS> Get-PSHostProcessInfo

ProcessName     ProcessId AppDomainName    MainWindowTitle
-----------     --------- -------------    ---------------
powershell           4244 DefaultAppDomain C:\test
powershell_ise       4624 DefaultAppDomain C:\test
```

You can then connect to the relevant host. In this case we're connecting to the ISE from the PowerShell console:

```
PS> Enter-PSHostProcess -Id 4624
[Process:4624]: PS C:\Users\Richard\Documents>
```

The prompt changes to show you've connected to a particular process. If the PowerShell host to which you need to connect is on a remote system, enter a PowerShell remoting session to that system and then use Enter-PSHostProcess. In either case, use Debug-Runspace, as shown earlier, to perform your debugging. Exit-PSHostProcess is used to leave the PowerShell runspace.

15.6 *Summary*

- The Write-* cmdlets can provide diagnostic information during script execution.
- The preference variables control the output of the Write-* cmdlets.

- Scripts can write diagnostic information to the event logs.
- You can create your own event log to store information from PowerShell scripts.
- Strict mode captures some errors before the script runs.
- Use the latest version of strict mode for maximum effect.
- Scripts can be statically analyzed for errors.
- PSScriptAnalyzer contains many rules that may identify problems in your code.
- Transcripts of the output of a PowerShell session are now available from the ISE and other hosts as well as the console.
- The PowerShell debugger is available in the console and the ISE.
- The PowerShell debugger uses the same keyboard shortcuts as Visual Studio.
- You can execute non-debugger commands in the debugger because the debugger is a full reentrant PowerShell session.
- You can set a breakpoint in a script to force entry to the debugger when it's reached based on arbitrary conditional logic.
- You can set breakpoints on lines, variables, or commands.
- PowerShell v5 introduces the capability of debugging workflows, PowerShell jobs, scripts on remote machines, and scripts in other runspaces.

You've seen how to manage errors and debug your code in the last two chapters. In the next chapter, you'll start to put PowerShell to use when we investigate how to work with PowerShell data providers, files, and CIM classes.

Working with providers, files, and CIM

Outside of a dog, a book is man's best friend. Inside of a dog, it's too dark to read.

—Groucho Marx

No matter how hard you try to avoid it, you'll have to work with data at some time while using PowerShell. The great news is that PowerShell can work with data in about any format you care to name. The not-so-good news is that you'll have to learn a bunch of new techniques to work with that data.

In this chapter, we're going to concentrate on using PowerShell to

- Work with flat files, including XML
- Access COM objects
- Use the Common Information Model (CIM) classes to perform administration tasks

In addition, PowerShell can expose data stores, such as the registry, SQL Server, or Active Directory, in the same way as it exposes the file system through PowerShell providers. This means that once you've learned how to work with one provider you have a minimal learning curve to work with the others. This is huge boost to your productivity and makes you immediately effective with new technologies.

We'll start by looking at the providers built in to PowerShell before moving on to the other types of data.

16.1 PowerShell providers

PowerShell does a lot of work to promote a consistent user experience when navigating through hierarchical namespaces. This consistency allows you to use the same commands to work with the file system, the registry, and other stores. The core mechanism that PowerShell uses to accomplish this is the PowerShell *provider model*. A PowerShell provider is a software component, loaded through modules or snap-ins, that's used to produce a file system–like experience for other data stores, such as the registry.

NOTE Providers can't be written in PowerShell; you have to use C# or another compiled language.

PowerShell installs a number of providers by default. You can view the installed providers by using `Get-PSProvider`, as shown in figure 16.1.

```
Administrator 64 bit C:\MyData\SkyDrive\Data\scripts                    —   □   X
PS> Get-PSProvider

Name                Capabilities                           Drives
----                ------------                           ------
Registry            ShouldProcess, Transactions            {HKLM, HKCU}
Alias               ShouldProcess                          {Alias}
Environment         ShouldProcess                          {Env}
FileSystem          Filter, ShouldProcess, Credentials     {C}
Function            ShouldProcess                          {Function}
Variable            ShouldProcess                          {Variable}
Certificate         ShouldProcess                          {Cert}
WSMan               Credentials                            {WSMan}


PS> Get-PSDrive | Format-Table

Name       Used (GB)     Free (GB) Provider    Root                     CurrentLocation
----       ---------     --------- --------    ----                     ---------------
Alias                              Alias
C            143.90         87.52 FileSystem   C:\                      MyData\SkyDrive\Data\scripts
Cert                               Certificate \
Env                                Environment
Function                           Function
HKCU                               Registry    HKEY_CURRENT_USER
HKLM                               Registry    HKEY_LOCAL_MACHINE
Variable                           Variable
WSMan                              WSMan


PS> _
```

Figure 16.1 The default PowerShell providers and PSDrives

A provider will expose a data store as one or more named drives. These are referred to as *PSDrives* to avoid confusion with the system drives. You can use `Get-PSDrive` to view the available drives, also shown in figure 16.1.

We'll look at PSDrives in more detail later in this section, but first we need to deal with the cmdlets that you use to work the data exposed through PSDrives.

16.1.1 PowerShell core cmdlets

A PowerShell *provider* is an installable component usually packaged as part of a PowerShell module or snap-in. The basic architecture of the provider module aligns with what are called the *core cmdlets*. These cmdlets provide the common (or core) activities and are grouped by noun: `Item`, `ChildItem`, `ItemProperty`, `Content`, `Location`, `Path`, `PSDrive`, and `PSProvider`, as shown in table 16.1.

Table 16.1   PowerShell core cmdlets

Noun	Cmdlets	Purpose
Item	Clear-Item; Copy-Item; Get-Item; Invoke-Item; Move-Item; New-Item; Remove-Item; Rename-Item; Set-Item	Work directly with an item in a data store
ChildItem	Get-ChildItem	Access and manipulate items that are children of a particular item
ItemProperty	Clear-ItemProperty; Copy-ItemProperty; Get-ItemProperty; Move-ItemProperty; New-ItemProperty; Remove-ItemProperty; Rename-ItemProperty; Set-ItemProperty	Access and manipulate the properties of an item
Content	Add-Content; Clear-Content; Get-Content; Set-Content	Access and manipulate content of text files
Location	Get-Location; Pop-Location; Push-Location; Set-Location	Access and manipulate location within a PSDrive
Path	Convert-Path; Join-Path; Resolve-Path; Split-Path; Test-Path	Access and manipulate, paths within a PSDrive
PSDrive	Get-PSDrive; New-PSDrive; Remove-PSDrive	Access and manage PSDrives
PSProvider	Get-PSProvider	Access PowerShell providers

NOTE   The help files `about_Core_Commands` and `about_providers` supply further information.

Many of the core cmdlets have dynamic parameters, that is, parameters that are only available in one or more PSDrives. A help file is available for each of the built-in providers that details the dynamic parameters on each core cmdlet. These can be accessed using the Provider name. For example:

```
PS> Get-Help Registry
```

Providers are the heart of the namespace mechanism, but you don't usually work directly with them. Instead, you work through named *drives* that allow you access to the provider's capabilities.

16.1.2 *Working with PSDrives*

PowerShell providers are typically accessed through named drives. This means that each provider will have at least one drive associated with it. The drives that a provider exports needn't correspond to things like system disk drives (though the file system provider usually has one drive name exported for each physical drive on the computer). Their names can also be longer than the single character permitted in drive letters.

The provider-exported named drives are called *PSDrives*. Similarly, a path that contains a PSDrive is called a *PSPath*, and a path that contains a physical drive is called a *provider-specific path*. A PSPath must be translated into the provider-specific path form before it can be processed by the system.

Another useful feature supported by many providers is the ability to create your own drive names. That means you can, for example, create a PSDrive as a shortcut to a common resource such as a test folder on your machine:

```
PS> New-PSDrive -Name Test -PSProvider FileSystem `
-Description 'Test area' -Root C:\test\

Name    Used (GB)    Free (GB) Provider    Root     CurrentLocation
----    ---------    --------- --------    ----     ---------------
Test         0.00        89.62 FileSystem  C:\test\
```

You're able to access this drive only from the PowerShell session in which you created it. If you need this drive in all sessions, add the creation command to your profile. You can create persistent mapped network drives using the `-Persist` parameter.

> **Accessing the documents folder**
>
> If you want to work with folders in your user area, use the ~ as a shortcut. For instance:
>
> ```
> Get-ChildItem -Path (Resolve-Path -Path ~)
> Get-ChildItem -Path (Resolve-Path -Path ~\documents)
> ```
>
> That will access your user area and your documents folder, respectively. The call to `Resolve-Path` converts the PSPath to an absolute provider path. Note that ~ refers to the home directory of the current provider, so if you've performed a change directory action into the Registry, ~ won't refer to your user area any longer.

You can move into the new drive or access it using the core cmdlets from table 16.1. PowerShell enables you to create appropriate items in the new drive (you couldn't create a file if you'd used the registry provider for the new drive) and access the content of those items:

```
PS> Add-Content -Value 'Hello There' -Path test:\junk.txt
PS> Get-Content -Path Test:\junk.txt
Hello There
```

Using non-PowerShell applications with a PSDrive

Non-PowerShell applications don't understand PSDrives and therefore can't use paths containing PSDrives directly. If you're in the PSDrive, the system automatically sets the current directory properly on the child process object to the provider-specific path before starting the process. You need to use the provider-specific path as supplied by Resolve-Path:

```
cmd /c type (Resolve-Path test:/junk.txt).ProviderPath
```

rather than

```
cmd /c type test:/junk.txt
```

PowerShell has another couple of tricks for working with paths.

16.1.3 Working with paths

Most of the time paths work, but there are special cases to consider.

- Hidden files aren't normally displayed by the file system provider; force is required to see hidden files.
- The PowerShell provider infrastructure has universal support for wildcards, though [and] need special care.
- The -LiteralPath parameter suppresses pattern-matching, which makes dealing with paths containing wildcard characters much easier.

HIDDEN FILES

By default, Get-ChildItem doesn't show hidden files, and the item files won't access them either. You need to use the -Force parameter. Try this:

```
PS> Get-ChildItem -Path C:\ -Filter *.sys
```

You'll see nothing returned. Use the -Force parameter

```
PS> Get-ChildItem -Path C:\ -Filter *.sys -Force

    Directory: C:\

Mode                 LastWriteTime         Length Name
----                 -------------         ------ ----
```

```
-a-hs-      15/05/2017      09:37      6843224064 hiberfil.sys
-a-hs-      12/05/2017      14:10      2550136832 pagefile.sys
-a-hs-      12/05/2017      14:10        16777216 swapfile.sys
```

and everything is visible.

The `Get-ChildItem` cmdlet also has the `-Attributes`, `-Hidden`, `-ReadOnly`, and `-System` dynamic parameters on the file system provider for dealing with particular file attributes. The file system provider also supports the `-Directory` and `-File` dynamic parameters for restricting output to directories and files, respectively.

PATHS AND WILDCARDS

You can use wildcards any place you can navigate to, even in places such as the PSDrive you created earlier:

```
PS> Get-ChildItem -Path test:\*.txt | Format-Table -AutoSize

    Directory: C:\test

Mode          LastWriteTime Length Name
----          ------------- ------ ----
-a----  31/01/2017     20:09     57 ac.txt
-a----  16/05/2016     10:46     52 data.txt
-a----  09/05/2017     19:54    804 err.txt
-a----  08/02/2016     18:52     34 My New File [1].txt
-a----  08/02/2016     18:52     34 My New File [2].txt
-a----  08/02/2016     18:52     34 My New File [3].txt
-a----  15/05/2017     11:11     13 junk.txt
```

We might all agree that this is a great feature, but there's a down side. Suppose you want to access a path that contains one of the wildcard metacharacters: ?, *, [, and]. In the Windows file system, * and ? aren't a problem because you can't use these characters in a filename or directory name. But you *can* use [and]. Working with files whose names contain [or] can be quite a challenge because of the way wildcards and quoting work. Square brackets are used a lot in filenames that applications create where they avoid collisions by numbering the files. Some examples are shown in the output immediately preceding this.

If you want only the files that contain [or], you need some special processing because the [is being treated as part of a wildcard pattern. Clearly you need to suppress treating [as a wildcard by quoting it. The backtick is the obvious candidate, but a single backtick is insufficient. If you keep adding backticks, you'll eventually get a result:

```
PS> Get-ChildItem -Path  test:\*`````[*.txt

    Directory: C:\test

Mode          LastWriteTime             Length Name
----          -------------             ------ ----
-a----      08/02/2016     18:52            34 My New File [1].txt
```

```
-a----        08/02/2016      18:52              34 My New File [2].txt
-a----        08/02/2016      18:52              34 My New File [3].txt
```

But if you want all the numbered versions of a particular file, you'll end up with something like this:

```
PS> Get-ChildItem -Path  "test:\My New File ````[*````].txt"
```

You have to use double quotes and four backticks each for the [and]. Much of the complication arises because you want some of the metacharacters to be treated as literal characters, whereas the rest still do pattern-matching. Trial and error is usually the only way to get this right.

> **NOTE** As we've said before, this stuff is hard. It's hard to understand and it's hard to get right. Unfortunately, no one has yet to come up with a better mechanism. This problem occurs in any language that supports pattern-matching. Patience, practice, and experimentation are the only ways to figure it out.

You can avoid a lot of the trial and error by using the -LiteralPath parameter.

THE -LITERALPATH PARAMETER

The -LiteralPath parameter is available on most core cmdlets. Say you want to copy a file from the previous example. If you use the regular path mechanism in Copy-Item

```
PS> Set-Location -Path C:\test\
PS> Copy-Item 'My New File [1].txt'  C:\test1\junk.txt
PS> Get-ChildItem -Path C:\test1\junk.txt
Get-ChildItem : Cannot find path 'C:\test1\junk.txt' because it does not exist.
At line:1 char:1
+ Get-ChildItem -Path C:\test1\junk.txt
+ ~~~~~~~~~~~~~~~~~~~~~~~~~~~~~~~~~~~~~~~
    + CategoryInfo          : ObjectNotFound: (C:\test1\junk.txt:String) [Get-
   ChildItem], ItemNotFoundException
    + FullyQualifiedErrorId : PathNotFound,Microsoft.PowerShell.Commands.
   GetChildItemCommand
```

the copy fails because the square brackets were treated as pattern-matching metacharacters. Now try it using -LiteralPath:

```
PS> Copy-Item -LiteralPath 'My New File [1].txt'  C:\test1\junk.txt
PS> Get-ChildItem -Path C:\test1\junk.txt

    Directory: C:\test1

Mode                LastWriteTime         Length Name
----                -------------         ------ ----
-a----        08/02/2016      18:52           34 junk.txt
```

This time it works properly.

PowerShell 5.0 enhancement

In PowerShell v5 on Windows 10, the PSReadline module is automatically loaded and brings a number of enhancements to the PowerShell console. One enhancement deals with escaping metacharacters in filenames. If you type

```
PS> Remove-Item -Path C:\test1\junk.txt
PS> Copy-Item my
```

and then press the Tab key, you'll find that the filename is expanded with the required escape characters:

```
PS> Copy-Item '.\My New File `[1`].txt'
```

You can then perform the copy:

```
PS> Copy-Item '.\My New File `[1`].txt' C:\test1\junk.txt
PS> Get-ChildItem -Path C:\test1\junk.txt

    Directory: C:\test1

Mode                LastWriteTime         Length    Name
----                -------------         ------    ----
-a----          08/02/2016        18:52       34  junk.txt
```

The -LiteralPath parameter is still necessary for PowerShell versions 4.0 and earlier.

When you pipe the output of a cmdlet such as Get-ChildItem into another cmdlet like Remove-Item, the -LiteralPath parameter is used to couple the cmdlets so that metacharacters in the paths returned by Get-ChildItem (including aliases dir or ls) don't cause problems for Remove-Item. If you want to delete the files we were looking at earlier, you can use Get-ChildItem to see them:

```
PS> Get-ChildItem 'My New File ``[*'

    Directory: C:\test

Mode                LastWriteTime         Length  Name
----                -------------         ------  ----
-a----       23/01/2016     17:37             12  My New File [1].txt
-a----       23/01/2016     17:37             12  My New File [2].txt
-a----       23/01/2016     17:37             12  My New File [3].txt
```

Now pipe the output of Get-ChildItem into Remove-Item

```
PS> Get-ChildItem 'My New File ``[*' | Remove-Item
```

and verify that they've been deleted.

This covers the issues around working with file paths. From here we can move on to working with the file contents after a quick look at the Registry provider.

16.1.4 *The Registry provider*

PowerShell uses paths to access many types of hierarchical information on a Windows computer. Probably *the* most important type of hierarchical information is the Registry, a store of hierarchical configuration information, much like the file system. But there's one significant difference—in the Registry, a container has two axes: children and properties or, as you're more used to calling them from hashtables, keys and values. This is one of the more complex scenarios that the provider model addresses.

In the Registry provider, it's no longer sufficient to have only the path; you also need to know whether you're accessing a name or a property. Let's take a look. Start by cd'ing to the PowerShell hive in the Registry:

```
PS> cd hklm:\software\microsoft\powershell
```

Let's see what's there:

```
PS> Get-ChildItem

    Hive: HKEY_LOCAL_MACHINE\software\microsoft\powershell

Name                          Property
----                          --------
1                             Install : 1...
3                             ConsoleHostShortcutTarget : C:\..
```

Unfortunately, the default display for a Registry entry is a bit cryptic, and for once using Format-List doesn't make it any more comprehensible. But you found an item named 1, which we can dig into:

```
PS> Get-ChildItem ./1

    Hive: HKEY_LOCAL_MACHINE\software\microsoft\PowerShell\1

Name                          Property
----                          --------
0409                          Install : 1
PowerShellEngine              ApplicationBase  : C:\Win...
PSConfigurationProviders
ShellIds
```

You see information about the subkeys, but what about accessing the properties? First, you need to determine if there are any subkeys:

```
PS> Get-Item ./1 | select Property

Property
--------
{Install, PID}
```

You then use the `Get-ItemProperty` cmdlet to access the property:

```
PS> Get-ItemProperty -Path ./1 -Name PID

PID           : 89383-100-0001260-04309
PSPath        : Microsoft.PowerShell.Core\Registry::
                HKEY_LOCAL_MACHINE\software\microsoft\
                PowerShell\1
PSParentPath  : Microsoft.PowerShell.Core\Registry::
                HKEY_LOCAL_MACHINE\software\microsoft\
                PowerShell
PSChildName   : 1
PSDrive       : HKLM
PSProvider    : Microsoft.PowerShell.Core\Registry
```

Notice that you need to specify both the path and the name of the property to retrieve. Properties are always relative to a path. There's another somewhat annoying thing about how `Get-ItemProperty` works: It doesn't return the value of the property—it returns a new object that has the property value as a member. Before you can do anything with this value, you need to extract it from the containing object:

```
PS> (Get-ItemProperty -Path ./1 -Name PID).PID
89383-100-0001260-04309
```

By using the `.` operator to extract the member's value, you can get the value. You could also use this:

```
PS> Get-ItemProperty -Path ./1 -Name PID | select -ExpandProperty  PID
89383-100-0001260-04309
```

> **NOTE** This is another one of those design trade-offs the PowerShell team encountered as they developed this environment. If only the value was returned, you'd lose the context for the value (where it came from and so on). In order to preserve this information, the team ended up forcing people to write what appears to be redundant code. A better way to handle this might've been to return the value with the context attached as synthetic properties.

So far, we've looked at accessing the HKEY_CURRENT_USER and HKEY_LOCAL_ MACHINE Registry hives. These are the only two hives for which PowerShell drives are created by default. How do you access the other hives? The answer is to fall back on the provider:

```
PS> Get-ChildItem -Path Registry::

    Hive:

Name                            Property
----                            --------
HKEY_LOCAL_MACHINE
HKEY_CURRENT_USER
```

```
HKEY_CLASSES_ROOT                    EditFlags : {0, 0, 0, 0}
HKEY_CURRENT_CONFIG
HKEY_USERS
HKEY_PERFORMANCE_DATA                Global : {80, 0, 69, 0...}
                                     Costly : {80, 0, 69, 0...}
```

You can follow the paths through the Registry starting with the provider rather than a drive:

```
PS> Get-ChildItem -Path registry::HKEY_CURRENT_CONFIG\System\
   CurrentControlSet\SERVICES\TSDDD\

   Hive: HKEY_CURRENT_CONFIG\System\CurrentControlSet\SERVICES\TSDDD

Name                                 Property
----                                 --------
DEVICE0                              Attach.ToDesktop : 1
```

> **NOTE** Other PowerShell drives are also accessible via their providers using similar syntax.

Now that you're more familiar with PowerShell providers, let's look at how you can work with files and their content.

16.2   *Files, text, and XML*

You saw earlier in the chapter how to work with the file system provider. In this section, we'll show you how to read and write file content. We'll then cover how to work with unstructured text as well as XML structured text. Let's start by discovering how to read file content and how to write to files.

16.2.1   *File processing*

In PowerShell, files are read using the Get-Content cmdlet. This cmdlet allows you to work with text files using a variety of character encodings and lets you work efficiently with binary files. Writing files is a bit more complex, because you have to choose between Set-Content (or Add-Content) and Out-File. The difference here is whether the output goes through the formatting subsystem.

It's important to point out that there are no separate open/read/close or open/write/close steps to working with files. The pipeline model allows you to process data and never have to worry about closing file handles—the system takes care of this for you.

READING TEXT FILES

The Get-Content cmdlet is the primary way to read files in PowerShell. In fact, it's the primary way to read any content available through PowerShell drives. Figure 16.2 shows this cmdlet's syntax.

```
non-Administrator 64 bit C:\test                                            —    □    ✕
Get-Content [-Path] <string[]> [-ReadCount <long>] [-TotalCount <long>] [-Tail <int>] [-Filter <stri
g>] [-Include <string[]>] [-Exclude <string[]>] [-Force] [-Credential <pscredential>] [-UseTransacti
n] [-Delimiter <string>] [-Wait] [-Raw] [-Encoding <FileSystemCmdletProviderEncoding>] [-Stream <str
ng>] [<CommonParameters>]

Get-Content -LiteralPath <string[]> [-ReadCount <long>] [-TotalCount <long>] [-Tail <int>] [-Filter
string>] [-Include <string[]>] [-Exclude <string[]>] [-Force] [-Credential <pscredential>] [-UseTran
action] [-Delimiter <string>] [-Wait] [-Raw] [-Encoding <FileSystemCmdletProviderEncoding>] [-Stream
<string>] [<CommonParameters>]

PS>
```

Figure 16.2 `Get-Content` **syntax**

Reading text files is simple. The command

```
PS> Get-Content -Path myfile.txt
```

will send the contents of myfile.txt to the output stream. Notice that the command signature for -Path allows for an array of path names. This is how you concatenate a collection of files. Let's try this. First, create a collection of files:

```
PS> Set-Location -Path C:\test\
PS> 1..3 | foreach { "This is file $_" > "file$_.txt"}
```

And now display their contents:

```
PS> Get-Content -Path file1.txt,file2.txt,file3.txt
This is file 1
This is file 2
This is file 3
```

NOTE PowerShell uses Unicode encoding by default. If you want to read PowerShell-created files using cmd.exe utilities, you have to use ASCII encoding.

Heads or tails?

You've seen that the -TotalCount parameter can be used to control how many lines are read from a file. This parameter has an alias of -Head to fit with other file-reading utilities (Get-Content has aliases of type and cat). Create a file with a number of lines:

```
PS> 1..10 | foreach { "This is line $_" |
Add-Content -Path multifile.txt}
```

You can read the beginning of the file:

```
PS> Get-Content -Path .\multifile.txt -Head 3
```

(Continued)

or you can read the end of the file:

```
PS> Get-Content -Path .\multifile.txt -Tail 3
```

This won't work though:

```
PS> Get-Content -Path .\multifile.txt -Head 3 -Tail 3
```

`-Head` and `-Tail` are mutually exclusive.

`Get-Content`, by default, reads a line at a time, so you get an array of lines if you do this:

```
PS> $v1 = Get-Content .\multifile.txt
PS> $v1.Count
10
```

If you want the text in the file to be a single string, you use the `-Raw` parameter:

```
PS> $v2 = Get-Content .\multifile.txt -Raw
PS> $v2.count
1
```

That's about it for text files. Reading binary files takes a little more work than simple text files.

READING BINARY FILES

The function in the next listing can be used to display the contents of a binary file. It takes the name of the file to display, the number of bytes to display per line, and the total number of bytes as parameters.

Listing 16.1   Get-HexDump

```
function Get-HexDump {
    param (
        [Parameter(Mandatory)]
        [string]$path,
        [int]$width=10,
        [int]$total=-1
    )
                                                         ❶ Set $OFS to
    $OFS=''                                                empty string
    Get-Content -Encoding byte -Path $path -ReadCount $width `
        -TotalCount $total |
    foreach {
        $record = $_
        if (($record -eq 0).count -ne $width)          ❷ Skip record if
                                                           length is zero
```

```
    {
        $hex = $record | foreach {
            ' ' + ('{0:x}' -f $_).PadLeft(2,'0') }
        $char = $record | foreach{
            if ([char]::IsLetterOrDigit($_))
                { [char] $_ } else { '.' }}
        "$hex $char"
    }
  }
}
```

❸ Format data

The function takes a mandatory path parameter and optional parameters for the number of bytes per line and the total number of bytes to display. You're going to be converting arrays to strings and you don't want any spaces added, so you'll set the output field separator character ❶ to be empty.

The Get-Content cmdlet does all the hard work. It reads the file in binary mode (indicated by setting -Encoding to byte), reads up to a maximum of -TotalCount bytes, and writes them into the pipeline in records of length specified by -ReadCount. The first thing you do in the foreach scriptblock is save the record that was passed in, because you'll be using nested scriptblocks that will cause $_ to be overwritten.

If the record is all zeros ❷, you won't bother displaying it. It might be a better design to make this optional, but we'll leave it as is for this example. For display purposes, you're converting the record of bytes ❸ into two-digit hexadecimal numbers. You use the format operator to format the string in hexadecimal and then the PadLeft() method on strings to pad it out to two characters. Finally, you prefix the whole thing with a space. The variable $hex ends up with a collection of these formatted strings.

Now you need to build the character equivalent of the record. You'll use the methods on the [char] class to decide whether you should display the character or a dot (.). Notice that even when you're displaying the character, you're still casting it into a [char]. This is necessary because the record contains a byte value, which, if directly converted into a string, will be formatted as a number instead of as a character. Finally, you'll output the completed record, taking advantage of string expansion to build the output string (which is why you set $OFS to ''). Example output is shown in figure 16.3.

```
PS> Get-HexDump -path C:\Windows\Web\Wallpaper\Windows\img0.jpg -width 12 -total 84
 ff d8 ff db 00 84 00 02 02 02 02 02 ÿØÿÛ........
 02 02 02 02 02 03 02 02 02 03 04 03 ............
 02 02 03 04 05 04 04 04 04 04 05 06 ............
 05 05 05 05 05 06 06 07 07 08 07 ............
 07 06 09 09 0a 0a 09 09 0c 0c 0c 0c ............
 0c 0c 0c 0c 0c 0c 0c 0c 0c 0c 0c 01 ............
 03 03 03 05 04 05 09 06 06 09 0d 0a ............
PS>
```

Figure 16.3 Example Get-HexDump output

In this example, you're using `Get-HexDump` to dump out the contents of one of the Windows bitmap files, specifying that it display 12 bytes per line and stop after the first 84 bytes. The first part of the display is the value of the byte in hexadecimal, and the portion on the right side is the character equivalent. Only values that correspond to letters or numbers are displayed. Nonprintable characters are shown as dots.

> **NOTE** You may find that PowerShell performs slowly when reading large files. One option in that case is to use the .NET I/O classes.

That covers reading files, but what about writing to a file?

WRITING FILES

You have two major ways to write files in PowerShell—by setting file content with the `Set-Content` cmdlet and by writing files using the `Out-File` cmdlet. The big difference is that `Out-File`, like all the output cmdlets, tries to format the output. `Set-Content` writes the output as is. If its input objects aren't already strings, it will convert them to strings by calling the `ToString()` method. This isn't usually what you want for objects, but it's exactly what you want if your data is already formatted or if you're working with binary data.

The other thing you need to be concerned with is how the files are encoded when they're written. In an earlier example, you saw that by default text files are written in Unicode. Let's rerun this example, changing the encoding to ASCII instead:

```
PS> 1..3 | foreach{ "This is file $_" |
Set-Content -Encoding ascii file$_.txt }
```

The `-Encoding` parameter is used to set how the files will be written

> **NOTE** You use `Set-Content` rather than `Out-File` because `Out-File` adds extra processing overhead that you don't need when writing primitive data such as text. And be aware that `Out-File` and `Set-Content` use different default encodings. A standard default encoding may be used in PowerShell v6.

16.2.2 *Unstructured text*

Although PowerShell is an object-based shell, it still has to deal with text. In chapter 3, we covered the operators that PowerShell provides for working with text. In this section, we'll cover some of the more advanced string-processing operations. We'll discuss techniques for splitting and joining strings using the `[string]` and `[regex]` members and using filters to extract statistical information from a body of text.

USING SYSTEM.STRING TO WORK WITH TEXT

PowerShell has the `-split` operator to separate elements of a string. The `Split()` method on the `[string]` class provides a few more options. The `Split()` method with no arguments splits on spaces. In this example, it produces an array of three elements:

```
PS> 'Hello there world'.Split().length
3
```

In fact, it splits on any of the characters that fall into the `WhiteSpace` character class. This includes tabs, so it works properly on a string containing both tabs and spaces:

```
PS> "Hello`there world".Split()
Hello
here
world
```

Notice the second element! The characters `` `t `` are interpreted as a tab character.

Although the default is to split on a whitespace character, you can specify a string of characters to use to split fields:

```
PS> 'First,Second;Third'.Split(',;')
First
Second
Third
```

Here you specify the comma and the semicolon as valid characters to split the field.

There is, however, an issue; the default behavior for "split this" isn't necessarily what you want. The reason is that it splits on each separator character. This means that if you have multiple spaces between words in a string, you'll get multiple empty elements in the result array, for example:

```
PS> 'Hello there    world'.Split().length
6
```

In this example, you end up with six elements in the array because there are three spaces between `there` and `world`. Looking at the MSDN documentation for the `Split()` method, you'll see that there are options to use `StringSplitOptions`. You can test what the options do by casting a string into the options:

```
PS> [StringSplitOptions]'abc'
Cannot convert value "abc" to type "System.StringSplitOptions".
Error: "Unable to match the identifier name abc to a valid
enumerator name. Specify one of the following enumerator names
and try again:
None, RemoveEmptyEntries"
At line:1 char:1
+ [StringSplitOptions]'abc'
+ ~~~~~~~~~~~~~~~~~~~~~~~~~~
    + CategoryInfo          : InvalidArgument: (:) [], RuntimeException
    + FullyQualifiedErrorId :
  SubstringDisambiguationEnumParseThrewAnException
```

`RemoveEmptyEntries` looks like it might solve your problem:

```
PS> 'Hello there    world'.split(' ',[StringSplitOptions]::RemoveEmptyEntries)
Hello
there
world
```

It works as desired. Next, you can apply this technique to a larger problem.

ANALYZING WORD USE IN A DOCUMENT

Given a body of text, say you want to find the number of words in the text as well as the number of unique words and then display the 10 most common words in the text. For our purposes, we'll use one of the PowerShell help text files: about_ Assignment_operators.help.txt. Remember that Get-Content creates an array where each element is a line from the file. You want a single string so you have to use the -Raw parameter:

```
PS> $s = Get-Content `
-Path $PSHOME\en-US\about_Assignment_Operators.help.txt `
-Raw
PS> $s.length
22780
```

$s contains a single string containing the whole text of the file. Next, split it into an array of words:

```
PS> $words = $s.Split(" `t", [stringsplitoptions]::RemoveEmptyEntries)
PS> $words.Length
3453
```

The text of the file has 3453 words in it. You need to find out how many unique words there are. The easiest approach is to use the Sort-Object cmdlet with the -Unique parameter. This code will sort the list of words and then remove all the duplicates:

```
PS> $uniq = $words | sort -Unique
PS> $uniq.count
719
```

The help topic contains 719 unique words. Using the Sort-Object cmdlet is fast and simple, but it doesn't give the frequency of use. Luckily, PowerShell includes a cmdlet that's useful for this kind of task: Group-Object. This cmdlet groups its input objects into collections sorted by the specified property. This means you can achieve the same type of ordering with the following:

```
PS> $grouped = $words | group | sort count
```

The most frequently used word is, unsurprisingly, "the":

```
PS> $grouped[-1]

Count Name                          Group
----- ----                          -----
  335 the                           {the, the, the, the...}
```

You can display the 10 most frequent words with this:

```
PS> $grouped[-1..-10]

Count Name                          Group
----- ----                          -----
```

```
335 the          {the, the, the, the...}
134 to           {to, to, to, to...}
121 a            {a, a, a, a...}
110 ...          {...
 97 value        {value, value, value, value...}
 94 $a           {$a, $a, $a, $a...}
 85 C:\PS>       {C:\PS>, C:\PS>, C:\PS>, C:\PS>...}
 80 of           {of, of, of, of...}
 74 =            {=, =, =, =...}
 55 variable     {variable, variable, variable...}
```

The code creates a nicely formatted display courtesy of the formatting and output sub-system built into PowerShell. In the world of unstructured text, you'll quickly run into examples where simple splits aren't enough. As is so often the case, regular expressions come to the rescue.

Regular expressions are a domain-specific language (DSL) for matching and manipulating text. We covered a number of examples using regular expressions with the -match and -replace operators in chapter 3. This time, you're going to work with the regular expression class itself.

SPLITTING STRINGS WITH REGULAR EXPRESSIONS

There's a type accelerator, [regex], for the regular expression type. The [regex] type also has a Split() method, but it's much more powerful because it uses a regular expression to decide where to split strings instead of a single character:

```
PS> $s = "Hello-1-there-22-World!"
PS> [regex]::split($s,'-[0-9]+-')
Hello
there
World!
```

In this example, the fields are separated by a sequence of digits bound on either side by a dash. This pattern couldn't be specified with simple character-based split operations.

When working with the .NET regular expression library, the [regex] class isn't the only class that you'll run into. You'll see this in the next example, when we look at using regular expressions to tokenize a string.

TOKENIZING TEXT WITH REGULAR EXPRESSIONS

Tokenization, or the process of breaking a body of text into a stream of individual symbols, is a common activity in text processing; for instance, the PowerShell interpreter has to tokenize a script before it can be executed. In the next example, we're going to look at how you can write a simple tokenizer for basic arithmetic expressions you might find in a programming language. First, you need to define the valid tokens in these expressions. You want to allow numbers made up of one or more digits; allow expressions made up of any of the operators +, -, *, or /; and also allow sequences of spaces. Here's what the regular expression to match these elements looks like:

```
PS> $pat = [regex] "[0-9]+|\+|\-|\*|/| +"
```

This is a pretty simple pattern using only the alternation operator | and the quantifier +, which matches one or more instances. Because you used the [regex] cast in the assignment, $pat contains a regular expression object. You can use this object directly against an input string by calling its Match() method:

```
PS> $m = $pat.match("11+2 * 35 -4")
```

The Match() method returns a Match object (the full type name is System.Text .RegularExpressions.Match). You can use the Get-Member cmdlet to explore the full set of members on this object at your leisure, but for now you're interested in only three members. The first member is the Success property. This will be true if the pattern matched. The second interesting member is the Value property, which will contain the matched value. The final member you're interested in is the Next-Match() method. Calling this method will step the regular expression engine to the next match in the string and is the key to tokenizing an entire expression. You can use this method in a while loop to extract the tokens from the source string one at a time. In the example, you keep looping as long as the Match object's Success property is true. Then you display the Value property and call NextMatch() to step to the next token:

```
PS> while ($m.Success)
{
    $m.value
    $m = $m.NextMatch()
}

11
+
2

*

35

-
4
```

In the output, you see each token, one per line, in the order in which they appeared in the original string.

SEARCHING FILES WITH THE SELECT-STRING CMDLET

The Select-String cmdlet allows you to search through collections of strings or collections of files. It's similar to the grep command on UNIX-derived systems and the findstr command on Windows. Figure 16.4 shows the parameters on this cmdlet. Select-String is optimized for searching through files.

```
Administrator 64 bit C:\test                                                    —  □  ×
PS> Get-Command Select-String -Syntax

Select-String [-Pattern] <string[]> [-Path] <string[]> [-SimpleMatch] [-CaseSensitive] [-Quiet] [-List] [-Include <str
ng[]>] [-Exclude <string[]>] [-NotMatch] [-AllMatches] [-Encoding <string>] [-Context <int[]>] [<CommonParameters>]

Select-String [-Pattern] <string[]> -InputObject <psobject> [-SimpleMatch] [-CaseSensitive] [-Quiet] [-List] [-Include
<string[]>] [-Exclude <string[]>] [-NotMatch] [-AllMatches] [-Encoding <string>] [-Context <int[]>] [<CommonParameters
]

Select-String [-Pattern] <string[]> -LiteralPath <string[]> [-SimpleMatch] [-CaseSensitive] [-Quiet] [-List] [-Include
<string[]>] [-Exclude <string[]>] [-NotMatch] [-AllMatches] [-Encoding <string>] [-Context <int[]>] [<CommonParameters
]

PS>
```

Figure 16.4 Syntax of Select-String

Let's search through all of the "about_*" topics in the PowerShell installation directory to see if the phrase "wildcard description" is there:

```
PS> Select-String  -Path $pshome/en-US/about*.txt `
-Pattern 'wildcard description'

C:\Windows\System32\WindowsPowerShell\v1.0\en-US\about_Wildcards.help.txt:21:
   Wildcard Description         Example
Match              No match
```

You see that there's exactly one match, but notice the uppercase letters in the matching string. If you rerun the search using the -CaseSensitive parameter

```
PS> Select-String  -Path $pshome/en-US/about*.txt `
-Pattern 'wildcard description' -CaseSensitive
```

nothing is found. Searching through files this way can sometimes produce more results than you need.

Normally Select-String will find all matches in a file. The -List switch limits the search to the first match in a file. The -Quiet switch returns $true if any of the files contain a match and $false if none do. You can also combine the two switches so that the cmdlet returns the first match in the set of files.

If you want to search a more complex set of files, you can pipe the output of Get-ChildItem into the cmdlet and it will search all of these files. Let's search all the log files in the system32 subdirectory:

```
PS> Get-ChildItem -Recurse -Filter *.log -Path $env:windir\system32 |
Select-String -List -Pattern 'fail' | Format-Table path
```

Only the path to a log file containing a record with "fail" in it will be displayed.

The MatchInfo object produced by Select-Object has a context property. This property allows you to have Select-String include the lines before and after the matching line. You can specify two numbers to the -Context parameter. The first number is the length of the prefix context and the second is the suffix context; for instance, to get only the matching line and the four following lines, you have to specify a prefix context of 0 and a suffix of 4:

```
PS> Get-Help Select-String |
Out-String -Stream |
Select-String -Pattern 'syntax' -Context 0,4

> SYNTAX
    Select-String [-Pattern] <String[]> [-Path] <String[]> [-AllMatches]
    [-CaseSensitive] [-Context <Int32[]>] [-Encoding
    {unicode | utf7   |  utf8   | utf32 | ascii |
    bigendianunicode  |default | oem}]
    [-Exclude <String[]>] [-Include <String[]>]
    [-InformationAction {SilentlyContinue | Stop | Continue |
    Inquire |  Ignore | Suspend}] [-InformationVariable <System.String>]
    [-List] [-NotMatch] [-Quiet] [-SimpleMatch] [<CommonParameters>]
```

GETTING ALL MATCHES IN THE LINE

Another property on the MatchInfo object is the Matches property. This property is used when the -AllMatches switch is specified to the cmdlet. It causes all matches in the line to be returned instead of only the first match. You'll use this switch to perform the same type of tokenization that you did with regular expressions in section 16.2.2. You'll pipe the expression string into Select-String with the -AllMatches switch and the same regular expression you used earlier:

```
PS> '1 + 2 *3' |
Select-String -AllMatches -Pattern '[0-9]+|\+|\-|\*|/| +' |
foreach { $_.Matches } | Format-Table -AutoSize

Groups Success Captures Index Length Value
------ ------- -------- ----- ------ -----
{1}      True   {1}        0     1   1
{ }      True   { }        1     1
{+}      True   {+}        2     1   +
{ }      True   { }        3     1
{2}      True   {2}        4     1   2
{ }      True   { }        5     1
{*}      True   {*}        6     1   *
{3}      True   {3}        7     1   3
```

You use the Foreach-Object cmdlet to isolate the Matches property and then format the output as a table. You can see each of the extracted tokens in the Value field in the Matches object. Using this mechanism, you can effectively and efficiently process things like large log files where the output is formatted as a table.

> **NOTE** If you're using PowerShell v5.1 on Windows 10 with the Creators update (build version 10.0.15063.413 or later) you'll see {0} for all entries in the Groups and Captures columns.

All the text so far in this chapter has been *unstructured text* where there's no rigorously defined layout for that text. As a consequence, you've had to work fairly hard to extract the information you want out of this text. There are, however, large bodies of structured text, where the format is well defined in the form of XML documents.

16.2.3 *XML structured text processing*

XML (Extensible Markup Language) is used for everything from configuration files to log files to databases. PowerShell uses XML for its type and configuration files as well as for the help files. For PowerShell to be effective, it has to be able to process XML documents effectively. Let's look at how XML is used and supported in PowerShell.

> **NOTE**   This section assumes you possess some basic knowledge of XML markup.

We'll look at the XML object type, as well as the mechanism that .NET provides for searching XML documents.

USING XML AS OBJECTS

PowerShell supports XML documents as a core data type. This means that you can access the elements of an XML document as though they were properties on an object. For example, let's create a simple XML object. Start with a string that defines a top-level node called top. This node contains three descendants: a, b, and c, each of which has a value. Let's turn this string into an object:

```
PS> $d = [xml] '<top><a>one</a><b>two</b><c>3</c></top>'
```

The [xml] cast takes the string and converts it into an XML object of type System.XML.XmlDocument. This object is then adapted by PowerShell so you can treat it as a regular object. Let's try this out. First, display the object:

```
PS> $d

top
---
top
```

As you expect, the object displays one top-level property corresponding to the top-level node in the document. Now let's see what properties this node contains:

```
PS> $d.top

a   b   c
-   -   -
one two 3
```

Three properties correspond to the descendants of top. You can use conventional property notation to look at the value of an individual member:

```
PS> $d.top.a
One
```

Modifying this node is as simple as assigning a new value to the node. Let's assign the string "Four" to node a:

```
PS> $d.top.a = 'Four'
PS> $d.top.a
Four
```

You can see that it's been changed. But there's a limitation: you can only use a string as the node value. The XML object adapter won't automatically convert non-string objects to strings in an assignment, so you get an error when you try it. All the normal type conversions apply, so you can use a node value in arithmetic actions if it can be converted to a suitable type.

Adding elements to an XML document isn't a simple assignment operation.

ADDING ELEMENTS TO AN XML OBJECT

Let's add an element d to this document. To do so, you need to use the methods on the XML document object. First, you have to create the new element. Then you set the element text, the "inner text," to a value and finally append the new element to the document:

```
PS> $el= $d.CreateElement('d')
PS> $el.Set_InnerText('Hello')
PS> $d.top.AppendChild($el)
```

Notice that you're using the property setter method here. This is because the XML adapter hides the basic properties on the XmlNode object. The other way to set this would be to use the PSBase member:

```
PS> $ne = $d.CreateElement('e')
PS> $ne.InnerText = 'World'
PS> $d.top.AppendChild($ne)
```

Now that you know how to add children to a node, how can you add attributes? The pattern is the same as with elements. First, create an attribute object. Next, set the value of the text for that object. Finally, add it to the top-level document:

```
PS> $attr = $d.CreateAttribute('BuiltBy')
PS> $attr.Value = 'Windows PowerShell'
PS> $d.DocumentElement.SetAttributeNode($attr)
```

You can't cast the document back to a string and see what it looks like instead; you have to save the document as a file and display it:

```
PS> $d.Save('C:\test\new.xml')
PS> Get-Content -Path C:\test\new.xml
<top BuiltBy="Windows PowerShell">
  <a>one</a>
  <b>two</b>
  <c>3</c>
  <d>Hello</d>
  <e>World</e>
</top>
```

You've constructed, edited, and saved XML documents, but you haven't loaded an existing document yet, so that's the next step.

LOADING AND SAVING XML FILES

In the previous section, you saved an XML document to a file and read it, as text, using `Get-Content`. If you want to work with an XML document, you need to cast the output of `Get-Content` into an XML document:

```
PS> $nd = [xml] (Get-Content -Path C:\test\new.xml)
```

> **Speedier XML reading**
>
> By default, `Get-Content` reads one record at a time. This process can be quite slow. When processing large files, you should use the `-ReadCount` parameter to specify a block size of –1. Doing so will cause the entire file to be loaded and processed at once, which is much faster. Alternatively, here's another way to load an XML document using the .NET methods:
>
> ```
> PS> ($nd = [xml]'<root></root>').Load('C:\test\new.xml')
> ```
>
> Note that this does require that the full path to the file be specified.

Let's verify that the document was read properly:

```
PS> $nd.top

BuiltBy : Windows PowerShell
a       : one
b       : two
c       : 3
d       : Hello
e       : World
```

Everything is as it should be. Even the attribute is there.

Although this is a simple approach and the one you'll probably use most often, it's not necessarily the most efficient approach because it requires loading the entire document into memory. For large documents or collections of documents, loading all the text into memory may become a problem. In the next section, we'll look at alternative approaches that, though more complex, are more memory efficient.

USING THE XMLREADER CLASS

Our previously discussed method for loading an XML file is simple but not too efficient. It requires that you load the file into memory, make a copy of the file while turning it into a single string, and create an XML document representing the entire file using the XML Document Object Model (DOM) representation. The DOM allows you to treat an XML document as a hierarchy of objects, but to do so it consumes a lot of memory.

A much more memory-efficient way to process XML documents is to use the `System`
`.Xml.XmlReader` class. This class streams through the document one element at a time
instead of loading the whole thing into memory. You need a function that will use the
XML reader to stream through a document and output it properly indented—an XML
pretty-printer, if you will.

First, you need a more complex document where there are more attributes and
more nesting on which you can test your document.

Listing 16.2   Creating the text XML document

```
@'
<top BuiltBy = "Windows PowerShell">
    <a pronounced="eh">
        one
    </a>
    <b pronounced="bee">
        two
    </b>
    <c one="1" two="2" three="3">
        <one>
            1
        </one>
        <two>
            2
        </two>
        <three>
            3
        </three>
    </c>
    <d>
        Hello there world
    </d>
</top>
'@ > c:\test\fancy.xml
```

The function to read XML documents will be called `Format-XmlDocument` to keep within
the PowerShell naming conventions.

Listing 16.3   The `Format-XmlDocument` function

```
function global:Format-XmlDocument {
    param
    (
        [string]$Path = "$PWD\fancy.xml"
    )
    $settings = New-Object System.Xml.XmlReaderSettings      ①  Create
    $doc = (Resolve-Path -Path $Path).ProviderPath               settings
    $reader = [System.Xml.XmlReader]::Create($doc, $settings)    object
    $indent=0
    function indent {
        param
```

```
            (
                [Object]$s
            )
        '    '*$indent+$s                    ❷  Define formatting
    }                                           function

    while ($reader.Read())                              ❸  Process
    {                                                      element
        if ($reader.NodeType -eq [Xml.XmlNodeType]::Element)  nodes
        {
            $close = $(if ($reader.IsEmptyElement) { '/>' } else { '>' })
            if ($reader.HasAttributes)
            {
                $s = indent "<$($reader.Name) "
                [void] $reader.MoveToFirstAttribute()
                do
                {
                    $s += "$($reader.Name) = `"$($reader.Value)`" "
                }
                while ($reader.MoveToNextAttribute())
                "$s$close"
            }
            else
            {
                indent "<$($reader.Name)$close"
            }                                              ❹  Increase
            if ($close -ne '/>') {$indent++}                  indent level
        }
        elseif ($reader.NodeType -eq [Xml.XmlNodeType]::EndElement )
        {
            $indent--
            indent "</$($reader.Name)>"
        }
        elseif ($reader.NodeType -eq [Xml.XmlNodeType]::Text)
        {
            indent $reader.Value                       ❺  Format text
        }                                                  element
    }
    $reader.close()
}
```

Format-XmlDocument is a complex function, so it's worthwhile to take it one piece at a time. Let's start with the basic function declaration, where it takes an optional argument that names a file. Next, you create the settings object ❶ you need to pass in when you create the XML reader object. You also need to resolve the path to the document, because the XML reader object requires an absolute path. Now you can create the Xml-Reader object itself. The XML reader will stream through the document, reading only as much as it needs, as opposed to reading the entire document into memory.

You want to display the levels of the document indented, so you initialize an indent-level counter and a local function ❷ to display the indented string. Now you read through all of the nodes in the document. You choose different behavior based on the type of the node. An element node ❸ is the beginning of an XML element. If the element has attributes, then you add them to the string to display. You use the Move-ToFirstAttribute() and MoveToNextAttribute() methods to move through the attributes. If there are no attributes, display the element name.

At each new element, increase ❹ the indent level if it's not an empty element tag. If it's the end of an element, decrease the indent level and display the closing tag. If it's a text element, display the value of the element ❺. Finally, close the reader. You always want to close a handle received from a .NET method. It'll eventually be discarded during garbage collection, but it's possible to run out of handles before you run out of memory.

The function and its output are illustrated in figure 16.5.

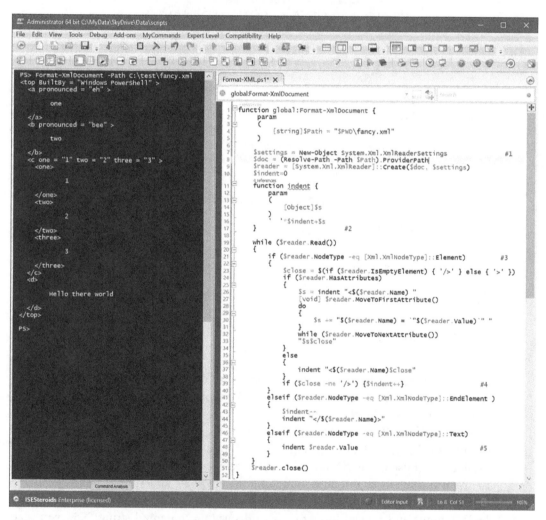

Figure 16.5   Format-XmlDocument **displaying the test document in the ISE. Note that the ISE looks slightly different because ISEsteroids (www.powertheshell.com/isesteroids/) is in use.**

The obvious next question is: How do you process XML documents on the pipeline?

PROCESSING XML DOCUMENTS IN A PIPELINE

Pipelining is one of the signature characteristics of shell environments in general and PowerShell in particular. Because the previous examples didn't take advantage of this feature, we'll look at how it can be applied. You're going to write a function that scans all the PowerShell help files, both the text about topics and the XML files, for a specified pattern. The code for the function is shown in the following listing.

> **Listing 16.4** `Search-Help` function scans help files for a pattern

```
function Search-Help
{
    param (
        [Parameter(Mandatory)]
        $pattern
    )

    Select-String -List $pattern -Path $PSHome\en-us\about*.txt |
    foreach {$_.filename -replace '\..*$'}

    Get-ChildItem $PSHOME\en-us\*dll-help.*xml |
    foreach { [xml] (Get-Content -ReadCount -1 -Path $_) } |
    foreach{$_.helpitems.command} |
    Where-Object {$_.get_Innertext() -match $pattern} |
    foreach {$_.details.name.trim()}
}
```

The `Search-Help` function takes one parameter to use as the pattern for which you're searching. The `$pattern` parameter is set as mandatory so the user will be prompted if the parameter isn't provided.

First, you search all the text files in the PowerShell installation directory and return one line for each matching file. Then you pipe this line into the `ForEach-Object` (or, more commonly, its alias `foreach`) to extract the base name of the file using the `-replace` operator and a regular expression. This operation will list the filenames in a form that you can type back into `Get-Help`.

Next, you get a list of the XML help files and turn each file into an XML object. You specify a read count of `-1` so the whole file is read at once. You extract the command elements from the XML document and then see whether the text of the command contains the pattern you're looking for. If it does, then you emit the name of the command, trimming off unnecessary spaces.

As an example of using the function, try this:

```
PS> Search-Help scriptblock
```

As well as being a handy way to search help, this function is a nice illustration of using the divide-and-conquer strategy when writing scripts in PowerShell. Each step in the pipeline brings you incrementally closer to the solution.

Another way to extract information from an XML document involves using XPath queries with `Select-Xml`.

XPATH AND SELECT-XML

XML Path Language, also known as XPath, is a *path-based pattern language*, which means it's like the collision of paths, wildcards, and regular expressions. It's useful because it gives you a fast, concise way to select pieces of information from an XML document. An XPath expression can be used to extract nodes, content, or attributes from a document. It also allows calculations to be used in the expressions to get even greater flexibility. Things get a bit more complex because XML allows for multiple nodes with the same name and allows attributes on nodes.

Next, you'll set up a test document and explore these more complex patterns. The following script fragment creates a string you'll use for the examples. It's a fragment of a bookstore inventory database. Each record in the database has the name of the author, the book title, and the number of books in stock. Save this string in a variable called `$inventory`, as shown here.

Listing 16.5   Creating the bookstore inventory

```
$inventory = @"
  <bookstore>
    <book genre="Autobiography">
      <title>The Autobiography of Benjamin Franklin</title>
      <author>
        <first-name>Benjamin</first-name>
        <last-name>Franklin</last-name>
      </author>
      <price>8.99</price>
      <stock>3</stock>
    </book>
    <book genre="Novel">
      <title>Moby Dick</title>
      <author>
        <first-name>Herman</first-name>
        <last-name>Melville</last-name>
      </author>
      <price>11.99</price>
      <stock>10</stock>
    </book>
    <book genre="Philosophy">
      <title>Discourse on Method</title>
      <author>
        <first-name>Rene</first-name>
        <last-name>Descartes</last-name>
      </author>
      <price>9.99</price>
      <stock>1</stock>
    </book>
    <book genre="Computers">
      <title>Windows PowerShell in Action</title>
      <author>
```

```
            <first-name>Bruce</first-name>
            <last-name>Payette</last-name>
          </author>
          <price>39.99</price>
          <stock>5</stock>
        </book>
      </bookstore>
"@
```

We'll work through examples of using XPath with `Select-Xml` on the `$inventory` string from listing 16.5. Let's start with something simple—getting the bookstore node at the root of the document:

```
PS> Select-Xml -Content $inventory -XPath /bookstore

Node                    Path                    Pattern
----                    ----                    -------
bookstore               InputStream             /bookstore
```

Unfortunately, the output doesn't look promising. The node object you're after is mixed in with the context of the query: where the processed text came from and what the query was. To extract the node object, you have to reference it as a property:

```
PS> (Select-Xml -Content $inventory -XPath /bookstore).Node

book
----
{book, book, book, book}
```

This output shows that there are four child nodes under bookstore. Extend your query to get these child items in a similar manner to how you could get the contents of a directory in the file system:

```
PS> Select-Xml -Content $inventory -XPath /bookstore/book

Node                    Path                    Pattern
----                    ----                    -------
book                    InputStream             /bookstore/book
book                    InputStream             /bookstore/book
book                    InputStream             /bookstore/book
book                    InputStream             /bookstore/book
```

Here's the nested-node issue again. Again you have to use the . operator to retrieve the content. For each of the nodes, you need to extract the Node property, so you apply the foreach cmdlet:

```
PS> Select-Xml -Content $inventory -XPath /bookstore/book |
foreach { $_.node }

genre  : Autobiography
title  : The Autobiography of Benjamin Franklin
author : author
price  : 8.99
stock  : 3
<output truncated for brevity>
```

This time you see the properties of all four nodes. If you want to extract only the title nodes, add `title` to the end of the path:

```
PS> Select-Xml -Content $inventory -XPath /bookstore/book |
foreach { $_.node.title }

The Autobiography of Benjamin Franklin
Moby Dick
Discourse on Method
Windows PowerShell in Action
```

At this point, using `foreach` all the time is getting tedious, so let's define a filter to simplify this:

```
PS> filter node { $_.node }
```

Now let's look at more advanced examples. So far, you've returned the entire set of nodes, but when querying for information, you usually want to get part of that information. You can do this quite easily with the `Where-Object` cmdlet:

```
PS> Select-Xml -Content $inventory -XPath /bookstore/book |
node | where { [double] ($_.price) -lt 10}

genre   : Autobiography
title   : The Autobiography of Benjamin Franklin
author  : author
price   : 8.99
stock   : 3

genre   : Philosophy
title   : Discourse on Method
author  : author
price   : 9.99
stock   : 1
```

This example retrieves all the books priced less than $10. XPath has built-in functionality that's similar to the `Where-Object` cmdlet: *predicate expressions*. These expressions appear in the path surrounded by square brackets and can contain a simple logical expression. Nodes where the expression evaluates to true are returned. Here's the previous example using a predicate expression instead of the `Where-Object` cmdlet:

```
PS> Select-Xml -Content $inventory -XPath '/bookstore/book[price < 10]' |
node
```

You get the same result in both cases. Notice that in the predicate expression you were able to reference `price` directly as opposed to `[double] ($_.price)` the way you did in the `Where-Object` case. Because the expression is being executed by the XPath engine, it can make these optimizations, simplifying the reference to the `price` item and treating it as a number automatically.

In the previous example, the `price` item was a path relative to the current node. You can use `..` to reference the parent node. Now write your expression so that it returns only the titles of the books whose price is less than $10:

```
PS> Select-Xml -Content $inventory `
-XPath '/bookstore/book/title[../price < 10]' |
node

#text
-----
The Autobiography of Benjamin Franklin
Discourse on Method
```

The path selects the title node but filters on the path `../price`, which is a sibling to the `title` node.

As we discussed earlier, elements aren't all that an XML document can contain. Another major item is the attribute. XPath allows an attribute to be referenced instead of an element by prefixing the name with `@`, as you see here:

```
PS> Select-Xml -Content $inventory -XPath '//@genre' | node

#text
-----
Autobiography
Novel
Philosophy
Computers
```

This example shows the `genre` attribute for each of the book nodes. You can also use attributes in predicate expressions in the path:

```
PS> Select-Xml -Content $inventory `
-XPath '//book[@genre = "Novel"]' |
node

genre  : Novel
title  : Moby Dick
author : author
price  : 11.99
stock  : 10
```

This example uses the `@genre` attribute in the node to return only books in the `Novel` genre. Note that, unlike the PowerShell relational operators, XPath operators are case-sensitive. If you specify `novel` for the genre instead of `Novel`, nothing is retrieved, whereas doing the same thing with the `Where-Object` cmdlet works fine.

NOTE Remember that XPath is its own language and doesn't necessarily behave the same way as the equivalent expression in PowerShell.

Now let's do some processing on the data in the document instead of only retrieving the node. In this example, you'll calculate the total value of the inventory, which is the sum of the product of multiplying the `price` node and the `stock` node:

```
PS> Select-Xml -Content $inventory -XPath '//book' | node |
foreach {[double] $_.price * $_.stock } |
Measure-Object -Sum | foreach { $_.sum }
```

```
356.81
```

This code uses XPath to extract the relevant nodes and then uses PowerShell to perform the calculations.

The examples in this section illustrate the basic mechanism for using XPath to extract data from documents. They're far from comprehensive, though. There's a lot more to learn about the details of the XPath language—the functions it supports, how to do calculations, and so forth—but this level of detail is probably not needed for most scenarios because PowerShell can do all of these things in a much more flexible way.

RENDERING OBJECTS AS XML

Up to this point, you've been working with XML as objects. Now you're going to switch it around and render objects into XML using cmdlets. PowerShell provides two cmdlets for rendering objects as XML, each with slightly different purposes. The ConvertTo-Xml cmdlet renders objects with relatively simple but verbose format. This cmdlet is useful for interoperating between PowerShell and other environments. Conversions using Export-Clixml are much more complex but also more compact and are intended for efficiently passing data between instances of PowerShell.

> **NOTE**   ConvertTo-XmL doesn't automatically create an output file, but Export-CliXml does.

We'll start with the simpler of the cmdlets: ConvertTo-Xml which takes an object as an argument or (more commonly) as pipeline input and generates an XML document from it. Let's use it to produce XML from a list of Windows services. You'll get the list using the Get-Service cmdlet, but you'll limit the number of services you'll work with to three for brevity's sake:

```
PS> $doc = Get-Service | select -First 3 | ConvertTo-Xml
PS> $doc

xml                             Objects
---                             -------
version="1.0" encoding="utf-8" Objects
```

The collection of objects is rendered into an XML document with the top node Object, which, in turn, contains a collection of Object elements as shown:

```
PS> $doc.Objects.Object

Type                             Property
----                             --------
System.ServiceProcess.ServiceCo... {Name, RequiredServices, CanPau...
System.ServiceProcess.ServiceCo... {Name, RequiredServices, CanPau...
System.ServiceProcess.ServiceCo... {Name, RequiredServices, CanPau...
```

Here you see that each `Object` element has the type and properties of the source object included in the output document. But this representation doesn't show the document format effectively, so use the `-As` parameter to display the document as a single string:

```
PS> Get-Service | select -First 1 | ConvertTo-Xml -As String

<?xml version="1.0" encoding="utf-8"?>
<Objects>
  <Object Type="System.ServiceProcess.ServiceController">
    <Property Name="Name" Type="System.String">AJRouter</Property>
    <Property Name="RequiredServices" Type="System.ServiceProcess.
ServiceController[]" />
    <Property Name="CanPauseAndContinue" Type="System.Boolean">False</
Property>
    <Property Name="CanShutdown" Type="System.Boolean">False</Property>
    <Property Name="CanStop" Type="System.Boolean">False</Property>
    <Property Name="DisplayName" Type="System.String">AllJoyn Router
Service</Property>
    <Property Name="DependentServices" Type="System.ServiceProcess.
ServiceController[]" />
    <Property Name="MachineName" Type="System.String">.</Property>
    <Property Name="ServiceName" Type="System.String">AJRouter</Property>
    <Property Name="ServicesDependedOn" Type="System.ServiceProcess.
ServiceController[]" />
    <Property Name="ServiceHandle" Type="SafeServiceHandle">SafeServiceHand
le</Property>
    <Property Name="Status" Type="System.ServiceProcess.ServiceControllerStat
us">Stopped</Property>
    <Property Name="ServiceType" Type="System.ServiceProcess.
ServiceType">Win32ShareProcess</Property>
    <Property Name="StartType" Type="System.ServiceProcess.
ServiceStartMode">Manual</Property>
    <Property Name="Site" Type="System.ComponentModel.ISite" />
    <Property Name="Container" Type="System.ComponentModel.IContainer" />
  </Object>
</Objects>
```

Now the structure of the saved data is much clearer. The type name of the original object is included as an attribute on the `Object` tab. The child elements of `Object` are a collection of `Property` objects with the property name and type as attributes and the value as the element content.

One thing we didn't mention was the serialization depth. The default depth is 2. You see this in the `RequiredServices` property, whose content is two additional nested properties. You can override the default depth using the `-Depth` parameter on the cmdlet.

> **NOTE** You might be tempted to set the depth to a larger value to preserve more information, but be aware that the size of the document can explode with deep nesting. For example, saving the process table with the default depth of 2 produces a 700 KB file, which is already quite large. Increasing the depth to 3 explodes the file to 7 MB—a tenfold increase in size!

The other parameter on the cmdlet that we haven't talked about is -NoTypeInformation. When you specify this parameter, no type information is included in the generated document:

```
PS> Get-Service | select -First 1 |
ConvertTo-Xml -As String -NoTypeInformation

<?xml version="1.0" encoding="utf-8"?>
<Objects>
  <Object>
    <Property Name="Name">AJRouter</Property>
    <Property Name="RequiredServices" />
    <Property Name="CanPauseAndContinue">False</Property>
    <Property Name="CanShutdown">False</Property>
    <Property Name="CanStop">False</Property>
    <Property Name="DisplayName">AllJoyn Router Service</Property>
    <Property Name="DependentServices" />
    <Property Name="MachineName">.</Property>
    <Property Name="ServiceName">AJRouter</Property>
    <Property Name="ServicesDependedOn" />
    <Property Name="ServiceHandle">SafeServiceHandle</Property>
    <Property Name="Status">Stopped</Property>
    <Property Name="ServiceType">Win32ShareProcess</Property>
    <Property Name="StartType">Manual</Property>
    <Property Name="Site" />
    <Property Name="Container" />
  </Object>
</Objects>
```

This simplifies the output even further. It makes sense if the target consumer for the generated document isn't a .NET-based application and therefore won't be able to do much with the type names.

The ConvertTo-XML cmdlet is useful for interoperation with non-PowerShell applications, but for PowerShell-to-PowerShell communication, too much information is lost. For the PowerShell-to-PowerShell scenario, a much better solution is to use the Export-Clixml and Import-Clixml cmdlets, which provide a way to save and restore collections of objects from the PowerShell environment with higher fidelity (less data loss) than the ConvertTo-Xml cmdlet.

The encoding the *-Clixml cmdlets use is what PowerShell remoting uses to send objects between hosts. To recap our discussion, we mentioned that only a small set of types serialize with fidelity and that other types are shredded into property bags. With the *-Clixml cmdlets, you can see what the encoding looks like. Let's try this out. First, create a collection of objects: a hashtable, a string, and some numbers. Then serialize them to a file using the Export-Clixml cmdlet:

```
PS> $data = @{a=1;b=2;c=3},"Hi there", 3.5
PS> $data | Export-Clixml -Path C:\test\out.xml
```

Let's see what the file looks like:

```
PS> Get-Content -Path C:\test\out.xml
<Objs Version="1.1.0.1" xmlns="http://schemas.microsoft.com/
  powershell/2004/04">
  <Obj RefId="0">
    <TN RefId="0">
      <T>System.Collections.Hashtable</T>
      <T>System.Object</T>
    </TN>
    <DCT>
      <En>
        <S N="Key">c</S>
        <I32 N="Value">3</I32>
      </En>
      <En>
        <S N="Key">b</S>
        <I32 N="Value">2</I32>
      </En>
      <En>
        <S N="Key">a</S>
        <I32 N="Value">1</I32>
      </En>
    </DCT>
  </Obj>
  <S>Hi there</S>
  <Db>3.5</Db>
</Objs>
```

You can use `Import-Clixml` to re-create the data. To show that the resultant object is identical to the original test with `Compare-Object`, do this:

```
PS> Compare-Object -ReferenceObject $data `
-DifferenceObject (Import-Clixml -Path C:\test\out.xml) `
-IncludeEqual

InputObject SideIndicator
----------- -------------
{c, b, a}   ==
Hi there    ==
3.5         ==
```

These cmdlets provide a simple way to save and restore collections of objects, but they have limitations. They can load and save only a fixed number of primitive types. Any other type is "shredded," which means it's broken apart into a property bag composed of these primitive types. This allows any type to be serialized but with some loss of fidelity. Objects can't be restored to exactly the same type they were originally. This approach is necessary because there can be an infinite number of object types, not all of which may be available when the file is read back. Sometimes you don't have the original type definition. Other times there's no way to re-create the original object, even with the type information, because the type doesn't support this operation. By restricting the set of types that are serialized with fidelity, the `Clixml` format can always recover objects regardless of the availability of the original type information.

There's also another limitation on how objects are serialized. An object has properties. Those properties are also objects that have their own properties, and so on. This chain of properties that have properties is called the *serialization depth*. For some of the complex objects in the system, such as the `Process` object, serializing through all the levels of the object results in a huge XML file. To constrain this, the serializer traverses only to a certain depth. The default depth is 2. You can override this default either on the command line using the `-Depth` parameter or by placing a `<Serial-izationDepth>` element in the type's description file. If you look at $PSHome/types.ps1xml, you can see some examples of where this has been done.

So far, we've discussed manipulating files, strings, and text data. Now we need to discuss how to convert text data into objects.

16.2.4 *Converting text output to objects*

One of the first things everyone learns about PowerShell is it works with objects. You can execute legacy command-line applications in the PowerShell console but you get text output, as shown in figure 16.6.

Converting the output from text to objects is possible, but it requires a lot of work and the results can be quite fragile if the application's output changes. Power-Shell v5 has a cmdlet—`ConvertFrom-String`—that makes these conversions much simpler. Referring to figure 16.6 as you progress through this section will clarify the code.

If you start by passing the output of `netstat` through `Convert-String`, you'll discover the first issue:

```
PS> netstat -n | ConvertFrom-String | Select-Object -First 5

P1      P2
--      --
Active Connections
        Proto
        TCP
        TCP
        TCP
```

The header line `Active Connections` is split to create two properties, `P1` and `P2`. The default delimiter is whitespace. The contents of the `Proto` (protocol) field are assigned to `P2` and all other data is dropped. Not quite what you wanted!

Let's skip the first three lines:

```
PS> netstat -n | select -Skip 3 | ConvertFrom-String
```

```
Administrator 64 bit C:\MyData\SkyDrive\Data\scripts                    —    □    ×

PS> netstat -n

Active Connections

  Proto  Local Address          Foreign Address         State
  TCP    10.10.54.200:49723     10.10.54.201:3389       ESTABLISHED
  TCP    192.168.0.5:49695      157.56.124.172:443      ESTABLISHED
  TCP    192.168.0.5:49744      157.56.194.8:443        ESTABLISHED
  TCP    192.168.0.5:50605      213.199.179.159:40026   CLOSE_WAIT
  TCP    192.168.0.5:50615      91.190.217.44:12350     CLOSE_WAIT
  TCP    192.168.0.5:50793      40.101.1.82:443         ESTABLISHED
  TCP    192.168.0.5:50800      91.190.219.143:443      ESTABLISHED
  TCP    192.168.0.5:50897      157.55.236.165:443      ESTABLISHED
  TCP    192.168.0.5:51105      157.56.194.7:443        ESTABLISHED
  TCP    192.168.0.5:51400      157.56.194.24:443       ESTABLISHED
  TCP    192.168.0.5:51578      54.230.9.20:443         CLOSE_WAIT
  TCP    192.168.0.5:51579      54.230.9.20:443         CLOSE_WAIT
  TCP    192.168.0.5:51582      54.230.9.20:443         CLOSE_WAIT
  TCP    192.168.0.5:51583      23.43.75.27:80          CLOSE_WAIT
  TCP    192.168.0.5:51586      23.202.173.98:80        ESTABLISHED
  TCP    192.168.0.5:51602      23.96.240.104:443       TIME_WAIT
  TCP    192.168.0.5:51610      204.79.197.200:443      ESTABLISHED
  TCP    192.168.0.5:51611      204.79.197.200:443      ESTABLISHED
  TCP    192.168.0.5:51612      204.79.197.200:443      ESTABLISHED
  TCP    192.168.0.5:51615      204.79.197.200:443      ESTABLISHED
  TCP    192.168.0.5:51880      132.245.226.242:443     ESTABLISHED
  TCP    192.168.0.5:51995      132.245.27.34:443       ESTABLISHED
  TCP    [::1]:51608            [::1]:51609             ESTABLISHED
  TCP    [::1]:51608            [::1]:51616             ESTABLISHED
  TCP    [::1]:51608            [::1]:51617             ESTABLISHED
  TCP    [::1]:51608            [::1]:51618             ESTABLISHED
  TCP    [::1]:51609            [::1]:51608             ESTABLISHED
  TCP    [::1]:51616            [::1]:51608             ESTABLISHED
  TCP    [::1]:51617            [::1]:51608             ESTABLISHED
  TCP    [::1]:51618            [::1]:51608             ESTABLISHED
PS>
```

Figure 16.6   Output of the netstat.exe legacy application

Each line of `netstat` output looks something like this:

```
P1 :
P2 : TCP
P3 : 10.10.54.200:49723
P4 : 10.10.54.201:3389
P5 : ESTABLISHED
```

The first set of outputs is the field headers. Notice that the properties are given consecutive names: P1, P2, P3, and so on. The next step is to discard the field header row and assign useful names to the properties:

```
PS> netstat -n | select -Skip 4 |
ConvertFrom-String -PropertyNames Protocol,
LocalAddress, ForeignAddress, State
```

The output is a number of objects of this form:

```
Protocol         :
LocalAddress     : TCP
ForeignAddress   : 10.10.54.200:49723
State            : 10.10.54.201:3389
P5               : ESTABLISHED
```

The properties are assigned incorrectly because there are multiple whitespaces at the beginning of each line. One way to deal with that is to assign a dummy property:

```
PS> netstat -n | select -Skip 4 |
ConvertFrom-String -PropertyNames Blank, Protocol,
LocalAddress, ForeignAddress, State
```

The output looks like this:

```
Blank            :
Protocol         : TCP
LocalAddress     : 10.10.54.200:49723
ForeignAddress   : 10.10.54.201:3389
State            : ESTABLISHED
```

You should filter out the `Blank` property because it's not required:

```
PS> netstat -n | select -Skip 4 |
ConvertFrom-String -PropertyNames Blank, Protocol,
LocalAddress, ForeignAddress, State |
Select-Object Protocol, LocalAddress, ForeignAddress, State
```

This will produce the output shown in figure 16.7.

Figures 16.6 and 16.7 look similar. The important point is now that you can convert the `netstat` output to objects, you can apply standard PowerShell techniques to filter the data. For example:

```
PS> $nso = netstat -n | select -Skip 4 |
ConvertFrom-String -PropertyNames Blank, Protocol, LocalAddress,
   ForeignAddress, State |
Select-Object Protocol, LocalAddress, ForeignAddress, State

PS> $nso.where({$_.State -eq 'ESTABLISHED'})
PS> $nso | sort State
PS> $nso | where LocalAddress -like '192.168.0.5*' | sort ForeignAddress
```

That closes our look at files and working with text data. It's time to turn your attention to the older COM object model and how you can work with it in PowerShell.

```
Administrator 64 bit C:\MyData\SkyDrive\Data\scripts            —    □    ×

PS> netstat -n | select -Skip 4 | ConvertFrom-String -PropertyName ^
rotocol, LocalAddress, ForeignAddress, State | Select-Object Proto
Address, ForeignAddress, State

Protocol LocalAddress         ForeignAddress        State
-------- ------------         --------------        -----
TCP      10.10.54.200:49723   10.10.54.201:3389     ESTABLISHED
TCP      192.168.0.5:2869     192.168.0.1:38129     TIME_WAIT
TCP      192.168.0.5:2869     192.168.0.1:38130     TIME_WAIT
TCP      192.168.0.5:49695    157.56.124.172:443    ESTABLISHED
TCP      192.168.0.5:49744    157.56.194.8:443      ESTABLISHED
TCP      192.168.0.5:50605    213.199.179.159:40026 CLOSE_WAIT
TCP      192.168.0.5:50615    91.190.217.44:12350   CLOSE_WAIT
TCP      192.168.0.5:50800    91.190.219.143:443    ESTABLISHED
TCP      192.168.0.5:50897    157.55.236.165:443    ESTABLISHED
TCP      192.168.0.5:51105    157.56.194.7:443      ESTABLISHED
TCP      192.168.0.5:51578    54.230.9.20:443       CLOSE_WAIT
TCP      192.168.0.5:51579    54.230.9.20:443       CLOSE_WAIT
TCP      192.168.0.5:51582    54.230.9.20:443       CLOSE_WAIT
TCP      192.168.0.5:51586    23.202.173.98:80      CLOSE_WAIT
TCP      192.168.0.5:51717    54.192.9.49:443       CLOSE_WAIT
TCP      192.168.0.5:51718    54.192.9.49:443       CLOSE_WAIT
TCP      192.168.0.5:51719    54.192.9.49:443       CLOSE_WAIT
TCP      192.168.0.5:51720    54.192.9.49:443       CLOSE_WAIT
TCP      192.168.0.5:51721    54.192.9.49:443       CLOSE_WAIT
TCP      192.168.0.5:51722    54.192.9.49:443       CLOSE_WAIT
TCP      192.168.0.5:51724    104.16.24.216:80      CLOSE_WAIT
TCP      192.168.0.5:51725    104.16.26.216:80      CLOSE_WAIT
TCP      192.168.0.5:51771    132.245.68.242:443    ESTABLISHED
TCP      192.168.0.5:51798    157.56.194.24:443     ESTABLISHED
TCP      192.168.0.5:51816    132.245.27.34:443     ESTABLISHED
TCP      192.168.0.5:51846    13.69.159.30:443      TIME_WAIT
TCP      192.168.0.5:51851    104.46.1.211:443      ESTABLISHED
TCP      192.168.0.5:51852    104.66.246.11:443     ESTABLISHED
TCP      192.168.0.5:51854    40.113.22.47:80       ESTABLISHED
TCP      192.168.0.5:51855    192.168.0.1:56688     TIME_WAIT
TCP      192.168.0.5:51856    192.168.0.1:56688     TIME_WAIT
TCP      192.168.0.5:51857    192.168.0.1:56688     TIME_WAIT
TCP      192.168.0.5:51858    192.168.0.1:56688     TIME_WAIT
TCP      192.168.0.5:51860    192.168.0.1:56688     TIME_WAIT
TCP      192.168.0.5:51861    192.168.0.1:56688     TIME_WAIT
TCP      192.168.0.5:51862    192.168.0.1:56688     TIME_WAIT
TCP      192.168.0.5:51863    192.168.0.1:56688     TIME_WAIT
TCP      192.168.0.5:51864    192.168.0.1:56688     TIME_WAIT
TCP      192.168.0.5:51866    192.168.0.1:56688     TIME_WAIT
TCP      192.168.0.5:51867    192.168.0.1:56688     TIME_WAIT
TCP      192.168.0.5:51868    192.168.0.1:56688     TIME_WAIT
TCP      192.168.0.5:51880    132.245.226.242:443   ESTABLISHED
```

Figure 16.7 Result of processing `netstat` **output with** `ConvertFrom-String`

16.3   *Accessing COM objects*

COM is an interface specification describing how to write libraries that can be used from multiple languages or environments. Prior to technologies like COM, each programming language required its own set of libraries. The COM specification allowed the creation of libraries of *components* that could be accessed from multiple languages. But beyond sharing library code, COM allowed running applications to expose automation interfaces that external programs could use to remotely control them. In this section, we'll introduce COM and show you how to leverage COM classes using PowerShell. COM provides easy (and in some cases trivial) access to many Windows features. We'll work through a number of examples in a variety of application scenarios, and we'll complete our COM coverage by examining some of the issues and limitations the PowerShell scripter may encounter.

CREATING COM OBJECTS

The first thing you need to know if you want to work with COM (or any other object system for that matter) is how to create instances of COM objects. As with .NET objects, you use the New-Object cmdlet, but for COM objects you have to specify the -ComObject parameter:

```
PS> $word = New-Object -ComObject 'Word.application'
```

Unlike .NET objects, COM doesn't have a way to pass arguments to the object's constructor, making it hard to initialize the object. As a workaround for this, in PowerShell v2 (and later) you use the -Property parameter on New-Object to initialize properties on the constructed object before returning it.

Unique to the COM parameter set is the -Strict switch. This switch tells the cmdlet to generate an error if a .NET/COM Interop library is loaded. In chapter 2, we talked about how the PowerShell type system uses *adaptation* to give the user a consistent experience with different kinds of objects. COM objects are one of these adapted types, but the way the PowerShell adapter works is affected by the presence or absence of a COM Interop library.

In effect, this Interop library is .NET's own adaptation layer for COM. The net effect is that the PowerShell COM adapter will project a different view of a COM object if an Interop library is loaded versus when there's not one. This becomes a problem because, for any given COM class on any given machine, there may or may not be an Interop library, so you may or may not get the doubly adapted COM object. If you want to be able to write scripts that behave consistently everywhere, you need a way to control how the adaptation is done. The -Strict parameter allows you to detect this when an Interop library is loaded. Once you know what's happening, you can decide whether you want to fail or continue but along a different code path. This kind of portability issue is something to keep in mind when you're writing a script using COM that you plan to deploy on other machines. But for now, let's move on to our next topic and see how to find out which COM classes are available.

IDENTIFYING AND LOCATING COM CLASSES

Officially, all COM classes are identified by a globally unique ID (GUID). This isn't a particularly friendly way to identify, well, anything. As far as PowerShell is concerned, COM objects are identified by a much more usable name called the *ProgID*. This is a string alias that's provided when the class is registered on the system. Using the ProgID is the most human-friendly way of identifying the object. By convention, the ProgID has the form

```
<Program>.<Component>.<Version>
```

which (at least according to the MSDN documentation) should be fewer than 39 characters in length.

> **NOTE** Although this format is the recommended way to create a ProgID, there's no real way to enforce it, resulting in some interesting interpretations of what each of the elements means. Generally, it seems in practice that <Program> is the application suite, toolset, or vendor that installed it; <component> is the COM class name; and the version number is normally not used in calls, though it may exist in even a multipart form.

COM objects are registered in (where else?) the Registry. This means that you can use the Registry provider to search for ProgIDs from PowerShell.

Listing 16.10 Discovering ProgIds

```
function Get-ProgId
{
    param (
        $filter = '.'
    )
    Get-ChildItem -Path 'REGISTRY::HKey_Classes_Root\clsid\*\progid' |
    foreach {if ($_.name -match '\\ProgID$') { $_.GetValue('') }} |
    Where-Object {$_ -match $filter}
}
```

Using the function with the default search filter

```
PS> Get-ProgId | Sort-Object
```

will return all available ProgIds. If you want to restrict the search—for instance, for the ProgId for Internet Explorer—use the filter:

```
PS> Get-ProgId -filter internet
```

> **NOTE** The CIM class Win32_ProgIDSpecification will return some but not all ProgIds. The safest option is to use the function in listing 16.10.

As with everything else in PowerShell, examples save thousands of words, so we'll show you examples of working with COM objects, starting with how to automate some Windows basic features.

AUTOMATING WINDOWS WITH COM

The `Shell.Application` class provides access to Windows Explorer and its capabilities. It allows automation of many shell tasks, like opening file browser windows, launching documents or the help system, finding printers, computers, or files, and so on. The first thing you need to do is create an instance of this class:

```
PS> $shell = New-Object -ComObject Shell.Application
```

As always in PowerShell, COM objects, like any other object type, can be examined using `Get-Member`. It's worth exploring the available methods; for instance, the `Explore()` method , which will launch an Explorer window on the path specified:

```
PS> $shell.Explore('C:\Temp\')
```

At this point, you should see something like figure 16.8. This method call opened an Explorer window in the Temp directory of the C: drive.

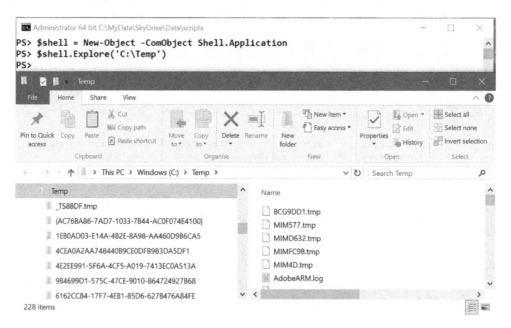

Figure 16.8   Launching Windows Explorer on C:\Temp

Here's a handy function for laptop users who move around a lot. Many laptops have docking stations that allow you to easily connect multiple peripherals. This is great except that you need to undock the laptop before heading to a meeting. Depending on the laptop, this can be annoying, so here's a quick one-line function to undock a laptop:

```
PS> function eject { ( New-Object -ComObject Shell.Application ).EjectPC()}
```

This function gets an instance of the `Shell.Application` object and then calls the `EjectPC()` method to undock the laptop.

The `Windows()` method on `Shell.Application` allows you to get a list of the Explorer and Internet Explorer windows that are currently open:

```
PS> $shell.Windows() | select Name, LocationURL
```

or you can index directly into the collection of Windows:

```
PS> $shell.Windows()[0] | select Name, LocationURL

Name            LocationURL
----            -----------
File Explorer   file:///C:/Temp
```

PowerShell 5.0 changes

Prior to PowerShell v5 you'd have received an error when trying to index into the collection of Windows:

```
PS> $shell.Windows()[0]
Unable to index into an object of type System.__ComObject.
At line:1 char:18
+ $shell.Windows()[0 <<<< ]
```

The error occurred because the PowerShell interpreter didn't know how to index these collections, because they consisted of the COM object inside a .NET wrapper, which was then adapted by PowerShell. You had to use this syntax:

```
PS> $shell.Windows().Item(0)
```

A number of changes were made to the way COM objects are processed during the development of PowerShell v5, including being able to understand the wrappers and so index into the collection.

The other big improvement was in processing speed. Utilizing COM objects could be glacially slow, in particular the Excel objects when writing to a spreadsheet. Power-Shell v5 shows a significant increase in processing speed for COM objects.

Closing a window requires the `Quit()` method:

```
PS> $shell.Windows()[3].Quit()
```

You can even close a set of windows in one pass:

```
PS> $shell.Windows() | where LocationURL -match 'amazon' |
foreach {$_.Quit()}
```

There are many other methods for you to explore using the Shell.Application class. But for now, we'll turn our attention to Microsoft Word.

USING MICROSOFT WORD FOR SPELL CHECKING

Wouldn't it be great if every environment you worked in had spell checking, like word processors do? With PowerShell and COM, you can get at least part of the way there. You're going to write a script that will use Microsoft Word to spell check the contents of the clipboard and then paste them back. You'll call this script Get-Spelling.ps1. Try this in both the PowerShell console and the ISE.

Let's see how it's used. First, put some text, with errors, on the clipboard:

```
PS> Set-Clipboard -Value 'Some text with errros'
```

Now run the function from listing 16.11:

```
PS> Test-Spelling
```

You'll see the Word Spelling dialog box pop up, as shown in figure 16.9.

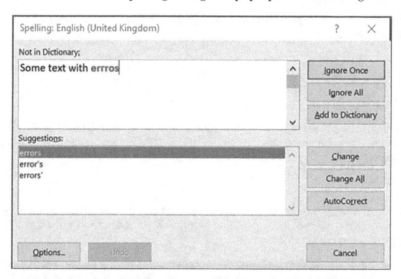

Figure 16.9   The Microsoft Word spell checker launched by the Test-Spelling function shows the misspelled text that was copied from the clipboard.

You need to go through all the spelling errors and fix them as appropriate. Once all the errors are fixed, the dialog box will disappear, and the pop-up box will be displayed, indicating that the revised text is available in the clipboard.

NOTE   The *-Clipboard cmdlets were introduced in PowerShell v5.

You can view the changed text:

```
PS> Get-Clipboard
Some text with errors
```

and you're finished. The text is correctly spelled. Now that you know how to use this script, let's look at the Test-Spelling code.

Listing 16.11   The Test-Spelling function

```
function Test-Spelling {
    $wshell = New-Object -ComObject WScript.Shell
    $word = New-Object -ComObject Word.Application
    $word.Visible = $false
    $doc = $word.Documents.Add()
    $word.Selection.Paste()

    if ($word.ActiveDocument.SpellingErrors.Count -gt 0)
    {
        $word.ActiveDocument.CheckSpelling()
        $word.Visible = $false
        $word.Selection.WholeStory()
        $word.Selection.Copy()
        $wshell.PopUp( 'The spell check is complete, ' +
        'the clipboard holds the corrected text.' )
    }
    else
    {
        [void] $wshell.Popup('No Spelling Errors were detected.')
    }

    $x = [ref] 0
    $word.ActiveDocument.Close($x)
    $word.Quit()
}
```

The first thing you do is create the object instances you're going to use. You need an instance of WScript.Shell to pop up a message box and the Word.Application object for the bulk of the work. Once you have the Word.Application object, you make the Word window invisible and then add an empty document to hold the text you want to spell-check.

Next, you copy the contents from the clipboard to the Word document you created and see if you need to spell check the text. If you do, you present the Spelling dialog box. When the spell check is complete, you select all the text and copy it back to the clipboard so you can paste it into the original document and inform the user that the corrected text is available. If there were no spelling errors, you'd display a message box confirming this. The last step is to discard the document you created and close the application. With this script, you can add spell-checking capabilities to any application that lets you select and copy text.

NOTE Obviously, if Microsoft Word isn't your word processor of choice, it should be simple to modify the script to work with any word processor that exports a similar automation model.

Using COM in PowerShell lets you automate applications, but there are also issues with COM support, which we'll cover in the next section.

ISSUES WITH COM

Support for COM in PowerShell is good but not perfect. In part, this is because Power-Shell depends on .NET, and .NET's support for COM is also not perfect. In this section, we'll explore a few problems that you may run into when using COM from PowerShell, including more information on the Interop assembly issue.

One problem that arises is that some COM objects are available only to 32-bit applications. On 64-bit systems, the 64-bit PowerShell binaries are run by default, so if you need to use a 32-bit–only COM object, you'll have to explicitly start the 32-bit version of PowerShell. This can also be an issue when using remoting because the default remoting configuration on 64-bit systems is 64-bit as well. To remotely run a script that requires a 32-bit COM object, you'll have to connect to the 32-bit configuration on the remote machine, regardless of whether the local system is 32- or 64-bit.

Another thing that can potentially cause problems has to do with the way the COM object has been wrapped or adapted. There are three possible categories of COM objects you may encounter: a COM object that has a .NET Interop library, a COM object that has a type library (commonly called a typelib) but no Interop assembly, and a COM object that has neither.

In the first category, you get a COM object that has been wrapped in a .NET Interop wrapper. This wrapper may introduce changes in the object's interface or behavior that affect how you work with that object compared to the raw COM object. For this reason, the New-Object cmdlet's ComObject parameter set has an additional parameter, -Strict, that causes a nonterminating error to be written if an Interop assembly is loaded. Let's look at examples. Start by creating an instance of the Word.Application object you used earlier:

```
PS> $word = New-Object -ComObject Word.Application
```

Now try it again but with the -Strict parameter:

```
PS> $word = New-Object -ComObject Word.Application -Strict
New-Object : The object written to the pipeline is an instance of the type
    "Microsoft.Office.Interop.Word.ApplicationClass"  from the component's
    primary interoperability assembly. If this type exposes different members
    than the IDispatch members, scripts that are written to work with this
    object might not work if the primary interoperability assembly is not
    installed.
At line:1 char:9
+ $word = New-Object -ComObject Word.Application -Strict
+         ~~~~~~~~~~~~~~~~~~~~~~~~~~~~~~~~~~~~~~~~~~~~~~~~
```

```
  + CategoryInfo           : InvalidArgument: (Microsoft.Offic...pplication
Class:ApplicationClass) [New-Object], PSArgument
Exception
  + FullyQualifiedErrorId : ComInteropLoaded,Microsoft.PowerShell.Commands.
NewObjectCommand
```

You get a detailed error message explaining that the object that was loaded is a wrapped object. Note that this is a nonterminating error message, so the object is still returned and execution proceeds. Here's how to use this feature to write a script that can adapt its behavior appropriately.

First, you don't want the error message to appear in the output of your script, so redirect it to $null. But even when you do this, the $? variable, which indicates whether the last command executed was successful, is still set to $false so you know that an error occurred:

```
PS> $word = New-Object -ComObject Word.Application -Strict 2> $null
PS> $?
False
```

A script should check this variable and take an alternate action for the wrapped and nonwrapped cases. Investigating further, let's see what was returned by the call to New-Object:

```
PS> $word.GetType().Fullname
Microsoft.Office.Interop.Word.ApplicationClass
```

The output shows that the object is an instance of the Interop assembly mentioned earlier.

Next, look at an object for which there's no Interop assembly and see how that behaves differently. Create an instance of the Shell.Application class you worked with earlier:

```
PS> $shell = New-Object -ComObject Shell.Application
PS> $shell | Get-Member

   TypeName: System.__ComObject#{efd84b2d-4bcf-4298-be25-eb
542a59fbda}

Name              MemberType Definition
----              ---------- ----------
AddToRecent       Method     void AddToRecent (Varian...
BrowseForFolder   Method     Folder BrowseForFolder (...
:
```

In this situation, you see that the type of the object is System.__ComObject followed by the GUID of the registered type library. This type library allows you to see the members on the object but doesn't affect the object's behavior.

There is another type of object you need to consider: those created using CIM.

16.4   *Using CIM*

CIM is an industry standard (a set of related standards) created by Microsoft, HP, IBM, and many other computer companies with the goal of defining a common set of management abstractions. By creating interoperable *common models* for managed elements like services, processes, or CPUs, you can start to build management tools and processes that can be applied universally. WMI is Microsoft's original implementation of CIM.

> **NOTE**   In this section we'll show you how the CIM cmdlets work. If you want to dig deeper into CIM (WMI), you should read *PowerShell and WMI* by Richard Siddaway (Manning Publications, 2012), which covers the WMI and CIM cmdlets and how to use them to administer Windows systems.

There are standard ways of wrapping bits of management data in a well-defined package so you can work with this data across different vendors and environments in a consistent way; these are the standard or base CIM classes. To support environment-specific extensions, CIM also allows vendors to create derived classes of the CIM base classes that can surface nonstandard features as a set of extensions while still preserving the common base characteristics of the model. The goal of all this is to make it easier to create system administration tools (and, by corollary, system administrators) that can work effectively in heterogeneous environments. In the next section, we'll look at how the CIM/WMI infrastructure facilitates these goals.

CIM and WMI

One point of confusion that needs to be cleared up immediately is the difference between CIM and WMI. The short and simple answer is that there isn't any difference.

CIM is a standard created by the Distributed Management Task Force (DMTF) to provide a common definition of management information across computers, networks, applications, and services; see www.dmtf.org/standards/cim. The DMTF defines CIM like this:

"CIM provides a common definition of management information for systems, networks, applications, and services, and allows for vendor extensions. CIM's common definitions enable vendors to exchange semantically rich management information between systems throughout the network."

WMI is the name Microsoft gave its original implementation of the CIM standard.

The new API and cmdlets introduced with PowerShell v3 use the CIM prefix to distinguish them from the WMI cmdlets introduced in PowerShell v1 and v2. The WMI cmdlets use DCOM (Distributed Component Object Model) to connect to remote machines. The newer CIM cmdlets use WS-MAN for remote connectivity in a similar way to PowerShell remoting.

PowerShell has supported CIM since version 1.0; in fact, `Get-WmiObject` was the only cmdlet in the original PowerShell version that had the capability to access remote machines. The level of CIM support in PowerShell has increased with subsequent versions. This section will explain what CIM is, how to access it from PowerShell, and what you can do with CIM once you have this access. You'll work through a number of examples to see how things work, exploring the sorts of tasks that can be accomplished.

PowerShell v3 introduced a new API and cmdlets for working with WMI. Usually referred to as the CIM cmdlets, they have the ability to create and use connections to remote machines in a similar manner to PowerShell remoting. We'll concentrate on the CIM cmdlets in this section rather than the older WMI cmdlets. The CIM cmdlets support both the original WMI providers and the newer APIs, as shown in figure 16.10.

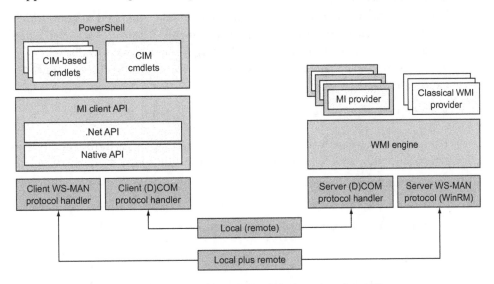

Figure 16.10 CIM cmdlet support for original WMI providers and modern API

16.4.1 The CIM cmdlets

The CimCmdlets module supplies a number of cmdlets for working with CIM, as shown in table 16.2. The equivalent WMI cmdlet is provided where applicable.

Table 16.2 The CIM cmdlets and their purpose compared with the WMI cmdlets

CIM cmdlet	Purpose	Equivalent WMI cmdlet
`Get-CimClass`	Retrieves CIM class structure	None
`Get-CimInstance`	Retrieves objects from CIM	`Get-WmiObject`
`Get-CimAssociatedInstance`	Retrieves associated CIM instances	None
`Invoke-CimMethod`	Invokes a method on a CIM class	`Invoke-WmiMethod`
`New-CimInstance`	Creates a new instance of a CIM class	None

Table 16.2 The CIM cmdlets and their purpose compared with the WMI cmdlets *(continued)*

CIM cmdlet	Purpose	Equivalent WMI cmdlet
Register -CimIndicationEvent	Subscribes to events surfaced through CIM	Register-WmiEvent
Remove-CimInstance	Removes a CIM instance from the repository	Remove-WmiObject
Set-CimInstance	Sets the properties of a CIM instance	SetWmiInstance

FINDING CIM CLASSES

Before you can use Get-CimInstance to retrieve data, you need to know which class to use. CIM is a *self-describing* technology, which means it provides ways for a client application to ask the object manager on the target system what's available. Get-CimClass leverages these mechanisms. For example, to see all of the classes with BIOS in their name, use this:

```
PS> Get-CimClass -ClassName *bios*
```

The output shows each of the available class names along with the methods and properties defined by those classes. Let's look at a specific class:

```
PS> Get-CimClass -ClassName Win32_Bios

   NameSpace: ROOT/cimv2

CimClassName CimClassMethods CimClassProperties
------------ --------------- ------------------
Win32_BIOS   {}              {Caption, Description ...}
```

As you saw with .NET, the amount of information returned from the commands is frequently enough for your purposes, but all the standard classes that Microsoft includes with Windows are well documented on MSDN: http://mng.bz/43Da.

This documentation includes many examples showing how to use classes. Many of the examples are written in VBScript, although this is becoming less true over time. CIM classes are arranged in namespaces. In the previous output, you saw

```
   NameSpace: ROOT\cimv2
```

indicating that the classes listed were located in this namespace. Because this is PowerShell's default namespace, you haven't needed to use the -Namespace parameter yet. All classes are identified by a path of this form:

```
\\<computer>\<namespace>\<namespace>:<class>
```

> **NOTE** The vast majority of CIM classes that you'll use on a regular basis live in the root\cimv2 namespace. PowerShell treats this as the default namespace,

which is why you don't force the use of the `-Namespace` parameter. Because the `-ClassName` parameter is positional, many CIM commands can be written as `Get-CimInstance Win32_Bios`.

Namespaces can contain nested namespaces and classes. The set of CIM namespaces and classes available on a machine depends on what's installed on that machine (both applications and operating system).

SELECTING CIM INSTANCES

Table 16.2 shows that `Get-CimInstance` (equivalent to the older `Get-WmiObject`) is used to retrieve data from the CIM repository. If you're dealing with the default namespace, the cmdlet is used like this:

```
PS> Get-CimInstance -ClassName Win32_Bios

SMBIOSBIOSVersion : 2.05.0250
Manufacturer      : American Megatrends Inc.
Name              : 2.05.0250
SerialNumber      : 036685734653
Version           : OEMA - 1072009
```

To run this same command against a remote computer, you have to add the `-Computer-Name` parameter to the command. You get this:

```
PS> Get-CimInstance -ClassName Win32_Bios -ComputerName W510W16

SMBIOSBIOSVersion : 6NET61WW (1.24 )
Manufacturer      : LENOVO
Name              : Ver 1.00PARTTBLX
SerialNumber      : R81BG3K
Version           : LENOVO - 1240
PSComputerName    : W510W16
```

CIM cmdlet connectivity

The CIM cmdlets use different protocols to connect to systems depending on the scenario:

- Local machine (no use of `-ComputerName`) = COM
- Local machine using `-ComputerName` = WS-MAN
- Remote machine using `-ComputerName` = WS-MAN
- Remote machine using CIM session = WS-MAN
- Remote machine using CIM session using DCOM protocol = DCOM

If you want to restrict the data returned from a CIM call, the most efficient way is to use the `-Filter` parameter:

```
PS> Get-CimInstance -ClassName Win32_NetworkAdapterConfiguration `
-ComputerName W510W16 -Filter "DHCPEnabled = $true"
```

This is the equivalent of using a WMI Query Language (WQL) query:

```
PS> Get-CimInstance -ComputerName W510W16 `
-Query "SELECT * FROM Win32_NetworkAdapterConfiguration
WHERE DHCPEnabled = $true"
```

The -Filter parameter takes the part of the WQL query after the WHERE keyword.

Like .NET and COM objects, WMI objects have methods. You'll see how to invoke these methods in the next section.

INVOKING CIM METHODS

CIM classes can have both static or class members and object or instance members. Static methods are the easier types to call because you only need the class name, method name, and arguments to call. Instance methods are more complex because you need to specify additional information to identify which instance of the target class to invoke the method on.

As our test case for static methods, let's use the static Create() method on the Win32_Process class to create an instance of (start) a process—in this case, calc.exe. The command to do that looks like this:

```
PS> Invoke-CimMethod -ClassName Win32_Process -MethodName Create `
-Arguments @{CommandLine = 'calc.exe'}

ProcessId ReturnValue PSComputerName
--------- ----------- --------------
     3620           0
```

If the method call is successful, then the ReturnValue will be 0, indicating success. Any other value indicates failure and the error. The ProcessID will contain the process ID or handle of the new process. The arguments for the method are supplied as a hashtable. If you have multiple arguments, separate them with a semicolon (;):

```
PS> Invoke-CimMethod -ClassName Win32_Process -MethodName Create `
-Arguments @{CommandLine = 'notepad.exe'; CurrentDirectory = 'C:\test'}
```

The easiest way to invoke an instance method is to get the instance and pass it to Invoke-CimMethod:

```
PS> Get-CimInstance -ClassName Win32_Process -Filter "Name='calculator.exe'"
   | Invoke-CimMethod -MethodName Terminate
```

A filter identifies the individual process, which is then passed to Invoke-CimMethod, and the Terminate() method is called. The process is shut down.

DELETING CIM INSTANCES

The Remove-CimInstance cmdlet can be used to delete instances. You could use this instead of calling the Terminate() method:

```
PS> Get-CimInstance -ClassName Win32_Process -Filter "Name='calculator.exe'" |
Remove-CimInstance
```

The final action you may need to take on a CIM instance is to modify its properties.

MODIFYING CIM INSTANCES

Many of the properties on CIM classes are read-only; you can't alter them. You can check if an individual property is read-only like this:

```
PS> (Get-CimClass -ClassName Win32_OperatingSystem).
CimClassProperties['Manufacturer']

Name                : Manufacturer
Value               :
CimType             : String
Flags               : Property, ReadOnly, NullValue
Qualifiers          : {MappingStrings, read}
ReferenceClassName  :
```

If you want to see all the read-only properties, use this:

```
PS> Get-CimClass -ClassName Win32_OperatingSystem |
select -ExpandProperty CimClassProperties |
where Flags -like '*ReadOnly*' |
select Name, CimType
```

Conversely, if you want to see the properties, you can change the `-like` operator to `-notlike` in the previous code. This shows that on the `Win32_OperatingSystem` class you can modify the `Description` and `ForegroundApplicationBoost` properties.

How do you modify a property value on a CIM instance? The clue is in the question. You use `Set-CimInstance`. Let's start by creating an environment variable:

```
PS> New-CimInstance -ClassName Win32_Environment -Property @{
Name = 'PiAvar';
VariableValue = 'PiA 2017';
UserName = "$($env:COMPUTERNAME)\bpayette"}

Name            UserName                    VariableValue
----            --------                    -------------
PiAvar          LAPTOPO2\bpayette           PiA 2017
```

Modify the value assigned to the variable:

```
PS> Get-CimInstance -ClassName Win32_Environment `
-Filter "Name = 'PiAvar'" |
Set-CimInstance -Property @{VariableValue='What about next year?'} `
-PassThru

Name            UserName                    VariableValue
----            --------                    -------------
PiAvar          LAPTOPO2\bpayette           What about next year?
```

The majority of the time when you're accessing CIM data, you're going to be working with remote machines. When using PowerShell remoting to access remote machines (see chapter 11) you can create connections (remoting sessions) that can be used many times. An analogous situation exists when using the CIM cmdlets.

16.4.2 CIM sessions

Creating and destroying links from your administration machine to a remote machine is an expensive proposition. You need to get the maximum return from creating that connection. PowerShell remoting enables you to create a persistent session you can reuse. In a similar manner, the CIM cmdlets have an option to use a CIM session.

> **NOTE** You can't copy files over a CIM session as you can in a PowerShell v5 remoting session.

A CIM session is similar to a PowerShell remoting session in that it's based on WS-MAN (by default) but is designed to be utilized by the CIM-based cmdlets and connects to a different endpoint (the WMI provider).

You create CIM sessions by passing one or more computer names to the `New-Cim-Session` cmdlet:

```
PS> $computers = 'W16DSC01', 'W16AS01'
PS> $cs = New-CimSession -ComputerName $computers
```

The CIM session object contains the computer name and the protocol:

```
PS> Get-CimSession -ComputerName W16DSC01

Id           : 1
Name         : CimSession1
InstanceId   : 864bb2cf-3b08-4d65-8d0f-00f857f0a7a9
ComputerName : W16DSC01
Protocol     : WSMAN
```

The session information is passed to the cmdlet through the `-CimSession` parameter:

```
PS> Get-CimInstance -CimSession $cs -ClassName Win32_OperatingSystem |
select SystemDirectory, BuildNumber, Version, PSComputerName

SystemDirectory     BuildNumber Version PSComputerName
---------------     ----------- ------- --------------
C:\Windows\system32 9600        6.3.9600 W16DSC01
C:\Windows\system32 9600        6.3.9600 W16AS01
```

CIM sessions need WS-MAN 3.0 (introduced with PowerShell v3). If you try to access a machine running PowerShell v2 (which used WS-MAN 2.0), you'll get an error:

```
PS> $cs2 = New-CimSession -ComputerName W8R2STD01
PS> Get-CimInstance -CimSession $cs2 -ClassName Win32_OperatingSystem |
select SystemDirectory, BuildNumber, Version, PSComputerName

Get-CimInstance : The WS-Management service cannot process the request. A
    DMTF resource URI was used to access a non-DMTF class. Try again using a
    non-DMTF resource URI.
At line:1 char:1
+ Get-CimInstance -CimSession $cs2 -ClassName Win32_OperatingSystem | s ...
+ ~~~~~~~~~~~~~~~~~~~~~~~~~~~~~~~~~~~~~~~~~~~~~~~~~~~~~~~~~~~~~~~~~~~~~~~~
    + CategoryInfo          : NotSpecified: (root\cimv2:Win32_
```

```
OperatingSystem:String) [Get-CimInstance], CimException
  + FullyQualifiedErrorId : HRESULT 0x80338139,Microsoft.Management.
Infrastructure.CimCmdlets.GetCimInstanceCommand
  + PSComputerName        : W8R2STD01
```

The problem is that PowerShell v2 used WS-MAN 2.0. You can overcome this issue by creating a DCOM-based CIM session:

```
PS> $opt = New-CimSessionOption -Protocol Dcom
PS> $csd = New-CimSession -ComputerName W8R2STD01 -SessionOption $opt
PS> $csd

Id          : 4
Name        : CimSession4
InstanceId  : 2de6064f-f018-4b71-8d80-95fe2413089c
ComputerName : W8R2STD01
Protocol    : DCOM
```

The DCOM-based CIM session is used in exactly the same manner as a WS-MAN session:

```
PS> Get-CimInstance -CimSession $csd -ClassName Win32_OperatingSystem |
select SystemDirectory, BuildNumber, Version, PSComputerName

SystemDirectory     BuildNumber Version  PSComputerName
---------------     ----------- -------  --------------
C:\Windows\system32 7601        6.1.7601 W8R2STD01
```

Once you have a CIM session created, the CIM cmdlets will use WS-MAN- and DCOM-based sessions together:

```
PS> Get-CimInstance -CimSession ($cs + $csd) `
-ClassName Win32_OperatingSystem |
select SystemDirectory, BuildNumber, Version, PSComputerName

SystemDirectory     BuildNumber Version  PSComputerName
---------------     ----------- -------  --------------
C:\Windows\system32 7601        6.1.7601 W8R2STD01
C:\Windows\system32 9600        6.3.9600 W16DSc01
C:\Windows\system32 9600        6.3.9600 W16AS01
```

NOTE You can create a DCOM-based CIM session to machines running WS-MAN 3.0 if required.

Many of the cmdlets in Windows 8.0 and later are created using Cmdlet Definition XML (CDXML). The cmdlets in the NetAdapter and NetTCPIP modules are good examples.

NOTE CDXML-based cmdlets are created using the cmdlets-over-objects technology introduced in PowerShell v3. In this case, you wrap the CIM class in the appropriate XML and publish as a PowerShell module. The CIM class must be on the remote machine for these cmdlets to work remotely.

If you look at the syntax of those cmdlets, you'll see that they have a -CimSession parameter but don't have a -ComputerName parameter. This is an artifact of the way they're created. You have to use CIM sessions when using these cmdlets against remote machines. You can use a computer name as a value to the -CimSession parameter—it creates a session to the remote machine, executes the command, and then removes the session. If you're making multiple CIM calls to the same machine, it's more efficient to use a CIM session.

That concludes our investigation of using CIM through PowerShell and closes this chapter.

16.5 *Summary*

- PowerShell providers supply a file system–like experience for other data stores.
- Providers are exposed as PowerShell drives.
- Core cmdlets work across providers.
- The LiteralPath parameter suppresses pattern-matching behavior.
- Use the *Content cmdlets to work with text files.
- Get-Content has -Head and -Tail parameters to read the beginning and end of files.
- Advanced string handling can be performed using the [string] and [regex] classes.
- Use Select-String to search string data.
- XML documents have to be created manually.
- Select-Xml uses XPath queries.
- ConvertFrom-String can convert text output from legacy applications to objects.
- COM objects can be accessed from PowerShell.
- COM processing speed is greatly increased in PowerShell v5.
- The CIM cmdlets should be used in preference to the older WMI cmdlets.
- Use Get-CimClass to discover CIM classes, methods, and properties.
- CIM sessions provide a persistent connection to remote machines.
- CIM sessions use WS-MAN by default; DCOM is available as an option for connecting to PowerShell v2 systems.

In the next chapter, we'll continue our investigation of how PowerShell works with data when we look at using .NET and events.

17

Working with .NET and events

This chapter covers

- .NET and PowerShell
- Real-time events

I love it when a plan comes together!

—Col. John "Hannibal" Smith, The A-Team

The good news is that PowerShell is .NET -based and works with .NET objects. The not-quite-so-good news is that not all of .NET is immediately available when you open PowerShell. Some .NET functionality is available through cmdlets—for the rest you need to access the .NET classes in your code. PowerShell doesn't load the entire .NET framework, so you'll need to load assemblies before you can use them. Once an assembly is loaded, you have access to the rich .NET functionality, including creating graphical applications in PowerShell.

> **NOTE** PowerShell v6 uses .NET core which has further restrictions as described in the appendix.

Windows is an event-based system. You can use PowerShell to access events from a number of sources. Your scripts can then either display information about the event or take action based on the event.

We'll start with .NET before moving on to events.

17.1   .NET and PowerShell

The original PowerShell concept was to have cmdlets for every task, but that goal wasn't achievable in the time frame available for the release of PowerShell v1. Instead, the team made the decision to make it easier to work directly with the .NET Framework. That way, although it might not be as easy to do everything the way the team wanted, at least it would be possible.

In retrospect, this may have been one of the best things to happen to PowerShell. Not only did the team backfill their original scenarios, but the set of problem domains (such as creating GUIs) in which PowerShell was applicable greatly exceeded original expectations.

17.1.1   Using .NET from PowerShell

We're assuming that you have a basic understanding of .NET. If you're new to .NET or need a refresher, we recommend you read http://mng.bz/RIvK before reading the rest of this chapter. The basic arrangement of entities in .NET is as follows: members (properties, methods, and so on) are contained in types (classes, structs, and interfaces) which are, in turn, grouped into namespaces.

The arrangement of types into classes and namespaces is called *logical type* containment. You also need to understand *physical type* containment. Where do these collections of types live on a computer? This organization is done through the assemblies we mentioned earlier. An *assembly* is a file stored somewhere so that the program loader can find it when needed. Each assembly contains the definitions for one or more types. Because a set of types is contained in an assembly, clearly the set of assemblies that's loaded determines the complete set of types available to you. PowerShell loads most of the assemblies you'll need for day-to-day work by default when it starts, but sometimes (like when you want to do GUI programming) you'll have to load additional assemblies.

VERSIONING AND ASSEMBLIES

With .NET, Microsoft tried to solve some of the problems with assemblies, in particular the issue of versioning of DLLs. In effect, an assembly is a DLL with additional metadata in the form of an *assembly manifest.*

This assembly manifest lists the contents of the DLL as well as the name of the DLL. The full (or strong) name for an assembly is a complex beast and warrants some discussion. To try to solve some of the identity and versioning problems, .NET introduced the idea of a *strong name.* As well as the assembly filename, a strong name uses public key cryptography to add information that will allow you to validate the identity of the DLL author. When a .NET program is linked against a strong-named assembly, it will run only if *exactly the same assembly* it was linked against is present. Replacing the file won't work, because the strong name will be wrong.

One more thing that's included in the strong name is the version number. The result is that when the DLL is loaded, the correct version must always be loaded even if later versions are available. But it also means that to service the assembly to fix bugs, you can't change the version number of the assembly because the version number is part of the strong name. You end up with two versions of an assembly with the same version number. The net effect of all of this is that .NET didn't solve the versioning problem—it merely moved things around a bit.

THE DEFAULT POWERSHELL ASSEMBLIES

Now let's talk about how PowerShell finds types and assemblies. All compiled programs contain a list of assemblies needed for the program to execute. This list is created as part of the linking phase when the program is compiled. When the program executes, the referenced assemblies are loaded automatically as needed. When the system tries to locate a required assembly, the loader performs a process called *probing* to find that assembly. It looks in a number of places automatically; the most important one is the global assembly cache (GAC). If an assembly has been installed in the GAC, you don't have to care where it is—the system will find it for you as long as you know its name.

Because the PowerShell interpreter is a compiled program, it also contains a list of required assemblies. Through the automatic loading mechanism, all these assemblies and the types they contain are available to PowerShell scripts by default.

You can view the assemblies PowerShell loads by default by opening a new Power-Shell console (ensures only defaults are loaded) and running:

```
PS> [System.AppDomain]::CurrentDomain.GetAssemblies() |
sort Fullname | select Fullname
```

The `AppDomain` class is .NET's way of encapsulating an isolated execution environment. It's similar in some ways to PowerShell sessions but even more isolated. For example, each `AppDomain` can have its own set of assemblies, whereas `PSSessions` all share the same assemblies. The static `CurrentDomain` property lets you access the domain you're executing in, and `GetAssemblies()` gives you the list of assemblies currently loaded into the `AppDomain`.

> **NOTE** You'll see an extended set of assemblies if you run the code in PowerShell ISE as opposed to the console.

Once you have the list of assemblies, you can use the `GetTypes()` and `GetExported-Types()` methods on each assembly object to get all the types in that assembly. The `Get-ExportedTypes()` method gives you all the public types, which is usually what you want. `GetTypes()` returns both public and private types, which is primarily useful for exploring how things are organized below the public façade. The function in the following listing gets the full names of all of the public types in each assembly and matches them against the pattern provided in the function argument (which defaults to matching everything).

Listing 17.1   Getting exported types from .NET assemblies

```
function Get-Type {
    [CmdletBinding()]
    param (
        [string]$Pattern='.'
    )
```

```
        [System.AppDomain]::CurrentDomain.GetAssemblies() |
        Sort-Object FullName |
        foreach{
            $asm = $psitem
            Write-Verbose $asm.Fullname

            switch ($asm.Fullname) {
                {$_ -like
            'Anonymously Hosted DynamicMethods Assembly*'}{break}
                {$_ -like
            'Microsoft.PowerShell.Cmdletization.GeneratedTypes*'}
            {break}
                    {$_ -like  'Microsoft.Management.Infrastructure.
              UserFilteredExceptionHandling*'}
              {break}
                    {$_ -like 'Microsoft.GeneratedCode*'}{break}
                    {$_ -like 'MetadataViewProxies*'}{break}
                    default {
                        $asm.GetExportedTypes() |
                        Where-Object {$_ -match $Pattern} |
                        Select-Object @{N='Assembly';
                        E={($_.Assembly -split ',')[0]}},
                        IsPublic, IsSerial,FullName, BaseType
                    }
                }
            }
        }
}
```

Use the function like this:

```
PS> Get-Type -Pattern '^system\.timers' |
Format-Table Assembly, IsPublic, Fullname

Assembly IsPublic FullName
-------- -------- --------
System        True System.Timers.ElapsedEventArgs
System        True System.Timers.ElapsedEventHandler
System        True System.Timers.Timer
System        True System.Timers.TimersDescriptionAttribute
```

Add the -Verbose switch on Get-Type to see the list of assemblies that are scanned as well as the results.

DYNAMIC ASSEMBLY LOADING

Automatic loading applies only to compiled programs like Notepad.exe or PowerShell .exe because it depends on the required assembly list contained in the executable. PowerShell scripts are interpreted and have no compile or "static" link phase, so if you want to make sure that an assembly you need is loaded, you have to explicitly load it. In chapter 10, you saw how to do this with module manifests; you add the list of required assemblies to the RequiredAssemblies manifest element. In effect, module manifests are the dynamic equivalent to the static manifest found in an assembly. But with simple scripts you don't have a manifest, so in this case you'll use the `Add-Type` cmdlet—the "Swiss Army knife cmdlet"—for dealing with assemblies and compiled code.

> **NOTE** You'll see numerous examples where `[system.reflection.assembly]` `::LoadWithPartialName` is used to load an assembly. This is a hangover from PowerShell v1 and shouldn't be used because the `LoadWithPartialName` method is obsolete.

You can dynamically load assemblies by name. You can even use wildcards in the assembly name (but an error is generated if more than one assembly filename matches the pattern). For example, to load the Windows Forms assembly (`winforms`) that's in `System.Windows.Forms`, instead of the full name, you can use:

```
PS> Add-Type -AssemblyName System*forms
```

This works because `Add-Type` has a fixed list of short names that correspond to specific versions of the .NET Framework assemblies. `Add-Type` will allow you to use the short name only for assemblies that are on this list. If it's not on the list, you have to use the strong name for the assembly. For `winforms`, the strong name looks like

```
"System.Windows.Forms, Version=2.0.0.0, Culture=neutral, PublicKeyToken=b77a5
   c561934e089"
```

which is a bit unwieldy. Still, as long as you stick to the assemblies Microsoft ships with Windows, you can use the short names and a wildcard. If you choose a non-Windows assembly, you have to use the full name.

Creating your own types

You can create your own types using C#, Visual Basic, or JScript and then use `Add -Type` to compile them into your PowerShell session.

In PowerShell v5 you can create classes in PowerShell, which we cover in chapter 19.

CREATING INSTANCES OF TYPES

Now that you can find types, you generally need to create instances of these types to use their properties and methods (although there are some types such as `[System .Math]` that have only static members and so don't require instantiation). For example, before you can search using the `[regex]` type, you need to create an instance of that type from a pattern string. As you saw in earlier chapters, you can use the `New-Object` cmdlet to create instances of types in PowerShell.

This cmdlet takes the name of the type to create, a list of parameters to pass to the type's constructor, and a hashtable of property name/values to set on the object once it has been constructed.

THE NEW-OBJECT -PROPERTY PARAMETER

The -Property parameter allows individual properties to be set on the object after it has been constructed. In many cases, doing so can greatly simplify the code needed to completely initialize an object. For a simple example, let's create a Timer object:

```
PS> New-Object -TypeName System.Timers.Timer -Property @{
 AutoReset = $true
 Interval = 500
 Enabled = $true
}

AutoReset           : True
Enabled             : True
Interval            : 500
Site                :
SynchronizingObject :
Container           :
```

In this example, you're creating the object and then setting three properties—Auto-Reset, Interval, and Enabled—in a single statement. Without -Property, you'd have to create an intermediate variable and use four statements. We need to explain some more cautions.

A WORD OF CAUTION ABOUT USING NEW-OBJECT

Although the signature for the New-Object cmdlet is pretty simple, it can be more difficult to use than you might think. People who are accustomed to programming in languages such as C# have a tendency to use this cmdlet like the new operator in those languages. As a consequence, they tend to write expressions like this:

```
PS> $x = 'a', 'b', 'c', 'd', 'e', 'f', 'g', 'h'
PS> New-Object string($x,1,3)
```

Unfortunately, writing the expression this way obscures the fact that it's a cmdlet, making things confusing. It'll work fine, but it looks too much like a function call in other programming languages, and that leads people to misinterpret what's happening. The syntax for New-Object is as follows:

```
New-Object [-TypeName] <String> [[-ArgumentList] <Object[]>]
```

That means the previous example could be written like this:

```
PS> New-Object -TypeName string -ArgumentList $x,1,3
```

The comma notation indicates an argument that's passed as an array. This is equivalent to

```
PS> $constructor_arguments= $x,1,3
PS> New-Object string $constructor_arguments
```

NOTE You're not wrapping `$constructor_arguments` in yet another array. If you want to pass an array as a single value, you need to do it yourself and write it in parentheses with the unary comma operator.

WORKING WITH GENERIC TYPES

With version 2.0 of .NET, a feature was added to the CLR type system called *generic types* (or *generics*). Generics introduce the idea of a *type parameter*. Instead of passing objects as arguments when creating an instance of type, generics also require you to pass in *type parameters* that are used to determine the final types of some part of the object. This concept is rather confusing if you haven't encountered it. As usual, an example should make things clearer.

Generics are easiest to understand when you talk about creating collections. Before the introduction of generics, if you wanted to create a collection class, you had to either write a new version of the class for each type of object you wanted it to store or you had to allow it to hold any type of object, which meant you had to do your own error checking. With generics, you can write a collection that can be constrained to contain only integers or strings or hashtables. Let's look at examples.

We'll start by creating a list—specifically, a list of integers. To do this, you need to know the base type of the collection and the type parameter you need to pass when creating an instance of the collection. The base type you're going to use is `System .Collections.Generic.List`, which takes a single type argument. To create an instance of the collection, you pass the closed type name to `New-Object`. By *closed*, we mean that a concrete type has been specified as the type parameter. For a collection of integers, this looks like

```
PS> $ilist = New-Object System.Collections.Generic.List[int]
```

where the name in the square brackets is the type parameter. You can use other types as well. To create a list of strings, you'd write

```
PS> $slist = New-Object System.Collections.Generic.List[string]
```

You can even use generics in the type parameter:

```
PS> $nlist = New-Object `
System.Collections.Generic.List[System.Collections.Generic.List[int]]
```

This example defines a list of lists of integers. In general, nested generic types are discouraged because they quickly become difficult to understand.

So far, we've dealt with only a single type parameter, but generics can take as many type parameters as are needed. For example, a generic dictionary, which is similar to our old friend the hashtable, takes two type parameters: the type of the key and the type of the value. This looks like

```
PS> $stoi = New-Object 'System.Collections.Generic.Dictionary[string,int]'
```

Notice that this time you have to put quotes around the type name—otherwise, the comma between the two type parameters would cause the type name to be treated as separate parameters.

With all this time we've spent playing the .NET trivia challenge game, we're sure heads are buzzing and coffee is being desperately sought. In the remainder of this section, we'll look at how you can apply some of the things you've learned to build more interesting applications.

17.1.2 PowerShell and GUIs

The full name of the PowerShell package is *Windows PowerShell*. In this section, we'll look at the *Windows* part of the name. You can do GUI programming with PowerShell, as you'll see.

We're going to look at both WinForms and Windows Presentation Foundation (WPF) because the framework used in a particular scenario will depend on a number of criteria. First and foremost, WPF can't be used with PowerShell v1 because v1 doesn't support the single-threaded apartment (STA) threading model which allows a thread waiting on a time-consuming operation to allow another thread to run. If you need to write a UI for use in an STA environment, WinForms is your only choice.

> **NOTE** PowerShell v5 starts the shell using STA by default. This change was introduced in PowerShell v3.

Second, the tools you have available will influence your choice. There are now GUI designers that support using WinForms with PowerShell. This may make WinForms the better, easier, and faster way to do things. WPF, conversely, makes it much easier to create rich, modern UIs. It also supports clean separation of business logic and presentation, allowing the look of the application to be changed without requiring changes to the underlying scripts. You'll see more of these details as we look at each framework. Finally, WinForms has been part of .NET since the beginning, whereas WPF was added with .NET 3.0. If you need your GUI to run on a .NET 2.0–only system, you should look at using WinForms.

Each of these libraries provides a framework and collection of utility classes for building graphical application UIs. Let's see what you can do with these libraries. We'll begin by looking at WinForms.

POWERSHELL AND WINFORMS

The core concepts in WinForms are controls, containers, properties, and events. A *control* is an element in a UI—buttons, list boxes, and so on. Most controls, like buttons, are visible controls that you interact with directly, but there are some controls, such as timers, that aren't visible yet still play a role in the overall user experience. Controls have to be laid out and organized to present a GUI. This is where containers come in. *Containers* include things such as top-level forms, panels, splitter panels, tabbed panels, and so on. Within a container, you can also specify a layout manager which determines how the controls are laid out within the panel. *Properties* are regular properties, except that they're used to set the visual appearance of a control. You use them to set things such as the foreground and background colors or the font of a control.

The final piece in the WinForms architecture is the event. *Events* are used to define the behavior of a control both for specific actions, such as when a user clicks the Do It button, as well as when the container is moved or resized and the control has to take some action. Like everything else in .NET (and PowerShell), events are represented as objects. For WinForms, the most common type of event is `System.EventHandler`. For PowerShell, anywhere an instance of `System.EventHandler` is required you can use a scriptblock. If you want a particular action to occur when a button is clicked, attach a scriptblock to the button click event.

EventHandler arguments

For an event handler to do its job, it requires information about the event that caused it to be invoked. You saw a similar pattern with `ForEach-Object` and `Where-Object`, where the value the scriptblock operated on was passed using the automatic variable `$_`. The `EventHandler` integration in PowerShell follows the same basic pattern. In .NET, when an `EventHandler` is invoked, it's passed two arguments: the object that fired the event and any arguments that are specific to that event. The signature of the method that's used to invoke an event handler looks like this:

```
void Invoke(System.Object, System.EventArgs)
```

These values are made available to the scriptblock handling the event using the automatic variables `$this` and `$_`. The variable `$this` contains a reference to the object that generated the event, and `$_` holds any event-specific arguments that might have been passed. In practice, you don't need these variables most of the time because of the way variables in PowerShell work. With global, script, and module scopes, you can usually access the objects directly. Still, it's good to be aware of them in case you need them.

Many elements in building a Windows Forms application are repeated over and over. If you're working in an environment such as Visual Studio, the environment takes care of generating the boilerplate code. But if you're building a form using Notepad, you need to be a bit more clever to avoid unnecessary work. Let's build a module containing a number of convenience functions that make it easier to work with WinForms. We'll call this module WPIAForms. If this module is placed somewhere in your module path, then you can use it by including the line

```
Import-Module WPIAForms
```

at the beginning of your script.

Listing 17.2   The WPIAForms.psm1 module

```
Add-Type -Assembly System.Drawing, System.Windows.Forms        ◄── ❶ Load required
                                                                      assemblies
function New-Size                                              ◄──
{
  param (                                                         ❷ Create Size
    [Parameter(mandatory=$true)] $x,                                objects
    [Parameter(mandatory=$true)] $y
  )
  New-Object System.Drawing.Size $x,$y
}

function New-Control                                          ◄── ❸ Create
{                                                                   controls
  param (
    [Parameter(mandatory=$true)]
    [string]
      $ControlName,
    [hashtable] $Properties = @{}
  )

  $private:events = @{}                                           ❹ Extract events
  $private:controls = $null                                         and controls from
                                                                    the hashtable
  foreach ($pn in "Events", "Controls")                        ◄──
  {
    if ($v = $Properties.$pn)
    {
      Set-Variable private:$pn $v
      $Properties.Remove($pn)
    }
  }
                                                                ❺ Construct a
  $private:control = if ($Properties.Count) {              ◄──┘    control object
    New-Object "System.Windows.Forms.$ControlName" `
      -Property $Properties }
        else {
          New-Object "System.Windows.Forms.$ControlName" }
                                                                ❻ Add child
  if ($controls) {                                          ◄──    controls
    [void] $control.Controls.AddRange(@(& $controls)) }

  foreach ($private:en in $events.keys)                     ◄──
  {                                                             ❼ Bind event
    $method = "add_$en"                                         handlers
    $control.$method.Invoke($events[$en])
  }
                                                                ❽ Ensure the
  if ($control -eq "form") {                                ◄──    form is visible
    $c.add_Shown({ $this.Activate() }) }

  $control                                                  ◄──
}                                                             ❾ Return the
                                                               configured control
```

The first thing a WinForms module should do is make sure that the necessary assemblies are loaded ❶. (Remember that trying to load an assembly multiple times is harmless.)

Next, you define a convenience function ❷ for creating `Size` objects. Like many helper functions, it hides the long type names used to construct the objects.

Then you come to the heart of the module: the `New-Control` function ❸. This function is used to construct all the controls for your UI. It takes as arguments the name of the WinForms control class to instantiate and a hashtable containing three types of entries:

- Simple properties to set on the control
- An `Events` hashtable specifying which control events you want to handle
- A scriptblock used to create the child controls for this form

The function iterates over the keys in the hashtable ❹, looking to extract the `Controls` and `Events` members because they aren't simple properties on the object you're creating. The scriptblock in the `Controls` member will be evaluated, and any control objects it returns will be added as children of the current control. The `Events` member requires more complex processing. It's also a hashtable, but in this case the keys are the names of control events, and the values are the scriptblocks to bind to those events.

Once the two special members have been extracted, the function passes the cleaned-up hashtable to the `-Property` parameter on `New-Object` ❺ to initialize the control. Unfortunately, there's an annoying limitation on `-Property`: If the value passed to `New-Object` is either `$null` or empty, it will error out. This necessitates wrapping the call to `New-Object` in an `if` statement so that `-Property` gets used only when the hashtable is *not* empty.

Now that the control object exists, add any child controls that were extracted ❻ and bind any event handlers that were specified ❼. One additional event handler is added to ensure that the window is visible ❽. Finally, the completely configured control object is returned ❾.

Although there doesn't seem to be much to this library, it can significantly clarify the structure of the application you're building. Try it out by re-implementing the one-button example and see what it looks like. The result is shown in figure 17.1.

```
Import-Module WPIAForms.psm1
$form = New-Control -ControlName form -Properties @{
    Text = 'Hi'
    Size = New-Size -x 100 -y 60
    Controls = {
        New-Control -ControlName button -Properties @{
            Text = 'Push Me'
            Dock = 'Fill'
            Events = @{
                Click = {$form.Close()}
            }
        }
    }
}
$form.ShowDialog()
```

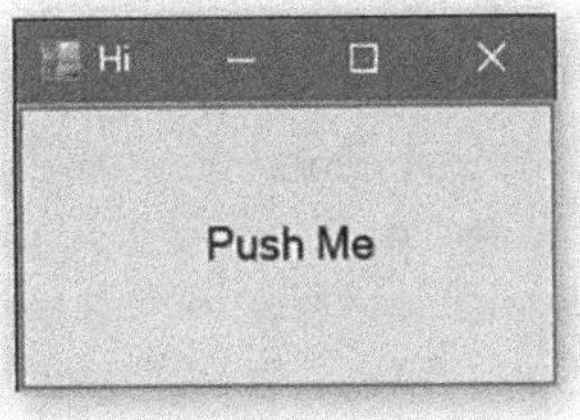

Figure 17.1 An example using the WPIAForms module. Both the code and the resulting window are shown here.

The resulting code isn't any shorter, but the hierarchical structure of the form is much more obvious. The top-level form is created using `New-Control` and sets the title to "Hi" and the size of the form to 100 x 60. The `Controls` member script-block creates the child controls for the form. In this case you're adding a `Button` object, and again you use `New-Control` to create the object, set the `Text` and `Dock` properties, and define the `Click` event handler. Notice that at no point did you have to write any conditional loops—instead of describing how to build the form, you've declared what you want. In effect, you've created a simple DSL for defining WinForms-based UIs.

> **NOTE** A number of GUI builders on the market support building WinForms UIs in PowerShell, including SAPIEN Technologies PowerShell Studio and iTripoli's Admin Script Editor (which has an integrated PowerShell forms designer and is now unsupported freeware). Both of these tools provide sophisticated PowerShell authoring environments as well as (or with) the forms designer. GUI builders eliminate most of the manual layout and UI construction code.

Let's see where you've ended up. In the previous example, you invented a rather limited DSL for building GUIs in a declarative way. Clearly the ability to separate UI *structure* from the implementation logic is compelling, so it would be nice if, rather than inventing your own language, you could use an existing GUI definition language. In practice, this is exactly what the WPF is. Therefore, we're going to spend time seeing how WPF can simplify building UIs in PowerShell.

POWERSHELL AND THE WPF

In this section, you'll learn how to use WPF from PowerShell to construct GUIs. WPF takes a different approach to constructing a GUI compared to WinForms. With WPF the UI is written *declaratively* using an XML-based markup language called XAML (Extensible Application Markup Language). The approach used in WPF is similar to the DSL you wrote as well as to the way HTML works: you describe the basic components, and the framework handles all the construction details. An important aspect of the design of WPF is that the UI description is *decoupled* from the UI logic. This separation of appearance and behavior aligns with well-established best practices for UI design (such as coders write code and design specialists do design).

You'll see how this all works by building a simple GUI front end to some Power-Shell commands. We'll cover only a fraction of the features of WPF—just enough to accomplish our goal of quickly building a simple UI. First, you'll have to satisfy a few prerequisites before you can use WPF from PowerShell.

Although WPF has been around as long as PowerShell, in PowerShell v1 you weren't able to use WPF without a lot of tricks. That's because WPF can only be called from an STA-mode thread (yes, here it is again). With PowerShell v2 and later, this limitation ceased to be an impediment. (And in the ISE, which is a WPF application, you always run in STA mode, so by default everything will work.)

The other thing you need to do to use WPF in your scripts is to load the WPF assemblies, `PresentationCore` and `PresentationFramework`, using `Add-Type`. With these prerequisites out of the way, you can start working on our example project.

The goal of this exercise is to create a GUI front end to the `Get-ChildItem` and `Select-String` cmdlets using WPF. You want novice users to be able to execute a file search without having to be experts in PowerShell. A screen shot of the desired UI is shown in figure 17.2.

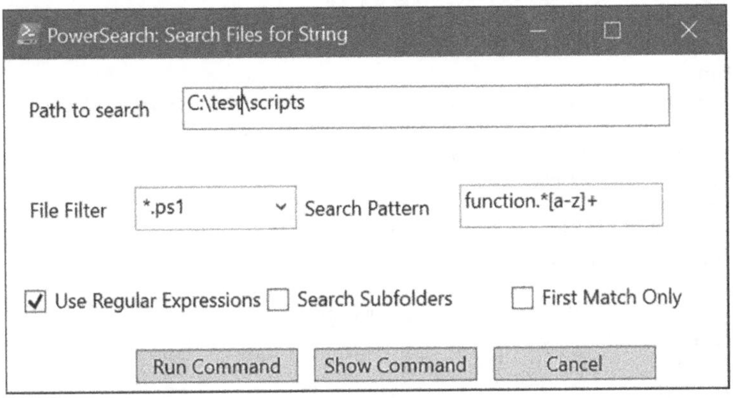

Figure 17.2 A dialog box that front-ends the PowerShell `Get-ChildItem` and `Select-String` cmdlets, allowing users to search with PowerShell even if they don't know the language

In this form, the user can specify the path to search (defaulting to the current directory), the extension of the files to search, and the pattern to use when searching the file text. By default, regular expressions will be used in the text search, but an option is provided to suppress this. There are also options to indicate that subfolders should be searched as well and that only the first match in each file may be returned. At the bottom of the dialog box are buttons to run or cancel the search. There's also a button that will display the command to be run before executing it—a useful mechanism for learning PowerShell.

Although this is a simple dialog box, it would be annoying to implement with WinForms because of the manual control layout required. WPF uses XAML to describe the interface. The XAML text for the interface you're going to create is shown next.

Listing 17.3 The search.xaml file declaring the file search interface

```
<Window
  xmlns="http://schemas.microsoft.com/winfx/2006/xaml/presentation"
   xmlns:x="http://schemas.microsoft.com/winfx/2006/xaml"
    Title="PowerSearch: Search Files for String"
     SizeToContent="WidthAndHeight" >
  <DockPanel>
    <StackPanel HorizontalAlignment="Left" Orientation="Horizontal"
      Width="425" DockPanel.Dock="Top" Margin="10,17,10,17">
       <Label Width="100" >Path to search</Label>
```

Create the top-level window.

Create a StackPanel to hold controls.

Add a Label to the StackPanel.

```
<TextBox Name="Path" Width="300" >Add Row</TextBox>
  </StackPanel>
<StackPanel HorizontalAlignment="Left" Orientation="Horizontal"
  Width="425" DockPanel.Dock="Top" Margin="10,17,10,17">
  <Label Width="70" >File Filter</Label>
  <ComboBox Name="FileFilter" Width="100" IsEditable="True">
    *.ps1
  </ComboBox>
  <Label Width="100" >Search Pattern</Label>
  <TextBox Name="TextPattern" Width="125" >
    function.*[a-z]+
  </TextBox>
</StackPanel>
<StackPanel HorizontalAlignment="Left" Orientation="Horizontal"
  Width="425" DockPanel.Dock="Top" Margin="10,17,10,17">
  <CheckBox Name="UseRegex" Width="150" >
    Use Regular Expressions
  </CheckBox>
  <CheckBox Name="Recurse" Width="150" >
    Search Subfolders
  </CheckBox>
  <CheckBox Name="FirstOnly" Width="150" >
    First Match Only
  </CheckBox>
</StackPanel>
<StackPanel HorizontalAlignment="Left" Orientation="Horizontal"
  DockPanel.Dock="Top" Margin="75,5,5,5">
  <Button Width="100" Name="Run" Margin="5,0,5,0" >
  Run Command
  </Button>
  <Button Width="100" Name="Show" Margin="5,0,5,0" >
  Show Command
  </Button>
  <Button Width="100" Name="Cancel" Margin="5,0,5,0" >
  Cancel
  </Button>
</StackPanel>
  </DockPanel>
</Window>
```

Create another StackPanel for the next row.

Add a named TextBox to the StackPanel.

Add a ComboBox for the file filter.

Add dialog buttons to the bottom.

Looking through the XAML code, you see many things that are familiar from the Win-Forms examples: Label controls, TextBoxes, Buttons, and so on. This means you don't have to learn a lot of new concepts, rather a new way to describe how they should be put together. In this UI description, the dialog box is constructed as a set of rows of controls. A StackPanel layout control is used to arrange the elements in each row, and a DockPanel holds all the rows.

Let's look at one of the control declarations in detail. The XAML that declares the Run button looks like this:

```
<Button Width="100" Name="Run" Margin="5,0,5,0" >
  Run Command
</Button>
```

By inspecting the text, you can see that you're creating a `Button` control, setting the `Width` property on that control to 100, and setting the control `Margin` property with values for left, top, right, and bottom margins. Of particular importance is the `Name` property, which lets you associate a unique name string with the control. You'll need this information later when you're binding actions to the controls.

This XAML document describes what your form will look like but doesn't say anything about how it behaves.

> **NOTE** At this point, the XAML experts in the audience will be shouting that, in fact, many elements in XAML *do* let you describe behaviors (animations, triggers, and such). These features are beyond the scope of this exercise, but you're encouraged explore all the things that can be done with XAML. It's amazing how much you can accomplish using markup.

You now have to attach your business logic to this markup. To display your form, you must load the XAML into the session and use it to create an instance of `System.Windows`. `.Window`. The WPF framework includes utility classes to do most of the heavy lifting for this task. Once you have the UI object, you have to attach PowerShell actions to the controls. The following listing shows the script that does both of these things for you.

Listing 17.4 search.ps1: defining the file search behavior

```
Add-Type -Assembly PresentationCore,PresentationFrameWork      <──  Load
                                                                    the WPF
trap { break }                                                      assemblies.

$mode = [System.Threading.Thread]::CurrentThread.ApartmentState
if ($mode -ne "STA")
{
  $m = "This script can only be run when powershell is " +
    "started with the -sta switch."
  throw $m
}
                                                          Compute the path
function Add-PSScriptRoot ($file)               <──       to the XAML file.
{
  $caller = Get-Variable -Value -Scope 1 MyInvocation
  $caller.MyCommand.Definition |
    Split-Path -Parent |
      Join-Path -Resolve -ChildPath $file
}
                                                          Load the XAML that
$xamlPath = Add-PSScriptRoot search.xaml       <──        constructs the UI.
$stream = [System.IO.StreamReader] $xamlpath
$form = [System.Windows.Markup.XamlReader]::Load(
      $stream.BaseStream)
$stream.Close()
                                                  Find and set the Path
$Path = $form.FindName("Path")                 <──  control to $PWD.
$Path.Text = $PWD
```

```
$FileFilter = $form.FindName("FileFilter")
$FileFilter.Text = "*.ps1"
```
◁── **Set the default file
filter extension.**

```
$TextPattern = $form.FindName("TextPattern")
$Recurse = $form.FindName("Recurse")

$UseRegex = $form.FindName("UseRegex")
$UseRegex.IsChecked = $true
```
◁── **Set up the
CheckBox controls.**

```
$FirstOnly = $form.FindName("FirstOnly")

$Run = $form.FindName("Run")
$Run.add_Click({
    $form.DialogResult = $true
    $form.Close()
})
```
◁── **Bind the button
Click actions.**

```
$Show = $form.FindName("Show")
$Show.add_Click({Write-Host (Get-CommandString)})

$Cancel = $form.FindName("Cancel")
$Cancel.add_Click({$form.Close()})

function Get-CommandString
{
```
◁── **Build the
command string.**

```
  function fixBool ($val) { '$' + $val }
  "Get-ChildItem $($Path.Text) `
    -Recurse: $(fixBool $Recurse.IsChecked) `
    -Filter '$($FileFilter.Text)' |
      Select-String -SimpleMatch: (! $(fixBool $UseRegex.IsChecked)) `
        -Pattern '$($TextPattern.Text)' `
        -List: $(fixBool $FirstOnly.IsChecked)"
}
```
◁── **Format Booleans so
"True" becomes $true.**

```
if ($form.ShowDialog())
{
  $cmd = Get-CommandString
  Invoke-Expression $cmd
}
```
◁── **Show the form
and wait.**

As was the case with the contents of the XAML file, many elements in this script should be familiar from the WinForms examples. To add an action to a button, you use the add_Click() event method, as you did with WinForms. You use the Text property on TextBox controls to get and set the contents of those controls. CheckBoxes have an IsChecked property, as was the case with WinForms. The biggest difference here is that, instead of binding actions as you construct the form, the XAML loader does all the construction and returns the completed object. You then have to find the controls by name to be able to access them. In practice, this turns out to be pretty simple. Once you've located the control objects, everything else is much the same as it was with Win-Forms. The Get-CommandString function is used to generate a string containing the PowerShell command that will perform the search. This function uses the retrieved control objects along with string expansion to produce a complete command.

ADVANTAGES OF USING WPF

The biggest advantage of using WPF is the separation of UI description from UI behavior. By not mixing code and markup, each piece becomes simpler and can be modified fairly independently. For example, because you're identifying the controls by name, it doesn't matter where they get moved around in the form—you'll still get the correct control when you ask for it by name.

The other big advantage to this separation of concerns is that you can now use all the WPF XAML GUI builders with PowerShell. Unlike WinForms, where the tools needed to know PowerShell to work, XAML is XAML, so the programming language (for the most part) doesn't matter, and the UI can be designed independently, decoupled from any code. This also means that the UI can be designed by an expert UI designer and the code added by an expert scripter. Finally, the higher-level nature of the WPF framework means that more effective PowerShell GUI frameworks can be created.

POWERSHELL FRAMEWORKS FOR WPF

Inspired by possibilities that arise from the combination of PowerShell and WPF/ XAML, the PowerShell community has created a high-level library for building WPF GUIs in PowerShell. The library is called ShowUI and is a free download from https:// github.com/showui/showui. As of this writing, the latest version is 1.5.

ShowUI is the result of merging the WPK library written by James Brundage (who was a member of the PowerShell team) and the PowerBoots library, originally written and coordinated by Joel "Jaykul" Bennett (who is a PowerShell MVP). ShowUI is packaged as a PowerShell module and provides a multitude of useful features.

And with that, we've finished our tour of .NET and what you can do with it. It's time to turn our attention to working with events.

17.2 *Real-time events*

An *event* is exactly what it sounds like: something happens; for example, a file is changed, a button is clicked, or a process is started. Events on a Windows machine can be *synchronous* or *asynchronous*. In this section, we'll spend more time working with synchronous events, but the majority of the material will focus on asynchronous *events*. Asynchronous event handling allows scripts to respond to real-world events in a timely manner. We'll also explore the basic concepts of *event-driven* scripting, the PowerShell eventing model and infrastructure, and how to apply this feature.

17.2.1 *Foundations of event handling*

PowerShell supports three major categories, or *sources*, of events: .NET object events, CIM events, and engine events (events generated by PowerShell itself). But before we go into specific discussions on any of these topics, you need a common understanding of the concepts and terminology used in event-based programming.

In the .NET Framework (and therefore in PowerShell), events are tangible objects represented using classes. When you look at any class in the .NET Framework, you'll see that, along with methods and properties, each class also exposes some events. These event members are the focus of our discussion of .NET eventing.

Now let's talk about what an event is, and what makes event-based scripting different from traditional procedural scripting. The key difference with event-based scripting is that instead of an activity being executed as a result of an action in the *script*, a script (or at least a portion of it) is executed as a result of an action by the *system*. This pattern is sometimes called *inversion of control*, but it can be expressed more colorfully as *don't call me, I'll call you.*

> **NOTE** This way of characterizing event-based programming captures the essence of the model perfectly. Crispin Cowan (Linux Security and now Windows Security Guru Extraordinaire) suggested the "*don't call me, I'll call you*" definition as he and Bruce were hiking through the Cougar Mountains in Washington. Clearly, inspiration can arrive anywhere.

The traditional and event-driven flow control patterns are shown in figure 17.3.

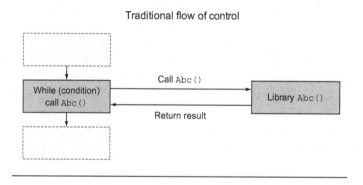

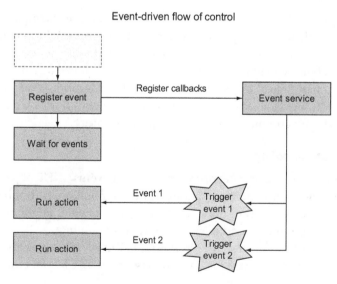

Figure 17.3   The normal flow of control in a script is compared to the flow in an event-based script. In the normal flow of control, the main thread of execution always retains control, calling library routines as needed. In event-based programming, the mainline registers a set of callback actions that will be executed when the specified event occurs. The event service then controls the flow of execution.

Look at the traditional flow of control illustrated in figure 17.3. In the traditional model, the flow of control always belongs to the mainline of the program. If an action is required, the mainline program directly invokes that action. In contrast, with the eventing pattern, rather than directly initiating actions, the mainline program registers the set of actions with an event source and then goes to sleep. It never initiates any actions on its own. Instead, the event source is responsible for initiating actions as required. In this scenario you are, in effect, turning control over to the event service.

> **NOTE** In practice, we've been using this callback pattern all along, not only in GUIs. This is how the `ForEach-Object` and `Where-Object` cmdlets work: You pass action scriptblocks to the cmdlets, and the cmdlets take care of calling your code when it's needed.

In other situations, the event service may be an active entity like another thread or process. In practice, real programs rarely restrict themselves to a single model but instead use different models at different times as appropriate.

17.2.2 *Synchronous events*

The defining characteristic of synchronous eventing is that there's never more than one action occurring at any given time. All the event-driven actions are *synchronized*, and no action is ever interrupted. This is the event-handling pattern used in most GUI frameworks like Windows Forms or Windows Presentation Foundation.

SYNCHRONOUS EVENTING IN GUIS

In synchronous GUI frameworks, you create a collection of GUI elements and then register actions with these elements so that when the user does something like click a button, your actions will be executed. Once you've finished creating the GUI and registering the event actions, you hand control over to the framework, which will call the actions you defined when it needs to.

In PowerShell, for defining synchronous event handlers, you can usually attach a scriptblock directly to the event member on the object. In fact, you've already applied this pattern many times, as in the following, familiar example from chapter 1:

```
Add-Type -AssemblyName System.Windows.Forms
$form = New-Object -TypeName System.Windows.Forms.Form
$button = New-Object -TypeName Windows.Forms.Button
$button.text='Push Me!'
$button.Dock='fill'
$button.add_Click({$form.close()})
$form.Controls.Add($button)
$form.ShowDialog()
```

By now, you know that this code creates a button that will close its containing form when clicked. The line `$button.add_Click({$form.close()})` is where the event handler is attached, or bound, to the control. The `Button` object has a `Click` event, which fires when the button is clicked. To add the `Click` event handler, you call the add_Click() method, passing in the scriptblock to execute. Because the add_Click() method requires an argument of type System.EventHandler, PowerShell automatically wraps the scriptblock with a generated subclass of System.EventHandler. The System.EventHandler class is an example of what is called a *delegate* in .NET terminology.

DELEGATES AND DELEGATION

In the GUI examples you saw in section 17.1, you set up control actions in the GUI by attaching event handlers to the controls in the UI. When you set up event handlers like this, you are, in effect, delegating the execution of that code to the UI and depending on it to call the code at the right time. Because this involves delegated actions, a logical name for these event handlers would be delegates—which is what they're called in .NET.

Events are represented as members on a class. The delegate values you assign to event members are represented by types that derive from a common base type. In this case, the common base type is System.Delegate. Depending on the argument type for the target event member, the required event handler argument will be a specific subclass of Delegate. In the PowerShell world, the role of the delegate is always played by scriptblocks. But because scriptblocks don't derive from System.Delegate, the Power-Shell runtime has to synthesize Delegate *wrapper classes* for the scriptblock that match the argument type required by the event member. Let's see how this works in a non-GUI example.

> **NOTE** PowerShell v1 supported only the single subclass of delegate, System.EventHandler, because of time restrictions. This type was chosen because it's widely used in the .NET framework, in particular by the GUI frameworks. This meant that there were many useful things you could do even though you had only the one type. In v2 and later, the delegate-wrapping support is generalized to cover all types of delegates, so you no longer have to deal with the limitations of only one delegate type.

A NON-GUI SYNCHRONOUS EVENT EXAMPLE

Although the use of System.EventHandler is common in .NET, additional synchronous delegate types in the .NET Framework don't follow the System.EventHandler pattern. PowerShell v2 and later versions have greatly improved support for delegate types, and the PowerShell runtime can automatically generate wrappers for any type of delegate.

> **NOTE** You can generate a wrapper for any event type, but you can't always automatically infer what type to generate in all scenarios. For those cases, the use of an explicit cast is required to disambiguate things. When you cast a scriptblock to the target type, the correct wrapper can be synthesized.

In this example, we'll look at how PowerShell's enhanced delegate handling works. You're going to use a scriptblock as the MatchEvaluator in a call to the static Replace() method on the [regex] class. View the overloads for the Replace() method by using this:

```
PS> [regex]::Replace
```

The overload of `Replace()` you're interested in uses a delegate to do custom transformations during the replace operation. The signature for this method is

```
static string Replace(
    string input,
    string pattern,
    System.Text.RegularExpressions.MatchEvaluator evaluator)
```

The first two arguments are the string to act on and the pattern to search for. The final argument is a delegate of type

```
[System.Text.RegularExpressions.MatchEvaluator]
```

Now, examine this type:

```
PS> [System.Text.RegularExpressions.MatchEvaluator] |
Format-List Name,FullName,BaseType

Name     : MatchEvaluator
FullName : System.Text.RegularExpressions.MatchEvaluator
BaseType : System.MulticastDelegate
```

You can see that it derives from `System.MulticastDelegate`. Because delegates are invoked using the `Invoke()` method, by looking at this method's signature you can see what parameters your scriptblock requires. Let's see what this method looks like for the `MatchEvaluator` delegate (note the leading space in the `' Invoke'` pattern, which reduces the set of matched members):

```
PS> [System.Text.RegularExpressions.MatchEvaluator] |
foreach {[string] ($_.GetMembers() -match ' Invoke')}

System.String Invoke(System.Text.RegularExpressions.Match)
```

You see that the delegate takes a single parameter representing the matched text, so the scriptblock will look like this:

```
{param($match) ... }
```

Note that in this scriptblock definition, we omitted the type attribute for simplicity, and in practice it isn't needed. The delegate signature guarantees that the scriptblock will never be called with the wrong argument types.

And now that you have the signature figured out, let's find out what this method does. Looking up the `MatchEvaluator` class on MSDN, you see the following:

> *You can use a `MatchEvaluator` delegate method to perform a custom verification or manipulation operation for each match found by a replacement method such as `Regex .Replace(String, Match-Evaluator)`. For each matched string, the `Replace` method calls the `MatchEvaluator` delegate method with a `Match` object that represents the match. The delegate method performs whatever processing you prefer and returns a string that the `Replace` method substitutes for the matched string.*

For your purposes, this means that whatever the scriptblock returns will replace the matched substring. Let's try it out. Write an expression that will replace all the characters in a string with their corresponding hex representation:

```
PS> $inputString = 'abcd'
PS> [regex]::replace($inputString, '.',
    [System.Text.RegularExpressions.MatchEvaluator] {
        param($match)
            '{0:x4}' -f [int] [char]$match.value
    }
)

0061006200630064
```

Inside the scriptblock, you take each argument character and then use the format operator to turn it into a set of four hexadecimal digits.

By now, you should be comfortable with synchronous events. Asynchronous events introduce a number of considerations that make handling them more complicated. But because asynchronous events are a much more realistic way to model the world, the ability to handle them in PowerShell is important in scenarios such as responding to alerts. Beginning with the next section, you'll spend quite a bit of time mastering these event patterns and learning how to apply them to solve real problems.

17.2.3 *Asynchronous events*

Asynchronous events are much trickier to deal with than their synchronous cousins. A synchronous event effectively runs on the same thread of execution as everything else. At no point are there ever two actions occurring at the same time. Everything happens deterministically, eliminating any collisions or consistency/coherency issues.

Unfortunately, that model doesn't match the way much of the real world works. Real-world events don't occur in a strict deterministic order—they happen when they happen, interrupting whatever else might be going on at that time. This type of concurrent operation makes life difficult for scripters because it means things may possibly get changed out of order or in unanticipated ways, resulting in inconsistencies and errors.

In PowerShell v1, there was no support for the asynchronous pattern, which made it pretty much impossible to handle asynchronous events. To allow for robust handling of asynchronous events, PowerShell v2 added an eventing subsystem that uses a centralized event manager to ensure that this occurs in a rational sequence. This subsystem takes care of all the bookkeeping and synchronization needed to ensure a stable and consistent system without a lot of work on the part of the script author.

> **NOTE** PowerShell is single threaded, so when it's busy executing something it can't handle events. They are queued and executed once PowerShell is available again.

SUBSCRIPTIONS, REGISTRATIONS, AND ACTIONS

The scripting model PowerShell uses for handling asynchronous events involves a few core concepts. The first is the idea of an *event subscription*, where you select the type of events you want to know about and then subscribe to be notified when they occur. These subscriptions are registered with a source identifier, which allows you to give a friendly name to each subscription. Once registered, the event subscription will be notified about relevant events as soon as they occur and will continue to receive notifications until the subscription is cancelled by explicitly unregistering it. Each event subscription may optionally specify an action to be taken.

THE EVENTING CMDLETS

The PowerShell eventing cmdlets, shown in table 17.1, allow you to register and unregister event subscriptions and list the existing subscriptions. You can also list pending *events* (as opposed to subscriptions) and handle or remove them as desired. There is also a cmdlet that allows scripts to generate their own events.

Table 17.1   The PowerShell eventing cmdlets

Cmdlet name	Description
`Register-ObjectEvent`	Registers an event subscription for events generated by .NET objects.
`Register-CimIndicationEvent` `(Register-WmiEvent)`	Registers an event subscription for events generated by WMI objects
`Register-EngineEvent`	Registers an event subscription for events generated by PowerShell itself.
`Get-EventSubscriber`	Gets a list of the registered event subscriptions in the session.
`Unregister-Event`	Removes one or more of the registered event subscriptions.
`Wait-Event`	Waits for an event to occur. This cmdlet can wait for a specific event or any event. It also allows a timeout to be specified limiting how long it will wait for the event. The default is to wait forever.
`Get-Event`	Gets pending unhandled events from the event queue.
`Remove-Event`	Removes a pending event from the event queue.
`New-Event`	Allows the script to add its own events to the event queue.

When handling events, you need to be able to register actions in response to these events. You do so using cmdlets, but because there are several types or sources of events, there are also several event registration cmdlets, as you saw in the table. The event subscription registration cmdlets are `Register-EngineEvent`, `Register-ObjectEvent`, `Register-CimIndicationEvent`, and `Register-WmiEvent`. PowerShell-specific events are handled using the `Register-EngineEvent` cmdlet, asynchronous events on .NET objects are handled using `Register-ObjectEvent`, and WMI events are addressed with `Register-CimIndicationEvent` or `Register-WmiEvent`.

17.2.4 *Working with asynchronous .NET events*

You use the `Register-ObjectEvent` cmdlet to create subscriptions for asynchronous events on .NET objects. First, you need to identify the event you're interested in. For .NET events, this means that you need an object and the name of the event member on that object to bind. This is the same pattern you've already seen with Windows Forms and WPF, where, for example, a `Button` object has a `Click` event accessed through the `add_Click()` member.

Once you've decided on the event to handle, you need to specify what to do with it. The `-Action` parameter on the cmdlet allows you to provide a scriptblock to execute when an event fires. This scriptblock will receive a lot of information about the event when it's run, but there may be additional, custom data that you want to pass to the event handler. You can do this with the `-MessageData` parameter.

Finally, when you're working with a number of events, the ability to attach a friendly name to the subscription will make things easier to manage. This is what `-Source` `-Identifier` is for: It allows you to name the event registration or *event source*.

There's one last parameter we haven't discussed yet: `-SupportEvent`. In larger event-driven scripts, there may be a number of event registrations that exist only to support higher-level constructs within the application. In these scenarios, it's useful to be able to hide these supporting events much like the rationale behind the way you hide supporting functions in modules. This event-handler hiding is accomplished using the `-SupportEvent` switch. As was the case with modules, if you do want to see the hidden events, you can specify the `-Force` switch on `Get-Event-Subscriber`.

WRITING A TIMER EVENT HANDLER

Okay, enough talk—let's start doing something with .NET events. One of the most obvious examples of an asynchronous event is a timer. A *timer* event fires at regular intervals regardless of what else is going on. Let's see how you can set up subscription events generated by the .NET `System.Timers.Timer` class.

> **NOTE** These cmdlets can be used *only* for asynchronous .NET events. It's not possible to set up event handlers for synchronous events using the PowerShell eventing cmdlets. That's because synchronous events all execute on the same thread and the cmdlets expect (require) that the events will happen on another thread. Without the second thread, the PowerShell engine will block the main thread and nothing will ever get executed.

CREATING THE TIMER OBJECT

The first thing you need for our example is a `Timer` object. You use `New-Object` to create it:

```
PS> $timer = New-Object -TypeName System.Timers.Timer
```

Events exist as members on a class, so you can use `Get-Member`, filtering the results on the `Event` member type, to see what events this object exposes:

```
PS> $timer | Get-Member -MemberType Event

   TypeName: System.Timers.Timer

Name          MemberType Definition
----          ---------- ----------
Disposed      Event      System.EventHandler Disposed(System.Objec...
Elapsed       Event      System.Timers.ElapsedEventHandler Elapsed...
```

From this output, you can see that the `Elapsed` event is what you're looking for—it fires when the timer period has elapsed.

SETTING THE TIMER EVENT PARAMETERS

But you need to know more about this object than the events—you need to know how to set the timer interval and start and stop the timer. Again, you can use `Get-Member` to find this information. (Note that, for brevity, the output shown here has been trimmed to the interesting members.)

```
PS> $timer | Get-Member

   TypeName: System.Timers.Timer

Name                    MemberType Definition
----                    ---------- ----------
Disposed                Event      System.EventHandler Disp...
Elapsed                 Event      System.Timers.ElapsedEve...
Close                   Method     System.Void Close()
Start                   Method     System.Void Start()
Stop                    Method     System.Void Stop()
ToString                Method     string ToString()
AutoReset               Property   System.Boolean AutoReset...
Enabled                 Property   System.Boolean Enabled {...
Interval                Property   System.Double Interval {...
```

When you look at the output, the way to start and stop the timer is obvious. The `AutoReset` property determines if the timer fires only once (`AutoReset = $false`) or fires repeatedly every interval (`AutoReset = $true`). Finally, the `Interval` property controls the firing interval. Because the value is a double, you can guess that it's specified in milliseconds.

> **NOTE** Yes, you could've gone to the MSDN documentation. But why bother? With `Get-Member` and a reasonably decent understanding of .NET, `Get-Member` is often all you need. This makes PowerShell a useful tool for developers as well as IT professionals. Even in Visual Studio, sometimes we'll still flip over to a PowerShell window to search for information about a type. Simple text and typing is still faster sometimes.

BINDING THE EVENT ACTION

Let's register for an event on this object, which you do with the following command:

```
PS> Register-ObjectEvent -InputObject $timer `
-EventName Elapsed -Action { Write-Host '<TIMER>' } |
```

```
Format-List Id, Name, PSJobTypeName, State, HasMoreData,
Location, Command

Id              : 4
Name            : d1d302c6-7297-4c0b-b6c7-fc9f02195a2c
PSJobTypeName   :
State           : NotStarted
HasMoreData     : False
Location        :
Command         :  Write-Host '<TIMER>'
```

This command attaches a scriptblock to the event that will write out the phrase `'<TIMER>'` when it fires. You have to use `Write-Host` in this scriptblock because the output from a triggered event action is discarded.

Using Register-ObjectEvent

As a handy way to remember how to use the `Register-ObjectEvent` cmdlet, think of assigning the scriptblock to the event member. If PowerShell supported this, it would look something like this: `$timer.Elapsed = { Write-Host "<TIMER>" }`.

The `Register-ObjectEvent` command allows positional parameters in the same order, so the command would look like

```
PS> Register-ObjectEvent $timer Elapsed { Write-Host "<TIMER2>" }
```

where the order of the elements is the same: object/member/action.

Now you'll wait a minute—and nothing happens. That's because you haven't done all the other things to the `Timer` object to make it start firing (though, obviously, binding the event handler beforehand is usually a good idea).

ENABLING THE EVENT

Let's complete the remaining steps needed to start the timer triggering. Set the interval to 500 ms so the timer will fire in half a second:

```
PS> $timer.Interval = 500
```

You want it to fire repeatedly, so set the `AutoReset` property to `$true`:

```
PS> $timer.AutoReset = $true
```

Next, enable the timer by setting the `Enabled` property to `$true` (or by calling the `Start()` method, which also sets `Enabled` to `$true`):

```
PS> $timer.Enabled = $true
<TIMER>
<TIMER>
```

The timer starts running, and you see the output you expected. Next comes the hard part: getting it to stop. The command is easy: type `$timer.Stop()` and press Enter. But in the console shell, the timer is writing to the screen at the same time you're typing. This results in scrambled output, looking something like this:

```
<TIMER>
$timer.Stop()<TIMER>
<TIMER>
```

(Here's another place where the ISE works better—the timer output doesn't interfere with the ability to run commands.) Once you've stopped the timer, you can restart it by calling the `Start()` method a second time:

```
PS> $timer.Start()
<TIMER>
<TIMER>
<TIMER>
<TIMER>
PS> $timer.Stop()<TIMER>
```

Now that you know how to register a basic event subscription, we'll look at how to manage these subscriptions.

MANAGING EVENT SUBSCRIPTIONS

In this section, you'll see how to find your event subscriptions and how to remove them when you've finished with them. Being able to remove them is important because event subscriptions persist in the session until explicitly removed.

Before you can remove a subscription, you have to find it. PowerShell provides the `Get-EventSubscriber` cmdlet to do this. Let's use it to look at the subscription you registered in the previous section:

```
PS> Get-EventSubscriber

SubscriptionId   : 2
SourceObject     : System.Timers.Timer
EventName        : Elapsed
SourceIdentifier : d1d302c6-7297-4c0b-b6c7-fc9f02195a2c
Action           : System.Management.Automation.PSEventJob
HandlerDelegate  :
SupportEvent     : False
ForwardEvent     : False
```

The `Get-EventSubscriber` cmdlet returns `PSEventSubscriber` objects, which have complete information about the registration: the object generating the event, the action to execute, and so on. There are a couple of interesting properties to note in this output.

Because you didn't give the subscription a friendly name using `-SourceIdentifier` when you created it, the `Register-ObjectEvent` generated one for you. This autogenerated name is the string representation of a GUID, so you know it's unique (but not that friendly). The other thing to notice is that the action shows up as a PowerShell `Job` object. Because the relationship between events and jobs is a somewhat longer discussion, we'll defer it to section 17.2.14.

Now that you can list the event subscriptions, you can set about removing them. You registered event subscriptions with `Register-ObjectEvent`, so what you need to do is *unregister* the subscription, which you'll do with `Unregister-Event`. The cmdlet noun in this case is `Event`, not `ObjectEvent`, because you can use a common mechanism to unregister any kind of event. It's only the registration part that varies. The rest of the eventing cmdlets remain the same.

When you're unregistering an event subscription, there are two ways of identifying the event to unregister: by the `SubscriptionId` property or by the `SourceIdentifier`. The subscription ID is an integer that's incremented each time an event subscription is created. Because you didn't give your event registration a friendly name, you'll use the `SubscriptionId` to unregister it:

```
PS> Unregister-Event -SubscriptionId 2 -Verbose
VERBOSE: Performing the operation "Unsubscribe" on target "Event subscription
    'd1d302c6-7297-4c0b-b6c7-fc9f02195a2c'".
```

Note that you include the `-Verbose` flag in this command so that you can see something happening. If you try running the command again, it will result in an error. The `Unregister-Event` cmdlet is silent as long as nothing goes wrong. If something does go wrong, you get an error.

We've covered the basics of creating and managing event subscriptions. But before the handlers for these events can do much useful work, they'll need access to additional information. In the next section, you'll write more sophisticated handlers and see how they can use the automatic variables provided by the eventing subsystem.

17.2.5 Asynchronous event handling with scriptblocks

In this section, we'll look at the automatic variables and other features that PowerShell provides to allow scriptblocks to be used as effective event handlers.

17.2.6 Automatic variables in the event handler

In PowerShell eventing, the scriptblock that handles the event action has access to a number of variables that provide information about the event being handled. These variables are described in table 17.2.

Table 17.2 The automatic variables available in the event handler scriptblock

Variable	Description
`$event`	This variable contains an object of type `System.Management` `.Automation.PSEventArgs` that represents the event being handled. It allows you to access a wide variety of information about the event, as you'll see in an example. The value of this variable is the same object that the `Get-Event` cmdlet returns.

Table 17.2 The automatic variables available in the event handler scriptblock *(continued)*

Variable	Description
$eventSubscriber	This variable contains the PSEventSubscriber object that represents the event subscriber of the event being handled. The value of this variable is the same object that the Get-EventSubscriber cmdlet returns.
$sender	The value in this variable is the object that generated the event. This variable is a shortcut for $EventArgs.Sender.
$sourceEventArgs	Contains objects that represent the arguments of the event being processed. This variable is a shortcut for $Event.SourceArgs.
$sourceArgs	Contains the values from $Event.SourceArgs. Like any other scriptblock, if there is a param statement, the parameters defined by that statement will be populated and $args will contain only leftover values for which there were no parameters.

Let's write a quick test event handler to see what's in the object in $Event. You'll use the timer event again:

```
PS> $timer = New-Object -TypeName System.Timers.Timer -Property @{
Interval = 1000; Enabled = $true; AutoReset = $false }
```

In the event subscription action, you'll display the contents of the event object:

```
PS> Register-ObjectEvent $timer Elapsed -Action {$Event | Out-Host}

Id Name                              PSJobTypeName State      HasMore
                                                              Data
-- ----                              ------------- -----      -------
3  54b59faf-5fea-45ff-b086-5c5d3b1eb4c5             NotStarted False
```

You'll start the timer to generate the event:

```
PS> $timer.Start()

ComputerName     :
RunspaceId       : cd66f2a6-d112-4d09-851d-e02c3f6e459b
EventIdentifier  : 1
Sender           : System.Timers.Timer
SourceEventArgs  : System.Timers.ElapsedEventArgs
SourceArgs       : {System.Timers.Timer, System.Timers.ElapsedEventArgs}
SourceIdentifier : 54b59faf-5fea-45ff-b086-5c5d3b1eb4c5
TimeGenerated    : 16/05/2017 14:30:01
MessageData      :
```

In this output, you see the properties on the PSEvent object that correspond to the variables listed in table 17.2. The Timer object that generated the event is available through the Sender property on the object and the $sender variable in the scriptblock. The PSEvent object also includes context data about the event, such as the time the event occurred, the event identifier, and the RunspaceId this event is associated with.

The `ComputerName` property is blank because this is a local event, but in the case of a remote event, it would contain the name of the computer where the event occurred.

17.2.7 *Dynamic modules and event handler state*

Because an event can fire at any time, you might never know what variables were in scope, and this in turn could make it hard to know what state will exist when the action is executed. Instead, you want to be able to run the event handlers in a well-defined, isolated environment. This objective aligns with the design goals for PowerShell modules, so you can leverage this feature by creating a *dynamic module* (section 10.4) for the action scriptblock. The eventing subsystem does this by calling the `NewBoundScript-BlockScriptblock()` method to attach a dynamic module to the handler scriptblock.

Beyond ensuring a coherent runtime environment for your event handler scriptblock, the module also allows it to have private state. This ability can be quite useful when you're monitoring a system's behavior over time. You can accumulate the information privately and then process it once you've gathered enough samples. Let's look at how this state isolation works. The following is a trivial example where you maintain a count of the number of timer events fired. Once you reach a predetermined limit, the timer will be stopped. Let's walk through the example. First, you create the `Timer` object:

```
PS> $timer = New-Object System.Timers.Timer -Property @{
Interval = 500; AutoReset = $true}
```

As usual, you subscribe to the `Elapsed` event on the timer:

```
PS> Register-ObjectEvent -InputObject $timer `
-MessageData 5 -SourceIdentifier Stateful `
-EventName Elapsed -Action {
    $script:counter += 1
    Write-Host "Event counter is $counter"
    if ($counter -ge $Event.MessageData)
    {
        Write-Host 'Stopping timer'
        $timer.Stop()
    }
} > $null
```

In the handler scriptblock for this event, you're updating a script-scoped variable `$script:counter`, which holds the number of times the event has fired. This variable will be visible only within the dynamic module associated with the event, preventing your `$counter` from colliding with any other users of a variable called `$counter`. After the variable is incremented, you print the event count and then check to see whether the limit has been reached. Notice that you're making use of the `-MessageData` parameter to pass the limit to the event handler, which it retrieves from the `MessageData` property on the `Event` object. Now start the timer running to see it in action:

```
PS> $timer.Start()
Event counter is 1
Event counter is 2
```

```
Event counter is 3
Event counter is 4
Event counter is 5
Stopping timer
```

As intended, the timer message is displayed five times and then the timer is stopped. This example can easily be modified to, for example, monitor CPU usage or process working sets over a period of time.

Setting up action scriptblocks for asynchronous events allows you to efficiently handle events in the background. This, in turn, lets the main thread of your script continue execution in the foreground or, in interactive sessions, allows you to continue entering commands at the shell prompt. There are, however, many monitoring scenarios where there's no main thread and all you want to do is wait for events to happen. If a service process crashes or faults, you want to be notified so you can take action to restart it. Otherwise, you wait for the next event to arrive. This "wait for an event" pattern is addressed using the Wait-Event cmdlet.

17.2.8 Queued events and the Wait-Event cmdlet

As an alternative to setting up numerous individual event handler actions, you can use the Wait-Event cmdlet to process events in a loop. This cmdlet allows you to block the PowerShell session, waiting until an event or events happen. When the event arrives, you can take whatever action is required and then loop and wait for the next event. This event loop pattern is common in GUI programming. The syntax for the Wait -Event command is simple:

```
Wait-Event [[-SourceIdentifier] <string>] [-Timeout <int>]
```

By using the -SourceIdentifier parameter, you can wait for a specific named event. If you don't use it, then any unhandled event will unblock you. By using the -Timeout parameter, you can limit the length of time you'll wait for the event. This allows you to take remedial actions if the event you're waiting for failed to occur in the prescribed time.

> **NOTE** You can either register an action for an event or wait for an event, but you can't do both. If an action has been registered, when the event fires the event object will be removed from the queue and passed to the action scriptblock for processing. As a result, any Wait-Event calls listening for this event will never receive it and will block forever.

Let's experiment with this cmdlet using something other than the timer event. In this example, you'll work with the file system watcher class: System.IO.FileSystemWatcher. This class is used to generate events when changes are made to monitored portions of the file system. Let's look at the events exposed by this type:

```
PS> [System.IO.FileSystemWatcher].GetEvents() | Select-String .

System.IO.FileSystemEventHandler Changed
System.IO.FileSystemEventHandler Created
```

```
System.IO.FileSystemEventHandler Deleted
System.IO.ErrorEventHandler Error
System.IO.RenamedEventHandler Renamed
System.EventHandler Disposed
```

Using this class, you can register for notifications when a file or directory is created, changed, deleted, or renamed. You can create a `FileSystemWatcher` object that will monitor changes to your desktop. First, you need to get the resolved path to the desktop folder:

```
PS> $path = (Resolve-Path ~/desktop).Path
```

You have to do this because, as discussed previously, when you use PowerShell paths as arguments to .NET methods (including constructors), you must pass in a fully resolved path because .NET doesn't understand PowerShell's enhanced notion of paths.

Now, construct the file watcher object for the target path:

```
PS> $fsw = [System.IO.FileSystemWatcher] $path
```

Set up an event subscription for the `Created` and `Changed` events:

```
PS> Register-ObjectEvent -InputObject $fsw –EventName Created `
-SourceIdentifier fsw1
```

```
PS> Register-ObjectEvent -InputObject $fsw –EventName Changed `
-SourceIdentifier fsw2
```

Finally, enable event generation by the object:

```
PS> $fsw.EnableRaisingEvents = $true
```

At this point, when you call `Get-Event`, you should see nothing:

```
PS> Get-Event
```

This assumes that no other process is writing to the desktop while you're doing this. Let's perform an operation that will trigger the event. Create a new file on the desktop:

```
PS> Get-Date | Out-File -LiteralPath ~/desktop/date.txt
```

You didn't set up an action for either of the event registrations, so you won't see anything happen immediately. The events, however, haven't been lost. Unhandled events are added to the session *event queue* where they can be retrieved later. Let's see what's in the queue at this point:

```
PS> Get-Event | select SourceIdentifier

SourceIdentifier
----------------
fsw1
fsw2
```

In the output, you see that two events have been added: one for the creation of the date.txt file and a second indicating that a change to the containing directory has occurred. Note that reading the events doesn't remove them from the queue. You need to use the `Remove-Event` cmdlet to do this—otherwise, you'll keep rereading the same event objects. The `Remove-Event` cmdlet allows events to be removed either by `SourceIdentifier` or by `EventIdentifier`. To discard all the events in the queue, pipe `Get-Event` into `Remove-Event`:

```
PS> Get-Event | Remove-Event
```

The queue is now empty, so you can call `Wait-Event` and the session will block until a new event is generated (or you press Ctrl-C):

```
PS> Wait-Event
```

To trigger an event, from another PowerShell session update the date.txt file:

```
PS> Get-Date > ~/desktop/date.txt
```

This code will cause an event to be added to the queue, terminating the `Wait-Event`, which will write the terminating event object to the output stream:

```
ComputerName     :
RunspaceId       : cd66f2a6-d112-4d09-851d-e02c3f6e459b
EventIdentifier  : 12
Sender           : System.IO.FileSystemWatcher
SourceEventArgs  : System.IO.FileSystemEventArgs
SourceArgs       : {System.IO.FileSystemWatcher, date.txt}
SourceIdentifier : fsw2
TimeGenerated    : 16/05/2017 17:07:56
MessageData      :
```

Although you're unblocked, the event hasn't technically been handled, so it still exists in the queue and you still have to manually remove it from the queue:

```
PS> Get-Event | Remove-Event
```

If you use the `-Timeout` parameter on `Wait-Event` and no event is generated, the session will automatically unblock. This makes it easy to distinguish between a timeout and an event.

Now let's move on to the second type of events that can be handled by the Power-Shell eventing infrastructure: CIM events.

17.2.9 *Working with CIM events*

In this section, we're going to cover how to work with CIM (WMI) events in Power-Shell. As was the case with .NET events, you handle CIM events using a cmdlet to register actions associated with the events: the `Register-CimIndicationEvent` cmdlet.

NOTE Register-CimIndicationEvent is a replacement for Register-WmiEvent and should be used in preference to the older WMI cmdlet.

All the other eventing cmdlets remain the same as you saw for object events and will also be the same for any new object sources that might be added in the future.

CIM EVENT BASICS

CIM events are, in some ways, considerably more sophisticated than .NET events. First, CIM events are represented as CIM objects and so, like all CIM objects, can be retrieved from either a local or remote computer in a transparent way. Second, because CIM event subscriptions can take the form of a WQL query, event filtering can take place at the event source instead of transmitting all events to the receiver, which is forced to do all the filtering. This is important if you're monitoring a small set of events on a large number of computers. By doing the filtering at the source (remote) end, far less data is transmitted to the receiver and much less processing needs to be done by the receiver, allowing for the overall monitoring task to scale to far more computers than would otherwise be possible.

NOTE Unlike object events, there's no notion of synchronous CIM events, so all event handling must go through the eventing subsystem.

We'll begin our exploration of CIM events by looking at the Win32_*Trace classes, which are much simpler to deal with than the full query-based event subscriptions.

17.2.10 *Class-based CIM event registration*

Before jumping into the full complexity of query-based event subscriptions, we'll look at some predefined CIM event classes. These classes hide a lot of the complexity required by query-based event registration, making them easier to use. You can use the following command to get a list of these classes—you'll also display their superclasses to see the relationships between the classes:

```
PS> Get-CimClass Win32_*trace | select CimClassName, CimSuperClassName

CimClassName             CimSuperClassName
------------             -----------------
Win32_SystemTrace        __ExtrinsicEvent
Win32_ProcessTrace       Win32_SystemTrace
Win32_ProcessStartTrace  Win32_ProcessTrace
Win32_ProcessStopTrace   Win32_ProcessTrace
Win32_ThreadTrace        Win32_SystemTrace
Win32_ThreadStartTrace   Win32_ThreadTrace
Win32_ThreadStopTrace    Win32_ThreadTrace
Win32_ModuleTrace        Win32_SystemTrace
Win32_ModuleLoadTrace    Win32_ModuleTrace
```

By inspecting the class/superclass relationships, you can see that these classes form a hierarchy of event sources, where the farther you go from the root, the more specific the event becomes. This hierarchy is illustrated in figure 17.4.

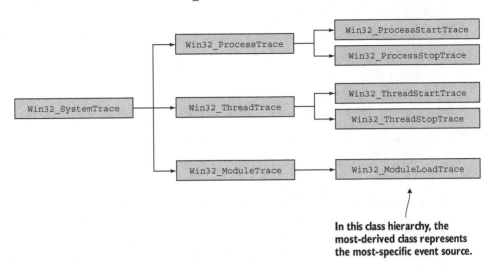

Win32_*Trace event class hierarchy

In this class hierarchy, the most-derived class represents the most-specific event source.

Figure 17.4 This figure shows the hierarchy of classes representing simplified WMI event sources. The most-derived class matches the most-specific event. `Win32_ProcessStartTrace` will fire only for process starts, whereas `Win32_ProcessTrace` will fire for both process starts and process stops.

Let's work through an example that shows how this works.

> **NOTE** Because these event sources fire for *any* process event, regardless of who starts them, these commands must be run from an elevated shell on Windows Vista and later. Also, be aware that because you're recording all process events in the first set of examples, you may see additional output from other processes starting and stopping.

USING THE WIN32_PROCESSTRACE EVENTS

You'll use the `Win32_Process*Trace` classes in this experiment. First, you'll set up an event subscription to the `Win32_ProcessStartTrace`, which will fire every time a process starts:

```
PS> Register-CimIndicationEvent -ClassName Win32_ProcessStartTrace -Action {
    'Process Start: ' +
    $event.SourceEventArgs.NewEvent.ProcessName |
    Out-Host
}
```

You can assign an action scriptblock to these event subscriptions, as you did with object events. In the scriptblock body, you'll write a message indicating what type of event was fired along with the process name. You'll set up similar event handlers for the

`Win32_ProcessStopTrace` and `Win32_ProcessTrace` events, again displaying the type of the event and the process name:

```
PS> Register-CimIndicationEvent -ClassName Win32_ProcessStopTrace -Action {
    'Process Stop: ' +
    $event.SourceEventArgs.NewEvent.ProcessName |
    Out-Host
}

PS> Register-CimIndicationEvent -ClassName  Win32_ProcessTrace -Action {
    'Process Any: ' +
    $event.SourceEventArgs.NewEvent.ProcessName |
    Out-Host
}
```

From the hierarchy (and the names of the events), you know that `Win32_ProcessStart-Trace` fires when a process starts, `Win32_ProcessStopTrace` fires when a process is terminated, and `Win32_ProcessTrace` fires on either kind of process event. To test these subscriptions, run the following command, which will start and stop an instance of the `calc` process a number of times (on Windows 10 – earlier versions of Windows called the process calc:

```
PS> & {
    Start-Process calc
    Start-Sleep 3
    Stop-Process -Name Calculator
    Start-Sleep 3
    Start-Process calc
    Start-Sleep 3
    Stop-Process -Name Calculator
    Start-Sleep 3
}
```

In this command, you're using `Start-Process` to start the `calc` process. After three seconds, you use `Stop-Process` to terminate the `calculator` instance. This pattern is repeated two times, and the whole thing is wrapped in a scriptblock to cause it to be executed as a single command, so you avoid having your commands mixed in with the output and cluttering things up. Here's the output produced by this command (Windows 10 also refers to `calc.exe` as `calculator.exe`):

```
Process Start: calc.exe
Process Start: Calculator.exe
Process Any: calc.exe
Process Any: Calculator.exe
Process Any: calc.exe
Process Stop: calc.exe
Process Stop: Calculator.exe
Process Any: Calculator.exe
Process Start: calc.exe
Process Any: calc.exe
Process Start: Calculator.exe
```

```
Process Any: Calculator.exe
Process Any: calc.exe
Process Stop: calc.exe
Process Stop: Calculator.exe
Process Any: Calculator.exe
```

The first two records were generated by the first `calc` process starting. You get both `Win32_ProcessStartTrace` and `Win32_ProcessTrace` firing, but not `Win32_ProcessStop-Trace`. The `calc` process is then stopped, resulting in two more records, and this is repeated one more time for a total of eight records. (The order in which the specific and general events are fired is nondeterministic, so the exact order will change with different runs of the start/stop command.)

The final step in this experiment is to clean up the event subscriptions you created. Here's the easiest way to do that:

```
PS> Get-EventSubscriber | Unregister-Event
PS> Get-Job | Remove-Job
```

> **NOTE** This code removes all event subscriptions for this session. That's fine for experimentation, but you should be careful doing this in a production environment and be selective about what is removed.

This completes the easy part of CIM event handling. Although setting up event handlers this way was easy, it was also limited. When you retrieve CIM object instances using `Get-CimInstance`, you're able to perform sophisticated filtering and can be precise about the objects you retrieve. You can be as precise with events, but doing so requires the use of WQL queries. We'll cover that in the next section.

QUERY-BASED CIM EVENT REGISTRATIONS

In chapter 16, you used the WMI Query Language to select and filter CIM objects. The format of those instance-based WQL queries was

```
SELECT <propertyList> FROM <ObjectClass> WHERE <predicateExpression>
```

With a little bit of additional syntax, WQL can also be used to select and filter CIM events.

> **NOTE** In CIM parlance, what you filter is called a *notification,* not an event. CIM defines an event as something that happens at a particular time like a process starting or a user logging on. Notifications are the object representation (or model) for these event occurrences. For simplicity, we're going to stick to using *event* for both cases in the rest of this chapter.

The core syntax for event queries is the same as for instance queries but with some additional features. We'll look at these features in the next couple of sections.

THE WITHIN KEYWORD

The first of the additional keywords we'll discuss is WITHIN. This keyword is used in a query as follows:

```
SELECT <propertyList> FROM <EventClass> WITHIN <Seconds> WHERE
  <predicateExpression>
```

The WITHIN keyword is used to specify the *polling interval* that the WMI service should use to monitor and relay event data. The polling interval is the frequency with which the monitored resource is checked. The smaller the polling interval, the more often the monitored resource will be checked. This results in faster and more accurate event notifications, but it also places a greater burden on the monitored system. The argument to the WITHIN keyword is a floating-point number. This means you could theoretically specify polling intervals of less than one second. But specifying a value that's too small (like 0.001 seconds) could cause the WMI service to reject a query as not valid due to the resource-intensive nature of polling. The polling interval should be chosen based on the type of event being monitored. If the event doesn't require instant action, it's generally recommended that the polling interval be greater than 300 seconds (5 minutes).

THE CIM INTRINSIC EVENT CLASSES

The objects you query for are also a bit different. With object events, you create an instance of an object and then subscribe to an event on that object. With CIM event queries, you subscribe to the type of event and then specify the event-generating class you're interested in. Some of the most useful of these intrinsic-event classes are _Instance-CreationEvent, _InstanceDeletionEvent, and _InstanceModificationEvent, which are all derived from _InstanceOperationEvent. These classes and their relationships are shown in figure 17.5.

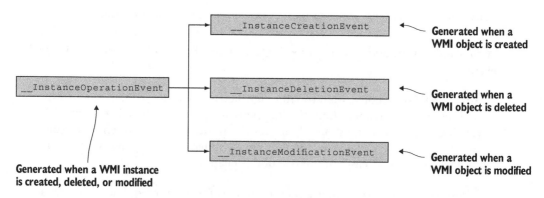

Figure 17.5   The class hierarchy for the CIM instance operation event class. These events are generated when a CIM is object is created, deleted, or modified. The base event class is triggered for all three.

These classes mirror the pattern you saw in the previous section, where `Win32_Process-Trace` was the root event with `Win32_ProcessStartTrace` and `Win32_ProcessStopTrace` as derived events. The difference here is that there's no class like Win32_Process mentioned in these events. They are general-purpose events generated by all objects. When you want to register an event subscription for one of these events, you use the `ISA` operator to select which class you're interested in receiving instance notifications from. Let's see what a query using the `WITHIN` keyword and these instance notifications events looks like:

```
PS> $svcQuery = @"
   SELECT * FROM __InstanceOperationEvent WITHIN 1
   WHERE TargetInstance ISA 'Win32_Service'
   AND TargetInstance.Name='BITS'
"@
```

This query says to retrieve all events from `InstanceOperationEvent` with a polling interval of 1 second (this is an experiment, so you use a small value) where the object generating the event is an instance of the `Win32_Service` class and the `Name` property on the instance is `BITS` (Background Intelligent Transfer Service). You want to generate an event anytime something happens to the BITS service.

Use the `Register-CimIndicationEvent` cmdlet to subscribe to this event. In the action field, display a message indicating the source of the event and then print out the contents of the $event variable:

```
PS> Register-CimIndicationEvent -Query $svcQuery -Action {
   Write-Host 'Got instance operation event on Win32_Service'
   $Event | Format-List * | Out-Host
}
```

With the event subscription set up, trigger the event by starting the BITS service:

```
PS> Start-Service BITS
Got instance operation event on Win32_Service
ComputerName      :
RunspaceId        : 2e7fa8de-aa03-4061-bce7-edf3a58d846d
EventIdentifier   : 1
Sender            : Microsoft.Management.Infrastructure.CimCmdlets.
   CimIndicationWatcher
SourceEventArgs   : Microsoft.Management.Infrastructure.CimCmdlets.
   CimIndicationEventInstanceEventArgs
SourceArgs        : {Microsoft.Management.Infrastructure.CimCmdlets.
   CimIndicationWatcher, }
SourceIdentifier : 2587f4cc-fea5-4711-8a6d-4ae648e2524d
TimeGenerated     : 16/05/2017 17:20:20
MessageData       :
```

After a second or so, you see the message printed out by the action scriptblock. Stop the service and you get a second message because the event you've subscribed to fires for any change.

In the next section, we'll look at additional features for improving the network behavior of the system by grouping events instead of sending them one at a time.

AGGREGATING EVENTS WITH GROUP

The next keyword we'll cover is GROUP. The GROUP clause is used to *aggregate* the events based on certain criteria. This means that instead of generating one notification per event, the WMI service will group them together with a count and a representative instance. This is another way to reduce the load on the client and the network:

```
SELECT * FROM EventClass [WHERE property = value]
    GROUP WITHIN interval [BY property_list]
    [HAVING NumberOfEvents operator integer]
```

You create a query-based WMI event registration using the -Query parameter set on Register-CimIndicationEvent. Let's set up this new event subscription. First, save your query in a string and set up a counter that will record the total number of events:

```
PS> $GroupQuery = @"
  Select * From __InstanceOperationEvent Within .5
  Where TargetInstance Isa 'Win32_Service'
  and TargetInstance.Name='BITS'
  Group Within 20
"@
PS> $global:TotalEvents = 0
```

Now register this event subscription:

```
PS> Register-CimIndicationEvent -Query $GroupQuery -Action {
    Write-Host 'Got grouped event'
    $ne = $Event.SourceEventArgs.NewEvent
    $ti = $ne.Representative.TargetInstance
    $global:TotalEvents += $ne.NumberOfEvents
    $msg = 'Type: ' + $ne.__CLASS +
      ' Num Evnts: ' + $ne.NumberOfEvents +
      ' Name: ' + $ti.Name +
      ' (' + $ti.DisplayName + ')' |
    Out-Host
}
```

In the body of the event action scriptblock, you'll format a string containing some of the more interesting fields (at least for the purpose of this experiment). You'll show the type of the event class, the number of events that have been aggregated, and then the Name and DisplayName for the matched service. You'll generate a series of events using a foreach loop to cause the event aggregation to fire:

```
PS> foreach ($i in 1..3){
    Start-Service -Name BITS
    Start-Sleep 2
    Stop-Service -Name BITS
    Start-Sleep 2
}
```

These events will all be accumulated in the event group, and when the group interval expires, you should get an event notification. Use the `Start-Sleep` command to wait for the timeout to expire:

```
PS> Start-Sleep 10
Got grouped event
Type:  Num Evnts: 6 Name: BITS (Background Intelligent Transfer Service)
```

The event count shows your total:

```
PS> "Total events: $TotalEvents"
Total events: 6
```

Now that you have your event, let's clean up the event subscription:

```
PS> Get-EventSubscriber | Unregister-Event
```

In this example, you've seen how you can use the GROUP keyword to further reduce the number of events that need to be sent to the monitoring script.

This completes our look at CIM eventing, so let's move on to something a bit different. Up until now, we've only been talking about how to respond to events. In the next section, you'll see how to generate some events of your own.

17.2.11 Engine events

The last category of events we're going to look at is *engine events*. With engine events, the notifications are generated by the PowerShell engine itself, either through one of the predefined engine events or by explicitly generating an event in a script using the `New-Event` cmdlet.

PREDEFINED ENGINE EVENTS

There's currently only one predefined engine event identified by the string "Power-Shell.Exiting". This string can also be retrieved using a static method as follows:

```
PS> [System.Management.Automation.PsEngineEvent]::Exiting
PowerShell.Exiting
```

This event is triggered when the PowerShell engine is shutting down and allows you to perform actions before the session exits. Here's an example event registration:

```
PS> Register-EngineEvent `
  -SourceIdentifier PowerShell.Exiting `
  -Action {
    "@{Directory='$PWD'}" > ~/pshState.ps1
  }
```

This command registers an action to take when the PowerShell session ends. This action writes a hashtable to the file pshState.ps1 in the user's directory. The hashtable captures the user's current directory at the time the session was exited. Let's use this in an example. You'll create a child `PowerShell.exe` process to run your script so you don't have to exit the current process. PowerShell recognizes when a scriptblock is passed to the `PowerShell.exe` command and makes sure that everything gets passed to the command correctly. Let's run the command:

```
PS> powershell {
      Register-EngineEvent `
        -SourceIdentifier PowerShell.Exiting `
        -Action {
          "@{Directory='$PWD'}" > ~/pshState.ps1
          } | Format-List Id,Name
        cd ~/desktop
        exit
    }
Id   : 3
Name : PowerShell.Exiting
```

Now look at the content of the file:

```
PS> Get-Content ~/pshState.ps1
@{Directory='C:\Users\brucepay.REDMOND\desktop'}
```

You see that the file contains a hashtable with the current directory recorded in it. This example can easily be expanded to include things like the user's history or the contents of the `function:` drive, but adding those extensions is left as an exercise for the reader.

The other class of engine events is script-generated events. We'll look at those next.

17.2.12 *Generating events in functions and scripts*

The last of the core eventing cmdlets to look at is the `New-Event` cmdlet. This cmdlet allows a script to generate its own events. Let's use this cmdlet in an example to see how it works. First, you create the timer object:

```
PS> $timer = New-Object System.Timers.Timer -Property @{
  Interval = 5000; Enabled = $true; AutoReset = $false }
```

Then you register the event subscription:

```
PS> Register-ObjectEvent $timer Elapsed -Action {
  Write-Host '<TIMER>'
  New-Event -SourceIdentifier generatedEvent -Sender 3.14
} > $null
```

In the handler scriptblock, as well as writing out a message, you're calling `New-Event` to generate a new event in the event queue. Finally, start the timer

```
PS> $timer.Start() > $null
```

and wait for the event. Pipe the object returned from `Wait-Event` into the `foreach`
cmdlet for processing:

```
PS> Wait-Event -SourceIdentifier generatedEvent |
foreach {
    'Received generated event'
    $_ |
    Format-Table -AutoSize SourceIdentifier, EventIdentifier, Sender
    $_ | Remove-Event
}

Received generated event

SourceIdentifier EventIdentifier Sender
---------------- --------------- ------
generatedEvent                 2    3.14
```

You see the output from `Wait-Event`. In the `foreach` block, you display the source
identifier of the event generated by `New-Event`, and the `Sender` field shows the number
you passed to the cmdlet. When you've finished with this example, you'll remove the
event subscription:

```
PS> Get-EventSubscriber | Unregister-Event
```

This pretty much completes the local event-handling story. But with PowerShell's
remoting capabilities, obviously your eventing infrastructure needs to work in a distributed environment as well. In the next section you'll see how to work with events in
remote scenarios.

17.2.13 Remoting and event forwarding

Being able to set up local event handlers is useful, but you also need to be able to process events generated on remote computers to manage distributed datacenters. The
PowerShell eventing subsystem, by building on top of PowerShell remoting, makes this
surprisingly easy. In figure 17.6 notice the `-Forward` parameter. This parameter does
exactly what you might expect: it forwards the subscribed event to a remote session.
This is where the `-SourceIdentifier` parameter becomes critical. The source identifier name that's specified at the event source end becomes the name of the event to
process on the receiving end. This process is illustrated in figure 17.6.

Here's where the engine events come into play. The forwarded events are handled
using engine event processing. `Register-EngineEvent` lets you register subscriptions
that trigger the event handler based on the subscription identifier sent from the remote
end. The events generated by `New-Event` in the previous section are also engine events.
In the next section, we'll look at a detailed example where you forward an event from
one machine for processing on another.

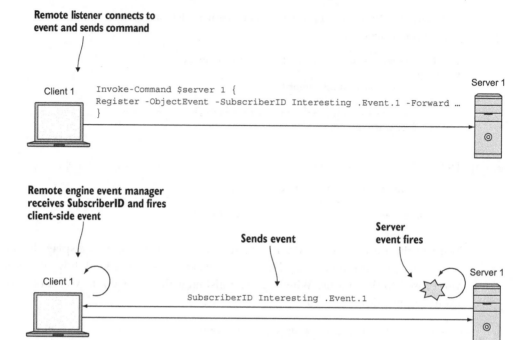

Remote listener connects to event and sends command

Client 1

```
Invoke-Command $server 1 {
Register -ObjectEvent -SubscriberID Interesting .Event.1 -Forward ...
}
```

Server 1

Remote engine event manager receives SubscriberID and fires client-side event

Sends event

Server event fires

Client 1

```
SubscriberID Interesting .Event.1
```

Server 1

Figure 17.6 The second-hop authentication changes when credential delegation is used. Without delegation, the second hop from server 1 to server 2 authenticates as the user that the service is running under. With credential forwarding enabled, server 1 can use the client credentials to authenticate to server 2 as the client user.

HANDLING REMOTE EVENTLOG EVENTS

In this section, you're going to apply what you've learned. Your goal is to be notified locally every time an event is written into the event log on a remote computer. The .NET EventLog class exposes such an event: EntryWritten. To set this up, you must establish event forwarding on the remote machine and then register a load event handler. You'll also need to maintain a connection to the remote end using the duration of time you want to get events because the events are being forwarded over this channel.

The first thing you need to do is to establish a connection to the target computer. You do so with the New-PSSession cmdlet, passing credentials if needed:

```
PS> $s = New-PSSession -ComputerName W16DSC01
```

This is the session you'll use to set up the event forwarding and then transfer the forwarded events. Next, you'll use Invoke-Command to set up the event-forwarding registration. The code to do that looks like this:

```
PS> Invoke-Command -Session $s {
    $myLog = New-Object System.Diagnostics.EventLog application
    Register-ObjectEvent `
```

```
        -InputObject $myLog    `
        -SourceIdentifier EventWatcher1 `
        -EventName EntryWritten `
        -Forward

    $myLog.EnableRaisingEvents = $true
}
```

Inside the scriptblock passed to `Invoke-Command`, you're creating an `EventLog` object associated with the `Application` event log. Then you use `Register-ObjectEvent` to set up event forwarding for events that occur on the `EntryWritten` event. You'll use the source identifier name `EventWatcher1`. Finally, you enable raising events on the event log object.

With the remote end configured, it's time to set up the local end. This task is much simpler. You register an engine event handler that will trigger on the source ID matching the remote end:

```
PS> Register-EngineEvent -SourceIdentifier EventWatcher1 -Action {
    param($sender, $event)

    Write-Host "Got an event: $($event.entry.message)"
}
```

And you're finished. Now whenever an entry is added to the Application event log on the remote computer, you'll see the entry message displayed on your console. If you're impatient, you can trigger an event yourself. Use the .NET `FailFast()` API to cause a "Watson" event to be generated by crashing a PowerShell process on the remote machine:

```
PS> powershell "[System.Environment]::FailFast('An event')"
```

After a short time, you'll see something like the following displayed on the console:

```
Got an event:
```

Well, this sort of worked. The event did trigger the event handler, and you got the part of the event you wrote. Unfortunately, the most interesting piece—the message in the event itself—is mysteriously absent. You'll see what happened in the next section.

SERIALIZATION ISSUES WITH REMOTE EVENTS

The serialization mechanism used by remoting can sometimes cause problems when using remote events. Because the event is being sent over the remoting channel, it has to be serialized by the PowerShell serializer. By default, the serialization depth is only 1. This means you get the top-level properties but not the second-level properties. To preserve the message content in `$event.Entry.Message`, you need to change the serialization depth for this type of object to 2. You need an XML document that you can pass to `Update-TypeData` to change the serialization depth for

`System.Diagnostics.EntryWrittenEventArgs` to 2. Save this XML in a variable as a string for now:

```
$typeSpec = @'
<Types>
    <Type>
        <Name>System.Diagnostics.EntryWrittenEventArgs</Name>
        <Members>
            <MemberSet>
                <Name>PSStandardMembers</Name>
                <Members>
                    <NoteProperty>
                        <Name>SerializationDepth</Name>
                        <Value>2</Value>
                    </NoteProperty>
                </Members>
            </MemberSet>
        </Members>
    </Type>
</Types>
'@
```

Now before you use this to set up new events, you should remove the existing event registrations on both the local and remote ends of the connection:

```
PS> Invoke-Command $s { Unregister-Event EventWatcher1 }
PS> Unregister-Event EventWatcher1
```

You have the XML in a local variable but you need to update the type metadata on the remote end. You need to get the content of the $typeSpec variable over to the remote machine, which you'll do by passing it as an argument to the Invoke-Command scriptblock:

```
PS> Invoke-Command -ArgumentList $typeSpec -Session $s {
        param ($typeSpec)

        $tfile = New-TemporaryFile
        $newfilename = $tfile.FullName -replace '\.tmp$', '.ps1xml'
        Rename-Item -Path $tfile.FullName -NewName $newfilename
        Set-Content -Value $typeSpec -Path $newfilename

        Update-TypeData -PrependPath $newfilename
        Remove-Item -Path $newfilename -Force
}
```

Let's go over what's happening in this scriptblock. First, you're using the PowerShell v5 cmdlet New-TemporaryFile to create a temporary file in your TEMP folder. Because the default extension on the filename that's returned is .tmp and you need it to be .ps1xml, you use the -replace operator to change the extension and rename the file. Then you write $typeSpec to the file using Set-Content, call Update-TypeData to load the file, and clean up by removing the temp file.

With the type metadata updated, you can set up the remote event registration as before:

```
PS> Invoke-Command $s {
    $myLog = New-Object System.Diagnostics.EventLog application
    Register-ObjectEvent `
        -InputObject $myLog `
        -SourceIdentifier EventWatcher1 `
        -EventName EntryWritten `
        -Forward

    $myLog.EnableRaisingEvents = $true
}
```

then set up the local event subscription:

```
PS> Register-EngineEvent -SourceIdentifier EventWatcher1 -Action {
    param($sender, $event)

    Write-Host "Got an event: $($event.entry.message)"
}
```

And finally, you're ready to try your event trigger on the remote machine again:

```
PS> powershell "[System.Environment]::FailFast('An event')"
```

This time, you'll see the event messages including the text from the call to `FailFast()` as written into the event log on the remote system.

Congratulations! We've pretty much reached the end of our eventing discussion and you're still with us. Event processing is an advanced topic, even for full-time programmers. Understanding how multiple actions are going to interoperate can be mind-boggling. PowerShell's approach to eventing is designed to make this as simple as possible, but understanding how it works under the hood can go a long way toward helping you figure things out. Let's take a peek.

17.2.14 How eventing works

The eventing infrastructure relies on two other components of PowerShell: modules (for isolation, as discussed earlier) and jobs (for managing subscriptions). When you registered an event subscription, you saw that an object was returned. This object is, in fact, a job object, with the same base class as the object you get back from `Start-Job` or the `-AsJob` parameter on `Invoke-Command`. Once an event subscription is created, it will show up in the `Job` table, which means you can use the `Get-Job` cmdlet as another way to find this subscription. Let's go back to our timer event subscription and see what this looks like:

```
PS> $timer = New-Object -TypeName System.Timers.Timer
PS> Register-ObjectEvent -InputObject $timer `
  -EventName Elapsed -Action { Write-Host '<TIMER>' }
```

```
PS> Get-Job | Format-List

Module          : __DynamicModule_c83413eb-bad9-47eb-88b0-e4d38ff2aa7f
StatusMessage   :
HasMoreData     : False
Location        :
Command         :  Write-Host '<TIMER>'
JobStateInfo    : NotStarted
Finished        : System.Threading.ManualResetEvent
InstanceId      : 1f73bb6b-5fe0-4ce4-8d2e-f750f3a4c1ed
Id              : 4
Name            : d49bc9da-dfd5-4b5a-9cc9-5b44b508415c
ChildJobs       : {}
PSBeginTime     :
PSEndTime       :
PSJobTypeName   :
Output          : {}
Error           : {}
Progress        : {}
Verbose         : {}
Debug           : {}
Warning         : {}
Information     : {}
State           : NotStarted
```

Let's start the timer running again, setting the interval to something large so you can still type:

```
PS> $timer.Interval = 60000
PS> $timer.Start()
```

Now when you run Get-Job after the timer has started (you may need to wait a little while)

```
PS> Get-Job | Format-Table State,Command -AutoSize

State    Command
-----    -------
Running  Write-Host '<TIMER>'
```

you see that the job state has been changed to Running. The other thing you should be able to do if it's a Job is to stop it by calling Stop-Job. It works. But this code has done more than stop the job—it's also removed the event subscription!

Because event handlers are effectively running in the background, it seems logical to manage an active subscription as a Job. You should note that, although the executing event handler is represented as a Job, it wasn't started using Start-Job and, unlike PowerShell jobs, still runs in process with the session that set up the subscription.

At the beginning of our discussion on events, we talked about the issues involved in dealing with asynchronous events. Because these events can occur in any order, great care is required to make sure that the integrity of shared data structures is maintained. To maintain this integrity, you have to make sure that programs synchronize access to the shared objects, and doing so turns out to be difficult. In fact, this is one of the most common reasons that a program stops responding and appears to be hung. If two actions are trying to update a synchronized object at the same time, they can end up blocking each other, each trying to get exclusive access to the resource. This type of contention is called a *deadlock*.

PowerShell deals with this problem by imposing a strict order on the actions instead of on individual data objects. When an asynchronous event occurs, the eventing subsystem adds that event object to the event queue. Then, at various points in the PowerShell runtime, the engine checks to see if there are any events posted to the event queue. If there are, the engine suspends the mainline activity, pulls an event off the queue, switches to the module context for that event handler, and then executes the event scriptblock. This queuing mechanism is illustrated in figure 17.7.

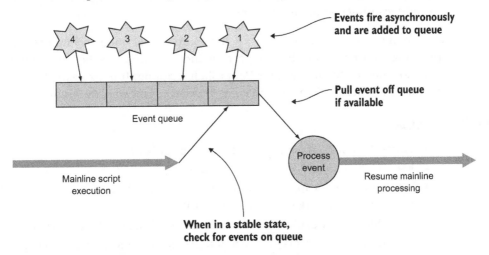

Figure 17.7 How asynchronous event processing is handled in PowerShell. As events occur, they're added to the queue asynchronously. At various stable points, the engine checks the queue and pulls events off to execute. Once the event execution is complete, normal processing resumes.

Events are added to the queue as they arrive and then are pulled off the queue by the engine and processed when a convenient spot is reached.

To make sure events are processed in a timely manner, the engine needs to check the queue fairly often, but if it checks too often, it will substantially slow down the interpreter. In PowerShell, the engine checks for events in all calls that write objects, including between each stage in a pipeline. It also checks between each statement in a script and anywhere the engine might loop for a long time. This provides a good trade-off between event latency and overall performance. In the case where multiple events are pending on the queue at the time of the check, the engine will use a throttling policy to decide how many of the pending events will be processed before returning to the mainline so that the foreground activity isn't "starved." (As an aside, the places where the event queue is checked are the same places that the engine checks to see if it has been requested to stop executing, such as when the user presses Ctrl-C.)

If the event has an action block associated with it, that scriptblock executes until it's completed. Once the event action is finished, the mainline activity is resumed. Because the engine processes events only when it knows the system state is stable, problems related to inconsistent system state don't arise, and all activity is effectively synchronous.

> **NOTE** An event action runs until it's complete. As long as it's running, no other events are processed, and the mainline activity is suspended. This means that event handlers shouldn't be written to execute for a long time. The same consideration exists when writing GUIs. If a control's event handler runs on the UI thread for a long time, the UI will be blocked, unable to respond to events, causing it to appear to hang.

This architecture isn't as efficient as the more fine-grained techniques, so it's not appropriate for programs that are performance-sensitive. It is, however, simple, effective, and completely sufficient for PowerShell scripting. It makes asynchronous event handling in PowerShell a reasonable if somewhat advanced proposition.

17.3 Summary

- PowerShell doesn't load all .NET classes by default.
- Use Add-Type to load additional assemblies.
- You can write GUI applications in PowerShell, but that doesn't mean you should.
- PowerShell can work with WinForms or WPF.
- PowerShell can work with events from .NET, CIM, and the PowerShell engine.
- Synchronous events occur one at a time—for instance, a button click in a GUI application.
- Asynchronous events can occur at any time and can interrupt other actions.
- Events are registered in a PowerShell session. If the session is closed, the registrations are lost.
- Use a source identifier to identify events.
- Use scriptblocks to define the action to be taken if an event is triggered.
- New-Event is used to create events from within scripts and functions.
- Events work with the job system.
- Events can be forwarded from a remote machine to the local machine.
- Serialization can cause problems with remote events—you need to change serialization depth to 2.

It's time to investigate some of the newer features in PowerShell. We'll start with Desired State Configuration in the next chapter.

18
Desired State Configuration

This chapter covers
- The need for Desired State Configuration (DSC)
- Configuration management theory
- DSC architecture
- DSC modes: push and pull
- Local configuration manager
- Partial configurations

Make it so!

—*Captain Jean-Luc Picard,* USS Enterprise-D

The need to build and configure servers quickly in a consistent, repeatable manner has been a longstanding problem in IT. One solution is to adopt Desired State Configuration (DSC), a PowerShell extension introduced with Windows Server 2012 R2 (PowerShell v4) and extended in Windows Server 2016 (PowerShell v5). DSC provides a mechanism to manage the configuration of your server estate, including:

- Add or remove Windows features
- Manage registry, files, and folders
- Manage processes and services
- Install and manage software packages

711

In addition, DSC can monitor the server configuration you've applied and, if necessary, reset the configuration to the desired state if the current configuration has been modified so that it doesn't match the desired state. DSC can also be configured to manage reboots required by configuration changes.

In this chapter, we'll introduce you to DSC. We'll start by explaining the need for DSC and going over the underlying theory of configuration management. After reviewing the architecture of DSC, we'll demonstrate how it works with examples.

DSC can work in two modes: push and pull. In *push* mode, you're responsible for delivering the configuration to the server. In *pull* mode, the target server pulls its configuration from the DSC server. We'll explain how to set up both options and why push mode scales better to the enterprise.

We'll also explore the Local Configuration Manager, a DSC component local to each target server. The chapter closes with a look at how configurations can be broken into parts that can be managed by different teams, called *partial configurations*.

First let's look at the theory.

18.1   *DSC model and architecture*

In this section, we'll look at why you need DSC, then examine the DSC model and architecture. First, let's recap why we need configuration management in general and DSC in particular.

18.1.1   *The need for configuration management*

The number of servers in an organization has grown significantly over the years, and continues to grow. The introduction of virtualization, containers, and programming methodologies such as Agile programming, means that servers can and must be created quickly to meet the changing business needs of the organization. Organizations are moving new applications into production with increasing frequency; sometimes multiple new builds are issued in a day, all needing new servers.

The "traditional" method of manually configuring servers fails for a number of reasons:

- *It's a slow process*—Installing and configuring the operating system and required software can take a minimum of several hours.
- *The process is error prone*—Even with checklists it's easy to miss a step.
- *It's non-repeatable*—You can't guarantee that two servers will be configured identically. Different administrators may have differing views about how a server should be configured or be working from different versions of the build instructions.
- *Undocumented changes are made*—Configurations drift from the baseline with time.

This situation is also summed up in figure 18.1, where the requirement is to build six identical servers. In reality, even if the same person builds each server, there will be differences. The potential differences become greater if the servers are built by different people.

Requirement

Reality

Figure 18.1 A common requirement of six identically configured servers. The reality is that each will be different.

One approach is to script your builds. Scripting has a number of drawbacks, including the fact that not all administrators are comfortable with it. Also, ensuring that a common version of the script is used can be problematic. Some configuration tasks require advanced scripting skills that may not be available in the organization.

The server configuration problem becomes twofold: first, you need the processes in place to manage configuration management, and second, you need the tools to perform configuration management. Configuration management is part of a wider DevOps framework and should be introduced into your organization as part of your adoption of DevOps processes. How you move your organization to embracing the DevOps principles is outside of our scope.

A number of tools have been created in recent years for managing configurations. Some examples are Puppet (https://puppet.com), Chef (www.chef.io), Salt (https://saltstack.com), and Ansible (www.ansible.com). These tools are all from the UNIX/Linux world and so require a Linux system to install them on. As a consequence of their origin, Puppet, Chef, and the other tools work well in the Linux space. But when it came to implementing their toolsets on Windows, they've struggled. This was partly because Windows is an API-driven operating system, as opposed to the document-driven nature of Linux. Also, many Windows administrators have been reluctant to learn Linux merely to bring configuration management into their environment.

Enter DSC. It is intended to supply a basic configuration management framework for Windows that can be used directly by Windows administrators. It's also intended to make it easier for the manufacturers of existing configuration tools to work with Windows by enabling them to use DSC.

Now you know why you need DSC. Before we look at its architecture, let's look at the DSC model of configuration management.

18.1.2 *Desired State Configuration model*

Creating a PowerShell script to configure one or more servers builds on the knowledge and skills you already possess. Everything you've learned in the book so far can help you create those scripts.

DSC introduces you to a different way of thinking. You're telling the system how you want it to be configured, you're not necessarily worried about how it gets to the desired state. You are in effect creating a model of the desired state and applying that model. In practice, this means that you create a configuration that is transported and applied to the target server. The sequence of operations is:

1 A configuration is created.
2 A MOF file is generated from the configuration.
3 The MOF file is transported to the target server.
4 The target server implements the configuration.

MOF files

DSC uses Managed Object Format (MOF) files to transfer configuration information to the target machine. MOF is part of the DMTF CIM standard (originally implemented on Windows as WMI—see chapter 16). The MOF file generated from a configuration is a fully resolved pure-data representation of the configuration. There are no unresolved variables in the MOF file. MOF was chosen because it's a format that allows you to represent the classes defining an object as well as instances of those objects.

In this section, we'll discuss these concepts and explain how DSC differs from the PowerShell scripting you know and love.

DECLARATIVE PROGRAMMING

One of the exercises from our English lessons in school was having to write a set of instructions to perform a task. Think about making a cheese sandwich. You have to perform a number of discrete steps:

- Remove two slices of bread from packet
- Butter one side of each slice
- Put one slice on plate butter side up
- Cut cheese into slices
- Place slices on bead
- Put second slice on top of cheese, butter side down
- Cut sandwich in half

That list shows the major steps. The process could easily run to 30 or more steps if each were broken down further. You may not realize it, but this is how your PowerShell scripts work—you provide a set of instructions that PowerShell (hopefully) executes to completion. This approach is known as *procedural*, or *imperative*, programming. You tell the system how to perform the tasks.

DSC doesn't work this way. DSC is declarative. You tell the system how you want it to be configured, and it goes off and performs the task *without* your having to provide all the intermediate commands. Captain Picard doesn't tell his subordinates how to do things. He tells them what they have to do, and when they're ready to proceed he says, "Make it so." Applying that philosophy to our cheese sandwich example, we'd have a single step that stated, "Make a cheese sandwich."

Now that you understand how you'll be thinking about things in a different way, let's look at the DSC model.

DSC MODEL BREAKDOWN

The DSC model requires three things:

1   An external representation of the desired state of the system, called a configuration
2   A way to get and set the system state
3   A way to compare the desired state against the current state and enact the changes that need to be made to bring the system into compliance with the desired state

This model is illustrated in figure 18.2.

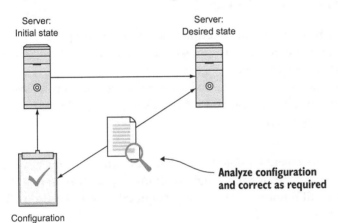

Server:
Initial state

Server:
Desired state

Analyze configuration
and correct as required

Configuration

Figure 18.2   DSC model showing the initial and desired state

Let's examine the individual model parts. We'll be covering each in greater depth later in the chapter. The most important point is that you need a representation of the desired state that exists independently from the current state of the system. This allows you to compare the desired state against the current state, compute the differences, and then perform the necessary steps to bring the current state into compliance with the desired state.

DSC CONFIGURATION

The representation of the desired state of the system is called a *configuration*. In DSC, a configuration is made up of components called *resources*, which represent concrete aspects of the system, like files, processes, or services. An example of a DSC configuration containing a single resource looks like this:

```
Configuration AddFile {
    File TestFolder {
        Ensure = 'Present'
        Type = 'Directory'
```

```
        DestinationPath = 'C:\TestFolder'
        Force = $true
    }
}
```

The configuration checks whether a folder called TestFolder is present on the C: drive of the target machine. If the folder isn't found, it is created. We'll cover creation of DSC configurations in more detail later in this chapter.

Once you have a configuration, you need a way to apply it against the target machine. Doing that involves testing the current configuration and making any changes to bring it in line with the desired configuration.

NOTE DSC requires the ability to uniquely identify a resource on the system: the *key* property. (In some cases, such as the WindowsProcess resource, this had to be fudged by the PowerShell team).

A DSC configuration represents a *single* terminal state for the target machine. That's why you can't have a document that says a resource is both 1 and 0, because that's a temporally impossible terminal state.

The DSC agent is *monotonic* in operation—each resource moves you closer to the desired terminal state. It never moves you farther away (though the resource implementation may do that internally).

DSC RESOURCES

DSC configurations are created using DSC resources. The previously mentioned configuration uses the `File` resource, though we didn't explicitly state this. The `File` resource is one of a small number of DSC resources installed with PowerShell. These resources enable you to

- Manage files and folders
- Manage the registry, event logs, processes, and services
- Manage Windows operating system roles and features
- Manage local users and groups

There are many more resources on the PowerShell Gallery—over 900 at the time of writing. You can find the available resources using

```
PS> Find-DscResource

Name                        Version  ModuleName      Repository
----                        -------  ----------      ----------
Group                       2.3.0.0  PSDscResources  PSGallery
GroupSet                    2.3.0.0  PSDscResources  PSGallery
Registry                    2.3.0.0  PSDscResources  PSGallery
Script                      2.3.0.0  PSDscResources  PSGallery
Service                     2.3.0.0  PSDscResources  PSGallery
xDefaultGatewayAddress      3.1.0.0  xNetworking     PSGallery
xDHCPClient                 3.1.0.0  xNetworking     PSGallery
xDnsClientGlobalSetting     3.1.0.0  xNetworking     PSGallery
```

```
cNtfsPermissionEntry         1.3.0    cNtfsAccessControl PSGallery
cNtfsPermissionsInheritance 1.3.0    cNtfsAccessControl PSGallery
```

NOTE This is a small sample of the available resources.

You'll notice that some of the resources have a *c* or an *x* as a prefix. These prefixes indicate that a resource is supplied by the PowerShell community (*c*) or is a Microsoft-supplied resource that's classed as experimental (*x*, meaning it may change).

Resources are delivered as modules. To use a resource from the gallery, download and install the module that contains the resource, as discussed in chapter 9. If you can't find a ready-made resource, you can write your own—we'll show you how to do that in chapter 19 when we discuss PowerShell classes.

IDEMPOTENT OPERATION

What happens if you run an imperative script that changes your server's configuration and then rerun it at some future time? If you're lucky, nothing bad happens during the rerun, but it's quite possible for the server configuration to be damaged so that the server becomes unusable.

DSC (like all good configuration management systems) is *idempotent*—the configuration can be applied multiple times without changing the result beyond the initial application. For a simple example, multiplying by 1 is an idempotent operation:

```
PS> 9*1
9
PS> 9*1*1
9
PS> 9*1*1*1
9
PS> 9*1*1*1*1
9
```

You can multiply a number by 1 as many times as you want, and you'll always get the same result.

Applying a DSC configuration multiple times to the same target gives the desired configuration. DSC checks whether the server is compliant with the configuration and, if so, doesn't make any changes . We'll show this in action in section 18.2.

DSC VERSIONS

DSC was originally introduced with Windows Server 2012 R2. Since that time, a number of changes have been made to DSC that produce different versions. The major changes occurred as follows:

- Windows 2012 R2 RTM, July 2013
- Windows 2012 R2 General Availability, October 2013
- Windows 2012 R2 Update, November 2014
- DSC for Linux, versions 1.0 and 1.1, May 2015 and September 2015 respectively
- WMF 4.0 update for Windows 2012 and 2008 R2, January 2016

- WMF 5.0 RTM, December 2015
- Windows 2016 and WMF 5.1, October 2016

In practical terms, this means there are potential conflicts in the MOF file (usually the introduction of new properties) between these versions. The versions are backward-compatible; old versions work with new versions, but not vice versa. You need to either be consistent between the DSC versions on the machine on which you create the configuration and the machine to which you apply it, or modify the MOF as applicable to accommodate the differences. We recommend consistency between DSC versions as the safest approach.

18.1.3 *DSC architecture*

The architecture of DSC is illustrated in figure 18.3.

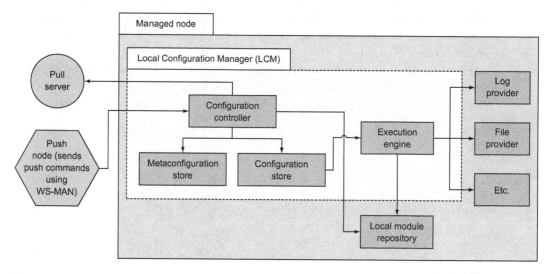

Figure 18.3   DSC architecture

The important point in the DSC architecture is the separation of the managed node (the large box in figure 18.3) from the source configuration (written in PowerShell) on the pull server or the push node (on the left-hand side of the figure). The server passes a static, intermediate representation of the configuration (a MOF file) to the Local Configuration Manager (LCM) on the managed node.

The LCM takes each resource in the MOF file and passes it to the corresponding resource provider. The resource providers are pieces of PowerShell code contained in modules that are responsible for ensuring that the system is compliant with the resources in the configuration.

The configuration controller does a couple of things: It validates the MOF file (valid syntax schema is correct, and so on) and it checks to see if all the necessary resource providers are available. If there are missing providers, and a pull server is configured, then the resources are downloaded. If it's not configured to download resources, then it fails the validation process. The execution engine is only responsible for interpreting the configuration and calling the providers. If you push the configuration to the managed node, you have to ensure that the required modules are also installed on the managed node.

On Windows, the resources can be written in PowerShell or in unmanaged code as WMI providers, though that's not encouraged—resources should be written *only* in PowerShell. On Linux, they are currently written in Python. Generalizing the LCM-to-resource-provider interface to allow the providers to be written in pretty much any language has been discussed by the PowerShell team, but that won't happen in the near future.

This architecture and set of abstractions let Windows administrators manage Linux without needing any special knowledge of Linux, and vice versa. In the case of simple configurations, they can be written without even knowing much about PowerShell!

Enough theory—it's time to see how this works in practice.

18.2 Push mode to a single node

Push mode is the simplest way to use DSC. You can construct configurations that apply to single nodes or multiple nodes. In a single configuration file, you can set one or many configuration items with interlocking dependencies, based on the complexity of your configuration. Installing a single Windows feature may require only a single configuration item, whereas installing and configuring multiple features could require a number of configuration items.

> **NOTE** You'll get most benefit from this chapter by trying these examples in your *test* environment. Viewing the output from the application of a configuration is useful and educational.

Push mode is the ideal place to start with DSC, but it has issues—and limitations—you need to understand. We'll start by showing you how to create a DSC configuration for a single node.

18.2.1 Create configuration

In section 18.1 we showed you an example configuration that creates a folder:

```
Configuration AddFile {

    File TestFolder {
        Ensure = 'Present'
        Type = 'Directory'
        DestinationPath = 'C:\TestFolder'
        Force = $true
    }
}
```

Let's use another option: create the folder and add a file to the folder, as shown here.

Listing 18.1   A simple push configuration

```
Configuration AddFile {                        ❶  Define
    Node W16TGT01 {                                target name

        File TestFile {                                   ❷  Define file
            Ensure = 'Present'                                configuration
            Type = 'File'
            DestinationPath = 'C:\TestFolder\TestFile1.txt'
            Contents = 'My first Configuration'
            Force = $true
        }
    }
}
                                               ❸  Create
AddFile -OutputPath .\MOF                           MOF file
```

The configuration is named `AddFile`. Configuration names are arbitrary. The `Node` keyword ❶ defines the computer to which the configuration will be applied. If you don't use `Node`, the configuration will be applied to the local machine (the MOF file will be named `localhost.mof`).

The configuration item ❷ uses the `File` resource to ensure that a file named Test-File1.txt is present in the folder and has `'My first configuration'` set as its contents. If the folder structure you specify in the path for your file isn't present, the configuration will create the appropriate path.

The configuration is run ❸, and a MOF file is created in the MOF subfolder of the current folder.

> **NOTE** If you don't use `-OutputPath` when you run the configuration, your MOF file will be created in a subfolder with the same name as the configuration. How you organize your MOF files is up to you, but we recommend you decide on a method and stick with it.

18.2.2 *MOF file contents*

Running the configuration produces the following output:

```
PS> AddFile -OutputPath .\MOF

WARNING: The configuration 'AddFile' is loading one or more built-
    in resources without explicitly importing associated modules. Add
    Import-DscResource -ModuleName 'PSDesiredStateConfiguration' to your
    configuration to avoid this message.

    Directory: C:\Scripts\MOF

Mode                LastWriteTime         Length Name
----                -------------         ------ ----
-a----        05/02/2017     11:09          2868 W16TGT01.mof
```

You can stop the warning message appearing by adding this line of code immediately before the Node keyword:

```
Import-DscResource -ModuleName PSDesiredStateConfiguration
```

See listing 18.4 for an example.

> **NOTE** You need to import any resou.rces you use other than the built-in resources, so this is a good habit to get into.

Here is the MOF file you generated.

Listing 18.2 MOF file created by listing 18.1

```
/*
@TargetNode='W16TGT01'
@GeneratedBy=Richard
@GenerationDate=05/02/2017 11:09:03
@GenerationHost=W16DSC01
*/

instance of MSFT_FileDirectoryConfiguration as $MSFT_
   FileDirectoryConfiguration1ref
{
ResourceID = "[File]TestFile";
 Type = "File";
 Ensure = "Present";
 Contents = "My first Configuration";
 DestinationPath = "C:\\TestFolder\\TestFile1.txt";
 Force = True;
 ModuleName = "PSDesiredStateConfiguration";
 SourceInfo = "C:\\Scripts\\PIA3e\\Listing18.1.ps1::3::5::File";

ModuleVersion = "1.0";
 ConfigurationName = "AddFile";
};
instance of OMI_ConfigurationDocument
                    {
 Version="2.0.0";
                    MinimumCompatibleVersion = "1.0.0";
                    CompatibleVersionAdditionalProperties=
   {"Omi_BaseResource:ConfigurationName"};
                    Author="Richard";
                    GenerationDate="05/02/2017 11:09:03";
                    GenerationHost="W16DSC01";
                    Name="AddFile";
                    };
```

> **NOTE** We've removed some blank lines from listing 18.2 to save space.

The MOF file starts with a header block that includes information on the target node and the machine and user that generated the file. Each resource instance has a corresponding block in the MOF file that starts

```
instance of MSFT_FileDirectoryConfiguration
```

You can compare the information in these blocks directly with the corresponding configuration item. The CIM classes given in the MOF file can be found in the ROOT\ Microsoft\Windows\DesiredStateConfiguration namespace.

The last block in the MOF file starts

```
instance of OMI_ConfigurationDocument
```

The contents of this block vary, depending on the version of PowerShell used to generate the MOF file. If you don't have matching DSC versions on your target machines and the machine you use to generate the MOF file, you may get an error when you apply the MOF file. The best approach is to ensure the PowerShell versions match—otherwise, you may need to edit the MOF file to remove lines that earlier versions of PowerShell can't handle. The error message should indicate the line in the MOF file causing the problem.

The next step is to apply the MOF to the target computer.

18.2.3 *Applying the configuration*

Once you've generated the MOF file, you can apply the configuration to your target machine:

```
PS> Start-DscConfiguration -ComputerName W16TGT01 -Path .\MOF\ `
-Wait -Verbose

VERBOSE: Perform operation 'Invoke CimMethod' with following parameters,
  ''methodName' = SendConfigurationApply,'className' =
MSFT_DSCLocalConfigurationManager,'namespaceName' = root/Microsoft/Windows/
  DesiredStateConfiguration'.
VERBOSE: An LCM method call arrived from computer W16DSC01 with
user sid S-1-5-21-759617655-3516038109-1479587680-1104.
VERBOSE: [W16TGT01]: LCM:  [ Start  Set       ]
VERBOSE: [W16TGT01]: LCM:  [ Start  Resource  ]  [[File]TestFile]
VERBOSE: [W16TGT01]: LCM:  [ Start  Test      ]  [[File]TestFile]
VERBOSE: [W16TGT01]:                              [[File]TestFile] The system
  cannot find the path specified.
VERBOSE: [W16TGT01]:                              [[File]TestFile] The related
  file/directory is: C:\TestFolder\TestFile1.txt.
VERBOSE: [W16TGT01]: LCM:  [ End    Test      ]  [[File]TestFile]  in 0.0320
  seconds.
VERBOSE: [W16TGT01]: LCM:  [ Start  Set       ]  [[File]TestFile]
VERBOSE: [W16TGT01]:                              [[File]TestFile] The system
  cannot find the path specified.
VERBOSE: [W16TGT01]:                              [[File]TestFile] The related
  file/directory is: C:\TestFolder\TestFile1.txt.
```

```
VERBOSE: [W16TGT01]: LCM:    [ End     Set      ] [[File]TestFile]   in 0.0000
   seconds.
VERBOSE: [W16TGT01]: LCM:    [ End     Resource ] [[File]TestFile]
VERBOSE: [W16TGT01]: LCM:    [ End     Set      ]
VERBOSE: [W16TGT01]: LCM:    [ End     Set      ]   in  0.3590 seconds.
VERBOSE: Operation 'Invoke CimMethod' complete.
VERBOSE: Time taken for configuration job to complete is 0.738 seconds
```

There are a few things to note before we discuss the output:

- The MOF file doesn't have to be specified, just the path to it. Start-DscConfiguration figures out the correct MOF file to use based on the name of the machine you specify.
- The MOF file is transported to the target machine over WS-MAN. You can specify the target machine through the -ComputerName parameter or you can create a CIM session to the target machine. If you have a folder that contains MOF files for *only* the machines you want to configure, you can supply the -Path.
- You don't need to use -Verbose all the time, but it's a good idea when you're testing a configuration because you can see what's happening as the configuration is applied.
- If you don't specify -Wait, the configuration is applied by a PowerShell job of job type ConfigurationJob. You can manage the jobs created by DSC with the standard PowerShell job cmdlets (see chapter 13).

As you read through the output from Start-DscConfiguration, you'll notice that you're invoking a CIM method. The LCM on the target machine receives the configuration and tests whether the configuration matches the configuration document. In this case, the LCM is testing for the existence of the file C:\TestFolder\TestFile1.txt.

The configuration item isn't found, so the configuration is applied—look for Start Set and End Set pairs. It's confusing, but the application of the configuration will generate a message that the item can't be found. It makes sense when you think that the configuration wouldn't be applied if it already existed!

Now would be a good time to show that DSC is idempotent. Reapply the configuration:

```
PS> Start-DscConfiguration -ComputerName W16TGT01 -Path .\MOF\ `
-Wait -Verbose

VERBOSE: Perform operation 'Invoke CimMethod' with following parameters,
   ''methodName' = SendConfigurationApply,'className' =
MSFT_DSCLocalConfigurationManager,'namespaceName' = root/Microsoft/Windows/
   DesiredStateConfiguration'.
VERBOSE: An LCM method call arrived from computer W16DSC01 with user
sid S-1-5-21-759617655-3516038109-1479587680-1104.
VERBOSE: [W16TGT01]: LCM:    [ Start  Set      ]
VERBOSE: [W16TGT01]: LCM:    [ Start  Resource ] [[File]TestFile]
VERBOSE: [W16TGT01]: LCM:    [ Start  Test     ] [[File]TestFile]
VERBOSE: [W16TGT01]:                             [[File]TestFile] The
   destination object was found and no action is required.
VERBOSE: [W16TGT01]: LCM:    [ End    Test     ] [[File]TestFile]   in 0.0310
   seconds.
```

```
VERBOSE: [W16TGT01]: LCM:   [ Skip    Set       ]  [[File]TestFile]
VERBOSE: [W16TGT01]: LCM:   [ End     Resource  ]  [[File]TestFile]
VERBOSE: [W16TGT01]: LCM:   [ End     Set       ]
VERBOSE: [W16TGT01]: LCM:   [ End     Set       ]   in  0.3440 seconds.
VERBOSE: Operation 'Invoke CimMethod' complete.
VERBOSE: Time taken for configuration job to complete is 0.543 seconds
```

You'll receive messages stating `'The destination object was found and no action is required'`, and you'll see `Skip Set` statements

You can test whether a server is configured to match the configuration document.

18.2.4 *Testing the configuration application*

One test is to see if the configuration item is present:

```
PS>  Invoke-Command -ComputerName W16TGT01 -ScriptBlock {
         Get-Content -Path c:\testfolder\testfile1.txt
         }
My first Configuration
```

Unfortunately, that doesn't test whether the configuration is correct. The correct test is to use `Test-DscConfiguration`:

```
PS>  Test-DscConfiguration -ComputerName W16TGT01
True
```

It would be nice to see a bit more information, so you can include the MOF file in the test:

```
PS>  Test-DscConfiguration -ComputerName W16TGT01 `
-ReferenceConfiguration .\MOF\W16TGT01.mof |
Format-List

InDesiredState             : True
ResourcesInDesiredState    : {[File]TestFile}
ResourcesNotInDesiredState :
ReturnValue                : 0
PSComputerName             : W16TGT01
```

Alternatively, you can use the `-Verbose` parameter:

```
PS>  Test-DscConfiguration -ComputerName W16TGT01 -Verbose

VERBOSE: Perform operation 'Invoke CimMethod' with following parameters,
    ''methodName' = TestConfiguration,'className' =
MSFT_DSCLocalConfigurationManager,'namespaceName' = root/Microsoft/Windows/
    DesiredStateConfiguration'.
VERBOSE: An LCM method call arrived from computer W16DSC01 with user sid S-1-
    5-21-759617655-3516038109-1479587680-1104.
VERBOSE: [W16TGT01]: LCM:   [ Start   Test       ]
VERBOSE: [W16TGT01]: LCM:   [ Start   Resource  ]  [[File]TestFile]
VERBOSE: [W16TGT01]: LCM:   [ Start   Test       ]  [[File]TestFile]
VERBOSE: [W16TGT01]:                                [[File]TestFile] The
    destination object was found and no action is required.
```

```
VERBOSE: [W16TGT01]: LCM:  [ End     Test     ]  [[File]TestFile] True in
   0.0310 seconds.
VERBOSE: [W16TGT01]: LCM:  [ End     Resource ]  [[File]TestFile]
VERBOSE: [W16TGT01]: LCM:  [ End     Test     ]    Completed processing test
   operation. The operation returned True.
VERBOSE: [W16TGT01]: LCM:  [ End     Test     ]    in  0.0630 seconds.
VERBOSE: Operation 'Invoke CimMethod' complete.
True
VERBOSE: Time taken for configuration job to complete is 0.201 seconds
```

The output shows that the configuration items were found and the configuration is correct.

18.2.5 *Viewing the current configuration*

You can view the current configuration of the target machine. In this case we'll use a CIM session:

```
PS>  $cs = New-CimSession -ComputerName W16TGT01
PS>  Get-DscConfiguration -CimSession $cs
```

> **CimSession and ComputerName**
>
> You may want to use a CIM session if you're going to be performing multiple actions against the target machines—for instance, setting, testing, and getting the configuration.
>
> You can simplify the approach because the -CimSession parameter on Get-Dsc-Configuration (and other cmdlets that have a -CimSession parameter) will take an array of computer names (or a single computer name) instead of a CIM session object. If you use a computer name, a CIM session will be created, used, and destroyed in the background. This is approach is fine if you're performing a single action, but a CIM session is recommended if you're performing multiple actions because it's a more efficient technique.

For each configuration item in the configuration document, you'll see output of this form:

```
ConfigurationName    : AddFile
DependsOn            :
ModuleName           : PSDesiredStateConfiguration
ModuleVersion        :
PsDscRunAsCredential :
ResourceId           : [File]TestFile
SourceInfo           :
Attributes           : {archive}
Checksum             :
Contents             :
CreatedDate          : 02/05/2017 11:09:47
Credential           :
DestinationPath      : C:\TestFolder\TestFile1.txt
Ensure               : present
```

```
Force                 :
MatchSource           :
ModifiedDate          : 02/05/2017 11:09:47
Recurse               :
Size                  : 25
SourcePath            :
SubItems              :
Type                  : file
PSComputerName        : W16TGT01
CimClassName          : MSFT_FileDirectoryConfiguration
```

Don't forget to remove the CIM session if you don't need it:

```
PS> Remove-CimSession -CimSession $cs
```

You've seen how to apply and test a configuration. The last part of the lifecycle is to remove the configuration.

18.2.6 *Removing a configuration*

There will come a time when you need to remove the configuration items from your target because you're repurposing the machine or the configuration is no longer appropriate. In the case of a file, you could perform a deletion, but it's better practice to reverse the configuration. This shows the reversal of the configuration from listing 18.1.

Listing 18.3   Removing a configuration

```
Configuration AddFile {
  Node W16TGT01 {
    File TestFile {
        Ensure = 'Absent'
        Type = 'File'
        DestinationPath = 'C:\TestFolder\TestFile1.txt'     ❶ Ensure item
        Force = $true                                           removal
    }

    File TestFolder {
        Ensure = 'Absent'
        Type = 'Directory'
        DestinationPath = 'C:\TestFolder'
        Force = $true                          ❷ Remove file
        DependsOn = '[File]TestFile'              before folder
    }
  }
}
AddFile -OutputPath .\MOF
```

Two important points to note. First, the `Ensure` parameter is set to `Absent` ❶. This ensures that the item is removed if present. Second, the folder removal should be dependent ❷ on the file removal. Once the MOF file is created you can apply it:

```
PS> Start-DscConfiguration -ComputerName W16TGT01 -Path .\MOF\ -Wait
```

Use `Test-DscConfiguration` to determine if the file has been removed. As a second check, you can use `Test-Path`:

```
PS> Test-Path -Path \\W16TGT01\C$\TestFolder\TestFile1.txt
False
```

We've spent quite a long time walking you through creating, applying, testing, and deleting a configuration. This only applied to a single machine. It's more likely that you'll want to apply a configuration to multiple machines—preferably simultaneously.

18.3 *Pushing to multiple nodes*

If you need to apply the same configuration to multiple machines, you could run listing 18.1 a number of times, changing the computer name each time. That's inefficient, not to mention boring and error-prone, so we'll show you how to parameterize your configurations. First, we'll show how to change only the nodes to which you'll apply the configuration. Then we'll show you how to use configuration metadata to change the configuration being applied based on the machine name.

18.3.1 *Parameterizing the computer name*

If you have a number of machines you need to apply exactly the same configuration to, the easiest approach is to parameterize the computer name.

Listing 18.4 Parameterizing the computer name

```
Configuration AddFile {
  param (
    [Parameter(Mandatory=$true)]          ❶ Parameter
    [string[]]$ComputerName                  block
  )
  Import-DscResource -ModuleName PSDesiredStateConfiguration

  Node $ComputerName {                    ❷ Node uses
                                             parameter
    File TestFile {
        Ensure = 'Present'
        Type = 'File'
        DestinationPath = 'C:\TestFolder\TestFile1.txt'
        Contents = 'My first Configuration'
        Force = $true
    }
  }
}                                         ❸ Computer
                                             names
                                             supplied
AddFile -OutputPath .\MOF -ComputerName 'W16TGT01', 'W16DSC02'
```

The configuration is an evolution of listing 18.1. The parameter block ❶ defines a single mandatory parameter—`ComputerName`—which is an array of strings, each element of which is a computer name. A statement to explicitly import the resources being used has been added:

```
Import-DscResource -ModuleName PSDesiredStateConfiguration
```

This will stop the warning messages being issued that we saw with listing 18.1. The Node ❷ is modified to use the `ComputerName` parameter name rather than having a hardcoded computer name.

When the configuration is run ❸, the `-ComputerName` parameter is used to supply the names of the computers you'll apply the configuration to. You'll see output similar to this:

```
    Directory: C:\scripts\MOF

Mode                LastWriteTime         Length Name
----                -------------         ------ ----
-a----        02/05/2017     14:50          2128 W16TGT01.mof
-a----        02/05/2017     14:50          2128 W16DSC02.mof
```

A MOF file is produced for each computer name that you supply to the configuration. Notice that you didn't have to create any looping structures in your code to manage multiple machines—it's all done for you.

NOTE   If you think the parameter block looks like that used in functions and scripts, you're correct.

You can now apply your configuration:

```
PS> Start-DscConfiguration -ComputerName W16TGT01, W16DSC02 `
-Path .\MOF\ -Wait
```

If you don't use the `-Wait` parameter, you'll only see a single job managing the application of the configuration. But if you look at the child jobs

```
PS> Get-Job -IncludeChildJob

Id Name   PSJobTypeName      State      HasMoreData Location         Command
-- ----   -------------      -----      ----------- --------         -------
22 Job22  ConfigurationJob   Completed  True        W16TGT01,W16DSC02 Sta…
23 Job23  ConfigurationJob   Completed  True        W16TGT01         Sta…
24 Job24  ConfigurationJob   Completed  True        W16DSC02         Sta…
```

you'll see that there is one child job per machine to be configured. The parent job manages the creation and running of the child jobs.

Test the application of the configuration:

```
PS> Test-DscConfiguration -ComputerName W16TGT01, W16DSC02
True
True
```

If you need more details on the applied configurations:

```
PS> Get-DscConfiguration -CimSession W16TGT01, W16DSC02 |
Format-Table PSComputerName, ConfigurationName, Ensure, Type -AutoSize

PSComputerName ConfigurationName Ensure  Type
-------------- ----------------- ------  ----
W16TGT01       AddFile           present file
W16DSC02       AddFile           present file
```

We'll leave the creation of the configuration to remove the folders and file to you (hint: modify listing 18.3). A version of the code is available in the book's download file: RemoveListing18.4.ps1.

As well as parameterizing the computer names, you can also supply other information to the configuration, including the parts of the configuration to apply.

18.3.2 Using configuration data

You can parameterize your configurations beyond the computer name by supplying configuration data in the form of hashtables. In fact, you can configure anything you want using parameters. But the purpose of configuration data is to allow you to easily separate configuration (also known as *environment* configuration) from topology (*structural* configuration). You can also think of it as separating the *what* (topology) from the *where* (configuration). This is an important point that people seem to miss. The canonical example is http://mng.bz/3LsX. It defines three roles (configurations) and then uses configuration data to map those roles to physical machines. All three roles can be on one machine, or each role can be on a discrete machine or on multiple machines for High Availability scenarios.

This example modifies the contents of the text file depending on the machine being configured.

Listing 18.5 Using configuration metadata

```
$ConfigurationData = @{                                              ◄─────  Configuration
  AllNodes = @(                                                      ❶       data
    @{NodeName = 'W16TGT01';FileText='Configuration for Role 1'},
    @{NodeName = 'W16DSC02';FileText='Configuration for Role 2'}
  )
}

Configuration AddFile {
  Import-DscResource -ModuleName PSDesiredStateConfiguration

  Node $AllNodes.NodeName {                        ◄─────  Setting
                                                   ❷       node name
    File TestFile {
        Ensure = 'Present'
        Type = 'File'
        DestinationPath = 'C:\TestFolder\TestFile1.txt'    ❸  Setting
        Contents = $Node.FileText                      ◄─────  text
        Force = $true
    }
  }
```

```
    }
}
AddFile -OutputPath .\MOF -ConfigurationData $ConfigurationData  ◄──┘
```
④ **Running configuration**

Configuration data ❶ is supplied as a hashtable that must have one key named All-Nodes. Other keys are permitted, though seldom used. AllNodes is an array of hashtables; each hashtable defines the configuration for a single machine and must have a key named NodeName (name of the machine to be configured). Again, other keys are permitted.

You can define the configuration data hashtable in a .psd1 file and access it as

```
AddFile -OutputPath .\MOF -ConfigurationData ./confdata.psd1
```

> **NOTE** Forgetting to include the -ConfigurationData parameter and the hashtable is a common error when you start using this approach.

When the configuration is run, $AllNodes.NodeName ❷ is accessed to process each individual machine affected by the configuration. As the configuration is processed, other elements of the machine's hashtable, as defined in the configuration data, are accessed—for instance, $Node.FileText ❸ to set the file's contents.

The configuration data is linked to the configuration when it's run using the -ConfigurationData parameter ④ and passing the variable containing the configuration hashtable. A MOF file is produced for each machine listed in the configuration data, as you would expect.

Applying the configuration is performed in the usual way—supply the computer names or a CIM session together with the path to the MOF files:

```
PS> Start-DscConfiguration -ComputerName W16TGT01, W16DSC02 `
 -Path .\MOF\ -Wait -Verbose
```

You can test the configurations individually:

```
PS> Test-DscConfiguration -ComputerName W16TGT01
True
PS> Test-DscConfiguration -ComputerName W16DSC02
True
```

or simultaneously:

```
PS> Test-DscConfiguration -ComputerName W16TGT01, W16DSC02
True
True
```

The final test is to view the content of the files:

```
PS> Invoke-Command -ComputerName W16TGT01, W16DSC02 `
-ScriptBlock {Get-Content -Path C:\TestFolder\TestFile1.txt}

Configuration for Role 1
Configuration for Role 2
```

You can remove this configuration, if required, using the RemoveListing18.4.ps1 script in the download code.

So far, you've seen how to apply a configuration to multiple machines. There are many situations where you need to create a set of machines, each of which has its own unique requirements.

18.3.3 *Configuration data and roles*

Imagine that you're creating the infrastructure for an internet-facing system such as an e-commerce site. You'd need to create a number of identical web servers, a server to run your business logic, and possibly a database server. Also, you'll need to rebuild this infrastructure on a frequent basis as new versions of the software are released.

You could set up a single configuration for each server type and run that. In fact, that's how you would probably start for development purposes. But you should look at a single configuration that works with all your servers and applies the correct configuration based on the *role* of the server.

This is easier to grasp with an example. This listing shows a role-based configuration.

Listing 18.6   Role-based configurations

```
$ConfigurationData = @{                              Configuration
    AllNodes = @(                                  ❶ metadata
        @{NodeName = 'W16TGT01';Role = 'Hyper-V'},
        @{NodeName = 'W16CN01';Role = 'AD'}
    )
}

Configuration RoleConfiguration                      Composite
{                                                  ❷ resource
    param ($Role)
    switch ($Role) {
      'Hyper-V' {
          Import-DscResource -ModuleName PSDesiredStateConfiguration
          WindowsFeature Hyper-V {
              Ensure = 'Present'
              Name = 'Hyper-V-PowerShell'
          }
      }
      'AD' {
          Import-DscResource -ModuleName PSDesiredStateConfiguration
          WindowsFeature AD {
              Ensure = 'Present'
              Name = 'RSAT-AD-PowerShell'
          }
      }
    }
}
                                                   ❸ Main
Configuration ToolsConfig                            configuration
{
    Import-DscResource -ModuleName PSDesiredStateConfiguration
    node $allnodes.NodeName
```

```
    {
        RoleConfiguration ServerRole
        {
            Role = $Node.Role
        }
    }
}

ToolsConfig -ConfigurationData $ConfigurationData `
-OutputPath .\MOF
```

❹ **Run configuration**

We start with the configuration metadata ❶ held within the `$ConfigurationData` hashtable. The metadata defines the server name and the role it will take. The role controls the configuration applied to the server.

> ### Composite resources
>
> A *composite resource* is a DSC configuration that's used as a resource in another configuration. In the case of listing 18.6, the configuration `RoleConfiguration` performs the task of configuring the target based on the role assigned to that system. `RoleConfiguration` is used as a composite resource by the `ToolsConfig` configuration.
>
> In this case, the composite configuration is contained in the same file as the top-level configuration. If you wanted to reuse the composite resource in many other different configurations, you could save it with a .schema.psm1 extension. You'd also need to create a module manifest that defined the .schema.psm1 file as the root module.
>
> A worked example of using composite resources in this manner is available at http://mng.bz/1e6G.

A configuration called `RoleConfiguration` ❷ performs the configuration. It takes a role as a parameter, and using a switch parameter determines which Windows feature—Hyper-V PowerShell module or Active Directory PowerShell module—is installed. You could have further nesting at this point by calling additional configurations. As with all nesting options, achieving the correct balance between granularity and maintainability will depend on your exact circumstances and the scenarios you're working with.

The `ToolsConfig` configuration ❸ is the master configuration that calls `RoleConfiguration`. `ToolsConfig` is the configuration that's run ❹ and to which the configuration data is passed.

Once the MOF files are created, the configuration can be applied:

```
PS> Start-DscConfiguration -ComputerName W16TGT01, W16CN01 `
-Path .\MOF\ -Wait -Verbose
```

If you watch the output, you'll see these two lines:

```
VERBOSE: [W16CN01]:                              [[WindowsFeature]
  AD::[RoleConfiguration]ServerRole]
Successfully installed the feature RSAT-AD-PowerShell.
```

```
VERBOSE: [W16TGT01]:
[[WindowsFeature]Hyper-V::[RoleConfiguration]ServerRole]
Successfully installed the feature Hyper-V-PowerShell.
```

They indicate that the configuration has been successfully applied.

Testing the configuration is a little more difficult:

```
PS> Invoke-Command -ComputerName W16TGT01, W16CN01 -ScriptBlock {
Get-WindowsFeature -Name Hyper-V-PowerShell, RSAT-AD-PowerShell
} | sort Name |
Format-Table Name, DisplayName, Installed, PSComputerName

Name                  DisplayName        Installed  PSComputerName
----                  -----------        ---------  --------------
Hyper-V-PowerShell    Hyper-V Module...  True       W16TGT01
Hyper-V-PowerShell    Hyper-V Module...  False      W16CN01
RSAT-AD-PowerShell    Active Directo...  True       W16CN01
RSAT-AD-PowerShell    Active Directo...  False      W16TGT01
```

You can see from the output that the correct configuration has been applied to each machine.

Even with parameterization, push mode has a number of issues that limit its usefulness.

18.3.4 *Issues with push mode*

You've been introduced to DSC in push mode and the benefits you gain in terms of managing your server configurations. DSC push mode is a huge step forward compared to manually configuring servers, but as with most things, it has its minuses.

Here are the main drawbacks to using push mode:

- *Doesn't scale*—Using push mode on 10 servers is manageable. At a scale of hundreds or thousands of servers, manual processes break down. A situation with frequent builds required by new application versions also causes push mode to be unsatisfactory.
- *Delivering resource modules to target*—The PowerShell module containing the DSC resources used by a configuration has to be installed on the target machine. When using push mode, it's your responsibility to ensure this (hint: copying files over a PowerShell remote session is a great way to perform this action).
- *Fire and forget*—Monitoring and reporting are manual processes. Once you've pushed the configuration to the target node, that's it. All finished. If you want to monitor the configuration and correct any configuration drift, it's your job to figure out how to do that and create the required scripts.

These points bring us to the conclusion that DSC push mode is great for development and testing. It's also adequate for small environments. But if you have a large environment to manage through DSC, or you have frequent software releases for which you need to build new infrastructure each time, you need something more. That something is DSC pull mode.

18.4   DSC in pull mode

In the DSC examples you've seen so far, the configuration has been *pushed* to the target server. As you saw in section 18.3.4, push mode doesn't scale well. In this section, we'll cover DSC in *pull* mode, where the target server contacts the pull server and *pulls*—and then applies its configuration.

We'll start by covering the pull server architecture and then move on to showing you how to create a pull server using DSC. When the pull server is running, you need to create your configuration and publish the MOF file (together with any required modules) to the pull server.

The final part of the picture is to configure the target machine's LCM to work with the pull server, which we'll postpone to section 18.5.

What does DSC look like in pull mode?

18.4.1 Pull server architecture

The architecture of DSC in pull mode is illustrated in figure 18.4.

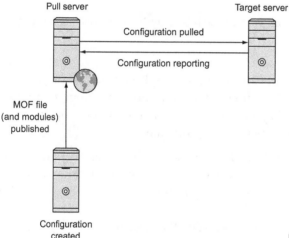

Figure 18.4   DSC in pull mode

A DSC configuration is created. This is usually on a separate machine from the pull server—development on a production server is a bad thing in many organizations. The configuration is run to create a MOF file. The MOF file, together with any required DSC resource modules, is published to the pull server.

> **NOTE** The pull server protocol specification is available through the Microsoft Open Specifications program. Its designation is MS-DSCPM. See http://mng. bz/TzY3 for the specification of the protocol.

The target server is configured via the LCM to periodically poll the pull server for its configurations. When a configuration is found, it and any associated resource modules are downloaded to the target server and applied.

NOTE LCM configuration is covered in section 18.5.

The target server can be configured to report the status of its configuration to the pull server. The LCM can also be configured to reapply the configuration if the target server's configuration drifts from the desired state (you can also do this in push mode, but it's rare to see that done). These mechanisms provide a compliance regime for your environment. You can confidently state what a server's configuration should be and prove that its state matches the desired state. PowerShell 1, Auditors 0.

The next big question is: How do you create a pull server?

18.4.2 Creating a pull server

The best way to create a DSC pull server is to use DSC. In this section, we'll show you how to create a web-based pull server.

> **Pull server on SMB Share**
>
> You can set up a DSC pull server based on an SMB share instead: http://mng.bz/uWRh.
>
> Our simple advice is *don't*.
>
> An SMB share–based pull server isn't as versatile as the full pull server we're going to show you and should only be used for testing the pull concept or for situations where it's impossible to use an HTTP-based pull server.

If you have a machine you're using as a push server, then you can create the configuration and push it to the relevant server. If you have a pull server already in your environment and want to create another one, get the new pull server to pull its configuration from the original pull server.

Before you can create the pull server, you need to take care of a few prerequisites.

PULL SERVER PREREQUISITES

There are two main prerequisites. First, if you want to secure and encrypt the web traffic to and from your pull server, you need to install an SSL certificate on the machine. This will be used during the creation of the pull server. You'll need to know the thumbprint of the certificate:

```
PS> Get-ChildItem -Path Cert:\LocalMachine\My\

   PSParentPath: Microsoft.PowerShell.Security\Certificate::LocalMachine\My

Thumbprint                                Subject
----------                                -------
FF24E1BA4B32D2F75A8F9648DECC1D070F1F2B13  CN=W16DSC02
```

Second, you'll need to install the modules containing the DSC resources you require to install and configure the pull server. These modules can be found on the Power-Shell Gallery.

The following modules are required:

```
PS C:\Scripts> Find-Module xPSDesiredStateConfiguration

Version Name                                   Repository Description
------- ----                                   ---------- -----------
5.1.0.0 xPSDesiredStateConfiguration PSGallery  The xPSD...

PS> Find-Module xWebAdministration

Version  Name                    Repository Description
-------  ----                    ---------- -----------
1.16.0.0 xWebAdministration PSGallery  Module w...
```

Both `xPSDesiredStateConfiguration` and `xWebAdministration` are classed as experimental and as such are subject to change, *including breaking changes*, with no notice. If the versions you find are different from those mentioned, you'll need to test the code we use to ensure there haven't been any breaking changes.

These two modules need to be installed on the pull server and any system you use for creating configurations:

```
PS> Install-Module -Name xPSDesiredStateConfiguration, xWebAdministration `
    -Force
```

The modules will be installed to C:\Program Files\WindowsPowerShell\Modules, as are all modules obtained from the PowerShell Gallery.

Now it's time to create the configuration for your pull server.

Pull server and Local Configuration Manager

You need to do three things to configure your DSC environment to use a pull server:

1 You need to configure a pull server—which we'll be covering in a moment.
2 You'll need to create a configuration to operate in pull mode and publish it to the pull server. That will be covered in section 18.4.3
3 You'll need to configure the LCM on the target machine(s) to use the pull server. We'll postpone that discussion until section 18.5, where we cover all aspects of the LCM.

CREATING THE PULL SERVER

Using a DSC configuration to create a DSC pull server is a fitting way to proceed.

Listing 18.7   Creating a pull server

```
$ConfigurationData=@{                          Configuration
    AllNodes = @(                           ❶  data
    @{
        NodeName = 'W16DSC02'
        Role = @('Web', 'PullServer')
```

```
      CertThumbPrint = Invoke-Command -Computername 'W16DSC02' -ScriptBlock {
      Get-Childitem -Path Cert:\LocalMachine\My |
      where Subject -Like 'CN=W16DSC02*' |
      Select-Object -ExpandProperty ThumbPrint}
    }
);
}
```

```
Configuration Pullserver {
  Import-DscResource -ModuleName PSDesiredStateConfiguration
  Import-DscResource -ModuleName xPSDesiredStateConfiguration
  Import-DscResource -ModuleName xWebAdministration

  Node $AllNodes.where{$_.Role -eq 'Web'}.NodeName {
  WindowsFeature IIS {
    Ensure = "Present"
    Name = "Web-Server"
  }

  WindowsFeature NetExtens4 {
    Ensure = "Present"
    Name = "Web-Net-Ext45"
    DependsOn = '[WindowsFeature]IIS'
  }

  WindowsFeature AspNet45 {
    Ensure = "Present"
    Name = "Web-Asp-Net45"
    DependsOn = '[WindowsFeature]IIS'
  }

  WindowsFeature ISAPIExt {
    Ensure = "Present"
    Name = "Web-ISAPI-Ext"
    DependsOn = '[WindowsFeature]IIS'
  }

  WindowsFeature ISAPIFilter {
    Ensure = "Present"
    Name = "Web-ISAPI-filter"
    DependsOn = '[WindowsFeature]IIS'
  }

  WindowsFeature DirectoryBrowsing {
    Ensure = "Absent"
    Name = "Web-Dir-Browsing"
    DependsOn = '[WindowsFeature]IIS'
  }

  WindowsFeature StaticCompression {
    Ensure = "Absent"
    Name = "Web-Stat-Compression"
    DependsOn = '[WindowsFeature]IIS'
  }

  WindowsFeature Management {
    Name = 'Web-Mgmt-Service'
```

2 Required resource modules

3 Install IIS

4 IIS sub-features to install

5 IIS sub-features to block

6 IIS management

```
      Ensure = 'Present'
      DependsOn = @('[WindowsFeature]IIS')
    }

    Registry RemoteManagement {
      Key = 'HKLM:\SOFTWARE\Microsoft\WebManagement\Server'
      ValueName = 'EnableRemoteManagement'
      ValueType = 'Dword'
      ValueData = '1'
      DependsOn = @('[WindowsFeature]IIS','[WindowsFeature]Management')
    }

    Service StartWMSVC {
      Name = 'WMSVC'
      StartupType = 'Automatic'
      State = 'Running'
      DependsOn = '[Registry]RemoteManagement'
    }

    xWebsite DefaultSite {
      Name = "Default Web Site"
      State = "Started"
      PhysicalPath = "C:\inetpub\wwwroot"
      DependsOn = "[WindowsFeature]IIS"
    }
  }

Node $AllNodes.where{$_.Role -eq 'PullServer'}.NodeName {
  WindowsFeature DSCServiceFeature {
    Ensure = "Present"
    Name   = "DSC-Service"
  }

  xDscWebService DSCPullServer {
    Ensure = "Present"
    EndpointName = "PullServer"
    Port = 8080
    PhysicalPath = "$env:SystemDrive\inetpub\wwwroot\PullServer"
    CertificateThumbPrint =  $Node.CertThumbprint
    ModulePath = "$env:PROGRAMFILES\WindowsPowerShell\DscService\Modules"
    ConfigurationPath = "$env:PROGRAMFILES\WindowsPowerShell\DscService\
  Configuration"
    State = "Started"
    UseSecurityBestPractices = $false
    DependsOn = "[WindowsFeature]DSCServiceFeature"
  }

  xDscWebService DSCComplianceServer {
    Ensure = "Present"
    EndpointName = "ComplianceServer"
    Port = 9080
    PhysicalPath = "$env:SystemDrive\inetpub\wwwroot\ComplianceServer"
    CertificateThumbPrint = "AllowUnencryptedTraffic"
    State = "Started"
    UseSecurityBestPractices = $false
```

7 Registry configuration

8 Install DSC

```
    DependsOn = ("[WindowsFeature]DSCServiceFeature","[xDSCWebService]
  DSCPullServer")
   }
 }
}

Pullserver -ConfigurationData $ConfigurationData -outputPath .\MOF
```

This long configuration breaks down into a number of chunks. The first chunk ❶ is the configuration data. In this example, we're setting two roles—Web and PullServer— for our server, called W16DSC02 in this case. The certificate thumbprint for the SSL certificate on the pull server is recovered through a script rather than hardcoding. This makes your code more portable and saves the error-prone exercise of typing in the thumbprint. Let PowerShell do the work for you.

Moving on to the configuration itself, the first step ❷ is to import the modules required by the configuration.

> **NOTE** You should have installed these modules in the previous section. If you haven't, make sure they're installed on both the authoring server and the machine that will become your pull server.

Creating a pull server requires IIS and DSCServiceFeature to be installed. We'll start with IIS ❸ and install the basic web server Windows feature. Unfortunately, this won't give us quite what we need, so we have to ensure that a number of the IIS sub-features are present. ❹ These sub-features include ISAPI and ASP. Likewise, there are a number of IIS features we don't want installed—ever. These include ❺ Directory Browsing and Static Compression.

> **NOTE** We've shown only a few features that we don't want installing. Your organization may have others that it thinks shouldn't be installed. The pattern shown in listing 18.7 is infinitely adaptable. You can add more configuration items as required.

It's always a good idea to be able to manage your servers remotely, so make sure that you install the management service ❻ and set the registry keys ❼ to enable this scenario. The IIS configuration concludes by setting the IIS service (WMSVC) startup to automatic and ensures that the default website—which DSC uses—will be started when IIS starts.

The DSC configuration ❽ is simpler. The first part ensures that the DSC service is installed. The pull server— DSCPullServer—is then configured. Most of the settings should be self-explanatory by now. The port that the pull server clients will use to connect is set to 8080. This is arbitrary; you can use another port if required. A specific port is specified to separate traffic if another application is using the default website. The ModulePath and ConfigurationPath settings control where the pull server stores configurations and modules that its clients need to pull. If you don't put them in that place, the client won't find them.

It may seem odd to set UseSecurityBestpractices to $false. Setting this property to $true will reset registry values, which in this case will be controlling SSL, under "HKLM:\SYSTEM\CurrentControlSet\Control\SecurityProviders\SCHANNEL". This environment change enforces the use of a stronger encryption cypher and may affect legacy applications. More information can be found at http://mng.bz/U3dr and http://mng.bz/747N.

> **NOTE** You'll have noticed the heavy use of DependsOn in listing 18.7. It's worth tracing the dependencies and the interaction of the IIS and DSC configurations with each other and the configuration data. This is a complicated configuration, and if you can understand this, you're well on the way to mastering DSC.

The final part of the DSC configuration is for the compliance server. This provides reporting and compliance information on the configuration of the pull server's client machines. For now, we're only configuring the compliance server. The configuration of the compliance server is similar to the pull server, but we're allowing unencrypted traffic to use the compliance server and we're configuring a different port.

The last line of listing 18.7 runs the configuration and creates the MOF file as usual. You then need to push the configuration to the machine you're creating a pull server on:

```
PS> Start-DscConfiguration -ComputerName W16DSC02 -Path .\MOF\ `
-Wait -Verbose
```

Expect it to run a while. Restart the new pull server:

```
PS> Restart-computer -ComputerName W16DSC02 -Wait -Force
```

Your DSC pull server should now be ready for use. Before jumping into using the pull server, we should test the configuration:

```
PS> Test-DscConfiguration -ComputerName W16DSC02
```

You should also test the pull server by connecting to the web service. From your authoring server (or another machine in the domain):

```
PS> Start-Process `
-FilePath iexplore.exe https://W16DSC02:8080/PSDSCPullServer.svc
```

You should see something like figure 18.5.

Notice the name of the service: PSDSCPullServer.svc. It's hardcoded into the DSC resource. If you need to modify that, check carefully that you find all the places it's specified.

Your pull server is up and running. It appears to be working correctly. The next step is creating and publishing a MOF file to the pull server.

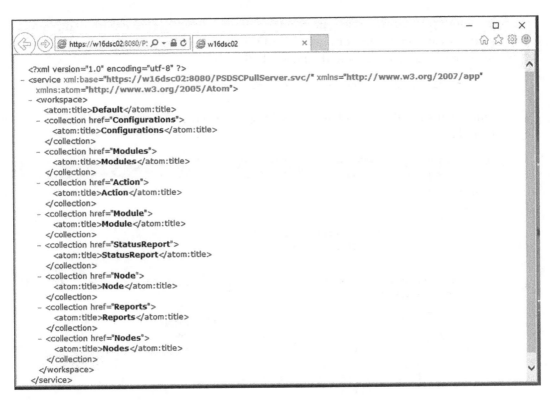

```xml
<?xml version="1.0" encoding="utf-8" ?>
- <service xml:base="https://w16dsc02:8080/PSDSCPullServer.svc/" xmlns="http://www.w3.org/2007/app"
    xmlns:atom="http://www.w3.org/2005/Atom">
  - <workspace>
      <atom:title>Default</atom:title>
    - <collection href="Configurations">
        <atom:title>Configurations</atom:title>
      </collection>
    - <collection href="Modules">
        <atom:title>Modules</atom:title>
      </collection>
    - <collection href="Action">
        <atom:title>Action</atom:title>
      </collection>
    - <collection href="Module">
        <atom:title>Module</atom:title>
      </collection>
    - <collection href="StatusReport">
        <atom:title>StatusReport</atom:title>
      </collection>
    - <collection href="Node">
        <atom:title>Node</atom:title>
      </collection>
    - <collection href="Reports">
        <atom:title>Reports</atom:title>
      </collection>
    - <collection href="Nodes">
        <atom:title>Nodes</atom:title>
      </collection>
    </workspace>
  </service>
```

Figure 18.5 Testing the pull server

18.4.3 Publishing a MOF file

When you're working with DSC in push mode, you create a MOF file and manually push it to the target server. You're implicitly assuming that the server is running and ready to receive its configuration. When working in pull mode you don't care about the state of the target server because you publish the MOF file to the pull server and leave the target server to pull its configuration when it's ready.

A number of steps are required to create a configuration to pull:

1 Create the configuration.
2 Copy to the pull server.
3 Ensure resources are on the pull server.
4 Force pull (for demo or testing). In production, wait for the target machine to be ready to pull its configuration.

Examples are everything, so we'll demonstrate this process by creating a MOF file that'll configure the target server with a file share. The configuration is shown in listing 18.8.

Before you start to create the configuration file, you need to ensure that required resources are on the authoring server. In this case, you'll need to download the xSmb-Share resource module from the PowerShell gallery:

```
PS> Install-Module -Name xSmbShare -Force
```

Once that's installed, you have everything you need to create the configuration to be pulled.

Listing 18.8   Configuration to be pulled

```
Configuration stdShare {
    param
        (
            [Parameter(Mandatory=$true)]
            [string[]]$ComputerName

        )
    Import-DscResource -ModuleName PSDesiredStateConfiguration    ❶ Import
    Import-DscResource -ModuleName xSmbShare                          resources

    Node $ComputerName {
                                                    ❷ Create
        File TestFolder {                              folder
            Ensure = 'Present'
            Type = 'Directory'
            DestinationPath = 'C:\TestFolder'
            Force = $true
        }
                                                    ❸ Create
        File TestFile {                                file
            Ensure = 'Present'
            Type = 'File'
            DestinationPath = 'C:\TestFolder\TestFile1.txt'
            Contents = 'My first Configuration'
            Force = $true
        }

        xSmbShare StandardShare
        {                                           ❹ Create
            Ensure = "Present"                         share
            Name    = "Standard"
            Path = 'C:\TestFolder'
            Description = "This is a test SMB Share"
            ConcurrentUserLimit = 0
        }
    }
}

stdShare -ComputerName W16TGT01 -OutputPath .\MOF
```

You've already seen this configuration earlier in the chapter. Creating a file in a folder was our first simple configuration example. The configuration starts by importing the required resources ❶. Creating the folder ❷ and its associated file ❸ are performed in two steps this time. Creating the share is equally straightforward ➍. A name for the share and the path to the folder are required. The description and concurrent user limits are optional.

Run the configuration to create your MOF file. If you were using push mode, you'd use `Start-DscConfiguration` to push the MOF file to the target machine (assuming you'd remembered to copy the required resource module to the target). With push mode, you have a few more hoops to jump through.

You need to rename the MOF file so that it matches the identification of the target server. A GUID is used as the identifier. You generate a new GUID by using `New-Guid`:

```
PS> $psclientid = New-Guid | select -ExpandProperty guid
PS> $psclientid
5827c542-20bb-487c-89cb-484cbe5f0b1f
```

Getting the GUID in production

The important thing is that the same GUID is used for the target machine's configuration ID and the data sent to the pull server. If your target machine has already been configured to use the pull server, it'll have a configuration ID, so you can find the GUID like this:

```
PS> $pscs = New-CimSession -ComputerName <target machine>
PS> $psclientid = Get-DscLocalConfigurationManager -CimSession $pscs |
select -ExpandProperty ConfigurationID
```

We'll use this GUID to rename the MOF file:

```
PS> Get-ChildItem -Path  C:\scripts\MOF\W16TGT01.mof |
Rename-Item -NewName "C:\scripts\MOF\$psclientid.mof"
```

You then need to create a checksum of the MOF file:

```
PS> New-DscChecksum -Path "C:\scripts\MOF\$psclientid.mof" -Force
```

The MOF and checksum files

```
5827c542-20bb-487c-89cb-484cbe5f0b1f.mof
5827c542-20bb-487c-89cb-484cbe5f0b1f.mof.checksum
```

need to be transferred to the pull server.

> **NOTE** The checksum files are used by the target machine when it pulls its configuration, and any required resource modules, to ensure that the integrity of those items hasn't been compromised.

The ability to copy files across a PowerShell remoting session makes life easier here:

```
PS>  $s = New-PSSession -ComputerName W16DSC02
PS>  Get-ChildItem -Path .\MOF\ -Filter "$psclientid.*" |
```

```
Copy-Item -Destination "C:\program Files\WindowsPowerShell\DscService\
  Configuration" `
-ToSession $s -Force
```

The last step in preparing the configuration is to get a copy of the resource module onto the pull server. This has to be archived into a zip file with a name that includes the module version. It's always advisable to use the module you've installed on your authoring server to ensure there are no compatibility issues. First, get the module path and version:

```
PS> $module = Get-Module -ListAvailable xSmbShare
PS> $modulepath = "$(Split-Path -Path $module.Path)\*"
PS> $moduleversion = $module.Version.ToString()
```

Then create a zip file and generate a checksum:

```
PS> Compress-Archive -Path $modulepath `
-DestinationPath "C:\scripts\ModuleZips\xSMBShare_$moduleversion.zip" `
-Force

PS> New-DscChecksum `
-Path "C:\scripts\ModuleZips\xSMBShare_$moduleversion.zip" `
-Force
```

The destination isn't important. Keeping the zip files together helps organize the files.

NOTE   The archive cmdlets were introduced in PowerShell v5. The archive module is now part of the PowerShell open source projects on GitHub.

Your final step is to copy the module's zip and checksum files to the pull server:

```
PS> Get-ChildItem `
-Path "C:\scripts\ModuleZips\xSMBShare_$moduleversion.*" |
Copy-Item `
-Destination "C:\Program Files\WindowsPowerShell\DscService\Modules\" `
-ToSession $s -Force
```

The pull server has now been configured and has a configuration ready to be pulled. It's now time to configure the target machine to use the pull server, but before moving on to that, don't forget to remove any unwanted PowerShell remoting sessions you created in this section.

18.5   *Configuring the Local Configuration Manager*

The previous sections in this chapter have been concerned with supplying the configuration you'll apply to your target server, either through push or pull mode. In this section, we'll concentrate on the target machine and, more specifically, on the LCM.

NOTE   This section is specifically targeted at PowerShell v5. For LCM configuration in PowerShell v4, see http://mng.bz/A84O.

Every target machine has an independent LCM. It is DSC's local engine with responsibility for applying the configurations received by the machine. It also controls the following:

- Setting how the machine receives configurations—push or pull mode
- Timing with which the machine pulls and applies configurations
- Controlling pull servers used by the machine
- Controlling reporting servers used by the machine
- Managing partial configurations (see section 18.6)

We'll look at the default LCM settings and see what can be changed and how those changes can be applied. Then we'll show you how to use DSC to configure the LCM to use a pull server.

18.5.1 *LCM settings*

All machines running Windows PowerShell v4 and above have a copy of the LCM running. It's part of the operating system—or it's installed through the Windows Management Framework if you've upgraded PowerShell on an older copy of Windows. We'll show you the default LCM settings in this section and then see how to change them.

DEFAULT LCM SETTINGS

The default LCM settings can be viewed on a newly created machine (or one you can guarantee hasn't been modified):

```
PS> $cs = New-CimSession -ComputerName W16TGT01
PS> Get-DscLocalConfigurationManager -CimSession $cs

ActionAfterReboot              : ContinueConfiguration
AgentId                        : CBE8E714-C86B-11E6-841F-00155D36C90B
AllowModuleOverWrite           : False
CertificateID                  :
ConfigurationDownloadManagers  : {}
ConfigurationID                :
ConfigurationMode              : ApplyAndMonitor
ConfigurationModeFrequencyMins : 15
Credential                     :
DebugMode                      : {NONE}
DownloadManagerCustomData      :
DownloadManagerName            :
LCMCompatibleVersions          : {1.0, 2.0}
LCMState                       : Idle
LCMStateDetail                 :
LCMVersion                     : 2.0
StatusRetentionTimeInDays      : 10
SignatureValidationPolicy      : NONE
SignatureValidations           : {}
MaximumDownloadSizeMB          : 500
PartialConfigurations          :
RebootNodeIfNeeded             : False
RefreshFrequencyMins           : 30
RefreshMode                    : PUSH
```

```
ReportManagers                   : {}
ResourceModuleManagers           : {}
PSComputerName                   : W16TGT01
PSComputerName                   : W16TGT01
```

You can also run `Get-DscLocalConfigurationManager` locally if required.

> **NOTE** You can use the machine name with the `-CIMSession` parameter if accessing the target machine once. We're using a CIM session here because we'll be accessing the machine multiple times.

The most important point to note is the `RefreshMode` property. By default, it's set to PUSH. This makes it easy to push configurations to a machine, but it means you have to do some work to convert to a pull environment.

Most of the properties are self-explanatory. Documentation for the LCM properties can be found at http://mng.bz/e7n8. We need to call out a few of the properties.

`ConfigurationModeFrequencyMins` controls how often (in minutes) the current configuration is checked and applied. It's ignored if `ConfigurationMode` is set to `ApplyOnly`.

`RefreshFrequencyMins` controls how often (in minutes) the LCM checks a pull server to get updated configurations. This is ignored if LCM isn't configured to use a pull server.

> **NOTE** `ConfigurationModeFrequencyMins` must be a multiple of `RefreshFrequencyMins`, or `RefreshFrequencyMins` must be a multiple of `ConfigurationModeFrequencyMins`.

`ConfigurationMode` has a number of possible settings:

- `ApplyOnly`—DSC applies the configuration. No further action is taken until a new configuration is available.
- `ApplyAndMonitor`—Default value. In this mode, the LCM applies any new configurations, and if the configuration of the machine drifts from the desires state (due to a manual change possibly), the change is logged.
- `ApplyAndAutoCorrect`—New configurations are applied. Any drift in configuration is logged, and the current configuration is reapplied.
- `RefreshMode`—Can be PUSH (default) or PULL. If set to PULL, a pull server must be configured through the `ConfigurationRepositoryWeb` property.
- `ConfigurationID`—A GUID used to identify the machine to a pull server.

Now that you've been introduced to the LCM properties, let's look at changing the LCM settings.

CHANGING LCM SETTINGS

You use `Get-DscLocalConfigurationManager` to view the LCM settings, so it's probably not a big surprise that you use `Set-DscLocalConfigurationManager` to change the LCM settings. You can't use the cmdlet directly. You first need to provide a configuration.

Listing 18.9 Changing the LCM settings

```
[DSCLocalConfigurationManager()]
Configuration LCM {
    Param (
        [Parameter(Mandatory=$true)]
        [string[]]$ComputerName
    )

    Node $Computername
      {
        Settings
        {
         ConfigurationMode = 'ApplyAndAutoCorrect'
         RebootNodeIfNeeded = $true
        }
      }
    }
}

LCM -computername W16TGT01 -OutputPath .\MOF
```

The first thing to notice is the `[DSCLocalConfigurationManager()]` decorator. This is required if you're working with the LCM—otherwise, DSC will assume you're using a normal resource. A parameter block is used to supply the computer names to which the configuration will be applied.

The `Settings` resource is used to modify the basic LCM settings. You'll see other options that can be used for controlling pull servers in the next section. In this example, we're changing the LCM so that it automatically corrects configuration drift and allows the machine to reboot if needed during the application of a configuration.

Running the configuration produces a MOF file, as expected:

```
PS>  C:\Scripts\Listing18.9.ps1

    Directory: C:\scripts\MOF

Mode                LastWriteTime        Length Name
----                -------------        ------ ----
-a----       13/02/2017     12:48          1166 W16TGT01.meta.mof
```

But notice the name of the MOF file: W16TGT01.meta.mof. The .meta.mof extension is used to differentiate MOF files used to configure the LCM from standard configuration MOF files used to configure the server.

NOTE This file is commonly known as the *metaconfiguration* because it contains information that configures the local configuration manager.

`Set-DscLocalConfigurationManager` applies the LCM configuration rather than `Start -DscConfiguration`:

```
PS>  Set-DscLocalConfigurationManager -CimSession $cs -Path .\MOF\ -Verbose

VERBOSE: Performing the operation "Start-DscConfiguration:
  SendMetaConfigurationApply" on target "MSFT_DSCLocalConfigurationManager".
```

```
VERBOSE: Perform operation 'Invoke CimMethod' with following parameters,
   ''methodName' = SendMetaConfigurationApply,
 'className' = MSFT_DSCLocalConfigurationManager,
 'namespaceName' = root/Microsoft/Windows/DesiredStateConfiguration'.
VERBOSE: An LCM method call arrived from computer W16TGT01 with user sid S-1-
   5-21-759617655-3516038109-1479587680-1104.
VERBOSE: [W16TGT01]: LCM:  [ Start   Set      ]
VERBOSE: [W16TGT01]: LCM:  [ Start   Resource ]   [MSFT_DSCMetaConfiguration]
VERBOSE: [W16TGT01]: LCM:  [ Start   Set      ]   [MSFT_DSCMetaConfiguration]
VERBOSE: [W16TGT01]: LCM:  [ End     Set      ]   [MSFT_DSCMetaConfiguration]
   in 0.0470 seconds.
VERBOSE: [W16TGT01]: LCM:  [ End     Resource ]   [MSFT_DSCMetaConfiguration]
VERBOSE: [W16TGT01]: LCM:  [ End     Set      ]
VERBOSE: [W16TGT01]: LCM:  [ End     Set      ]    in  0.7620 seconds.
VERBOSE: Operation 'Invoke CimMethod' complete.
VERBOSE: Set-DscLocalConfigurationManager finished in 1.105 seconds.
```

Let's check our change:

```
PS> Get-DscLocalConfigurationManager -CimSession $cs |
select ConfigurationMode, RebootNodeIfNeeded

ConfigurationMode    RebootNodeIfNeeded
-----------------    ------------------
ApplyAndAutoCorrect             True
```

and our target machine's LCM shows the settings we desire.

Now that you know how to modify the LCM settings, it's time to discover how to configure the LCM to use a pull server.

18.5.2 *Configuring LCM to use a pull server*

Configuring a machine's LCM to use a pull server involves modifying the LCM settings and providing the data the LCM needs to find the pull server. An example configuration to enable the use of the pull server we created earlier is shown in the following listing.

Listing 18.10   Configuring LCM to use the pull server

```
[DSCLocalConfigurationManager()]
Configuration LCMpull {
  param (
    [Parameter(Mandatory=$true)]
    [string[]]$ComputerName,

    [Parameter(Mandatory=$true)]
    [string]$guid,

    [Parameter(Mandatory=$true)]
    [string]$ThumbPrint
  )
  Node $ComputerName {              ❶ LCM settings
    Settings {
```

```
        AllowModuleOverwrite = $True
        ConfigurationMode = 'ApplyAndAutoCorrect'
        RefreshMode = 'Pull'
        ConfigurationID = $guid
    }

    ConfigurationRepositoryWeb DSCHTTPS {
        ServerURL = 'https://W16DSC02:8080/PSDSCPullServer.svc'
        CertificateID = $thumbprint
        AllowUnsecureConnection = $false
    }

    ReportServerWeb RepSrv {
        ServerURL = 'http://W16DSC02:9080/PSDSCPullServer.svc'
        CertificateID = 'AllowUnencryptedTraffic'
        AllowUnsecureConnection = $true
    }
  }
}

#$guid = New-Guid | select -ExpandProperty Guid
$guid = '5827c542-20bb-487c-89cb-484cbe5f0b1f'

$thumbprint=Invoke-Command -Computername W16DSC02 {
Get-Childitem Cert:\LocalMachine\My |
where Subject -Like 'CN=W16DSC02*' |
Select-Object -ExpandProperty ThumbPrint}

LCMpull -computername W16TGT01 -Guid $guid `
-Thumbprint $thumbprint -OutputPath .\MOF
```

❷ Pull server settings

❸ Report server settings

❹ Setting GUID

❺ Certificate thumbprint

❻ Create MOF

The configuration starts with the [DSCLocalConfigurationManager()] decorator to ensure it targets the LCM. The important changes to the LCM settings ❶ are to change the RefreshMode to PULL and to supply the GUID that'll be used for the ConfigurationId.

The pull server configuration ❷ includes the URL of the server and its certificate thumbprint. The reporting server ❸ is configured to use unencrypted traffic (HTTP instead of HTTPS). In a production environment, you'll want to encrypt all traffic.

In this case, the GUID ❹ for the ConfigurationId is supplied. The alternate option is to generate a new GUID.

NOTE Configuring the target node or creating the first configuration to be pulled is a chicken-and-egg scenario: which is first? The correct answer is whichever works for the problem you're trying to solve.

The pull server's certificate thumbprint ❺ can be retrieved directly from the pull server. Running the configuration ❻ produces a .meta.mof file.

The LCM modifications are applied:

```
PS> Set-DscLocalConfigurationManager -ComputerName W16TGT01`
 -Path .\MOF\ -Verbose
```

Testing the LCM has to be done over a CIM session:

```
PS> Get-DscLocalConfigurationManager -CimSession $cs

ActionAfterReboot              : ContinueConfiguration
AgentId                        : CBE8E714-C86B-11E6-841F-00155D36C90B
AllowModuleOverWrite           : True
CertificateID                  :
ConfigurationDownloadManagers  : {[ConfigurationRepositoryWeb]DSCHTTPS}
ConfigurationID                : 5827c542-20bb-487c-89cb-484cbe5f0b1f
ConfigurationMode              : ApplyAndAutoCorrect
ConfigurationModeFrequencyMins : 15
Credential                     :
DebugMode                      : {NONE}
DownloadManagerCustomData      :
DownloadManagerName            :
LCMCompatibleVersions          : {1.0, 2.0}
LCMState                       : Idle
LCMStateDetail                 :
LCMVersion                     : 2.0
StatusRetentionTimeInDays      : 10
SignatureValidationPolicy      : NONE
SignatureValidations           : {}
MaximumDownloadSizeMB          : 500
PartialConfigurations          :
RebootNodeIfNeeded             : False
RefreshFrequencyMins           : 30
RefreshMode                    : Pull
ReportManagers                 : {[ReportServerWeb]RepSrv}
ResourceModuleManagers         : {}
PSComputerName                 : W16TGT01
PSComputerName                 : W16TGT01
```

The machine is now configured to use the pull server.

You can either wait for the DSC refresh cycle to pull the configuration, or if you're impatient, you can force a refresh:

```
PS> Update-DscConfiguration -CimSession $cs -Verbose -Wait
```

As always you should test the configuration:

```
PS>  Test-DscConfiguration -CimSession $cs
True
```

You can also test that the share exists:

```
PS> Get-SmbShare -CimSession $cs
```

Name	ScopeName	Path	Description	PSComputerName
ADMIN$	*	C:\Windows	Remote Admin	W16TGT01
C$	*	C:\	Default share	W16TGT01
IPC$	*		Remote IPC	W16TGT01
Standard	*	C:\TestFolder	This is a test SMB Share	W16TGT01

And that the file can be accessed:

```
PS> Get-Content -Path "\\W16TGT01\Standard\TestFile1.txt"
My first Configuration
```

So far, you've created configurations as a complete unit. In some circumstances, you may need to adopt a more granular approach—which leads us to the use of partial configurations.

18.6 Partial configurations

Partial configurations were introduced in PowerShell v5. They allow you to deliver fragments of the configuration to your target rather than a complete configuration. The LCM on the target machine will combine the fragments before applying as a single configuration. In this section, we'll examine your options for using partial configurations, when you should use them, and, possibly more importantly, when you shouldn't. We'll close with an example.

18.6.1 Partial configurations: yes or no

In this section, we'll examine the reasons why you might want to use partial configurations and issues you may encounter when using partial configurations.

PARTIAL CONFIGURATION USE CASE

Why would you want to use partial configurations? Isn't life complicated enough without splitting your configurations into a number of pieces?

The assumption behind partial configurations is that your environment isn't managed by a single team (or single person, in smaller environments). You might have a team that manages the operating system on your servers, but other teams manage the applications, such as SQL Server, Exchange, or SharePoint. Alternatively, developers creating a new application may split the management of the configuration. In either case, a single configuration can't be created to manage the target server due to permissions, skillset, or even office politics!

Partial configurations enable each team to create the configuration to manage *their part of the environment*. The server team creates a configuration to manage the operating system, and then other teams create configurations to manage the applications such as SQL Server, Exchange or your inhouse developed application. This also has the advantage of reducing the size of the individual configuration scripts.

The partial configurations can be pushed to the target machine, or the target can obtain the partial configurations from a pull server. If required, you can even use a mixture of push and pull modes to deliver the partial configurations.

Partial configurations could also be useful even if you have a team responsible for configuration work. You could use them to split up a large configuration and make it more manageable.

ISSUES WITH PARTIAL CONFIGURATIONS

On the surface, partial configurations seem like an ideal solution to managing an environment with diverse responsibilities. But a number of potential pitfalls lie in wait. For example, does the server team's standard settings for the server match the requirements of the application that'll run on the server? You may find that both teams try to configure the same things in different ways and end up with errors.

There is a way to overcome these issues—it's called communication. If you're going to use partial configurations, you're going to have to get the various people involved talking to each other. And you need someone with overall ownership of the whole configuration who can define the allowed configuration fragments.

Let's see how partial configurations work, starting with push mode.

18.6.2 *Pushing partial configurations*

Using partial configurations in push mode is broadly similar to using standard configurations in push mode: you create the configurations and push them to the target. There are a few differences:

- You need to configure the LCM to accept the partial configurations.
- The partial configurations are pushed to the target using `Publish-DSCConfiguration`.
- The configuration is run using `Start-DSCConfiguration`.

This will be easier with an example. To keep it simple, we'll only use built-in resources. Let's use a configuration that has two tasks:

- Create an environmental variable and set its value
- Create a registry key

Here's the configuration for creating an environmental variable.

Listing 18.11   Configuration to create environmental variable

```
Configuration EnvVarConfig {
  param (
    [string]$ComputerName
  )

  Import-DscResource -ModuleName PSDesiredStateConfiguration

  Node $ComputerName {
    Environment EnvironmentPC {
      Ensure = 'Present'
      Name = 'PCtestvar'
      Value = 'PIA 3e'
    }
  }
}

EnvVarConfig -ComputerName W16CN01 -OutputPath .\MOF\Env\
```

The `Environment` resource is used to create an environmental variable called `PCtest-var`, which is given a value of `'PIA 3e'`.

The important point is the output path that's used when the configuration is run. You need to separate the MOFs for the partial configurations—otherwise they'll overwrite each other because they have the same name. In practice, because the fragments are being created by different owners there will be no overlap if they're created on different machines. This is only a problem when doing an example like this.

NOTE If you ever find that one owner is authoring two fragments in production, you shouldn't be using partial configurations.

In this case, we'll create a subfolder in the MOF folder for the environmental variable configuration.

The next job is to generate the configuration that'll create the registry key, as shown in the following listing.

Listing 18.12 Configuration to create the registry key

```
Configuration RegConfig {
  param (
    [string]$ComputerName
  )

  Import-DscResource -ModuleName PSDesiredStateConfiguration

  Node $ComputerName {
    Registry RegistryPC {
      Ensure = 'Present'
      Key = 'HKEY_LOCAL_MACHINE\SOFTWARE\RegTestKey'
      Valuename = 'PCTestVar'
      ValueData = 'PIA 3e'
      ValueType = 'String'
    }
  }
}

RegConfig -ComputerName W16CN01 -OutputPath .\MOF\Reg\
```

String is the default registry type, but you should specify the data type for completeness and for debug purposes—and so that you'll understand what you were trying to achieve when you look at the configuration in the future. A subfolder called Reg is used for the MOF file to ensure we don't accidentally overwrite a partial configuration.

The last piece of the configuration is the control portion that defines the allowed partial configurations listing.

Listing 18.13 Control configuration

```
[DSCLocalConfigurationmanager()]
Configuration PCTest1 {
  param (
```

```
      [string]$ComputerName
   )

   Node $ComputerName {
      PartialConfiguration EnvVarConfig {
        Description = 'Sets the environmental variable'
        RefreshMode = 'Push'
      }

      PartialConfiguration RegConfig {
        Description = 'Sets the registry key'
        RefreshMode = 'Push'
      }
   }
}

PCTest1 -ComputerName W16CN01 -OutputPath .\MOF
```

This will configure the LCM on the target machine, so it needs the [DSCLocal-Configurationmanager()] decorator. Each partial configuration needs to be listed in the control configuration using a block like this:

```
      PartialConfiguration EnvVarConfig {
        Description = 'Sets the environmental variable'
        RefreshMode = 'Push'
      }
```

The PartialConfiguration resource is used. The name that's applied must match the configuration names used in the partial configuration scripts. A description helps explain what is happening.

You can apply the control configuration:

```
PS> Set-DscLocalConfigurationManager -Path .\MOF\ -ComputerName W16CN01
```

If you examine the LCM settings on the target machine

```
PS> $cs = New-CimSession -ComputerName W16CN01
PS> Get-DscLocalConfigurationManager -CimSession $cs
```

this line is of interest:

```
PartialConfigurations   : {[PartialConfiguration]EnvVarConfig,
   [PartialConfiguration]RegConfig}
```

It shows the two partial configurations we want to apply. Let's look at the Partial-Configurations setting in more detail:

```
PS> Get-DscLocalConfigurationManager -CimSession $cs |
select -ExpandProperty PartialConfigurations

ResourceId            : [PartialConfiguration]EnvVarConfig
SourceInfo            : C:\Scripts\Listing18.13.ps1::8::6::PartialConfiguration
ConfigurationSource   :
```

```
DependsOn               :
Description             : Sets the environmental variable
ExclusiveResources      :
RefreshMode             : Push
ResourceModuleSource    :
PSComputerName          : W16CN01

ResourceId              : [PartialConfiguration]RegConfig
SourceInfo              : C:\Scripts\Listing18.13.ps1::13::6::PartialConfiguration
ConfigurationSource     :
DependsOn               :
Description             : Sets the registry key
ExclusiveResources      :
RefreshMode             : Push
ResourceModuleSource    :
PSComputerName          : W16CN01
```

You can see the SourceInfo is set to the script containing the control configuration. The description and name of each partial configuration are also stored.

The next step is to publish the MOF files to the target machine:

```
PS> Publish-DscConfiguration -Path .\MOF\Env\ `
-ComputerName W16CN01 -Verbose

VERBOSE: Perform operation 'Invoke CimMethod' with following parameters,
    ''methodName' = SendConfiguration,'className' =
MSFT_DSCLocalConfigurationManager,'namespaceName' = root/Microsoft/Windows/
    DesiredStateConfiguration'.
VERBOSE: An LCM method call arrived from computer W16DSC01 with user sid S-1-
    5-21-759617655-3516038109-1479587680-1104.
VERBOSE: [W16CN01]: LCM:  [ Start  Set       ]
VERBOSE: [W16CN01]: LCM:  [ End    Set       ]      Saved configuration
    document into the partial configuration store.
VERBOSE: [W16CN01]: LCM:  [ End    Set       ]
VERBOSE: Operation 'Invoke CimMethod' complete.
VERBOSE: Publish-DscConfiguration finished in 0.213 seconds.

PS>  Publish-DscConfiguration -Path .\MOF\Reg\ -ComputerName W16CN01 -Verbose

VERBOSE: Perform operation 'Invoke CimMethod' with following parameters,
    ''methodName' = SendConfiguration,'className' =
MSFT_DSCLocalConfigurationManager,'namespaceName' = root/Microsoft/Windows/
    DesiredStateConfiguration'.
VERBOSE: An LCM method call arrived from computer W16DSC01 with user
sid S-1-5-21-759617655-3516038109-1479587680-1104.
VERBOSE: [W16CN01]: LCM:  [ Start  Set       ]
VERBOSE: [W16CN01]: LCM:  [ End    Set       ]      Saved configuration
    document into the partial configuration store.
VERBOSE: [W16CN01]: LCM:  [ End    Set       ]
VERBOSE: Operation 'Invoke CimMethod' complete.
VERBOSE: Publish-DscConfiguration finished in 0.11 seconds.
```

Because the LCM on the target machine is expecting the partial configurations, they don't overwrite, as would normally happen if you sent multiple MOF files with the same name to the target.

Now it's time to apply the configuration. The `-UseExisting` parameter on `Start-DSCConfiguration` tells the LCM to use the configurations it already has rather than push a new configuration to the target machine:

```
PS> Start-DscConfiguration -ComputerName W16CN01 `
-UseExisting -Wait -Verbose

VERBOSE: Perform operation 'Invoke CimMethod' with following parameters,
   ''methodName' = ApplyConfiguration,'className' =
MSFT_DSCLocalConfigurationManager,'namespaceName' = root/Microsoft/Windows/
   DesiredStateConfiguration'.
VERBOSE: An LCM method call arrived from computer W16DSC01 with
user sid S-1-5-21-759617655-3516038109-1479587680-1104.
VERBOSE: [W16CN01]:                                [] Starting consistency engine.
VERBOSE: [W16CN01]: LCM:   [ Start   Resource ]  [[Environment]EnvironmentPC]
VERBOSE: [W16CN01]: LCM:   [ Start   Test     ]  [[Environment]EnvironmentPC]
VERBOSE: [W16CN01]:                               [[Environment]EnvironmentPC]
   (NOT FOUND) Environment variable 'PCtestvar'
VERBOSE: [W16CN01]: LCM:   [ End     Test     ]  [[Environment]EnvironmentPC]
   in 0.3120 seconds.
VERBOSE: [W16CN01]: LCM:   [ Start   Set      ]  [[Environment]EnvironmentPC]
VERBOSE: [W16CN01]:                               [[Environment]EnvironmentPC]
   (CREATE) Environment variable 'PCtestvar' with value 'PIA 3e
VERBOSE: [W16CN01]: LCM:   [ End     Set      ]  [[Environment]EnvironmentPC]
   in 0.2030 seconds.
VERBOSE: [W16CN01]: LCM:   [ End     Resource ]  [[Environment]EnvironmentPC]
VERBOSE: [W16CN01]: LCM:   [ Start   Resource ]  [[Registry]RegistryPC]
VERBOSE: [W16CN01]: LCM:   [ Start   Test     ]  [[Registry]RegistryPC]
VERBOSE: [W16CN01]:                               [[Registry]RegistryPC] Registry
   key 'HKLM:\SOFTWARE\RegTestKey' does not exist
VERBOSE: [W16CN01]: LCM:   [ End     Test     ]  [[Registry]RegistryPC]  in
   0.3750 seconds.
VERBOSE: [W16CN01]: LCM:   [ Start   Set      ]  [[Registry]RegistryPC]
VERBOSE: [W16CN01]:                               [[Registry]RegistryPC] (SET)
   Create registry key 'HKLM:\SOFTWARE\RegTestKey'
VERBOSE: [W16CN01]:                               [[Registry]RegistryPC] (SET)
   Set registry key value 'HKLM:\SOFTWARE\RegTestKey\PCTestVar'
   'PIA 3e' of type 'String'
VERBOSE: [W16CN01]: LCM:   [ End     Set      ]  [[Registry]RegistryPC]  in
   0.3440 seconds.
VERBOSE: [W16CN01]: LCM:   [ End     Resource ]  [[Registry]RegistryPC]
VERBOSE: [W16CN01]:                               [] Consistency check completed.
VERBOSE: Operation 'Invoke CimMethod' complete.
VERBOSE: Time taken for configuration job to complete is 2.841 seconds
```

Finally, test that the configuration worked:

```
PS> Test-DscConfiguration -ComputerName W16CN01
True
```

Partial configurations in push mode are more complicated than pushing a single, large configuration, but may be useful if you need to split your configurations to control their size. Production environments are more likely to be using a pull server, so we'll see how partial configurations work with a pull server next.

18.6.3 *Pulling partial configurations*

A pull server offers scalability for a production environment compared to using push mode, but partial configurations bring additional complexity.

To configure a target machine using partial configurations in pull mode you need to

- Modify the LCM of the target machine to use pull mode and tell it which partial configurations to use
- Create the configurations, rename them, and copy to the pull server
- Wait for the target machine refresh cycle to apply the configurations or force an immediate refresh cycle

The first job is to modify the LCM. Use listing 18.10 to originally configure the target machine to use a pull server. That listing can be modified, as shown in the following listing, to also include the definition of the partial configurations to use.

Listing 18.14 Modifying the LCM to use partial configurations in pull mode

```
[DSCLocalConfigurationManager()]
Configuration LCMpull {
  param (
    [Parameter(Mandatory=$true)]
    [string[]]$ComputerName,

    [Parameter(Mandatory=$true)]
    [string]$guid,

    [Parameter(Mandatory=$true)]
    [string]$ThumbPrint
  )
  Node $ComputerName {
    Settings {
      AllowModuleOverwrite = $True
      ConfigurationMode = 'ApplyAndAutoCorrect'
      RefreshMode = 'Pull'
      ConfigurationID = $guid
    }

    ConfigurationRepositoryWeb DSCHTTPS {
      ServerURL = 'https://W16DSC02:8080/PSDSCPullServer.svc'
      CertificateID = $thumbprint
      AllowUnsecureConnection = $false
    }

    ReportServerWeb RepSrv {
      ServerURL = 'http://W16DSC02:9080/PSDSCPullServer.svc'
      CertificateID = 'AllowUnencryptedTraffic'
      AllowUnsecureConnection = $true
    }

    PartialConfiguration EnvVarConfig {
      Description = 'Sets the environmental variable'
      ConfigurationSource = '[ConfigurationRepositoryWeb]DSCHTTPS'
      RefreshMode = 'Pull'
    }
```

❶ Environmental variable partial configuration

```
      PartialConfiguration RegConfig {
        Description = 'Sets the registry key'
        ConfigurationSource = '[ConfigurationRepositoryWeb]DSCHTTPS'
        RefreshMode = 'Pull'
      }

    }
}

#$guid = New-Guid | select -ExpandProperty Guid
$guid = '5827c542-20bb-487c-89cb-484cbe5f0b1f'

$thumbprint=Invoke-Command -Computername W16DSC02 {
Get-Childitem Cert:\LocalMachine\My |
where Subject -Like 'CN=W16DSC02*' |
Select-Object -ExpandProperty ThumbPrint}

LCMpull -computername W16TGT01 -Guid $guid `
-Thumbprint $thumbprint -OutputPath .\MOF
```

Registry
key partial
❷ configuration

The changes involve adding the partial configuration definitions. The environmental variable configuration ❶ uses the name of the configuration (exactly as we did for partial configurations in push mode). The configuration information includes a description, a reference to the pull server to be used, and the refresh mode—in this case, push.

A similar partial configuration definition is used for the registry key ❷. Both partial configuration definitions are based on the name of the configuration. You'll need those names in a moment.

You need to push the LCM configuration to the target machine:

```
PS> Set-DscLocalConfigurationManager -Path .\MOF\ `
-ComputerName W16TGT01 -Force
```

You can view the configuration over the same CIM session:

```
PS> Get-DscLocalConfigurationManager -CimSession W16TGT01 |
Format-List ConfigurationDownloadManagers, ConfigurationID,
  ConfigurationMode, PartialConfigurations, RefreshMode

ConfigurationDownloadManagers : {[ConfigurationRepositoryWeb]DSCHTTPS}
ConfigurationID               : 5827c542-20bb-487c-89cb-484cbe5f0b1f
ConfigurationMode             : ApplyAndAutoCorrect
PartialConfigurations         : {[PartialConfiguration]EnvVarConfig,
                                 [PartialConfiguration]RegConfig}
RefreshMode                   : Pull
```

Notice that the partial configurations are registered, and the refresh mode is set to pull.

Now create the partial configurations. You can use the code from listings 18.11 and 18.12. You'll need to change the computer name when creating the MOF files:

```
PS> EnvVarConfig -ComputerName W16TGT01 -OutputPath .\MOF\Env\
PS> RegConfig -ComputerName W16TGT01 -OutputPath .\MOF\Reg\
```

If you remember, when we created a pull configuration we needed to rename the MOF file using the configuration ID of the target server.

> **NOTE** In PowerShell v5, the requirements for configuration ID were relaxed. It can now be any string. It doesn't have to be a GUID. Semantically, it's equivalent to a Role ID now. Originally it was supposed to be a NodeID, but people kept using it for roles, so the PowerShell team repurposed it and added a separate property to identify the node.

When you use partial configurations in pull mode, the naming convention is

```
<configuration name>.<configuration id>.mof
```

Let's quickly work through the steps to get your partial configurations to the pull server. First, you need to get the configuration ID of the target server:

```
PS> $cid = Get-DscLocalConfigurationManager -CimSession $cs |
select -ExpandProperty ConfigurationID
```

then use the GUID to rename the MOF files:

```
PS> Rename-Item -Path C:\Scripts\MOF\Env\W16TGT01.mof `
-NewName "EnvVarConfig.$cid.mof"

PS> Rename-Item -Path C:\Scripts\MOF\Reg\W16TGT01.mof `
-NewName "RegConfig.$cid.mof"
```

Each MOF file needs to have a checksum file generated:

```
PS> New-DscChecksum -Path .\MOF\Env\EnvVarConfig.5827c542-20bb-487c-89cb-
    484cbe5f0b1f.mof -Force

PS> New-DscChecksum -Path .\MOF\Reg\RegConfig.5827c542-20bb-487c-89cb-
    484cbe5f0b1f.mof -Force
```

Then you can copy the MOF files and the checksum files to the pull server:

```
PS> Get-ChildItem -Path .\MOF\Env -Filter "*$cid*" | Copy-Item -Destination
    'C:\Program Files\WindowsPowerShell\DscService\Configuration\'
-ToSession $s -Force

PS> Get-ChildItem -Path .\MOF\Reg -Filter "*$cid*" | Copy-Item -Destination
    'C:\Program Files\WindowsPowerShell\DscService\Configuration\'
-ToSession $s -Force
```

The new configurations will be applied at the next refresh—or if you're impatient (or in testing mode), you can force a refresh of the configuration:

```
PS> Update-DscConfiguration -ComputerName W16TGT01 -Wait -Verbose
```

Partial configurations introduce a level of complexity and extra management that you may not need. The only valid scenario for partial configurations is when the fragments of configuration are being supplied by separate area owners. If you have complex configurations, you could break them down into a set of composite resources and use a master configuration that references the composite resources rather than trying to use partial configuration. We recommend that you only use partial configurations if you have to.

18.7   Summary

- You can use DSC to manage the configuration of your server estate.
- DSC is declarative and idempotent.
- DSC is standards-based.
- A DSC configuration uses DSC resources to define the configuration parameters.
- DSC can work in push and pull modes.
- A DSC configuration can be parameterized to manage one machine or many machines.
- Configuration data can be separated from the topology of the environment.
- When using pull mode, the MOF file generated by the configuration must be renamed using the target machine's configuration ID.
- You must also generate a checksum of the MOF file, for a configuration to be used in pull mode, and copy both files to the pull server.
- Partial configurations enable you to split your configuration, and they can be created by different teams.

The one part of DSC we haven't shown you yet is how to create your own DSC resources. We'll cover that in chapter 19, where we discuss another new feature in PowerShell v5: PowerShell classes.

Classes in PowerShell

19

This chapter covers
- The basic ideas underlying classes in PowerShell
- PowerShell class and enumeration creation
- Detailed discussion of properties and methods in PowerShell classes
- Method overloading and inheritance
- Class initialization and construction
- DSC resources based on PowerShell classes

> *Oh brave new world that has such people in it!*
>
> Miranda in William Shakespeare's The Tempest

PowerShell has always been a .NET language in that it worked with and consumed the types in the .NET framework, but it was always a kind of second-class citizen compared to other .NET languages because you couldn't create new types directly in PowerShell. This has been fixed in PowerShell v5, which now supports the ability to define new classes as well as extend existing .NET classes.

> **NOTE** The `class` keyword was reserved in the earliest versions of Power-Shell with the intent that the team would eventually add this capability to

PowerShell. It only took a little under 10 years to do it because the PowerShell team didn't want to rush into something as important as this.

In this chapter, we're going to look at what defining classes allows you to do as a PowerShell scripter/programmer. Also, one of the primary drivers for introducing classes in v5 was to make it easier to define DSC management resources. In the latter part of the chapter, we'll look at how this is done.

19.1   Writing classes in PowerShell

The ability to write classes in PowerShell was introduced in PowerShell v5. In this section, we'll show you how to create and use methods and properties in PowerShell classes.

> **NOTE** If you've done any programming in C#, while reading this chapter you should notice that PowerShell class syntax is a close subset of the C# syntax. The things that are missing from the subset include interface definition, property getters/setters, and the `const`, `private`, `protected`, and `internal` member attributes. Also, the new and `overload` attributes are not supported because all class members in PowerShell are virtual. This subset was specifically chosen to balance language complexity against expressive power, aligning PowerShell to the feature set available in other popular dynamic languages such as Python and Ruby. On the flip side, if you don't program in C#, then learning PowerShell classes will also help you to learn C#.

The addition of classes to PowerShell is something of a game changer; it means that you can now *program* in PowerShell with all the capabilities present in mainstream dynamic programming languages. Classes also add a new level of reliability to programming in PowerShell. Many of the new features allow PowerShell to check your code for errors statically—while you're writing the code instead of waiting until runtime. To maximize your experience using classes in PowerShell, it's recommended that you use a PowerShell-aware editor like the PowerShell Integrated Scripting Environment (PowerShell ISE) or Microsoft Visual Studio Code (a free open source editor from Microsoft.) These tools can show you code errors while you're editing your programs.

Now let's dive in and see what PowerShell classes have to offer. We'll start our exploration by looking at simple classes that contain only data members—properties.

19.1.1 Using properties in a PowerShell class

All the way through this book you've been using properties on objects. Properties are data members on objects and are fundamental to how PowerShell performs selecting, sorting, and formatting work. In this section, you'll see how to define properties in your own classes in PowerShell. Let's start with the simplest possible example:

```
PS> class Point
{
    $x
    $y
}
```

In this example, you use the `class` keyword, followed by the name of the class and a list of variable names that are to be the properties of the class. You could also write it this way on a single line:

```
PS> class Point { $x; $y }
```

This example shows how, with a small amount of text, you can define your first class. This is about as simple as it can get. To create an instance of this class, use either `New-Object` (a mechanism introduced way back in v1)

```
PS> New-Object Point
x y
- -
```

or, preferably, the `new()` method introduced in v5:

```
PS> [Point]::new()

x y
- -
```

> **NOTE** For code written for version 5 or above, when explicitly creating an object instance, you're much better off using the PowerShell v5 `[type]::new()` method. It's significantly faster than using `New-Object` and it's easier to get array arguments correct. (Try passing a single argument that's an array to `New-Object`, and you'll quickly figure out how hard that is to do.)

Now use `Get-Member` on the instance of the `Point` class to make sure everything is as expected:

```
PS> $p = [Point]::new()
PS> $p | Get-Member

   TypeName: Point

Name        MemberType Definition
----        ---------- ----------
Equals      Method     bool Equals(System.Object obj)
GetHashCode Method     int GetHashCode()
GetType     Method     type GetType()
ToString    Method     string ToString()
x           Property   System.Object x {get;set;}
y           Property   System.Object y {get;set;}
```

You'll see all the characteristics you'd expect from a regular .NET type. Along with the members you defined (x and y), you also see the default .NET members `GetType()`, `ToString()`, and so on. This happens because `Point` is a regular .NET type. PowerShell classes are full .NET classes, which allows them to participate fully in the .NET ecosystem.

> **NOTE** For C# users, even though PowerShell 5+ doesn't support the getter/setter syntax from C#, data members in PowerShell classes are properties, not fields. At some point in the future, the getter/setter syntax will likely be added.

Okay, let's move along and see what else you can do with class properties. In the output from the previous examples, the values of the x and y members were empty (null). That's because they're untyped members. Let's update the class to add type constraints to the members. It doesn't take a lot more work to do this:

```
PS> class Point
    {
       [int] $x
       [int] $y
    }
PS> [Point]::New()
x y
- -
0 0
```

Now that you've added a type constraint [int] to each of the members, when you print out the instance, the values are 0 (the default value for integers) rather than null as they were in the earlier example.

But what if you want to have a specific initial value? The following example shows how to do this:

```
PS> class Point {
       [int] $x = 1
       [int] $y = 2
}
```

It's as simple as assigning an initial value to the member. (At this point, this may seem familiar—it's the same syntax used to initialize function parameters.)

Now let's look at a way to create and initialize an instance all in one step by using *cast initialization*. To do this, you take a hashtable and cast it into the desired type:

```
PS> $p = [Point] @{ x=1; y=2 }
PS> $p

x y
- -
1 2
```

When you print out the value of $p, you can see that 1 has been assigned to x and 2 has been assigned to y. This is a powerful technique because you can take unschematized data in the form of hashtables or PSObjects and convert it into strongly typed objects. Let's create a second class, Square, to see how this works. The Square class looks like this:

```
PS> class Square {
       [Point] $c1
       [Point] $c2
}
```

It's another simple class, but this time the members are typed as being of the `Point` class you defined earlier. Let's use the cast constructor to create an instance of this out of nested hashtables:

```
PS> $sq = [square] @{c1 = @{x=1; y=2}; c2 = @{x=3; y="4"}}
PS> $sq.c1.x
1
PS> $sq.c2.y
4
```

In this example, the top-level hashtable had two members, c1 and c2, each of which was defined in terms of x and y. In the cast construction, the constructor walked through the nested hashtable converting each element to the desired type, including converting the string "4" to the number 4. The same thing can be done with, for example, JSON documents. The following string is equivalent to the hashtable from the previous example:

```
PS> $jstr = '{"c1":  {"x":  1, "y":  2}, "c2":  { "x":  3, "y":  "4"}}'
```

Now let's convert it first into PSObjects using `ConvertFrom-JSON` and then cast the result into a `[Square]`:

```
PS> $sq = [square] ($jstr | ConvertFrom-Json)
PS> $sq.c1.x
1
PS> $sq.c2.y
4
```

And again, the cast initialization works all the way down, converting each piece to the required type. What happens if something is wrong in one of the source elements? Let's find out. You'll change the c2 element in the data to have x and z instead of x and y. Here's what happens:

```
PS> $jstr = '{"c1":  {"x":  1, "y":  2}, "c2":  { "x":  3, "z":  "4"}}'
PS> [square] ($jstr | ConvertFrom-Json)
Cannot convert value "@{c1=; c2=}" to type "Square".
Error: "Cannot convert value "@{x=3; z=4}" to type "Point".
Error: "Cannot convert the "@{x=3; z=4}" value of type "System.Management.
   Automation.PSCustomObject" to type "Point".""
At line:1 char:1
+ [square] ($jstr | ConvertFrom-Json)
+ ~~~~~~~~~~~~~~~~~~~~~~~~~~~~~~~~~~~~
    + CategoryInfo          : InvalidArgument: (:) [], RuntimeException
    + FullyQualifiedErrorId : InvalidCastConstructorException
```

The cast fails, and you get a somewhat informative message indicating what went wrong in the conversion process. With PowerShell v5, if you need to validate a JSON document, you have to create a set of classes that represents the schema of the JSON document.

19.1.2 *Class member attributes*

Members in PowerShell classes can optionally have the keyword attributes: `hidden` and `static`. Let's learn a bit about them.

THE HIDDEN ATTRIBUTE

The `hidden` attribute makes a member, well, hidden. This means you won't ever see the member by default; `Get-Member` won't show it. You can force it to be shown by using `-Force`. Why would you want to hide a member? `Hidden` is intended to be used on class members that are used internally by the class but aren't part of the end-user (public) signature of the class. In essence, these members are *private* to the class.

> **NOTE** Why not make them private like they are in C#? Because in the compiled language world, the debugger is a separate program from the compiler that has special access to everything. In contrast, the debugger in PowerShell is PowerShell—a reentrant session of the interpreter that lets you inspect the system. Because it's only PowerShell, anything that makes members inaccessible to PowerShell makes them inaccessible to the debugger (because it's PowerShell). In effect, the `hidden` attribute is a compromise between completely public members and private members. You don't see them unless you explicitly ask for them.

THE STATIC ATTRIBUTE

The `static` attribute allows you to define static members in a PowerShell class. You saw static members previously when we discussed method invocation. Now you'll see how to create these members. Here's an example showing a class with a static member:

```
PS> class myclass {
    static $foo = 123
}
```

In this example, you can see that all you need to do to create a static member is to prefix the member with the keyword `static`. Now you can access this member as follows:

```
PS> [myclass]::foo
123
```

Because the property is static, there's no need to create an instance of the object in order to access the member. You can have hidden static members too. That looks like the following:

```
PS> class myclass2 {
    static $foo = 123
    hidden static $bar = 3.14
}
```

As mentioned in the previous section, you can still access the member

```
PS> [myclass2]::bar
3.14
```

but when you use `Get-Member` to look at the static members on the class

```
PS> [myclass2] | Get-Member -Static -Type Properties

   TypeName: myclass2

Name MemberType Definition
---- ---------- ----------
foo  Property   static System.Object foo {get;set;}
```

you don't see the bar property. If you want to see it, you use the `-Force` parameter on `Get-Member`, which looks like this:

```
PS> [myclass2] | Get-Member -Static -Type Properties -Force

   TypeName: myclass2

Name MemberType Definition
---- ---------- ----------
bar  Property   static System.Object bar {get;set;}
foo  Property   static System.Object foo {get;set;}
```

MEMBER VALIDATION ATTRIBUTES

Along with the keyword attributes (`hidden` and `static`), you can use the data transformation and data translation attributes you're familiar with from advanced function parameters (see section 7.2.6) on class members. Let's see an example of a class using these attributes. The following example uses the `[ValidateRange()]` and `[Validate-Set()]` attributes to constrain the allowed values on the class members:

```
PS> class ApartmentPets
{
    [int]
    [ValidateRange(1,88)]
    $UnitNumber

    [string]
    [ValidateSet("cat", "dog", "bird")]
    $Type

    [int]
    [ValidateRange(0,3)]
    $Count
}
```

This class could be used to keep track of the type and number of pets in each apartment of a building. But this goes beyond merely keeping track; the attributes on the class members prevent an entry from containing more than three (or fewer than zero) pets as well as restricting the type of pet and ensuring that the apartment number is valid. You can create a valid instance of this class by casting a hashtable into an instance of [ApartmentPets]:

```
PS> [ApartmentPets] @{ UnitNumber = 22; Type = "cat"; Count = 2 }

UnitNumber Type Count
---------- ---- -----
        22 cat      2
```

Running this code creates an instance for apartment unit 22, which has two cats. But let's try increasing the count a bit:

```
PS> [ApartmentPets] @{ UnitNumber = 22; Type = "cat"; Count = 10 }
Cannot create object of type "ApartmentPets". The 10 argument is greater than
    the maximum allowed range of 3. Supply an argument that is less than or
    equal to 3 and then try the command again.
At line:1 char:1
+ [ApartmentPets] @{ UnitNumber = 22; Type = "cat"; Count = 10 }
+ ~~~~~~~~~~~~~~~~~~~~~~~~~~~~~~~~~~~~~~~~~~~~~~~~~~~~~~~~~~~~~~~~~
    + CategoryInfo          : InvalidArgument: (:) [], RuntimeException
    + FullyQualifiedErrorId : ObjectCreationError
```

Trying to create an entry with 10 cats, results in an exception being thrown instead of creating an invalid instance. This ability to constrain the allowed values for members in a class provides a powerful way to ensure that all the objects you're dealing with have valid data.

That's enough about data members for now. Let's take a short detour to look at how enumeration types are defined in PowerShell.

19.1.3 PowerShell enumerations

The .NET framework provides a user-definable data type related to classes called an *enumeration* (usually shortened to *enum*) that defines a closed set of named constant values. For example, there's a predefined enum type in the .NET framework for the days of the week, which you can access using a number or a name:

```
PS> [System.DayOfWeek] 0
Sunday

PS> [System.DayOfWeek] "Saturday"
Saturday
```

In either case, the string containing the name of the day of the week is returned. In practice, the underlying type for enums is Int32, allowing them to be cast to integers:

```
PS> [int] [System.DayOfWeek] "Saturday"
6
```

> **NOTE** C# supports both long and int for the underlying type for enums. PowerShell currently supports only int.

Finally, you can view the list of values in an enumeration:

```
PS> [enum]::GetNames([System.DayOfWeek]) -join ', '
Sunday, Monday, Tuesday, Wednesday, Thursday, Friday, Saturday
```

Let's look at how you can create your own enums in PowerShell. Use the enum keyword to define the start of the enum. Supply a name and the list of values, and it's done:

```
PS> enum foo { one; two; three }
```

As before, you can access the enum using numerical values, a static member reference, or a cast:

```
PS> [foo] 0
one

PS> [foo] "one"
one

PS> [foo]::one
one
```

Note that we didn't specify any values when we defined the enum. If no explicit values are provided, the compiler assigns integer values in order, starting at 0. Specifying explicit values looks like this:

```
PS> enum foo { one = 1; two = 2; three = 3 }
```

Note that the values must be constant, which means you can't, for example, use variables as the value for an enum member. The constant values, however, can be in any order, don't need to be consecutive, and don't even need to be unique:

```
PS> enum foo { one = 3; two = 20; three = 3 }
```

If you try to use a value that isn't part of the enum, you'll get an error:

```
PS> [foo]5
Cannot convert value "5" to type "foo" due to enumeration values that are not
   valid. Specify one of the following enumeration values and try again. The
   possible enumeration values are "three,one,two".
At line:1 char:1
+ [foo]5
+ ~~~~~~
    + CategoryInfo          : InvalidArgument: (:) [], RuntimeException
    + FullyQualifiedErrorId : UndefinedIntegerToEnum
```

Notice that you helpfully get a list of legal values. If you use a name that isn't in the list of values, you'll be ignored:

```
PS> [foo]::five
PS>
```

FLAGS ENUMERATIONS

Another way to use enumerations is as a bit field or set of flags, where each element of the enumeration represents a unique bit or flag. This is done by adding the [flags()] attribute to the enum definition, like so:

```
PS> [flags()] enum mybitfield {one = 0x1; two = 0x2; three = 0x4; all = 0x7}
```

This example defines three individual bits using hex values for each element, one per bit, and a fourth element, all, that's the bitwise AND of all three bits. You can use this with casts as follows:

```
PS> [int] [mybitfield] "one,three"
5

PS> [int] [mybitfield] "one,two,three"
7

PS> [int] [mybitfield] "all"
7
```

USING ENUMS

Now that you know all about enums, you may be wondering where to use them. They're typically used in functions and parameters, method parameters, and class properties. For example, the following function uses the `[DayOfWeek]` enum we looked at earlier:

```
PS> function foo {
        param([dayofweek] $bf)
        "$bf is day $([int] $bf) in the week"
    }
```

This function takes a single parameter constrained to be the `[DayOfWeek]`. Let's run it:

```
PS> foo tuesday
Tuesday is day 2 in the week
```

Running the function automatically converts the string "Tuesday" into the enumerated type. Casing the enum value, you get the corresponding number of the day in the week. You also get type checking for invalid values. If you pass in a month instead of a string, it errors out:

```
PS> foo september
foo : Cannot process argument transformation on parameter 'bf'. Cannot
   convert value "september" to type "System.DayOfWeek". Error: "Unable to
   match the identifier name september to a valid enumerator name. Specify
   one
of the following enumerator names and try again:
Sunday, Monday, Tuesday, Wednesday, Thursday, Friday, Saturday"
At line:1 char:5
+ foo september
+     ~~~~~~~~~
    + CategoryInfo          : InvalidData: (:) [foo],
   ParameterBindingArgumentTransformationException
    + FullyQualifiedErrorId : ParameterArgumentTransformationError,foo
```

Notice that the error message contains a complete list of the valid values. Also, with IntelliSense in the PowerShell ISE or Visual Studio Code, you'll see the values in a drop-down menu when entering your code.

We're finished with enumerations so we can finally move on to methods. Let's begin.

19.2   *Methods in PowerShell classes*

At long last, we're going to look at how to add methods (behaviors) to your classes. You'll learn many new things, but all the material in the previous sections in this chapter still applies. For example, `static` and `hidden` apply to methods as well as properties. Before we get started, there's some basic information you need to learn. It's summarized in the next section.

19.2.1 Method basics

Although methods in PowerShell classes are, in many ways, similar to PowerShell advanced functions, you must be aware of a number of important differences. When the PowerShell team was designing the class' features, it wanted to facilitate building larger programs with PowerShell. To that end, they made the following changes to the way things work:

- If a method is to have a return value, the type of that value must be specified as part of the method signature—for example, `[int]`. If no value is to be returned, then the return type of the method must be `[void]`.
- When returning a value, you must use the `return` statement. You can't allow a value to be written to the pipeline. Any values that are emitted directly to the pipeline are discarded. Although this might occasionally feel inconvenient, enforcing formal returns eliminates a common source of errors where objects are unintentionally leaked into the output stream, contaminating the output.
- Within a method, a variable must explicitly be assigned a value before it can be used in the method body. Using an unassigned variable will result in a compile-time error.
- Methods use *lexical scoping*, which means that the only variables you can use in the method body are ones that are defined in the method body. If you want to use global or script scope variables, you must use scope-qualified names; for example, `$global:myvar` or `$script:myvar`.
- Class member variables must be referenced as `$this.myVariable`. Likewise, if a method wants to reference other methods in the class, then it must also prefix the name with `$this`, as in `$this.mymethod(2, 3)`.
- Static members of the class, both properties and methods, are referenced using the class name and the `::` operator, as in `[myclass]::MyStaticProperty` or `[myclass]::MyMethod(2, 3)`.

Reading through that list is a bit dry, so in the next few sections we'll look at practical examples that illustrate these principles, starting with static methods.

19.2.2 Static methods

We'll start with static methods because these are the simplest method type. You'll see that they resemble PowerShell functions in many ways.

Like static properties, static methods don't require an instance of the class to be able to use them. Here is an example PowerShell class containing a static method.

Listing 19.1   A static method in a PowerShell class

```
class utils {
  static [int] Sum([int[]] $na){
    $result = 0
    if ($na -eq $null -or $na.Length -eq 0) {
      return $result
    }
    foreach ($n in $na) {
      $result += $n
    }
    return $result
  }
}
```

In this class, the Sum() method takes an integer array as its argument and returns the result of adding all of the values in the array together. Following the requirements spelled out in the previous section means that the syntax of a method declaration is a bit more complex than that of a function. Let's break the signature into pieces, as shown in figure 19.1.

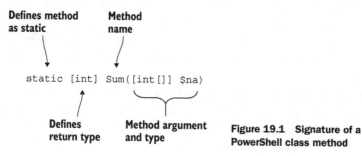

Figure 19.1   Signature of a PowerShell class method

Looking at the code in listing 19.1, you can see that the method is still similar to a function, but there are a couple of fundamental differences:

- The code defining the method is a scriptblock that has only an end block. You can't use Begin, Process, and End blocks in methods.
- You must use the return keyword to return the results and exit the method. You can't only emit the results to the pipeline the way you can with a PowerShell function.

Because Sum is a method, it's invoked like other static methods you've seen throughout the book using static method invocation syntax:

```
PS> [utils]::Sum(1..10)
55
```

As a comparison, the code in listing 19.1 can be converted to the more or less equivalent function as follows:

```
PS> function Sum {
  param ([int[]] $na)
```

```
      $result = 0
      if ($na -eq $null -or $na.Length -eq 0) {
        $result
      }
      foreach ($n in $na) {
        $result += $n
      }
      $result
}
```

and you use the function version as normal:

```
PS> sum -na (1..10)
55
```

You now have two ways to create reusable pieces of code: static methods and functions. Both have their advantages: Functions provide the most natural command-line experience, whereas static methods are more programmer friendly and make it possible to write large PowerShell programs more reliably.

> **NOTE** There's one other interesting advantage to static methods (at least at the time this book was written): Static method dispatch is orders of magnitude faster than function dispatch. Normally this doesn't make much difference, but if you're writing a tight, performance-sensitive loop that calls other code, you may consider writing that code as a static method rather than as a function. (In fact, method dispatch is fast for all methods, but static methods can most easily be used in place of functions, providing broader opportunities for performance enhancement in regular scripts.)

Now let's look at instance methods, which require that you create an instance of the class before you can use them. That's the topic of the next section.

19.2.3 Instance methods

Let's start by modifying listing 19.1. First, you'll rename the static Sum() method from listing 19.1 to ISum(), indicating that it specifically sums integers. Then you'll add a new method to perform the summation of an array of doubles.

Listing 19.2 Static and instance methods

```
class utils {
  static [int] ISum([int[]] $na){
    $result = 0
    if ($na -eq $null -or $na.Length -eq 0) {
      return $result
    }
    foreach ($n in $na) {
      $result += $n
    }
    return $result
  }
```

```
    [double] DSum([double[]] $da){
      $result = 0
      if ($da -eq $null -or $da.Length -eq 0) {
        return $result
      }
      foreach ($n in $da) {
        $result += $n
      }
      return $result
    }

}
```

The only change to the Sum() method was the name change. The big difference from listing 19.1 is that you've added a second method, DSum(), which sums an array of doubles. DSum() doesn't have the static keyword and so is an instance method. The return type and the argument type are set to [double] and [double[]], respectively, and the variable $na is changed to $da—otherwise the code is the same as ISum().

Having created your class, you can use the static ISum() method as before:

```
PS> [utils]::ISum(1..10)
55
```

If you want to create an instance of the class, you can use the ::new() static method:

```
PS> $ui = [utils]::new()
```

> **NOTE** The new() method is a sort of extension method. It doesn't exist on the object but is understood by the PowerShell language to mean that you want to create a new object. One consequence of this is that the new() method isn't shown in the output of Get-Member.

Use the Get-Member cmdlet to view the class methods and properties for your new instance:

```
PS> $ui | Get-Member

   TypeName: utils

Name        MemberType Definition
----        ---------- ----------
DSum        Method     double DSum(double[] da)
Equals      Method     bool Equals(System.Object obj)
GetHashCode Method     int GetHashCode()
GetType     Method     type GetType()
ToString    Method     string ToString()
```

Notice that the DSum() method is visible, but not the static ISum() method. If you want to see the static members of an object, you need to use the -Static parameter on Get-Member:

```
PS> $ui | Get-Member -Static

   TypeName: utils
```

```
Name              MemberType Definition
----              ---------- ----------
Equals            Method     static bool Equals(System.Object...
ISum              Method     static int ISum(int[] na)
ReferenceEquals   Method     static bool ReferenceEquals(Syst...
```

Having created the class instance, you can now use the method to sum a list of floating-point numbers:

```
PS> $ad = 1.1,2.2,3.3,4.4,5.5
PS> $ui.DSum($ad)
16.5
```

Our class has separate named methods defined for summing integers and doubles. Now let's add properties to the class that will be used by the methods you've defined. You'll add two new properties to the list: a static $ISumTotal property for the ISum() method and an instance property called $DSumTotal for the DSum() method. These properties will hold the running total of all of the summations.

Listing 19.3 Static and Instance methods with properties

```
class utils {                                ❶ Static sum variable
  static [int] $ISumTotal = 0      ◄┘           used by ISum()
  static [int] ISum([int[]] $na){
    $result = 0
    if ($na -eq $null -or $na.Length -eq 0) {
      return $result
    }
    foreach ($n in $na) {
      $result += $n
    }
    [utils]::ISumTotal += $result
    return $result
  }                                            ❷ Instance variable
  [double] $DSumTotal = 0.0         ◄┘           used by DSum()
  [double] DSum([double[]] $da){
    $result = 0
    if ($da -eq $null -or $da.Length -eq 0) {
      return $result
    }
    foreach ($n in $da) {
      $result += $n
    }
    $this.DSumTotal += $result
    return $result
  }
}
```

In a static method, you reference the property ❶ by using the name of the type, as in

```
[utils]::ISumTotal += $result
```

This isn't new; it's the same way you've always accessed static properties in a class. But the instance member introduces something new:

```
$this.DSumTotal += $result
```

Here you see a new variable, $this, being used to reference the specific instance ➋ of the object in the method. You saw this before in section 10.2.2, with script methods. Script methods also have an automatic $this pointer to refer to the instance of the object that the method is accessing.

You've looked at static and simple instance methods. Now let's look at the most sophisticated variation on instance methods. The PowerShell language allows for typed method parameters, which means that you can distinguish same-named methods by their list of parameters. This mechanism is called *method overloading*, which we'll look at next.

> **NOTE** Obviously, PowerShell also allows type constraints on function parameters, but still you can't have more than one function with the same name. For functions, the effective equivalent of overloads is parameter sets. There are advantages to both approaches. Overloading is expected and traditional for class methods. Parameter sets give you the expected and traditional command-line experience. The problem spaces are related but differ in significant ways, and so you have two different solutions.

19.2.4 *Method overloads*

A method overload occurs when a method has two or more versions, which differ only by their input definitions. The combination of name plus input definitions is called the *method signature*. The next listing shows the utils class rewritten to utilize method overloads. Instead of having separate ISum() and DSum() methods, you can have two methods called Sum that have different signatures.

Listing 19.4 Using method overloads

```
class utils {

    [int] Sum([int[]] $na){
    $result = 0
    if ($na -eq $null -or $na.Length -eq 0) {
      return $result
    }
    foreach ($n in $na) {
      $result += $n
    }
    return $result
  }
    [double] Sum([double[]] $na){
    $result = 0
    if ($na -eq $null -or $na.Length -eq 0) {
      return $result
    }
```

```
    foreach ($n in $na) {
      $result += $n
    }
    return $result
  }

}
```

Instead of having the ISum() and DSum() methods as in listing 19.3, this time you have two copies of the Sum() method, both of which are instance methods. They could have as easily been defined as two static methods, but you can't have one be static and the other be instance. As we've discussed, the only difference between the two lies in the method signatures:

```
[int] Sum([int[]] $na)
[double] Sum([double[]] $na)
```

The first version has integer input and output. The second version works with doubles. Create an instance of the class so you can look at it:

```
PS> $ui = [utils]::new()
```

Using Get-Member, you see two signatures for the Sum method:

```
PS> $ui | Get-Member

   TypeName: utils

Name        MemberType Definition
----        ---------- ----------
Equals      Method     bool Equals(System.Object obj)
GetHashCode Method     int GetHashCode()
GetType     Method     type GetType()
Sum         Method     int Sum(int[] na), double Sum(double[] na)
ToString    Method     string ToString()
```

You can also get the overloads for a method by using the method name without the parentheses:

```
PS> $ui.Sum

OverloadDefinitions
-------------------
int Sum(int[] na)
double Sum(double[] na)
```

From the perspective of the person using them, both methods are invoked with identical syntax but different parameter types. You start with summing an integer array, which looks like this:

```
PS> $ui.Sum(1..10)
```

Then you define and sum an array of doubles:

```
PS> $ad = 1.1,2.2,3.3,4.4,5.5
PS> $ui.Sum($ad)
16.5
```

The PowerShell runtime looks at the name of the method to get the available overloads and then compares the signature of each overload against the parameters to decide which one to invoke. When distinguishing overloads, the runtime does a best-match comparison. It's entirely possible to have two overloads that would work (in fact, the [double] variant would be perfectly happy with integers and convert them to doubles). When looking at an overload, the runtime picks the one with the closest match. If you pass in integers, the integer signature method is the closet match, even though the double signature method would work.

The methods you've seen so far have been visible to Get-Member and the user. As was the case with properties, at times you may want to hide internal methods from your users.

19.2.5 *Hidden methods*

As discussed in section 19.1.2, all PowerShell class members (both methods and properties) are public; private members are not supported. As was the case for properties, you can use the hidden keyword to create methods that are hidden from the default Get-Member results and PowerShell IntelliSense, even though the method's still a public member of the class. Typically, hidden is used to hide implementation details of the class, as shown in the following listing.

Listing 19.5   Using hidden methods

```
class HasLogging
{
  [int] Add($x, $y)
  {
    $this.Log("add $x $y")
    return $x + $y
  }
  [int] Subtract($x, $y)
  {
    $this.Log("subtract $x $y")          ❶ Call to hidden
    return $x + $y                          logging method
  }
  hidden [void] log($msg)                ❷ Hidden method
  {                                         used for logging
    # logging code goes here
  }
}
```

In this example class, a common method, log(), ❶ is used by the two other methods in the class. This is an internal logging method used by that class and is not intended to be called directly. As a consequence, it's marked hidden ❷ so as not to clutter up the user's experience with the class. Let's construct an instance of the class and see what Get-Member returns:

```
PS> [haslogging]::new() | Get-Member

    TypeName: HasLogging

Name        MemberType Definition
----        ---------- ----------
Add         Method     int Add(System.Object x, System.Object y)
Equals      Method     bool Equals(System.Object obj)
GetHashCode Method     int GetHashCode()
GetType     Method     type GetType()
Subtract    Method     int Subtract(System.Object x, System.Object y)
ToString    Method     string ToString()
```

As expected, the log() method isn't shown in the output.

Speaking of constructors, this is something we haven't discussed yet. The next section covers object construction in detail.

19.2.6 *Constructors in PowerShell classes*

A *constructor* is code used by the runtime to initialize an instance of a class. The constructor can populate some or all of the properties of a class. If you don't specify a constructor, a class automatically gets a default constructor that creates an instance with all properties set to their default values, as you saw in the earlier examples.

Let's return to our apartment pets example class:

```
PS> class ApartmentPets
{
    [int]
    [ValidateRange(1,100)]
    $UnitNumber

    [string]
    $Type

    [int]
    [ValidateRange(0,3)]
    $Count
}
```

This class has only the default constructor it gets automatically. This means that you have to create an instance explicitly and then assign it to each member:

```
PS> $petEntry = [ApartmentPets]::new()
PS> $petEntry.Count = 2
PS> $petEntry.Type = "cat"
PS> $petEntry.UnitNumber = 7
```

The alternative is to use the cast constructor:

```
PS> [ApartmentPets] @{ UnitNumber = 22; Type = "cat"; Count = 2 }
```

This works great in many cases but doesn't address all circumstances—like, say, you can have up to 3 cats but only 2 dogs or up to 10 fish. That logic can't be captured using attributes on the members. Instead, you'll have to write a constructor. You can add one or more constructors to your class, again overloaded by having different signatures. A constructor has the same name as the class, as shown next.

Listing 19.6   Using a non-default constructor

```
class ApartmentPets
{
    [int]
    $UnitNumber

    [string]
    $Type

    [int]                                                          Constructor to      ①
    $Count                                                         populate object
                                                                   properties
    ApartmentPets(){}

    ApartmentPets([int] $UnitNumber, [string] $Type, [int] $Count)
    {
        if ($UnitNumber -lt 1 -or $UnitNumber -gt 100)
        {
            throw [InvalidOperationException]::new(
            "Unit number $UnitNumber is invalid. Must be in range 1-100")
        }

        $maxPets = switch ($Type)
        {
            cat  { 3; break }
            dog  { 2; break }
            fish { 10; break }
            default {
                throw [InvalidOperationException]::new(
                "The allowed pets are dogs, cats & fish. A $type is not
                allowed")
            }
        }
        if ($count -gt $maxPets)
        {
            throw [InvalidOperationException]::new(
            "You are only allowed to have up to $maxPets pets of type $Type")
        }
        $this.Count = $Count
        $this.Type = $Type
        $this.UnitNumber = $UnitNumber
    }
}
```

The list of properties in the class is identical to listing 19.5. A constructor has the same name as the class and can take zero or more arguments in the parentheses ①. Arguments are separated by commas. The code to populate the properties is found between the braces, {}.

NOTE As soon as you add an explicit constructor to the class, the class no longer has a default constructor. If you still want a default constructor, you'll have to add it yourself; you no longer get it for free. That said, if you write a constructor like the one in listing 19.6, you don't want a default constructor because that would allow the class user to bypass the very checks you're trying to enforce in the explicit constructor.

You have to use $this to refer to the property name within the constructor:

```
$this.Type = $Type
```

$this indicates you're dealing with the current object. To create a new object you still use the new() pseudo-static method:

```
PS> [ApartmentPets]::new(22, 'cat', 2)

UnitNumber Type Count
---------- ---- -----
        22 cat      2
```

Error handling during object construction is managed by the constructor:

```
PS> [ApartmentPets]::new(22, 'cat', 4)
You are only allowed to have up to 3 pets of type cat
At line:27 char:13
+             throw [InvalidOperationException]::new(
+             ~~~~~~~~~~~~~~~~~~~~~~~~~~~~~~~~~~~~~~~~~~
    + CategoryInfo          : OperationStopped: (:) [],
   InvalidOperationException
    + FullyQualifiedErrorId : You are only allowed to have up to 3 pets of
   type cat
```

or

```
PS> [ApartmentPets]::new(22, 'parrot', 4)
The allowed pets are dogs, cats & fish. A parrot is not allowed
At line:21 char:17
+             throw [InvalidOperationException]::new(
+             ~~~~~~~~~~~~~~~~~~~~~~~~~~~~~~~~~~~~~~~~~~
    + CategoryInfo          : OperationStopped: (:) [],
   InvalidOperationException
    + FullyQualifiedErrorId : The allowed pets are dogs, cats & fish. A
   parrot is not allowed
```

Using new() with .NET classes

You can also use the new() option directly with .NET classes. For instance:

```
PS> [datetime]::new(2017,12,25)

25 December 2017 00:00:00
```

(Continued)

In this case you're using the first constructor listed at http://mng.bz/uV9G. The integers supplied to the constructor represent year, month, and day, respectively.

This is equivalent to using the `-ArgumentList` parameter on `New-Object`:

```
PS> New-Object -TypeName datetime -ArgumentList 2017, 12, 25

25 December 2017 00:00:00
```

You've seen how to create and use properties, methods, and constructors on a new class, but what about the case where you want to modify an existing class?

19.3 *Extending existing classes*

The act of creating a class that extends any existing class is called *inheritance*. The original class is known as the *base* class. The new class, known as the *derived* class, inherits all of the methods and properties of the base class.

> **NOTE** This section is included to complete the coverage of PowerShell classes. Class inheritance is a programmer topic and not something we'd expect many IT pros to use.

This topic is something that's definitely best explained through examples. We'll show you how to create a new class based on an inherited class, how to override the methods of the base class, and how to access the methods and constructor of the base class.

The first item is to create a derived class.

19.3.1 *Creating a derived class*

Before you can create a derived class, you need a base class. The following listing shows the base class we'll use for these examples.

Listing 19.7   The base class

```
class utils {

    [int] Sum([int[]] $na){
    $result = 0
    if ($na -eq $null -or $na.Length -eq 0) {
      return $result
    }
    foreach ($n in $na) {
      $result += $n
    }
    return $result
  }

}
```

You've seen this code several times already. The class has one method, Sum(), that sums an array of integers. Assume that you also want a method that will sum doubles. You could add a method overload as you did in section 19.2.3, but in this case, we've decided that you need a new class.

Here's how to derive a new class from your base class.

Listing 19.8 The derived class

```
class utils {
    [int] Sum([int[]] $na){
      $result = 0
      if ($na -eq $null -or $na.Length -eq 0) {
        return $result
      }
      foreach ($n in $na) {
        $result += $n
      }
      return $result
    }
}
class newutils : utils {
    [double] Sum([double[]] $na){
      $result = 0
      if ($na -eq $null -or $na.Length -eq 0) {
        return $result
      }
      foreach ($n in $na) {
        $result += $n
      }
      return $result
    }
}
```

❶ The base class

❷ Derived class start

❸ Method signature for derived class

The base class ❶ is as shown in listing 19.8 and earlier examples in the chapter. The new class's relationship ❷ to the base class is shown by the first line of the class definition:

```
class newutils : utils
```

The derived class name follows the class keyword. A colon followed by the base class name shows the class from which the new class is inheriting members. The version of the Sum() method that sums doubles ❸ is part of the new class.

An instance of the new class is created in the same way as for any PowerShell class:

```
PS> $ui = [newutils]::new()
```

If you examine $ui with Get-Member

```
PS> $ui | Get-Member

   TypeName: newutils
```

```
Name         MemberType Definition
----         ---------- ----------
Equals       Method      bool Equals(System.Object obj)
GetHashCode  Method      int GetHashCode()
GetType      Method      type GetType()
Sum          Method      double Sum(double[] na), int Sum(int[] na)
ToString     Method      string ToString()
```

you'll see both method overloads. In this case, both method overloads are available to the new class:

```
PS> $ad = 1.1, 2.2, 3.3, 4.4, 5.5
PS> $ui.Sum($ad)
16.5

PS> $ui.Sum(1..10)
55
```

In this example, you've extended the base class by providing an extra method overload. What about the situation where you want to override the method in the base class?

19.3.2 *Overriding members on the base class*

In this example you'll override the Sum() method of the base class. You override the method by creating a method in the derived class that has the same signature: name, return (output) type, and arguments as a method in the base class.

Listing 19.9   Overriding the base class

```
class utils {                                          ◁──┐  Base
                                                        ❶  class
    [int] Sum([int[]] $na){
    $result = 0
    if ($na -eq $null -or $na.Length -eq 0) {
      return $result
    }
    foreach ($n in $na) {
      $result += $n
    }
    return $result
  }
}
                                              ❷  Derived
class newutils : utils {                   ◁──┘  class
    [int] Sum([int[]] $na){
    $result = 0
    if ($na -eq $null -or $na.Length -eq 0) {
      return $result
    }
    $result = 1
    foreach ($n in $na) {               ❸  Change to
      $result *= $n              ◁──┘      method
    }
```

```
        return $result
    }
}
```

The base class ❶ is as in the previous section. The derived class ❷ has a method with the same signature as the base class. This means it will override, or replace, the method from the base class. The method in the derived class is different in that it calculates the product of the input array ❸ rather than the sum. Notice that $result is set to 1 before the calculations start. Multiplying by zero gives zero!

Creating an instance of the derived class hasn't changed, but when you examine the instance of the class, you'll see that the Sum() method has only a single overload:

```
PS> $ui = [newutils]::new()
PS> $ui | Get-Member

    TypeName: newutils

Name        MemberType Definition
----        ---------- ----------
Equals      Method     bool Equals(System.Object obj)
GetHashCode Method     int GetHashCode()
GetType     Method     type GetType()
Sum         Method     int Sum(int[] na)
ToString    Method     string ToString()
```

When you create an instance of the class and call the Sum() method, you now get the product of the numbers in the array rather than the sum:

```
PS> $ui = [newutils]::new()
PS> $ui.Sum(1..10)
3628800
```

You can still access the Sum() method in the base class if required.

ACCESSING THE BASE CLASS

You saw how to override a method in the base class in listing 19.9. If you need to use the method in the base class, you can do so. When you create your derived class, add a call to the base class's method:

```
PS> class newutils2 : utils {
  [int] Sum([int[]] $na){
      return ([utils]$this).Sum([int[]] $na)
  }
}
```

You're casting to the base class so that you can access the method. When you create an instance and use it, you get the sum of the array:

```
PS> $ui = [newutils2]::new()
PS> $ui.Sum(1..10)
55
```

19.3.3   *Extending .NET classes*

Because PowerShell classes are full .NET classes, it's possible for PowerShell classes to extend existing, compiled .NET classes.

> **NOTE**   There are limitations on this. Because PowerShell classes don't currently support the protected member keyword, it's not possible to extend classes that require overriding protected members.

Here's an example where you overload one of the classes in the PowerShell code base.

Listing 19.10   Inheriting from a .NET class

```
using namespace System.Management.Automation

class FixCase : ArgumentTransformationAttribute          ❶ Class that derives from
{                                                           an existing .NET class
    [object] Transform(
        [EngineIntrinsics] $engineIntrinsics,            Overload the abstract
        [object] $inputData)                             Transform() method
    {                                                    ❷ on that class
        [string] $data = $inputData -as [string]
        if (-not $data) {
            throw [PSArgumentNullException]::new("inputData")
        }
        return $data.SubString(0,1).ToUpper() +
            $data.Substring(1).ToLower()
    }
}

function AutocapPet
{
    param (                          ❸ Apply the attribute to
        [FixCase()]                     a function parameter
        [string]
            $petType
    )
    return $petType
}
```

The class that you're overloading is ArgumentTransformationAttribute ❶, which is the base class for the argument transformation attributes that can be applied to function parameters. Inheriting from this class requires us to introduce another new concept called an *abstract method*. Abstract methods are part of a class's signature that implies that the class can't be used directly. A class with an abstract method is called an *abstract class*. You can have abstract classes without any abstract methods, but there isn't much point to that. Abstract methods must be overloaded in the derived class to provide a concrete implementation.

That's what you're doing here with the ❷ Transform method. The concrete Transform method overloads the abstract method in the base class. Listing 19.10 also defined the function `AutocapPet` ❸ that uses the `[FixCase()]` attribute. Call this function with an all-lowercase argument:

```
PS> AutocapPet gEorGE
George
```

The result is returned correctly cased, which is rather handy.

19.4 *Classes, modules, using, and namespaces*

Now you know a lot about classes, but you still need to see how they're organized for use and reuse. The fundamental element of reuse is, as always, the PowerShell module. You'll organize your classes into modules and then use those modules in your scripts. The difference comes in how you use those modules. This is where another significant difference with classes shows up.

Whereas most things in PowerShell are resolved at runtime, PowerShell classes are processed at compile time. When you want to get all the type-checking benefits that classes provide, particularly IntelliSense support, it's necessary for PowerShell to know about classes ahead of runtime. Unfortunately, the usual way modules are referenced is the `Import-Module` cmdlet, which is a runtime thing. The environment knows nothing about the contents of a module until the `Import-Module` cmdlet is run, loading the module (and executing any code the module contains). This doesn't work for classes. Instead, PowerShell v5 introduced a new keyword, `using`, that does a superset of the things that `Import-Module` does.

> **NOTE** The implication here is that in PowerShell v5 scripts, you should generally prefer `using` over `Import-Module` because it provides better semantics for importation. There are still cases where you'll need to use `Import-Module`, like deciding which module to load at runtime, but those are fairly rare. For the most part, you should use `using` in scripts and modules targeting PowerShell v5.

THE USING ASSEMBLY PATTERN

The `using` keyword has three basic forms. The first form allows you to reference an assembly in your script. This form looks like this:

```
using assembly <assemblyName>
```

So, for example, to use the `Windows.Forms` assembly in your script, you would specify

```
using assembly System.Windows.Forms
```

at the top of the file. This will cause the `Windows.Forms` assembly to be loaded when you run your script. Now, because `using` is processed at compile time instead of runtime, the PowerShell ISE can show you mistakes as you're typing rather than waiting until runtime. If you type an incorrect name in the ISE, you'll see the error indicated by a red squiggle under the invalid name, as shown in figure 19.2.

```
1
2    using assembly System.Windows.XXX
```

**Figure 19.2   The PowerShell ISE shows
using assembly name errors while editing.**

Like many of the features associated with classes, this will help you catch errors while you're writing your code rather than waiting until you run it.

THE USING NAMESPACE PATTERN

The second variant for using is like this:

```
using namespace <namespace>
```

This variant will allow you to specify namespace prefixes that are used when Power-Shell tries to resolve a type name. This can greatly simplify things when you have a long namespace, like System.Windows.Forms. Figure 19.3 builds on the previous example, adding a namespace declaration for System.Windows.Forms, and then builds a small form example.

```
1
2    using assembly  System.Windows.Forms
3    using namespace System.Windows.Forms
4
5    $myform = [Form] @{ Name = "form1"; Text = "My First Form" }
6    $myButton = [Button] @{ Name = "btn1"; Text = "Push Me"; Dock = "Fill"}
7    $myForm.Controls.Add($myButton)
8    $myform.ShowDialog()
```

Figure 19.3   An example showing the use of using namespace to simplify using forms controls

In figure 19.3, because you add the namespace directive, the code can be written to reference the type [Form] directly instead of as [System.Windows.Forms.Form]. Likewise, buttons can be referred to as [Button]. This certainly makes the code tidier.

THE USING MODULE PATTERN

The final variant of the using directive is:

```
using module <moduleName>
```

This is the one you've been waiting for. It allows you to include a module in your script. Again, as with using assembly, the PowerShell ISE (or VSCode) will show an error (red squiggle) if the module name you specified to using module can't be found.

The using keyword should *always* be used to load modules containing classes. That's because classes are processed at compile time. All references to a class are resolved when the text referencing that class is scanned by the PowerShell parser. A class is visible only within the block of text defining it or in a block of text using a module with a defined class.

This block of text is called a compile unit. Let's look at an example. You'll take our friend the pets example from listing 19.6 and move it into a module called apartment-pets.psm1. Now you can use using to reference this module in another script. You'll create a new script called usingpets.ps1. This script will extend the class defined in apartmentpets to create a new class called `apartmentpets2` and add a new member, `Notes`, to the class. This new class is shown in this listing.

Listing 19.11 `apartmentpets2` **class inheriting from the** `apartmentpets` **class**

```
using module apartmentpets                    ◄───┐   Using apartmentpets brings
                                                   │   the base class into the
class apartmentpets2 : apartmentpets      ◄────┐   ❶   compile unit scope
{                                              │
    [string]                                   │   The new class extends
    $Notes                                     │   ❷   the existing one
}

$apEntry = [apartmentpets2] @{            ◄───┐
             Type = "dog"                      │   Create an instance
             Count = 1                         ❸   of the new type
             UnitNumber = 66
             Notes = "very friendly"
         }
                                          ❹   Display that
$apEntry | Format-List                 ◄──┘   instance as a list
```

In this listing, you can see the using statement ❶ that brings the base class, defined in the module apartmentpets, into the current compile unit. Then you create a new class ❷ that extends the base class with a new member, $Notes. Once you have the new class defined, you can create an instance out of it using a cast initialization. You display it as a list ❹. The output of this script looks like this:

```
PS> .\usingpets.ps1

Notes       : very friendly
UnitNumber  : 66
Type        : dog
Count       : 1
```

That's exactly what you'd expect. But what happens if the using statement isn't there and you put in an Import-Module instead? You'll get the following error:

```
PS> .\usingpets.ps1
At C:\Users\bgpay\documents\usingpets.ps1:5 char:24
+ class apartmentpets2 : apartmentpets
+                        ~~~~~~~~~~~~~~
Unable to find type [apartmentpets].
    + CategoryInfo          : ParserError: (:) [], ParseException
    + FullyQualifiedErrorId : TypeNotFound
```

This error occurs because you need to know the base type at compile time, and Import-Module doesn't get called until runtime, when it's too late. If you're using the ISE, you'll see an error as you're typing, as shown in figure 19.4.

This should make it clear that you should always import modules containing classes with the using module statement.

```
1   #using module apartmentpets
2   Import-Module apartmentpets
3
4   class apartmentpets2 : apartmentpets
```

Unable to find type [apartmentpets].

```
8   }
9
0   ⊟$apEntry = [apartmentpets2] @{
```

Figure 19.4 The error message when the base class module is not imported with the `using` **module statement**

USING MODULES AND NAMESPACES

The last thing we need to talk about with `using` is how modules and namespaces interact. You were able to simplify the use of the Windows Forms classes with a using namespace statement. Why didn't you need to do this with the module? Because when you use a module, the `using module <mymodule>` statement also has an implicit `using namespace <mymodule>` to simplify using the module. In practice, you could have written the new class as

```
using module apartmentpets

class apartmentpets2 : apartmentpets.apartmentpets
{
    [string]
    $Notes
}
```

but the implicit `using` namespace saves you the trouble and makes the most common scenario easier. To summarize: Every class defined in a module, lives in a namespace whose name corresponds to the module's name. But because there is an implicit `using` namespace in the `using` module, you don't have to worry about the namespace. The only time this will become a problem is when you import two different modules, m1 and m2, each of which contains a class with the same name, foo. In that case, you'd have to refer to the individual types using namespace-qualified names, as in [m1.foo] and [m2.foo].

At long last, we've finished our discussion of modules. But there's one more point for the classes discussion. Chapter 18 promised to show you how much easier it was to write a DSC resource using classes rather than MOF and scripts. The last section of this chapter covers that topic.

19.5   *Writing class-based DSC resources*

We said in chapter 18 that the easiest way to create your own DSC resource is to write it as a PowerShell class-based resource. Now that you know how to use PowerShell classes, it's time we showed you how to write a DSC resource.

The process for creating class-based resources is:

1   Create a script module containing one or more class-based resources. This involves writing a class and annotating it with a specific set of attributes.
2   Copy the module to a directory in your module path, typically something like C:\Program Files\WindowsPowerShell\Modules\. Double-check to make sure that

the module is in the right place. If it isn't, you'll get errors when trying to use it in a configuration. Again, smart editors like the ISE or VSCode will help you with this, calling out errors while you're writing the configuration that uses the resource. It isn't recommended that you put DSC modules in your personal module directory because that's not available to the local configuration manager—the LCM runs as Local System.

3 Create a module manifest that loads the script module and exports the resources defined in the script module using the DscResourcesToExport module manifest member.

4 Import the module into your configuration script and use it like any other resource.

We'll work through these steps in an example where you'll create a DSC resource to control the Windows firewall; you'll set it on or off for individual profiles.

The first step is to create the module with the class-based resource, as shown in the following listing. The class has a number of properties, corresponding to the resource properties, and three methods: Get(), Set(), and Test().

Listing 19.12 Class-based DSC resource

```
enum FWprofile {                    ◄──┐  Enum
    Domain                           ❶  definition
    Private
    Public
}

enum Ensure {
    Absent
    Present
}

[DscResource()]
class FireWallStatus {               ◄──┐  Start of class
                                      ❷  definition
    [DscProperty(Key)]
    [FWprofile]$profileName

    [DscProperty(Mandatory)]
    [Ensure]$ensure

    [DscProperty(NotConfigurable)]
    [bool]$enabled                                              ❸  Start of Get()
                                                                    method
    [FireWallStatus]Get() {          ◄──┘
        $fwp = Get-NetFirewallProfile -Name $this.profileName
        $test = [Hashtable]::new()
        $test.Add('ProfileName',$fwp.Name)
        $test.Add('Ensure', $this.Ensure)

        if ($fwp.Enabled) {$test.Add('Enabled', $true)}
        else {$test.Add('Enabled',$false)}

        return $test
    }
```

```
    [void] Set () {                                              ┌──◄
        $fwp = Get-NetFirewallProfile -Name $this.profileName    ❹  Start of Set()
        if ($this.ensure -eq [Ensure]::Present) {                   method
            if (-not $fwp.Enabled) {
                Set-NetFirewallProfile -Name $this.profileName -Enabled True
            }
        }
        else {
            if ($fwp.Enabled) {
                Set-NetFirewallProfile -Name $this.profileName -Enabled False
            }
        }
    }
                                                               ❺  Start of Test()
    [bool] Test () {                                     ┌──◄      method
        $fwp = Get-NetFirewallProfile -Name $this.profileName
        if ($this.ensure -eq [Ensure]::Present) {
            if ($fwp.Enabled) {
                return $true
            }
            else {
                return $false
            }
        }
        else {
            if ($fwp.Enabled) {
                return $true
            }
            else {
                return $false
            }
        }
    }
}
```

The enums at the top of the listing ❶ define the firewall profile names and the list of acceptable values for the Ensure option in the configuration (remember from chapter 18 that Ensure is set to Present to apply the configuration and Absent to remove the configuration).

The class definition ❷ has a [DscResource()] decorator. This marks the class as a DSC resource. Your class *must* have this decorator if you want it to work as a DSC resource. The class properties have the [DscProperty()] decorator, so they're also recognized by DSC. You'll notice that DscProperty is modified for each property. The values have the following meanings:

- Key—This property is used to identify the instance to which the configuration will be applied. You must define a key property in a PowerShell class-based resource. In this case, it's the firewall profile name.
- Mandatory—This property must have a value. In this case, Ensure controls whether the configuration is applied.
- NotConfigurable—This property isn't configurable by the DSC resource. It's populated in the Get() method to return additional information on the resource.

A PowerShell class-based resource must have three methods: `Get()`, `Set()`, and `Test()`. The class can have other helper methods if needed. The `Get()` ❸ method returns an object showing the current state of the configuration. A hashtable is populated to be the return object. Notice that the `Enabled` nonconfigurable property is used to return the current state of the firewall profile. This method is called when `Get-DscConfiguration` is used.

The `Set()` method ❹ is used by `Start-DscConfiguration` to apply the configuration. The method tests the current state of the configuration and enables or disables the firewall profile based on the combination of the values of `Ensure` and the current `Enabled` value.

`Test()` is the final method ❺. This method returns a Boolean value to indicate whether the configuration of the firewall profile matches the desired configuration. `Test-DscConfiguration` uses this method.

Once written, the module is placed in C:\Program Files\WindowsPowerShell\Modules\ and a module manifest is created:

```
PS> New-ModuleManifest -Path 'C:\Program Files\WindowsPowerShell\Modules\
    FirewallStatus\firewallstatus.psd1' `
-RootModule firewallstatus.psm1 -Guid ([GUID]::NewGuid()) `
-ModuleVersion 1.0 -Author 'Bruce & Richard' `
-Description 'Class based resource to toggle Windows firewall' `
-DscResourcesToExport 'FirewallStatus'
```

The `-DscResourcesToExport` parameter is used to create the list of resources available through the module. You must explicitly export the DSC resources from your module.

> **NOTE** The `DscResourcesToExport` module manifest member was added to improve the speed of resource discovery in a large set of modules. With this member, the resource discovery routines only need to scan the module manifest. Without it, the routines would have to scan all the .psm1 files, making the discovery process prohibitively slow. The down side is that if you forget to add it, your resource won't be discovered, which can be hard to debug.

Your new DSC resource is now ready to use, so it's time to create a configuration.

Listing 19.13 Configuration using a class-based resource

```
Configuration fwstatus {
    param (
        [Parameter(Mandatory=$true)]
        [string[]]$computername,

        [Parameter(Mandatory=$true)]
        [string]$profilename,

        [Parameter(Mandatory=$true)]
        [bool]$enabled
    )

    Import-DscResource -ModuleName firewallstatus
```

```
        if ($enabled) {$ens = 'Present'}
        else {$ens = 'Absent'}

        Node $computername {
            FirewallStatus fwstoggle {
                ProfileName = $profilename
                Ensure = $ens
            }
        }
    }
}

fwstatus -computername W16TGT01 -profilename Domain `
-enabled $true -OutputPath C:\Scripts\MOF
```

The script defines the configuration. The DSC resource is imported as usual. The value of Ensure is set based on the Boolean value of the configuration's enabled parameter. You only need the profile name and Ensure to define the configuration for the node. The script runs the configuration to generate the MOF file.

Create a CIM session to the target computer and test the current setting of the firewall profile:

```
PS> $cs = New-CimSession -ComputerName W16TGT01
PS> Get-NetFirewallProfile -CimSession $cs | select Name, Enabled

Name      Enabled
----      -------
Domain    False
Private   True
Public    True
```

You've cheated and switched off the domain firewall profile. Use Start-DscConfiguration to apply your new configuration; the Set() method of your class performs the action of configuring the firewall.

```
PS> Start-DscConfiguration -CimSession $cs -Path .\MOF -Wait
```

You can determine the setting again:

```
PS> Get-NetFirewallProfile -CimSession $cs | select Name, Enabled

Name      Enabled
----      -------
Domain    True
Private   True
Public    True
```

The standard DSC cmdlets can be used to test the configuration (call the Test() method)

```
PS> Test-DscConfiguration -CimSession $cs
True
```

and get the current configuration (use the Get() method):

```
PS > Get-DscConfiguration -CimSession $cs

ConfigurationName     : fwstatus
DependsOn             :
ModuleName            : FirewallStatus
ModuleVersion         : 1.0
PsDscRunAsCredential  :
ResourceId            : [FireWallStatus]fwstoggle
SourceInfo            :
enabled               : True
ensure                : Present
profileName           : Domain
PSComputerName        : W16TP5TGT01
CimClassName          : FireWallStatus
```

Using PowerShell classes greatly simplifies the creation of DSC resources. This concludes our coverage of PowerShell classes.

19.6 *Summary*

- Classes can be written in PowerShell starting in version 5.0.
- Along with classes, PowerShell v5 or greater allows you to define your own enumerations (enums).
- Properties and methods in PowerShell classes can be static- or instance-based.
- All members of a PowerShell class are public, but members can be hidden from general users. Get-Member -Force will make hidden members visible.
- A method must use return rather than placing objects on the pipeline and must declare its return type. If it returns nothing, then its return type must be [void].
- Methods can be overloaded based on the types of their arguments—on their method signatures.
- Objects, both PowerShell and .NET classes, can be instantiated using New-Object or the ::new() pseudo-static method. For scripts targeting PowerShell v5 or higher, the use of ::new() is strongly recommended for performance and reliability reasons.
- PowerShell classes have a default constructor, but you can create additional constructors.
- PowerShell classes can inherit from .NET classes or other PowerShell classes.
- DSC resources can be created using PowerShell classes. These classes must be stored in modules and imported with the Import-DSCResource keyword like MOF-based resources.
- A class-based DSC resource must have proper annotations and implement Get(), Set(), and Test() methods.

So far, we've shown you how to use the features of the PowerShell language. In the next— and last—chapter, we'll show you how to extend the way you use PowerShell through the use of the PowerShell APIs.

The PowerShell and runspace APIs

This chapter covers

- The PowerShell Application Programming Interface (API)
- How to perform isolated and concurrent operations
- Runspaces and runspace pools
- Out-of-process and remote runspaces
- Basic runspace management techniques

Here's a rule I recommend: never practice two vices at once.

—Tallulah Bankhead

So far, we've been dealing with PowerShell as a shell and scripting environment. In this chapter, we're going to look at it as an Application Programming Interface (API). An API is a set of functions, data structures, and classes that let you build applications on top of the software exposing that API. For example, the PowerShell ISE is an application that uses the PowerShell API. Normally, the PowerShell API is used by other programs for accessing PowerShell functionality, but it also turns out to be useful from within PowerShell itself. In effect, PowerShell scripts can act as host applications for other PowerShell engine instances, allowing you to perform advanced operations like dynamic pipeline construction, isolated execution, and concurrent operations.

20.1 *PowerShell API basics*

In this section, we'll look at the basic use patterns and structure of the PowerShell API. We'll look at how to construct instances of the core API objects and how to compose those objects into executable pipelines.

The PowerShell API is accessed using the class `System.Management.Automation` `.PowerShell`. That's a bit long to type, so a type accelerator `[PowerShell]` is provided to simplify access to the class. This class provides a factory method `Create()` that creates instances of the `[PowerShell]` object.

> **NOTE** In object-oriented design, the *factory method pattern* is a way of constructing objects using a method instead of directly calling a specific type's constructor. This abstracts the details of exactly which object is constructed and also allows the factory method to perform operations such as bookkeeping or object tracking before and after an object is created.

Once you have the `[PowerShell]` object instance, you can add commands to it using the `AddCommand()` method and finally invoke it using the `Invoke()` method. Let's look at the simplest example using the API. You're going to create an instance of the `[Power- Shell]` object, add one command, `Get-Date`, to the object's command collection, and then invoke it. This looks like the following:

```
PS> [PowerShell]::Create().AddCommand("Get-Date").Invoke()
19 May 2017 11:23:20
```

Take a look at this command and compare the English description to what you typed at the command line. Ignoring punctuation, they're identical. The PowerShell API is an example of what's known as a *fluent API*. A fluent API is one where the human-language representation and the code representation map one-to-one, item by item. This semantic mapping makes it easier for users to turn their intentions into executable code.

In the first example, the command you added, `Get-Date`, required no parameters, so you could add it and then invoke the command. Now let's see how to handle a command that does take parameters. You'll use the command `Get-CimInstance` with the argument `Win32_BIOS`. In pure PowerShell, the command would be entered as

```
PS> Get-CimInstance -ClassName Win32_BIOS
```

Using the PowerShell API, it looks like this:

```
PS> [PowerShell]::Create().AddCommand("Get-CimInstance"). `
AddParameter("ClassName", "Win32_BIOS").Invoke()

SMBIOSBIOSVersion : 90.1380.768
Manufacturer      : Microsoft Corporation
```

```
Name             : 90.1380.768
SerialNumber     : 004393254157
Version          : MSFT   - 0
```

Again, following the fluent API pattern, the method to add a parameter is `AddParameter()`. Now, suppose you only wanted to add a positional argument instead of the parameter name/value pair. As you can probably guess, the method to add an argument is `AddArgument()`. Here's the same example but adding an argument instead of a parameter:

```
PS> [PowerShell]::Create().AddCommand("Get-CimInstance"). `
AddArgument("Win32_BIOS").Invoke()

SMBIOSBIOSVersion : 90.1380.768
Manufacturer      : Microsoft Corporation
Name              : 90.1380.768
SerialNumber      : 004393254157
Version           : MSFT   - 0
```

In this example, the parameter-binding logic figures out what parameter to bind the value `Win32_BIOS` to, as it does in a PowerShell script.

Now that you have a basic understanding of the PowerShell API, commands, arguments, and parameters, let's work on some more advanced examples.

20.1.1 *Multi-command pipelines*

So far, you've been working with only simple commands, but one of PowerShell's greatest strengths is the ability to build pipelines of commands. In this section, we're going to look at how to do that with the PowerShell API.

To create a pipeline with more than one command, all you need to do is to make a subsequent call to `AddCommand()` for each additional command you want to add to the pipeline. Each command you add becomes the next stage in the pipeline. Let's see how this works with another example. In this example, you're going to convert this pipeline

```
PS> Get-Process -Name Power* | sort HandleCount -Descending
```

in PowerShell syntax into a `[PowerShell]` object. You start by creating the pipeline and adding parameters to it, as you've done previously:

```
[PowerShell]::Create().AddCommand("Get-Process").
AddParameter("Name", "Power*").
```

Then you add the `sort` command along with its parameters to the pipeline. This requires a second call to `AddCommand()`, followed by calls to `AddArgument()` and `AddParameter()`:

```
AddCommand("sort").
AddArgument("HandleCount").
AddParameter("Descending").
```

NOTE Switch parameters can either be added using the `AddParameter()` overload that takes only a parameter name or by passing the parameter name along with a Boolean value.

Finally, you call `Invoke()` to cause the command to be executed. The complete command, equivalent to the original PowerShell expression, looks like this:

```
PS> [PowerShell]::Create().AddCommand("Get-Process"). `
AddParameter("Name", "Power*"). `
AddCommand("sort"). `
AddArgument("HandleCount"). `
AddParameter("Descending"). `
Invoke()
```

Handles	NPM(K)	PM(K)	WS(K)	CPU(s)	Id	SI	ProcessName
579	33	84744	62784	13.89	17484	1	powershell
481	29	62852	55724	14.33	36460	1	powershell

Again, because you're using a fluent API, the transformation is pretty direct, with `AddCommand()` replacing the | pipe operator. This extends to as many stages in the pipeline as you need. Let's look at a more complex example with four stages in the pipeline. This example counts the number of processes with more than 1000 handles. The PowerShell expression to do this is

```
PS> Get-Process | where HandleCount -GT 1000 |
Measure-Object | foreach Count
```

and the [PowerShell] API equivalent is

```
PS> [PowerShell]::Create(). `
AddCommand("Get-Process"). `
AddCommand("where"). `
AddArgument("HandleCount").AddParameter("GT").AddArgument(1000). `
AddCommand("Measure-Object"). `
AddCommand("foreach").AddArgument("Count"). `
Invoke()
18
```

The converted expression has four calls to `AddCommand()`—one for each stage in the pipeline.

NOTE One thing to note in this example is that when specifying parameter names, you don't need to specify the dash before the parameter name. The fact that you're calling `AddParameter()` makes the intent clear.

20.1.2 Building pipelines incrementally

So far, all the examples have been showing the use of a single statement to create a [PowerShell] object. The fact that you can do this is one of the benefits of the fluent API design, but it's not required. You could choose to build the pipeline incrementally across a series of statements. Let's redo the final example in the last section. First, you need to get the [PowerShell] object into a variable:

```
PS> $p = [PowerShell]::Create()
```

Next, you add a command to that object:

```
PS> $p.AddCommand("Get-Process")

Commands           : System.Management.Automation.PSCommand
Streams            : System.Management.Automation.PSDataStreams
InstanceId         : ffff110b-677a-4d72-9036-6f7d28d6803c
InvocationStateInfo : System.Management.Automation.PSInvocationStateInfo
IsNested           : False
HadErrors          : False
Runspace           : System.Management.Automation.Runspaces.LocalRunspace
RunspacePool       :
IsRunspaceOwner    : True
HistoryString      :
```

Wait—you get a whole bunch of output from this command, so clearly an object is being returned from the AddCommand() method! This is the same object you've stored in the variable $p. You haven't seen this before because you've always been calling Invoke() at the end of your expressions. You can confirm that it's the same object by adding another command to the object and comparing the return value to what's stored in $p:

```
PS> $p -eq $p.AddCommand("where")
True
```

The result of the comparison shows that it always returns the same object. Next, you need to add the parameters and arguments to the object. Calls to AddParameter() and AddArgument() also return the same [PowerShell] object:

```
PS> $p -eq $p.AddArgument("HandleCount")
True
```

Now add the remaining parameters for the where command:

```
PS> $p = $p.AddParameter("GT").AddArgument(1000)
```

This time you're assigning the result of the method calls back to $p. This is sensible because the object returned is the same as the object being assigned and it eliminates unnecessary objects in the output stream.

> **NOTE** In PowerShell scripts, expressions in statements return values that are placed in the output stream. To avoid getting objects you don't want in the output stream, cast the expressions to [void] or assign the result to a variable. If you're a C# programmer, this behavior would be unexpected because statements in C# discard any results that are explicitly consumed. Because the

[PowerShell] API is used in both PowerShell and C#, it's important to remember this difference in behavior when switching languages.

This is how the fluent API works: Each method call returns the original object so it can be used for the next method call. Now add the remaining commands from the example to the object in $p:

```
PS> $p=$p.AddCommand("Measure-Object").AddParameter("Sum"). `
AddCommand("foreach").AddArgument("Count")
```

The complete pipeline object is now available in $p ready to invoke. Let's invoke it now:

```
PS > $p.Invoke()
18
```

Because the expression is still available in $p, you can invoke it again and again:

```
PS > $p.Invoke()
18
```

This way, you build the [PowerShell] object only once, regardless of how many times you need to invoke it.

The ability to incrementally build up pipelines is useful because you can do other processing or conditional logic between the steps to decide how to proceed. For example, within a script, you may want to dynamically add filters to the output of the script. Listing 20.1 shows an enhanced file list example demonstrating how this can be useful. Feel free to skip forward and take a look, but for the next section, we're going to switch to an extremely important topic we've glossed over so far: error handling.

20.1.3 *Handling execution errors*

So far, everything we're tried has worked perfectly. But we live in an imperfect world and so need to look at how to deal with errors. Remember that PowerShell has two types of errors: terminating, which halt execution, and nonterminating, which are reported. In the simplest case, a terminating error that occurs when you invoke a [PowerShell] object will result in an exception being thrown. Let's see what happens with a command-not-found error:

```
PS> [PowerShell]::Create().AddCommand("foobar").Invoke()
Exception calling "Invoke" with "0" argument(s): "The term 'foobar' is not
    recognized as the name of a cmdlet, function, script file, or operable
    program. Check the spelling of the name, or if a path was included, verify
    that the path is correct and try again."
At line:1 char:1
+ [PowerShell]::Create().AddCommand("foobar").Invoke()
+ ~~~~~~~~~~~~~~~~~~~~~~~~~~~~~~~~~~~~~~~~~~~~~~~~~~~~~~~
    + CategoryInfo          : NotSpecified: (:) [], MethodInvocationException
    + FullyQualifiedErrorId : CommandNotFoundException
```

You can trap this exception using the `try/catch` statement (see section 14.2.1) as follows:

```
PS> try { [PowerShell]::Create().AddCommand("foobar").Invoke() }
catch { "Caught exception: $_" }
Caught exception: Exception calling "Invoke" with "0" argument(s): "The term
    'foobar' is not recognized as the name of a cmdlet, function, script file,
    or operable program. Check the spelling of the name, or if a path was
    included, verify that the path is correct and try again."
```

This solution is good for terminating errors, but what about nonterminating errors that are written to the error stream? Let's try this by writing an explicit error:

```
PS> [PowerShell]::Create().AddCommand("Write-Error"). `
AddArgument("An error").Invoke()
```

And you get . . . nothing? Correct—nothing because the command succeeded in that it wasn't terminated, but there was still an error. Let's see how you can handle this case. The most important point is to assign the [PowerShell] object to a variable before invoking it. That's because the [PowerShell] object has a number of fields that you'll need to examine after the invocation completes. Let's set this up

```
PS> $p = [PowerShell]::Create().AddCommand("Write-Error"). `
AddArgument("An error")
```

and invoke the command

```
PS> $p.Invoke()
```

As in the earlier example, execution completes successfully with no indication of an error. Instead, you have to check properties on the [PowerShell] object. First, to see if any errors occurred, terminating or otherwise, you'll check the HadErrors property. If any errors were generated during execution, terminating or otherwise, this property will be true. Let's look:

```
PS> $p.HadErrors
True
```

Yes, an error did occur. Okay, you want to see what that error was. To do that, you need to look at the Streams property on the [PowerShell] object. The Streams property has one member for each of the streams PowerShell supports, as shown here:

```
PS> $p.Streams | Get-Member -Type Property | foreach Name
Debug
Error
Information
Progress
Verbose
Warning
```

Check the count on the `Error` stream, which, per the example, should contain one record:

```
PS> $p.Streams.Error.Count
1
```

and it does. Finally, we can dump out the error:

```
PS> $p.Streams.Error
Write-Error : An error
    + CategoryInfo          : NotSpecified: (:) [Write-Error],
   WriteErrorException
    + FullyQualifiedErrorId : Microsoft.PowerShell.Commands.
   WriteErrorException,Microsoft.PowerShell.
   Commands.WriteErrorCommand
```

As you might expect, anything written to the other streams during execution will be available in the respective stream property. Now create a `[PowerShell]` object that will emit a warning:

```
PS> $p = [PowerShell]::Create(). `
AddCommand("Write-Warning").AddArgument("A warning")
PS> $p.Invoke()
PS> $p.Streams.Warning
A warning
```

and, to check, examine the `HadErrors` property:

```
PS> $p.HadErrors
False
```

This confirms that no errors occurred during execution.

At this point, we've now looked at adding commands and parameters to `[Power-Shell]` objects and how to handle errors with the PowerShell API. This completes our discussion of the basic use of the PowerShell API. In the next section, we'll look at additional capabilities the API provides.

20.1.4 *Adding scripts and statements*

In the previous section we covered only the use of simple commands with the `[Power-Shell]` object. In this section, we'll look at two additional types of content you can add to the object: scripts and statements. Let's start with scripts.

ADDING SCRIPTS TO THE PIPELINE

We've looked at adding single commands, with or without parameters, and arguments to build pipelines using the PowerShell API. Now we're going to look at another way of adding executable content to the `[PowerShell]` instance. As well as commands, the PowerShell API allows you to add scripts to an instance. As you might expect by now, this is done through the `AddScript()` method.

> **NOTE** Using the word *script* in this context is a bit confusing because scripts are technically commands. If you want to invoke a script named myscript.ps1, then you should call AddCommand("myscript.ps1") because myscript.ps1 is a simple command—it's implemented as a script. The AddScript() method is about adding expressions to the pipeline, not commands. A much better name for the AddScript() method would have been AddExpression(), so in the same way that AddCommand() parallels Invoke-Command, AddExpression() would have paralleled Invoke-Expression. Unfortunately, no one thought of that at the time!

As always, we'll start by looking at a basic example. You're going to pass in a simple expression, 2+2, to be evaluated:

```
PS> [PowerShell]::Create().AddScript{2+2}.Invoke()
4
```

This example executes the expression 2+2. In many ways, AddScript() is the easiest method to use—just pass in the PowerShell code and execute it.

> **NOTE** This example showed passing a scriptblock to AddScript(). You can pass a string and get the same result. The advantage of using a scriptblock is that you get syntax checking on the code passed to the API when the object is created instead of deferring it to runtime.

Moving on, let's try something more complex with a script that contains three statements that emit the numbers 1, 2, and 3:

```
PS> $p = [PowerShell]::Create().AddScript{1;2;3}
PS> $p.Invoke()
1
2
3
```

This gives you the expected response. Now let's use a foreach loop to square these values:

```
PS> $p = [PowerShell]::Create(). `
AddScript{ foreach ($i in 1,2,3) { $i * $i }}
PS> $p.Invoke()
1
4
9
```

This illustrates that you can use any PowerShell construct with AddScript(). Anything that can go in a scriptblock can be used with AddScript(). This implies that you can also deal with input in the script you're adding to the [PowerShell] object. In a function or scriptblock, you can process input in two ways: by using $input in the end block or by creating a process block in the script. Both approaches work with AddScript().

By default, the script that's passed to the AddScript() method is run as if it was the end block in the script. This means you can use $input to get the input from the pipeline:

```
PS> $p = [PowerShell]::Create().  `
AddCommand("Get-Process").  `
AddScript{ $input |
            where { $_.name -like "csr*" } |
            foreach name
        }
PS > $p.Invoke()
csrss
csrss
```

This example takes the output of Get-Process, filters for processes matching "csr*", and then returns the name of the process. Note that, because this is running in the end block, there's no streaming. The prior command is run to completion before the added script is run. You can fix this by using a process block in the script. Create a new example that looks for process names in the process block:

```
PS> $p = [PowerShell]::Create().  `
AddCommand("Get-Process").  `
AddScript{process {
                if ($_.name -like "csr*")
                {
                    $_.name
                }
            }
        }
PS> $p.Invoke()
csrss
csrss
```

This example uses $_ to get the current pipeline object so it doesn't have to do any stream processing. Thus, a simple if statement is all that's needed. Now try a script that both returns values and writes errors:

```
PS> $p = [PowerShell]::Create().  `
AddScript{ 1; Write-Error "@ is an error"; 3 }
PS> $p.Invoke()
1
3
```

Invoking the example returns the output of the first and third statements. You need to check the [PowerShell] object for the error. First, verify that the error occurred:

```
PS > $p.HadErrors
True
```

and then dump out the error itself:

```
PS > $p.Streams.Error
  1; Write-Error "@ is an error"; 3  : @ is an error
    + CategoryInfo          : NotSpecified: (:) [Write-Error],
  WriteErrorException
```

```
    + FullyQualifiedErrorId : Microsoft.PowerShell.Commands.
WriteErrorException
```

NOTE This last example illustrates that just because the call to `Invoke()` returned a value doesn't mean that there wasn't an error. When using the `[PowerShell]` API, you should always check `HadErrors` and the streams to see if there were any errors.

We've now covered pretty much everything about scripts, so let's look at the last type of content you can add to a `[PowerShell]` object.

ADDING STATEMENTS TO THE PIPELINE

The last element type that can be added to a `[PowerShell]` object is a "statement." This term is in quotes because it doesn't mean *statement* quite the same way as we do in PowerShell script; we're not talking about `if` statements or `while` loops. What the `AddStatement()` does is add a second *pipeline* to the `[PowerShell]` object, resulting in a collection of pipelines that are executed one after the other. The output of all the pipelines/statements is aggregated and returned from the `Invoke()` method. This is easiest to understand with an example. You're going to create a `[PowerShell]` object that has three statements, each of which is a script that returns the number corresponding to the statement. First, create the `[PowerShell]` object and store it in the variable $p:

```
PS> $p = [PowerShell]::Create()
```

Next, add the first script, which returns the value 1.

```
PS> $p = $p.AddScript{1}
```

Now call the `AddStatement()` method to indicate that you're starting a new statement:

```
PS> $p = $p.AddStatement()
```

Now add the second script returning 2 as the content of the second statement:

```
PS> $p = $p.AddScript{2}
```

Finally, add the third statement and script in one step:

```
PS> $p = $p.AddStatement().AddScript(3)
```

You now have a complete object containing three statements that execute one after the other. Let's call `Invoke()` and see the result:

```
PS> $p.Invoke()
1
2
3
```

As expected, you get the three numbers corresponding to each of the statements.

ADDING STATEMENTS VS. ADDING SCRIPTS

Using the `AddStatement()` method may seem like an awkward way to execute multiple pipelines, particularly when you could call `AddScript()`. The primary scenario for `AddStatement()` is sending a series of commands to a remote runspace in `NoLanguage` mode, as described in section 11.6.4. Runspaces in `NoLanguage` mode won't accept script elements in the pipeline, so the only way to perform multiple actions in a single batch in this scenario is to use `AddStatement()`.

So far, we've talked about runspaces in a fairly peripheral manner. In the next section, we're going to look at them directly.

20.2 Runspaces and the PowerShell API

In this section, we'll look at how runspaces, which are PowerShell engine instances, interact with the PowerShell API. A runspace is a container that holds everything needed to execute PowerShell code. This container holds all variables, drives, commands, and the like that are used during the execution of a `[PowerShell]` object invocation. A runspace is *always* required when you want to execute PowerShell code, regardless of the mechanism used to execute that code, either API or script. A script user, however, typically isn't aware that there is a runspace because it was created by the host (for example, the PowerShell console host or the PowerShell ISE) application at startup. And so far, we as API users, haven't dealt with runspaces directly because the way we've been using the API allows the runtime to take care of the runspace requirement by creating a new one every time we call the API. This simplifies the API user's experience but comes with constraints and significant execution overhead.

The major constraint coming from a new runspace on each execution is that you can't incrementally build up state over a series of API calls. Conversely, a new runspace each time means that there is no cross-contamination between calls. This isolated execution is useful in its own right—for example, in creating uncontaminated test environments—and is something we'll cover in more detail in the next section before moving on to the more general cases.

20.2.1 Existing runspaces and isolated execution

In order for the `Invoke()` method on the `[PowerShell]` object to work, it needs an instance of the PowerShell runtime, namely a runspace. In all earlier examples, we didn't worry about this because the runtime took care of it for us by creating a new runspace for every call to `Invoke()`. By creating a new runspace each time, we get *isolated execution* where side effects of one call can't affect the operation of subsequent calls—at least as long as those side effects are restricted to runspace state. From an interactive user's perspective, this includes isolation from the interactive PowerShell session.

Let's walk through some examples to illustrate this behavior. You'll do this by creating and assigning variables in the different environments. First, create a variable $x in the interactive session:

```
PS> $x = 123
```

then use the API to try to retrieve that value:

```
PS> [PowerShell]::Create().AddScript{$x}.Invoke()
```

Nothing is returned because the variable $x exists only in the interactive session, not in the new runspace created by the API. Now use the API to set the variable:

```
PS> [PowerShell]::Create().AddScript{$x=456}.Invoke()
```

and again, try to retrieve it:

```
PS> [PowerShell]::Create().AddScript{$x}.Invoke()
```

Nothing is returned because the assignment was made only in the transient runspace created by the API. Finally, you can verify that the original value of $x in the interactive session hasn't changed:

```
PS> $x
123
```

REUSING THE CURRENT RUNSPACE

Creating a runspace each time has some obvious limitations—sometimes you do want to preserve side effects across commands. Consider trying to preconfigure an isolated test environment. You'd execute a series of API calls to configure the environment before executing the test code with a separate API call. This scenario can't work if you get a new environment every time you call the API.

The PowerShell API provides two mechanisms to accomplish durable state changes. The first allows you to say that the command should be run using the current runspace. The second involves your creating a durable environment in which to execute your commands (see section 20.2.2).

Let's start with using the current runspace. If you're in an interactive session, this would be the session's runspace. This is done by passing an argument of type `System.Management.Automation.RunspaceMode` to the `Create()` method. This enum provides two values: `CurrentRunspace` and `NewRunspace` (the default). Let's see an example using `CurrentRunspace` to change the value of $x you set up earlier:

```
PS> $x
123

PS> [PowerShell]::Create("CurrentRunspace").AddScript{$x=456}.Invoke()
PS> $x
456
```

This time, invoking the `[PowerShell]` object changes the value of $x in the session runspace. This is effectively equivalent to assigning the variable directly in the script. Given this, it's not obvious why you'd want to use this version of the API—it certainly doesn't provide any isolation. Where this can be useful is when you want to build up a pipeline dynamically and then execute it in the current runspace. Listing 20.1 shows the implementation of a fancy file list, or `fls`, command built on top of `Get-ChildItem`. It allows you to sort files by newest first, selecting the first N files to list and setting the output to return only the full name of the item.

Listing 20.1 A fancy file list command

```
function fls
{
    param (
        [Parameter()]
        [switch]
            $New,
        [Parameter()]
        [int]
            $First = -1,
        [Parameter()]
        [switch]
            $NameOnly
    )
    $p = [PowerShell]::Create("CurrentRunspace").        ← Create the base
            AddCommand("Get-ChildItem")                     [PowerShell] object
    if ($New)
    {                                                    ← If -New specified
        [void] $p.AddCommand("Sort-Object").               add sort command
            AddParameter("Descending").
            AddParameter("Property", "LastWriteTime")
    }
    if ($First -gt 0)
    {                                                    ← Restrict output
        [void] $p.AddCommand("Select-Object").             to $First N items
            AddParameter("First", $First)
    }
    if ($NameOnly)
    {                                                    ← Change output and
        [void] $p.AddCommand("ForEach-Object").            return only filename
            AddParameter("MemberName", "Fullname")
    }
    $p.Invoke()
    if ($p.HadErrors)                                    ← Check to see if
    {                                                       there were errors
        $p.Streams.Errors
    }
}
```

This listing shows how commands can be built up incrementally and then be executed in the current runspace. Execution in the current runspace is necessary for the command to have access to the runspace's current directory.

So far, we've been either dealing with runspaces that already exist or are automatically created on demand. Both of these cases limit what you can do with the runspace. In the next section, we're going to look at how to explicitly create your own runspaces.

20.2.2 *Creating runspaces*

Executing in your current session is useful, but a more interesting scenario would be to create a durable environment in which to execute your commands. This is core to the isolated test environment scenario we discussed earlier. Creating a durable execution environment is accomplished by explicitly creating a runspace and then using that runspace with the [PowerShell] API. Runspace creation is done using the System .Management.Automation.Runspaces.RunspaceFactory class, which has the type accelerator [runspacefactory]. This class provides methods that allow you to create a variety of runspace types. Let's start with the simplest case.

Getting a usable runspace requires a couple of steps. First you create the runspace and then you open it:

```
PS> $rs = [runspacefactory]::CreateRunspace()
PS> $rs.Open()
```

Once the runspace is ready, you can create a [PowerShell] object and set the Runspace property on that object:

```
PS> $p = [PowerShell]::Create()
PS> $p.Runspace = $rs
```

By setting the runspace on the [PowerShell] object, you let the runtime know to use that runspace for execution rather than create a new one. With the runspace assigned, add a script to the [PowerShell] object in $p and invoke it:

```
PS> $p.AddScript{$x = 123}.Invoke()
```

The script that's passed assigns a value to the variable $x in the associated runspace and so returns no value. Now you're going to execute another command in that runspace. You could create a new [PowerShell] object and associate the runspace, but let's look at an alternative way of doing this. Rather than creating a new [PowerShell] object each time, you can reuse the existing object by clearing the Commands property on the object. This removes all the previously added commands so you can start from scratch adding new commands:

```
PS> $p.Commands.Clear()
```

Now add a new script to return the value assigned to $x in the runspace you created. This will verify that its value is what you set it to in the first command:

```
PS> $p.AddScript{$x}.Invoke()
123
```

The output of the call to Invoke() confirms that the variable was set as intended.

By explicitly creating a separate runspace you now have two isolated execution environments for [PowerShell] commands. This is great for preventing cross-contamination, but another implication of two runspaces is that you should be able to do two things at once. You'll see how this works in the next section.

20.2.3 *Using runspaces for concurrency*

Concurrent execution is important for real-world tasks where more than one thing happens at a time. PowerShell provides limited concurrent operations with Invoke -Expression fan-out (see section 11.2.2) and background jobs (see section 13.1.2). In this section, we're going to look at how to perform concurrent operations using runspaces and the PowerShell API. The primary difference is in how you invoke the [PowerShell] object. In all earlier examples, you've been calling the Invoke() method. This is a *synchronous* method that starts execution and then waits for it to complete, returning the result of the execution. This prevents the caller's runspace thread (the *foreground* thread) from doing anything until the second runspace (the *background* thread of execution) has completed. In order to execute operations concurrently, you need a way to begin an *asynchronous* thread of execution. With the [PowerShell] object, this is done using the BeginInvoke() method.

Whereas the Invoke() method blocks until the execution completes and returns the result of that execution, the BeginInvoke() method immediately returns an object of type IASyncResult. This IASyncResult object provides a way for you to interoperate with the asynchronous operation you started. The most basic signature for Begin-Invoke() is System.IASyncResult BeginInvoke(). Let's look at an example to see what the IASyncResult object tells us about the background execution. Create a [Power-Shell] object with a single command and call BeginInvoke():

```
PS> $ia = [PowerShell]::Create().AddCommand("Get-Date").BeginInvoke()
```

> **NOTE** In this example, you're being a bit lazy and letting the runtime create the background runspace for you. Though simple, this doesn't allow for runspace reuse and so is not generally recommended as a best practice.

In the example, you're capturing the IASyncResult from the execution into the variable $ia so you can work with it later on. Let's display the object formatted as a list:

```
PS> $ia | Format-List

CompletedSynchronously : False
IsCompleted            : True
AsyncState             :
AsyncWaitHandle        : System.Threading.ManualResetEvent
```

The most important property for your immediate purposes is the IsCompleted property. This lets you know that the background execution has completed. In this simple example, the IsCompleted property is true immediately because the background execution was short. Now try running a command that takes longer. The Start-Sleep command is a good choice because you can specify fairly precisely how long you want the command to run:

```
PS> $ia = [PowerShell]::Create().AddCommand("Start-Sleep"). `
AddParameter("Seconds",5).BeginInvoke()
PS> $ia.IsCompleted
False
```

This time when you examine `IsCompleted`, you can see that the execution has not completed. Checking again in a few seconds, you'll see that it has completed:

```
PS> Start-Sleep -Seconds 5 ; $ia.IsCompleted
True
```

With commands other than `Start-Sleep`, the amount of time the command will take to complete is harder to predict. Clearly there has to be a better solution to waiting for completion than continuously checking (polling) the `IsCompleted` property. This is where the `EndInvoke()` method on the `[PowerShell]` object comes in. You pass the `IASyncResult` object returned from `BeginInvoke()` to `EndInvoke()`, and the foreground thread of execution will block until the background execution has completed. To do this, you need to store the `[PowerShell]` object in a variable in order to call `End-Invoke()` on that object. This looks like the following:

```
PS> $p = [PowerShell]::Create().AddCommand("Start-Sleep"). `
AddParameter("Seconds",5)
PS> $ia = $p.BeginInvoke();   $p.EndInvoke($ia)
PS> $ia.IsCompleted
True
```

If you check the value of `IsCompleted` after calling `EndInvoke()`, it will always be true. In effect, the `BeginInvoke()`/`EndInvoke()` pair are equivalent to the synchronous `Invoke()` except both threads run in parallel until `EndInvoke()` is called. Let's look at an example (listing 20.2) where you can see that both the foreground and background execution threads are running concurrently.

> **NOTE**   This example calls the Windows `[console]` API to print messages on the screen so you can see that they're both operating. The implication is that if you run it in the ISE, it won't work as expected.

Listing 20.2   Concurrent execution example

```
$r = [runspacefactory]::CreateRunspace()        ◁——  Create a background
$r.Open()                                             runspace

$p = [PowerShell]::Create().AddScript{          ◁——  Define the
    foreach ($i in 1..4) {                            background task
        [console]::WriteLine(">>> BACKGROUND $i")
        Start-Sleep 1
    }
```

```
        [console]::WriteLine("Background is done")
}
$p.Runspace = $r                              Start the
$a = $p.BeginInvoke()              ←┐         background task
foreach ($i in 1..3) {
        [console]::WriteLine("foreground $i <<<")
        Start-Sleep 1
}
[console]::WriteLine("Foreground is done")    Wait for the
                                   ←┐         background task
$p.EndInvoke($a)
"Called EndInvoke."
```

Running this script from the PowerShell console host produces the following output:

```
foreground 1 <<<
>>> BACKGROUND 1
foreground 2 <<<
>>> BACKGROUND 2
foreground 3 <<<
>>> BACKGROUND 3
Foreground is done
>>> BACKGROUND 4
Background is done
Called EndInvoke.
```

The messages from the foreground and background runspaces are interleaved. Because the background task does four iterations and the foreground task does only three, the foreground task completes first and then waits for the background task by calling `EndInvoke()`.

This is a trivial example. A more realistic example would be to perform several related, long-running operations concurrently, such as large file copies, formatting a disk, or creating virtual machines. In these scenarios, there may be a fairly large number of operations that could be performed in parallel. Manually creating and managing a large number of runspaces for these scenarios could be quite complex. It would be nice if PowerShell took care of all this bookkeeping is some way. That's exactly what runspace pools are all about. We'll look at those objects in detail in the next section.

20.3 Runspace pools

In all examples so far, you've been creating individual runspaces for each of the tasks you're performing. This results in numerous runspaces being created. Explicit reuse will reduce the number of runspaces that are created but there may still be a lot of work tracking all of them.

PowerShell provides a mechanism called runspace pools to take care of this bookkeeping automatically. A single runspace pool is made up of a number of individual runspaces. The runspace pool API allows you to set a number of constraints on the pool, allowing for automatic management of the amount of resources consumed. This is called throttling. For example, a runspace pool will allow you to limit (or throttle) the number of concurrent operations without having to explicitly code what's going on. You can start as many tasks as you need without worrying about running out of resources on the host machine. The runspace pool does this by limiting the pool of runspaces from a minimum to a maximum number of runspaces. Here's an example showing the creation of a runspace pool with a minimum of one and a maximum of three runspaces:

```
PS> $pool = [runspacefactory]::CreateRunspacePool(1, 3)
PS> $pool.Open()
PS> $pool.GetAvailableRunspaces()
3
```

When the pool is opened, it will have one runspace open and available. Now let's start a command running and see how the runspace count changes:

```
PS> $p1 = [PowerShell]::Create().AddCommand("Start-Sleep").AddArgument(30)
PS> $p1.RunspacePool = $pool
PS> $ia1 = $p1.BeginInvoke()
PS> $pool.GetAvailableRunspaces()
2
```

Add two more tasks:

```
PS> $p2 = [PowerShell]::Create().AddCommand("Start-Sleep").AddArgument(30)
PS> $p2.RunspacePool = $pool
PS> $ia2 = $p2.BeginInvoke()

PS> $p3 = [PowerShell]::Create().AddCommand("Start-Sleep").AddArgument(30)
PS> $p3.RunspacePool = $pool
PS> $ia3 = $p3.BeginInvoke()
PS> $pool.GetAvailableRunspaces()
0
```

The number of available runspaces drops to zero. But you can still add tasks to the pool even though there are zero available runspaces at that time:

```
PS> $p4 = [PowerShell]::Create().AddCommand("Start-Sleep").AddArgument(30)
PS> $p4.RunspacePool = $pool
PS> $ia4 = $p4.BeginInvoke()
PS> $pool.GetAvailableRunspaces()
0
```

When there are no available runspaces in the pool, new tasks are placed in a queue of tasks waiting to be executed. When a running task completes and its runspace becomes available, the next task in the queue is removed and invoked on the newly available runspace. The pool will continue to execute the maximum concurrent tasks allowed until the task queue is empty.

And now back to reality. Runspace pools are efficient mechanisms for handling concurrent operations, but you still need to deal with errors, which means you need to keep track of all the PowerShell objects you're creating. This listing shows how to do this.

Listing 20.3   **Foreach in parallel**

```
$pool = [runspacefactory]::CreateRunspacePool(1, 3)   ⟵  Limit to three
                                                          concurrent tasks
$pool.Open()
$tasks = foreach ($i in 1 .. 10)                ⟵  Capture the information
{                                                  for each task
    $p = [PowerShell]::Create()
    $p.RunspacePool = $pool
    $p = $p.AddScript{          ⟵  Set the code
        param ($iteration)         for the task
                                                        Each task writes
        foreach ($i in 1..5)                            iteration*2 stars
        {                                               to the console
            [console]::WriteLine("*" * ($iteration * 2))  ⟵
            Start-Sleep -Milliseconds 200
        }                                     The third iteration
        if ($iteration -eq 3)             ⟵  will write an error
        {
            Write-Error "ITERATION ERROR"
        }                              Capture [PowerShell],
    }.AddArgument($i)                  await object and
    $ia = $p.BeginInvoke()             iteration number
    @{p=$p; ia=$ia; iteration=$i}   ⟵
}
foreach ($t in $tasks)
{
    $t.p.EndInvoke($t.ia)                Check each iteration
    if ($t.p.HadErrors)              ⟵  for errors
    {
        Write-Error "Task iteration $($t.iteration) had errors"
        $t.p.Streams.Errors
    }
    $t.p.Dispose()
}
```

This example starts 10 tasks. Each task writes a line of stars to the console five times, where the number of stars written corresponds to the index of the task in the list of tasks being executed. The number of stars to write is passed as an argument to the task scriptblock, which is the same for each task.

NOTE In parallel processing terminology, this is called single instruction, multiple data (SIMD). Other variations would be passing both a unique scriptblock and a unique piece of data to each task, called *multiple instruction, multiple data* (MIMD), and finally passing multiple scripts but always using the same piece of data, or *multiple instruction, single data* (MISD).

To make sure at least one error is produced, there is special logic so that when the task index is 3, an error message is written.

To track all this information, as each task is started its [PowerShell] object, IASync-Handle, and task index are put into a hashtable that is then written to the output stream of the foreach statement. This output is captured in a variable, $tasks, and once all the tasks have started, a second `foreach` loop takes the complete list of tasks, waits for each task to complete, and then checks to see if any errors occurred during the execution of that task. Running this script will produce output similar to the following:

```
PS > .\foreachparallel.ps1
**
****
******
******
****
**
**
******
****
******
****
**
****
**
******
*******
************
*********
C:\Users\brucepay\documents\foreachparallel.ps1 : Task iteration 3 had errors
At line:1 char:1
+ .\foreachparallel.ps1
+ ~~~~~~~~~~~~~~~~~~~~~~
    + CategoryInfo          : NotSpecified: (:) [Write-Error],
    WriteErrorException
    + FullyQualifiedErrorId : Microsoft.PowerShell.Commands.WriteErrorExcepti
    on,foreachparallel.ps1

*********
<output truncated for brevity>
```

Note that the error message was printed before that last line of stars. The tasks are waited for in the order in which they were started, and so an individual task will complete before all the tasks have completed. If you wanted to defer error checking until all the tasks have completed, you would process the contents of $tasks twice—the first time to make sure all the tasks have completed, and then a second time to make sure all the errors have been accounted for.

To apply concurrent techniques successfully, you need to be careful about tracking the task objects and the associated errors. Taking advantage of the natural flow of the PowerShell pipeline makes this easy. The alternative—explicitly creating a collection and adding each task to the collection—makes the resulting code significantly more complex. For concurrent techniques to be successful, you need to take a disciplined approach that minimizes complexity and, in particular, approaches error handling in a structured way.

All the techniques we've looked at so far have used in-memory runspaces. In-memory runspaces have lower overhead than out-of-process executions like the jobs created with `Start-Job`, but there are cases where you want to have that extra layer of isolation.

With in-memory runspaces, if one of the tasks causes the process to terminate, all the other tasks will also be terminated. With process isolation, a task that crashes the process crashes only its host process. In the next section, we'll look at using process isolation with runspaces.

20.4 *Out-of-process runspaces*

Let's revisit the idea of isolation with runspaces. In section 20.2.1, we talked about how a runspace isolates all the PowerShell-specific data structures. This means that any process-wide pieces of data are still shared by all the runspaces. It also means that a catastrophic error—one that will cause the host process to exit—will also terminate all the runspaces in the process.

To provide an even greater layer of isolation, you can create an out-of-process runspace. An out-of-process runspace is created in a new process that is a child of the calling process and uses the PowerShell remoting protocol to communicate between the two processes. This is somewhat similar to the way Start-Job jobs work, but an out-of-process runspace lifecycle is different. With Start-Job, a new process is created when the job begins. The process exists for the duration of the job and then terminates when the job has completed. With out-of-process runspaces, the process is started when the runspace is opened and isn't terminated until the runspace is closed. This means you can run many tasks in the same process by reusing the runspace. It also means out-of-process runspaces are quite a bit more capable than background jobs but aren't significantly more complex than in-memory runspaces.

Creating an out-of-process runspace is straightforward: call the CreateOutOfProcess-Runspace() method to create the runspace and then open it like any other runspace:

```
PS> $ooprs = [runspacefactory]::CreateOutOfProcessRunspace($null)
PS> $ooprs.Open()
```

> **NOTE** The first argument to CreateOutOfProcessRunspace() is a pointer to an optional custom type table to use when communicating with that runspace. If this argument is null, the default PowerShell type table is used. PowerShell's default type files are loaded into the runspace just as if you'd started an instance of PowerShell. This default is fine in the majority of cases, but sometimes you may want specific control over how objects are serialized when passed between the processes. Custom type files allow this custom serialization information to be used by the remoting protocol. For information on how to create a type table instance, see http://mng.bz/46M0.

Once the runspace is open, you can send commands to it, like any other runspace. As an example, let's verify that the runspace is hosted in a separate process. You'll use the process identifier (PID), which is unique to each process, to distinguish parent from child. You'll be sending a command to the runspace that will return the process's ID using the $PID variable. First, create the [PowerShell] object for the command:

```
PS> $p = [PowerShell]::Create().AddScript{"child PID is $PID"}
```

Then set the runspace on the [PowerShell] object and invoke the command:

```
PS> $p.Runspace = $ooprs
PS> $p.Invoke()
child PID is 196
```

Now that you have the runspace PID, get the interactive host process id:

```
PS> "Local pid is $pid"
Local pid is 8368
```

On examination of the two PIDs, you can verify that the runspace is running in a different process.

So far, we've covered in-process and out-of-process runspaces. The last type of runspace we're going to cover is the remote runspace.

20.5 Remote runspaces

So far, all our runspace work has been done on the local computer. Now we're going to look at working with runspaces running on remote computers. But first a quick word about sessions and runspaces.

20.5.1 Sessions and runspaces

In chapter 11, when talking about remoting, we always talked about remote connections requiring *sessions* but never about remote runspaces. In the early design of PowerShell remoting, there were no PSSession objects, only runspaces. But when the team did usability studies, people were much more comfortable with the notion of a remote session because the term was already commonly used. The team introduced the PSSession object to be the script user-facing term, with the Runspace being relegated to advanced scenarios.

> **NOTE** Now that PowerShell is open source, you can see this session-versus-runspace legacy in the source itself. The file that contains the code for the New-PSSession command is still named newrunspacecommand.cs.

Fortunately, obtaining the underlying runspace from a session is quite simple because it's available as a property on the PSSession object:

```
PS> $s = New-PSSession localhost
PS> $s.Runspace

 Id Name          ComputerName   Type     State    Availability
 -- ----          ------------   ----     -----    ------------
 35 Runspace35    localhost      Remote   Opened   Available
```

20.5.2 Creating remote runspaces

Creating a remote runspace follows the same pattern you've used all along: You call the [runspacefactory]::CreateRunspace() method to the runspace. The difference between creating a remote versus a local runspace is that you must supply information about how to connect to the remote computer. This is done using the System.Management.Automation.Runspaces.WSManConnectionInfo class. Here's an example. Create the WSManConnectionInfo object by calling the constructor on it:

```
PS> $ci =
[System.Management.Automation.Runspaces.WSManConnectionInfo]::new()
```

Let's look at a subset of the information contained in the connection information object:

```
PS> $ci | Format-List scheme,computerName,port,appname

Scheme       : http
ComputerName : localhost
Port         : 80
AppName      : /wsman
```

This shows that you want to connect to the WS-MAN application on computer localhost using port 80 and HTTP for the base transport. You can now use this object to create a remote runspace by passing it to the CreateRunspace() method:

```
PS> $rrs = [runspacefactory]::CreateRunspace($ci)
PS> $rrs.GetType().FullName
System.Management.Automation.RemoteRunspace
```

Checking the type, you can see that the method has returned a RemoteRunspace instead of a regular Runspace. As always, before you can use a runspace to execute any code, it needs to be opened:

```
PS> $rrs.open()
```

Now create a [PowerShell] object and set its Runspace property to the remote runspace you created:

```
PS> $p = [PowerShell]::Create()
PS> $p.Runspace = $rrs
```

Add a scriptblock to the [PowerShell] object to print out the computer's hostname and the PID of the process hosting

```
PS> $p = $p.AddScript{
  "I am on host $(hostname)"
  "My PID is $pid"
  }
```

and invoke it:

```
PS> $p.Invoke()
I am on host brucepaybook
My PID is 17356
```

The output shows that the remote PID is 17356 whereas the local PID is 1132

```
PS> "Local PID is $PID"
Local PID is 1132
```

confirming, as we did in the out-of-process runspace case, that different processes are being used to host the runspaces.

> **NOTE** You may now be wondering how this scenario differs from the out-of-process case. In that case, the two processes are communicating directly over anonymous pipes. In the remoting case, the local session is communicating to the WS-MAN application, which creates the remote process and manages communication between the local and remote processes. Because there is an intermediary (WS-MAN), remote runspaces can support more features, including disconnected runspaces. In the out-of-process case, if the parent process terminates, then the child process is also terminated. In the remote runspace case, the local session can terminate, but the remote can remain active because the WS-MAN service manages the lifecycle of the remote session.

This concludes our rather brief discussion of remote runspaces. For more detailed information, consult the MSDN pages for the APIs, in particular the [WSManConnection-Info] class. See http://mng.bz/BCPq. The final section of this chapter looks at some basic hygiene principles with managing runspaces.

20.6 *Managing runspaces*

One last topic before we go: runspace management. We've been proceeding along, opening runspaces as needed. What we haven't always been doing is cleaning up the runspaces that we've been creating. Once a runspace is created and opened, it will remain in the current process until it's explicitly closed. You can find out how many runspaces you have going with the Get-Runspace command. Let's examine this further. Starting from a new session, create and open two runspaces:

```
PS> $r1 = [runspacefactory]::CreateRunspace()
PS> $r1.Open()
PS> $r2 = [runspacefactory]::CreateRunspace()
PS> $r2.Open()
```

Now use Get-Runspace to list all the runspaces in the session:

```
PS > Get-RunSpace
```

Id	Name	ComputerName	Type	State	Availability
1	Runspace1	localhost	Local	Opened	Busy
2	Runspace2	localhost	Local	Opened	Available
3	Runspace3	localhost	Local	Opened	Available

Notice that there are three runspaces in this session. That's because of the default runspace (Id 1) that handles the interactive commands passed to the session. Each runspace has a set of properties associated with it. The State property is fairly obvious; it's the current state of the runspace. In the formatted output this shows up as State, but note that state is a computed property in the format information that's equivalent to

```
PS> (Get-Runspace)[0].RunspaceStateInfo.State
Opened
```

The other property to be aware of is Availability. This property indicates whether there's a pipeline currently running in the runspace.

> **NOTE** Availability is also an alias used in formatting so things will fit on the screen. The property name is RunspaceAvailability.

Note that the default runspace will always be busy when you run a command because that runspace is used to run the command you typed. To close a runspace you need to call the close method on that runspace. The trick is not to close the default runspace, because that will end your session. You can do this by filtering on the RunspaceAvailability property as follows:

```
PS> Get-Runspace |
     where { $_.RunspaceAvailability -eq "Available" } |
     foreach Close
```

Now when you rerun the Get-Runspace command, all the non-default runspaces are closed:

```
PS> Get-RunSpace
```

Id	Name	ComputerName	Type	State	Availability
--	----	------------	----	-----	------------
1	Runspace1	localhost	Local	Opened	Busy
2	Runspace2	localhost	Local	Closed	None
3	Runspace3	localhost	Local	Closed	None

Runspace management isn't a major concern when working interactively, but if you have a long-running script that continually opens new runspaces without closing old ones, eventually you'll consume all the available resources. A much better strategy when using runspaces in a script is to create the necessary number of runspaces and then reuse them as needed. If you don't know how many runspaces you'll need, then the best solution is runspace pools, as discussed in section 20.3.

20.7 Summary

- The [PowerShell] API is a programmatic mechanism for creating and invoking PowerShell commands.
- This API can be used to build up multistage pipelines, both in fluent expressions and incrementally.

- This API also provides mechanisms for handling errors and exceptions in the pipelines you're building.
- Scriptblocks and statements can be added to your [PowerShell] expressions.
- Runspaces are created using the [runspacefactory] API.
- Runspaces can be used to create isolated execution environments and to perform concurrent operations.
- Runspace pools make it easier to deal with concurrent scenarios where there are many threads of execution.
- Out-of-process runspaces provide an additional level of isolation for tasks.
- Remote runspaces are used with the [PowerShell] API to execute commands on remote machines.

appendix
PowerShell 6.0 for Windows, Linux, and macOS

The PowerShell community was stunned (not too dramatic a word) in August 2016 when Microsoft announced that the core of PowerShell was going to be open source. Not only that, but PowerShell would now be available on Linux and Apple operating systems as well as Windows. Jeffrey Snover had been hinting in presentations at the PowerShell Summit (https://powershell.org/summit/) and other venues for a few years that he'd like to see PowerShell as an open source project, but it wasn't expected to happen so soon.

> **NOTE** The open source project includes the core PowerShell engine. Many of the non-core modules will also be ported. Many existing modules should work with PowerShell v6 due to the use of .NET standard 2.0.

In this appendix, we'll give you an overview of the open source project, explain the differences between PowerShell Core and the PowerShell you find on your Windows machine, and demonstrate the differences between running PowerShell on Linux/macOS compared to the experience you have on Windows.

The PowerShell open source project

The open source PowerShell project is hosted on Github at https://github.com/PowerShell/PowerShell and is open for anyone to join and contribute. PowerShell

823

6.0 includes versions for Windows, most major Linux distributions, macOS, and Docker. The list of supported platforms is evolving. You can see a complete list of supported platforms at the GitHub site. You can install PowerShell 6.0 side by side on Windows with an existing instance of PowerShell.

> **PowerShell 6.0 code status**
>
> At the time of writing PowerShell v6 is in development. It should be considered test code until it's formally released. Check the project website for the current state of the project before using.

Terminology

PowerShell v6 has introduced new terminology. Table 1 summarizes the terminology and explains the various editions of PowerShell.

Table 1   PowerShell terminology

Term	Meaning
Windows PowerShell	This is the edition of PowerShell that ships with Windows (or in a WMF download). It's built in, and requires, the full .NET CLR. Windows PowerShell is only available on the Windows platform. `$PSVersionTable.PSEdition` is set to `Desktop`.
PowerShell Core (PSCore)	This edition of PowerShell is built on the .NET Core CLR (see next section). PowerShell Core will be available on all supported platforms. `$PSVersionTable.PSEdition` is set to `Core`.
PowerShell on ?	PowerShell Core built for a specific platform, for instance: PowerShell on Linux or more specifically PowerShell on Centos 7.
PowerShell	A generic term that covers any and all editions. PowerShell can be used to refer to the language, framework, default cmdlets, and so on.

We've mentioned .NET Core a few times. It's time to explain what it is and how it's different from the .NET you've seen and used on Windows.

.NET Core

Throughout this book we've said that PowerShell is based on the .NET framework. This remains true for all editions of PowerShell. However, not all editions of PowerShell use the full .NET framework. The use of .NET is as follows:

- Windows PowerShell uses the full .NET CLR.
- PowerShell Core (PowerShell on Linux and so on) uses .NET Core.

The full .NET framework is described on Microsoft's MSDN site at http://mng.bz/PTPZ. All the examples in chapters 1–20 are based on Windows and therefore on the full .NET CLR.

PowerShell Core is based on .NET Core, which is a cross-platform implementation of the Windows .NET framework.

NOTE .NET Core is technically a subset of the full .NET CLR, but the .NET Standard 2.0 release of .NET Core has dramatically reduced the delta between the full CLR and Core. There will also be an ability to load full CLR assemblies into Core processes.

.NET Core is available for Windows, Linux, and macOS. This means that scripts written on Windows accessing the full .NET framework may not run on a non-Windows platform due to functionality not being present in .NET Core. You can view the .NET Core DLLs supplied with PowerShell Core and get a good idea of the .NET functionality available:

```
PS /home/richard> Get-ChildItem -path $pshome/*.dll
```

References for .NET Core can be found at http://www.dotnetfoundation.org/netcore and http://www.microsoft.com/net/core/platform.

PowerShell Core doesn't port all the PowerShell functionality you're used to, so there will be some issues (covered when we look at PowerShell on Linux). For an existing PowerShell user, probably the best place to start is by installing PowerShell Core onto an existing Windows system.

Installing on Windows

Installation on Windows uses a standard Windows .msi. Download the latest release for your version of Windows from https://github.com/PowerShell/PowerShell/releases. It'll be named something like PowerShell-6.0.0-beta.3-win10-win2016-x64.msi. After unblocking the file, double-click the .msi and follow the instructions. PowerShell 6.0 installs into C:\Program Files\PowerShell by default. An entry is also created on the Start menu.

You can run PowerShell 6.0 side by side with Windows PowerShell (v5.1 in this case), as shown in figure 1. Notice the differences between the two sets of output, especially the value of PsEdition.

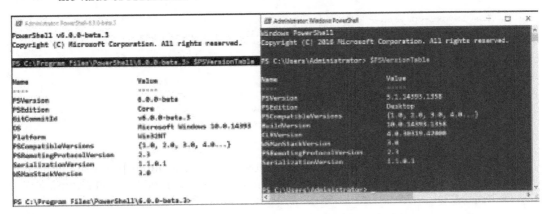

Figure 1 PowerShell 6.0 on the left and PowerShell 5.1 on the right. The background and text colors have been reversed from the default in the PowerShell 6.0 console for clarity.

You get a limited number of modules, and therefore cmdlets, available in PowerShell v6 on Windows:

```
PS> Get-Module -ListAvailable | select name

Name
----
CimCmdlets
Microsoft.PowerShell.Archive
Microsoft.PowerShell.Diagnostics
Microsoft.PowerShell.Host
Microsoft.PowerShell.LocalAccounts
Microsoft.PowerShell.Management
Microsoft.PowerShell.Security
Microsoft.PowerShell.Utility
Microsoft.WSMan.Management
PackageManagement
Pester
PowerShellGet
PSDesiredStateConfiguration
PSDiagnostics
PSReadLine
```

You can create a remote session to a machine running a copy of Windows PowerShell (in this case, PowerShell 5.1):

```
PS> $s = New-PSSession -ComputerName W16DSC01

PS> Invoke-Command -Session $s -ScriptBlock {Get-Process l*} |
Format-Table -AutoSize

NPM(K) PM(M) WS(M) CPU(s)   Id SI ProcessName PSComputerName
------ ----- ----- ------   -- -- ----------- --------------
    23 10.09 32.87   0.59  740  1 LogonUI        W16DSC01
    30  5.77  8.96   1.22  524  0 lsass          W16DSC01
```

Cmdlets that aren't part of PowerShell Core can be accessed on the remote machine:

```
PS> Invoke-Command -Session $s `
-ScriptBlock {Get-WmiObject -Class Win32_OperatingSystem}

SystemDirectory : C:\Windows\system32
Organization    :
BuildNumber     : 14393
RegisteredUser  : Windows User
SerialNumber    : 00376-30816-46802-AA030
Version         : 10.0.14393
PSComputerName  : W16DSC01
```

Within the limitations described earlier, PowerShell on Windows is very similar to the PowerShell you've seen throughout this book. What about PowerShell on Linux and macOS?

PowerShell on Linux and macOS

The introduction of PowerShell for Linux/macOS is a big step forward for managing heterogeneous environments. Windows administrators can now manage these systems using the same tool—PowerShell—they're used to using on their Windows systems. In this section, we cover installing PowerShell on Linux and the differences between PowerShell on Windows and PowerShell on Linux.

PowerShell is built on the assumption that you'll be administering your systems remotely. We examine remoting from Windows to Linux and Linux to Windows systems. DSC brings a huge change in the way you manage the configuration of your servers. You can manage Linux systems as well as Windows with DSC.

There are some differences, and issues, between Windows PowerShell and PowerShell on Linux/macOS.

Known issues

As you would expect, there are a number of issues with porting a 10-year-old .NET-based application—PowerShell—to non-Windows platforms. The PowerShell project team maintains a list of known issues as part of the project documentation at http://mng.bz/8j3L.

Some of these issues are flagged to be addressed during the development of PowerShell v6. Other issues are differences that are inherent to the various platforms to which PowerShell is being ported, and users will need to be aware of the issues and manage them.

Issues that may cause current Windows-based PowerShell users problems on non-Windows platforms or that may cause issues for non-Windows users learning PowerShell include the following:

- *Case sensitivity*—PowerShell, like Windows, is case-insensitive. Linux and macOS are case-sensitive, so the correct case must be used for filenames, paths, and environment variables. Running scripts, loading modules, and filename tab completion all depend on the correct case being used. Cmdlet names are case-insensitive!
- *File path delimiters*—Windows can use \ or /, but on non-Windows you must use /.
- *File extensions*—PowerShell uses file extensions—for instance, .ps1 for scripts and .psm1 for modules. Non-Windows platforms don't usually use file extensions. You need to use the correct extension for PowerShell to correctly interpret the file type.
- *Command aliases*—A number of aliases—ls, cp, mv, rm, cat, man, mount, ps—have been removed from the Linux and macOS implementations, as they hide the platform-native commands. These aliases are still present in PowerShell for Windows.
- *JEA*—JEA support is not available on Linux or macOS and is not in scope for PowerShell v6.

- *Sudo*—PowerShell doesn't support sudo directly. You need to start a new instance of PowerShell using sudo.
- *Missing cmdlets*—A number of cmdlets don't work properly or aren't available on Linux and macOS, including `*-Service`, `*-Acl`, `*-AuthenticodeSignatue`, `Wait-Process`, `*-PSSessionConfiguration`, `*-Event`, `Set-ExceutionPolicy`, `New-PSSession`, `New-PSSessionOption`, `New-PSTransportOption`, and `*-Job`. Some of these issues will be resolved in future releases.

One other thing to be aware of is that none of the PowerShell Core implementations includes the PowerShell ISE. If you need an editor for use with PowerShell Core, especially on non-Windows machines, we recommend using Visual Studio Code (VSC). VSC is a free download from https://code.visualstudio.com/ with versions available for Windows, various Linux distributions, and macOS. PowerShell and many other programming languages are supported through plugins that can be installed from within Visual Studio Code.

Before you can do anything, though, you need to get PowerShell onto your Linux system.

Installation

PowerShell on Linux is available on a large number of Linux distributions, but in this appendix we'll just be looking at PowerShell on Centos 7.

> **NOTE** We'll be assuming that you have a working Linux system and have sufficient Linux skills to follow this discussion.

You can find instructions for installing PowerShell on CentOS 7 at http://mng.bz/7fa8. Instructions for other Linux types and macOS are also available. Follow the download instructions and install the PowerShell package.

You may find that you see a message about a yum lock, as shown in figure 2.

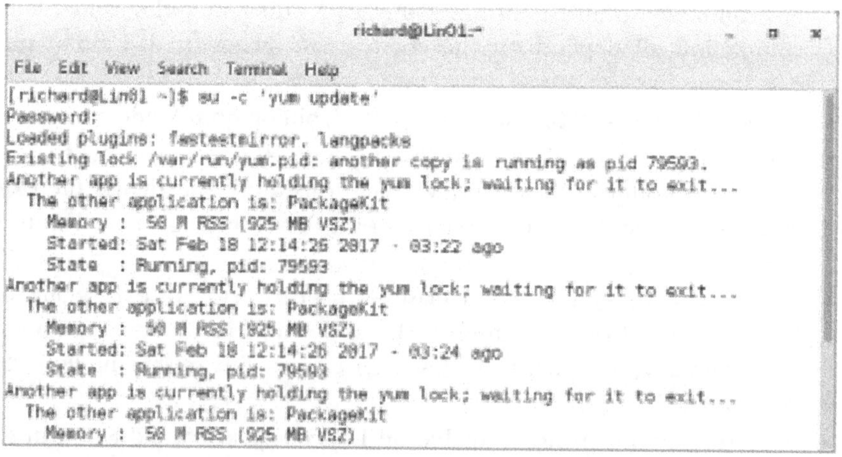

Figure 2   Yum error message due to lock held by PackageKit

If you get such a message, follow the instructions to disable packagekit (which manages updates) that you'll find at http://mng.bz/5co7. The PowerShell package can then be installed.

The PowerShell project has started releasing the install packages to the appropriate repositories so that you can use Linux's built-in package management systems to install and update PowerShell. First, you need to enter super user mode and register the Microsoft repository:

```
sudo su
curl https://packages.microsoft.com/config/rhel/7/prod.repo > /etc/yum.
  repos.d/microsoft.repo

exit
```

You can then install PowerShell:

```
sudo yum install -y powershell
```

Starting PowerShell is a simple call to the application:

```
powershell
```

The advantage of this approach is that when new releases of PowerShell 6.0 are made available, you can easily update your installation:

```
sudo yum update powershell
```

Now that you've installed PowerShell for Linux, how do you use it?

Using PowerShell v6 on Linux

Using the PowerShell core language is essentially identical to the examples we've shown in the rest of the book. One obvious difference is the modules that are available. You saw the modules available for PowerShell on Windows earlier. Figure 3 shows the modules available to a new PowerShell on Linux installation.

A number of modules that are available in PowerShell for Windows aren't available in PowerShell for Linux:

- CimCmdlets
- Microsoft.PowerShell.Diagnostics
- Microsoft.PowerShell.LocalAccounts
- Microsoft.WSMan.Management
- PSDiagnostics

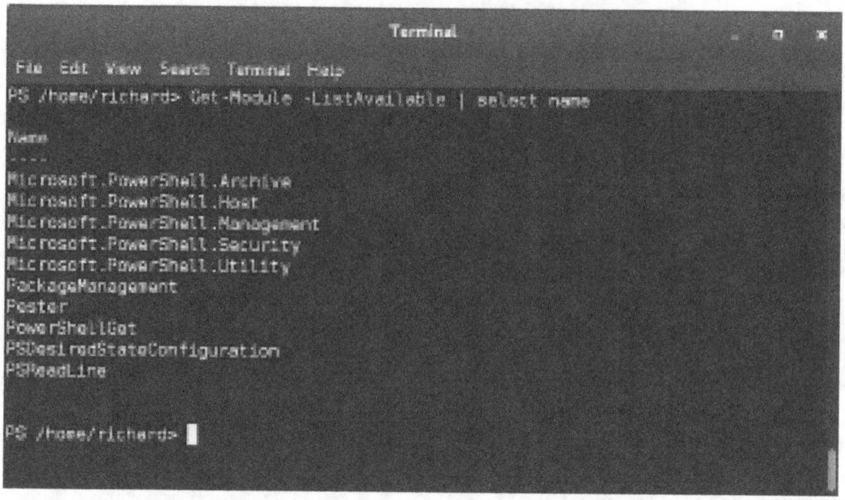

Figure 3   A list of default modules for PowerShell on Linux

These modules contain functionality that is directly related to the Windows platform and so can't be ported to Linux and other platforms. Linux/macOS versions of these modules may become available in the future. There are some possible issues with other modules. Script modules will load but may not work properly if they make Windows-centric assumptions about the file system or access Windows-specific functionality. Binary modules won't load if they depend on functionality that isn't present in .NET Standard 2.0.

A number of the Windows PowerShell providers are also not available on Linux/macOS:

- Registry
- WSMan
- Certificate

PowerShell v6 being available on a number of platforms means you can write scripts that are portable across platforms. Your script needs to know which platform it's running on to avoid errors due to missing functionality. The $PSVersionTable contains detailed operating system information. On Windows, you'll see this:

```
PS> $PSVersionTable

Name                         Value
----                         -----
PSVersion                    6.0.0-beta
PSEdition                    Core
GitCommitId                  v6.0.0-beta.3
OS                           Microsoft Windows 10.0.14393
Platform                     Win32NT
PSCompatibleVersions         {1.0, 2.0, 3.0, 4.0...}
PSRemotingProtocolVersion    2.3
SerializationVersion         1.1.0.1
WSManStackVersion            3.0
```

On Linux you'll see this:

```
PS /home/richard> $PSVersionTable

Name                        Value
----                        -----
PSVersion                   6.0.0-beta
PSEdition                   Core
GitCommitId                 v6.0.0-beta.3
OS                          Linux 3.10.0-514.6.1.el7.x86_64
                            #1 SMP Wed Jan 18 13:06:36 UTC 2017
Platform                    Unix
PSCompatibleVersions        {1.0, 2.0, 3.0, 4.0...}
PSRemotingProtocolVersion   2.3
SerializationVersion        1.1.0.1
WSManStackVersion           3.0
```

The Platform field or the OS field (if you require more detailed tests) can be used to
determine the operating system the code is running on.

PowerShell v6 includes variables, shown in listing 1, to help with this:

- $IsCoreCLR
- $IsLinux
- $IsOSX
- $IsWindows

Listing 1 Cross-platform scripting

```
$dt = @{
  '3' = 'Fixed'
  '5' = 'CD-Rom'
}

$hlth = @{
  '0' = 'Healthy'
  '1' = 'Scan Needed'
  '3' = 'Full Repair Needed'
}

if ($IsCoreCLR) {
  if ($IsLinux){
    df -T
  }
  elseif ($IsWindows) {
    Get-CimInstance -Namespace 'ROOT/Microsoft/Windows/Storage' `
    -ClassName MSFT_Volume |
    select DriveLetter, FileSystemLabel, FileSystem,
    @{N='DriveType'; E={$dt["$($_.DriveType)"]}},
    @{N='HealthStatus'; E={$hlth["$($_.HealthStatus)"]}},
    @{N='SizeRemaining(GB)'; E={[math]::Round($_.SizeRemaining / 1GB, 2)}},
    @{N='Size(GB)'; E={[math]::Round($_.Size / 1GB, 2)}}
  }
}
```

```
else {
  Get-Volume
}
```

The script starts by defining two hash tables, $dt and $hlth, that will be used to decode the values returned from a CIM class. The variable $IsCoreCLR is used to determine whether the script is running on an instance of PowerShell Core or Windows PowerShell.

If the script is running on PowerShell Core, the next test determines if it's running on Linux or Windows. The Linux command df -T is used to return disk information if the script is running on Linux. Get-CimInstance with a call to the MSFT_Volume class is used for a Windows machine running PowerShell Core. The hash tables are used to supply readable values for the drive type and health status. The disk size information is converted to GB with the result converted to two decimal places.

If the script isn't running on PowerShell Core, it assumes Windows PowerShell and uses the Get-Volume cmdlet. Get-Volume also uses the MSFT_Volume CIM class.

> **NOTE** The Get-Volume cmdlet and the MSFT_Volume CIM class are only available on Windows 8/2012 and later. If you're using Windows 7, you can modify the script to use Win32_Volume instead.

The results of running the script are shown in figure 4.

So far, you've seen PowerShell running directly on Linux. What about remoting between instances of PowerShell running on Windows and Linux?

PowerShell remoting and Linux

You saw in chapter 11 how PowerShell remoting works using WS-MAN as its transport mechanism. PowerShell for Linux doesn't include a WS-MAN provider. Traditionally, Linux has used SSH (Secure Shell) for remote access. PowerShell for Linux performs remote access using SSH.

> **NOTE** The plan is that eventually there will be a single mechanism for PowerShell remoting regardless of the client and target. Until that time, you need to use SSH if Linux machines are involved and WS-MAN if only Windows machines are involved.

If you want to perform PowerShell remoting between Windows machines and Linux machines, you need to have SSH installed at both ends. PowerShell on Windows uses OpenSSH. You can run this code to find the links to the latest releases of OpenSSH:

```
$url = 'https://github.com/PowerShell/Win32-OpenSSH/releases/latest/'
$request = [System.Net.WebRequest]::Create($url)
$request.AllowAutoRedirect=$false
$response=$request.GetResponse()
$([String]$response.GetResponseHeader("Location")).Replace('tag','download')
    + '/OpenSSH-Win64.zip'
$([String]$response.GetResponseHeader("Location")).Replace('tag','download')
    + '/OpenSSH-Win32.zip'
```

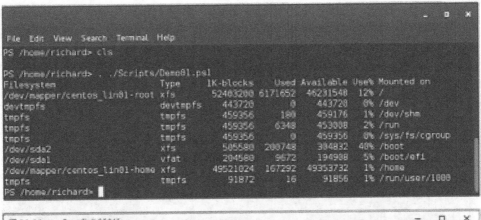

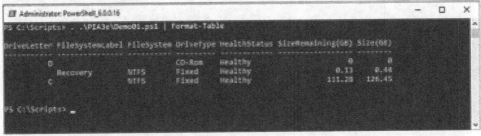

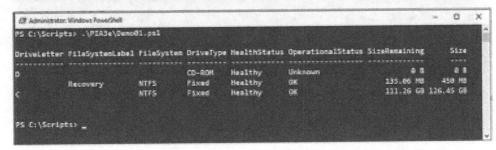

Figure 4   The results of running listing 1 on PowerShell on Linux (top), PowerShell on Windows (middle), and Windows PowerShell (bottom).

You'll see results like this:

```
https://github.com/PowerShell/Win32-OpenSSH/releases/download/v0.0.17.0/
   OpenSSH-Win64.zip
```

```
https://github.com/PowerShell/Win32-OpenSSH/releases/download/v0.0.17.0/
   OpenSSH-Win32.zip
```

Download the appropriate version. Instructions for installing a Windows version of OpenSSH are available at http://mng.bz/n48S. The instructions don't explicitly state it, but ensure that all instances of PowerShell or CMD are started with elevated privileges when installing OpenSSH. When OpenSSH is installed, perform the additional configuration steps for Windows machines at http://mng.bz/10iL.

OpenSSH is available for most Linux distributions. Install, or update, both client and server versions of OpenSSH and configure as described at the SSHRemoting URL given earlier.

You also need to ensure that the Linux and Windows machines can find each other on the network. Either ensure that your DNS contains entries for all relevant machines or add appropriate entries to the hosts file on your machines.

PowerShell remoting from Linux to Windows works in a similar manner to Windows to Windows remoting. An example of a remoting session from a Linux machine to a Windows machine is shown in figure 5.

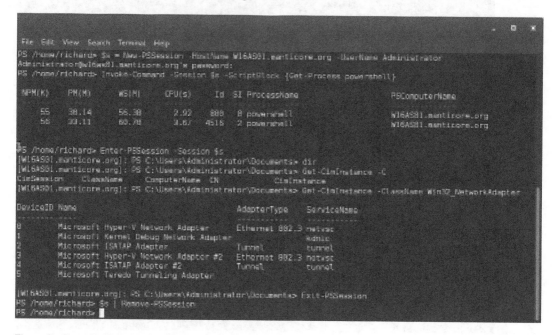

Figure 5   Remoting session from Linux to Windows

NOTE   PowerShell remoting between Linux and Windows machines works only with PowerShell v6 because it's the only version that supports the use of SSH.

Create a remoting session from the Linux machine to the Windows machine:

```
$s = New-PSSession -HostName W16AS01.manticore.org
-UserName Administrator
```

You'll be prompted for the password of the user account you specify. Invoke-Command can then be used, as with the remoting sessions you've already seen:

```
Invoke-Command -Session $s -ScriptBlock {Get-Process}
```

A PowerShell remoting session from Linux to Windows can also be used interactively. Notice the prompt change in figure 5. Within the remoting session, you can access the functionality on the Windows machine that's not present on the Linux machine, such as the CIM cmdlets.

You can also create a remoting session from Windows to Linux:

```
PS> $sl = New-PSSession -HostName Lin01.manticore.org -UserName root
root@lin01.manticore.org's password:
```

You'll be prompted for the password. Commands can be run over the session:

```
PS> Invoke-Command -Session $sl -ScriptBlock {Get-Process -Name powershell}

NPM(K)  PM(M)  WS(M)  CPU(s)     Id   SI ProcessName PSComputerName
------  -----  -----  ------     --   -- ----------- --------------
     0   0.00   0.02   11.21   5863 5809 powershell  Lin01.manticore.org
     0   0.00   0.02    4.07   7898 7898 powershell  Lin01.manticore.org
```

or you can enter the session:

```
PS> Enter-PSSession -Session $sl
[Lin01.manticore.org]: PS /root> $PSVersionTable

Name                         Value
----                         -----
Name                         Value
----                         -----
PSVersion                    6.0.0-beta
PSEdition                    Core
GitCommitId                  v6.0.0-beta.3
OS                           Linux 3.10.0-514.6.1.el7.x86_64 #1 SMP Wed Jan
   18 13:06:36 UTC 2017
Platform                     Unix
PSCompatibleVersions         {1.0, 2.0, 3.0, 4.0...}
PSRemotingProtocolVersion    2.3
SerializationVersion         1.1.0.1
WSManStackVersion            3.0

[Lin01.manticore.org]: PS /root> Exit-PSSession
```

You can copy a file from a Windows machine to a Linux machine:

```
PS> Copy-Item -Path .\test.txt `
-Destination "/home/richard/Scripts/" -ToSession $sl -Force
```

and vice versa:

```
PS> Copy-Item -Path "/home/richard/Scripts/*.txt" `
-Destination .\PIA3e\ -FromSession $sl -Force
```

You can even use a WS-MAN-based session to a Windows machine and a SSH session to a Linux machine together:

```
PS> $sw = New-PSSession -ComputerName W16DSC01
PS> Get-PSSession
```

```
Id Name    ComputerName   ComputerType   State   ConfigurationName
-- ----    ------------   ------------   -----   -----------------
 1 SSH1    Lin01.ma...    RemoteMachine  Opened  DefaultShell
 2 WinRM2  W16DSC01       RemoteMachine  Opened  Microsoft.PowerShell
PS> Invoke-Command -Session $sl, $sw `
-ScriptBlock {Get-Process -Name PowerShell}

NPM(K) PM(M) WS(M) CPU(s)    Id   SI ProcessName PSComputerName
------ ----- ----- ------    --   -- ----------- --------------
    27 53.44 62.52   1.22  1740    2 powershell  W16DSC01
     0  0.00  0.02  12.18  5863 5809 powershell  Lin01.manticore.org
     0  0.00  0.02   7.70  7898 7898 powershell  Lin01.manticore.org
```

PowerShell remoting between Linux and Windows machines enables you to perform your administration on whichever platform you prefer. Whatever your mix of Linux and Windows machines, you can administer them using the same PowerShell tools.

> **NOTE** PowerShell v6 remoting over SSH is a possible answer to the issue of accessing non-domain Windows machines remotely. The use of SSH bypasses the Kerberos-related issues that make non-domain remoting difficult and is an alternative to the use of certificate-based remoting, which is the current recommendation.

In chapter 18 we showed you how to use DSC. What we didn't cover was that DSC is also available for Linux machines.

DSC and Linux

The agent side of DSC for Linux has been available since PowerShell v4. You need to install a number of pre-requisite packages on the Linux target machine to support the DSC for Linux agent. Also, you'll need to download the modules from the PowerShell gallery that provide the resources for configuring Linux.

The client side—Start-DSCConfiguration—isn't going to be supported in PowerShell v6. You can compile configurations on Linux but you can't use any of the DSC cmdlets because they're CIM based.

> **NOTE** DSC agent for Linux isn't dependent on PowerShell 6.0, but we're combining the Linux-based material into this appendix for ease of reference.

We briefly cover installing DSC for Linux and then show you a DSC for Linux configuration.

Installing DSC for Linux

Installing the DSC agent on Linux is a multi-stage process. First, you install the Open Management Infrastructure (OMI), which is a CIM server for Linux. Then you ensure that prerequisite packages are installed, and then you can install the DSC package on the Linux machine. The final step is to download the DSC resource modules to your Windows authoring machine.

DSC uses CIM, as we showed in chapter 18. Linux doesn't have a native CIM provider, so you need to install OMI.

INSTALL OMI ON A LINUX MACHINE

OMI is an open source project—https://github.com/Microsoft/omi—to develop a portable and highly modular CIM Object Manager (CIMOM). It can be built and installed on most UNIX and Linux systems. It's also used in network switches, including those from Arista and Cisco.

Before you install OMI, ensure you have OpenSSL—at least version 0.9.8 and preferably 1.0.x—on the Linux system. Download OMI from https://github.com/Microsoft/omi/releases and install. You should also download and install the appropriate package for your system from http://mng.bz/SPAg so that OMI can use the PowerShell Remoting Protocol over WS-MAN. With this package installed, you can create CIM sessions to the Linux system from a Windows machine.

You should check that OMI is running by using the following:

```
sudo /opt/omi/bin/omicli ei root/omi OMI_Identify
```

You'll see a listing of all instances of the OMI_identify class in the root/omi namespace.

Now it's time to install DSC for Linux.

INSTALL DSC FOR LINUX ON A LINUX MACHINE

DSC for Linux is also an open source project at https://github.com/Microsoft/PowerShell-DSC-for-Linux. The pre-requisites for installing DSC for Linux (descriptive name and package name) are as follows:

- *GNU C Library*—glibc
- *CURL http client library*—libcurl
- *Python*—python
- *Python Ctypes library*—python-ctypes
- *Open Management Infrastructure*—omi
- *OpenSSL libraries*—openssl

The installation package for DSC for Linux is available from http://mng.bz/7Z39. Download and install. The last step is to download the DSC resource modules.

INSTALL DSC FOR LINUX MODULE ON A WINDOWS MACHINE

If you remember from chapter 18, DSC resources are used to create configurations. The DSC resources for configuring Linux are available on the PowerShell gallery. Their names start with the prefix *nx*:

```
PS> Find-Module nx* | Format-Table Version, Name, Description

Version Name                  Description
------- ----                  -----------
```

```
1.0    nx                  Module with DSC Resources for Linux
1.1    nxNetworking        Module with DSC Networking Resources for Linux
1.1    nxComputerManagement Module with DSC Computer Management Resources
                           for Linux
```

You can install all three modules in one pass:

```
PS> Find-Module nx* | Install-Module -Force
```

The DSC resources currently available for configuring Linux include the following:

```
PS> Get-Module -ListAvailable nx* |
foreach {Get-DscResource -Module $_.Name} |
Format-Wide -Column 4

nxArchive                nxEnvironment  nxFile      nxFileLine
nxGroup                  nxPackage      nxScript    nxService
nxSshAuthorizedKeys nxUser                 nxComputer  nxDNSServerAddress
nxFirewall               nxIPAddress
```

Linux administration is performed by configuring the contents of numerous files. If a resource isn't available to configure a particular aspect of your Linux machine, you should be able to complete the task by modifying the contents of the appropriate file.

Before attempting to configure the Linux machine, you should test that you can connect to OMI.

TEST CIM ON A LINUX SYSTEM

The easiest way to test connectivity to CIM on your target machine is to create a CIM session to that machine:

```
PS> $cred = Get-Credential root

PS> $sopt = New-CimSessionOption -UseSsl -SkipCACheck `
-SkipCNCheck -SkipRevocationCheck

PS> $sl = New-CimSession -Credential $cred -Authentication Basic `
-ComputerName Lin01 -SessionOption $sopt
```

Create a PowerShell credential object for the root account on the Linux system. You then need to create a set of options for the CIM session. In this case, you're telling the system to use SSL (encrypt the connection) but to skip all the tests on the machine's SSL certificate. You can then create the session using the credential and options you set earlier and configuring the session to use Basic (user name/password) authentication.

The resultant CIM session looks identical to a similar session established to a Windows machine:

```
PS> $sl

Id          : 1
Name        : CimSession1
InstanceId  : 6dd1b519-db6e-4fbf-b26e-91b86bcb79e7
ComputerName : Lin01
Protocol    : WSMAN
```

OMI doesn't install any useful classes for configuring your Linux machine directly, but you can display some basic information as a test:

```
PS> Get-CimInstance -CimSession $s1 -ClassName OMI_Identify `
-Namespace root/omi

InstanceID              : 2FDB5542-5896-45D5-9BE9-DC04430AAABE
SystemName              : Lin01
ProductName             : OMI
ProductVendor           : Microsoft
ProductVersionMajor     : 1
ProductVersionMinor     : 1
ProductVersionRevision  : 0
ProductVersionString    : 1.1.0-0
Platform                : LINUX_X86_64_GNU
OperatingSystem         : LINUX
Architecture            : X86_64
Compiler                : GNU
ConfigPrefix            : GNU
ConfigLibDir            : /opt/omi/lib
ConfigBinDir            : /opt/omi/bin
ConfigIncludeDir        : /opt/omi/include
ConfigDataDir           : /opt/omi/share
ConfigLocalStateDir     : /var/opt/omi
ConfigSysConfDir        : /etc/opt/omi/conf
ConfigProviderDir       : /etc/opt/omi/conf
ConfigLogFile           : /var/opt/omi/log/omiserver.log
ConfigPIDFile           : /var/opt/omi/run/omiserver.pid
ConfigRegisterDir       : /etc/opt/omi/conf/omiregister
ConfigSchemaDir         : /opt/omi/share/omischema
ConfigNameSpaces        : {root-omi, interop, root-Microsoft-
   DesiredStateConfiguration, root-Microsoft-Windows-
   DesiredStateConfiguration}
PSComputerName          : Lin01
```

This is pretty much the same information you saw when you tested that OMI was running from the Linux machine.

Now it's time to create a configuration.

Using DSC for Linux

Using DSC to configure a Linux machine is the same as configuring a Windows machine:

- Create a configuration file
- Create a MOF file from the configuration
- Apply the MOF file to the target machine

The configuration file is first.

CREATING A CONFIGURATION FILE

A configuration file for a Linux machine is identical to that for a Windows machine, except that a different set of resources, defined in the nx*, modules must be used.

We'll repeat our first configuration from chapter 18—to create a file and set its contents as an example, as shown in the following listing.

Listing 2   DSC for a Linux configuration file

```
Configuration LxDSCConfig
{
 param ([string]$node)

  Import-DSCResource -Module nx

  Node $node
  {
    nxFile myTestFile
    {
      Ensure = "Present"
      Type = "File"
      DestinationPath = "/tmp/dsctest"
      Contents="This is our DSC on Linux Test!"
    }
  }
}

LxDSCConfig -node Lin01 -OutputPath .\MOF
```

The configuration starts with the Configuration keyword and the configuration name. A single parameter, $node, is accepted by the configuration. The module containing the Linux DSC resources is imported, and the nxFile resource is used to configure the file and its contents.

A MOF file is created in the location defined by -OutputPath. You can now apply the configuration.

APPLYING A CONFIGURATION

Pushing a configuration to a Linux machine is identical to pushing to a Windows machine if you're pushing the configuration from a Windows machine. Start-DSCConfiguration isn't supported on Linux yet and won't be for the PowerShell v6 release.

NOTE You can compile configurations into MOF files on Linux—you just can't deploy them from the Linux machine.

Let's push the configuration to our Linux machine:

```
PS>  Start-DscConfiguration -CimSession $sl -Path .\MOF\ -Verbose -Wait

VERBOSE: Perform operation 'Invoke CimMethod' with following parameters,
  ''methodName' = SendConfigurationApply,'className' =
MSFT_DSCLocalConfigurationManager,'namespaceName' = root/Microsoft/Windows/
  DesiredStateConfiguration'.
VERBOSE: Operation 'Invoke CimMethod' complete.
VERBOSE: Time taken for configuration job to complete is 0.655 seconds
```

You'll need to use a CIM session (the one we created earlier) to push your configuration. You can test the configuration:

```
PS>  Test-DscConfiguration -CimSession $sl
True
```

and view the configuration:

```
PS>  Get-DscConfiguration -CimSession $sl

DestinationPath : /tmp/dsctest
SourcePath      :
Ensure          : present
Type            : file
Force           : False
Contents        : This is our DSC on Linux Test!
Checksum        :
Recurse         : False
Links           : follow
Group           : root
Mode            : 644
Owner           : root
ModifiedDate    : 23/02/2017 20:09:34
PSComputerName  : Lin01
CimClassName    : MSFT_nxFileResource
```

DSC for Linux performs and operates in the same way as DSC against Windows that you saw in chapter 18. You can also configure a Linux machine to utilize a pull server and even mix and match Linux and Windows configurations in the same file.

NOTE Hint: use roles to separate the two types of machine.

Summary

- PowerShell core engine is now an open source project.
- Powershell v6 will be available for Windows, Linux, and macOS.
- PowerShell v6 is built on .NET Core.
- PowerShell remoting uses SSH for Windows to Linux or Linux to Windows connections. Windows to Windows can use WS-MAN or SSH.
- PowerShell for Linux is still in its infancy compared to Windows PowerShell but is already capable of performing basic management tasks on your systems.
- The porting of PowerShell and DSC to Linux means you can manage your heterogenous environments with a single set of tools.
- Windows Powershell will continue to be the version that ships OOB with Windows and will continue to evolve through its ecosystem of modules.

index